Socialist Unemployment

Socialist Unemployment

THE POLITICAL ECONOMY OF YUGOSLAVIA, 1945–1990

Susan L. Woodward

PRINCETON UNIVERSITY PRESS

PRINCETON, NEW JERSEY

Copyright © 1995 by Princeton University Press
Published by Princeton University Press, 41 William Street,
Princeton, New Jersey 08540
In the United Kingdom: Princeton University Press, Chichester, West Sussex

Library of Congress Cataloging-in-Publication Data

Woodward, Susan L., 1944–
Socialist unemployment : the political economy of Yugoslavia,
1945–1990 / Susan L. Woodward.
p.   cm.
Includes bibliographical references and index.
ISBN 0-691-08645-1 (alk. paper)
1. Unemployment—Yugoslavia.   2. Full employment policies—
Yugoslavia.   3. Yugoslavia—Economic conditions—1945–1992.
4. Socialism—Yugoslavia.   I. Title.
HD5811.6.A6W66   1995
331.13′79497—dc20   94-46153
                                                            CIP

This book has been composed in Caledonia

Princeton University Press books are printed on acid-free paper
and meet the guidelines for permanence and durability of the
Committee on Production Guidelines for Book Longevity of the
Council on Library Resources

Printed in the United States of America

1   3   5   7   9   10   8   6   4   2

To Peter Vincent Woodward

In Memoriam

Child of unemployed man: "Why don't we have heat?"
Mother: "Because there is no coal."
Child: "Why is there no coal?"
Mother: "Because your father is out of work."
Child: "Why is my father out of work?"
Mother: "Because there is too much coal."
      —Dr. Dieter Steifel, Austria, 1931

One gets the impression that as a society we are quite
   inert when it comes to solving the problem of
unemployment. We have difficulty accepting facts if
they do not conform to our conceptions or plans. A
progressive, and particularly a socialist society, cannot
  wait "optimistically" for so important and delicate a
   problem to be resolved spontaneously and cannot
  expect its members not to be exposed to great social
and economic risk as a result. Security of employment
  is one of the significant contributions of socialism,
highly valued and popular, particularly in the ranks of
the working classes of capitalist countries, something
that we ought not allow ourselves to question. We are
  aware of the fact that it is difficult to harmonize
economic necessity and political opportunity, but we
should not allow those difficulties to demobilize us.
    —Tripo Mulina, Yugoslavia, 1968

CONTENTS

List of Figures and Tables xi

Preface xiii

CHAPTER 1
Introduction: The Paradox of Socialist Unemployment 3

CHAPTER 2
The Making of a Strategy for Change 31

CHAPTER 3
Creating a State for Socialist Development 64

CHAPTER 4
Military Self-Reliance, Foreign Trade, and the Origins
of Self-Management 98

CHAPTER 5
A Republic of Producers 164

CHAPTER 6
Unemployment 191

CHAPTER 7
The Faustian Bargain 222

CHAPTER 8
Slovenia and Foča 260

CHAPTER 9
Divisions of Labor 310

CHAPTER 10
Breakdown 345

EPILOGUE 371

Appendix: Statistical Data 375

Bibliography 393

Index 427

FIGURES AND TABLES

FIGURES

Figure 1-1.	Map of Former Yugoslavia	2
Figure 6-1.	Employment Growth, 1962–1975	192
Figure 6-2.	Unemployment, 1952–1988	193
Figure 6-3.	Rate of Unemployment, 1959–1988	193
Figure 6-4.	Unemployment: Gross and Net Rates	199
Figure 6-5.	Job Seekers and Yugoslavs Working Temporarily Abroad	200
Figure 6-6.	Length of Time Waiting to Be Employed	202
Figure 6-7.	Length of Time Waiting to Be Employed (proportions)	202
Figure 6-8.	Women among the Registered Unemployed	203
Figure 6-9.	Unemployment Rates by Republic: The North	204
Figure 6-10.	Unemployment Rates by Republic: The South	204
Figure 6-11.	Economically Active Population by Republic	205
Figure 6-12.	Unemployment by Age Category	206
Figure 6-13.	Unemployment by Age Category (proportions)	206
Figure 6-14.	Women, New Entrants, and the Educated	207
Figure 6-15.	Women, New Entrants, and the Educated (proportions)	208
Figure 6-16.	Youth Unemployment Rates: The North	209
Figure 6-17.	Youth Unemployment Rates: The South	209
Figure 8-1.	Employment in the Social Sector by Republic	292
Figure 9-1.	Rate of Unemployment: Kosovo, Slovenia, and Bosnia-Herzegovina	340
Figure 9-2.	Rate of Youth Unemployment: Kosovo, Slovenia, and Bosnia-Herzegovina	340
Figure 9-3.	Rate of Employment: Kosovo, Slovenia, and Bosnia-Herzegovina	341

LIST OF FIGURES AND TABLES
TABLES

Table 1-1.   International Comparison of the Sectoral   25
            Distribution of Employment

Table 1-2.   Level of Employment in Socialist and Market   27
            Capitalist Countries, 1974

Table 6-1.   Rate of Employment by Republic or Province   205

PREFACE

BETWEEN THE Great Depression of the 1880s and the Great Depression of the 1930s, the political systems of modern states were created. Inseparable from that development was unemployment. Mass political parties, governmental activism in the economy, systems of public welfare—all were a response to the phenomenon of mass, industrial unemployment and the efforts by working-class organizations to protect against it. By the 1980s, the solutions that had been in use had failed. Unemployment began to take on serious proportions even in the wealthiest, most technologically advanced nations of the world. Countries celebrated as models of full employment—Sweden, Austria, even Japan—were dismantling the systems of political decision making in the economy that had managed their success.

At the same time, the socialist alternative, which had once inspired political action and a remedy against unemployment, was also under attack. The global defeat of both Keynesian and Marxian programs had its crowning glory in the political revolutions in central and eastern Europe in 1989–90 and their open declaration that the "natural price" for liberal democracy and the prosperity of market economies was large-scale unemployment. In eastern Germany, the seat of social democracy—where the Yugoslav socialist story begins—that unemployment was conservatively estimated at 50 percent on the first anniversary of German reunification.

Guided by the older verity—that unemployment was the great, unresolved affliction of capitalism, and socialism was a movement to make it unnecessary—I began this book with what seemed an obvious paradox: a socialist country with high and unremittingly rising unemployment. In the early 1980s, when my research began, socialist Yugoslavia had the highest rate of registered unemployment in Europe. The country was acclaimed for its maverick approach to socialism—for defying the ideological blocs of the cold war, helping to organize the nonalignment movement, and creating a domestic order of economic democracy and decentralized, market socialism. But those few who noticed its unemployment—part of the paradox was the great silence toward this unemployment in the Yugoslav public as well as in scholarship on the country—identified the cause as the system of "workers' control." According to this theory, economic democracy gave workers the right to manage their firms, and they chose to maximize their incomes at the expense of new investment. Yugoslavs had made the syndicalist dilemma into an organizing principle of society.

Before the alternative explanation in this book could appear, the country died. To explain the paroxysm of killing and territorial war that followed, a new exceptionalism—of ancient ethnic hatreds and a Balkan culture of blood revenge—replaced the fame of Yugoslavia's "third way." Yugoslav socialism was ascribed a role in the tragedy for failing to allow political democracy and for repressing national identities and the historical aspirations of the country's peoples for national self-determination. But for the most part, its experiment was assigned to the overnight oblivion of the rest of European socialism. The branch of scholarship claiming that Yugoslav politics was always about the national question and ethnic conflict seemed vindicated.

In fact, neither the disintegration of Yugoslavia nor the character of its wars can be understood apart from the political-economic and social system created by the Yugoslav League of Communists or the effect of rising unemployment on that system. The leaders' approach to employment was a core element of the system. The dynamic of governmental policy alternated between two models, which I have labeled (after contrasting wartime administrations in 1941–45) "Slovenia" and "Foča." The first model represented the approach to economic growth—and the economic and political institutions to implement that approach—of the dominant ideology of liberal, or reform, communism. The second model represented the policies and institutions periodically required by the strategic considerations of national defense and of a foreign-trade strategy in contractual markets, or in market conditions where revenues depended on supply increases instead of price competition. A central element in both approaches was the country's foreign economic and strategic relations and its domestic adjustment to international conditions.

In the breakup of Yugoslavia, an extreme version of this dynamic played out with the initial, almost surgical secession of Slovenia (to pursue the Slovene model independently in central Europe) and the prolonged, bloody agony of Bosnia-Herzegovina (where the Foča model had its earliest and most developed expression). The ability of Slovenia to exit was inseparable from the political consequences of the republic's nearly forty years of full employment. The characteristics of the war in Bosnia-Herzegovina were, likewise, inseparable from the political consequences of nearly 25 percent unemployment in the 1980s, at the start of another liberalizing, "efficiency-oriented" economic reform for international adjustment. Both were the product, as was the broader path of disintegration, of a political system based on the liberal, or reform-communist, model of socialism and on the leaders' system of social protection against unemployment—a system that structured the labor force into high-productivity and subsistence sectors of the economy, with corresponding differences in property rights and political participation: one socialist (or public), the other independent (or private).

The understandable focus on the collapse of Yugoslavia and the human tragedy of its wars diverts attention, unfortunately, from the resemblance between its strategy and the one eventually followed in other socialist states. If not a prelude to war, the economic reform of socialist societies for the purposes of global economic integration and economic recovery in a period of worldwide stagflation and then recession has left in its wake a type of social organization and attitudes—described in this book—about social status, economic rights, and welfare that will shape the path of postcommunist regimes. The dismissal of a century of human experience in the case of the Soviet Union and nearly fifty years in the case of European socialist states also cannot erase the problems socialism arose to solve or its more generally shared dilemma of the declining relevance of the responses to agrarian and industrial unemployment in the 1920s and 1930s to conditions in the 1990s and beyond. Structural unemployment among urban youth, both unskilled and university-educated, and within the administrative and service sectors poses a different problem for economic policy. Nationalism is only a negative manifestation of the political problem it poses; it remains uncertain who will organize the unemployed (and those threatened with unemployment in these conditions) and therefore what economic ideologies and political systems will result.

At the very time the Yugoslav socialist system was disintegrating, its key elements were the rage in Western theory: decentralization, rising labor productivity as the route to higher employment, the political and economic incentives of property rights, and social alternatives to budgetary expenditures on welfare. The underlying tension of the Austrian paradox in the epigraph to this book—the aggregate paradox of Keynes's ideological revolution, the dilemmas of secondary uncertainty and market failure, the relation between individual and social interests, the role of government—was the source of Yugoslavia's most highly contested and unsolved political, as well as ideological, predicament.

Like the former Yugoslav state, I have accumulated a very heavy burden of debts in the course of writing this book that can never be fully repaid. Beginning with those who helped financially, I acknowledge with particular gratitude the International Research and Exchanges Board, for enabling my research sojourn at the Zagreb Institute of Economics (Ekonomski Institut) during 1982; the American Council of Learned Societies and Williams College, for making possible a research leave at the Russian Research Center at Harvard University in 1981–82, when I began to think about the project; Yale University, for a social science faculty research grant and a glorious leave in California in 1987, where I was able to do the archival work and write undisturbed in the true ivory tower of the Hoover Institution and its supporting fellowship from the U.S. Department of State's discretionary grant program under the Soviet–

Eastern European Research and Training Act of 1983 (P.L. 98-164), Title
VIII, 97 Stat. 1047-50; and, finally, the National Fellows program of the
Hoover Institution, for the sanctuary in 1989–90 that gave me the addi-
tional quiet needed to complete the manuscript.

Even then, without the supportive work environment of the Brookings
Institution, the editing necessary to turn a book on a topic I considered of
burning interest—in the face of troubles far more serious—into a work of
history might never have been completed. Raghbendra Jha first suggested the topic and reignited an earlier interest in economic development discovered under the remarkable professional nurturance of Robert
T. Holt. No one who studied Yugoslavia escaped its spell of hospitality
and endless complexity; no one can escape the painful sense of loss over
its tragic death. Among my many hosts, I note especially Olga Supek,
Silva Mežnarić, Branko Horvat, Josip Županov, Zagorka Golubović, Radmila Nakarada, the librarians at the Zagreb Institute of Economics, Nikola
Uzunov, Boro Škegro, Tripo Mulina, and the late Kiril Miljovski. My
gratitude also goes to the many, many experts—economists, sociologists,
planners, historians, labor-bureau officials, and retired party officials—
who gave freely of their time and knowledge to make this book possible.

Daniel Turner produced the charts and graphs for the book, and Mil-
jenko Horvat provided informed research assistance. Judith Shapiro,
Louka Katseli, Gerry Arsenis, Deborah Milenkovitch, and Shirley Gedeon combined unquestioning friendship with invaluable support on economic issues; Elizabeth Brett, Sara and Nick Ohly, Pat Tracy, Martha
Lampland, Gail Kligman, and, above all, Vann Woodward and Don and
Betty Lampland sustained me.

Socialist Unemployment

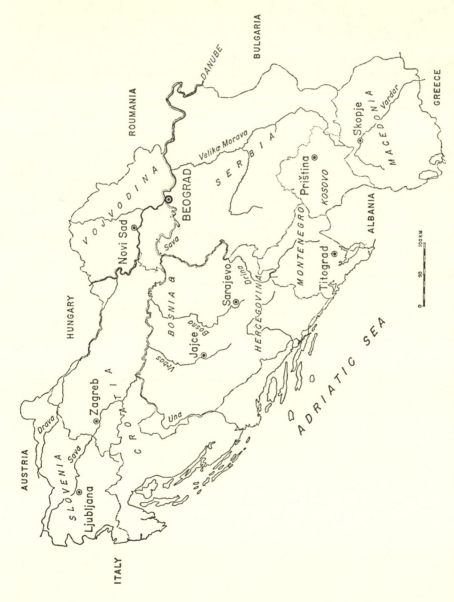

Figure 1-1. Map of Former Yugoslavia. *Source:* Hondius, *The Yugoslav Community of Nations.*

Chapter 1

INTRODUCTION: THE PARADOX
OF SOCIALIST UNEMPLOYMENT

UNEMPLOYMENT plays a pivotal role in the Marxist analysis of capitalism. At the symbolic level, unemployment exposed the myths of capitalism—its claims of economic growth and prosperity and of individual equality and justice through free markets and political rights. Labor organizers needed few arguments to convince workers who found their very survival dependent on employers' decisions to hire and fire that their vulnerability to unemployment reflected a constitutional inequality. The legal equality of citizenship could readily appear superficial to workers who saw privileges granted to profit makers while they themselves faced a trade-off between lower wages and unemployment. And despite the promise of continuous prosperity, economic growth was cyclical, and labor-shedding business downturns and periodic economic crises with mass unemployment were said to be necessary. At the analytical level, the irrationality of capitalist decision making was most easily demonstrated by citing unemployment—the waste of periodically idle human energy, plant, and equipment that seemed to be necessary to the dynamic equilibrium of free-market economies. At the political level, the threat of unemployment demonstrated that capitalism was not just a system of organizing the production and exchange of goods but a system of power, in which the fear of unemployment provided the essential discipline to keep labor in its place: to keep workers continually increasing their effort and output despite the limits on their share of realized profits and to keep them politically malleable even when their economic interests lay in radical change.

Among all the objectives of Marxist political movements, which sought political power in order to create an economic and social alternative to the evils of capitalist society, the end of unemployment was therefore a minimal condition—a *sine qua non*—of socialist society. This was so axiomatic that the achievement of full employment seemed unremarkable in countries governed by Marxist political parties. Few questioned the critics of socialist economies in their central focus on full employment and its guarantee of job security as the primary explanation for the decline of these economies in the 1980s (the fact that capitalist countries were experiencing a sharp rise in unemployment at the same time was not taken into account). It made sense that leaders of working-class parties would attempt to go even further than full employment, to design a world that would recognize human labor as central to individual identity and social interaction, the calculation of value in the economy, and human welfare and creativity. For all the euphoria over the collapse of the Berlin Wall in the former German Democratic Republic, the palpable sense of loss there over the disappearance of work-centered community in the year that followed reflected what socialists considered fundamental: that "work is how one makes sense of one's life, makes sense of one's place in nature."[1]

Socialist Yugoslavia was an exception to this world of full employment. The leadership of the Communist party acknowledged officially in 1950 that unemployment could exist under socialism, and the number of people registered as unemployed and as seeking work became ever larger as the years went by. In 1952, the newly reopened employment bureaus recorded a rate of unemployment at least two points above the 5 percent then considered the *normal rate*[2] in Western Europe; in 1985, when the number of Yugoslavs looking for work went above one million, the rate surpassed 15 percent, ranging from 1.5 percent in Slovenia to more than 30 percent in Kosovo and Macedonia.[3] Yet the Yugoslav leadership, more explicitly than in any other socialist state, had designed its society around the concept of community through labor, in which the core unit of social, economic, and political organization was the socialist workplace (called an *organization of associated labor*). The meaning of unemployment thus extended beyond the loss of potential wealth for society and the loss of income and identity for the unemployed that we associate with capitalist countries.[4] To be unemployed was to be excluded from full membership in society—a loss of full citizenship rights, a second-class status, a disenfranchisement.

The only theoretical attempt to explain Yugoslav unemployment—an analysis proposed in 1958 but accepted without question even in the late 1980s—identified the culprit as that organization of work and its concept of community. According to this theory, the country's system of decision making in labor-managed firms (called "worker self-management") gave employed workers too much power over the share of net profit going to

[1] John Berger, cited in Marzorati, "Living and Writing the Peasant Life," 50.

[2] This is the rate at which neoclassical economists consider market economies to be at full employment. It represents frictional unemployment caused by the job-search process, usually 4 or 5 percent.

[3] Mencinger, "Privredna reforma i nezaposlenost"; *Statistički godišnjak Jugoslavije*, 1990. Yugoslav newspapers and journals paid some attention to the symbolism of the one million mark.

[4] See Sen, *Employment, Technology, and Development*, on the three aspects of employment (production of some output or service; remuneration for work done; and reputation—a social status and identity associated with that work) and their measurement (4–5).

wages.[5] For the large number of scholars who studied and advocates who praised this experiment in economic democracy, unemployment was simply the price of allowing workers genuine participation in the life of their workplaces, analogous to the price paid by the unemployed under capitalism for society's economic prosperity.[6] For critics from the socialist camp (particularly economic reformers who wanted to introduce market socialism without accepting that the Yugoslav troubles were its result), as well as ones from the capitalist or anticommunist camp, it was obvious that the problem of Yugoslav socialism was its system of "workers' control." When high inflation also became a persistent problem, the analysis seemed doubly correct: if there were no worker participation, there would be no unemployment.

The denouement to Yugoslav socialism appears to be explained by this analysis. By legislative fiat, as the central plank in a program of radical economic reform, the government of prime minister Ante Marković in 1989 declared an end overnight to worker self-management on the grounds that it prevented the rational allocation of labor and the incentives necessary to higher productivity. No escape was possible from a decade of economic crisis, the argument went, unless unemployment became a threat to workers, managers were free to hire and fire, and potential foreign investors were assured of full private-property rights. But this economic paradox—that more unemployment is necessary to reduce unemployment—appears to ignore the more fundamental role of unemployment in socialist theory and practice.

The purpose of social ownership was not to provide job security but to reorganize economic activity and social relations fundamentally in order to make unemployment economically unnecessary and to deprive it of its political role. In that reorganization, job security was intended to be a direct incentive to effort and rising productivity of the kind attributed to systems with private ownership, while full employment was a political choice (if the literature on actual socialist countries is correct) on which the party's political legitimacy came to rest. Even analyses of unemployment in actual capitalist societies had shifted focus from the allocative and incentive roles of unemployment and a market-driven wage to the political and societal factors. The primary finding of the vast literature on coun-

[5] Ward, "The Firm in Illyria."

[6] Although most of the widespread theoretical and political writings on the system of self-management were positive and considered the price of unemployment (if they gave it consideration) worth paying, there were some who placed both the unemployment and the system of labor management and syndicalism into a broader revisionist critique, arguing that the leadership had simply restored capitalism; see, for example, Carlo, "Capitalist Restoration and Social Crisis in Yugoslavia."

tries that have achieved full or nearly full employment since World War II, in comparison with those where unemployment and labor-shedding recessions govern the economy, is that there is an explicit political commitment by the governing party to the goal of full employment.[7] The Keynesian revolution in the advanced industrial democracies after the Great Depression of the 1930s was an ideological revolution: a recognition that a market economy required macroeconomic management by governmental policies if it was to eliminate nonfrictional unemployment. The question in both market and planned economies was not whether the economy alone could prevent unemployment or what policies to adopt, but whether there was the political will and the political institutions necessary to implement those policies.[8] In both cases, the commitment came from labor-oriented parties that emerged to fight the consequences for labor of business-oriented, orthodox economic policy.

THE PARADOX

The Yugoslav exception to the rule of full employment in socialist states thus presents a political paradox—not as an economic problem but as a *political* fact. How could a ruling Communist party, claiming to represent the interests of labor and the theoretical analysis of Marx, ignore the political consequences of persistent and rising unemployment for almost forty years? The commonplace view of Communist party rule as a system of political repression, organized to give the party a monopoly on political power without its having to be accountable to a voting public or respond to political pressure from society, hardly explains how a system of rule can last forty years without attending to its legitimacy, if full employment was indeed the basis of that legitimacy. It does not explain why the party leadership did not at least experience a crisis of ideology or identity. On the contrary, it would suggest that the party had sufficient political power to implement its commitment to full employment.

Equally paradoxical was the great silence about Yugoslav unemployment in general. Most portraits of the Yugoslav system simply ignored its existence. From the common citizen to policymakers and politicians, analysts, critics, and protesters, a great public indifference to unemployment seemed to prevail.

This book represents an attempt to resolve this political paradox. What it proposes is that the models that have been used to analyze socialist

---

[7] Therborn, *Why Some Peoples Are More Unemployed than Others*, provides a good summary; he emphasizes that this political commitment must be present before the onset of economic crises induced by international conditions, such as that experienced by most countries in the late 1970s and the 1980s.

[8] See, for example, Weir and Skocpol, "State Structures."

societies are tied to a particular understanding of market economies and competitive politics that has little relation to the ordering principles of socialist states and societies. In the dominant model, people organized according to their economic interests. Those interests are defined above all by the institution of private property and its fundamental division between capital and labor, which defines individuals' political identities. Economic interests motivate people to enter public life, seeking to persuade others, organize collectively, and influence government to take courses of action that will further those interests.[9] Public policy is a result of such organized pressure, in which the competition among groups and the relative success of their demands depend on the balance of economic and organizational resources among them. Individuals may choose to organize on moral rather than economic grounds; but where there is a conflict between economic interest and ethical impulse, the model assumes that the former will win out. Whatever the short-term outcome of this competitive struggle to control government office, moreover, the long-term stability of a political system depends on its legitimacy. Policies and their outcomes must convince citizens that their government is acting in their interest, or is at least subject to being influenced accordingly. But it is short-term competition, not long-term legitimacy, that produces this accountability. The prevailing model of modern political life, in other words, imitates an ideological (theoretical) model of a market economy.

Expectations about the political role of unemployment have also been based on this model. Market economies, according to the model, are based on the fundamental conflict between profits and wages—in the aggregate, between price inflation and unemployment (the Phillips curve). In human terms, the conflict is between employers and workers: employers present workers with the choice between wage restraint and dismissal when profits are threatened. Because the political organization of interests reflects this "trade-off," so, too, do public policies. The distinction between governments that promote full employment and those that do not, scholars have found, is in the class basis of its ruling party. Proemployment governments tend to represent laboring constituents; political parties oriented to business interests are, as a rule, more concerned with price stability.[10] The difference between governing conservative and labor parties (when the particularities of national histories are removed by aggregate statistical analysis) is thus defined by their voters' economic interests on the issue of unemployment.

---

[9] Hirschman, *The Passions and the Interests*, analyzes the origins of this model in Western thought during the seventeenth century.

[10] Kirschen, *Economic Policy in Our Time*, first identified this correlation; see also Hibbs, "Political Parties and Macroeconomic Policy," for econometric evidence.

The paradox of unemployment in a socialist country thus arises from the historical fact that it was only when political parties representing the interests of labor won control over governments that explicit policies to promote employment and reverse the causes of unemployment were actually carried out. Wartime or business-oriented governments might achieve full employment, but only as a side effect rather than as a goal that could be politically sustained. Socialist and social democratic countries, on the other hand, explicitly aimed at full employment.

The very idea of unemployment, as something publicly recognized and distinct from the condition of poverty, vagabondage, and homelessness with which it was bound once public responsibility for poor relief began in the seventeenth century, began with the political pressure for government action in the second half of the nineteenth century from industrial unions, social movements, and political parties representing the interests of workers.[11] One of the best-organized, most conspicuous interest groups in modern societies—industrial workers, and wage earners more broadly—organized first in the early stages of industrialization into social-action leagues and craft unions in order to control access to employment, bargain more effectively for job rights, and provide mutual insurance during periods of unemployment. The appearance of mass unemployment in industrial societies after the 1880s increasingly pushed workers directly into the political arena because it became clear that atomized skirmishes with individual employers and local control over access to employment were insufficient.

The problem of unemployment was not only economic but political as well. Workers' wages and jobs depended on their capacity to bargain in the labor market, and that bargaining power depended on the level of employment; economic position and political strength rose and fell together. Unemployment thus had a *dual face*. As long as there was unemployment, workers' attempts as individuals or unions to improve their economic position were threatened by the right of employers to fire workers and dispose of their capital as they wished. Political organization to counteract that threat with an equal threat to withhold labor and disrupt production was always vulnerable to defection from members who could not risk being replaced by an unemployed worker willing to work for less. As long as workers' organizations could not promise their members protection against this competition, they found it difficult to exact the discipline that successful protest requires.

This meant that workers' economic interests were inevitably bound

[11] See, for example, Garraty, *Unemployment in History;* Hattam, "Economic Visions and Political Strategies"; and Tilly, Tilly, and Tilly, *The Rebellious Century*. But see also Keyssar, *Out of Work,* for sources of variation in the social context of work.

with the interests of the unemployed in escaping unemployment. Workers might choose to unite in craft or professional unions in order to raise incomes and protect jobs by policing artificial scarcities within sectors of the labor market, at the cost of unemployment for other workers; but the shortsightedness of this "trade-union consciousness" would be revealed when the anarchy of capitalist decision making produced another downturn in the business cycle (or even an economic crisis) and their rising wage share became the focus of cuts they did not have the power to fight. Only if they could unify and sustain such organization could they hope to overcome the trade-off through collective bargaining, political rights, and governmental policy.

Studies of the consequences of mass unemployment during the depression of the 1930s by social psychologists in Austria and Poland revealed another aspect of the link between the fate of individual workers and that of all wage earners, this time from the point of view of the unemployed. The researchers discovered that the psychological effects of unemployment made organization by the unemployed in their own behalf a rare event. Their time occupied by the struggle for survival and their efforts increasingly discouraged and diverted to the search for explanations of their own inadequacy, unemployed persons tended to become apathetic and to personalize the cause of their plight, responses that worked against collective action for change.[12] The link between their economic interest and the political organization to translate that interest into effective demand had to be made by people who had jobs and who understood that their long-term self-interest lay in common cause with all who live by their labor. Conversely, later studies suggest, where political organization in behalf of the unemployed comes from people motivated not by their own economic interest but by moral conviction or sympathy, their organizations do not have the staying power and cohesion necessary to be effective.[13]

Labor-oriented governments, in successfully promoting full employment, built on this recognition of the link between economic and political interests, between what happens to individual workers and to workers collectively, and between workers' position in the labor market and their political power. In addition to making an explicit political commitment to aim at full employment, parties representing the economic interests of laboring and small-property constituencies were able to reverse the slide

---

[12] Jahoda, Lazarsfeld, and Zeisel, *Marienthal*, 22–25; Jahoda, *Employment and Unemployment*. Later explanations of political organization, led by Olson in *The Logic of Collective Action*, reverted to the economic school.

[13] Schlozman and Verba, *Injury to Insult*; but see Rivers, "Micro-Economics and Macro-Politics," for ways that a solidarity of interests on unemployment may emerge among people of different economic interests without explicit political organization.

into ever-greater unemployment and in many cases to achieve full employment because of their attitude toward the role of the state. Governmental policy was viewed as a positive instrument to counterbalance the cycles of market activity or to make up for market failures, and labor-oriented governments had the political capacity to implement such economic policies at both the macroeconomic and microeconomic levels. Indeed, the literature on advanced industrial economies, independent of a political motivation of economic interest, identifies success in minimizing unemployment with the political capacity to employ an active, countercyclical policy of demand management and an active labor-market policy that permits flexible adjustment in wages and labor mobility without the economic and psychological costs of unemployment.[14]

The political factors necessary to this capacity, according to the literature, are a broad consensus on the need for a macrosystems approach to the economy;[15] a set of economic institutions appropriate to countercyclical demand management and effective exchange-rate policy;[16] and centralized institutions of bargaining between organized labor and capital that enable labor to negotiate trade-offs between wage restraint and some socialization of the risk of unemployment (through social welfare and active labor-market assists).[17] Labor-oriented governments tend to be most successful because they are more likely to be not only politically committed to macroeconomic regulation, but also tied to strong, peak unions that have won the right to represent labor in centralized collective bargaining and that have the power over their membership to guarantee labor's discipline in implementing agreements, including wage restraint (a system often referred to as corporatism). In the language of this school of explanation, the *power resources* with which wage earners translate their interests into effective aggregate demand are critical.[18]

The best demonstration of this argument seemed to be the socialist states of the Soviet mold. Instead of counteracting market forces with governmental policy, working-class political parties used their organizational power to create, through social ownership and economic planning, a permanent capacity to achieve full employment. Indeed, full employment was portrayed by supporters as one of the primary achievements of

[14] See especially Scharpf, "Economic and Institutional Constraints of Full-Employment Strategies."

[15] Lehmbruch, "Liberal Corporatism and Party Government."

[16] Weir and Skocpol, "State Structures."

[17] See Katzenstein, *Corporatism and Change;* Cameron, "Social Democracy"; and Esping-Andersen, *Politics against Markets.*

[18] The literature on European social democracies is rich with these findings. See Korpi and Shalev, "Strikes, Power, and Politics"; Korpi, *The Democratic Class Struggle;* Scharpf, "Economic and Institutional Constraints"; Cameron, "Social Democracy"; and Katzenstein, *Corporatism and Change.*

socialism. Even critics saw it as the basis of socialism's political legitimacy. A functional equivalent of the electoral mechanism was said to
exist in a *social contract* between government and people, in which citizens were guaranteed job and income security in exchange for their political support. Internal critics who saw this as state paternalism nonetheless
agreed that the state defined and provided for citizens' economic interests
in exchange for limits on their political expression of demands.[19]

Thus, according to the history of working-class organizations in capitalist societies and the experience of socialist states, unemployment should
never have reached the proportions it did in socialist Yugoslavia. Governed throughout its forty-five-year history by a Marxist party, the
League of Communists of Yugoslavia, the country should have had the
political will to achieve full employment. Because the ruling party also
created institutions within each workplace and locality where workers'
representatives decided jointly with management on all business and employment matters, it should have had the political capacity as well. Unemployment should have led to declining legitimacy and a rejection of the
pact on political passivity. The country should have experienced waves of
organized protest as the party's own working-class constituency demanded a change in policy. Nothing of the sort happened.

EMPLOYMENT AND THE POLITICAL MODEL OF SOCIALIST STATES

The industrial model with its trade-union trade-off between wages and
jobs came to dominate the understanding and study of political behavior
in socialist states as well in the late 1970s, after the totalitarian model was
discredited. The dynamic of socialist societies was defined by the absence
of restraint that was provided in capitalist market economies by the economic interests and political power of private capital—restraint on the
"investment hunger" of firms and on the "paternalism" of governments,
which aimed at job security but led to a shortage economy;[20] and the
restraint imposed by the threat of unemployment to keep workers' demands in check. The full employment that provided these systems' re-
puted legitimacy was illusory, according to internal critics. A vast "hidden
unemployment" or "overfull employment"[21] concealed a "gross underuti-
lization of labor"[22] that both limited the potential for economic growth and
repressed living standards. The only difference between socialist states of

---

[19] Pravda, "East-West Interdependence and the Social Compact in Eastern Europe";
Hauslohner, "Gorbachev's Social Contract."

[20] Kornai, *The Economics of Shortage.*

[21] Granick, *Job Rights in the Soviet Union*, 1.

[22] Adam, *Employment Policies in the Soviet Union and Eastern Europe*, xiii.

the Soviet model and Yugoslavia was that unemployment in the latter was open not hidden.

The open-unemployment variant was due to the consequences of worker self-management, according to Benjamin Ward's model to explain Yugoslav unemployment—which he appropriately labeled not market socialism but market syndicalism. Ward argued that because workers in labor-managed firms in Yugoslavia had the power to choose between new investment and individual incomes, they would limit the hiring of additional workers among whom net profit would have to be distributed. The conflict of interest between individual workers' wages and other workers' jobs was greater, in Ward's model, under social ownership than under capitalism because workers' power over labor-market questions had no contraints.[23]

In Hungary and Poland, unemployment took the form instead of declining standards of living and eventually economic crisis, but the explanation was the same. According to Charles Sabel and David Stark, full employment gave Hungarian workers substantial shop-floor bargaining power. Because the objective function of managers was to fulfill output targets on time, they conceded to workers' demands for higher wages in order to prevent them from leaving for higher wages elsewhere. To meet their expanding wage bill, managers then bargained with higher authorities for exceptions and subsidies. Whether they obtained subventions on plan targets, supplies from industrial ministries, or money advances from banks for the wage bill, the result was to reduce the resources available for new investment and eventually, when government authorities tackled the consequences for growth rates, to produce investment cycles that looked very much like their capitalist counterparts.[24] Alex Pravda and George Feiwel argue that the Polish case of declining growth and hidden unemployment resulted from the political power of workers in a socialist state rather than the economic power of workers in firms operating under full employment. Because the legitimacy of a Communist party government depended on the active support of workers, workers who organized to demand higher wages or lower consumer prices trapped political authorities into an affirmative response. These wage or price concessions created inflation, to which authorities also had to respond; the result in Poland was a political cycle of strike waves and bargaining between government and workers over incomes policy (wages and prices) that led to

---

[23] See chapter 6 for a fuller discussion of Ward's model.

[24] Sabel and Stark, "Politics, Planning, and Shop-floor Power." Other studies of the Hungarian labor market insist that workers' bargaining power and managers' strategies varied substantially, depending on workers' skill levels; but this refinement fits better with the argument that will be developed in this book. See Kertesi and Sziráckzi, "The Institutional System, Labour Market, and Segmentation in Hungary."

"premature consumerism." Resources were diverted from investment to workers' consumption, lowering the economy's potential for long-term growth and creating a new round of goods shortages, price inflation, and successful demands for higher wages.[25]

Thus, according to these theses, the economic crisis of socialist countries and their political collapse by the end of the 1980s—beginning in Poland and Hungary and spreading throughout the region—were the result of workers' interest in higher wages and their bargaining power. In some cases the pressure was political, exerted through wage strikes and demonstrations that threatened the core of the governments' legitimacy; in other cases it was economic, as workers took advantage of tight labor markets to bargain with managers in their firms and the managers in turn bargained with economic authorities. The normative conclusion was increasingly being drawn: that nothing short of political revolution would make possible real economic reform. The property rights of workers to a job, its compensations, and its status were seen as traditional (in the sense of outmoded).[26] For a modern, effective economy, these rights had to be replaced by mechanisms for more efficient allocation of resources: market wages, the disciplinary threat of unemployment, and a renegotiation of the social contract to replace governments' labor constituency with entrepreneurs. Privatization, market economies, and parliamentary governments with limits on their authority to respond economically to workers' demands were the only way out of the soft budget constraints[27] and shortages due to excess demand that had brought these countries to economic crisis.

Even those who still held to socialist values argued that any peaceful, parliamentary transition to socialism was a utopian dream that would necessarily be interrupted by economic crisis because the election of a socialist government would remove existing restraints on popular expectations. Demands for improved standards of living would rise faster than the capacity of the economy to produce results, leaving the government with a choice between economic crisis or abandoning both its wage-earning constituency and democracy for repression. Such new governments would be

---

[25] Pravda, "Poland 1980"; Feiwel, "Causes and Consequences of Disguised Industrial Unemployment in a Socialist Economy."

[26] Although Walder's argument in *Communist Neo-Traditionalism* was based on China, East European social scientists received it enthusiastically as a portrait of their regimes as well.

[27] The term *soft budget constraints* in regard to socialist economies was introduced by the Hungarian economist János Kornai in *The Economics of Shortage*. Although he argued that bailouts of large firms in capitalist countries also represented such "softness," and that in socialist countries cooperatives and private sector firms did have to operate by "hard budget constraints," the term came close to becoming an explanation for most of the economic and social ills of late socialism.

too politically fragile to manage the trade-off between investment and consumption in the face of populist demands and would collapse.[28]

The idea that socialist states had not created full employment but only a perverse, upside-down version of capitalist societies—where workers' excess power placed limits on growth, job security pushed the cost onto wages, and states were too weak to resist workers' pressure—was politically very persuasive. It fit well with the prevailing model of politics based on economic interests and their political organization. It did not challenge the prevailing orthodoxy of conservative reaction in the 1980s, which explained the global stagflation of the 1970s as a result of trade-union power and rising wage shares that had to be reversed. And it was a satisfactory replacement for the totalitarian model, demonstrating not only that there was political life in socialist states but also that, contrary to the argument that states were too strong, they were in reality too weak.

This idea also provided an answer to the question of legitimacy in the political paradox of socialist unemployment, which the revolutionary events of 1989–90 in Eastern Europe had appeared to question. The massive exodus from the German Democratic Republic (GDR) in the east, as citizens left secure jobs and incomes for the Federal Republic of Germany in the west, where unemployment was high and publicized, clearly seemed to belie the model's assumptions that workers' interests lie with full employment and that in socialist states they had been willing to trade political passivity and grant legitimacy in exchange for that full employment. The political revolutions in the East began where full employment reigned—in Hungary, Poland, Czechoslovakia, the GDR, and Romania. In Yugoslavia, democratization and the fatal attack on the constitutional position of the Communist party occurred in Slovenia, which enjoyed full employment, instead of in Serbia, Macedonia, or Bosnia-Herzegovina, where even officially recorded unemployment captured a quarter of the potential labor force or more. These events had also revived the totalitarian model, with its assumption of a hierarchy of values in society according to which people universally prefer freedom above economic security—even though its adherents did not explain why the desire for freedom lay dormant for most of the postwar period or why it was capable of radical action only in 1989. For most scholars, however, the model of economic interest, political demand, and the economic trade-offs of market economies fit these events better. An economic crisis resulting from too much worker power had motivated this upsurge out of political apathy or passivity.

The difficulty with this argument in the case of Yugoslavia was its fairy-

---

[28] Przeworski, *Capitalism and Social Democracy*, 43–46; idem, *Democracy and the Market*, chap. 4.

tale relation to the facts. Workers' wages declined as rapidly as unemployment rose during the stagflation of the 1970s and the economic crisis of the 1980s. Workers' self-management had been introduced in 1950 exactly at an early-revolutionary point of political fragility in order to obtain wage restraint. It was scarcely a system of worker control, even though it may have in some aspects created a labor aristocracy among those employed in labor-managed firms.[29] Ward's elegantly persuasive model was never intended to be a description of Yugoslavia and could not be verified there empirically.[30] As in the case of the Eastern bloc countries, the application of ideological assumptions based on capitalist market economies to critique a socialist system suggests a political purpose more than a trustworthy analysis. Moreover, Ward's model of labor-managed firms said nothing about government policy; and it lacked an analysis of political dynamics, which would have been necessary to explain the reality and the political paradox of open socialist unemployment.[31]

The Key Role of Economic Ideology in Shaping Socialist States

The assumption guiding this book on Yugoslav socialism is that the economic crisis of the 1980s and the revolutionary end to Marxist states in Europe were not sufficient to explain away the political paradox of unemployment in a socialist country. The explanation of that paradox offered here leads to a different accounting for the economic crisis and political revolutions. In providing an answer, this study has more in common with another political model of socialist states—the model of Leninist regimes—and its basis in ideology, an explanatory variable out of favor for market economies.[32] But the concept of Leninist regimes used here re-

[29] This is the implication of Estrin's study *Self-Management: Economic Theory and Yugoslav Practice.*

[30] See Smith, "Does Employment Matter to the Labour-Managed Firm?" Ward himself cautioned against seeing his model of the firm in "Illyria" as an analysis of the Yugoslav system, although he did come to believe that the Yugoslav system would tend to have more unemployment than an equivalent capitalist country (personal communication, fall 1989).

[31] Comisso, *Workers' Control under Plan and Market*, provides one possible political dynamic for a society composed of labor-managed firms—an alternation between pressures for greater autonomy and demands for governmental regulation, or between what she calls "market" and "plan." But this does not explain the choice of economic policies relating to unemployment or the absence of political pressures to address unemployment.

[32] The concept of Leninist regimes was an offshoot of the totalitarian school, developed primarily by Jowitt in *Revolutionary Breakthroughs and National Development* (and more explicitly in "An Organizational Approach to the Study of Political Culture in Marxist-Leninist Systems" and "Inclusion and Mobilization in European Leninist Regimes") on the basis of Selznick, *The Organizational Weapon*; and Schurmann, *Ideology and Organization in Communist China.*

fers only to a subset of socialist states known as regimes of the reform-communist persuasion. And while that concept gives priority to a revolutionary party's organizational principles and democratic centralism, the concept in this book begins with economic ideology.

The political system and politics of Yugoslav society did mirror its economy, in the way seen in capitalist market economies. But the ideology behind that economy was different, as was the society it shaped. The primary characteristic of socialist societies is that they originate with a political project, the project of a political elite. That project begins in the same way as did the model of liberal market economies—with an economic analysis of existing society, the political organization of economic interests, and policy choices that reflect the organizational and economic resources of a party's potential constituents and allies. But at the point at which we encounter the ideology—when the leadership achieved power and attempted to create a new society—it was a platform and an explicit *strategy* for change.

When studies of Communist regimes emphasize ideology, they tend to mean by *Marxism-Leninism* an attitude toward political power or a political structure—usually an unresponsive dogmatism or an organizational rigidity, as implied in the concepts of Leninism, totalitarianism, and democratic centralism. *Ideology* is here used instead as in capitalist regimes, to mean a set of economic ideas and the social and political relations appropriate to them. Those ideas defined goals, but also ways of thinking and perception. The ideology was built around a conception of economic growth and the social organization of labor—of employment in production and administration—that it implied. To understand the political responses to socialist unemployment, by both policymakers and those threatened by unemployment, one must begin with that ideology.

The central focus on economic growth served two purposes for Communist parties in power—one socialist, the other nationalist. The first goal was to increase capital so as to overcome the burden of underdevelopment, in ways that avoided the costs—including mass unemployment—that the capitalist way entailed for people who labor in factory, farm, or office. The second was to end the cycles of foreign economic and political dependence to which second-class status in the international arena had condemned these countries. The failure of previous governments to industrialize and to secure national independence was portrayed as a form of betrayal—as a consequence of antipopular and antilabor policies. According to the leader of the Yugoslav Communist party, only a prolabor party would put the interests of the Yugoslav peoples above foreign interests. They based their legitimacy as a ruling party on their commitment to the individual benefits of this economic growth—rising standards of living, secure subsistence, and national pride.

Industrialization and political independence of the state did not come easily. In contrast to the Marxist focus on the dynamics of capitalism and the subsequent stages of evolution toward socialism, Communist parties came to power in agrarian societies at early stages of capitalist and industrial development in countries outside the economic and political core of the global system. No fact was of greater consequence for Marxist revolutionary strategy and policy than these political origins because the parties' goals (particularly as defined by the influential German Social Democratic party in the late nineteenth century) had presumed the most advanced stages of capitalism, "bourgeois" political development, and internationalism. The states they created became developmentalist states instead. Paradoxically, these parties representing labor found that their most pressing problem was the shortage of capital—of machines, financial capital (domestic savings and access to global capital markets), and the human skills and mentality appropriate to industrial and technologically advanced society. Because they came to power through war in areas formerly ruled by the Russian, Habsburg, and Ottoman empires (and later by the British, French, and Americans) where the national question was still not settled, and because they faced a hostile international environment, internationalism was not the political result of the globalization of capital but a defensive response against its consequence for nations on the economic periphery. The issues of national identity, vulnerability, and territorial defense loomed far larger.

Marxist parties were not alone in their developmentalism, however. They shared it with all "latecomers" to the process of industrialization and nation-state formation.[33] The model of economic development based on the English experience of the seventeenth century occurred nowhere else, despite initial steps in Italy, the Netherlands, and India. Even in England, the spontaneous emergence of merchants and manufacturers depended on particular international conditions, and they succeeded in their mutual competition to influence state policy in their favor, as Joyce Appleby argues, only after they discovered an economic theory—an ideology—that was appropriate to those interests.[34]

The process of interstate competition that gave developmentalism its force was aided by the rise of economics as a profession and economists as a power in the nineteenth century, and by the mid-twentieth century no leaders of any state or aspiring state could ignore the temptation to use rational designs to enhance both power and authority. Theorists of socialist states in Europe claim Weber's fourth type of authority legitimation,

---

[33] Levy, *Modernization: Latecomers and Survivors;* Gerschenkron, *Economic Backwardness in Historical Perspective;* Kitching, *Development and Underdevelopment in Historical Perspective;* Berend and Ránki, *The European Periphery and Industrialization.*

[34] Appleby, *Economic Thought and Ideology in Seventeenth-Century England.*

Wertrationalität, as their particularity.[35] But it was common to many
states after the mid-nineteenth century, as the perception of their "backwardness" in relation to "more-developed" societies led states to use economic ideas and reasoned, *ex ante* designs in the service of a project to
catch up with the rich and powerful.[36] Socialist states, beginning with the
Bolshevik Revolution in 1917, only perfected and expanded this idea of
directed change to fully *societal* projects on the lines of grand strategy,
copying from the military tactics that the revolutionary parties had
chosen.

In contrast with the neoclassical economic model (and its Keynesian
variant) that informs the prevailing political model of modern societies,
this developmentalist project in Marxist-Leninist states was based in classical thought and its emphasis on structural change. The object of economic activity was to produce goods that would satisfy the needs of
consumers (the use value of final goods), but this required above all an
increase in society's productive capacity. Unemployment was not a theoretical problem for Marxists any more than it was for other classical theorists, but it was a political problem. A properly functioning economy
would have no unemployment; it would be self-regulating and would
need no external adjustments. But unemployment could occur if there
was insufficient capital to employ labor productively. The capacity to employ society's members was dependent on increases in productive capacity and was therefore hostage to who made investment decisions and by
what criteria. For liberal theorists, the rightful decision-makers were producers as property owners. Producers were also at the center of socialist
theory, but investment decisions could not be left to private prerogatives
and the motive of private gain alone, or to the secondary uncertainty
resulting from autonomous decision making in a market economy that
often made it unprofitable to invest in the infrastructure, producers'
goods, and even raw materials that were necessary to expanding productive capacity (industrialization).[37]

The crucial concept in this Marxian societywide project for capital formation and sustainable growth was *productive labor*. According to the
classical notion (whether physiocratic or cameralist, Marxian or Ricardian), growth occurred only through increases in real value—*net*, or *surplus*, value accumulated from production where the yield from human
labor exceeded that which was necessary to reproduce both that labor and

[35] See Fehér, Heller, and Márkus, *Dictatorship over Needs*.

[36] For a good example in a country that later adopted socialism for the same reason, see
Janos, *The Politics of Backwardness in Historical Perspective: Hungary, 1825–1945*.

[37] T. C. Koopmans coined the phrase "secondary uncertainty"; see Dobb's exposition in
Welfare Economics and the Economics of Socialism, 121–52.

all other, unproductive uses of human labor in society.[38] Value added in production was not only a monetary category of revenue above costs of production, but necessarily a real category: the wages of those whose labor created value represented *wage goods* (goods that workers would consume in the course of producing other goods, the level of which was based on a conception of subsistence that was set culturally and in social interaction). The *subsistence fund* for society defined the limit to economic growth. It depended not only on how many were consuming that fund in relation to how many were creating it (the calculation of this ratio incorporated both Malthusian considerations of population growth in which economic growth encouraged birthrates to rise, and classical analyses of class structure in which there were unproductive parasites such as landlords, lawyers, clergy, and aristocrats' servants living off the product of others), but also on the productivity of the industries producing those basic consumption goods and on the price of the goods.

There were two ways to increase growth. One was to encourage bringing as much of society's resources as possible into productive use and to reduce to a minimum the drain of resources into unproductive endeavors. In the colorful language of the physiocrats, for example, merchants' profits were "leeches sucking off" agricultural and industrial producers. All but essential administrators, preferably chosen by examination for professional skill, were "sterile"; bureaucrats only rarely contributed to the increase of productive output.[39] Naturally, the way a society *organized* its activities, including the offices and activities of the state, could be more or less wasteful. The second way to increase growth was to "capitalize" labor itself—by increasing individuals' capacity to raise their marginal output through use of machinery, application of science, new production techniques, organizational rationalizations, and education ("human capital"). Labor's reward should include incentives to higher productivity and capitalization; people would thus be defined in terms of their relative productivity—for example, according to skill, experience, output, or managerial abilities.

The goal of increasing the net output of society meant that rights to ownership and to the organization of economic activity should be handed to producers. By reuniting the functions of labor, commerce, manufacturing, and finance into a single association of workers, they would save on costs while work incentives would rise. A rational economic plan to coordinate the activities of individual associations and avoid the problems of secondary uncertainty would guide producers' economic decisions. The

[38] J. Roemer, *Free to Lose*, is a particularly lucid presentation of this guiding concept.
[39] Appleby, *Economic Thought and Ideology in Seventeenth-Century England*, 107, 134; Dobb, *Theories of Value and Distribution since Adam Smith*, 41.

crises of capitalism had taught that the separate role of money—the separation of production from finance, and autonomous decision making coordinated only by the price mechanism—could independently depreciate the value added by labor, whether through falling real wages, unemployment, or state debt and financial crises that prolonged resolution of the problem.[40] It was in society's interest to ensure a balance between the goods necessary to production (both producers' goods and wage goods) and the goods that represented an increase in its standard of living, and to prevent an autonomous role for money and finance.

From this economic ideology there also followed a view of the state and political relations. As a political organization in capitalist societies, Marxist parties argued, government took the guise of a neutral intermediary in the conflict between forces separated by the institution of private ownership; but its actions were not those of a disinterested arbiter, and so it actually served to mask the real structure of power in society. As an economic organization, it also imposed an additional layer of exploitation (rents and taxes) on labor's surplus, wasting resources on the coercive instruments necessary to maintain the power of both employers and rulers. Social ownership, on the other hand, would eliminate the need for such an organization. It could therefore eliminate the coercive power of taxation and police and the wastefulness of unproductive consumption by bureaucracies. The state would become less and less necessary. Economic and social functions could be reintegrated into associations of workers (producers), and although this would not eliminate all disagreements or conflicts of interest, they would no longer reflect an unbreachable divide between capital and labor.

There remained disputes among socialist parties and schools of thought—as there were among schools of classical economists—over, for example, what constituted value in a monetized society and therefore over how to price labor.[41] A policy of industrialization and a system of differentiated economic incentives would create differences in a socialist society according to workers' individual "capital" or the economic branch in which they worked. Disagreements over the optimal scale of production, particularly in agriculture, and over the pace of development and its political implications—for consumption standards and investment preferences and for which groups would benefit more from the resulting policy choices—remained unresolved in the socialist legacy and laid the basis for

[40] Rucciardi, "Rereading Marx on the Role of Money and Finance in Economic Development," is a rare example of attention to the crucial role of money and the causes of financial crisis in Marx's political as well as economic analysis and also in later Marxian theorizing.

[41] See Dobb, *Theories of Value and Distribution*, 112–20; and Milenkovitch, *Plan and Market in Yugoslav Economic Thought*, 21–31, 44–50, 230–49.

factional disputes.[42] Even the Soviet model, despite its image as a dogmatic blueprint of development and organization forcibly imposed on other societies, contained within it alternative paths and choices on development strategy and its associated policies and organization that reflected these disputes. This was most obvious in the Soviet debates on strategy of the 1920s,[43] although the debates revived after World War II and every decade thereafter in competing schools of policy and their political factions.

But a major assumption of socialist theory was that no economic conflicts in a society with social ownership would be inevitably unreconcilable in the way that private ownership of property created truly antagonistic relations between classes. Individuals were supposed to be guided by their economic interests—the Smithian assumption was nowhere rejected—but social ownership removed the artificial obstacles to their natural cooperativeness. Conflict between individuals' incomes or jobs and their common interest in economic growth was only a matter of time horizons, and it could be handled by education and the feedback of real growth. The institutions for regulating conflict could presume cooperation.

The societies created on the basis of Marxist ideology were organized on principles different from those of market economies with private ownership. Their politics, therefore, did not follow the market logic. The political correlate of the dynamic concept of the trade-off between capital and labor, investment and employment, was not a contest between parties and organized interests representing private owners of capital on the one hand and people who labor on the other. It was instead a range of policies for economic growth and its distribution, proposed by economists and government ministries; these policies benefited certain groups, firms, sectors, and regions but did not result from pressure by them. The swings portrayed in most analyses of socialist policy between utopia and development, vision and reality, "red" and "expert,"[44] were alternations between

[42] For a good introduction to the agricultural debates, see Mitrany, *Marx against the Peasant*, 7–23; see also Cox, *Peasants, Class, and Capitalism*. On the debates over pace, A. Erlich, *The Soviet Industrialization Debate*, remains extremely useful; see also Lewin, *Political Undercurrents in Soviet Economic Debates;* Dobb, *Soviet Economic Development since 1917;* and V. Gligorov, *Gledišta i sporovi o industrijalizaciji u socijalizmu.* Kitching, *Development and Underdevelopment*, is particularly helpful in showing the tensions among the Ricardian socialist, Listian nationalist, and Marxian strands within the socialist movement.

[43] A. Erlich, *The Soviet Industrialization Debate;* Lewin, *Political Undercurrents;* and Dobb, *Soviet Economic Development since 1917*, are still particularly useful sources.

[44] Löwenthal, "Development vs. Utopia in Communist Policy," is the classic work of this very large genre (most analyses being based on the Chinese case).

particular approaches to economic growth and their corresponding party factions. To implement a shift in approach required organizational and regulatory reform, not only of production and exchange but also of the state. Political authorities attempted to capture savings and control allocation not for the purpose of dominance alone[45] (although such motives may be found in any system), but also for the purpose of executing a particular economic theory. The precondition, however, was to obtain and protect political independence over domestic economic decisions; to do so required protecting above all national sovereignty, then the system of social ownership of capital, and within that system jurisdictional distinctions in public authority over economic assets. Policy alternations occurred primarily, it turned out, in response to changing international conditions that affected capital accumulation, the capacity to trade, and national security.

The antimilitarism of liberal economists, from the physiocrats on through Marx, left them ill-equipped to conceptualize war readiness as a part of a functioning economy.[46] The part of their conceptual tradition that could do so—the mercantilist and cameralist legacy—included a vision of the state, however, that the Yugoslav party leaders rejected. Finding a modus vivendi in the cold-war international order to suit their precondition of independent choice in economic strategy, they devised a peculiar international balancing act among the three camps of that international order. But the adjustments required to maintain the country's balance of foreign payments and those required for defense were often in conflict; similarly, the leaders' ideological preferences for economic strategy and political organization often clashed with the requirements of national sovereignty and defense. The result was a domestic contradiction that had already emerged during World War II—between what I will call the "Slovene model" of the ruling strategy and the "Foča conditions" (see chapter 2) that made the strategy possible. That contradiction defined the country's political dynamic as it altered economic policy in response to changing international conditions.

The methods that replaced the market in allocating factors of production varied among socialist societies, and so, therefore, did political organization. In the Yugoslav case of the class of reform-communist states, policies were debated in elected assemblies of citizen-producers representing autonomous organizations of "associated labor" and among factions of the single political party (as tended to be true in hegemonic

[45] Verdery, *National Ideology under Socialism*, has a very useful summary of these "modes of control" (74–87).

[46] Even Alexander Erlich's otherwise highly respected analysis of the Soviet debates on development strategy in the 1920s ignores the central role that defense and the army played in these debates and subsequent policy—with the result of crucial misinterpretations, according to Mark von Hagen (personal communication).

parties of the same historical period, such as the Liberal Democrats of Japan and the Christian Democrats of Italy). In place of the competitive mechanisms and decision rules of electoral and pressure-group politics, the political system was based on consensual or proportional mechanisms for defining rules by which money, goods, and people would be allocated or redistributed among economic interests. Instead of a choice between wages and jobs, there was a more or less continuous (but not frictionless) adjustment of the methods of employing labor aimed at improving the conditions for increasing both wages and jobs; the reorganization of society to use labor more productively and rules defining labor incentives that aimed to increase productivity would together increase aggregate economic growth.

Because all individuals were defined by their labor (and their capacity to create capital, usually measured by their individual contribution to productivity), the way that employment was organized defined the structure of society and the main lines of political life and conflict. The mechanisms of what Claus Offe calls a second logic alongside that of capital—a countervailing political force that people vulnerable to unemployment can wield against those who have power over economic decisions, whether through labor's organization against capital or popular opposition against the state—did not exist in Yugoslavia.[47] Instead, individuals sought to prevent their own unemployment by increasing their personal capital and individual access to employment and by resisting a demotion in their regulated social status. Employers (firms and governments) in turn competed to retain as much autonomy as possible over their assets while increasing their access to additional funds. There were as a result three very separate spheres of political action within the country, as defined by the leaders' original political-economic strategy: property owners' strategies toward capital assets, individuals' strategies regarding employment and status, and the mass of people left outside this public sector of political activity, including the unemployed. Only the first influenced policy, but the actions of all three shaped the evolution of Yugoslavia and its similarities with and differences from other socialist states.

PLACING THE YUGOSLAV CASE: SINGULAR HISTORIES AND COMMON REFORM STRATEGIES

In their comparative project on the size and incidence of unemployment and the response to it in Western Europe, North America, and Australia during the Great Depression, Barry Eichengreen and T. J. Hatton find no

---

[47] Offe, "Two Logics of Collective Action."

common pattern across countries, except that world depression is indeed reflected in large-scale domestic unemployment. Both before and after the Depression, countries varied substantially in the rate of unemployment, in the economic and social groups that were unemployed, and in the social consequences of unemployment. "Only in the early 1930s is a common pattern evident," write Eichengreen and Hatton.[48] For the crisis decade of 1973–84, similarly, Goran Therborn finds no general pattern for rates and incidence of unemployment in countries of the Organization for Economic Cooperation and Development (OECD)—only country-specific, historically defined profiles.[49]

This case study of unemployment in socialist Yugoslavia from 1945 to 1990 is based on this finding that countries have their own specific profiles, particularly in patterns of work, employment, and unemployment. It is also intended as a theoretical case study, however, with its assumption that these profiles are based on variables that are common across countries. The variable of developmental ideology, discussed above, places Yugoslavia in the universe of other socialist states; they had much in common because they shared the same legacy of developmentalist thought, the socialist debates in nineteenth-century Europe, and (for states outside the USSR) experiences with Soviet policy. Thus, despite the attention paid to Yugoslavia's system of "workers' control" and "market socialism" as different from state-socialist systems of the Soviet type in Eastern Europe, the similarities in employment structure between Yugoslavia and those countries (with the exception of women's participation in the labor force—related, as will be seen, to the issue of unemployment) point to a fundamental commonality.

Their differences arose from adapting this common legacy to the local imperatives of political struggle. The socialist parties' search for allies outside the industrial working class (in agriculture and sections of the urban middle class) as they formed a social movement for revolution and identified a domestic enemy, in conjunction with Comintern policy regarding political alliances, defined the social basis of each party when it came to power. Differences also arose from the international conditions under which the party competed for power and from the country's geopolitical and global economic positions. The effect of these differences in the composition of the party's political constituency and in international position was substantial variation—within a common ideology—in governmental policy, just as among market economies. It is this variation in governmen-

[48] Eichengreen and Hatton, *Interwar Unemployment in International Perspective*, p. 51.
[49] Therborn, *Why Some Peoples Are More Unemployed than Others*. Boltho finds the same variation in European countries' experience with inflation (*The European Economy*). Scharpf uses this variation for his analysis of unemployment in "Economic and Institutional Contraints."

TABLE 1-1

International Comparison of the Sectoral Distribution of Employment (percentages)

	Manufacturing & Mining (1)	Construction & Transportation (2)	Trade, Catering, Banking & Insurance (3)	Other Services (4)	(1) + (2)	(3) + (4)
Yugoslavia	42.6	19.8	17.7	19.9	62.4	37.6
Bulgaria	44.8	20.8	11.0	23.4	65.6	34.4
Czechoslovakia	44.1	19.4	12.7	23.7	63.5	36.4
East Germany	47.1	16.4	11.5	25.0	63.5	36.5
Hungary	43.2	20.4	12.2	23.9	63.6	36.1
Poland	43.2	21.8	12.2	22.8	65.0	35.0
Romania	50.4	21.1	8.8	19.8	71.5	28.6
Average	45.5	20.0	11.4	23.1	65.5	34.5
Austria	35.0	17.0	23.7	24.3	52.0	48.0
Belgium	27.9	15.6	26.4	30.1	43.5	56.5
Denmark	24.0	16.7	22.3	37.2	40.7	59.5

(continued)

Table 1-1 (Continued)

	Manufacturing & Mining (1)	Construction & Transportation (2)	Trade, Catering, Banking & Insurance (3)	Other Services (4)	(1) + (2)	(3) + (4)
Finland	31.0	16.3	22.8	30.0	47.3	52.8
France	29.3	16.4	25.6	28.2	45.7	53.8
Great Britain	32.1	13.5	24.6	29.8	45.6	54.4
Ireland	29.2	18.4	24.4	28.0	47.6	52.4
Italy	32.4	18.2	24.7	24.8	50.6	49.5
Netherlands	23.7	17.9	27.4	31.0	41.6	58.4
Norway	24.0	18.1	25.0	32.9	42.1	57.9
Portugal	37.2	18.4	19.0	25.1	55.6	44.1
Spain	33.7	18.5	29.6	19.2	52.2	48.8
Sweden	26.3	14.2	21.1	38.4	40.5	59.5
Switzerland	35.7	13.3	29.8	21.2	49.0	51.0
West Germany	39.6	14.3	21.6	24.7	53.9	46.3
Average	30.7	16.5	24.5	28.3	47.2	52.8

Source: International Labor Organization, Yearbook of Labor Statistics (1981), cited in Mencinger, The Yugoslav Economy, 20.

TABLE 1-2
Level of Employment in Socialist and Market Capitalist Countries,
1974 (percentages)

Socialist Countries	Percentage	Market Capitalist Countries	Percentage
Yugoslavia	21.0	Austria	40.1
Bulgaria	39.3	Belgium	38.8
Hungary	48.5	France	40.3
East Germany	42.7	West Germany	41.4
Poland	51.6	United Kingdom	44.3
Romania	47.9	Japan	47.4
USSR	45.7	United States	40.6
Czechoslovakia	50.1	Sweden	48.6

Source: Davidović, "Nezaposlenost i društvena nejednakost u Jugoslaviji," 4.

tal policy, within different social and international contexts, that produces country-specific histories.

Among countries ruled by political parties whose social base among wage earners and alliances with small-property owners lead to a sustained commitment to full employment, the governmental policies that matter in achieving full employment, according to the literature on advanced industrial societies, are national strategies for international trade and adjustment. The fact that mass unemployment occurs during global depressions and that unemployment tends to rise about the same time in many countries because they participate in a global economy (for example, both Yugoslavia and the developed capitalist economies had increasing difficulty with employment in the global crisis after the late 1970s, just as countries showed a common pattern in the early 1930s) has led to an appreciation of the role of national policy in promoting economic growth and employment at home when recessions occur in primary trading partners or in reserve-currency countries. As James Alt demonstrates econometrically, so significant a portion of domestic unemployment in open economies can result from a contraction in the external environment that the influence of any macroeconomic policy on the level of domestic unemployment cannot be assessed without first measuring those external influences.[50] The regulation school takes such empirical findings to a theoretical level, by arguing that strategies for capital accumulation and their accompanying patterns of employment are international regimes.[51]

[50] Alt, "Political Parties, World Demand, and Unemployment."

[51] For example, this school characterizes the period after 1973 as one of "global overaccumulation of capital in relation to the supply elasticity of both labour-power and primary products" (Itoh, "The World Economic Crisis"). See also Noel, "Accumulation, Regulation, and Social Change."

A country's niche in the international economy matters critically in this regard, and for a small state dependent on trade for some necessities of industrial growth—such as Japan, Sweden, Switzerland, or Austria—the primary issue, according to the scholarship on full employment, is its political capacity to formulate, agree upon, mobilize support for, and implement a strategy of adjustment to the international economy—to changes in demand for the country's exports and in its relative terms of foreign trade—in ways other than by adjusting levels of unemployment.[52]

The key element of Yugoslav exceptionalism was not the country's system of worker self-management or its multinational state, but its international position—its attempt to retain socialism at home and a vigilant national independence while being open to the world economy, which required constant adjustments in the use of labor and organization of employment.[53] It was partly in order to make those adjustments at the level of workers' wages and benefits that workers' councils were introduced. Yugoslavia's trajectory differed from that of other socialist countries above all in its earlier move to the economic and political reforms associated with global market integration and export orientation—to what the Hungarians called the "new economic mechanism" and to what R. W. Davies called the "new orthodoxy" in the USSR in 1985, the policies of reform communism that most characterize Leninism.[54] Introduced in Hungary after 1959–61, intermittently in Poland, in Czechoslovakia after 1963, and in the Soviet Union most recently and explicitly under Mikhail Gorbachev in 1985, the program had its most sustained experience in Yugoslavia. This book is a study of the attempts to maintain and implement that reform program under changing international conditions. While the primary difficulty for employment lay with the effect of openness on the country's institutions of economic management—the central regulation of financial indicators based on the closed accounting system of Soviet monetary planning (though with origins in German cameralism)—Yugoslav experience suggests that, in analyses of countries that have successful national strategies toward external markets, their international position should receive as much attention as is currently paid to their political institutions for economic management. In contrast to Yugoslavia's position of national independence outside both the Eastern and Western blocs, the full-employment countries not only were advanced industrial democracies but were fully incorporated into Western trading

[52] Alt, "Political Parties, World Demand, and Unemployment"; Katzenstein, *Corporatism and Change*; Therborn, *Why Some People Are More Unemployed than Others*; Cameron, "Social Democracy"; Eichengreen and Hatton, *Interwar Unemployment*.

[53] William Zimmerman also sees the domestic-international linkage as critical to the understanding of socialist Yugoslavia, but his argument differs from the one presented here; see *Open Borders, Nonalignment, and the Political Evolution of Yugoslavia*.

[54] Davies, "Soviet History in the Gorbachev Revolution."

alliances, and they had made a choice for neutrality within Western security alliances and for conventional territorial defense.

In attempting to explain the political paradox of unemployment in socialist Yugoslavia, this study came upon a social organization and political dynamic entirely different from that common in most views of the country. It was as if the question of unemployment had unlocked doors to the Yugoslav system in the same pivotal way that Marx ascribed to it in the analysis of capitalism. That process of discovery began with an examination of the early choices on political and economic strategy made by the Yugoslav Communist party leadership in the course of revolution and early state-building. These choices are the subject of the next two chapters. The leaders' decision for political and economic independence from Moscow, although not their choice alone, made the party's process of consolidation particularly intertwined with international conditions. That process, prolonged until 1949–52, and the founding period are described in extensive detail in chapter 4 because they were critical to the system that emerged and because the argument presented here differs substantially from previous scholarship. Chapter 5 then summarizes the principles of the political system that were put in place in 1952 and that governed the periodic adjustments in subsequent constitutional reforms.

As a result of the choices made in that founding period, the Yugoslavs moved ahead of the other socialist states on a path they all eventually took. Incorporating openness into their economic strategy and treating foreign aid, imported machinery, advanced technology, cheaper wage goods, and eventually foreign investment as critical supplements to domestic resources, they accepted Western food and military assistance, asserted national sovereignty outside of secure cold-war alliances with an independent defense, and moved to integrate into international markets by opening their borders to labor migration, participating in Western capital markets, and joining global trade and financial institutions—the General Agreement on Tariffs and Trade, the International Monetary Fund, and the World Bank (they also had association agreements with the European Community and the Council for Mutual Economic Assistance). This openness in turn required domestic economic and political reforms. Governmental policy toward employment and unemployment, discussed in chapters 7 and 8 (after the characteristics and meaning of unemployment in socialist Yugoslavia are presented in chapter 6), was driven by the need to respond to changes in the country's international environment in the areas of both trade and defense. The result was an increasing ineffectiveness of the institutions of macroeconomic regulation essential to the leaders' strategy for employment growth, and a growing disjuncture between the labor policy adopted for international adjustment and the characteristics of the labor supply at home.

The political consequences of the policies of adjusting labor and employment to international conditions are discussed in chapters 9 and 10: why there was public silence on the subject of unemployment; why no collective action to change economic policy could be mounted; and how unemployment nonetheless had political effects by corroding the principles underlying the political system and leading to a rebellion against it by people who were threatened not by capitalist unemployment but by socialist unemployment—a loss of social status and political rights over economic assets. As in European social democracies, the most vexing employment problem in the 1980s was not with industrial workers but with civil servants, white-collar administrators and staff, and the social services[55]—in the language of Yugoslav socialist ideology, "unproductive" people on "guaranteed salaries" from "budgetary employment." Property owners in the socialist sector fought to retain their rights—either individual rights to their social status with its political rights and economic benefits, or the collective rights to control economic resources belonging to governments and enterprises. But unlike in market economies, their economic interests, under rapidly changing international conditions, were expressed not in political organization and demands for policy change but in the arena of, and the methods of, the system of employment: redistribution of labor (of individual incomes and people among jobs and property sectors) and autonomy over capital. The result was a competition over both citizenship rights and governments' jurisdiction over money and finance; those struggles led, by way of constitutional contest and its competing visions of the state, to the country's dissolution.

[55] See Tarschys, "Curbing Public Expenditure," on the "scissors crisis" in public finance in OECD countries since the mid-1970s. See also Esping-Andersen, *Politics against Markets*, on the significance for policy change of the political alliance forged by the Swedish Social Democrats with white-collar unions after the late 1960s and these unions' "wildcat" opposition when the process of European integration began to displace civil-service jobs abroad (the significance of the housing problem, also critical in the Yugoslav case, is discussed as well).

Chapter 2

THE MAKING OF A STRATEGY FOR CHANGE

THE POLITICAL and economic system in socialist Yugoslavia was the product of a *strategy in motion, in the process of becoming.* Its institutions never stablized in the sense that most analytical approaches to politics and policy—whether the pressure-group, competitive-party, bureaucratic, or rational-actor approach—take for granted, treating institutions as given conditions in no need of examination. To understand the country's social order and explain the policies adopted, therefore, one must be more aware of the assumptions and mentality of the leaders who guided policies and institutional reform in response to environmental pressure—assumptions that remained constant (if not fully visible) throughout the period of their rule, as I will argue in the course of this book. The leaders' strategy for change had much in common with those of other Marxist-Leninist parties in Europe, which in turn borrowed much from, or were in reaction to, the policies and institutions of developmentalist governments in Europe in the nineteenth century. But strategies were also shaped by the process of acquiring power, and therefore each was particular to its own locale—the political questions it had to face, the potential constituencies and political allies within the society, and the level and character of economic development. In contrast to the view that Marxist-Leninist political parties are dogmatic, obsessed with "totalitarian" control and obedience to the dictates of the center of some hierarchy of power, their strategies were—like the ideology of any other political party—a set of "beliefs or ideas materialized in action, often in political conflict."[1] They were not fixed beforehand, but shaped by the time and conditions in which they were formed.

The strategy that the Yugoslav Communist leadership pursued after World War II was a composite of political choices made between 1928 and 1949. Like the approach to unemployment that began to crumble and change in the 1980s in advanced industrial states, such as Sweden, the United States, or France, the Yugoslav system had its origins in the 1930s.[2] In making these political choices, the Yugoslav leaders confronted

---

[1] Verdery, *National Ideology under Socialism,* 9.

[2] The Swedish corporatist system formed by the Social Democratic party between 1932 and 1938 was dismantled during the 1980s, a process completed with the moves for accession to the European Community. On the alliances of the New Deal and its Employment

two tactical problems. The first was how to construct a single program for a country of such heterogeneity, where political parties, unions, and potential constituencies differed substantially across regions, where profound differences of industrial and capitalist development exacerbated the dilemma about how to apply Marxist theory to largely agrarian and pre-bourgeois conditions,[3] and where the country itself was engaged in great quarrels over how to integrate its preunification territories and sociopolitical orders. This chapter will argue that the early shift of ideological dominance to political forces from the more economically and organizationally developed areas of the country, reinforced by the Marxist predilection to favor that which was most progressive or most advanced, was decisive in defining such a program. The second tactical problem was the fact that the political struggle, to a far greater extent than electoral dynamics in developed economies, played out simultaneously on two fronts: within an international power structure and requirements for international recognition, and within a domestic contest. Equally decisive for ultimate choices was the fact that moments of decision were most often determined by international events, from the founding of the party in 1919 to the end of that formative period, when after 1949 the state-building process began to stabilize—because, as its architect Edvard Kardelj told the third party plenum on December 29, 1949, the "most important battle of socialism now," that of national independence through Western recognition, had been won.[4]

The resulting program for transformation did not eliminate the tensions and differences between alternatives and factions. That thorn was still felt by Marshal Tito near the end of his life in 1980; Ivo Banac cites the leader's reminiscences: "The struggle we began more than fifty years ago for the resolution of party affairs was very hard, since factionalism was deeply rooted, and it went on a long time, practically from the founding of the KPJ [Communist Party of Yugoslavia]."[5] Some elements within the package of tactical and strategic choices were mutually contradictory, while substantive differences tended to be submerged in arguments about the appropriate *pace* of change or hidden in name-calling against political enemies.

Act, enacted in 1946, see Richard Bartel's 1992 interview of James Tobin in "The Economic Pendulum." For France, see Piore's review of the Salais group study, in "Historical Perspectives and the Interpretation of Unemployment."

[3] See Hoston, *Marxism and the Crisis of Development in Prewar Japan*, as a good example of how central this problem was to the formation of strategy and tactics within Marxist parties in the twentieth century.

[4] Petranović, Končar, and Radonjić, *Sednice Centralnog komiteta KPJ (1948–1952)*, 474.

[5] *With Stalin against Tito*, 45. Shoup emphasizes this factionalism as well in his careful study, *Communism and the Yugoslav National Question*, especially 13–59.

In contrast to the tendency in the literature on Yugoslavia to character-ize conflict in terms of political power only, this analysis attempts to re-store attention to what it considers those conflicts to have been about—at base, about a search for the optimal development of material life and the corresponding organization of social life, then about control over eco-nomic resources, and only in that context about the political instruments necessary to those goals. For example, the literature interprets both ac-tual conflicts over domestic economic policy and contests by which strat-egy was formulated and redefined as fights among leaders for personal power (elite conflict);[6] among ethnic groups for dominance or autonomy (national conflict);[7] or among layers in the party and state hierarchy for the location of power (conflict between center and republics, statism and pluralism, plan and market, conservatives and liberals).[8] But none of these classifications can explain its political construction of the problem of unemployment. Turning points considered politically decisive turn out to be far more ambiguous if one focuses on political-economic strategy. For example, the argument that 1940 is critical because the party was then fully "bolshevized," meaning that Tito succeeded in consolidating his leadership and imposing iron discipline,[9] looks different in light of the material in this chapter. The year 1948, universally recognized as decisive because Tito secured independence for his leadership and his country in a contest with Stalin in the famous quarrel that established the principle of "national communisms" (the ability of countries governed by Communist parties to follow their own path independently of Moscow),[10] seems far less important than 1946, 1947, and 1949, according to the material in chapters 3 and 4. For some, the interlude of the world war in 1941–45 is

[6] See especially Burg, *Conflict and Cohesion in Socialist Yugoslavia.* Rusinow, *The Yugoslav Experiment,* is far more nuanced, though he does weave his story around the contest between liberals and conservatives.

[7] Most studies of postwar Yugoslav politics pay obligatory obeisance to the national ques-tion as the underlying character of the state. The most undiluted version is in Banac, *The National Question in Yugoslavia;* see also Ramet, *Nationalism and Federalism in Yugoslavia;* and Cohen and Warwick, *Political Cohesion in a Fragile Mosaic.*

[8] Comisso, *Workers' Control under Plan and Market;* Burg, *Conflict and Cohesion;* Milenkovitch, *Plan and Market in Yugoslav Economic Thought* (in her discussion of eco-nomic thought, not political factions); Rusinow, *The Yugoslav Experiment.*

[9] Banac, *With Stalin against Tito,* 78.

[10] See especially Campbell, *Tito's Separate Road;* Radonjić, *Sukob KPJ s Kominformom i društveni razvoj Jugoslavije, 1948–1950,* 108ff.; Ulam, *Titoism and the Cominform;* Clissold, *Yugoslavia and the Soviet Union, 1939–1973,* 42–43; Auty, "Yugoslavia and the Cominform"; and Banac, "Yugoslav Cominformist Organizations." A. Ross Johnson's study *The Transformation of Communist Ideology* is also based on the concept of ideology as being shaped and reshaped in the process of critical political conflicts, but his choice of timing and critical event—before and after the Cominform resolution of June 28, 1948—creates a pic-ture of a process very different from what I think occurred.

decisive because of the leadership's decision to organize a peasant, "all-national" following with the battle cry of national liberation from foreign oppressors[11] and because of the leaders' troubled relationship with Stalin, which provided the resources for their independence—a popular following at home and the doubt necessary to disobedience. But this interlude was far more important in defining the army's postwar role and the leaders' political tactics abroad than in granting the party legitimacy at home. In fact, the underlying theme in the entire literature on Yugoslavia of *national independence* and *difference* from the Soviet bloc distracts from all these countries' similarities in economic strategy and in the influence of their international position (in relation to Moscow as well as the West and the third world) on policy choices and political reform.

To get away from these characterizations of what will still be familiar pieces (though told from a different perspective), I propose a different labeling shorthand for, on the one hand, the dominant package of the leaders' chosen design for a state and a social order and, on the other hand, the tensions that remained unresolved in the conditions in which the leaders operated and the disagreements among them. In keeping with the territorial organization of economic and political power that was so critical to the postwar state and the influence of its wartime origins, I will call these two tendencies (after the Partisans' wartime rules of order) the Slovene and Foča models. We begin with the choices made before the war.

IDENTITY AND ORGANIZATIONAL BOUNDARIES

The most fundamental decisions for a party and its strategy are those about *identity:* Who are we? Where do we draw our boundaries territorially and socially? With whom will we ally? How do we view our role in history? It was critical that these questions were posed for the Yugoslav Communist party in the interwar period when the national question drove political conflicts and the language of conflicts even when they were about other matters. The new Yugoslav state joined territories and peoples with separate identities and social orders, and their commitment to the common state and some common identity varied.[12] In addition,

---

[11] C. Johnson, *Peasant Nationalism and Communist Power.*

[12] Because the government was identified with the Serbian monarchy and its seat in Belgrade, and because the country was multinational, it was common to fight government policy in terms of national assertion and charges of national discrimination. Since histories of that period tend to focus on the national question, it is difficult for scholars even fifty years later to see a different story, and the wars of 1991 and 1992 will reinforce this difficulty. See, for example, Banac, *The National Question;* and Cohen and Warwick, *Political Cohesion.* In *National Ideology under Socialism* (especially pt. 2), Verdery argues that in socialist Romania, this preoccupation of the intellectuals came, over time, to capture the discourse and ideology of the Communist party.

those party leaders who tried to maintain the Marxist position that national consciousness and nation-states were secondary to and even diverted from the class struggle came under the most criticism from the
Comintern, which focused on the national question as a resource for
revolution—such as when its tactics demanded the right to self-
determination of peoples and the anticolonial struggle of "oppressed nations" to break up empires in the cause of "workers' and peasants'
states."[13] The fact was that the Yugoslav party, from its founding in April
1919, was also an alliance of preunification socialist parties and left-wing
cultural clubs that had different political legacies (the German social democratic and Austromarxist influences in Slovenia, for example, were very
different from the Chernyshevskian Marxism of Svetozar Marković's party
in Serbia) and different national consciousnesses. Although Paul Shoup
and Walker Connor argue that the party's eventual success lay in its very
ambiguity on the national question,[14] the issue was decisive in the choice
of constitutional program for the new state and in the consequences of the
choice of party leaders, in contrast with the equally compelling but less
influential events of the agricultural crisis of the 1920s, the Great Depression of the 1930s, or the king's suspension of the democratic constitution
in 1929. Moreover, in the extensive literature on the party's frequent
shifts, quarrels, and attempts to avoid the question, the usual distinction
drawn between internationalists (who saw national identities as a useful
weapon in the service of revolution) and committed nationalists tells us
little about how nationalism was defined, recognized, and authorized in
the Yugoslav space.[15] For example, internationalists could follow Lenin or
Stalin, and nationalists could believe, with the Austromarxist Karl Renner, in a "democratic nationalities federal state" recognizing that cultural
identities were as fundamental as economic ones for social organization;[16]
or with the German social democrats of the 1875 (Gotha) program that
nation-states were the natural organizational unit for an economy; or with

[13] Connor, *The National Question in Marxist-Leninist Theory and Strategy*, 137–42 and
chap. 3; Carr, *The Bolshevik Revolution*, vol. 1, note B, "The Bolshevik Doctrine of Self-
Determination," 410–28.

[14] Shoup, *Communism and the Yugoslav National Question*, in the contrast he draws (in
the conclusion) between the relation of Communist rule and the national question in the
period of state formation and the relation that had evolved by the 1960s; Connor, *The National Question*, 168.

[15] Connor's statement that Tito was an internationalist, calling frequently on patriotism
but always subordinating national goals to that of the revolution (*The National Question*,
xiv), is disputable at many points in the leader's long career.

[16] Gulick, *Austria from Habsburg to Hitler* 2:1369. Convinced of the Austrian influence
on debates in the northwest of Yugoslavia, despite my critics, I was particularly grateful to
Benjamin Ward for suggesting this work and the relevance of the Second and a Half
International.

the Slovene Edvard Kardelj and many Croat Communists that the proletarian struggle was first of all a national struggle and the best way to
achieve national aspirations.[17]

The first major choice came with the rout of the right faction from the
party leadership (the faction was outvoted in 1924 and purged by the
Comintern in 1928) in favor of a revolutionary approach that was against
working within the state as then constituted. The shift in party leadership
from Serbian to non-Serbian (especially Croat and Slovene) dominance
was particularly decisive, because it forever after confirmed federalism for
both party and government, as well as a strongly anticentralist concept of
the state (often tinged with opposition to Great Serbianism or Serbs in
general). For example, despite the Comintern's shift to united-front tactics after 1935 and the party's attempt to build that front on a *Yugoslav*
identity for all sections of the party and for its revolutionary objectives,
the party followed through on its commitment in 1934 to national self-
determination: when the Slovenes applied for their own section in the
Comintern, the Yugoslav party gave full organizational autonomy to the
Communist party of Slovenia (in 1937) and then to the Croat party (in
1938).

The federal units of the constitution adopted provisionally in 1943 were
to be defined nationally, but the concept of national identity that emerged
and its meaning for political tactics were also a result of the influence on
party thinking of the intellectual milieu in Croatia and Slovenia in the
1920s and 1930s. As Silva Mežnarić recounts it, intellectuals from these
former Habsburg territories felt themselves trapped, in limbo in both
national and class terms: they were in a backward state that was using
mercantilist policies to protect the less competitive and less developed
Serbian bourgeoisie and thereby preventing the full domestic development of capitalist forces; and in European space, their reality of petty-
bourgeois peripherality and international "nonposition" due to the
stunted development of an indigenous bourgeoisie separated them from
the world of great nation-states and the advance of global capitalism.[18]
The proletarian revolution would be simultaneously a national revolution—
against the exploitative tax and foreign-trade policies of the Serbian state
and *čaršija*,[19] against its increasing dependence on foreign connections

---

[17] Basom, "Socialism as National Liberation," provides a useful analysis of Kardelj's writings and pronouncements on the national question.

[18] Mežnarić, "A Neo-Marxist Approach to the Sociology of Nationalism: A Quest for Theory" (published in *Praxis International* as "A Neo-Marxist Approach to the Sociology of
Nationalism, Doomed Nations, and Doomed Schemes").

[19] Political slang for the links among merchants, bureaucrats, and state-protected industries centered in Belgrade.

and capital to maintain that power at home, and against the political chains of absolutism that prevented those in the former Habsburg territories from completing their process of nation-building and the democratic, republican revolution that would make the bourgeois stage of development possible. But these intellectuals tended to define the problem of revolution largely as one of consciousness and political action.

Steeped in the tradition of Hegelian "positioning," they were aware that both Marx and Engels categorically dismissed the Slavic nations as "relics of peoples," "nonhistoric nations" that would disappear with the march of capitalism, "barbarians" incapable of civilization and without the right of self-determination that was due the great, historic nations.[20] In the intellectuals' interwar debates, as Mežnarić records them, many became obsessed with asking, "Who are we in Europe?" What role could a working-class party of Slavs in a land of "vagabonds, travelling salesmen, smugglers" play within this historical process, to escape their petty-bourgeois peripherality? Both their explanation for this economic and political reality and the source of their emancipation were to be found in the sphere of consciousness and cultural identity, with the "ideology of smallness," deference to the major "historic" nations and the latter's cultural hegemony in Europe, and a sense of community characterized by a *sklavenmoral* (slave culture) in subordination to this external *herrenmoral* (master culture). Cultural backwardness maintained and perpetuated their economic backwardness and global nonposition because it hindered any internal sources of innovation, whether economic or cultural, thus making them forever vulnerable to great-power designs on their territory. Economic weakness in turn brought political impotence and subjection and led to cultural insignificance, which then returned full circle to economic exploitation.[21]

For these activist intellectuals, the historic mission of the Communist party was to take on the creative, revolutionary role played elsewhere by the bourgeoisie: to overthrow the Serbian monarchy, build a republic, emancipate the mass of the population from their petty-bourgeois mentality of inferiority by making them conscious of their collective power to alter their fate with their own hands, and bring "national equality to Serbs, Croats, Slovenes, Macedonians, Montenegrins."[22] This substitute

---

[20] Mežnarić, "A Neo-Marxist Approach," 11–12; see also Connor, *The National Question;* and Shoup, *Communism and the Yugoslav National Question.*

[21] Mežnarić, "A Neo-Marxist Approach," 9. The terms of reference are shared throughout the region; for a slightly different approach, see Janos, *The Politics of Backwardness in Historical Perspective: Hungary, 1825–1945.*

[22] Josip Broz Tito, at the fifth party conference, October 19–23, 1940, cited in Connor, *The National Question,* 147.

bourgeoisie would begin the process of economic emancipation with cultural and political emancipation. The fight for national independence by all the Yugoslav peoples against imperial powers, foreign capital, and their domestic agents and collaborators would achieve self-determination for the working people as national communities.

The concept of a nation in this critique was first of all a historical one, implying a set of class stages and a view of progress for peoples (nations) that were defined by the *historical and territorial* characteristics of *states*. Nations were also *economic units* and *communities of common culture and language*—the mix so common to the German sphere of reflection, developmental thought, and critique to which Marx, Engels, Herder, List, and Hegel all contributed.[23] Whatever the permutations of the idea of self-determination in the shifting Soviet, Comintern, and Yugoslav positions (autonomy, self-rule, the right to secession, full sovereignty), it always meant self-government of territorial units that had historical consciousness as nations—"free cultural and economic development" of an "administrative character."[24]

From this perspective, however, the nations within multinational Yugoslavia were not at the same stage of development. This was a problem tactically; as late as 1940, delegates to the fifth party conference in Zagreb could not themselves fully agree on what level of national formation had been achieved by each.[25] Capitalist development was very unevenly spread over the Yugoslav territories—from Slovenia, where commercial agriculture, public education and roads, and light manufacturing had begun to develop with the mid-eighteenth-century Theresian reforms in the Habsburg empire, to Bosnia and Macedonia, where Ottoman-type feudal relations on the land still marked political as well as economic and social life in the 1930s. Smallholding dominated agriculture, with the exception of the large estates of the plains of Vojvodina and

[23] The attempt (as in Szporluk, *Communism and Nationalism*) to counterpose communism and nationalism, especially in the sense of Marxism and Listianism, as polar opposites does not work for central Europe. In the Yugoslav debates and perceptions in the interwar period, the two were opposite sides, perhaps, but of the same coin. Hroch, "How Much Does Nation Formation Depend on Nationalism?" and Kitching, *Development and Underdevelopment in Historical Perspective*, demonstrate the interaction and frequent interdependence of the two ideologies.

[24] Tito, discussing the character of the new Yugoslav federation in *Borba*, May 22, 1945, cited in Shoup, *Communism and the Yugoslav National Question*, 116n.

[25] In the notes on the debate that remain, Milovan Djilas appears to have taken a mediating role, arguing that "the Croatian national question still exists." Tito replied that "the Croatian question *is* solved as a bourgeois question. But it is not completely solved even for the bourgeoisie (who are fighting in treacherous ways). There exists a clique with great Croatian oppressive tendencies" (Damjanović, Bosić, and Lazarević, *Peta zemaljska konferencija KPJ*, 214).

Macedonia, but these were held by absentee foreign owners or the churches (especially Roman Catholic and Muslim). Each region had been governed until 1918 by a different regime (or by a mixture, as in Bosnia-Herzegovina, which had a layer of Austro-Hungarian on top of Ottoman institutions after 1878), and the differences persisted because nearly all efforts by the Belgrade government to integrate the country—in financial institutions, roads and communications, educational policy, and industrial investment—had foundered on interminable political conflicts, local obstruction, or heavy-handed imposition of state policies in response.[26]

Peoples in the south, such as in what would become the republics of Bosnia and Macedonia, were in many (but not all) instances still mired in precapitalist relations with respect to religion, colonial oppression, and the nation embodied in the feudal power of a landholding class. Kardelj's insistence that the basis for national divisions on the historical map of Europe lay with communication and language[27] made it possible to grant at least the Bosnians recognition as a nation, a matter subject to dispute throughout the interwar (and even postwar) period. Tito, intervening in the rancorous debate at the last party conference before the war (in October 1940) regarding the national status of Muslims and the basis of nationhood for the ethnically mixed population of Bosnia, insisted that "Bosnia is a single unit because of centuries of communal life, regardless of religious beliefs."[28] But the national position of the Macedonians was a source of continuing dispute, revealing clearly that the Croats' and Slovenes' view guiding their policies toward national identity reflected only one of many class realities, with direct political consequences.

The Macedonian party section's perspective in 1940 was not a nationally defined territory in relation to European power (as it was to be defined in the federal structure after the war), but of class divisions within the Macedonian territory along national lines, divisions created by the colonizing policies of the Serbian state. According to Metodija Šator Šarlo, the secretary of the temporary regional committee formed for Macedonia in February 1940,[29] the national question of Macedonia was primarily a question of land, and this was an issue of class exploitation, despite the party leadership's position that it was not. It divided the party section between Macedonians and Serbs—not only the Serbian "generals, gendarmes, and spies," but all colonists who were "given the best

[26] I am grateful to István Csillag for emphasizing (in relation to debates in the 1970s about the level of economic integration among the Yugoslav republics) the failure of the interwar royal government to integrate not only physical infrastructure but also the financial institutions necessary for a unified market.

[27] Mežnarić, "A Neo-Marxist Approach."

[28] Damjanović, Bosić, and Lazarević, *Peta zemaljska konferencija*, 214.

[29] Shoup, *Communism and the Yugoslav National Question*, 52–53.

land," all of it taken from Macedonian peasants and their common pastures and forests. In Šarlo's view, the Croat position (and thus that of the party program) was "sectarian, Trotskyist"—telling the Macedonians that they would resolve their national question only after the proletarian world revolution and taking Lenin's position on the solidarity of all nationalities—whereas the Macedonians had to proceed immediately with developing their national consciousness, through culture and language, and emancipating their land from Serb rule.[30] "We can't go to the Macedonian peasant and tell him that colonists are the brothers of the Macedonian peasant," Šarlo insisted. "Whoever knows the psychology of the Macedonian peasant knows that he is fighting for blood revenge against the colonists."[31] The same argument applied to the Albanians in Kosovo-Metohija, where the colonists were "the pillar of hegemony [Great Serbianism]," where "feudal remnants" were still large, and where the "struggle for national rights of the Arnauti [Albanians]" was just beginning.[32]

The provisional government of 1943 created a federal republic of "nations" that represented historical communities, territorially defined, with extensive economic and cultural administrative autonomy; it thus authorized the dominance of the "progressive" sections of the party from the more-developed northwest. The importance to them of retaining each nation's individuality at each stage of their common struggle even prevented the use of "Yugoslav" labels. The war, for example, was an "all-national liberation struggle" under the slogan of "brotherhood and unity." The Macedonian section of the party could be a united, "national-revolutionary" front "cooperating with liberal bourgeois groups" because of their role in questions of culture and language; the working class would lead the struggle for this cultural self-determination, but it was not to take land from colonists—"only from those who oppress the Macedonian nation."[33] This rejection of the Macedonian (and Albanian) national concept led Šarlo to take the Macedonian section to the Bulgarian party, where Georgi Dimitrov continued to hold Stalin's view; likewise, the Albanians from Kosovo-Metohija joined the Italians, who were also more limber in their use of the colonial argument. Moreover, it was only after the war, at the fifth party congress in July 1948, that the four "communities"— Bosnia, Macedonia, Montenegro, and Serbia—gained the full status of separate party organizations ("national committees") to conform with the nationally defined territories of the new federal state.

[30] Damjanović, Bosić, and Lazarević, *Peta zemaljska konferencija*, 210–11.
[31] Ibid., 210.
[32] Ibid., 213.
[33] Djilas, at the fifth party conference, ibid., 212.

DIVISIONS WITHIN UNITY: THE LABOR QUESTION

The political victory of the Communist party after World War II is usually attributed to its redefinition of the national question as peasant patriotism against foreign invaders and to its insistence on an all-Yugoslav program, operating in all areas of the country. The party was the sole *Yugoslav* organization that appealed to the peoples' common interest in a better life and in putting behind them the conflicts of the interwar period with the resulting wartime horrors. But the party's actual approach to the national question—recognizing the differences in national development by allowing economic, cultural, and political autonomy, and recognizing all the nations' right to self-determination with their voluntary (at least in theory) union in a common state after 1943–45 (what Connor calls "retroactive self-determination" on the Leninist reasoning)[34]—was the source of extraordinary difficulty. A working-class party committed to economic development and social revolution would necessarily have to have a single plan for all areas, while operating politically in the different contexts of each of the national territories. The differences in national consciousness across these territories paled in comparison to their differences in socioeconomic conditions and level of organizational development, and were in part a result of them.

The party's Marxist focus on what was most economically advanced and politically progressive—"the organization of the most advanced elements of the proletariat" as "the greatest productive force in society"[35]—did give a direction that would likely have prevailed even without the choice of leaders in 1928 and especially after 1937, with Josip Broz and his circle. The overwhelming portion of the organized working class and the strongest industrial unions with the longest tradition were in Slovenia and Croatia. The Slovene proposal for a constitution in the bitter conflict of 1919–21, although rejected, contained a replica of the social legislation of the Weimar constitution, including the Bismarckian social-insurance programs and the workers' councils favored by the German Social Democratic party.[36] The 1921 constitution and the 1922 Law on Workers' Social Insurance did incorporate for those workers who belonged to registered unions the benefits that Slovene and Croat workers had won under the

---

[34] *The National Question*, 161.

[35] Ranković, "Referat o sindikalnom pitanju," 49–50.

[36] Beard and Radin write: "Betraying perhaps the influence of the new German constitution, the Slovenian project declares that the age of the military and police state is over and that the time has come for the social state. Some industries are to be placed in the hands of an economic council representing employees, employers, and consumers. In certain selected industries, the workers are to be empowered by legislation to take part in administration and to share in the profits" (*The Balkan Pivot*, 49–50; see also 55–56).

Habsburgs (guaranteeing health care and material assistance for illness, injury, old age, and death, for insured workers and their dependents).[37] Zagreb workers gained notoriety for their militancy during the interwar period, which the government repressed quite severely on occasion.

There were important pockets of radical workers elsewhere, such as those employed in the munitions factories of Kragujevac (Serbia), the tobacco workers in Macedonia, the printers in Montenegro, and the members of the famous soccer club of Split, but the real strength of the party outside of Slovenia and Croatia was not in industry. In Belgrade, for example, its strength was in the state sector and services (postal workers and unionized white-collar employees in banking, insurance, commerce, and construction). As late as 1940, at the fifth party conference, a delegate from Serbia noted that their party cadres "still undervalue the unions" and had "not posed the question of unemployment, or the starvation it threatened, as sharply as they ought."[38] Even after a particularly successful period of organizing workers and militant protest, in 1936–40, the report on the trade-union question at the 1940 conference admitted that the party remained weak among "miners, monopoly-sector workers, transport workers, and the industrial proletariat."[39] While organized workers had the right to assistance during unemployment, and the government contributed public funds to that aid after 1937,[40] the approach to unemployment in Belgrade at the time consisted of police roundups of beggars to do what amounted to forced labor, in conditions closer to medieval than modern. Most cities became depots for abandoned children of unemployed and uninsured families, who lived by begging or in apprenticeship to master workmen under near slavery conditions.[41] The sense of degradation and powerlessness among apprentices from peasant homes pervades the memoirs and interviews of one of their kind who was to become the leader of the Yugoslav Communist party—Josip Broz.

[37] See Has, "Društveno-ekonomski osvrt na problem zaposlenosti," 135–36; and Parmalee, "Medicine under Yugoslav Self-Managing Socialism," 38–42.

[38] Damjanović, Bosić, and Lazarević, *Peta zemaljska konferencija*, 206.

[39] Ranković, "Referat o sindikalnom pitanju," 51.

[40] In 1927 the workers' chambers, responsible for unemployment insurance, were obliged to be "self-managing" (i.e., financially autonomous); but during the second wave of interwar unemployment after 1936 (in the first wave, in 1930–34, every fifth insured worker was thrown out of work, and the real incomes of those who kept their jobs dropped 20 percent), that compensation was so paltry that the government granted public funds. The number of registered unemployed grew from 139,382 in 1928 to 1,069,443 in 1940 (M. Radovanović, "Različita shvatanja uzroka i oblika nezaposlenosti," 47; Dukanac, *Indeksi konjunkturnog razvoja Jugoslavije, 1919–1941*, 27–28; Has, "Društveno-ekonomski osvrt," 134–36; Ranković, "Referat o sindikalnom pitanju"; Vuković, "Uticaj svetske privredne krize," 213–15).

[41] Kalember, "Siromaštvo i pitanje besposličenja," 440–44.

The rural population had declined only to 74 percent by the end of the interwar period, and this figure rose as one traveled south; in Macedonia, it was 90 percent.[42] It is true that this agricultural sea included areas of large landed estates with agricultural laborers, numbering 400,000 in the Vojvodina plain, for example. The cyclical industries of mining, construction, brickmaking, and timber continued to depend on the ancient tradition of seasonal migration by unskilled peasants called *polutani*,[43] who left their land temporarily to seek cash-paying industrial jobs; these composed more than half the industrial labor force (in 1929–34, only 46.5 percent of industrial workers were in full-time positions, and only half of those were insured). As the delegate from Dalmatia reported at the 1940 party conference, the land question was "as important as the union one."[44] The Macedonians' conflict with the party's definition of the national question, which Šarlo and others found impossible to separate from the agrarian question, arose from their view, with Stalin, that the oppressed, colonized peasants were the revolutionary force. But organization among agricultural workers and small farmers was greatest, too, in Croatia and Slovenia, where the cooperative tradition was well-developed and peasant parties were strong.

To simplify this complexity, the party leaders used three political ideologies. The first was a national one. In Croatia, such an ideology was hard to avoid because the Communists' main competitor, the Croat Peasant party (CPP), based its successful appeal on Croat nationalism and identifying the Croat rural population as the true "people" (*narod*). The Slovene Peoples' party was also nationalist and clerical, in the Austrian Christian Social tradition. But the largest of the Serbian parties, the Radicals, although originally a peasant party, had long since become a party of the Belgrade royal establishment and local notables; and the other major Serbian parties operated outside Serbia proper, in Croatia or Vojvodina.

For others, Lenin's analysis of rural class differentiation, between rich farmers and poor or middle peasants, served better. Confused over the Macedonian focus on colonial (Serbian) usurpation of the peasant's right to their land, one Montenegrin delegate at the party conference asked, "Are there peasants, poor ones, who are colonists?" Another criticized the state in Montenegro because the monies being spent to drain Lake Scutari would benefit the bourgeoisie, while the state paid no attention to the poor peasant and how he lived. The Serbian delegate used the Russian

---

[42] Kostić, *Seljaci-industriski radnici;* Metodija Šator Šarlo, in Damjanović, Bosić, and Lazarević, *Peta zemaljska konferencija*, 210, for Macedonia. The agricultural population in 1931, the year of the last prewar census, was 76.5 percent (Tomasevich, *Peasants, Politics, and Economic Change in Yugoslavia*, 303).

[43] The word connotes something second-rate or mixed-breed.

[44] Damjanović, Bosić, and Lazarević, *Peta zemaljska konferencija*, 212–13.

metaphor in his focus on the marketing cooperatives that enabled the kulak to hold a village in his fist by controlling the supply and marketing of grain and by retaining the entire profit from the rise in grain prices. Discussing Vojvodina, party members concentrated on the burden of the land tax and the dominance of rich farmers and other bourgeois elements in the credit and flood-control cooperatives. Delegates from Dalmatia also singled out the dominance of wealthy farmers over rural cooperatives, particularly where Communists faced legal obstacles to competing openly or to infiltrating the powerful village cooperatives (Gospodarska Sloga) and cultural organizations (Seljačka Sloga) of the CPP.[45]

The third ideology was actually a combination of two others and was meant to address the difficult task of forming alliances under these circumstances. It included the Leninist idea of a vanguard party, representing the most advanced elements of the working class at its core; and revisionism, with its idea of the solidarity of a popular front of exploited forces across poor and middle strata. Even the Slovene and Croat workers were divided among unions organized, in the manner of French ones, along religious, ethnonational, and ideological lines. Slovene workers tended to side firmly with the social democrats or the clericals (and Kardelj admitted at the 1940 party conference that the Slovene party had done little to prevent German-speaking workers from joining the German union and from there siding with Hitler). In Croatia, Catholic unions and the union affiliated with the CPP were strong. Where peasant parties had organized cooperatives, in the north, the Communists' attempt to create "peasant chambers" on the model of workers' chambers was unsuccessful. There were divisions between organized and unorganized workers (primarily women and youth, who faced legal prohibitions on organizing and who filled the classic niche of Marx's industrial reserve army as low-cost competitors because of their lower skills and the traditional attitudes of employers); between unemployed urban workers and the rising number of peasants kicked off the land by the agrarian crisis after the mid-1920s but blocked from their usual escape route by the anti-immigrant walls around the richer countries after 1923;[46] and between Communists and

[45] Ibid.

[46] The fall in world farm prices in the second half of the 1920s was followed by declining domestic demand during the 1930s because urban wages also fell; growing poverty, indebtedness to moneylenders (who were often also local politicians), increasing liquidation of peasant smallholdings, and even widespread malnutrition bordering on starvation hit all areas of the country (see Tomasevich, *Peasants, Politics, and Economic Change*, pt. 2, but particularly chaps. 19, 20, and 27 [especially pp. 667–80]). A searing portrait of those conditions in Croatia—and an explanation of why many who were exposed to them became politically radicalized—can be had from an ethonographic diary of the young Rudolf Bićanić, an influential economist in post–World War II Croatia who before the war was an activist in the CPP, which he kept during a tour of the countryside to get in touch with "the people" after

their former allies in the United Unions of Yugoslavia (Ujedinjenje Sindikata Jugoslavije), who benefited by collaborating with the corporatist regime after 1937 (in the view of the Communists, betraying the working class by accepting laws against the strike and by cooperating with bourgeois interests).[47] These divisions prevented any real action for workers' rights and demanded political unity as its precondition.

The common denominator of these political ideologies was that workers should be united—organized on branch principles instead of by trade and profession—into comprehensive unions with sections for youth and women, and unified at local, regional, and countrywide seats into one working class: one union per factory, one party for the country. And because the united-front strategy among progressive, opposition parties had failed, the party would shift (as the Comintern signaled in 1939) to a popular-front strategy "from below," organizing the unorganized against political leaders and creating a solidarity of protest with wage workers among the mass of the population, independent of party—peasants and villagers, small producers, and the liberal, petty bourgeoisie.[48] But on what programmatic basis would that unity and "mass line" arise?

The report on the trade-union question at the fifth party conference was written by the militant Zagreb branch of the United Unions organization of Croatia and Slavonia (although it was handed to the Serbian party

---

he was released from jail for political activity; an English version of his *Kako živi narod* (*How the People Live*) was published posthumously by his widow, Sonia Bićanić, and anthropologist Joel Halpern. Peasant indebtedness so threatened the social order that the king granted a moratorium on rural debt in 1932.

[47] Until 1932, the party followed the Comintern's "sectarian" line against cooperation with social democratic parties and unions. The brief interlude of joint action gave way during 1937–38 to increasing conflict between the Communists and the Social Democrats over control of the union movement and conflict with the CPP over the Croat constituency—in large part a result of the corporatist policies of the Stojadinović government, which sought to gain the upper hand in 1937–38 by separating the Communists from any possible legal cover or allies. The government banned the United Unions organization where Communists still had some influence; created business and government unions in which legal status for collective bargaining, insurance, and other workers' rights was obligatory and in which Social Democrats chose to collaborate; and took over the workers' chambers, offices for social insurance, and workers' inspectors in factories. In August 1939, the royal government gave Croatia autonomy over all internal administration except that of the military, foreign affairs, and joint finances, and gave control over local administration to the CPP—which also required membership in either the clerical organizations or the CPP cooperatives (Gospodarska Sloga) to participate in local government.

[48] The Communist party of Croatia resisted this shift, however, and ignored party discipline in order to maintain its alliance with the CPP, supporting the latter's party list against the list fielded by the Communists in elections in December 1938, supporting the August 1939 Cvetković-Maček Agreement (*Sporazum*) for Croatian autonomy, requiring the catechism in Croat Partisan territory during the war, and so forth. See Banac, *With Stalin against Tito*, 75–98; Irvine, "State Building and Nationalism"; and idem, "Tito, Hebrang, and the Croat Question, 1943–1944."

activist Aleksandar Ranković to read), and it was a classic Marxist analysis of the crises of capitalist accumulation. The Great Depression was one of underproduction, the depression after 1936 one of overproduction; and both crises gave rise to monopoly capital—the increasing merger of industrialists, financial capital, and the state to counteract the fall in profits by increasing surplus value, not only by intensification of production at the workplace and allowing rising unemployment despite underutilized capacity, but also by raising prices through cartels in markets for food and other necessities. The responsibility for unemployment, inflation, militarism, and the corporatist decrees that reduced workers' political rights, however, lay with the state. The enemy, said the report, was fascism, whereby the state guaranteed the power of an expansionist capitalist class—the "great bourgeoisie" of Serbia and Great Serbianism and for some, like Tito, also that of Croatia and Great Croatianism—with police repression and corporatist exclusion, with military expenditures from the state budget to revive production through rearmament, and with mercantilist exploitation of the entire population, especially the poor. Protective import duties, state monopolies on basic goods, and other indirect taxes (representing 65.6 percent of all tax receipts in the 1930s)[49] shifted part of the burden of achieving profits and capital accumulation to the backs of consumers. The cost of living for all working and poor people rose substantially as a result of rising taxes, government debt, and monopoly prices for matches, salt, tobacco, and protected manufactures.[50] Feeding into the international conjuncture of fascism only made it worse. Intensified international competition in trade had led to wildly fluctuating exchange rates and a more frequent resort to bilateral, tied trade on clearing agreements in which poorer states like Yugoslavia were reduced to producing stocks for war, such as food and textiles for imperialist powers.[51] Instead of improving the terms of trade for farmers or agricultural nations, however, the cartels that sprang up to organize this trade and to speculate further captured the profits, so that in the boom year of 1937, price ratios between Yugoslav farmers and industry were the same as in 1932—the depth of the depression—and 70 percent of farm households remained in terrible poverty.[52] Despite greater demand for skilled labor in defense-

[49] Mitrany, *Marx against the Peasant*, 103. The figures for Bulgaria and Romania were similar, at 64.0 and 72.5 percent (ibid.).

[50] Ranković, "Referat o sindikalnom pitanju," 93–95.

[51] Yugoslav treaties with Italy and Germany, and their political outcome in the secret nonagression pact that Prince Regent Paul signed with Hitler only months after the fifth party conference (a pact to which Yugoslav air force officers responded with a coup in April 1941, provoking Hitler to bomb Belgrade and bring the war to the Balkans), fit Hirschman's classic analysis of economic power in *National Power and the Structure of Foreign Trade*.

[52] Ranković, "Referat o sindikalnom pitanju," 79.

related branches of industry and rising wages as a result of workers greater militancy (including a guaranteed minimum wage for unionized workers), rising inflation sent real wages plummeting.

The royal government had failed to develop the domestic economy for the benefit of its citizens, and the result was a dependent position in the world economy. The report condemned the government for seeking to evade this failure by foreign borrowing that made this dependence worse and by inviting foreign capital into domestic production with special protections that exacerbated poverty and unemployment at home. Selling off Yugoslav mines, factories, and even state monopolies over basic commodities (tobacco, matches, salt) to French, British, Swedish, Czech, and German capitalists in order to line the pockets of Belgrade bureaucrats and merchants was as hostile an act to the Yugoslav people as the export of food to pay for imports, the protections for a weak Serbian bourgeoisie that could not compete abroad, and the collusion among the national bourgeoisies to protect their power over workers. This criticism reverberated with a history of experience and populist politics in Habsburg territories since the mid-nineteenth century—where first a land market and then commercialization of agriculture, under conditions of global markets for agricultural produce, had forced indebted smallholders to sell to foreigners similarly dispossessed in richer countries but able to afford land in poorer countries.[53] Foreign companies also subjected wage earners in agriculture and industry to foreign competition by recruiting skilled labor from more-developed countries (nationally distinct layers of labor by skill were particularly noticeable in the mines, but the foreign component was also high in urban labor forces in northern cities, such as Ljubljana, in the late nineteenth century)[54] while local artisans were forced to wander the world in journeymen's bands or emigrate permanently in search of work.

Despite the union report's radical critique of capitalism, the party was not ready to write a political program for social revolution. At the party conference, Ranković omitted the report's concluding attack on capitalism and its assessment that the developing conflict between proletariat and capitalist class obliged the party to "link the struggle for wages with the struggle against capitalist methods of production, for a socialist order."[55] Although Tito admitted in his report to the conference that it was "greater social revolution that we plan," he made it quite explicit that their current task was to forge solidarity between the party and the "mass of the people," mobilize them for political action, and fight against fascism and

---

[53] R. Bićanić, "Agrarna kriza od 1873–1895."
[54] Stane Saksida, analysis of the Ljubljana census of 1880, personal communication, 1975.
[55] Ranković, "Referat o sindikalnom pitanju," 94.

war.[56] The trade-union report proposed that action on unemployment be linked to the struggle of employed workers (including their demands for equal pay for equal work), the right to work, and the right of unemployed workers to unemployment compensation, rent forgiveness, soup kitchens, food staples, and shelters.[57] But even this was too radical for some; Kardelj insisted on the Comintern view at the time—that union activists within factories should remain narrowly focused on economic issues and union rights. Warning that this tactic underestimated the strength and treachery of the Social Democrats, Ranković had the support of the Montenegrin section and of Sreten Žujović (also a Serb, then active in Macedonia) in arguing that the only way to link the wage struggle with the struggle for peace, for workers' rights, and for the civil and democratic freedoms of which the people were deprived under the "total, open dictatorship of the bourgeoisie" and its corporative regime was for the party to take charge of all unions, labor inspectors, and workers' chambers; plan and coordinate all its activities; organize unions and youth societies; create correspondence and reading groups and newspapers in all shops and factories; and train union cadres.[58]

The cautionary position won. Greater engagement in the workers' struggle did not ensue. The party focused its political campaign on the monarchy and on the fascist state—the "leader of reaction not only in Yugoslavia but in the entire Balkans"—and the foreign exploitation it had invited.[59] The "mass line" of a popular front from below defined the party's social and economic program. The common denominators of such an alliance of peasants, workers, and liberal middle strata, an alliance far larger than any minimum winning electoral coalition, were the "struggle against the high cost of living," as Kardelj argued was most appropriate in Slovenia,[60] and the struggle for national self-determination. The Yugoslav Communists' revolutionary commitment on political tactics and apparent subservience to the Comintern can therefore be deceptive, for the program combined elements that were much closer to the revisionism of the Austromarxists—such as constitutional recognition of the nationality issue, the alliance with peasant and middle groups, and commitment to the

[56] Tito, in Damjanović, Bosić, and Lazarević, Peta zemaljska konferencija.
[57] Little had changed in the proposals since 1932. See Has, "Društveno-ekonomski osvrt," 136–39; and "Let's Organize the Struggle of the Unemployed," 263.
[58] Ranković, "Referat o sindikalnom pitanju," 93–98.
[59] Ibid., 51. As the trade-union report chose to view it, the government was nearly the last in Europe to recognize the Soviet Union—doing so only in 1940—and the first to assault the political, union, and cultural organizations of the working class after World War I (the report was referring to the government's ban on the party's electoral participation in 1921 and, with the royal dictatorship in January 1929, its suspension of all civil liberties and workers' organizations).
[60] Damjanović, Bosić, and Lazarević, Peta zemaljska konferencija, 210–14.

smallholders' right to land ownership.[61] The links between early Marxism and the Ricardian socialists, or between Leninists and the radical agrarians, would become far clearer in the program once the state stabilized internationally after 1950. The lineage is most obvious in the writings of Kardelj, the alliance of the Slovene National Liberation Front, and the program of the CPP (especially in the proposals for postwar reconstruction that were written during the war by many of its activists).[62] And until that postwar order began to unfold after 1946, until the conflicts on the pace of change revived (see chapter 4), one might also have seen this alliance in the one link Tito was able to forge for the party in Serbia (as early as June 1941)—the "joint struggle" against the occupiers, for Soviet power, against English agents and the old order, against incitement to national hatred through joint committees of the "worker-peasant alliance," with Dragoljub Jovanović and the agrarian-socialist offshoot he formed from the left wing of the Serbian Agrarian party.[63] One might even have read this alliance in the views of Ranković (despite his disagreements with Kardelj) regarding party successes before the war. Noting with pleasure in his report on the trade-union struggle the many instances in which villagers had come on their own initiative to support striking workers with food and even participate in their mass demonstrations, Ranković urged party cadres to take advantage of this sympathy by organizing mass organizations as a ring of support around the unified union movement and by teaching both unionized workers and unorganized women and youth about their mutual interest in problems of unemployment and the wage struggle.[64]

MILITARY ORIGINS OF THE STATE

Hitler's decision to invade Yugoslavia in April 1941 redefined rather dramatically the party's methods of domestic political competition. Moving within months from the political vise of fascist retrenchment and corporatist exclusion to the armed struggle to which it was committed in principle but which it had expected as part of a social revolution far in the future (a struggle delayed by the Comintern's imposed respect for the Hitler-Stalin

[61] Gulick, *Austria from Habsburg to Hitler*, vol. 2, especially 1366–82.

[62] See Mirković, *Jugoslav Postwar Reconstruction Papers*.

[63] Banac, *With Stalin against Tito*, 6; see also Jovanović, "Političke uspomene." Mitrany labeled Jovanović a "romantic populist" (*Marx against the Peasant*, 113; see also 125–131, 250).

[64] The earliest attempts to "ensnare the peasant" (Friedrich Engels, cited in Mitrany, *Marx against the Peasant*, 22) for the socialist movement in the 1890s led to the first of the great debates over reformism and to the first use of the term *revisionism*, decades before the split over revolutionary strategy vs. evolutionary parliamentarism.

pact), the party set out to organize an armed uprising of popular/national liberation. The war turned its political weaknesses in elections into a comparative advantage over other forces: its early rejection of political reformism in favor of revolution against a state that could not protect its people from war; the imposed clandestinity and reliance on underground, conspiratorial organization so necessary in guerrilla warfare against foreign occupiers; the experience of leaders still alive in 1940 with Stalin's purges, the Spanish civil war, or the ideological training of long prison sentences in Sremska Mitrovica; the intense personal bonding and loyalty these experiences bred; and early choice of a federal party composed of territorial units with substantial operational autonomy so well suited, it turned out, to resistance war. Thus the effect of the war was to reinforce many of the political choices made before it—choices about social alliances and identities, political organization and leadership tactics, and even the choice of caution on an economic and social program and the disagreements over tactics and pace among peoples facing different conditions.

The Communists' ideological understanding of the war as fascism—class warfare played out at the international level—gave them the confidence to mobilize broad support and non-ethnonational bases for interpreting the civil war within Yugoslavia. At the same time, the choice for a popular front "from below" against external foes, based on the solidarity of the oppressed (workers, peasants, national minorities) was a default position (like that in 1937–40) because they failed, except in Slovenia, to persuade other parties to join their antifascist front. Tito tried more than once in 1941 to negotiate an alliance with Draža Mihailović and the Chetnik forces (the reconstituted Serbian royal army, internationally recognized as the fighting force of the London government-in-exile until 1944); his efforts included two trips of personal diplomacy to Mihailović's camp and offers to play a subordinate role if necessary. The very real disappointment at this failure was repeated in Croatia, where Tito retained the hope throughout the war that he might yet persuade Vladko Maček, leader of the CPP, to cooperate in the Croatian Liberation Front (ZAVNOH).[65] The failure of the June 1941 uprising in Užice, Serbia, the ease with which the Germans could retaliate in urban areas, the tendency of the urban population to passivity until late in the war (refusing to "leave for the forests," as the decision to join the Partisan army was called), and the collaboration of the Croatian Ustashe and the Independent State of

---

[65] Interview with Vlatko Velebit (Tito's emissary during the war to numerous Allied posts, as well as to Šubašić's government in London during the winter of 1944), New Haven, Conn., November 12, 1987.

Croatia with the Axis all necessitated support from the mass of the population in the countryside.

As in the past, the organizational requirements of the contest—in this case war—were politically critical. The leaders' preference to subordinate internal disputes to the unity necessary for political action needed no theory of democratic centralism to justify it, given the very dangerous requirements of physical survival and military operations and the priority of military victory. But the party was also transformed by war. As a vanguard, it became a supreme military headquarters, and its leader became Marshal. Party cadres became officers in mobile fighting units, or military commissars in local and regional "national liberation front" governments or in soldiers' brigades. The unions in their role were replaced as the "most active elements of the working class" by the proletarian peoples' liberation brigades—the elite, mobile troops that bore the brunt of direct military encounters. The army became the "school for the working masses," just as the unions had been "schools for socialism." The core of the postwar governing party was no longer the trade-union movement or the interwar equivalent of old Bolsheviks (the "Spaniards"); it was now the "Club of '41"—the "first fighters" (*prvoborci*) to join the Partisan movement. Throughout the later decades of socialist rule, appeals to civic virtue in political campaigns were modeled on the "best sons of the nation (or people)" (*najbolji sinovi naroda*), a large number of whom gave their lives for the honor; those who survived the war, organized into the influential veterans' association SUBNOR,[66] felt themselves the legitimate guardians of the revolution and of contemporary political virtue.

Of all the elements of prewar political strategy, the true victor of the war was federalism, for this was the principle on which the party constructed wartime administration—the other half of the political instrument to wage war and gain power. As in 1934, the Slovenes took the initiative that secured the principle. On April 27, 1941 (two months before Germany's attack on the Soviet Union), they founded the first of the many regional liberation councils that would govern in liberated territory. The Slovene National Liberation Front was a true united front, linking the leaderships of political parties and other groupings in an antifascist coalition: the Christian Socialist wing of the Slovene Peoples' party, the Communists, Sokol clubs, and several cultural associations of left-wing intellectuals. By February 27, 1943, the secret Dolomite Agreement (declared publicly on May 1) gave to the Communist party the hegemony within this coalition that it had long considered essential to its revolution-

---

[66] Savez Udruženja Boraca Narodnog Oslobodilačkog Rata (League of Associations of Soldiers in the National Liberation War).

ary strategy. At the same time, Slovenia never integrated its partisan corps into the army structure.[67] Following on the Slovene example, and the lessons of the losses at Užice, the party leadership sent members of the central committee out to organize uprisings and similar regional liberation fronts in their home territories. By November 1942, the party leadership had gathered delegates from these fronts to meet in the first of annual assemblies (the first two in liberated territory in Bosnia) that would become the provisional government, the Antifascist Council for the National Liberation of Yugoslavia (AVNOJ).[68] By its second session, AVNOJ had declared a federal republic as the principle of the postwar state.

The primary characteristic of these territorial subdivisions was their autonomy and the decentralization of power to each regional headquarters. Each unit was responsible for waging the war on its territory, for fielding the territorially circumscribed and recruited Partisan brigades, and for founding local governments—people's liberation committees—as territory was liberated. Gathering local progressives and allied supporters into assemblies of delegates sympathetic to the Partisans' liberation struggle, these governments at all three levels—local, territorial, and central—were managed in the parliamentary interim by an elected executive board of party cadres. In most cases, the effective unit of government was the local committee; it was the vital link between party leadership, army, and popular support—"all we had, had to come from the people," Kardelj often said.[69] This lifeline required organizing Partisan units, feeding and clothing soldiers, giving aid to the wounded and to refugees, running messages and material, disabling the enemy, propagandizing for the antifascist alliance, keeping schools open, and ensuring survival of the civilian population. Whether one sees in these committees the socialist model of the "commune" of Paris 1871 and Lenin's State and Revolution, the "municipal socialism" of Austromarxist slogan, or the Balkan and South Slav tradition of local self-government, they were undeniably the practical base of a new state, a base on which both Kardelj and Ranković would draw after the war.

The task of war also meant that executive power at the center fused party and military functions; the Supreme Headquarters was both central military command and politbureau of the Communist Party of Yugoslavia (CPY). This executive created and controlled its own mobile brigades (to Stalin's dismay, called proletarian brigades from the moment of their founding in December 1941), which moved with the action and engaged

---

[67] Gow, Legitimacy and the Military, 37. The Slovene partisan corps was, however, subordinated to—without being incorporated into—the fourth army (of four) in May 1945.

[68] The Slovenes and Macedonians did not attend, however.

[69] Nešović, Privredna politika i ekonomske mere u toku oslobodilačke borbe naroda Jugoslavije, 29.

the enemy strategically. These parallel armies—the proletarian brigades of the center and the territorial armies of the regions—actually acknowledged and reinforced the basic administrative autonomy of the territorial councils.

Although there remained challengers to Tito's leadership of the party both during and after the war, his joint role as supreme military commander and party secretary, the dictates of military as well as party hierarchy, and the profound emotional power and symbolism of the war hero clearly made alternative choices nearly impossible. Tito held his leadership position, confirmed in 1940, until his death in 1980. His personal style of rule can be traced directly to the needs of guerrilla warfare and its principles of military organization; he saw insubordination as both personal affront and vital danger to effective operations, and he approached factional conflicts as a matter of personal disloyalty requiring a change in leadership and installation of persons who could be trusted. Habits of political calculation that many later attributed to the political culture of Tito's native region—the political "cleverness" (lukavost; literally, "foxiness") of the peasantry of the Zagrebačke Zagorje lying between Croatia and Slovenia—were necessary to survival in guerrilla war, where preemptive action against the external foe and, when necessary, temporary retreat were a source of strength under conditions of weakness. Although differences of opinion and theoretical interpretation were not always obviated by personal loyalty and Tito's inclination to restore discipline and political harmony by co-opting into the leadership younger followers of a challenger, many of these skills remained too useful to abandon in postwar circumstances.

This was particularly the case in international relations, where Tito's wily behavior can be seen in wartime relations with Stalin (and thus with the international workers' movement)—as opposed to the usual interpretation that the party leadership was practicing self-restraint of its revolutionary goals in deference to Stalin's fears that "premature" party radicalism would spoil his relations with Britain—and also in his November 1943 independent declaration of a new state and his demand for international recognition of the sovereignty of Yugoslavia as a republic, in order to preempt the Allied leaders as they met at Teheran. Tito had learned with growing astonishment and anger that Stalin continued to support the London government-in-exile despite accumulating evidence that its forces in the field, the Chetniks, were collaborating outright with the Germans, and then learned (erroneously) that the Allies were preparing a landing in Yugoslavia to reinstate the king and the émigré government waiting in Cairo. Tito devoted much effort to obtaining Allied recognition of the Partisans as the primary fighting force in Yugoslav territory and especially to securing arms and supplies; this, too, required self-assertive cleverness. Only in July 1943, after two long years of British missions to the Partisans and mutual negotiations, did Tito's forces begin to receive Churchill's material recognition of their contribution to the Allied cause, and the British delayed shifting political support from the London government-in-exile to the Partisans until the next year. Soviet aid never materialized. The decisions taken at the second session of AVNOJ on November 29, 1943—to found a republic and refuse recognition to the king and to any international agreements made thereafter by the government-in-exile—were made in consideration of external events. Perhaps the participants had in mind the fate of the first Yugoslav state, when parties to the Corfu Declaration in 1917 also felt forced by diplomatic negotiations to act before they had reached mutual concord. But by 1943, Tito and his circle were intent on taking the initiative and presenting a *fait accompli* of domestic resolve against Stalin's pleas for silence on these matters. They informed Stalin of the AVNOJ gathering less than twenty-four hours in advance through his Comintern emissary, who had only just arrived at Partisan headquarters. As Kardelj later reported, their shock the next October when they learned of the Stalin-Churchill talks about Eastern and Western spheres of influence in postwar Eastern Europe and the Balkans—the "percentage deal" that would split Yugoslavia fifty-fifty—as well as of British maneuvers to reinstate the king, similarly led Tito to sign forthwith the accord with the head of the government-in-exile, Ivan Šubašić, for a provisional coalition government that they had been negotiating for nearly five months. The timing of the formation of a new government, announced in March 1945, was likewise a peremptory strategy in the face of the Allies' meeting at Yalta and their renewed efforts to shape the Yugoslav state and Balkan relations by forcing international recognition of AVNOJ on terms agreed to in the Tito-Šubašić accord of November 1, 1944 (for example, a coalition cabinet that included prewar politicians and review and ratification of the provisional government's legislation by a constituent assembly).[70]

The wartime symbiosis between party and army, political and national fortunes thus strengthened the leaders' tendency to analyze political struggles in international terms and to define the national question in terms of unity in a joint cause and against external threat. The dynamic of political decisions followed these two imperatives. The timing of the political stages of the revolution in the course of the war came to be set in large part by Tito's reading of external events and the international "correlation of forces," a pattern that continued in domestic policy after the war. Posi-

---

[70] Kljaković, "The Legacy of the Anti-Fascist Council"; Petranović, *Politička i ekonomska osnova narodne vlasti u Jugoslaviji za vreme obnove*, 207. See also Clissold, *Yugoslavia and the Soviet Union*, 33–40.

tioning within the domestic political arena depended on prior positioning in the international arena. External military threats only reinforced the Yugoslav Communists' view that capital, both domestic and foreign, would choose *divide et impera* when it could, thus necessitating political unity for the strength to resist.

SLOVENIA AND FOČA

Many issues on which there was internal party disagreement also resurfaced in the course of war, however, especially the meaning of national autonomy and self-determination; the pace of social revolution; and the consequences of social and economic heterogeneity for a uniform, societywide program. Because the war brought the first application of the Communists' strategy to real conditions and the first stages of governance itself, these disagreements and differences under the umbrella of general political and organizational principles already foreshadowed the contradictions in economic policy and outcome that are essential to understanding the political paradox of Yugoslavia's postwar unemployment.

Despite the guiding principle that an appearance of domestic consensus was essential to international leverage, the continuing dispute over the meaning of national autonomy and national rights led to interminable conflicts between the central party and its national sections. The 1941 founding document of the Slovene National Liberation Front, in spite of the party line of a united front, declared "the right of self-determination, including the right of secession and uniting with other people!"[71] To recapture the rebel Macedonians after their section defected to the Bulgarian side, Tito sent an entirely new leadership team to rally dissident elements and organize a separate front under the fiery leadership of Svetozar Vukmanović-Tempo. In Croatia, too, Tito met the party's disloyalty over the 1938 elections with a sweep of its top leadership; but this turned out to be insufficient, and relations with the Croatian party took more of his attention than relations with any other area.[72]

The problem was that the alliance between the CPY and the more-progressive elements of the CPP—not those associated with Maček—in ZAVNOH was dominated by the CPP, while the Croat Communists argued that they could win its following away from Maček's "collaborationist" leadership and inherit its popular and national mantle. To do so, they ignored central orders and accepted a wartime platform written by CPP activists that emphasized Croat national feelings; it included catechism in schools, the goal of democratic revolution (the "bourgeois" task), and an

---

[71] Connor, *The National Question*, 156.
[72] See Irvine, *State Building and Nationalism*.

economic program scarcely distinguishable from the (liberal) republican-
ism and radical populism of Stjepan Radić's CPP during the 1920s. Instead of developing a separate Communist party organization and cadre,
they helped to revive CPP organizations and newspapers and set up governmental offices (such as courts and a telegraph agency) of a "free
Croatia."[73] This waywardness was the cause of endless trips to the Croat
camp by Tito's emissary, Edvard Kardelj, in order to discipline Andrija
Hebrang, its leader after the end of 1942. It even became a source of
trouble with the Slovene National Liberation Front, which found the
Croat platform so appealing that it chose to publish it—earning Kardelj's
public fury. Yet Tito sought time and again to accommodate the Croatian
front so as to retain Croatia for the Communist cause, even to the extent
of playing down the early dominance of Serbs in Partisan units in areas
where the genocidal Ustasha policies had pushed Serbs to organize resistance and seek Partisan protection (in mixed areas of Dalmatia, Kordun,
and Lika). The Communists therefore made a "chauvinist" calculation in
their political equation in Croatia, where conflicts were between nationalities within a federal unit—a course they had explicitly rejected in the
Macedonian case.

The contrast between the "nationalism" for which the central party took
the Croat leadership to task and that in Slovenia is instructive. The
Slovene party, too, pursued a united-front strategy that downplayed
class-based appeals and emphasized populist, liberal, and Slovene cultural elements; it was scarcely different from the idea of Croatia as a single
"Croat" unit, irrespective of ethnonational identities within its territory,
and a Croat national program for them all. The Slovene program was also
a maximizing strategy, in large part a reaction to the loss of popular support the Communists suffered as a result of a class-based program of political differentiation in the villages during the spring of 1941. But the
party's success in forging an early wartime alliance without losing its organizational integrity enabled it to use Slovene nationalism rather than become subordinate to it; and when it sensed popular support was moving
toward the Christian Socials in 1943, it was able to maneuver a secret
agreement for its hegemony within the front.[74]

In dealing with the question of property during the war, which was part
of the question of the pace of revolution, the party also reinforced a du-
ality similar to that of the revisionist compromise of 1940. Early radicalization in the countryside had tried to push the national revolution to a
social revolution—partly spontaneously, partly as a result of party
policy—and there were expropriations, violent confrontations over sei-
zures of land, and "class warfare" between rich and poor peasants soon

[73] Banac, *With Stalin against Tito*, 95–96.
[74] Koštunica and Čavoški, *Party Pluralism or Monism*, 52–54.

after the declaration of popular uprising in 1941 in Slovenia and in the winter of 1941–42 in Montenegro. Because these events appeared to be the cause of a dramatic shift of popular support to the camps of competing parties, the leadership reinforced its commitment not to touch the question of property in the countryside, disavowing local radicals as "left excesses" and "left errors." With respect to industry, finance, and large landholdings, on the other hand, the "advanced core" of Marxist thinking received a boost from the war. The expropriation of exploiting classes could there be equated (as many desired) with the national revolution, with returning to the people its *national patrimony* of what German and Russian Marxists called the "commanding heights" of the economy, exploited by foreign economic interests and protected by the royal government as "gendarme." The right of just revenge against a defeated enemy of king, collaborators, and occupiers legitimized its nationalization. The provisional government's first act, in fact, was to lay claim in November 1943 to areas contested between Slovenia and Italy—the Slovene littoral and islands as well as Istria—and settle scores with the World War I Allies, who had awarded them to Italy (a point of particular interest to Kardelj, whose treatises defending the Slovene character of Trieste and the surrounding countryside were written in the 1930s). The declaration of a republic, of national independence from the king, was in fact a declaration against all remaining feudal property, including the large estates of the Hungarian, German, and Catholic-church landlords of the northern plains of Vojvodina and Slavonia.

In October 1944, within days of the Tito-Šubašić agreement, the government began its nationalization of domestic property by transferring all property owned by enemy combatants to public ownership. Three weeks later, at the third session of AVNOJ, on November 21, 1944, the core of the postwar socialized-property sector was established by expropriating the property of the German state, of war criminals, and of obvious collaborators. This was all the easier because the Axis occupiers had themselves expropriated the core of Yugoslav mining and industry to support their war effort. For example, Germans owned the lead and zinc mines at Trepča (formerly British), the Allatini chrome mine (formerly British), the Bor copper mine (formerly French), the Zenica steel plant, the Bata leather works (formerly Czech), and many textile and cotton mills—a total of 55 percent of Yugoslav industry.[75] In August 1945, an agrarian re-

---

[75] Warriner, *Revolution in Eastern Europe*, 19–20. See the series of reports prepared by Tomasevich for the U.S. War Department on German holdings ("German Economic Penetration and Exploitation of Southeastern Europe," "German Penetration of Corporate Holdings in Serbia," and "German Penetration of Corporate Holdings in Croatia"); Petranović, *Politička i ekonomska osnova narodne vlasti*, pt. 3, chap 1; and Kaser and Radice, *The Economic History of Eastern Europe, 1919–1975*, chap. 20.

form in turn legalized the wartime expropriations—property taken into local control in order to wage the war, and the landed estates and capitalist farms of the enemy and collaborators that were nationalized by fiat in November 1944. Into this national "land fund" also went all landholdings in excess of one hundred hectares that had been owned by banks, industrial enterprises, monasteries, charitable trusts, and churches.

The third tension between a central, uniform policy and the variety of conditions the party leadership faced was a result of the self-sufficiency granted territorial authorities to execute daily administrative tasks. In these experiences of actual governing was the germ of later conflict over economic institutions and policies. Limited to regions where liberation fronts were established and where the Partisans managed to liberate territory over a sustained period, these experiences produced two fundamentally different models of administration according to the political tasks and economic conditions each faced, one in Slovenia, and the other in the two southern territories of Bosnia-Herzegovina and Montenegro with the Bay of Kotor.

Immediately upon forming its council of national liberation in April 1941, the Slovene front formulated a set of governing principles. It was aided in putting these principles into administrative practice and creating stable rule more than a year and a half before the end of the war by the success of the popular-front coalition for the Slovene Communists, the small numbers under arms,[76] the relatively early cessation of hostilities on Slovene territory (one part was incorporated into the German Reich so that industry continued and little destruction occurred, while in the part under the front's control the Italians had capitulated by September 8, 1943), and an effective governmental apparatus from two hundred years of local self-government as a result of the eighteenth-century Theresian reforms.

Government in what I will call the Slovene model was based on "people's power" expressed through local assemblies of voters. They elected an executive body, the people's liberation committee, from delegates of political activists within the liberation front and created a fund, a treasurer, and principles of taxation. The front insisted on civilian control of all economic matters, by local councils independent of military commanders; and it distributed circulars throughout the war to propagandize for maximum local and popular initiative. Essential to its concept of politi-

---

[76] According to Gow, the Partisan movement "was never as strong in Slovenia— throughout 1941, the total of individuals engaged in Partisan detachments in Slovenia did not exceed 700 or 800"; at the time of Italian capitulation, there were probably four to five thousand (but eight thousand in the collaborationist White Guard), and the figure remained low in relation to other to other areas until the end of the war. (*Legitimacy and the Military*, 35).

cal self-government and local initiative was the principle of regional economic self-sufficiency and thus autonomy in economic policy. The party's
actions since 1934 remained consistent on this principle.

The social element of Slovene economic policies lay in the character of
the committee's fund. Beginning in October 1941 with a "people's tax"
and a "Freedom Bond," the front chose to finance the war effort and social
assistance in a way that would also effect a more egalitarian distribution of
wealth in the population. It replaced the host of prewar taxes with a single, progressive tax on incomes and gave citizens the option of voluntary
contributions to the war effort by purchasing shares in the bond. People
could also contribute their labor. To bring all arable land under cultivation and maximize production, the committees organized the free civilian
population (mainly youth and women) into volunteer collective-labor
teams to aid peasant producers. By April 1942, the front had instructed
economic commissions and local committees to assume management of all
land that was abandoned or that belonged to enemies or estate owners
accused of collaborating with the enemy, and then to lease this land gratis
to those willing to work it. In November it declared this property to be
under public ownership, while reiterating the inviolability of private
property once communal needs were met. The skeleton of an apparatus
for economic planning appeared in May 1942. A Central Economic Commission was to set policies for essential production and distribution. An
Administrative Commission was to collect reliable economic data about
supply stores, economic needs, and potential sources of provisions; translate these data into basic production plans; and supervise the implementation of sowing plans. Athough interrupted by hostilities, this economic
apparatus was able to operate again by August 1943.

For social as well as economic reasons, the architects of this economy
placed particular importance on keeping inflation in check and on financial stability, accomplished primarily by regulating upper limits on agricultural prices. With the end of hostilities in September 1943, the
people's liberation committee moved rapidly to order the monetary system. Between September and March of 1944, the committee blocked all
bank accounts to prevent hoarding, issued a new Partisan currency, and
created a bank with all the functions of central finance—issuance and
regulation of the money supply, provision of savings deposits and lending
operations, crediting of producers who were willing to work for the army
and the home front, and regulation of foreign exchange for businesses. By
the end of June 1944, the Slovene Partisan money and its bank, the De-
narni Zavod, had become the currency and central bank, respectively, of
postwar Yugoslavia. As the standard for the rapid conversion of all other
wartime currencies, the Slovene currency's own stability made possible
the early and successful stabilization of the dinar that was to be an impor-

tant mark of early Yugoslav socialist policy (in contrast to, for example, the infamous inflation of 1945–46 in neighboring Hungary).

The Slovene principles were the basis for the governing rules adopted by central party headquarters for application in all liberated territories— areas that were almost entirely in the south, where Partisan engagements were concentrated for most of the war. These principles were elaborated by Moša Pijade, the party's ideological patriarch at the time, into the Foča Regulations of February 1942, named for the leadership's base in eastern Bosnia after their humiliating long march out of Serbia the previous fall. What I call the Foča model employed the same basic political principles as the Slovene model, but in the very different conditions and experience of Bosnia-Herzegovina, Montenegro and the Bay of Kotor, and the Sandžak.

The contrast is striking. In these impoverished, supply-deficit, and heavily embattled regions, where the constant threat of starvation among the rising numbers of landless, poor, orphans, and refugees competed with the demands of an army for food, supplies, and sanctuary, liberation councils confronted highly uncertain conditions and shortages, with few effective instruments. The pressure to increase agricultural production while preventing speculation and inflation from depriving the poorest of access to food demanded a particularly effective political and administrative apparatus, yet the councils had to work with local administrations or cooperatives that were weak even before the war and that were frequently disrupted by battles during the war. In most cases, there was little to do but fall back on the simplest methods: above all, that each household should provide for itself from its own land. But even family self-sufficiency required redistribution. Thus a moratorium on rents was declared, and an agrarian reform distributed "surplus" land belonging to the church, monasteries, and charitable trusts to the landless and land-poor, on the principle of "land to the tiller." Local committees were told to define this surplus and set local landholding maximums. Rich peasants could keep their land on the condition that they provide land for refugees and donate tools to the poor. At the same time, central headquarters ordered the people's committees not to tamper with the "question of ownership."[77] As in Slovenia and Croatia, private property of land was guaranteed; but sharecropping as a form of exploitation was also prohibited, and the people's committees requisitioned peasants' produce to build up stores for the army. These collections were based on the same simple, progressive principle as the income tax in Slovenia, but they were necessarily a tax in kind, based on local surveys of available supplies and estimates of survival minimums for each household. Citizens were handed

[77] Nešović, *Privredna politika*, 129.

receipts certifying that they had fulfilled their tax obligations and said to be redeemable with their local government after the war. As in Slovenia, citizens were encouraged to volunteer donations above their quota.

Conditions did not allow these authorities to effect economic policy through price regulation, as the Slovene front could. Efforts to set prices so as to control distribution and limit inflation only led farmers to withdraw their produce from peasant markets and to complain so loudly that on January 15, 1943, the all-national provisional government ordered that the principle of free markets should be protected and that committees should find political rather than economic remedies to the problem of price inflation. Persuasion rather than a money price had to govern in shortage conditions. In Montenegro, committees established commissions of three persons—two delegates from the army and one from the people's committee—to supervise peasant markets, reminding farmers of their "patriotic duty" to keep prices low. If that did not work, they would flood the market with money to effect a rapid local devaluation. In liberated areas of Serbia and Bosnia, committees also organized merchants into associations for the direct purchase and collection of produce at freely negotiated prices. Some efforts were made to organize marketing cooperatives among peasants themselves in the hope of stimulating production and achieving a marketed surplus without speculation, but the base for such efforts was far less developed than in the highly cooperativized political traditions of Slovenia and Croatia (as the party had discovered in the 1930s). As in Slovenia, the committees also attempted to increase production with public labor, organizing collective-labor teams to cultivate the land of families who could not do so themselves because of the war.

In contrast to the north, the countryside in the predominantly Partisan-held territories faced overwhelming demands arising from the war itself, a local economy that even in good times was far closer to subsistence, and less-developed public institutions for economic cooperation and administration—all exacerbated by enemy occupation of the towns. Committees understandably fell back on a natural economy, adjusted policies and demands to specific local circumstances, and interwove civilian and military needs and personnel in the basic tasks of governing. With fewer instruments, they had to accomplish more in their common "struggle for national defense and liberation," such as actually implementing an agrarian reform, rationing food, and creating supply depots. Distributive egalitarianism and cooperation might have been natural to this setting, but the ambitions of rational planning, monetary stability, popular assemblies, and civilian control belonged to another world.[78]

[78] It would be unwise to think of the situation in the southern theater of war and its Foča principles in terms of the system of war communism in 1919–23, for the communist element

CONCLUSION

In Scandinavian social democracy—the classic case of necessary political commitment to full employment—electoral victories and governmental coalitions under economic circumstances of mass unemployment (the Great Depression) were the conditions that led to the definition of a new approach to unemployment by governmental policies.[79] The conditions that defined most elements of the Yugoslav Communist party's strategy for economic and social transformation were different. The Yugoslav royal government had declared the party illegal in 1921 and prohibited electoral participation by its various front organizations. As a result, party membership declined, and leaders went into exile or underground conspiracy. A minuscule party of 6,600 members with an affiliated youth wing of 17,800 at the last party conference (in October 1940) before war intervened,[80] it had little opportunity to test its strategy against a voting public or to refine it in repeated electoral contests. In contrast, the Austrian Social Democrats, who also came to power after World War II committed to full employment, were largely trade unionists who won sizeable electoral space because of their postwar purge of Fascists, policy of neutrality, and close ties to the United States.[81] While the Austrian Social Democrats had won the contest against the Communist party by the 1920s and their formative political experiences were the struggle against mass unemployment in the 1930s (for which they were jailed) and the subsequent civil war, the Yugoslav Communist party was still engaged in the conflict with the Social Democrats in 1937–40 (with the state being a significant intermediary in the corporatist exclusions after 1937 and in the outright ban on the United Unions organization in 1940, when the Communists were making advances with labor militancy). Moreover, in contrast to Austria, the percent of the Yugoslav population classified as

---

was based in conditions, not ideology. But there are parallels in the debate over ideology and expedience in the Soviet case as well; see Malle, *The Economic Organization of War Communism*, introduction.

[79] Tilton, "A Swedish Road to Socialism." Esping-Andersen, *Politics against Markets*, is especially good on the importance of the particular moment, and therefore domestic and international conditions, of a political decision in the Social Democrats' choice of issues, policy, and social support. See also Hall, *Governing the Economy*, on this subject for England and France.

[80] Banac, *With Stalin against Tito*, 5. Avakumović lists 6,455 as the number of party members (*History of the Communist Party of Yugoslavia* 1:185). The youth wing was called the League of Communist Youth of Yugoslavia (Savez Komunističke Omladine Jugoslavije, generally referred to by its acronym, SKOJ).

[81] Attention is drawn to the Austrian contrast not only because it is another example of social democratic success at full employment, but also because many Yugoslav economists insisted through much of the country's socialist period that if only governmental economic policy were correct, it "could be Austria."

industrial workers was low—only 11 percent as late as 1939—and the unionized working class, designated as those covered by social insurance, was less than 5 percent.[82]

The party's victory came instead through armed struggle and mass mobilization in an antifascist war of national liberation. It confirmed the Communists' choice for federalism (based on national identities historically and territorially defined and on substantial operational autonomy), their choice for revolution against the state and foreign capital, and their inclination to read power in international as well as domestic terms and to put great stock in a strong military defense. It was also profoundly revealing, in a way that would reoccur, of the conditions (international as well as domestic) necessary to support their preferred Slovene model of political and economic institutions—rational planning, economic management through regulation of money and prices, civilian rule in local parliaments combined with the party's ideological (but not administrative) hegemony in a coalition of political forces, and regional self-sufficiency. In the years following the Communists' entry into Belgrade as liberators in October 1944, industrial unemployment was a social question (a question of poverty and survival) far more than an economic one amid the tasks of postwar reconstruction and demobilization. Indeed, wartime destruction left the country in 1945 even less industrialized and more rural than when it entered the war. The defining moments for the CPY on its road to power were instead the revolutionary strategies of the Comintern (particularly with respect to the national question) in the 1920s and 1930s; fascism; world war; and, as we will see in the next two chapters, the cold-war division of the postwar world.

[82] Dukanac, *Indeksi konjunkturnog razvoja Jugoslavije*, 27.

Chapter 3

CREATING A STATE FOR SOCIALIST
DEVELOPMENT

THE EARLY socialist period in Yugoslavia is universally identified with the Soviet model and is called, in the Yugoslav literature, its "administrative period," on the argument that Stalinist policies and a planned economy operated. According to this consensus, the period ended around 1950–52, with the introduction of workers' councils in industry, the abandonment of agricultural collectivization, and the rechristening of the Communist party as the League of Communists to signify its abdication from direct administration for the conscious force of volunteer activists. Furthermore, the view is that these changes that produced the Yugoslav "exception" were introduced in response to popular dissatisfaction and the leaders' need to find domestic bases of political support and legitimacy once they had been abandoned by Moscow and the Cominform, with its famous expulsion letter of June 28, 1948.[1]

This chapter and the next will challenge such a view on three grounds that are essential to understanding the Yugoslav system under Communist party rule that did emerge. First, new states and socioeconomic orders do not emerge fully formed, like the phoenix, especially out of the ashes of war. They have to be created, and this applies especially to the far greater authority and administrative capacity necessary for a planned economy or the centralized, authoritarian character implied by most discussions of an "administrative period." The Yugoslav leadership never had that capacity.

Second, this view does not conform to the facts on the ground. Political power in October 1944, when the Partisans entered Belgrade, came largely from the barrel of a gun, was distributed among many authorities, and was territorially incomplete. Military campaigns with devastating losses (including more than thirty thousand on the Srem front)[2] continued into the spring of 1945, and the borders of the state were not fully settled

---

[1] On the Cominform conflict, see Clissold, *Yugoslavia and the Soviet Union, 1939–1973;* Ulam, *Titoism and the Cominform;* Djilas, *Conversations with Stalin;* V. Dedijer, *The Battle Stalin Lost;* and Banac, *With Stalin against Tito.* For this characterization of the period, any work on postwar Yugoslavia will suffice.

[2] V. Dedijer, *Novi prilozi za biografiju Josipa Broza Tita* 3:143.

until 1954. International recognition of the new state and leadership (and thus both national independence and domestic authority) was not secure until the end of 1949, being contested repeatedly during this period by both West and East. The party's attempts to introduce a five-year plan for rapid industrialization and the apparatus necessary to it began only during 1947, after a period of reconstruction; the plan was not patterned after a Stalinist model, but rather based in the Leninism of the New Economic Policy—a choice confirmed in April 1946, not 1952; and it was never consolidated because of continual difficulties obtaining foreign assistance and because of growing fears of war (in late 1947) and the resulting policy change. The period saw a set of changing policies and priorities in the construction of the state, when difficult international conditions and quarrels within the top leadership over fundamental questions of strategy were most influential.

Third, this view makes assumptions about the political dynamic of such a state that are faulty—for example, that it was largely principles of party hierarchy and personal obedience that were at stake in the Tito-Stalin conflict, or that when leaders introduced new policies that seemed more friendly to the population, they did so in response to popular demand, in order to gain more political support. Instead, the political dynamic of the period was driven by the international difficulties of the leaders' attempt to combine political radicalism and social caution—difficulties in both East and West, at the level of national security and foreign trade and aid. It was the goal of national, not party, independence that consumed this initial period of state-building, whereas relations between party and population were defined by the leaders' attempt to obtain desired economic outcomes within the constraints of an inhospitable foreign environment and by their conceptions of the proper strategy (economic theory, state form, and social relations) for transformation. As we will see in the next chapter, this throws a different light on their policy of "workers' control" and policies toward agriculture.

Yet revision of Yugoslav historiography is not the primary purpose of these two chapters. It is instead to demonstrate that the institutions of the Yugoslav system (such as workers' councils) and the focus of political conflicts (such as center-republic or national conflict) were defined originally by the leaders' strategy for industrialization without capitalist unemployment, that those institutions changed frequently in order to keep that strategy on track in the face of changing international conditions, and that the oppositions usually postulated in the literature—such as between administrative and self-managing systems, plan and market, center and republics—do not distinguish between systems and policies. A broad conception of policies toward labor does make that distinction, for the state (in its new sense) remained a master employer that periodically reorganized the society in adjusting to problems of capital, although with means that were neither directive nor market.

The leaders' "ideas actualized in action"[3] yielded, in the first years after the war, the institutional pieces of the two levels of power critical to employment: in laying an organizational framework to implement their economic-growth strategy, the leaders created a state, while a new system for employing and remunerating labor emerged from a struggle on several fronts to replace the market wage and collective bargaining of capitalism. In both aspects, there were difficulties at the highest levels because of a major political quarrel over the source of capital for the industrialization drive and over its foreign implications, and because of unexpected difficulties in foreign relations. This chapter ends with the first phase of that process of institutionalization, toward the end of 1947, when Tito perceived the foreign disputes and environment as so threatening that he chose to shift to a policy of military self-reliance. Chapter 4 examines the second phase, between November 1947 and 1951, when the leadership pursued a wholesale, though temporary, adjustment of this original structure of state and society to meet the new demands of production and foreign trade—with a dizzying kaleidoscope of legislation, amendments, temporary transfers of authority and power over capital and labor, and changes in industrial relations and agricultural policy.

A Rational State

The primary problem for the Yugoslav leaders after 1944 was how to industrialize rapidly, to reverse both the very low capital capacity that limited any real rise in living standards, and the country's vulnerability to the greater economic and national strength of industrialized powers. Promising a life different than that under the prewar kingdom yet facing the extraordinary demands of postwar reconstruction, the leaders found that their need for capital was greatest when they had the least to spare and when their political position was most fragile. The conflict was not one of relative shares for investment/profits and consumption/wages, but of how to effect structural change that would increase the capacity to employ the labor surplus in agriculture without creating financial crises that would devalue industrial labor, through falling wages or outright unemployment.

In the leaders' conception of economic growth, society's capacity to employ was limited by the size of the subsistence fund. This limit varied according to the number of people consuming more than they produced, whether because they were unemployed, their productivity was low, they

---

[3] Verdery, *National Ideology under Socialism*, 9.

performed tasks that were necessary to growth but did not yield a consumable output (such as producing capital goods and raw materials or laying infrastructure and constructing new plant), or they were paid for work that produced no usable output or service at all. There were also political limits due to the composition of the leaders' political alliance of smallholders, wage earners, and salary earners because the growth of the three groups' jobs and incomes were potentially in mutual conflict—even assuming that social standards of consumption could be kept modest for a while. A rural-urban conflict related to the price of food could arise between the level of farmers' incomes—and thus the relative threat of their proletarianization—on the one hand, and the level of workers' consumption standards—and thus their cost of production and the threat of their unemployment—on the other. A conflict between production workers and administrative personnel and another between generations might pit the wages and jobs for industrial workers against the net value (profit) redistributed to create new jobs for peasants and to employ middle strata.

With the high level of agricultural "surplus" (this surplus, called "agricultural overpopulation" in the interwar period, was measured by the proportion of the rural population that made no marginal contribution to productive output on the farm and was thus de facto unemployed), overcoming these economic and political limits required more than marginal adjustments. In the period between 1921 and 1938, only one-twelfth of the natural population growth (then at 1.5 percent a year) had been absorbed by industrial employment (for a total of 180,000 new jobs). The agricultural labor surplus during that period was estimated at 60 percent. The number of persons recorded as actively seeking nonagricultural employment grew, in proportion to the number of insured industrial workers, from 9.6 percent in 1922 to 26 percent in 1931, and to more than 80 percent by 1938.[4] The "peasant question," in Kardelj's statement of the leadership's policy, was "not to be resolved primarily in agriculture but in industrialization of the country, with the transfer of a large part of the labor force from the village into industrial production and other economic activities."[5] But not at the cost of real growth; that would only force cuts in

[4] Macura, *Stanovništvo kao činilac privrednog razvoja Jugoslavije*, 38–39.

[5] Cited in Puljiz, *Eksodus poljoprivrednika*, 6. Tomasevich writes for the interwar period: "A realization of basic significance, which became clear during the 1930's to most Yugoslav economists and to some politicians and administrators, was that the problem of agricultural overpopulation was the central economic issue of the country and that it had far-reaching political and social significance and ramifications. . . . Since mass emigration was impossible, the only avenue of approach to a permanent solution . . . was through industrialization. . . . Furthermore, there was an almost unanimous opinion in support of planned industrialization and, generally, for a planned economy in which the leading criteria would be the needs and the interests of the large mass of the peasant population" (*Peasants, Politics, and Economic Change in Yugoslavia*, 338–40).

consumption and employment later. In the language of the leadership, the structural change to create new employment capacity could not ignore the "law of value," the necessity of maintaining the "equilibrium conditions of reproduction."[6]

The leaders' solution was to restructure all of society for the optimal use of economic resources. At its center would be socially owned assets in manufacturing and finance (the "commanding heights" of Marxist discourse), which would use existing capacity to the fullest, the most modern technology available, and rational calculation of production technique and work incentives to increase productivity. Invoking Trotsky, Boris Kidrič (who had moved from heading the Slovene National Liberation Front to controlling the chief federal economic portfolios) maintained that the plan would be the "brain" of the economy, gathering accurate economic data from producers and providing them with scientific information about aggregate trends and possibilities in return. Expansion of the public sector would occur where production could benefit from the industrial organization of labor and mechanization, such as with large landholdings in grain production, mines, and large-scale manufacturing; and where services, such as wholesale trade, could benefit from economies of scale and the reduction of transfer costs by handing administration and distribution to producers themselves within an industrial branch. Society itself would be reorganized to reduce waste and nonproductive bureaucracy, creating a lean public administration—in Lenin's words, a "parsimonious" state—where the rate of capital accumulation in society would rise in proportion as administrative (*režijski*) costs declined. The instructions and incentives to implement public decisions including investment, would be communicated through centrally set financial indicators (cash advances, prices, credit, wage rates), not a bureaucracy, and the entire public sector would be covered by uniform accounts for the economy.

Alongside this capital sector, the assets of the rest of society would be redistributed more equally so as to raise average consumption and guarantee all households the means necessary for subsistence. From this "individual" sector, persons would move gradually into industry as growth in the public sector—through ever-higher productivity—created economic demand for new employment. It was very important that this process also be rational, so that there would be no fall in consumption standards already attained and no threat to growth. It was better to keep down the demand for food for the urban and industrial population by limiting the pace of agrarian exodus than to employ extensive methods of capital accu-

---

[6] For the context of the same debate in the Soviet Union and on the Leninism of the Yugoslav leadership, see Sutela, "Ideology as a Means of Economic Debate," 200.

mulation that would delay proportionate decreases in the consumption fund and threaten macroeconomic stability.

Moreover, to avoid the bureaucratic costs of centralization and accommodate the vast cultural and economic differences across republics that the territorial self-government of the federal system presumed, operational management would be as decentralized as possible. Because social ownership of assets in the public sector made governments the "founders" of enterprises, with final rights to dispose, regulate, and tax firms in their jurisdiction, there needed to be a functional division of labor to distinguish among levels of government. Following Lenin's approach to the national question (although its basis in the three departments of the Marxian scheme of reproduction also had strong Habsburg roots, most recently evident in the jurisdictions granted Croatia by the Cvetković-Maček Agreement of 1939), this division gave the federal government jurisdiction over defense, foreign relations, the monetary instruments necessary to maintain a unified market for the country, and investment in developmental projects of consequence to the growth of the economy as a whole, such as the long-gestating and huge capital investment for producers' goods such as iron and steel and major infrastructure. The federal government did not *own* any of these assets, however, and as soon as federal projects were up and running, they were to be handed to the republics for management. Federal revenue would come from customs duties and the turnover tax, but any share in the tax on enterprise income would have to be granted by republics. Republican governments would have jurisdiction over Department II activities—production supplies, processing industries, manufacturing, agriculture, labor, and capital projects of a regional character. To the local governments went Department III—the sphere of household consumption, comprising both public and private activity, such as small consumer goods, services and trades, local roads, elementary schools, and retail shops. The concept of "socially necessary consumption" assumed that expectations and needs would vary and, given the great variety of circumstance and custom in Yugoslavia at the time, that matters of daily life were best resolved close to home. This principle of subsidiarity might be abrogated under special circumstances (such as the emergency need for a national food policy immediately after the war, which prescribed sowing plans and compulsory purchase quotas for both state farms and private farmers), but never abandoned entirely.

Putting this program into practice, the leadership began with the transfer of property to the public sector and the redistribution of wealth for "social" (welfare) purposes. The process occurred in stages, from November 1945 to April 1948. It began with the provisional government's legalization of the nationalization of enemy property discussed in chapter 2, which yielded 55 percent of large industry and 6 percent of arable land; another 27 percent of the industrial stock—property owned by foreigners or citizens who had fled the country—was placed under state management. Most of the transport sector and manufacturing of household necessities (matches, salt, tobacco, fuel oil) were already under state monopoly.[7] Justifying this transfer largely as an assertion of national sovereignty, the leadership had wide popular support, and talk in the assembly and in public life appeared almost euphoric over kicking out foreigners and escaping national dependency.[8]

In the private sector, agrarian and currency reforms reduced substantial previous inequalities, although their purpose was not equalization but social transformation—reducing opportunities for exploitation or dispossession of the tools and land necessary for rural and artisanal households to subsist independent of the state. Distribution of land to poor and landless peasants who would actually work it added two hectares each of the holdings of 316,435 rural households, with special privileges to veterans of the Partisan army. Courts set up to hear claims required applicants to "show their horny hands as proof" of eligibility.[9] The agrarian-reform legislation of August 1945 prohibited hired and tenant labor and set limits of 20 to 35 hectares on private landholdings (depending on land use). The goal of currency reform—to prevent inflation and reduce money wealth—was assisted politically by the need to convert occupation currencies into the dinar, although in this case the assembly's nationalizing fervor infected national relations at home. Croat leaders (especially Andrija Hebrang) objected to the terms of exchange given the Croat currency, reflecting the Croats' historical memory of being cheated as former Habsburg citizens by the Serb monarchy after World War I—a memory that had been revived in public debate over the negotiations for Croat autonomy in 1939.[10] Moreover, the currency and banking reform revealed most clearly the influence that the Slovene experience during the war would have on the new economy. By this currency conversion and then revaluation, the obligatory reporting of money holdings, blocked bank accounts, confiscation of fortunes above certain limits through a highly progressive tax, expropriation of war profits into a national fund for recon-

[7] Kaser and Radice, *The Economic History of Eastern Europe, 1919–1975* 2:65–67; Zeković, "Razvoj i karakteristike privrednog sistema FNRJ"; and Hondius, *The Yugoslav Community of Nations*.

[8] See the discussion in the federal council of the provisional assembly (Narodna Skupština FNRJ, *Drugo redovno zasedanje* [4th session, December 5, 1946], 97–112).

[9] Doreen Warriner, the agrarian economist on the UNRRA mission to Yugoslavia, in *Revolution in Eastern Europe*, 138.

[10] Hebrang, at the fourth session of the provisional assembly, February 3, 1945, in Antifašističko Veće Narodnog Oslobodjenja Jugoslavije (AVNOJ), *Zakonodavni rad*, 106.

struction, and a fixed exchange rate with gold and the U.S. dollar, the new authorities reduced the money supply tenfold, gained substantial revenues for the reconstruction budget, and prevented serious inflation such as that in neighboring Hungary and Romania.

But it was not until the spring of 1948 that wholesale trading firms and the property of many urban trade and service establishments were nationalized. According to a more populist than Marxist analysis by Kidrič, in a 1946 speech to the national assembly, commercial profit was the most "primitive form of exploitation"; its drain on national accumulation through state wholesale-trading firms was proportionately greater the lower the level of industrial development and organic composition of capital (as in Yugoslavia at the time).[11] National wealth and individual consumption would rise together only if growth occurred in real terms—by producers who lowered production costs and raised productivity, not by commerce, speculation, and debt that produced money profits and had the potential to dilute incentives and destabilize the economy. Although Kidrič attacked the limits that commercial profit, other forms of speculation, and the stimulus to a profiteering spirit placed on true surplus value, his audience was likely to associate such profit with the "leeches" of Adam Smith and the long tradition of viewing this idea of exploitation as the merchants' and bankers' "profit upon alienation" against small producers.

One of the first acts of the provisional government, at the end of 1944, was to unify all prewar workers' and employees' unions into the United Unions of Yugoslavia, with divisions according to industrial branch. Each factory and firm would have a single union and eventually party office. In April 1945, legislation also set countrywide minimum wage rates for each industrial branch, equalized wage rates for men and women, and authorized employers to grant wage increases in response to price rises. Technical normatives for wages in priority branches were worked out throughout 1945–47. A uniform accounting system and unification of the principles of economic calculation were essential, Hebrang told the provisional assembly in February 1945 in his maiden speech as commissar of industry to introduce this legislation (retroactive to January 1); they were necessary "so as to organize economic activity rationally and to oversee economically all our state and private firms. The situation we have inherited is neither contemporary nor rational, but a sign instead of our economic backwardness, which will brake movement in the direction of increased production."[12] The prewar multitude of decentralized, separate welfare funds, each with different sources of revenue and different provi-

[11] Kidrič, "Obrazloženje osnovnog zakona o državnim privrednim preduzećima" (July 1946), 10.
[12] Hebrang, in AVNOJ, *Zakonodavni rad*, 37–38.

sions (such as the funds for social insurance during unemployment, old age, illness, and incapacitation), was also to be unified and centralized. As minister of social policy Anton Kržišnik explained,[13] it would be far more "economically rational" to increase the number of members and thus lower the amount of their individual contributions, reducing the necessary size of the reserve fund as well as offices and staff.

Hebrang also told the provisional assembly in February 1945 that strict limits on government expenditures (which would fall over time as the state "withered away") and obligatory balancing of government budgets were essential to a "people's government" that would "no longer permit theft from the people or the state by means of fraudulent accounts" or earnings gained through "exaggerated exploitation of the labor force, speculation, state subventions, and high protective tariffs at the expense of the consuming masses."[14] At the same time, all financial accounts— from the government budget to public funds for social insurance or education—were sectioned by republic, with the aim of budgetary autonomy and self-financing. Expenditures were to be made where revenues were collected; where there were common funds, the principle was the right to draw on those funds in proportion to the amount contributed. The spirit of this economic federalism was captured in the assembly's discussion of social-insurance funds in July 1945, when Kržišnik explained that "if we are a communal house, our stomachs are not communal"—and then, hastening to allay the fears of poorer regions, that this "did not exclude the possibility of offering fraternal aid" to federal units in less fortunate circumstances.[15]

The organizational apparatus for the economic plan and the law on state enterprises went to the national assembly in June and July 1946.[16] Firms were operationally autonomous, but because of the great shortage of technical experts (such as engineers and accountants) for critical advice on production technique and technical improvements, the middle administrative level between the enterprises and their respective ministries (these branch administrative offices were called *direkcije*, or directorates), along with expediters specializing in locating the cheapest source of supplies, became in practice more important and was the basis for the

[13] Kržišnik, ibid., 205–9.

[14] Hebrang, ibid., 38.

[15] Kržišnik, ibid., 212.

[16] The principles of ownership and internal organization of enterprises and the apparatus for planning and implementing investment choices were set out in two fundamental laws: the Law on the General Economic Plan and State Organs for Planning, sent to the assembly on June 4, 1946; and the Law on State Economic Enterprises, sent July 24. The Law on Cooperatives, defining the private sector and its relations with the public sector, was sent on July 27.

cooperation among firms in the same industrial branch that would replace market allocation and competition.[17] Most important to the leaders' concept of planning, however, was the system of cash accounts by which the production plan (also subdivided by republic) would be made operational. Following the Soviet system of *khozraschët*, in which budgetary units were autonomous and obliged to balance their budgets quarterly, the finance ministry and its banks (and especially its staff accountants) were to ensure that the circulation of money was tied to increases in real wealth by allotting cash directly for the needs of production.[18] The branch ministries and the planning commission were subordinate to territorial authority; and the economy was governed not by the plan but by policy decisions of the Economic Council, which coordinated both federal policy and the policies and cooperation of the republican governments.[19]

But the nexus of the entire system was the local governments (still the people's committees of wartime administration)—above all where employment and consumption were concerned.[20] Although the organizational changes would seem to have been creating a highly centralized "administrative" system and planned economy, the localities were actually at the center. The five-year plan was an aggregate of local plans, and it could not be composed until enterprises had formulated their production plans and localities their social plans; delays in preparing the plan for 1947 led to frequent admonitions against local commissars of the republican ministries. Local taxation and investment in local industries would determine whether the population's standard of living rose or fell and whether the market links with the peasantry brought food to the towns or col-

[17] These *direkcije* were the equivalent of Soviet *glavki*. See Carr and Davies, *Foundations of a Planned Economy*, vol. 1, pt. 1:351–84.

[18] See Davies, *The Development of the Soviet Budgetary System*, 70–84, 297ff.; Dobb, *Soviet Economic Development since 1917*, chap. 15; Lavigne, "The Creation of Money by the State Bank of the USSR"; and Gedeon, "Yugoslav Monetary Theory and Its Implication for Self-Management," on the influence of the real-bills doctrine on Soviet (and Yugoslav) monetary theory.

[19] The Yugoslav leaders' Leninism was reflected in their preference for giving priority to the territorial principle of organization above the sectoral. Lenin was an expert on regional policy, and one can see this in the regionalization program of July 1923 (see Carr, *Socialism in One Country, 1924–1926* 2:273–303) and in Khrushchev's Leninist revival ("economic reform") in the *sovnarkhozy* (see Nove, *An Economic History of the U.S.S.R.*, 335–37, 352–61). According to Hamilton, the basis of the Yugoslav five-year plan was the comparative advantage of each republic, with supplemental state investment in capital industries in strategically secure, mineral-rich areas in the south and interior (*Yugoslavia: Patterns of Economic Activity*).

[20] The writer Miroslav Krleža, a longtime critic and sympathizer of the CPY and a Tito confidant, said, when asked by Milovan Djilas what he thought of the new regime, "It's really awkward being subject to a district committee" (Djilas, *Rise and Fall*, 52).

lapsed for lack of local goods that farmers wanted to buy. The careful mobilization of the true agricultural labor surplus without exceeding the capacity for intensive employment in industry and without inordinate social upheaval depended on the economic and political calculations of local governments. Because of the leaders' strategy for gradual incorporation of peasants and the private sector into the modern public sector, it was also at the local level that economic coordination between the two sectors and their separate principles of socialist and capitalist accumulation would take place. Without proper local accounting, the leaders' method of achieving macroeconomic stability would fail; there was thus, throughout the fall of 1946 (and for two more years), an urgency to the work of the finance ministry—the loyal, skilled accountants who would guarantee this was Hebrang's "people's government"—to teach local officials how to keep economic records and use profit-and-loss accounting to supervise their economies.

Political stability depended on local authorities as well. It was at the local level that the majority of the population in the private sector had political representation; the leaders' concept of democracy, as we saw in the wartime Slovene model, was local participation of citizens in economic tasks and the assemblies of popular government. The fulfillment of their long-term goal of social transformation would begin with cooperatives at the village level and voters' assemblies in which political participation in economic decisions was to be the vehicle for educating peasants and artisans away from a subsistence mentality (which set limits on effort once basic needs were satisfied) toward an industrial mentality of ever-increasing social wealth and a long time horizon. And it was at the local level that opponents to specific policies or to the revolution itself (as were many clerics, wealthy peasants, and party organizers from prewar agrarian parties) could do damage and had to be engaged. A measure of the importance of these local jurisdictions is the sheer volume and frequency of legislated local reorganization in these years.

QUARRELS OVER DEVELOPMENT STRATEGY

The institutional apparatus of this new economy and administration, at least on paper, borrowed heavily from Soviet experience, both of the 1920s and the 1930s. But the principles of growth and the combination of political radicalism with social and economic gradualism, as we saw also in the interwar period and the war, were decidedly Leninist rather than Stalinist. Political revolution, national independence, and an assertive posture to define borders and alliances in the region were combined with an economic policy that recalls the New Economic Policy of the 1920s—

through which, in Bukharin's familiar phrase, the "commanding heights [would] gradually absorb the backward economic units"[21] and through which the incentives of market production would lead small producers, especially in agriculture, to increase yields and marketed produce or services and to cooperate with or join the modern, lean public sector at their own pace. As in the Soviet debates on industrialization of the 1920s, this combination left unresolved the source of rapid capital accumulation. The targets of the five-year plan scheduled to begin in January 1947 made this contradiction in strategy apparent. Despite the derision in foreign circles that met Milovan Djilas's boast that Yugoslavia would catch up with England in industrial production within ten years, and despite the charge of "megalomaniacal" expectations for immediate increases in capacity and output, the plan's objective of quenching the country's "thirst for economic and political independence," as Tito told the national assembly in April 1947, was deadly serious.[22]

The quarrel came early, at the politbureau meeting of April 1946: would the initial organizational rationalizations, concentration of scarce resources, and even "released initiative" of the agrarian reform and "people's government" be sufficient for the rapid leap in new investment?[23] The opposition's case began with agriculture: on top of the demands of reconstruction and lowered productivity in farms and factories (compared to that achieved by 1939), farmers were likely to consume a greater proportion of their produce for some time, and the equalization of purchasing power among urban consumers would raise their aggregate consumption as well. Hebrang confided to Doreen Warriner, the English agricultural economist on the UNRRA (United Nations Relief and Reconstruction Administration) mission to Yugoslavia, that the policy could not work economically without more-rapid increases in agricultural productivity and therefore without rapid collectivization of the land.[24] Trade control would not be sufficient to gain access to farmers' surplus and to prevent an inflationary spiral when industrial output would also be delayed by capital investments. The opposition argued that this reliance on the "law of value" and nominal control over the public sector without more-basic changes in the sphere of production or a slower-growth path was, simply put, state capitalism, with all its known consequences.[25] The

[21] Cited in A. Erlich, *The Soviet Industrialization Debate*, 10.

[22] Tito, "Speech on the Five-Year Plan," pam. collection, Yale University Library.

[23] See the discussion in V. Dedijer, *Novi prilozi* 3:292. The partial minutes that remain of the politbureau meetings are printed in this work.

[24] Warriner, *Revolution in Eastern Europe*, 142.

[25] The policy meant combining control over finance and investment in the domestic economy with openness to foreign aid and trade with capitalist countries.

leaders' policy of "socialism in one country," especially, was "foolhardy."[26]
Their economic federalism placed limits on the state's capacity to capture
the surplus and to maintain a stable currency—which particularly concerned Sreten Žujović, as minister of finance. Not only did the federal
division of the budget defy the fundamental accounting principle of budgetary unity, he argued, but it also left in the republics' control resources
that the center needed for new investment, and it did not define final
authority over the inevitable conflicts that would arise between the republics and the center over access to capital (and, it turned out, to labor as
well). Since the budgetary resources would come largely from a tax on
public-sector firms, the fact that the most-profitable and best-established
firms were under republican jurisdiction and concentrated largely in the
more-developed areas left unclear where the revenues for federal responsibility for defense and development would be found.[27]

The leaders' responses are notable as much for the political weapons
they used to deflect criticism as for the economic solutions they proposed.
Kidrič (as proponent of their macroeconomic policy) took the political of-
fensive: the "theory" that the state and its companion, the cooperative
sector of the economy, were in essence capitalist, with the same laws and
forms, was "an opportunistic, ultimately reactionary theory, which denies
the revolutionary political, social, and economic changes in the new
Yugoslavia. . . . [Its proponents] forget that . . . the state sector of our
economy is the result of the fact that we have a *people's power, and not a
power of exploiting classes.*"[28] This political control was the crucial difference. The operation of the "law of value" was not just characteristic of
capitalism, he continued, for that law would hold until distribution could
occur according to need. The real issue was whether the accumulation
that resulted from it remained in the hands of capitalists to serve "private
goals, and not social ones" or was under the control of a people's power.[29]

The dual strategy was a matter of concern, Kidrič did admit (indeed, he
worried publicly), because of the problems for macroeconomic management that would arise from the coexistence in one system of two logics of
accumulation, one socialist and one capitalist, and the "stubborn perse-
verance and resourcefulness" of the latter.[30] But in his view, the problem

[26] Sreten Žujović, in V. Dedijer, *Novi prilozi* 3:383–85. Four and a half years later,
Žujović admitted that he, at least, had found the discussion on state capitalism "confusing"
and had been forced into silence by "Djilas's insults." See his confession, in the form of a
public letter demanded by the party leadership, printed in *Borba*, November 25, 1950, 1.

[27] The debate is apparent in the minutes of the politbureau meeting (V. Dedijer, *Novi
prilozi* 3:292–93).

[28] Kidrič, "O nekim principijelnim pitanjima naše privrede," 46.

[29] Ibid.

[30] Kidrič, "Obrazloženje osnovnog zakona," 9.

of agriculture lay not in production but in exchange, and in the ability of the state to capture its resources and to secure advantage to the principles of accumulation in the socialized sector. He saw the most worrisome obstacle as the "monopoly position" of rural traders over agricultural markets and its inflationary potential, which could destabilize the operation of the "law of value."

Attempting to shame opponents for "underestimating" the domestic capacity to undertake the plan, Kidrič also attacked their pessimism about the liberating potential of this new people's power:

> When we listen to the so-called expert "arguments" of those sages who undervalue the creative power of our working masses, we are reminded of similar "military experts," who in 1941 demonstrated "professionally" that partisan [guerrilla] warfare in Yugoslavia was not possible and that a regular army could not be created from a partisan army. Under the leadership of our Party and Comrade Tito, our national masses very quickly destroyed both the theory and the practice of such prophecies.[31]

The economic solution to this initial demand on both investment and consumption was to gain supplements to the capacity of the public sector, from two sources: unpaid, *voluntary labor* from the population, and *foreign aid*. In order to keep the monetary demand for goods limited when new investment in capital equipment and infrastructure would delay the production of consumer goods but demand new workers and greater effort, the leaders would follow the Soviet example of "socialist competition" in the capital sector and would prolong the wartime system of Partisan brigades outside it. Employed workers would be rewarded for surpassing labor norms and cutting costs with status, honor, and nonmonetary privileges. "Shock workers," who saved on materials or exceeded piecework rates; "innovators" who suggested organizational or technical improvements in the labor process; and inventors in the ranks of workers would be given titles, badges of honor, new suits of clothing, or vacations in the new workers' resorts, and their names and pictures would be prominently displayed in one of the many broadsheets that poured forth to publicize the industrialization drive. Extraordinary but short-term demands for labor for the initial push to industrialize would be met by mobilizing "all available hands" of the rest of the population into "volunteer brigades" (what critics called a "bare-hands" approach to industrialization). Housewives, youth, demobilized soldiers, even prisoners of

---

[31] Kidrič, "O nekim principijelnim pitanjima," 49. Kiro Gligorov, the party's appointee to be deputy under Žujović at the finance ministry, used similar arguments against Žujović, including an attack on "cameralistics," in "Neki problemi u vezi sa izvršenjem opšte državnog budžeta za 1947 god."

war would provide free labor for construction; the leaders would thus avoid an extensive labor mobilization that would undermine their long-run strategy for intensive labor use within the capital sector and worsen short-run pressures on monetary stability.

In this period, each republic and locality had its projects, from schools and hospitals to roads and bridges, steel mills and machine factories. Salaried office workers were required to devote part of their worktime (and manual labor) to local projects. Towns organized "shock weeks" throughout 1946 and 1947 to reconstruct villages in war-torn regions. The federal government's projects, in line with its jurisdiction over capital development, included the "Brotherhood and Unity" motor highway between Belgrade and Zagreb, the "youth rail line" between Banovići and Brčko in Bosnia, the expansion of the mine at Banovići-Živinice (Bosnia), and the hydroelectric power plants at Žirovnica (Macedonia), Maribor (Slovenia), and Dravograd (Slovenia). At the same time, socialist competition and labor brigades were organized to move political organizations and values in the direction the leaders sought. Of the brigades, for example, the most prestigious were the federal projects that selected youth from all regions on a competitive basis and that were organized by the League of Communist Youth of Yugoslavia (Savez Komunističke Omladine Jugoslavije, or SKOJ), whose radical proclivities were harnessed for many tasks of social transformation. In the projects' focus on the younger generation as the "heroes" of a new beginning, political loyalties to a new Yugoslavia and technical skills to increase society's productivity would be built as well as roads, with a mixture of political education, training in industrial skills and discipline, and cultivation of "brotherhood" among the nations and "all-national" bonds through patriotic and populist rituals in field camps far from home.

The new role of the unions began with the task of organizing socialist competition in factories and at construction sites, while the Popular Front (Narodni Front, the mass political organization tied to the party) was charged with mobilizing popular acts of solidarity and patriotism and organizing the local labor brigades. The importance of the local community was most apparent in the leaders' hope of encouraging local initiative by private citizens and volunteers in contributing to the reconstruction effort and in improving living standards. One of the purposes of the democratic assemblies that existed alongside the executive people's committees was to turn patriotism and democracy into motivations for "voluntary contributions" to bond issues and financing for specific local economic and cultural projects. In the tax reform of December 27, 1947, when the leadership faced the reality of budget deficits in the first phase of the five-year plan, certain towns and worker settlements were given the authority to introduce local excise taxes to balance their budgets.

The search for foreign aid, on the other hand, was clearly an admission that the great leap in capital requirements of the industrialization plan could not be accomplished at home by the leaders' strategy. Foreign aid was critical to that strategy and, like the war, defined much of the trajectory of the Communists' first decade of power. The idea was to obtain both cheaper wage goods and more-advanced technology on foreign markets, preferably by purchasing them on credit against future trade or by receiving outright assistance. Not fully self-sufficient in any case, the country also needed to import some raw materials, such as coking coal for steel production and cotton for textiles and clothing; and food aid was needed to help tide it over through the gradual reconstruction and transformation of agriculture. Also critical, however, was military aid—from strategic raw materials to weapons and hardware—so that the plan to develop defensive strength did not conflict too much with civilian needs.

The literature on the transition to socialism tends to downplay, even ignore, the international aspects of that transition, but the role of foreign trade and aid was central in the debates on industrialization strategy in the Soviet Union during the 1920s. All participants shared Marx's assumption (written to Vera Zasulich) that the demands of industrial take-off on the population could be "relaxed" with foreign capital, but they disagreed on the particular role of foreign trade. Should they follow an export-led path and, in view of their comparative advantage at the time, invest substantially in agriculture and labor-intensive primary products for export, which would impose a slower and potentially dependence-renewing path of industrialization? Or should they seek assistance from friendly powers to sustain an import surplus while they built up capital-intensive, infrastructural, and producers' goods industries, which would enable them to move sooner onto a higher-growth path and develop a comparative advantage in processed and manufactured goods? As portrayed, however, these debates tended to ignore the importance of defense and, in particular in the 1920s, the political pressure from the army, from soldiers being demobilized, and from military industries that they not be overlooked entirely.[32] The Yugoslav leaders could not but be aware of these Soviet debates, of the deep meaning of the opposition's charge that they were pursuing "socialism in one country," and of the consequences of the revolution's failure to spread to the West in 1919–20 for Yugoslav hopes of friendly assistance and for subsequent domestic policy.[33]

[32] Mark von Hagen, personal communication on the basis of his research. These issues of national defense and the military are strikingly absent from the discussions about economic-development strategy in the 1920s (including the otherwise splendid study by Alexander Erlich, *The Soviet Industrialization Debate*).

[33] Such assistance from Western powers was Lenin's major hope in 1919; although the

Thus, the inner Yugoslav leadership—Tito, Kardelj, Kidrič, Djilas, and others—at the time based its strategy and its assumption of foreign aid in part on the conviction that the international correlation of forces had changed fundamentally after World War II. First there was the Soviet Union, truly a friendly power as another socialist state that would aid them materially. But it had not aided them during the war, and its ability to assist others after the war—given its own serious task of domestic reconstruction—was likely to be severely limited; so it was important that the Partisans had also been part of the Allied fight against Germany. Although their efforts to secure Allied military and economic support during the war had been a painful, uphill battle, by mid-1944 they had nonetheless been recognized by Britain and the United States as the primary ally in the Balkans deserving of aid. This very fact also seemed to prove that an era of peaceful coexistence between socialist and capitalist countries had replaced international class antagonism and the threat of capitalist encirclement.[34] Because the real threat of war after the defeat of fascism, in the Yugoslav leaders' view, came from the gap between rich and poor nations, they began to broadcast widely on the necessity of redistribution of wealth through foreign aid as the primary weapon for peace. And in their own neighborhood, the defeat of Germany and the rise of progressive governments in Eastern Europe offered the hope (motivating Tito's wildly successful tour of its capitals in February and March 1946) that "Slavic solidarity" would also bring opportunities for favorable trade agreements and aid. These assumptions were wrong.

On the one hand, the Soviet leadership made no change in the policy it had pursued since 1940 toward the Yugoslav party. Yugoslav radicalism threatened Stalin's desire to protect the Soviet Union's alliance with Britain and the United States, whereas the goals of its own territorial security—the containment of Germany, reconstruction at home, and stable, mixed governments ("people's democracies") on its border—took priority over socialist internationalism in the region. The Yugoslavs' discussions of a Balkan alliance,[35] active involvement in Albania[36] and

---

consequences of its disappointment were well known, they were not sufficient to dissuade others from later holding the same hope.

[34] See Hahn, *Postwar Soviet Politics*, on the emergence of the same view in the USSR at the time and Andrey Zhdanov's special role in it.

[35] On the long history of this idea and on the dispute over inclusion (at Stalin's urging) of Bulgaria, see Connor, *The National Question in Marxist-Leninist Theory and Strategy*, 130–42. Kardelj appears to have been the most open opponent, arguing that they should not integrate with *poorer* states, such as Bulgaria and also Albania (see V. Dedijer, *Novi prilozi* 3:302).

[36] CPY emissaries helped organize the Albanian Communist party and its partisan resistance during the war. Ties deepened after the war, with discussions about integrated economic plans and armies, joint economic ventures, a Yugoslav military base at Korçë, and,

support for the Democratic Army of Greece in the brewing civil war,[37] and claims on lands occupied by South Slavs (especially those bordering Slovenia in Italy and Austria)[38] won them Stalin's fury rather than aid. Soviet technical and military advisers did arrive in the fall of 1944, and official recognition on April 15, 1945, brought promises of economic and military assistance; there were discussions of joint ventures that summer, a treaty of friendship, mutual aid, and postwar cooperation on April 11, 1946, and promises that June to provide weapons, munitions, and aid to defense industries. But as late as February 1947, little aid had arrived, and only two agreements—on shared control over Danube River traffic and Yugoslav civil aviation—had been concluded, on terms Yugoslavs found extremely unfavorable but agreed to "because they hoped for other investment."[39]

On the other hand, the British and the Americans also continued their wartime policy of using aid as a weapon of political influence. For example, in the negotiations over Allied Military Liaison Aid, they sought to influence the composition of the postwar government in favor of the king and the London government-in-exile. They provided no aid for a year after the aid agreement was signed April 3, 1944, while they negotiated a power-sharing arrangement between Tito and the former prime minister Šubašić; quarreled over the bill;[40] and were deadlocked over the Yugoslavs' requests for the return of their gold reserves ($47 million) deposited by the royal government in the Federal Reserve Bank of New York and over their Danube Fleet of two hundred river craft, which had been sequestered by Allied forces. In the year preceding the contentious politbureau meeting of 1946, the Yugoslavs' repeated requests for aid and trade with the United States encountered a policy aiming "to undermine the new regime with economic collapse."[41] For example, their request in June 1945, for a $300 million credit from the U.S. Export-Import Bank was repeatedly tabled as the United States nursed hopes of assisting the

---

when the USSR refused to assist Yugoslav plans to explore for oil in Vojvodina, access to Albania's petroleum reserves.

[37] Yugoslavia eventually provided training bases, sanctuary for refugees, and supplies of food, medicine, and weapons.

[38] Slovene national claims (which Kardelj felt intensely) on Trieste, parts of Istria and the Slovene littoral, the Julian March, and Austrian Carinthia led eventually to the Trieste crisis. It began in early 1945, as Yugoslavia sent four armed divisions (800,000 soldiers) to Zone A to preempt the decisions being made at Yalta (see Mugoša, "Odnosi Jugoslavije i SAD-a izmedju 1945 i 1949," chap. 1; and Clissold, *Yugoslavia and the Soviet Union*).

[39] Kidrič, quoted in V. Dedijer, *Novi prilozi* 3:322. On the quarrels over joint ventures and Soviet aid, see V. Dedijer, *The Battle Stalin Lost*, 73–95, 102; Kidrič, "Obrazloženje osnovnog zakona," 13; and Clissold, *Yugoslavia and the Soviet Union*, 230.

[40] Mugoša, "Odnosi Jugoslavije i SAD-a," 44.

[41] Ibid.

return of prewar Serbian parties (the Democrats and the Radicals) to power, then of obtaining higher compensation for Americans' property that had been nationalized and cessation of support for the Greek guerrillas.

Relations with Europe were no more successful, because of the competition on both sides of the emerging continental divide for capital and raw materials to repair war damage and because the destruction of German industry and eastern European agriculture laid waste to Europe's primary prewar sources of capital goods, food, and fuel.[42] Trade agreements with Poland and Czechoslovakia foundered on serious conflicts of national interest. These countries' reservations about Yugoslavia's plan, the likelihood that it could make good on its commitments of agricultural goods, ores, and timber, and the fact that they would be creating a competitor in foreign markets for processed goods and machinery were matched on the Yugoslav side with indignation that Slavic solidarity did not lead to more development assistance that would enable it to obtain machinery and pursue its development strategy of replacing exports of low-value-added primary goods with higher-value-added exports.[43] Like Stalin, the Poles and Czechs worried that Yugoslav foreign policy would antagonize the West and endanger their greater success at trade and credit relations.[44]

Although Yugoslavia was a founding member of the United Nations and the International Monetary Fund (IMF), the new government's disputes over the dinar-dollar exchange rate caused negotiations for IMF credits (and therefore access to World Bank loans as well) to break down in March 1945, and mounting tensions over Trieste made Yugoslavia the sole UN member to be refused the Lend-Lease aid it sought in order to repair transportation networks and obtain military hardware. The decisions on war reparations at the Paris Peace Conference in November–December 1945 that protected Germany from heavy war indemnities at the cost of Yugoslav (and other) claims were considered so damaging that Tito sought persistently after January 4, 1946, to secure an invitation to

---

[42] Hogan, *The Marshall Plan;* Milward, *The Reconstruction of Western Europe, 1945–51.*

[43] I am grateful to Carol Lilly for this discovery, from her exhaustive reading of the newspaper *Borba* at the time, that the Yugoslav leadership tried to use arguments about "Slavic unity" against Polish and Czechoslovak objections.

[44] Czechoslovak president Edvard Beneš reportedly told premier Klement Gottwald in March 1946 that "Yugoslav unpredictability [threatens] to drag us into conflict with the West as well. But you don't know them, they have always created disturbances with the West. They'll pull us into this. They are such a people that one does not know what they will do. A people that surprises" (V. Dedijer, *Novi prilozi* 3:223). It did not help that Americans had taken early to referring to Tito as a "Soviet agent" and to Yugoslavia as Stalin's "most loyal satellite."

Washington to press his case personally for an American loan.[45] Although also subject to frequent delays and U.S. objections, UNRRA assistance (finally agreed to on April 15, 1945) became the critical (and nearly the only) source of external support for reconstruction. In the two years between June 30, 1945, and June 30, 1947, the mission distributed approximately $415 million in food and grains (70 percent of the total assistance) in addition to clothing, textiles, medical equipment and medicines, agricultural machinery and livestock, industrial plant and tools to resume production in mines, sawmills, a steel mill, and a large quantity of trucks, jeeps, locomotives, and wagons, while earnings from the government sale of UNRRA goods were the main source of financing for the Fund for Reconstruction of War-Damaged Regions.[46]

The 1946 politbureau meeting at which the dispute over development strategy erupted had been called to mark the shift from reconstruction and the "social" (basic welfare) question to the institutional preparation for the industrialization plan; it took place five days, in fact, after the signing of the Soviet-Yugoslav treaty of friendship, mutual aid, and postwar cooperation. The consequences of the meeting were decisive. Hebrang was replaced as chair of the Economic Council and minister of industry by Kidrič, and then removed from the politbureau. The fact that he was kept on as head of the planning commission was, as many argue, due to his intellectual strengths and stature within the party (which were considerable); but a stronger reason was probably that many agreed with him and could have used his expulsion to coalesce into a more formal opposition. The competition of either Hebrang or Žujović for leadership of the party, which many saw as possible, and the challenge of their economic ideas to the policies of the Slovene model had one more stage to go through before their final purge in May 1948; but their marginalization on the choice of strategy began here.[47]

[45] In place of the $11 billion Yugoslavia asked of Germany, it received $35.8 million; in place of $1.3 billion from Italy, it got $125 million; and in place of $1.28 billion from Hungary, it was granted $70 million. None of these amounts had been received by April 1946, however, and the Yugoslavs renounced Bulgarian reparations of $25 million as part of their treaty of friendship, signed in August 1947 (see Mugoša, "Odnosi Jugoslavije i SAD-a," chap. 2).

[46] Ibid., chap. 1. On the continual quarrels with the United States—including the frustration of UNRRA's director, Fiorello La Guardia, with what he saw as unjustified interference with humanitarian aid to the Yugoslavs—see ibid.; and Warriner, *Revolution in Eastern Europe*. For a balanced, overall view, see Lampe's introductory chapter in Lampe, Prickett, and Adamović, *Yugoslav-American Economic Relations since World War II*.

[47] On the debate, see V. Dedijer, *Novi prilozi* 3:292–93. The view that both Hebrang and Žujović, and especially Hebrang, might be competition for Tito and that they might be political leaders with a separate constituency in their own right came up frequently in the course of the author's interviews in 1982 with people who had been present.

THE NEW SYSTEM OF LABOR

Without foreign assistance, economic growth would depend on maximal use of internal reserves, especially increased labor productivity in factories and on farms and the ability of the government to keep a lid on wages in relation to the supply and price of basic consumption goods (such as food). Despite Kidrič's attack on Hebrang in the debate on state capitalism, Hebrang, too, assumed that the political revolution alone would take them a long way toward releasing capital reserves. As he told the provisional assembly in 1945, "the new relations toward work will awaken in every Yugoslav worker a sense for rationalization."[48] But the unions, whose role would necessarily change, and particularly skilled workers, who had substantial bargaining power because of their new importance to the industrialization strategy and their very short supply, continued instead to fight for higher wages, until the introduction of workers' councils in 1950 finally eliminated their market power. Political liberation alone was not sufficient. While the introduction of economic planning centered on redefining property rights and teaching the system of economic accounting, there would be no results without reorganization of productive activity and incentives in industry and agriculture.

Tito made this clear in his version of the leadership's concept of economic growth during a contentious two-hour meeting with a delegation from the League of Railroad and Transport Workers and Employees in January 1946. As the union journal *Glas* reported, the league was protesting the firing of two hundred drivers from the state transport firm and the government's limits on union demands for higher wages. Tito's response was that higher wages were no longer the correct route to an improved standard of living; instead, it was ever-greater productivity on the one hand and better and cheaper food from increased yields and marketed produce of farmers' cooperatives on the other. The drivers lost their jobs, he explained, because of their "bureaucratism": they were not taking proper care of their cars, had even destroyed precious UNRRA trucks, and were trafficking with smugglers. But more to the point, he insisted, it was not good policy to centralize several thousand trucks; it was better to hand them over to those who would be *economically* responsible for their use and upkeep—namely, the republics and enterprises. The federal government's only task related to transport should be to guarantee the free transport of colonists (in the settlement of Vojvodina during 1946–47) and of food to starving regions.[49]

The first step in the leaders' project to replace the "wage struggle" with

[48] Hebrang, in AVNOJ, *Zakonodavni rad*, 37.
[49] *Glas*, January 4, 1946, 1.

a socialist concept of workers' interests was the reorganization of factory management in the new public sector. Early in 1945, in his role as commissar of industry and president of the Economic Council, Hebrang had created an open parliamentary confrontation over workers' "right to supervise production," a right outlined in the proposed law on workers' commissars (poverenici).[50] Defending the factory manager's authority against union proposals that the elected workers' commissars share in decisions on the organization of production, he turned the parliamentary vote around despite the opinion in favor of the unions on second reading of the legislative commission chaired by Moša Pijade. The problem was not the idea of worker participation itself, which "they surely would later" introduce, but the union's "avant-gardism." "Looking reality in the eye," given the low level of workers' expertise at the time and the fact that most factories were being managed by their former owners, Hebrang called the proposals impractical and sure to antagonize those managers "before they were ready," which would interfere with implementation of their plans.[51] By the time the law on state economic enterprises was proposed, in July 1946, Kidrič had presented a compromise.[52] The Soviet principle of edinochalie (one-man management), giving the director final authority (which Kidrič compared to the military system of unified command, avoiding reference to the Soviet example), would prevail within the enterprise as long as the director worked closely and consulted frequently with all groups concerned with production (the union, associations of production workers, organs of state management, and the professional-technical advisory council [stručni savjet]). At the same time, the unions were to be represented on the professional council and told to organize production conferences periodically so that the workers could be directed toward discussion about ways to improve production organization and away from the functions they had been usurping in 1945 and 1946, "such as interfering in the business of the enterprise, replacing managers, forcing salary increases, and improving work conditions beyond justified measures."[53]

The next step was to reform the unions. The main vehicle by which labor had attempted to control and raise its price in the Yugoslav lands since the 1880s was union control over employment. By the late 1930s, this consisted of two parallel systems. Organized workers had lost control

[50] Savezno Veće Narodne Skupštine FNRJ, Stenografske beleške, July 1945, 458–78. On the early system, see also A. Ross Johnson, The Transformation of Communist Ideology, 159ff.

[51] Hebrang, in AVNOJ, Zakonodavni rad, 467–68.

[52] Kidrič, "Obrazloženje osnovnog zakona."

[53] Petranović, Politička i ekonomska osnova narodne vlasti za vreme obnove, 81.

over the employment bureaus to local governments, but the unions were increasingly militant—using the strike especially—as the demand for skilled labor rose with rearmament. Under the corporatist regime, the unions shared trilateral responsibility with local governments and the workers' chambers (the corporatist, semipublic institutions of Austrian, German, and Italian tradition) for employment and collective bargaining over contracts. Social insurance was regulated by the state and funded by both employers' and employees' contributions, but only workers on permanent, legal contracts were eligible. Nonetheless, skilled workers could often do better by bargaining for permanent contracts directly with employers, who tried to evade the insurance regulations by circumventing the labor exchanges when hiring. Unskilled workers, unorganized and without such leverage, were forced to compete "on the street" by the conditions of surplus. In the first two years after the war, the provisional government continued this system—expanding the network of employment-service bureaus from thirty-five to sixty-five because of rising urban unemployment—and filled the employment bureaus with its own people, chosen by the Commissariat for Social Policy in consultation with the United Unions organization. The bureaus remained self-financing and self-managing, as they had been before the war. As registries of unemployed and generally unskilled persons, they mainly filled requests from local governments and the Popular Front organization for labor for public works—to repair property, stand guard over reconstruction projects, or assist in harvests and repairs on the state agricultural estates.[54]

The prewar system was abolished on April 23, 1946, in the first phase of organizational rationalizations in preparation for the industrialization plan, by giving the unions authority over the employment bureaus and title to their property. "Union mediation of labor" aimed to eliminate the "bureaucratic, passive, receiving-window" approach of local officials, who—unlike union officials—depended on government budgets for their salary.[55] As the wage was no longer the means to regulate employment but a direct incentive to increase productivity, however, the unions' role in collective bargaining over wages and employment contracts (now called "economism") would be replaced by legislated wage differentials and output norms, employment criteria, and work-safety and social-policy regulations. The unions' task was now the "struggle for increased productivity and development of new relations toward work, organization of competitions, self-sacrificial solutions to material difficulties, and the technical,

---

[54] Radmilović, "Karakter službe posredovanja rada i pitanje njene reorganizacije," 11–12.
[55] Ibid.

ideological, and political instruction of workers."[56] For that reason, the network of the new United Unions organization was expanded to every state enterprise, and these plant-based unions were joined into associations—one for each industrial branch—called union leagues (*savezi sindikata*). To safeguard workers' interests on questions outside the technical scope of production decisions, such as work safety and social policy, all workers and staff within a firm would elect workers' representatives (also an Austro-German inheritance) to represent these interests in workplace decision making, participating jointly with management, unions, and government authorities.[57]

Reorienting the unions and other workers' organizations to the workplace and replacing market wages with pay calculated as a direct incentive to productivity would not eliminate the upward pressure on wages from employers' competition for workers with industrial and technical skills; the shortage of such workers was the greater problem for macroeconomic stability and monetary control. Nor did legal specification of the union's new role put a stop to their attempts to bargain for wage gains for their members, so that in mid-November 1946, the minister of labor, Vicko Krstulović, called the executive board of the United Unions organization into plenary session in order to read it the riot act. Adding his voice, Kidrič, the economic minister, even warned obliquely of dire consequences if they did not accept the authority of the legislated wage norms and desist their continued militance over wage bargaining. In December, federal authorities organized a policy conference to discuss the problem of "labor," but its main theme was the "organizational difficulties" with the unions.[58]

At the conference, three views competed. Many urged greater regulation of the labor market. The majority wanted to make the unions responsible for employment, requiring all workers and employers to contract under union auspices and recruiting the social-insurance bureaus to police the employment and wage regulations by threatening the withdrawal of benefits. The leadership rejected both views in favor of retaining the current "initiative" of employers and managers in solving their own labor problems. The leaders wanted simultaneously to reduce unions' bargaining room over wages and to hold managers responsible for production despite managers' attempts to shift the blame to unions when production lagged and to get the central government to assign or mobilize labor polit-

[56] Has, "Društveno-ekonomski osvrt na problem zaposlenosti," 140.

[57] Ibid.; Krstulović, "Stalno podizanje proizvodnosti rada poboljšava radne i životne uslove radničke klase."

[58] V. Begović, "Problem obezbjedjenja radne snage i stručnih kadrova u petogodišnjem planu," 22–30; Radmilović, "Karakter službe posredovanja rada."

ically when they had difficulty attracting skilled industrial and professional workers. Only days after the conference, on December 13, a new
office of labor inspectors was created to relieve the unions of their oversight role on labor contracts and work safety and to replace the labor
commissars (the organs of revolutionary authority in the local people's
committees, many of whom were still soldiers in the liberation army) with
civil servants responsible to the branch ministry within their republic.
The protection of workers' interests fell solely to the worker inspectors in
the firm, whom workers elected annually.

The next step in replacing wage bargaining with direct productivity
incentives at the firm was to reduce the labor mobility that made wage
competition possible and prevented application of technical normatives
for wages and labor use. The population would thus be settled physically,
into jobs and between the two sectors of the economy. In January 1947,
peasants eligible to settle in the northern plains were given only two more
months to accept the offer or lose the right of resettlement.[59] These were
largely agricultural laborers from "passive" regions[60] in Bosnia, Herzegovina, southern Croatia, and Montenegro who had also been Partisan
soldiers; they had until then been encouraged to move to the state farms
in Vojvodina—where their labor was needed and their patriotism and
military experience important for the defense of the plain.[61] Vojvodinian
authorities, worried about social stability, began to rail against the explosion of "wild marriages" (common-law unions) among colonists,[62] campaigned for legalization of such cohabitations, and required new settlers
to arrive with their families or stay away. In March, workers in the public

[59] V. Petrović, *Razvitak privrednog sistema FNRJ posmatran kroz pravne propise*,
vol. 2.

[60] The phrase *pasivni krajevi* (passive regions), according to Tomasevich, referred to
"areas greatly deficient in food production as well as in other earning opportunities and
therefore depending for livelihood, to a large extent, on outside earnings" (*Peasants, Politics, and Economic Change*, 265). These were the areas of the karst, especially those near
the Adriatic coast, from the Gulf of Trieste to Ljubljana, then southeast to Kolašin and down
the Morača and Bojana rivers (largely what are now Monetenegro, Herzegovina, Dalmatia,
and southwestern Croatia).

[61] Of about 190,000 families (with about 500,000 members) of agricultural laborers (landless peasants) before the war, 70,701 families received one to two hectares of land in agrarian
reform; most of the rest went to the agricultural estates, although some went to industry or
other branches of the public-sector economy. They became the core (72 percent) of social-
sector agricultural labor (*Privreda FNRJ u periodu 1947–1956*, 164–65). This resettlement
was to become the source of political problems later (especially in the 1980s and in the civil
war that began in 1991) as Serbs reassessed the purpose of the loss of life on the Srem front
in 1945 and as non-Serbs charged that the royal government had used agrarian reform in the
interwar period to settle Vojvodina and Slavonia with Serbs.

[62] Kostić-Marojević, *Promena društvene sredine i promene u porodici*, 65 n. 129, citing
research by V. Djurić.

sector were issued labor books (*radne knjižice*, the *livrets* of French tradition without which one could not get a new job)[63] so that evidence about their wage and employment could be improved and so that legislated wage norms and employment rights could be implemented. Executives of district or town people's committees, or their labor commissions, were told to issue these books and record the worker's occupation, training, and length of employment; the books also contained a space for recording prizes, honors, inventions, and selection as a shock worker.

This settling process was particularly important in the countryside, where employers under pressure to cut costs but with authority to hire and fire would be inclined to perpetuate the existence of an "industrial reserve army." The idea behind the sector of "individual" property had been to guarantee subsistence to villagers who worked their own land or produced related services through smallholding rights. There was a strong element of radical republican and populist tradition in this view— that the concentration of assets on land and the resulting inequalities were unjust, destroyed communal solidarity, and produced unemployment, and that the initiative of private ownership and profit in consumers' markets, with the freed energies and civic virtue of those free to exploit their own labor rather than forced to sell it to others, would lead to rational use and increasing yields. These populist, or agrarian socialist, elements of the Slovene model prevailed despite limits on significant productivity gains due to parcelized landholdings, the shortage of agricultural machinery and working stock, and the prohibitively high capital costs of industrial inputs (such as fertilizers, advanced seeds, and tractors). There is also strong evidence that in the minds of policymakers responsible for the economy and for agriculture, who were overwhelmingly drawn from Slovenia and Croatia—such as Boris Kidrič, Edvard Kardelj, and Vladimir Bakarić—these smallholders were not the impoverished subsistence peasantry of the passive regions in the south and southwest (where soil was essentially unarable) but the successful middle-size, commercially oriented farmers of their northern regions who had emerged with the abolition of serfdom by the 1880s. These farmers had led in the adoption of new agricultural techniques, in contrast to the large landowners in Vojvodina, Bosnia, and Macedonia who had found cheap labor an easier route to profits than modernization; and they dominated the cooperative movement.[64]

Cooperation was the key to this sector—to protecting the individual holdings of producers while pooling assets such as machinery and exper-

[63] V. Petrović, *Razvitak privrednog sistema FNRJ* 2:50–65.

[64] On these farmers, see R. Bićanić, "Agrarna kriza od 1873–1895." Bakarić and his adviser Slavko Komar were particularly influential in defining agricultural policy in this period.

tise, and to the marketing links that could increase production for the market and provide an organizational link for direct contracts with the public sector firms, increasing their supplies and tying the private sector to the public sector's economic dynamic. The agrarian reform of August 1945 created the necessary legal machinery by permitting and regulating the voluntary formation of peasant cooperatives along the lines of Lenin's stages of cooperativization; but in line with Kautsky, technical possibilities were to determine the pace of cooperativization in production. Labor cooperatives called *seljačke radne zadruge* (peasant labor cooperatives), like the Soviet *kolkhoz*, were encouraged in areas of food-grain and export-crop production (primarily in the large estates of the northern plains of Vojvodina and partly in Slavonia—and not, it turned out, in the plains of Macedonia).[65] But authorities responded with benign neglect to the many labor cooperatives that demobilized Partisans and poor peasants set up (some say out of ideological fervor; others say the purpose was to pool scarce implements or avoid compulsory deliveries and state taxation) in regions that could not support such collective labor economically. The month before the decisive politbureau meeting of April 1946, in fact, contracts for membership in existing labor cooperatives were reduced from ten to three years.[66] Elsewhere, general farmers' cooperatives (*opće zemljoradničke zadruge*) were formed on the basis of prewar marketing and consumer cooperatives and Lenin's cooperative plan of 1921.

The primary purpose of cooperatives, in Kardelj's vision, was in fact far less economic than social and transformative. A cooperative would coextend with a village and become the basis of its social and public life as well as its economic exchange. Although cooperation would begin with marketing, as was the tradition of the cooperatives in Slovenia, Croatia, and Serbia that would be taken over politically ("from below"), these cooperatives would be territorially confined to a village or district, where mutual exchange would grow into more-extensive cooperation naturally and transform villages into full socialist communities. At the same time, given Kidrič's Bukharinite insistence that the primary problem in agriculture was not producers but traders, marketing cooperatives were the right vehicle for governmental policy. At first, when extreme shortages of food prolonged wartime methods, policies included the requisitioning (*otkup*) of a portion of a farmer's wheat, corn, pigs, and wool at government-set prices, and delegation of plainclothes policemen and party cadres to stroll farmers' free markets and cajole peasants into "patriotic" prices (tactics of the Foča model). With more normal conditions, essential produce such as

---

[65] Some would say these cooperatives were forced; but see the debate at the third plenum of the CPY central committee in December 1949 between Jovan Veselinov and party leaders (discussed in chapter 4).

[66] Tomasevich, "Collectivization of Agriculture in Yugoslavia."

grains and meat continued to be purchased at government prices as part of a national food policy, and cooperatives' stores were given monopoly over the sale of industrial goods to the villages so that the government could influence farmers' incentives to increase yields and market agricultural produce while leaving them free to make production decisions. This capacity to regulate the overall terms of trade between agriculture and industry, village and factory, private and public sectors was a crucial element of macroeconomic equilibrium between wage funds and wage goods.

Equally important at the time, by transferring control over cooperatives from private traders to local authorities (who were elected by cooperative members), the government was preparing to protect state firms from competition for labor with the private sector for the time when the state firms were ready to employ new workers from the villages. Also, local authorities could more rationally regulate the pace of that movement from agriculture to industry and from private to public sector by keeping data on the local labor supply and using means of recruitment that did not require outlays of cash.

Localization of cooperatives and limits on the economic power of private traders together had a political consequence that drew vehement opposition from former peasant-party allies in the assembly—above all the Communists' main front partner in Serbia, Dragoljub Jovanović. According to Kardelj, these autonomous socialist communities in the villages would be integrated vertically through obligatory membership in district business leagues (*poslovni savezi*),[67] by being represented in local assemblies and then indirectly up the governmental hierarchy, and through contracts with public-sector firms. This would be a direct blow, in Jovanović's view, to cooperation as a social movement (which he contrasted to the united-union movement for industrial workers) and to its economic potential through functional specialization and horizontal links among cooperatives over a wider territory than that of the district, operating in an all-Yugoslav market. In the parliamentary debate on the law on the cooperatives that took place on July 9, 1946, noncommunist village notables, such as the priest and clericalist don Ante Salacan, charged that the law destroyed the "autonomy" of the peasantry (evoking catcalls of

[67] *Poslovni savezi*, or business leagues, were organizations of agricultural producers along the same lines as the industrial-branch producers' associations (*privredne komore*) that organized wholesale trade and supply contracts for their members. Kidrič stated their purpose: "To strengthen general cooperatives, their joint provisioning and their ever-closer links with the state economy. . . . [They] will represent the greatest guarantee that the coops will perform the tasks assigned to them today to benefit the working masses in the village and the city and to raise the national product" ("Obrazloženje nacrta osnovnog zakona o zadrugama," 7–9).

"Reactionary!" from the floor). While Jovanović supported the cooperatives—"not the Czech kind but the Soviet"—he insisted that without a political party to give voice to the peasantry, their separate interests would have no defender and they would remain subordinate to the public sector and industrial workers.[68]

The economic consequences of localization also created a political problem, in this case with industrial ministries. Although the idea of two sectors, one public and one private, was to concentrate scare resources and attention on the public sector—compensating the individual sector with freedom and smallholding rights during the wait for public-sector jobs—Kardelj's vision began with the construction of cooperative centers in almost every village in the country. As with the volunteer brigades, the villagers, in building the physical infrastructure for communal activity with their own hands, would develop symbolic and practical commitment to their cooperative. In spite of the savings on wage costs, the diversion of budgetary funds and construction materials to these centers was loudly criticized by people from the ministry of mining and manufacturing whose requests for such resources to build housing at the mines had been ignored. Particularly vocal against the village cooperatives, whose aim was to settle labor in the villages, were mine directors already having great difficulty finding labor in the aftermath of war and agrarian reform and because of inadequate housing.[69]

Until the postwar nationalizations, the mines had been largely foreign-owned, and management imported skilled workers and technical staff, especially from Germany. As a rule, the mines were also undermechanized, because the supply of cheap, unskilled labor from the surrounding impov-

[68] Narodna Skupština FNRJ, *Prvo redovno zasedanje*, 416–24. Jovanović consistently held this position from his first negotiations with Tito during the war; see his "Političke uspomene." He was already in the parliamentary opposition after the fall of 1945; and, as with Hebrang, his position spelled the end of his career—though he was not arrested until the fall of 1947.

[69] Mulec and Glišič, "Problem radne snage u metalurgiji i rudarstvu." Opposition to the construction of these cooperative centers also came from traditional authorities in the village—demonstrating that Jovanović represented only one stream of opinion against governmental policy toward the countryside, as Kardelj's parliamentary speech on the 1948 budget (on April 25, 1948) suggests: "I know of the example of one village which recently finished the construction of its cooperative center. The village was, as they say, inclined toward reaction. Actually, a few wealthy owners succeeded in exerting influence on the mass of the peasants with small and medium-sized holdings. When the initiative for the building of a cooperatve center came from the People's Front, strong organized resistance was offered. The well-known rumors about common kitchens and common beds began to fly. One part of the peasants with small and medium-sized holdings, however, set to work, and when the first results were seen, a turn-about took place in the village. The whole village set to work" (cited by Wolff, *The Balkans in Our Time*, 327). By the end of 1947, four thousand cooperative centers were under construction, according to Kardelj (ibid., 326–27).

erished countryside seemed almost inexhaustible—particularly when the long-distance seasonal migrants supplemented day laborers from nearby villages. German wartime occupation simply added coercion by conscripting labor. Nationalization of the mines and the agrarian reform thus interrupted the mines' traditional labor supply. Peasants now preferred to remain at home on their small plots rather than enter mines with their horrendous conditions, whereas much of the agricultural "surplus" population had been moved as colonists to state farms in Vojvodina or Slavonia. The little housing available at the mines consisted of drafty, primitive barracks without sufficient supplies of blankets and other necessities. Far from the urban trade network, mine settlements had difficulty getting food, clothing, and industrial goods, which were in short supply. Even if government policy had been amenable, raising wages to attract more skilled labor made little sense if there was nothing to buy. For most workers, the alternative to these living conditions was commuting from home, which meant an exhausting addition to the workday of, on average, four to six hours on foot (bicycle tires were nonexistent and train fares were too high for an ordinary worker)—a circumstance that was unlikely to raise workers' productivity or leave time for training. Moreover, workers who commuted were more likely to remain at home during sowing and harvest seasons. Turnover, absenteeism, and other behavior contrary to industrial discipline followed; and because foremen and supervisers also came from the villages, such behavior was usually indulged. To compensate, one could hire more workers (if they could be found) or pay skilled workers extra for overtime, but both solutions raised rather than lowered costs of production and intensified conflicts among workers over wage differentials and with budgetary authorities charged with enforcing profit-and-loss accounts.[70] Mine managers made do with prisoners of war—German and Italian workers still interned in the mines—to relieve their shortages. Prisoners accounted for a majority of the workforce at the Sartia mine (near Smederevo), for example, and a third at the copper mine at Bor. In 1945, the government attempted to lure back Yugoslav "miners and other workers" who had migrated abroad before the war by approving the international convention on pension rights for migrant workers, but this step apparently met union resistance. The "inhospitable" union offices at the mines was the other cause of Kidrič's sharp rebuke at the United Unions plenum in November 1946.

Thus opposition to the policy on cooperatives and agriculture, and to the government's refusal to assume responsibility for recruiting labor where shortages interfered with essential tasks, came from the ministry of mining and from mine managers with an immediate practical problem

---

[70] On the situation in the mines, see Mulec and Glišič, "Problem radne snage."

concerning labor and the resources necessary to attract it from the villages. For these officials and party cadres, the policy did nothing to facilitate the move toward socialism—it was a waste, if the ultimate aim was socialization of agriculture; and it diverted scarce resources away from the socialized sector and its immediate needs of fuel and exports for the industrialization plan. Similar opposition arose to the assignment of final authority over labor to the republics, because of the great regional inequalities in the location of skilled and professional labor. Since government policy was relying on the immediate returns of increased productivity in existing plants, industries favored with publicly allocated resources were located largely in the more-developed regions of the country where industrialization had occurred much earlier, especially Slovenia and Croatia. Speakers in one public forum after another derided the "old" and the "backward" in their society to support this reversal of the policy of the prewar government; they identified that policy with a "logic of economic growth [based on] the more backward sectors and regions of the economy," in the words of the Croatian-based *Encyclopedia of Yugoslavia*,[71] that punished the more-developed regions with heavier taxation and economic discrimination from Belgrade to pay for it.

Difficulties finding labor to fulfill new tasks necessary to the plan, therefore, led to quarrels over priorities in investment and economic strategy among federal ministers, the party leadership, and some "national committees" (the republican party organizations) and republican governments. Factories in the more-developed north had advantages that their governments sought to protect, while the mines, new construction sites, and forests essential to exports tended to be located in the poorer interior (especially within Bosnia, Croatia, and Serbia). The policy of administrative rationalization for better utilization of scarce technical skills came in conflict with professionals who did not want to move and possibly lose status and cultural identity as well as comfort. Slovene authorities in particular came into frequent conflict with those responsible for federal tasks, such as raising export revenues to restore the balance of payments and new construction for defense and capital development, because Slovenia had proportionately the greatest number of skilled workers and professionals as well as the greatest resources to be able to retain them with higher pay. The central authorities' ongoing frustration in attracting doctors, teachers, and engineers to poorer regions and priority projects in isolated areas, even with higher salaries and material benefits, led to frequent calls on the floor of the assembly throughout 1945 to require obligatory service in these regions. Yet the party leadership strongly resisted these calls in order to protect republican authority over labor against the

---

[71] Cited in Bombelles, *Economic Development of Communist Yugoslavia*.

central government and to institute monetary incentives and normalized governmental rules as instruments of labor allocation.

WHAT PRICE FOREIGN AID?

To be able to maintain their strategy against domestic opposition of all kinds, the Yugoslav leaders counted on foreign assistance. By the fall of 1946, they faced severe balance-of-payments deficits, and UNRRA aid was drawing to a close. At the United Unions plenum in November, Kidrič warned, "It's an old truth that what one purchases in foreign countries one must first earn in blood at home."[72] Although the political and legal steps in preparation for the five-year plan were on course, it was late by nearly four months, appearing on April 26, 1947, rather than at the first of the year. The delay was blamed on obstruction from the federal planning commission, chaired by Hebrang; but politicians' public speeches reveal a preoccupation instead with difficulties in foreign trade. In early 1947, Yugoslavia felt the first serious pinch of the emerging U.S. policy of containment in Europe, against communism and its spread to Greece and Turkey. On January 25, even before the appearance of the Truman Doctrine (March 15) and the Marshall Plan (July)—the "two halves of the walnut" of U.S. policy[73]—President Truman removed Yugoslavia from the UN's list of those most in need of American food aid after UNRRA closed, where it had joined Austria, Italy, Hungary, Greece, and Poland and had been slated to receive $68.2 million of the total of $350 million. Accusing Yugoslavia of giving grain free to Romania and Albania and of allowing higher bread rations than in France, Czechoslovakia, Poland, or Switzerland, Truman prohibited the sale of any food before May or June (the prohibition was extended indefinitely in April). At that point, the export-control regime of the Cocom Accords went into effect to prevent the sale of any defense-related ("dual-use") goods to countries governed by Communist parties, with Yugoslavia at the top of the list (the ban affected cotton desperately needed for textiles and shoes, and several pending contracts with American engineering firms).[74] With conflicts over Soviet assistance as well, the leaders had no choice but to shift to trade; they negotiated seventeen bilateral agreements (including all countries of the future Eastern bloc and Sweden) between May and August 1947.

[72] Kidrič, "Govor na Petom plenumu centralnog odbora jedinstvenih sindikata Jugoslavije" (Belgrade, November 11, 1947).

[73] Hogan, *The Marshall Plan.*

[74] Mugoša, "Odnosi Jugoslavije i SAD-a." On Cocom, see Adler-Karlsson, *Western Economic Warfare.* For a balanced overview of these conflicts, see the article by Lampe in Lampe, Prickett, and Adamović, *Yugoslav-American Economic Relations.*

The political and economic contradictions of their strategy, as the opposition saw it, would now be exacerbated by the demands of export production. Extraction of primary commodities for export was labor-intensive and located primarily in the poorer regions, far from the developed and urban centers of settlement and modern industry. In his speech inaugurating the first five-year plan in April 1947, Tito alluded to the difficulties at the same time that he renewed a commitment to the leaders' chosen strategy. Against their goal of "economic and political independence," there were many critics, he said: critics of rapid industrialization, of priority for heavy industry, of a "planned agriculture." Some feared the plan would destroy artisanal trades, others that Yugoslavs would become dependent on American and English capital. But the issue was quite the reverse, Tito insisted. If they did not create their own domestic industry, they would return to the dependence on capitalist countries they had experienced under the old regime and to all the "heartless exploitation" and "ruthless pillage" that had meant. Because of "various difficulties in obtaining the necessary machinery," however, the plan would require "fulfilling all our obligations towards foreign countries." As long as trade credits and loans were not forthcoming, they had no choice but to produce the coal, timber, livestock, and ores they had committed in foreign-trade agreements to pay for the needed imports. Fulfilling these obligations would depend on the "greatest efforts" to improve and multiply the skills of the industrial workforce, for the "main source of greater accumulation and the chief means of raising the material and cultural standard of living of the working people is increased productivity of labor." The key to plan fulfillment lay in mechanization, rationalization, pay according to work, and socialist competition. Public-sector (wage) employment over the five-year planned period was projected to grow from 610,000 to 1,380,000, an increase equivalent *only* to the natural increase in the working-age population over the period.[75]

But, just as during the war, the institutions of the Slovene model conflicted with the demands facing the areas of the Foča model. The leaders' strategy for real economic growth and for the political support of a wide popular alliance continued to be based on capital-intensive manufacturing using skilled labor; limitation of the expansion of the "wage fund" (both in terms of the money supply and in the real terms of food production) by restricting new employment; cuts in the costs of administration (the "nonproducers"); and various incentives to individual effort to increase productivity, all supplemented by foreign aid and imports of capital and wage goods the country was not yet ready to produce. Their first adjustment in this strategy after the January blow was to concede, in February, the need

---

[75] Tito, "Speech on the Five-Year Plan," 8, 10, 17, 19, 33.

for *temporary* control over foreign exchange; all holders of foreign currencies were required to deposit them with the National Bank until the matter of foreign reserves was settled. Although Tito had spoken throughout 1946 on the need to end the volunteer brigades, unemployed workers and army units were now sent into the forests to cut timber and to the state farms to help in the harvest, while war prisoners still in the country who had lesser skills were impressed into work on the roads. In June the government came to the aid of the mine directors, despite Kidrič's concern for macroeconomic stability, and granted a 20 percent raise in miners' wages and somewhat smaller raises for workers in defense industries.[76] But by the end of 1947, the leaders could not maintain this program. Their fear of war and the increased tensions with the U.S. and Soviet leaderships led to a shift toward strategic self-reliance, a reversal of demobilization, and a breakdown in their policy toward labor, which was not restored until Western aid began to flow after August 1949. The next chapter will show how they adjusted to international conditions with their policy toward industrial and agricultural labor, and how that policy led in the end to the final stage of localizing labor and to the workers' councils that had appeared premature in 1945.

[76] V. Petrović, *Razvitak privrednog sistema FNRJ*, vol. 3.

Chapter 4

MILITARY SELF-RELIANCE, FOREIGN TRADE, AND THE ORIGINS OF SELF-MANAGEMENT

THE CONFLICT between domestic programs of economic recovery with rapid expansion through imports, programs motivated in most cases by the hope of avoiding the mass unemployment that followed World War I, and a shortfall of finance with rising trade deficits confronted most of Europe during 1947.[1] Although the Marshall Plan (initiated in July) is now viewed as having been the solution to that conflict in Western Europe, the political consequences in France, Belgium, and Italy of a return to orthodoxy had already occurred in May. Communist parties and organized labor chose to leave the postwar antifascist coalitions in order to side with workers' strike demands against the austerity policies of demand restriction—thus ending, Charles Maier argues, any possibility for the radical change in labor's role in economic management that had seemed possible only months before. It was in Britain that the choice was made after July; but there, too, Marshall Plan financing had the effect of restoring both the prewar strength of financial authorities and the Labour party's compromise, which was to help enforce stabilization so as to retain control over its voting constituency.[2]

The same problem faced the Yugoslav leaders. But the failure of foreign relations to normalize and the emerging cold war dashed their hopes of peaceful coexistence, while their socialist goals made the political calculations of a policy response more complex. Their economic strategy depended on imports, but because so little aid was forthcoming from either East or West, their trade deficits and falling reserves gave them no choice but to increase exports and reduce domestic demand. Yet their political revolution and the country's economic conditions did not allow the option of reversing course on the goal of rapid industrialization. Both elements of the leaders' political strategy posed a dilemma for policy: the military basis of national independence required them to increase stockpiles and

---

[1] Milward, *The Reconstruction of Western Europe, 1945–51.*

[2] Maier, "The Two Post-War Eras," especially 346. On the consequences for British politics, see Hall, *Governing the Economy*; on the "quid pro quo" for Marshall Plan aid, see Wexler, *The Marshall Plan Revisited*; Milward, *The Reconstruction of Western Europe*; and Hogan, *The Marshall Plan.* A reinterpretation of the reasons for the Marshall Plan's success is found in Eichengreen and Uzan, "The Marshall Plan."

production of strategic supplies and to build up defense industries and armaments at home at the same time that exports had to increase; and the promise of gradual improvements in living standards for the population on which they based their claim to power and their alliance of peasants, workers, and middle strata would make it extremely difficult to *reduce* domestic consumption even before power had been consolidated.

The dilemma was most immediate in the demands on labor policy. Increased production for foreign trade and defensive security would demand increased employment—particularly in mines, forests, heavy industry, and construction, where labor shortages were already a serious problem—and that increased employment would imply an expansion of the aggregate wage bill, not a contraction. This expansion in absolute numbers and in the proportion of workers consuming what others produced was in conflict with the chosen development strategy of rising labor productivity and declining relative consumption without inordinate economic, social, and political instability.

The new state and the Communist party's political power were consolidated in this period. Their shape emerged from the leaders' attempt to create an institutional and political capacity to implement their strategy for change while adjusting to international conditions they did not expect—not a collapse of foreign demand for domestic products and resulting unemployment, but inadequate finance for import needs and political barriers to trade that forced them to mobilize new labor when they did not want to pay either the economic or the political costs. As in the war, the Slovene model confronted Foča conditions. This process is followed in great detail in this chapter because it was so critical to the system that emerged and because the conventional accounts that this chapter revises have such a hold in both scholarship and general opinion.

The leadership confronted this dilemma from July 1947, when UNRRA aid ended and American hostility intensified, to the fall of 1950, when the promise of American aid began to relax the austerities of production for export and defense and to assure national sovereignty despite the embargo and propaganda war from the East. In contrast to the standard picture of a "break" in domestic policy after the Cominform resolution of June 28, 1948, the period saw five distinct shifts in policy as the leaders adjusted to changes in international conditions with alterations in their policy toward labor: (1) July to October 1947, when increasing difficulties with the West revived leadership quarrels over the strategy; (2) November 1947 to April 1948, when Tito shifted investment policy dramatically in anticipation of war; (3) May to December 1948, when political power was consolidated during a crisis in food and fuel and the drive for military self-reliance; (4) December 1948 to August 1949, when the labor mobilization to increase production for exports and defense and to cut imports

took on the character of a military campaign; and (5) August 1949 to June
1952, when Western aid, trade, and recognition allowed labor rationalization and a return to the countryside, despite rising military budgets; the
rulers then consolidated the "new strategic and tactical order" of their
original strategy. In each case, the leadership, trying to increase supplies
while keeping a lid on demand, revised not only policies but also the
institutional capacities to implement them.

In contrast to the dominant focus of the literature on Yugoslavia in this
period, the Tito-Stalin quarrel was only a part of the broader international
positioning that was taking place in Europe at the time. Its interpretation
as a battle for ideological conformity within international communism also
hides what is critical in this period: the creation of a state and a set of
institutional and policy habits, or tendencies, in responding to particular
international conditions. This chapter will argue that Yugoslavia's radicalization in agriculture between September 1948 and August 1949 was not
an attempt to prove itself sufficiently Stalinist to regain favor, as is usually
said, but a short-lived mobilization of labor and agricultural production
that sought to avoid the Stalinist path; and that both the reversal of that
policy and the introduction of workers' councils in 1950 were not an attempt to gain domestic political legitimacy in the face of international
isolation, but a return to the leaders' preferred focus on manufacturing
and engineering firms with use of economic incentives to raise labor productivity, and on macroeconomic stabilization by cutting employment instead of wages, by decentralizing administration, and by sending many
workers back to the countryside, under the pressure of trade reorientation to the West. By treating the policies of 1950 as a turn away from
internationalist obedience to a "democratic" response to popular demand,
the literature has ignored the real domestic conflicts as well as the remarkable similarity to the stages of Soviet policy change from 1921 to
1933. In that light, Western aid in 1949 (not the "Cominform break" in
1948) appears even more decisive, in contrast to the effect of rearmament
in Europe after 1936–37 on Soviet policy, because it supported a return
to the strategy the Yugoslav leadership had chosen in 1946.

The confusion stems largely from the leaders' behavior in foreign relations. For example, they seemed to go out of their way to antagonize both
the United States and the USSR in asserting their sovereignty in the region, while they continued throughout the period to seek aid and trade on
both sides. Despite shooting down two American airplanes in 1946, giving aid to Greek rebels (the Democratic Army of Greece), and pressing
claims to Trieste/Zone A, they relentlessly pursued their requests for a
World Bank loan, U.S. Export-Import Bank credits, and the return of
their gold reserves. Quarrels simmered with Stalin over their interference in Albania, the terms of Yugoslav-Bulgarian federation, defense
doctrine, the behavior of Soviet military officers in Yugoslavia, and de-

fense ties with Romania.[3] But in July 1947 a twelve-month bilateral trade agreement, and then Soviet credits and technical advisers for defense industries[4]—followed in early August by Tito's press conference angrily denouncing the United States for obstructing Yugoslavia's development plan and trade negotiations with Britain—seem to support (though somewhat after the fact) the U.S. argument that Tito was "Stalin's puppet." At the end of June, the Yugoslavs sent a note of serious interest in the European Recovery Program (Marshall Plan), only to reject membership on July 9.[5] At the first meeting of the new Communist Information Bureau, on September 22–27, 1947,[6] the Yugoslav leaders derided the French and Italian Communists for their "petty-bourgeois" concession to a parliamentary line, arguing that they had squandered the great resources of their wartime resistance and that as "parties which wait to jump into power," they were impotent to oppose the American interference that kicked them out of power and onto the road of isolated opposition. The Yugoslavs also attacked Władysław Gomułka for his moderate "Polish road."[7] At the same time, the Polish minister of the economy, Hilary Minc, attacked the Yugoslavs' economic program as some vain hope of a "third road" that would necessarily lead them back by the economic route to capitalism, and he argued that their unwillingness to accept the agreement among Eastern European Communists the previous February to hasten the pace of agricultural collectivization put them in the same camp as Gomułka.[8] The explanation for such apparently contradictory behavior lies on the ground, in the strategy the leaders had chosen earlier.

[3] There is a large literature on the Yugoslav-Soviet conflict. It is still worth beginning with V. Dedijer, *The Battle Stalin Lost;* and Djilas, *Conversations with Stalin.* See also Clissold, *Yugoslavia and the Soviet Union, 1939–1973.*

[4] The USSR committed itself to exchange "cotton, paper, cellulose, oil products, coal and coke, ferrous and non-ferrous metals, automobiles, tractors and other equipment, agricultural fertilizers, etc." for Yugoslav "lead, zinc and pyrite concentrates, copper, tobacco, hemp, plywood and agricultural goods," beginning retroactively on June 1. The defense pact granted Yugoslavia long-term credits of $135 million for equipment for the mining, metal, oil, chemical, and timber industries (Clissold, *Yugoslavia and the Soviet Union,* 43, 167).

[5] The United States was opposed to including Yugoslavia at the Paris negotiations, but an offical invitation came on July 4 after British and French ambassadors met with Yugoslav leaders at the Slovene resort of Bled to urge their participation.

[6] The Yugoslavs claimed to have initiated the idea, and the Cominform offices were to be located in Belgrade; but many argue that the September meeting was called precisely to exert control over the Yugoslav party.

[7] V. Dedijer, *Novi prilozi za biografiju Josipa Broza Tita* 3:276.

[8] Warriner, *Revolution in Eastern Europe,* 43–46. She cites Minc's April 1947 speech to the central committee of the Polish United Workers' party, published in the Cominform journal *For a Lasting Peace, for a People's Democracy* (August 1, 1948). On the Cominform meeting, see V. Dedijer, *Novi prilozi* 3:271–79. Many misinterpret the Yugoslav's position at these meetings because of their alliance with Zhdanov, but their position has been clarified by Werner Hahn's definitive account of Zhdanov's moderate position at the time (*Postwar Soviet Politics*).

July–October 1947: Rationalization

Within two months of the inauguration of the five-year industrialization plan, the problem of labor had become political. The local labor shortages, rapid labor turnover, and stubborn wage pressure were serious problems under the conditions of a trade deficit, limits on essential imports of machinery and food, and high production targets in order to fulfill the plan and increase exports. According to the planning commission's July 10 conference, called the very day after the rejection of the Marshall Plan invitation to attend the Paris negotiations, there was rising political discontent. Although production targets had been formulated and sent down, no one, from the ministries to the factory managers, had given a thought to labor supplies,[9] according to conference participants. Most believed that the source of the problem was the still-dominant "capitalist mentality" among managers and officials, which simply assumed that an inexhaustible reserve of willing workers among the unemployed and the agricultural surplus population would spontaneously yield itself up upon demand. But according to the commissioner of the plan, Andrija Hebrang, this view ignored the consequences of the agricultural policy. The issue remained what he had argued at the politbureau meeting in April 1946: the economic intensification and rationalizations since late 1946 would be insufficient to compensate for their moderate policy toward the countryside. In contrast to technically more advanced countries, he continued, where high levels of mechanization and little use of labor power made agriculture highly productive, Yugoslavia had to substitute labor for nonexistent machines. Unlike collectivized agriculture in the USSR, the agrarian reform had so parcelized holdings (there were now some two million farms) that they neither released what would in a modern economy be surplus labor nor produced enough to feed those already outside the rural sector. The shortage of skilled and professional labor— and, even worse, its uneven distribution in relation to economic needs— meant that such labor could not compensate for the absence of machinery in industry in raising productivity.

The party leaders, however, continued to view the cause of labor turnover, wage pressure, and food shortages as a matter of inadequate work incentives and state access to supplies, and wanted to pursue growth from existing capacity—which in their view was still underutilized. The principle of their system was to be "to each according to his work," accompanied by greater vigor in settling the labor force and, to relieve political discontent in the meantime, improved distribution of scarce consumer goods

---

[9] V. Begović, "Problem obezbjedjenja radne snage i stručnih kadrova u petogodišnjem planu," 18–32.

and elimination of speculators. As Tito told the youth brigade assembled in Sarajevo on November 16, 1947, to celebrate their completion of the Šamac-Sarajevo rail line, their example to the country on "how to work" was the spirit of a new Yugoslavia. "He who will not work has no right to use the results of another's labor, to benefit from the efforts of you who have contributed for the good of our community."[10]

The pace of work on elaborating the technical normatives for wage calculation and then legislating wage norms became feverish during the fall.[11] At the annual meeting of the union hierarchy in November 1947 (the fifth plenum), the federal Labor Minister, Vicko Krstulović repeated his warning of the previous November to unions and managers to cease plant-level wage bargaining and obey the legislated rules. Echoing the theme of politicians' speeches throughout the fall, he soberly insisted that planned, centrally regulated wage scales were essential to the production plan.[12] Federal regulations also used economic incentives to increase the supply of professionals and to get them to move: stipends for university education, graduated according to fields of social priority; honorariums for professionals willing to teach in night schools; and pay supplements for the costs of travel for professionals and administrators to job sites away from home. Enterprises and artisans' workshops willing to take on the training of more apprentices than their legal obligation (since 1946) of one for every three skilled workers they employed were also offered a subsidy.[13] A collective incentive encouraged "all workers and employees of the enterprise" to participate in raising productivity and "realizing profits" by reducing the cost-prices of production: enterprises that earned more than their planned revenue by cutting costs had the right to retain a portion of that revenue for a "managers' fund," which would "raise the social and cultural level of workers and employees" by building new apartments, canteens, libraries, or clubs (and, not incidentally, also cut these expenditures from public budgets).[14]

Reducing labor turnover also required more rational direction. Thus the planning commission instructed district people's committees to survey and record the true labor surplus in the towns and villages of their territory. At the November union plenum, Krstulović complained about

---

[10] Tito, "Govor na svečanosti prilikom puštanja u saobračaj omladinske pruge Šamac-Sarajevo," 160.

[11] V. Petrović, *Razvitak privrednog sistema FNRJ posmatran kroz pravne propise*, vol. 3.

[12] Krstulović, "Stalno podizanje proizvodnosti rada poboljšava radne i životne uslove radničke klase."

[13] This was an obligation that factory managers had nonetheless ignored; they saw such training as a "nonproductive" cost that only reduced their profit margins.

[14] Bjeladinović, "O privrednim preduzećima," 373.

the "irrationalities" of countrywide searches for labor. Serbian companies were seeking workers in the Croat regions of Dalmatia, Lika, and Medjumurje while Croatian companies were recruiting in Vojvodina and Serbia proper. What was the sense of identical construction firms' crossing republican borders to recruit new labor when they could find it nearby? Prejudice against the employment of women from both factory managers and union bureaus, he also argued, was a major obstacle to the obvious solution to local labor shortages—a solution that would at the same time keep down public expenditures for housing, child allowances, and transportation (it was rare at the time for a woman not to marry).[15] The many skilled emigrants who had returned to Yugoslavia in sympathy with the new political regime were still threatened, as he had complained the year before, because local people's committees were not helping them to settle.

To reduce labor turnover at industrial sites (particularly because of villagers who went home frequently to get supplies), to strengthen production incentives by linking access to supplies directly to productive labor, and to attract new labor, the ministry of trade and provisions began using coupons to ration necessities for wage and salary earners and their families, a system called guaranteed provisions (*obezbedjeno snabdevanje*). Redeemable in state stores at factories or in the new public trade network for food and other necessities, these coupons would also reduce the portion of wages paid in cash without cutting workers' consumption. The system would thus reduce the strain on enterprises' cash reserves, enable the National Bank to cut the supply of money it had to keep in circulation in order to implement plan directives, and undercut the prohibited but persistent wage bargaining between unions and managers.[16] Similarly, a series of experiments in the middle of 1947 moved more supply functions to the enterprise. Firms under federal and republican jurisdiction that employed more than two hundred workers were required to organize in-plant stores and canteens to supply their own workers, staff, and their families, while all factory administrators were told to order supplies of both rationed and nonrationed necessities, including food and clothing, directly from their republican ministries of trade and provisions according to the number of employees each month. Such an enterprise-based system of local stores could further cut cost-prices of production by cutting the costs of distribution, could possibly save fuel and scarce rolling stock, and certainly gave the government a weapon against managers who ig-

---

[15] The strident insistence of labor officials on increasing the employment of women suggests concern not only about ideological commitment and labor shortages, but also about depletion of the male labor force due to defense mobilization. They were up against powerful cultural prejudices, however, even from party members who opposed their wives' taking jobs. See Naljeva, "Neka pitanja partiskog rada medju ženama."

[16] Vujošević, "O nedostacima službe radničkog snabdijevanja"; Lompar, "O novom sistemu trgovine."

nored wage norms and hoarded labor by forcing such managers to keep employment records and standardized accounts of wages and costs. Finally, rather than rely totally on the peasants for food and raw materials, state enterprises and public institutions would grow their own. If they cultivated "workers' gardens" on land adjacent to their buildings or created their own farms by leasing land owned by local people's committees, they could become self-sufficient in vegetables, potatoes, pigs, and poultry and would be immune from market shortages. All manner of public persons, from factories to hospitals to farmers' marketing cooperatives, were encouraged to create these "community farms" (*zadružne ekonomije*) and to release employees part-time to work collectively on the land alongside the "devotion of all interested persons"—that is, volunteers who were otherwise unoccupied.[17]

The effect of the system of guaranteed provisions was, of course, to bias the direction of supplies toward workers in priority industries and in the socialized sector in general. Representatives for these industries would have said, however, that this bias would only redress the disadvantages their workers faced in competing for necessities on the market. In the drive for increased productivity in the public sector, after all, it was only *their* incomes that were limited, and those priority-sector firms tended to be far from the existing trade network (the offices of worker provisions in the cities and towns or the general farmers' cooperatives in the villages). Workers received wages at the end of a work cycle but had to pay for necessities in advance, while the sales period was so short that they lost days from production simply in driving from one local office to another in search of clothing. Despite legislated higher rations for miners, one official from the Ministry of Social Policy complained in January 1948 that many miners had not received clothing for five months, others had yet to receive any blankets, and there was very little in the way of bed linen, shoes, and clothing. Sandals for lumberjacks had been delivered in place of the promised boots, and on agricultural estates—the "young model farms that ought to create a new life in the village"—farm workers were often left with only chaff after grain had been exported to towns and foreign markets. If they got any flour or grain at all, it was less than their regulated allowance, and they frequently had to pay higher prices for food on the state farm than they would have paid in private farmers' markets. The farm canteens were poorly supplied, and rations of sugar, coffee, soap, and oil arrived a month later than scheduled, if at all. Summer clothing arrived in winter, winter clothing in summer.[18]

The immediate solution to shortages of food, raw materials, and exports, of course, still depended on farm production in the private sector.

---

[17] Bjeladinović, "O privrednim preduzećima," 373.
[18] Vujošević, "O nedostacima," 14.

The government permitted prices to rise in the markets where farmers sold their surplus after meeting their quotas for compulsory deliveries (*otkup*). This freedom was accompanied, however, by harsh penalties against those involved in trading activities—"speculators"—to prevent these wealthier and middle-size farmers from hoarding supplies, speculating with farm prices, and bidding up the price of rural labor. The rural poor in food-deficit regions received the right to guaranteed provisions, even if the household owned some land. The official explanation of this privilege was political—it was a just reward to those who had sacrificed so much to feed Partisan soldiers during the war—but it also sought to keep these peasants on the land to prevent proletarianization, undefended territory, and wage competition from private employers. Rhetoric was thick with Leninist slogans about the poor and middle peasants who labored on their smallholdings themselves (and with Kidrič's favorite, the "blight of speculation").

The line being drawn comes out clearly in a story recorded by Vladimir Dedijer of a lunch conversation at Tito's palatial office, Beli Dvor. Tito liked to consult a particular peasant from a village near Bjelovar, Croatia, on the "needs and mood of the people." But after Bujnah's tales of state injustices and mistakes toward the peasantry, Tito reminds him that as a "middle peasant," he must put the "general interest" before his personal views, and that all will be well in the new Yugoslavia for those who work. On the shortage of boots, Tito explains that "we must first equip our army . . . I have already taken steps to obtain leather and soles abroad . . . and if there aren't sufficient raw materials from abroad, in a year or two we'll have leather from our own cattle and we'll begin to set aside boots for our peasants, too." As for the rumors that the state will take land from the peasants, these are lies, "because who the devil would we give it to?" And they both agree that land lying idle is also wrong and that taking land from those who will not work it is justified. The low farm prices and guaranteed provisions are to prevent speculators from buying up cheap produce and making a profit when others go without: "Let those who want more than their rations pay more, [but] cement, bricks, pipe, and other peasant needs will gradually be allowed on the free market. And we'll import textiles from Poland and Czechoslovakia. I've told people traveling there to buy iron and banding for wagons. But they demanded corn, and we'll have to give them some corn."[19]

Governmental capacity to implement these policies remained focused on the self-sufficiency of localities, which were urged to open new industries that would generate revenues to free up republican federal budgets for new investment and that would produce local goods to attract farmers'

[19] V. Dedijer, *Novi prilozi* 3:242–43.

produce to the market; to improve local parsimony, especially by consolidating firms wherever feasible in order to cut their needs for administrative staff and to save on plant and equipment; and to adopt economic accounting (officials from the ministry of finance put ever more time into teaching it during the fall of 1947—often in words taken directly from Soviet speeches of the mid-1920s—through seminars for district officials in the techniques of accounting, economic supervision of enterprises, and budgetary discipline). As with the debate on supplies, the idea that the severe shortage of skilled labor and loyal agents would recommend economies of scale through concentration and centralized allocation was rejected in favor of local knowledge and binding people to land, employer, and locality, as the Tudor Statutes did in similar troubles.

The political campaign aimed at "nonproducers" who might take advantage of the market opening in the countryside. On September 26, 1947, at the second congress of the Popular Front, the Communist leadership withdrew its support from the Croat Peasant party; in early October, the CPP leader Josip Gaži and the Serb left agrarian Dragoljub Jovanović went to trial. During the fall, Kardelj began a reform of the local people's committees. From the frequent allusions to "reactionaries" and those "who sit in cafés and criticize rather than work," one can infer a campaign against prewar village political organizations and those who would oppose the new differentiation, including the shift in December away from the flat tax (which the ministry of finance continued to defend) to a steeply progressive income tax on private farmers.

November 1947–April 1948: Preparing for War

The problems with foreign trade were soon complicated by the growing conflict with the Soviet leadership over policy in the Balkans and military doctrine and authority.[20] Rejecting "fantasies" designed to "create insecurity in the nation" as a "very refined way to demobilize our people," Tito

---

[20] For example, there were quarrels over Yugoslav intervention in Albania, which by the end of 1947 so infuriated Stalin—because he believed it would give the Americans occasion for an attack—that he summoned Djilas, whom he thought he could influence, to Moscow; it also led to the suicide in November of Albanian politburo member Nako Spiru, allegedly as a protest against the stationing of a Yugoslav air force unit there and proposals to unify their armies. Other points of conflict included the November 27 mutual-defense treaty with Bulgaria, apparently intended to obstruct Stalin's plans for their federation; Tito's discussions with Gheorghe Gheorghiu-Dej on December 16–20 regarding Yugoslav-Romanian joint military doctrine (in follow-up talks in January with Svetozar Vukmanović-Tempo, the Romanians called the Yugoslav model "closer to Romania than to the USSR" because they both had only "just emerged from revolution" [V. Dedijer, *Novi prilozi* 3:225]); the escalation in February of the Greek civil war, in response to which the UN established a special investigatory commission on the Balkans; and the Tripartite Agreement of March 20 an-

criticized those "enemies in our country who now take advantage of the international situation to create a psychosis as if tomorrow will bring war, . . . saying: America is the strongest country in the world; it will change our situation back to the old ways, . . . bringing international reaction with an enormous military and atomic bombs." Tito told the youth brigade in Sarajevo on November 16 that "today's working world in capitalist countries is intelligent enough not to want to go to war for alien interests." Nonetheless, he added, "Let no one think that the people of Yugoslavia in their efforts, in their difficulties in constructing the country, in working to improve the living standard, are not at the same time taking care of their own security."[21] By March, he had summoned in secret the first meeting since 1940 of the surviving members of the party's central committee to announce that the refusal of the USSR to deliver promised military hardware and to negotiate indispensable trade left them with no other choice than to construct their army, air force, navy, and defense industries with domestic resources alone.[22] "We must orient ourselves alone, with our own forces," and for this "we will have to sacrifice much."[23]

This change meant that alongside exporting to reduce the trade deficit, they would shift investments and production to the needs of self-reliance: capital goods, transport, import substitutes, and strategic raw materials, including food and fuel. This shift, in turn, required temporary but fundamental readjustments in federal economic jurisdictions and far greater employment of labor.

The federal portion of the general state budget was already dangerously in deficit because revenues, defined by its sphere of jurisdiction over foreign affairs and the all-Yugoslav market, had fallen drastically with the exhaustion of war profits and UNRRA goods sales and with the effect of the austerity program and production delays on turnover-tax receipts. Ordering the strategic stockpiling of grain and the mandatory adoption of guaranteed provisions and workplace stores in December 1947,[24] Tito began to make the governmental adjustments necessary to gain for the

---

nouncing the intention to hand Trieste/Zone A to Italy, with which Stalin concurred despite Yugoslav claims. Although Tito's speeches during the fall of 1947 expressed concern over the growing threat of global war and the danger of tensions within the UN, in his speech marking Yugoslav Army Day (December 22), he acknowledged the conflicts with Soviet military officers over lines of authority.

[21] Tito, "Govor na svečanosti," 163–64.

[22] The Soviet Union had stopped deliveries from their July 1947 trade treaty and postponed negotiations over its renewal until December 1948. On March 18, it withdrew its military and civilian advisers and the promises of weapons made to Kardelj in early February.

[23] V. Dedijer, Novi prilozi 3:308.

[24] In an attempt to stop the managers' practice of bypassing the state trading network for more-beneficial barters with other firms, it was decided that enterprises close to trade net-

federal government the capital and labor that the new investment policy required. A governmental decree (*uredba*) on December 27 made a statutory exception for 1948 and 1949 to the rules governing transfers of ownership and dispersal of assets within the public sector. On January 8, the assembly was informed that the Ministry of Industry would be subdivided into three ministries—heavy industry and mining coming under federal jurisdiction alone and only light industry remaining a shared federal-republican competence—and the Ministry of Agriculture and Forestry into two, although they would continue under shared federal-republican jurisdiction. Tito assumed the dual authority of minister of defense and prime minister, adding to his growing personal power. In January 1948, the recommendations of the labor conference held the previous July appeared on the agenda of the politbureau; it was decided to transfer final authority over labor in plan execution from factory managers to the state, although the federal minister of labor was still obliged to respect republican jurisdiction over labor by working in full consultation with republican labor ministries. In summoning Jakov Blažević to Belgrade on December 29, 1947, to take over at the Ministry of Trade and Provisions, Tito explained that the world situation "wasn't rosy"—there could even be war and other "unpleasantness"—and thus they could not afford to create a united front of "embittered" peasants against them when they might have to depend on their fighting loyalty.[25] As a loyal member of the Croatian leadership, member of the central committee of the party since 1940, prosecuting attorney in the trial of Archbishop Stepinac, and organizer of the "uprising" in Lika (for which he was punished by Hebrang, the Croat party leader at the time), Blažević was selected, Tito explained, because the problem of supplies had become "a significant political issue." They needed a new policy toward the village.[26]

Kidrič announced the increase in expenditures of 45.2 percent—"in capitalist terms, difficult to comprehend"—in his annual speech on the budget in April. Although conspicuously silent on the increase in defense expenditures of 35 percent, he did explain that capital construction would grow 73 percent, industrial production 61 percent, and the output of coal, steel, and cement faster than the overall plan rate; and there would be an entire range of products never before produced at home, such as asphalt, light- and heavy-grade benzin, petrolcoke, charcoal briquettes, cylinder oil, transformers, ship engines, asbestos products, electrodes, drills, and their "rich but underutilized" domestic raw materials. Although "one of

---

works now had to get ministerial permission to create farms and stores, and rules on trade between firms were clarified.

[25] From Blažević's diary, printed in V. Dedijer, *Novi prilozi* 3:229–34.

[26] Ibid., 3:230.

the most basic, central planned tasks of the country" for 1948 was growth in exports, he insisted that there would be "no trade-off between living standards and growth in foreign trade." Sounding no less than ever like the Trotsky of the Soviets' twelfth party congress of October 1923 or the Bukharin of 1924–25, however, he promised that the increase in accumulation would come not from inflationary finance, lowered consumption, or exploitation of the peasantry, but from "production itself"—by utilizing the vast reserves still hidden within existing capacity, by eliminating waste, and by further lowering costs of production. In the first public statement of the leadership's policy toward labor, Kidrič told the national assembly: "It is well known how capitalists solve the question of a reserve army of proletarians. They solved it by means of pauperization and proletarianization of the village, by means of terrible economic and other pressure on the working peasant, above all on the poor and poorest. We cannot and will not take such a path to mobilizing the new labor power necessary for our industrialization."[27]

The primary focus of labor policy was still public sector firms, but the problem of productivity was now blamed on managers and government officials who cavalierly ignored regulations (in his own speech to the assembly the next day, Kardelj cited a long list from the year-end reports of inspectors on the State Control Commission, of which he was head). When told to gather data on the labor supply, for example, too many officials (Kidrič complained) only retorted that sufficient numbers of qualified personnel to draw up accurate labor plans would not be available for five more years, let alone months. Economic establishments "and even entire republics" responded to the shortages with "pseudoplanning" for more than seven times the labor they actually needed, "savage" competition among firms, hoarding and even kidnapping of labor, and the unconscionable overpayment of certain categories of workers at the expense of others, resulting in mounting chaos in their wage policy. Ministry staff were so lax in their inspections that managers were essentially free to hoard. Factory directors used the labor shortage as an excuse for failing to deliver planned output, and then tried to blackmail leaders who wanted the plan fulfilled into leaving them free to recruit their own labor and use overtime pay as needed. Union offices continued their unfriendliness to new workers (in the mines they wanted overtime work instead) and their general disregard for other causes of labor turnover, absenteeism (on average 23–27 percent in the first five months of 1948), and general lack of discipline, all of which increased the number of workers needed to meet assigned production targets. Many district people's committees refused to recruit new workers and were protected by their republican govern-

---

[27] Kidrič, "Govor na pretresu opštedržavnog budžeta za 1948 godinu," 239.

ments, while others contributed directly to the serious political tensions in the countryside by filling their labor quotas mechanically, without sensitivity to individual preferences for place and type of employment.[28]

Within factories, there would be a move to three shifts and continued emphasis on human capital as a substitute for machines. Research and development, the training of technicians and skilled labor, the authority of engineers, consultation between "work collectives" and scientists to improve production technique and work organization, and monetary rewards for shock workers and inventors were all critical to higher productivity and finding hidden reserves, but the state would no longer leave this to firms. On May 17, 1948, it announced a host of new federal offices for scientific research and development, such as one for developing a domestic raw-material base and an institute for electric energy, and federal schools for technical training, such as a secondary forestry school for the karst (to reforest this barren area along the Adriatic coast). Kidrič did not mention the decision to spend substantial resources on the rush to atomic (later nuclear) power and weaponry.[29]

The leaders would also introduce enterprise plans "of Soviet practice," legally obliging factory directors to rationalize their use of labor, tie production possibilities to financial means, and plan future needs for skilled labor and technicians so that appropriate training occurred on time. In January, social-insurance bureaus had received instructions to gather data on employment levels, the wage fund, and work hours, a move aimed at enforcing drafting of enterprise labor plans more promptly and more in line with actual needs of production. Republican and federal ministries would then combine these plans with surveys by district labor offices to formulate a countrywide plan for labor, including quotas for the temporary mobilization of unskilled labor into volunteer brigades for increased export production in the mines, forests, and agriculture and for capital construction projects. On May 29, 1948, a federal bureau of statistics was created under the office of the state president, and during the month of June census takers went into the field to gather the data on labor supply that it had been so difficult to get factory managers and the people's committees to gather. Some professionals would be transferred *temporarily* to Belgrade, "regardless of where they otherwise have their permanent employment and sphere of activity,"[30] and the federal minister of labor would assign skilled labor to federal priorities where there was continued difficulty in getting people to move. Kardelj was particularly impatient with professionals who wanted to keep their comfortable life in the city,

---

[28] Ibid., 253.
[29] See S. Dedijer, "Tito's Bomb."
[30] Kidrič, "Govor na pretresu opštedržavnog budžeta za 1948 godinu," 250.

given the tasks at hand: "Those who do not want to understand that it is their duty to work and to give of themselves wherever they are needed for building up our country are good-for-nothing sons of the people and good-for-nothing citizens of this country. Such people must understand that the community will behave the same way toward them."[31] As for workers' living standards, they would not fall, but it would be "pure demagogy" if the leaders pushed for a rise in living standards at this point. The "only healthy, solid guarantee of raising the living standard" was to continue the drive to raise labor productivity. A new wage system, officially inaugurated on May 29 and scheduled to be implemented by July, would replace the disparate wage norms devised the previous year for priority branches with a coordinated system of centrally set average wage norms based on progressive piece rates and bonuses for above-norm output.[32]

The political problem, however, was how to mobilize the "tens and tens of thousands of new forest, construction, and industrial workers who must be recruited from the village," without following either the capitalist path of "a reserve army of proletarians" or the Stalinist path that nearly destroyed agricultural production. In his explanation to Blažević when he began work in January of the need for a new policy toward the village, Tito did not mention that agricultural production had not yet recovered its prewar level and that the incentive of higher prices in farmers'-surplus markets during the fall of 1947 had made it increasingly difficult to enforce the compulsory-delivery quotas on which the system of guaranteed provisions depended. Arrests of farmers who resisted the required sales to the government had risen alarmingly. At the same time, party radicals complained that the policy benefited richer farmers over middle and poor peasants and favored the countryside in general over urban residents and industrial workers. But for Tito, it was the tax policy toward the village "imposed by the Ministry of Finance" (headed by Sreten Žujović) that was fueling political "oppositionists" and rural discontent.[33] Moreover, the problem with the kulaks was in their role as employers. With higher prices for their produce, rich farmers could afford to offer higher wages and better food to poor peasants than could the factories and mines of the public sector. This was already the case in all regions—except Macedonia.[34] In their mutual competition with the state over labor, the kulaks also had a cultural advantage: "opposition elements" in the villages were successfully frightening peasants with rumors that if they entered factory

[31] Kardelj, quoted in Arsov, "Mobilizacija nove radne snage za izvršenje privredcnog plana," 8. The unwillingness of doctors, engineers, and other technicians to move out of capital cities such as Belgrade into the newly industrializing areas was the subject of newspaper cartoons as well as leaders' derision from 1945 on.

[32] See V. Petrović, *Razvitak privrednog sistema FNRJ*, vol. 3.

[33] Tito, in V. Dedijer, *Novi prilozi* 3:229–34.

[34] Lazar Kološevski, the representative from Macedonia, at the second plenum of the

gates, they would return to find their land taken from them and their families transported.[35]

However harsh the measures to requisition produce and control trade were becoming because of the need for supplies, the leadership did *not* want to "hit the kulaks frontally"[36] but to find new, indirect ways to squeeze them economically. The aim was to undercut their market power—their ability to monopolize rural trade and labor markets—without eliminating them as individual producers. Thus on February 11 the government unveiled a new policy of farm-production incentives to replace the free markets, and it forbade trade in agricultural produce outside the official trade network.[37] According to this policy—called trade by linked, or interdependent, prices (*vezane cene*)—peasants in either the private or cooperative sector who sold their surplus above the compulsory-delivery quota to an agent in the state trading network would receive, in addition to cash, coupons with which they could purchase industrial goods under government monopoly at prices 16 percent lower than in retail markets. Guaranteed provisions would be given only to protect the livelihoods of the poorest and the efficacy of production incentives to workers. Tito's instructions to Blažević, on January 15, 1948, were to aid most the regions of greatest suffering during the war and to distinguish among poor, middle, and kulak peasantry in both taxation and requisitioning.[38] As Kidrič explained in April, the solution to the problem of agricultural production still lay with industry: they would be "disregarding internal economic links" if they did not first improve peasants' living conditions and produce the industrial inputs necessary for higher agricultural yields. "Naturally," Kidrič added, the provision cards, favorable fiscal measures, and other economic aid to protect the living standards of the "working peasant" would be withdrawn from those who take such assistance in place of working; and "of course the speculator's standard will fall!"[39]

CPY central committee, January 28–30, 1949, in Petranović, Končar, and Radonjić, *Sednice centralnog komiteta KPJ (1948–1952)*, 63.

[35] Arsov, "Mobilizacija nove radne snage," 10.

[36] Kardelj, in his report on the "policy of the CPY toward the village" (see also the reference in that report to Kidrič's position at a conference of the government's Economic Council on June 5, 1948), and Tito, at the second plenum of the CPY central committee, in Petranović, Končar, and Radonjić, *Sednice*, 23, 70.

[37] This *Uredba o prodaji poljoprivrednih proizvoda vezanoj sa pravom na kupovinu odredjenih industrijskih proizvoda po nižim jedinstvenim cenama* (Regulation on the sale of agricultural products in exchange for the right to purchase certain industrial products at lower, unified prices) was valid until April 1950, when it was replaced by the *Uredba o trgovini po vezanim cenama* (Regulation on trade by linked prices) and a version of the USSR's 1921 tax in kind and 1923 forward contracts. See Petrović, *Razvitak privrednog sistema FNRJ*, vol. 3; and Lompar, "O novom sistemu trgovine," 11.

[38] V. Dedijer, *Novi prilozi* 3:233.

[39] Kidrič, "Govor na pretresu opštedržavnog budžeta za 1948 godinu," 240.

The class struggle in "their way" in the new Yugoslavia was not that of Stalinist collectivization; it took place in commerce, and it was a "struggle against speculators" that was simultaneously a struggle against "administrative" measures. On the one hand, the state and cooperative trade network had to eliminate the side trading, private middlemen, and speculative practices that were feeding inflation. Anyone engaged in reselling goods without license would be prosecuted. Capitalist elements and "remnants of the former ruling class" would be deprived of their economic power. On the other hand, local officials had too often resorted to administrative measures in collecting and distributing goods when they should have been using financial measures—controlled prices—to influence allocation. Thus on April 2, a second domestic nationalization in urban areas—the "road to liquidating the urban bourgeoisie"— transferred to social ownership (either state or cooperative) the remainder of retail trade and all enterprises of local jurisdiction: smaller industrial and construction firms, all printers and warehouses, 500 hotels, 30 sanatoriums and hospitals, 100 cinemas, and 530 dairies. Overnight, 3,100 private shops and establishments closed down. Legislation also prohibited trade in fixed assets, most importantly the private sale of land of any amount—"even if the holding was below the 'so-called minimum.'" Private purchase of agricultural machinery was prohibited to "capitalist elements."[40]

The state would also enter the world of village labor for the first time. Anyone who wished to employ village labor—whether privately, for permanent industrial jobs, or in volunteer labor brigades—would now be required to go through local offices of the labor ministry (established in every district people's committee in September 1948). These offices would also conduct surveys of labor power in the district to improve identification of the true surplus—labor that could move permanently to the wage sector without threatening (largely private) agricultural production—and thereby reduce the problems of labor turnover in industry when recruitment occurred to fill the higher quotas set for industrial employment in 1948.

At the same time, Kardelj did begin in April to refer to the need for a "fundamental break" in agriculture (using Stalin's 1928 phrase) because, as Kidrič put it, "the social process taking place in our country . . . must be conceived as a unified whole. If that process, if the construction of socialism, were not to move with the tempo that conditions and the stage of development demand, then economic success would also fall behind."[41] The socialization of agriculture had to lay the groundwork for the

---

[40] Balog, "Uredbe vlade FNRJ u 1948 godini," 97. The regulations excluded the purchase of buildings for use as housing by workers, employees, civil servants, artisans, or working peasants in the towns.

[41] Kidrič, "Govor na pretresu opštedržavnog budžeta za 1948 godinu," 255.

agricultural machinery being produced by encouraging the formation of more cooperatives "of the new type" (peasant labor cooperatives)[42] with their industrial principles—land concentration, economic accounting, pay according to output, more efficient organization of work, and socialist competition. In fact, production cooperatives would be formed only where crops needed for defense stockpiles, export, and import substitution, such as grains and cotton, could be grown (in the Vojvodina plain but not necessarily in the Macedonian plains, for example; or, in the case of livestock, on otherwise unarable land in Bosnia). Moreover, as Vladimir Bakarić admitted later, the primary reason was not agricultural deliveries, but to release more labor "naturally" for industry and for volunteer brigades.[43]

This middle path on agriculture has been confusing to most analysts, particularly because its implementation in the following year did lead to local excesses in the rush to fill labor quotas. Already in Kidrič's defense against critics, one can see the political difficulty of even defining this course when political lines had been drawn historically in other ways. Thus, on April 12, behind closed doors, to critics on the left within the central committee, Kidrič used class-based arguments: "a superficial observer might think that the system of linked trade is a concession to capitalist elements"; on the contrary, "linked trade as such limits kulaks in getting rich" and, with upcoming measures against speculators and "capitalist elements" in the village, would strengthen the poor and middle peasants. The important points were that more than 90 percent of industry was in state hands, that wholesale trade had been liquidated, and that all of private retail trade would soon follow (as it seems to have done by the end of May).[44] However, in public debate before the national assembly ten days later, Kidrič sought to reassure those "elements" and to do what he could to keep the popular-front alliance together. The policy of linked trade would, he agreed, reduce farmers' cash revenue, but it would also improve the terms of trade between industrial and agricultural products in their favor. A comparison with average price ratios in the last years before the war would show that farmers' purchasing power was now greater by 12 percent, and to the extent that the terms of trade were still to agriculture's disadvantage, the gap represented an entirely new reality. Before the war, he explained, the high cost of industrial goods was due to the exploitation of foreign capitalists, who bought Yugoslavia's raw materials for much less than their worth and then sold Yugoslav consumers finished goods from those same raw materials at much higher prices— which they had no choice but to pay because those foreigners refused to

[42] *Seljačke radne zadruge.*

[43] Bakarić, in discussion at the third plenum of the CPY central committee, December 29–30, 1949, in Petranović, Končar, and Radonjić, *Sednice,* 415.

[44] Kidrič, in V. Dedijer, *Novi prilozi* 3:375–76.

produce the goods in Yugoslavia. Now, that gain would stay at home to develop the economy. Because the policy would also make possible lower food prices, urban residents would benefit and the end of rationing would reduce "administrative bureaucratism." To compensate, the policy would also cut the tax on "working peasants' incomes" more than 40 percent over the 1947 rate, and it would allow free sale at the higher official price of any surplus after the post-harvest collections for guaranteed provisions and linked trade.[45]

The approach to the problem of foreign trade was similar. The primary concern was the waste of foreign exchange because of the poverty of cadres in foreign-trade organizations and the inadequate commercial network—reflected in, for example, the "lousy" system of billing; foreign buyers were getting goods free because Yugoslavs viewed bills of lading as mere formalities. The "most important economic-organizational task," Kardelj argued in his April 25–26 speech on governmental reform and the economy, was to put "our socialist commerce . . . on its feet"; producers themselves needed to become "socialist traders," attentive to the commercial side of their work and the skills necessary to it. Inventories were piling up in industrial warehouses and deliveries of goods were "lagging terribly behind production" because public-sector managers attended only to production. Employees in the trade network who still thought with a "capitalist mentality" should be replaced by socialist cadres: those who could show initiative in moving goods; keep better records and follow the dictates of profit-and-loss accounting; and, under the pressure of the "wide participation of the masses," fight bureaucratism.[46] Most important was foreign trade, and Kardelj called on every person and enterprise in the country to assist:

> It is the ultimate in narrow-mindedness when some economic institutions refuse to release some staff to foreign trade. We emphasize that old Yugoslavia had more numerous and qualified foreign-trade cadres than we have with fewer tasks and less responsibility than has our foreign trade. Our economic institutions must end at once their harmful practice of holding onto cadres who are necessary for foreign trade, for if not, they will cause great damage to themselves and to their country.[47]

The effect of the January decisions was a severe food and fuel crisis that lasted throughout March and April.[48] The first signs of increased hardship were visible within days of the March 1 politbureau meeting, when Tito

[45] Kidrič, "Govor na pretresu opštedržavnog budžeta za 1948 godinu," 244.
[46] Kardelj, "The Struggle for the Fulfillment of the First Five Year Plan," 15, 22, 27.
[47] Ibid.
[48] Blažević mentioned the crisis frequently in discussion at the second plenum of the CPY central committee (in Petranović, Končar, and Radonjić, *Sednice*, 144).

announced the policy of building defense forces on their own (*na sopstvene snage*) in order to secure the approval of republic leaders for the shift in investment, cuts in imports at the expense of light industry (and therefore enterprises under republican jurisdiction), and tasks that this policy would require of the republics. Staple foods disappeared from local markets as stockpiling and military use increased[49] and exports rose (by the end of the year, exports of corn and wheat alone had increased tenfold over the 1947 figures).[50] Cuts in civil-aviation flights, freight movements, and automobile traffic reflected the decision to conserve petroleum fuels and increase the export of coal.[51] In March, whole villages in Slovenia rebelled against local officials over the changed quotas of ration cards allocated under the new policy of linked trade. Tensions between the Slovene and federal governments over who was to blame rose to such heights that Kardelj and Kidrič had to intervene personally.[52] Rules forbidding the traditional Easter slaughter of sacrificial animals so as to conserve livestock for export and food for workers' tables led to direct confrontations with churches in countless villages. The political backlash over the April 2 nationalization left such scars that for twelve to eighteen months thereafter, the leadership raised its specter whenever radicals argued for faster and more direct socialization.

Even before the first Cominform resolution, then, the policy on agriculture had begun to change in order to gain labor for production that leaders considered necessary to national sovereignty; the decisive political purge of the opposition to come had been defined; and out of the reorganization to implement the plan and their particular strategy toward labor there emerged a new state, the vision of which was fully conceptualized in Kardelj's April 25 speech.

The role of state power during the "socialist transition" (that is, when state power would still have a role) was to be the "integral coordinator" of society. Ceasing to be an instrument for fiscal exploitation and coercion "above" society, it would become (in Engels's famous phrase) the administrator of things, not of men. A republic of socioeconomic communities based on production and consumption, it would be held together by a set of central rules and offices of technical supervision, but would encourage as much decentralized execution, autonomous management, and demo-

---

[49] U.S. Ambassador Cavendish Cannon's telegram to the U.S. secretary of state, February 4, 1949; he also wrote that "in April 1948 security zones requiring special and unobtainable permit for all diplomats were greatly expanded" (*Foreign Relations of the United States, 1949* 5:862).

[50] Wolff, *The Balkans in Our Time*, 333–35.

[51] *Foreign Relations of the United States, 1948* 4:1067; minutes of the central committee meeting of March 1, 1948, in V. Dedijer, *Novi prilozi* 3:303–8.

[52] Blažević diary, in V. Dedijer, *Novi prilozi* 3:234–35.

cratic participation in firms and localities as possible. The bureaucratic state would be replaced with the efficiency of a technocratic democracy. While decentralization to encourage local initiative could result not in efficiency but in a systemic inefficiency of horizontal deals and collusion among factory managers, factories and farms, or local committees that circumvented technically efficient rules when it was in their particular interest, this could not be resolved by a bureaucratic apparatus that alienated working people and diverted surplus value to pay unnecessary administrative salaries. The answers to the economic waste and political power of "bureaucratism" were a lean state (of federal and republican administrations); financially autonomous communes (the name given to the unit of local administration); and "people's power"—supervision of central principles on issues affecting living standards (welfare, clothing, housing, health and safety measures, food, labor productivity) by assemblies of mass participation in factories, cooperatives, and communes.[53] This required turning the state into a staff of rule-making experts, decentralizing necessary administration to the locality, and perfecting the vertical chain of command between the two—the financial plan that would enforce the production plan, the rules and laws formulated by scientific institutes and engineers in the ministerial directorates to assist in production technique and development of resources, and the inspectors of the central control commission to oversee quality and safety standards.

The economic basis of this vision of the state received a very practical impetus in the spring of 1948. Financial and economic independence of localities was necessary to relieve the growing budgetary burdens on republican governments that resulted from the redirection of resources to defense, capital investment, and the foreign market. Subsidies to local governments would be cut, and district and urban people's committees would have to take greater initiative than they had in 1947 in developing their "local economies" and relying on local materials. Local assumption of the tasks of economic development and social change would permit the central government to concentrate on plan priorities. "Control from below" would replace paid officials with democratic voluntarism so that the shortage of cadres and budget deficits could be relieved. Popular initiative in expanding national wealth was a free commodity, and it engaged citizens in the new order.

Mass participation was also a powerful political instrument of class struggle. In the most critical task ahead, the rational recruitment of new

[53] A. Ross Johnson argues in *The Transformation of Communist Ideology* that the Yugoslav leaders developed their critique of bureaucracy out of their reassessment of Stalinism during 1949; in fact, they had made this critique and actively promoted it from the beginning of their rule, particularly in 1947 and 1948 (see, for example, Kidrič, "O nekim principijelnim pitanjima naše privrede").

labor, political care was essential; so it was handed to the mass political organizations—the Communist youth organization (SKOJ), the Antifascist Women's Front, the district party committee, and the United Unions branch. And the localization of governmental tasks was essential to the leaders' concept of national defense, just as their military strategy of territorial defense had developed during the war. Although the effect of the governmental reform was not to reduce but to increase the number of state offices and officials, these were primarily at the district level, not the center; and although economic policy was surely set in the most centralized and even secretive forums, the political struggle gave more effective authority to local commissariats and political organizations than to administrators.

Perhaps just as important to the evolution of Kardelj's design for the state was a repetition of the tactic of wartime and the April 1946 politbureau meeting: using patriotism to cover up substantive disputes over policy and justify a political purge. At the plenary session of the central committee that preceded Kardelj's April 1948 speech, held in the library of the former King Alexander's palace in Belgrade on April 12 and 13, the twenty-four members were presented with Stalin's letter of March 27 and the draft of a Yugoslav reply, and then given a choice—between "the policy of the CPY" and "Stalin and his theses." The internal debate was no longer over domestic policy; it was an issue of national loyalties. As Tito said in conclusion: "Comrades, remember that it is not a matter here of any theoretical discussion. . . . We must not allow ourselves to be forced into a discussion of such things. Comrades, the point here, first and foremost, is the relations between one state and another."[54]

This time voicing disagreement, Žujović called both the precipitate reply and the leadership's chosen policy of socialism in one country a "fatal mistake," because "we've isolated ourselves from the broader perspective under the burden of power."[55] But Tito's answer was "You, Crni [Žujović's *nom de guerre*], have taken for yourself the right to love the USSR more than me."[56] By May 5, when Tito announced the removal of Hebrang and Žujović to the national assembly, a thorough purge had begun of the ministry of finance (under Žujović) and of the ministry of heavy industry and the planning commission (both under Hebrang, whose view was also solicited after the meeting). Arrested four days later, these two of the most prominent prewar Communists and conceivable candidates for party leadership were charged by a party tribunal with betrayal. As Tito had instructed his colleagues on April 12, "We must do everything to

[54] V. Dedijer, *Novi prilozi* 3:338. See also Vukmanović-Tempo, *Revolucija koja teče* 2:71–72.

[55] V. Dedijer, *Novi prilozi* 3:370.

[56] Ibid., 382.

prevent people who want to destroy the unity of our Party from doing so."[57] In April alone, an "espionage trial" of twenty-seven prewar, non-communist leftists in Ljubljana removed many of the remaining members of the popular front from high governmental positions. Most "internationalists," such as the "Spaniards" (Spanish civil war veterans), and a large number of party intellectuals succumbed to exile, trial and prison, or suicide. Two waves of personnel change in federal ministries, in the spring and again in August, placed loyalists in the majority—above all in the ministries of labor, mining, and foreign affairs.

In Kidrič's April budget speech, where the shift in investment strategy was apparent, he criticized skeptics' charges as "enemy slander" and opponents as "experts educated in foreign technical schools, under the influence of monopolistic 'theories' of foreign financial capital" who were prejudiced against domestic production of raw materials and investment in metallurgy and metal-processing industries. At the same time, those who disagreed with the huge increase in capital investment were no better than wartime traitors, for "without the development of basic branches of our heavy industry, mining, electrification, etc. . . . our country would fall deeper and deeper into economic dependence on foreigners, and it would prevent the construction of socialism in the FPRY [Federative People's Republic of Yugoslavia]." The population would make the necessary sacrifices out of patriotism, he insisted:

> Dear people's delegates, we can compare the struggle for Tito's Five-Year Plan with the National Liberation struggle in many ways. Namely, in the current struggle for the Five-Year Plan, huge efforts are also needed, sacrifices are needed, because without effort and without sacrifice there are no great victories, just as without them there would have been none in the National Liberation struggle. And in this struggle as well there appear, just as there appeared in the National Liberation struggle, waverers, capitulators, enemies, who spread disbelief in success, disbelief in the powers of our land and our working nation. And just as the experience of the National Liberation struggle clearly showed that such people were in fact working against the independence and freedom of our land, the experience of the struggle for our Five-Year Plan and its success also demonstrates, and will demonstrate, that people who spread doubt in our economic powers are in fact enemies of the all-around strengthening of our fatherland, and are at the same time enemies of the construction of socialism in our country.[58]

[57] Ibid. According to Dedijer, the conflict aroused "excitement"; but the chargé d'affaires at the U.S. Embassy sent word to Washington of surprising apathy on May Day and on Tito's birthday (May 25)—in striking contrast to the previous year's celebrations. He also reported signs during May of a "drop in the regime's confidence and optimism" (*Foreign Relations of the United States, 1948* 4:1070–72).

[58] Kidrič, "Govor na pretresu opštedržavnog budžeta za 1948 godinu," 245.

Despite even Tito's insistence in 1946 that the volunteer labor brigades should end, these popular "contributions" to the extraordinary but short-run demands for capital construction and federal projects would continue. Similarly, the extraordinary budget expenditures would be covered in part by a "national bond for the five-year plan for development of the national economy of the FPRY," which would, like the bond for national liberation of January 1943 (which unfortunately would mature in 1948), offer the population another opportunity to participate in the defense of the country's independence.

MAY–DECEMBER 1948: THE POLITICS OF MILITARY SELF-RELIANCE

The leaders had never given up on efforts to obtain trade and assistance, unblock their gold reserves, and reverse a tourist ban with the United States; Tito even delegated Srdja Prica in early January 1948 to renew requests in Washington with an explanation of their difficulties with the USSR. The concessions they made in February on compensation for American property claims in hopes of reopening negotiations bore fruit by May, when they conceded ("precipitately," the Americans thought) to much of the U.S. position in order to get an agreement on June 11.[59] In June, they repeated their "interest in expanding Western trade" in conversations with U.S. and other Western diplomats, and several times during July Tito raised the idea of their participating in the Marshall Plan after all. By October, they had reduced the flow of supplies to aid the rebels in the Greek civil war—a sore point with Stalin and the primary complaint of the United States since late 1946—but probably because of the burden on their own economy. The United States began a tentative reassessment in light of these concessions, sensing an extraordinary propaganda opportunity that was emerging with the Cominform resolution of June 28. After July 6, the State Department and the National Security Council edged from a policy designed to undermine the Communist regime through economic hardship to one of "watchful waiting."[60] To replace the oil deliveries that Albania, Hungary, and Romania canceled in July (the first manifestations of the trade slowdown from the East, which were followed by Czechoslovakia's refusal to send more coking coal and machinery until the Yugoslavs upheld their part of the trade agreement),[61] the United States now gave Yugoslavia permission to purchase

[59] The Yugoslavs held up the signing until July 19, however, so that it would coincide with the opening of the fifth party congress two days later. The concessions included payment of $18 million for various claims out of the $57 million in dispute, and 47 million dinars for their obligations on Lend-Lease goods.

[60] Mugoša, "Odnosi Jugoslavije i SAD-a izmedju 1945 i 1949."

[61] Very little else occurred at this point, despite the standard view that there was an

oil from the Allied occupation authorities in Trieste. In September, a team from the IMF and the World Bank arrived in Belgrade to reopen negotiations on conditions for credits and loans, and the U.S. State Department allowed two American companies to submit preliminary requests for export licenses to sell Yugoslavia machinery forbidden by the strategic embargo in exchange for minerals and ores.[62] In his negotiations with the U.S. ambassador Cavendish Cannon, Kardelj confided their dire need of tires, fuel, and truck and tractor parts to relieve transportation bottlenecks. That request was rejected in December, but in October the World Bank did include Yugoslavia along with Austria, Poland, Czechoslovakia, and Finland in its offer of a loan for timber equipment because of the bank's special interest in encouraging timber exports from the East to Western Europe. The success of U.S.-Yugoslav negotiations over the gold reserves encouraged Western European governments to enter trade negotiations to gain similar leverage in their own claims against Yugoslavia. Between April and December 1948, the period in which the Soviet trade treaty had been postponed, Yugoslavia concluded bilateral treaties with Britain, Argentina, Italy, Belgium, the Netherlands, Sweden, Switzerland, Turkey, and France, among others.[63]

The supply of primary commodities for export and capital construction thus continued to dominate the home front, where Kidrič and Kardelj proceeded with additional institutional adjustments to improve incentives and enforce both real and accounting balances. On June 5, the day of the new bond subscription, the Economic Council held a conference of all persons involved with agricultural policy to discuss the results of the spring sowing and the prospects for the compulsory deliveries in the fall. Apparently resisting strong pressures for a direct confrontation with rich farmers, Kidrič instead conceded to much higher quotas, by changing the criteria used in 1947–48: instead of being based on the size of a farmer's cultivated land surface, the quota would be a steeply progressive proportion of the actual harvest (up to 85 percent) depending on the size of the holding, after deductions were made for household consumption, animal feed, seed, and forage. State farms had to sell their entire yield: labor

---

immediate blockade from the East. The trade blockade came into effect only during 1949; it was more or less complete by the end of June, except for the one-eighth of previous trade contracts that had been negotiated with the USSR in December 1948 (Ibid.; and *Foreign Relations of the United States, 1949*, vol. 5).

[62] The machinery included a steel-blooming mill worth $3 million, fifteen oil drills, five mobile machine-repair shops, Banbury mixers for a tire plant, and several thousand tractor tires; the minerals and ores included copper and lead worth $6 million for the steel mill alone (see, among others, Mugoša, "Odnosi Jugoslavije i SAD-a"; and Clissold, *Yugoslavia and the Soviet Union*).

[63] Mugoša, "Odnosi Jugoslavije i SAD-a"; *Foreign Relations of the United States, 1949* 5: 854–55 (cables from December 23–24, 1948).

cooperatives, between 10 and 50 percent; general farmers' cooperatives, between 20 and 28 percent; and peasants with less than two hectares, none. Farmers willing to conclude forward contracts (*kontrahiranje*)[64] with the state were promised prices 25 percent higher than the official price for both compulsory deliveries and free surpluses. The National Bank was instructed to shift credits for the cooperative sector from the 1947 emphasis on working capital to one encouraging investment. Local reforms also aimed at capturing savings, from the private sector in local savings associations established to administer the national bond, and from public-sector enterprises in the establishment of National Bank branches in every district to administer the system of cash planning[65] (legislated on August 14).

Insistence on local and settled sources of labor, probably of even greater concern because of the decision to develop the territorial militias, remained policy. Writing in the June issue of *Narodna Država*, the journal for government officials in economic administration, the new minister of labor, Ljubčo Arsov, urged particular care "to avoid as much as possible large transfers of working people from one region of the country to another." As he explained, "It is also necessary to keep in mind that people are separated from their environment with difficulty and that they wish in one way or another to keep in the closest contact with their own region."[66] He then reiterated his predecessor's stress on employment of women, arguing that the reasons for their low proportion in the employed labor force in 1947 (only 18.8 percent, though the figure varied greatly among sectors and regions) had to be acknowledged: women's "relative backwardness due to their subordinate position and education historically," the absence of cafeterias and day-care centers, and discrimination by some factory directors who objected to the rules equalizing women's pay rates with those of men.[67]

Nonetheless, the concern over food and fuel took on emergency proportions in early June; the response on the ground, as under the supply-strained, embattled conditions of Foča in the war, was military campaigns, political pressures, and even physical coercion to extract all available internal supplies. With coal reserves down to several days' sup-

---

[64] See V. Petrović, *Razvitak privrednog sistema FNRJ* 4:143–44. The system of forward contracts was also patterned after the Soviet system, which was introduced (at first on a voluntary basis and then, in 1933, by decree) between individual peasant farms and the collective-farm movement then developing, in order to secure supplies. "Credit facilities and supply of manufactured goods were coupled with a guarantee of certain minimum supplies of grain" (Dobb, *Soviet Economic Development since 1917*, 224; see also 285).

[65] *Kaseno planiranje*; see Dobb, *Soviet Economic Development since 1917*, 385–402.

[66] Arsov, "Mobilizacija nove radne snage," 6.

[67] Ibid., 4.

ply, Kidrič left Belgrade for a progress of the mines in the interior (by coal-consuming train!), perhaps consciously imitating Stalin's "Urals-Siberian method,"[68] to see what his personal touch could do to get supplies moving. At the end of June, Tito moved his tough troubleshooter since 1942, Svetozar Vukmanović-Tempo, from the standing army he had helped build after the war to the federal Ministry of Mining and Power. Despite Vukmanović-Tempo's penchant for blunt, shocking rhetoric, his memoirs for these months are probably not hyperbole:

> We began with "robbing" the mines and forests: we dug up the richest veins of ore, cut down entire complexes of forest. . . . All those products that were in demand on foreign markets and for which we had secured foreign exchange in order to purchase raw and intermediate materials for the needs of industrial production and supplying the population. To do this, it was necessary to secure sufficient labor or mechanization. We did not have the foreign exchange for the second, which left us with the single option of mobilizing labor. We did not waver: all unemployed in the towns—those who had no proof that they were employed in some socially useful work—were mobilized and sent to work in the mines. Peasants also had to work in the mines and at construction sites when they were not occupied in agricultural labor. Labor offices were created in the communes[69] for mobilization. The mobilization was forced; those who fled from work were punished with prison sentences lasting up to two months. In this universal mobilization of people, the country increasingly took on the character of one great construction site. . . . But it was not that magnificent effort of the entire population that characterized the period directly after liberation, when the entire population voluntarily set to work so that the country would emerge as soon as possible from the ruins of the four-year-long war. . . . Instead, there were elements of coercion. Working in the mines were miners and "unemployed" citizens and in some places even prisoners who had been sentenced to hard labor because of criminal activity.[70]

This mobilization was in effect by July, when the first revision of the plan for labor increased the quota that people's committees had to supply from the villages *fourfold*. Kidrič's April optimism in urging full utilization of capacity was no longer justified by August, as the combined pressure on production and the shortage of replacement parts began to take their toll on plant and equipment and thus on output in mining, timber, and public agriculture.[71] Because the harvest looked promising and the

---

[68] See Nove, *An Economic History of the USSR*, 153.

[69] Vukmanović-Tempo uses the word *opština*, a prewar Serbian term for local governments, although they were not created as such in the socialist period until 1955.

[70] Vukmanović-Tempo, *Revolucija koja teče* 2:102–3.

[71] Ibid.; *Foreign Relations of the United States, 1948* 4:1107.

bread ration had been officially raised, the fact that food shortages continued "thoroughly alarmed the populace."[72] Amid severe shortages of meat
and fats in consumer markets, moreover, the government requisitioned
hogs for export in early September. At the September 20 meeting of the
Economic Council, as reports from the harvest and purchasing boards
flowed in, Kidrič finally conceded to those who saw the kulak as the
source of the problem. Unleashing a campaign of political slogans against
the rich kulak, village magnate, remnants of "clericalism," speculators,
"saboteurs," and agents of foreign espionage, the leaders no longer attempted to stop rumors that collectivization was imminent.[73] Although the
party policy since July to "limit capitalist elements in the village in their
exploitative activities" was noncommittal on methods, party zealots now
pressured peasants into labor cooperatives. By November, work was being
reorganized at state farms along brigade principles copied from both Soviet
and wartime experiences, including a new title of socialist competition—
"fighters for high yields," because productivity had been singularly disap-
pointing and threatened these farms' role in export production.[74]

The reaction is not surprising. Many middle peasants apparently slack-
ened their harvest efforts, calculating that they would soon lose their land
anyway, whereas richer peasants used their linked-trade coupons not for
industrial goods, but as currency to obtain the labor services of poor peasants. Mothers in cities who could not obtain coupons for guaranteed provisions because they were not employed turned to "speculation" (illegal
trade) in order to feed their children (for which, Tito lamented in January
1949, "we lock them up and send them to labor camps, and don't pay any
attention at all to what will become of their children").[75] Factory managers pressed by shortages and under obligation to provide guaranteed
provisions for their workers ignored the rules and bargained directly with
farmers and their cooperatives: rubber boots in exchange for poultry, textiles for lard and meat, pigs' hair and electric motors for fuel wood, shoes
for textiles. Barter between factories (even factories in different republics), between factories and district people's committees, between the directorates of industrial ministries, republican governments, trade-union
branches, and all the way up to the level of ministries created an entire
system of unregulated commerce in kind. A "commercial apparatus," in
Kidrič's oxymoron, was emerging independent of state control, and it
kept for domestic consumption goods already committed for export in

[72] Cable to Washington from U.S. Embassy in Belgrade, August 22, 1948, in *Foreign
Relations of the United States, 1948* 4:1106.

[73] Bakarić, "O radu narodnog fronta na selu." *Foreign Relations of the United States, 1948*
4:1054–1118.

[74] Petranović, Končar, and Radonjić, *Sednice*, 696 n. 50.

[75] Ibid., 261.

trade agreements. By October, trains were stopped for lack of fuel, and a shortage of tires and parts sidelined trucks and tractors.

Contrary to the shift in January to state (federal) control over trade and labor plans, the May politbureau meetings began a drive to prepare the party to be the primary instrument of direction, using an active, militant core of workers (like the proletarian brigades during the war) against officials, managers, professionals, and other staff in both public and private sectors in the "battle to complete the plan." Government officials, many of them holdovers from the prewar government, and factory managers, engineers, and other professionals in the economy whose interests conflicted with the leaders' policy or whose skills lay not with political campaigning but with technical calculations and managerialism could no longer be trusted. The party was to consolidate its power as a governing political party and occupy the offices of the state in the context of emergency mobilization—to increase capital construction for military self-reliance and to extract from domestic consumption all the supplies needed for foreign-trade contracts made without credit.

On May 9, Tito began preparations within the surviving central committee for a party congress, although the final decision was not taken until May 22 and the public announcement was delayed until Tito's official birthday on May 25.[76] This congress signaled the official end to the period of the popular-front coalition and its ambivalence about the full role of the Communist party, during which party members had been instructed to keep their membership secret, radical action was led more often by the youth wing (SKOJ), and activists, because they still represented the party-as-army—the military commisars of the wartime proletarian brigades and the commissariats of the local people's committees during reconstruction—were (by the end of 1946) being demobilized and replaced by civilians. But the rising popular discontent, the political delicacy of administering a fourfold increase in labor for the new policy of "defense with our own resources," and the coming purge of those who would side with Stalin made loyal party cadres essential again as operatives.

The political space between May 25 and July 21, when the fifth congress convened in Belgrade, was filled with a host of precongress rituals and party meetings to elect delegates. Organizationally, the congress made two major changes: granting full status as national committees to what had so far been only provincial party organizations in Bosnia-Herzegovina, Macedonia, and Montenegro; and initiating a membership drive designed to shift the party's social base to the new working class.[77]

[76] V. Dedijer, *Novi prilozi* 3:228.

[77] Ljujić, "Primanje u partiji i poboljšavanje socijalnog sastava." However, Ljujić reports, many party organizations in factories were not implementing the new party line, aimed at

In fact, the mass-enrollment campaign that followed was a roll call on national loyalty. The criterion for new and old members alike was their answer to a single question, asked of each, standing alone in front of the others and without discussion: were they for Stalin or Tito?[78] Those who sided with Stalin (known since then as the *ibeovci*, or Cominform sympathizers)—in some cases entire party committees, especially in Montenegro—were expelled, and many were arrested. But this purge, which lasted from August 1948 to the end of 1950, was also a civil war. Alongside the arrest of a secret Bolshevik party faction in the Belgrade Faculty of Economics in late 1948, the publicized border escapes of many army generals (not all successful), and the large proportion—which was not publicized—of soldiers and air force officers in the resulting political emigration (estimated at 3,500), the disproportionate purge of Serbs and Montenegrins over Croats and Slovenes, as well as the countless private scores that were settled in the upheaval, reflected the national and regional dimensions of a partisan struggle that was concentrated in the interior borderlands and the southwest.[79] The industrial working class still predominated in Croatia and Slovenia, where industry was more developed and war damage less severe—although it was soon to be joined by the new workers employed in Bosnia-Herzegovina as investment in heavy industry was concentrated there in 1948 and 1949 for reasons of strategic safety and the location of mineral resources.

Because the party's primary task was to implement the economic policy, however, its activity would mirror the economy's dualism (and the party's political strategy of 1940). In the public sector, it would appear as the organized vanguard of a unified industrial working class integrated into production units. In the private sector and in the government that joined the two sectors, it would be a parallel force, mobilizing solidarity and overseeing officials in the government and the mass political organizations such as the Popular Front.

As early as August, the ruling came that the minister of foreign affairs had to be a member of the party politbureau, and three senior party leaders were made vice-presidents in the government—Kardelj, Aleksandar Ranković, and Blagoje Nešković. Labor recruitment was a matter of the greatest political sensitivity, requiring experts in agitation and propaganda to persuade potential workers of the contribution they would be making to the country's development and independence; at the same time, it could not be permitted to harm economic growth by increasing

---

reducing the proportion of peasants and improving the party's social composition by enrolling more production workers.

[78] My informant is Borislav Škegro, whose father experienced this in Bosnia.

[79] Discussions of the *ibeovci*, including data on who they were, are in Banac, *With Stalin against Tito;* and Petranović, Končar, and Radonjić, *Sednice,* 231–348.

employment in administration rather than production, as some republics had already begun to do when Kidrič complained about it the previous April. In the villages, the political agents of labor recruitment were still Popular Front activists acting "voluntarily . . . as a great patriotic duty."[80] But alongside the labor offices set up in each district on September 1, advisory councils (*savjeti*) were created representing all of the mass organizations (the Popular Front, the unions, the Antifascist Women's Front, the youth organizations, and others). Although Kardelj's reform to improve the vertical links in government had legislated district branches of the party's control commission on September 25, the commissariats (abolished in the move to civilian control in 1947) were also resurrected on October 18 to give party members in the militia and security forces (which the proletarian brigades had become by then) supervisory roles in the execution of federal tasks. The heads of each commissariat were, however, to be responsible to the executive boards of the local governments where they sat ex officio; the board's president and secretary had final authority within their territory. Each ministerial branch in the republican governments also created a section of each people's committee—for agriculture, trade and supplies, communal affairs, industry and crafts, finance, labor, education and culture, public health, social welfare, local transport, and, where relevant, for tourism, construction, forestry, and fishing. Planning commissions were set up in the district people's committees with the authority to create branch directorates where more than one enterprise in a branch of production operated locally. The republican governments were instructed to set up commissions for immediate administrative reorganization of the local people's committees—proposals were to be finished by December 1, internal conflicts resolved by the fifteenth, reorganization completed by the thirtieth, and new sessions convened no later than March 1, 1949.[81]

The separation of the party from its wartime coalition also gave formal autonomy to its allied organizations. This autonomy was celebrated in countrywide congresses between October 1948—with congresses of the United Unions, SKOJ, the Antifascist Women's Front, the league of engineers and technicians, the Serbian and Slovene academies of science, the federal academic council, and the physicians' association, as well as a countrywide youth festival—and April 1949, when the last of the republican, regional, and urban party congresses opened the way for the third congress of the Popular Front and the election of assemblies that would authorize the tax, labor, and requisitioning policies of the drive for self-reliance.

[80] Kidrič, "Govor na pretresu opštedržavnog budžeta za 1948 godinu," 253.
[81] Opće uputstvo no. 79, *Službeni List*, no. 770 (October 18, 1948): 1399.

December 1948–August 1949: The Price
of Trade Reorientation

The commodity-trade account in the Yugoslav balance of payments for 1948 was more favorable than in any other year after World War II until the late 1980s. The import cuts and forced exports did not, however, forestall a balance-of-payments deficit that year after two years of surplus, and the threat of a foreign-exchange crisis loomed for early 1949. The Yugoslavs' success in trade negotiations with the West only meant greater obligations of export commodities and foreign-exchange earnings to pay the interest on trade credits that had been negotiated on "beggar's terms" (up to 11 percent interest and repayment of principal in no more than four to five years).[82] On December 1, the trade protocol with the USSR for 1949 trimmed off seven-eighths of the value of their previous agreement, and by January 10, Ambassador Cannon was crowing in a telegram to the U.S. secretary of state that the trade deficit would "inevitably force Yugoslavia [to] divert [a] major volume[of] trade to [the] West [,] thereby unexpectedly further[ing] [an] important ERP [European Recovery Program] aim."[83] Early in 1949, the Yugoslavs intensified efforts to find new markets in the European Economic Community and the United States for their minerals (especially copper and lead) and timber; agreed to the dinar-dollar exchange rate that they had refused in 1945, so as to obtain IMF credits; used intermediaries (especially one Austrian bank) to buy coking coal and machinery incognito in the East; and applied for commercial-bank credits in the United States. By May, the deficit was $50 million and reserves were at $34 million (of which $23 million had been set aside for essential imports—such as coking coal, oil, cotton, and machinery—and payment of the IMF quota).

Reviving a wartime practice (which would become a postwar institution— usually called a *sastanak kod druga Tita,* a "meeting at the behest of Comrade Tito"), Tito summoned a "kitchen cabinet"[84] of trustworthy colleagues on December 8, 1948, to agree on policy prior to his New Year's speech to the assembly and the second plenum of the party's central committee on January 28–30, 1949.[85] Politically, they would not accept that the actions of the USSR and the people's democracies would "not be tem-

---

[82] Vukmanović-Tempo, *Revolucija koja teče,* vol. 2.

[83] *Foreign Relations of the United States, 1949* 5:854–55.

[84] This was Tito's own label, according to Adamić, *The Eagle and the Roots.*

[85] V. Dedijer, *Novi prilozi* 3:238–41. The second plenum was the first elected party forum to discuss party policy since October 1940. It met only days after party leaders learned that they would not be invited to the founding meeting of the Council for Mutual Economic Assistance, the idea for which they claimed (in their note of protest) to have originated.

porary," and should be fought in an ideological battle, considered as "sabotage" to prevent Yugoslavia "from constructing socialism."[86] Economically,
this decision meant reorienting their trade to hard-currency markets in
the West, seeking its aid to replace Soviet aid, and accepting the economic and political consequences of this shift.

In the six months since the Cominform resolution, they had been able
to increase requisitioning quotas. But now the additional demand was so
great as to require increases in output—and this attention to production
meant attention to labor. The continuing difficulty in attracting engineers
and skilled labor to federal projects in heavy industry and defense could
also no longer be ignored. Both the instruments of a policy to deal with
these problems and the propaganda campaign (the "war of the radio
waves"[87] begun in early December) took the leaders' political radicalism a
step further and exacerbated the tensions between it and Kidrič's economic methods. The conflict between principle and reality also led to a
confusing combination of centralization and decentralization. The quarrels between federal and republican authorities over investment and finance (especially foreign) led the center to assert ever-greater control; but
the tasks of production in industry and agriculture led to a radical democratization in factory, farm, and local government and (in contrast to the
rational calculations integral to the leaders' policy on labor) to campaign
methods and extraordinary mobilizations, as in the fall. These quarrels
had their personal side as well; the palpable tensions within the leadership over immediate policy measures—between Kidrič and Tito, Kardelj
and Ranković, Salaj and Vukmanović-Tempo—reflected deep differences
in assumptions and approaches, as well as their recognition of the consequences for long-term strategy and institutions.[88]

The primary problem of enforcement of policy in this period, as Tito
told his colleagues December 8, now lay with the republics. The foreign-
exchange crisis required the center to give priority to imports for projects
"that contribute to capital production—heavy industry, mining, transport, the army." This would require "iron discipline" among republican
authorities over "who is permitted to import what," but it also meant that
the leadership would stop food imports and even increase exports of agricultural products and other primary commodities to pay for critical imports and to pay the interest on loans. Any investment that did not
develop fuels, transport, or capital goods had to be postponed, and the

[86] Ibid., 239.

[87] Bakarić, in a speech to the Croatian parliament in January 1949 ("Vezana trgovina
poljoprivrednih i industrijskih proizvoda i njeno ograničavanje porasta kapitalističkih elemenata na selu").

[88] See the discussion, especially on Kidrič's report on economic policy and Nešković's
report on supplies and food, at the second plenum of the CPY central committee (in Petranović, Končar, and Radonjić, *Sednice*, 132–77).

republics would have to accept responsibility for the production of "basic accumulation" (supplying the basic needs of the population). It was no longer a matter of finance but of shortages in real factors of production—which was a consequence, Tito argued, of the refusal of republican governments to plan and develop agriculture; to obey central regulations on wages and their implicit limits on employment; or to balance their government budgets or accounts in their cash plans. "The republics cannot behave in 1949 as they did earlier," Tito warned.[89]

The central committee plenum at the end of January revealed raging conflicts of interest, in fact, between center and republics, when Tito, Kidrič, and Kardelj confronted republican delegates with their obligation to implement central directives. Republics had followed their own interests, producing machines rather than articles of mass consumption and housing and totally neglecting agriculture in their investment plans for 1949. Where federal authorities had taken temporary control—for example, on the grain-growing farms of Vojvodina—the results contrasted sharply with the inattention of republican ministers of agriculture and party cadres alike, who did not consider agriculture an important branch of a socialist economy.[90] The district and republican governments had not implemented the regulations on compulsory deliveries, tending instead to favor the rich peasant, hide data about yields and reserves from the federal authorities, complain loudly about the inequitable division of planned quotas among republics, and waste valuable time bargaining with the planning commission over quotas for labor and farm purchases when they should have been on the ground collecting grain and other produce. Nor did they lift a finger to stop the underground trade among factories, ministries, and unions. Budget deficits in the republics that disturbed macroeconomic balances and led republics to go begging for federal assistance in 1947 and 1948 could be traced directly to "irrationalities in labor use" in their state administrations and "antiplan increases in monetary authorizations" by republican ministries and enterprises; overemployment and the high salaries paid to civil servants were particularly glaring in the deficits of Slovenia and Bosnia during 1948. The minister of heavy industry, Franc Leskošek, complained that although the decision to guarantee engineers to heavy industry had been taken December 8, nothing had yet been done.[91]

The leaders' solution was a fundamental shift in the federal contract.

[89] V. Dedijer, *Novi prilozi* 3:239.

[90] Petranović, Končar, and Radonjić, *Sednice*, 81–83; see also pp. 55, 72.

[91] Ibid., 165. Adamić also reports, from his visit in 1949, that there was a great shortage of engineers and technicians; moreover, the construction of the Litostroj machine and die works—Leskošek's "dream" as a metalworker before the war—and of the Strnišče aluminum factory (both federal projects in Slovenia) still suffered from shortages of labor, which were alleviated with workers from Italy (*The Eagle and the Roots*, 176–81).

They insisted on "greater organization and planning, particularly in relations between republican and federal ministries,"[92] imposed a ceiling on new investment by the republics of 5 percent over 1948 figures and obligatory self-financing of that investment from enterprise profits and savings within the republic, and required republics to produce more wage goods—agricultural products and workers' apartments especially—and to rationalize employment and the supply system so as to make more internal reserves available for federal enterprises. To reduce bureaucracy further and ensure loyal execution, the national committees (republican party leaderships) were charged with cleaning house, improving the quality of ministry staffs, and placing "reliable" people in the governmental apparatus (especially in trade and commerce). The shortages of necessities and the unauthorized monetary expansion finally, the leaders said, gave them no choice but to centralize control over supplies and ration goods temporarily.

For Kidrič, centralized control over distribution posed a serious problem because it threatened the fundamental instrument of economic incentives to producers and the inextricable relation between production and distribution (the "law of value"). Nearly bursting with impatient anger and frustration at the second plenum, Kidrič lectured those "economic workers and leaders" who continued to believe mistakenly that "so-called distributive plans are the alpha and omega of a planned economy, that they represent the ultimate in socialist planning technique"; the "idiocy" of their "sterile pragmatism" was the primary obstacle to any solution to their daily breakdowns in production. "Comrades who think that everything can be resolved with distributive plans forget that the source of national income, the source of social wealth, of its ample assortment, is production and not distribution. . . . In short, not even the best planner of distribution can distribute what is not produced, no matter how great the consumption demand." Those who believed in materials balances and the administrative allocation of supplies "forget the role of *money* in a planned economy of socialism," while those who believed that raising wages would increase production "forget the role of the fund of supplies." The operation of economic laws—the relation between demand and supply—was, he insisted, "even more important in the period of building socialism" than it had been before. The system of planned distribution prevented progress in the quality and assortment of goods and the normalization of daily economic life, which only the release of "socialist free trade" could bring. Only with economic incentives to increase the supply of necessities and with strict adherence to planned wages would economic

---

[92] Tito, at the kitchen-cabinet meeting of December 8, 1948, in V. Dedijer, *Novi prilozi* 3:240.

laws function properly and "the direct influence of consumption, i.e., the *market*, on direct production" restore balance to the economy.[93]

The purpose of supply centralization (and the division of the Ministry of Trade and Provisions into two) was largely political: to "simplify" the system of guaranteed provisions and purge the "old merchants" who still managed nationalized firms in the state trade network and whose "business criteria" were feeding inflation. Now consumer goods in shortage would be provided only to those who contributed directly to "expanded reproduction" (capital investments) and "who realize the five-year plan" (essentially, workers in public-sector industry and agriculture). People with access to food at home would no longer receive any state provisions; what they could not provide for themselves they could buy through linked trade by selling their farm surplus to the state (and direct contracting between state firms and cooperatives would increase peasants' production of fat and meats). Better yet, they could join the general farmers' cooperatives; these had access to industrial goods through direct contracts with public-sector firms, and the leaders now encouraged them to invest their trade profits in small manufacturing and craft activities of the cooperative. Those who were unable to support themselves through agriculture, such as the rural poor rewarded for their Partisan service with barely cultivable parcels of land, should move permanently into industry or mining, where they would again be eligible for guaranteed provisions. The squeeze on the private sector and the increase of 30 percent in guaranteed provisions to those employed in state and cooperative production would act as economic incentives to join that public sector and increase its labor productivity. People would no longer "get things for free, as they did in 1945 and 1946," Tito almost barked at delegates to the second party plenum in January 1949. All commercial food establishments such as greengrocers, inns, and restaurants that were not absolutely essential had to be closed. In those few places where new inns were necessary (as for tourism), governments should supervise but management must be private.[94]

For Kardelj and Ranković, however, the moment required shifting far greater authority to the party. As Miha Marinko said at the second plenum in the discussion on Kidrič's report on the economy, "we need to have people whom one can discipline."[95] Although not all central committee members agreed with him, Kardelj insisted that the only solution to the lack of discipline over wages and labor was "to lead through the

[93] Petranović, Končar, and Radonjić, *Sednice*, 102–4.

[94] Tito, at the second plenum of the CPY central committee, ibid., 71; see also 58–59 and Nešković's report on provisions and distribution, 113–31.

[95] Ibid., 151.

Party."[96] To implement Tito's belief that "the faster our Party becomes capable, strong, and organized, the sooner problems and tasks presented to it will be executed rapidly and well, and the closer socialism will be,"[97] Ranković proposed a long list of reforms, including the system of *nomen-klatura* for nine thousand positions, obligatory party membership for the heads of the radio and press, and, taking even Tito by surprise, the recommendation that they create a new governmental level between the republic and the district—a region (*oblast*) along the lines of the wartime *okrug*—to improve economic coordination.[98] At the same time, the party's organizational improvements would be ineffectual without improved social standing in the community. Citing the miseries party cadres suffered in comparison with the status and privileges of government officials, Djuro Pucar urged better pay and apartments. Tito's vision of authority was less mundane, as he described the majesty of the new central committee building under construction in Belgrade.[99]

In the conception of the core leadership, the party was not a debating or authoritative forum, but a body of hands-on, loyal activists whose task was to work at the local level to coordinate the economy, supervise government execution, devote substantial effort to agitation and propaganda, manage the human and political side of the subtleties in their agricultural policy and the growing austerities, and provide the information that was not reaching the leadership about why policies were not being implemented correctly. Tito told the delegates in preface to Kardelj's plenary report on policy toward the village:

> I think, comrades, that you need not consider that you have come to give some theoretically formed definitions. What we need is for you to bring forth facts, to give us examples, concrete things. We know that some things will be

[96] Ibid., 169.

[97] Ibid., 251.

[98] Ibid., 202–6. On similar regionalization in the USSR between 1923 and 1926, see Carr, *Socialism in One Country, 1924–1926* 2:273–303. According to M. Kovačević, this further "territorialization" of the labor office and labor inspection was Kardelj's idea and was undertaken because republican ministries, especially in Croatia and Serbia, were not supervising sufficiently; to reduce apparatus and improve the planning and training of labor, *oblast* offices of ten to fifteen civil servants would link ministries and people's committees ("Pripreme za organizaciju oblasnih povereništava rada u NR Srbiji"). Labor inspectors, on the other hand, in groups of three to eleven, were elected by workers in the popular front and union, and their work was "voluntary, honorific, and free" (*Bulletin du Conseil Central de la Confédération des Syndicats de Yougoslavie* 4, nos. 6–7 [1949]: 14).

[99] Petranović, Končar, and Radonjić, *Sednice*, 252–53, 251. Djilas became known later for criticizing both the "grandiose plans" for palaces, opera houses, and state buildings and, especially, the privileges that the party elite were granting themselves in 1945–48. The critical analysis that established his global reputation was *The New Class (1957)*; a description of the grandiosity is in his later *Rise and Fall*, 62–69.

repeated, but there are so many varied ordinary things that are not known to us, and I would give I don't know what for us to know them. There, that's what is necessary here, at this plenum. No great speechifying is required, but facts that life brings forth daily.[100]

Ranković complained that party cadres spent all their time building up party committees instead of attending to economic matters as they should, and problems arose when party instructors and cadres traveled around the country. Party cadres had to be "settled" with a particular territory. With proprietary instincts like those they hoped to nurture among permanent employees in social-sector firms and farms, party officials in the localities would govern as *gazde*,[101] who knew their territory like the back of their hand and who responded to problems personally as they arose.[102] This policy made it essential that every village have a party organization—in Slovenia alone, one-third of all villages were outside the party network.

Alongside this decentralization of power in the party's operations, there was a democratizing impulse in its resort to the aid and solidarity of the population, as in analogous circumstances in 1938–40 and 1942–44. At the December 8 meeting, Tito reemphasized the critical importance of nurturing the "creative initiative" and "socializing potential" of mass participation and specified three political forms—public opinion, economic democratization, and the rule of law. Most important, local party committees should improve their information about and supervision over local conditions by developing criticism through the press, consulting people "from below" (ordinary people, not local influentials or party organizations) to ensure timely discovery of problems, listening to the "voice of the people," and subjecting the local executive of the people's committees to election by local assemblies. The formalization of this idea of consulting popular opinion in the next reform of local government was, Kardelj told the national assembly in June 1949, the "expression of deep democratic desires of the popular masses for self-management, for direct participation in the administration of the state."[103] The motivation for this earlier

[100] Petranović, Končar, and Radonjić, *Sednice*, 240.

[101] Originally meaning "landlord" or "head of household," the word carried the connotation of "boss."

[102] *Na licu mesta,* or "on the spot" (Petranović, Končar, and Radonjić, *Sednice*, 203). At the same time, the practice was introduced of delegating party members from the central committee for longer periods to important places of communication, industry, mining, and so forth, in order to assist the local party organization *na licu mesta* and to inform the central committee regularly about the actual state of implementation.

[103] Radonjić, *Sukob KPJ s Kominformom i društveni razvoj Jugoslavije, 1948–1950,* chap. 3, pt. 2. In his exposition of the new "state order" for the 1949 *Informativni Priručnik Jugoslavije,* Jovan Djordjević, a legal scholar and primary adviser to Kardelj, identified the

version of *glasnost* was the problem of ever-fewer goods in the markets, further "differentiation" between beneficiaries of government supplies and those left to fend for themselves, and the war against inflationary pressures and its natural scavengers, the "speculators" in goods markets. Under the circumstances, it was necessary to give people nonmonetary instruments for communicating their demands and to devise nondisruptive barometers of discontent.

In addition, working people would be mobilized in democratic forums to assert "control from below" against the wealthy and powerful of the previous order who might obstruct their path toward socialism. Management boards in the farmers' cooperatives and people's committees would continue to handle daily and technical matters, but their decisions would be subject to approval by elected assemblies. The general law on people's committees of June 6, 1949, added neighborhood voters' meetings and elected assemblies alongside the reformed executive branches, and the revised basic law on cooperatives of June 9 required the full membership of the general farmers' cooperatives to meet in assembly annually (in some republics, such as Croatia, twice yearly) to discuss and approve the distribution of total income for the year and the rule book that defined operations between sessions. An additional advantage of these vehicles of local democracy was, of course, their relatively low expenditure of economic resources. Salaries did not have to be paid or offices funded to mobilize the public's participation in the rituals of state power or to gain its help in keeping local politicians accountable in the use of public funds. This was also true of the rule of law that Tito ordered to increase the economic authority of the federal government.

The issue that focused attention on law was the shortage and uneven distribution of professionals, such as doctors, engineers, and veterinarians. Some leaders, like the Bosnian Pucar, thought that in the case of medical doctors they should solve the problem by conscription and forced relocation to communities in need. Tito's response at the second plenum was that coercion "will poison the people." When Pucar countered that "our people were completely satisfied with German doctors [who were] prisoners of war," Tito defined a more general political principle for the new state: "Nonetheless, we can't just gather them up as you suggest; one must pass a law."[104] Respect for the rule of law was essential to state authority, from those at the top all the way to the lowest rungs of the hierarchy, but peasant culture in Yugoslavia also demanded it. "We can't play around with the people's trust, because if we need anything—we

---

"essential character" of "local organs" as their capacity to be "self-managing" (*samouprav-nost*), adding that the scope of local self-management was, according to Lenin, the primary difference between socialist and bourgeois ("fictive") self-governance (144–45).

[104] Petranović, Končar, and Radonjić, *Sednice*, 253.

need that trust."[105] For example, party cadres who had filled their planned quotas of agricultural deliveries for 1948 but had broken the government's regulations of that June to do so were playing a dangerous game: "I think there is not a single people in Europe with such an attitude toward legal measures. They respect them and act in accordance with them. But when those laws are transgressed and when they are unjust, then [that people] cannot be reconciled. Then things cross over into jokes, jesting, and stories, and who knows where it can lead in the end?"[106]

The burning question for leaders was labor for federal projects. This was no longer only a matter of daily shortages, Kidrič told one audience after another, but of a change in the social structure itself. The faster tempo of socialist transformation is the policy most often associated with this period, but it is usually taken to mean the decision to collectivize agriculture for the purpose of proving loyalty to the international workers' movement and to Stalin. Policy toward the village was indeed the focus of the second plenum of the central committee, but the goal was to prevent the political errors of a "too-rapid, coercive" approach to socialization of the village that would result from a "mechanical, mistaken adoption of the Soviet line in collectivization."[107] As Tito told the delegates, "we can't go that route and we have no need to take that road."[108] At the end of December, Vladimir Bakarić (increasingly the party spokesman for agriculture, after Kardelj) also told a meeting of Croat popular-front activists of the problem with party members who tried to show their loyalty to *Tito* with "loud declarations" that "socialism had already arrived in the village." "The struggle against kulak pressure and influence in the village is, it is true, a component part of our policy of alliance of worker and peasant in this period," Bakarić said, "but it isn't its entire content, nor even its most significant part."[109]

That most significant part was to increase production, and this was a matter of production incentives and farming skills. Tito told the plenum delegates:

[105] Tito (ibid., 137).

[106] Tito (ibid).

[107] Mijalko Todorović (ibid., 84; see also 85).

[108] Ibid., 85. Tito was particularly concerned in this case about livestock for export and for urban consumption, producing data on the loss of cattle during the period of collectivization in the USSR and mentioning the differences "both politically and economically" between the Soviet and the Yugoslav situations. "We can avoid such losses by following the correct line of the central committee on the village," he added. "It's not a question," he had said moments earlier, "of our dreaming up something because we want to differentiate ourselves from the Soviet path; rather, we are solving that question in a manner that is best for us, taking into account particularly the current situation in our country" (75–76).

[109] "O radu narodnog fronta na selu," 90–91.

It wouldn't be difficult to say that this year we're going to liquidate capitalism in the village, but we would also liquidate the grain supply for next year—and not only the grain fund, but a wide range of other agricultural products. . . . We must find a more correct path for our work in the countryside so as not to cut off the branch we're sitting on, which means that the development of socialism in the countryside must proceed parallel with the possibilities of creating funds of foodstuffs for the population. Were it possible . . . to create reserves—that is, pay for food abroad so that we could make up for what the kulak would not give—then our situation would be different.[110]

Although the politbureau itself was not of one mind on agricultural policy, causing "frequent discussion" late into 1949,[111] the line Kardelj presented at the plenum was "Lenin's cooperative policy of 1921 . . . as has been our policy all along."[112] There were many routes to incorporating the kulak and middle peasant in the social sector, and the party would continue to encourage a variety of "transitional" forms of cooperation to attract them—especially the village-based general farmers' cooperatives, which would expand only gradually by investing their own trade profits into craft and industrial production. Membership in any type of cooperative would develop a cooperative consciousness and prepare peasants for higher stages of socialization later. It was just as important for the long run to win their political allegiance and overcome their reluctance to market their produce under uncertainty, reluctance they had amply demonstrated with cutbacks during 1948. A greater problem, according to Bakarić, were the "left-wing ideologues" in the party who refused to admit kulaks into labor cooperatives. This difficulty was compounded by the ministers of agriculture in Croatia and Serbia, who let applications to form labor cooperatives pile up on their desks and refused to provide funds that might make pay in the peasant labor cooperatives attractive to middle and rich farmers, and by the many party members (as village leaders, often rich peasants themselves) who refused to join. The consequence was that production cooperatives were dominated, as were the state farms, by people who had had little or no land before the war and therefore possessed few of the organizational and farming skills necessary to large-scale production. Those kulaks who wished to be a part of the new order must be allowed to join and, it they wished, to bring only part of their landholdings and stock with them, keeping the rest as private holdings. Although they would have "one foot in the capitalist sector," they would also have "one foot in the socialist sector," Kardelj said often. If the kulak joined,

---

[110] Petranović, Končar, and Radonjić, *Sednice*, 69.

[111] Kardelj, at the third plenum of the CPY central committee, in Petranović, Končar, and Radonjić, *Sednice*, 451.

[112] Ibid., 26.

then the wary middle peasant would, too.[113] The fact that there were more agronomists with secondary education employed in the federal ministry for light industry than in the federal agricultural ministry and all its institutes was only a ludicrous extension of the same disregard for agriculture and thus the skills needed to improve its productivity.[114]

In the first months of 1949, the leadership ordered the withdrawal into the interior of all defense-related industries (mills, warehouses, oil refineries) that were located in vulnerable northern borderlands such as Vojvodina and Medjumurje, including the removal of steel production from Slovenia to Bosnia. In this "strategically defined" sanctuary in the central mountains (above all in Bosnia), new steel mills and munitions plants were built and supply bunkers hidden. These areas, rich in ores and timber, were already the site of a large proportion of federal projects, and this shift led to the relocation of more than 100,000 workers.[115] The costs of transportation alone were huge. Operative labor plans for the first six months of 1949 called for more than 2.3 million new workers countrywide when employment stood at 1,126,891 in November 1948.[116] Although recruitment reached only 61.9 percent of this target, this was more than three times as many new workers as in the comparable period of 1948 (when the target of 750,000 was realized 60 percent).[117] Labor turnover severely harmed both the quantity and quality of production; the figures for 1949 argue that for every 100 workers employed in permanent positions, 587 workers had to be recruited and, on average, another 300 members of special Popular Front brigades and 70 members of the League of People's Youth (the party-linked organization for youth).[118] Factory managers seemed to think they had a "divine right to replace the plan with the competitive struggle for labor" and to bid for workers with ever-higher wages.[119] The new minister of finance, Dobrivoje Radosavljević, was particularly rankled by those who continued the traditional "thirteenth pay" (end-of-year holiday bonus) and by state officials who

[113] Ibid., 31. See Verdery, *Transylvanian Villagers*, 38–39, on the same approach in Romania in 1958–59.

[114] As Mijalko Todorović complained (Petranović, Končar, and Radonjić, *Sednice*, 82).

[115] Spasenija Babović, in discussion at the third plenum of the CPY central committee, ibid., 437.

[116] Tito's speech to the parliament on December 27, 1948 ("The Real Reasons behind the Slander of the Cominform Countries toward Yugoslavia"). The November 1948 employment figure was only 100,000 more than that for December 1947. Tito also said in his speech that 60,000 new workers would be needed for federal projects in 1949, and a total for the year of 100,000.

[117] Has, "Društveno-ekonomski osvrt na problem zaposlenosti," 142.

[118] Vujošević, "O nekim problemima radna snage."

[119] Kidrič, report to the second plenum of the CPY central committee, in Petranović, Končar, and Radonjić, *Sednice*, 103.

conceded to staff pay raises.[120] The severe shortage of manufactured goods led to a veritable nomadism[121] as workers went unpredictably from one factory to the next or between factory and farmstead in search of higher wages, food and clothing, and stores with goods on the shelves. Despite its public reservations, the leadership also continued to supplement the core of permanent industrial labor with volunteer brigades from the villages. Local people's committees, with the aid of Popular Front brigades, were able to mobilize more than a million people in response to the higher quotas, two-thirds of whom worked an entire month; a large number were called up many times and without warning, against all the written regulations.[122] Party organizations were required to form special "Communist brigades" to do two months' service in the mines and in construction. The many more ordered into the army, after conscription was renewed in 1949, found themselves doing much of the same—"voluntary" labor in the mines, at construction sites, in the forests, and in grain fields.[123]

Local party organizers found the assemblies and voters' meetings in villages a useful vehicle for mobilization. Although echoing Stalin's Urals-Siberian method, these assemblies were used not to arouse class tensions for dekulakization but to mobilize temporary labor power, and party cadres reported success not with slogans of class struggle but with appeals to patriotic conscience and village unity. For example, a report from Zenica, Bosnia-Herzegovina, is filled with surprised delight at the ease with which they turned the tide against recalcitrant villagers when they read President Tito's 1949 New Year's speech on the "real reasons" for the activities of the USSR and the people's democracies (they wished to sabotage Yugoslavia's revolution and industrialization).[124] Another report from a local party organization recommended that others try a tactic it had learned when it accepted villagers' desire to go altogether to worksites rather than individually: forming a brigade along village lines made everything go smoothly.[125] Many district committees, however, took easier

---

[120] At the second plenum of the CPY central committee, ibid., 156.

[121] Kidrič's quaint phrase was *seljakanje s posla* (ibid., 285).

[122] Has, "Društveno-ekonomski osvrt," 142.

[123] For example, the party organization in Tuzla oblast mobilized 5,250 new workers, of which 1,354 were Communists, for three mines in October 1949 (Spasojević, "Kako je partiska organizacija Tuzlanske oblasti izvršila zadatak uključenja radne snage u rudarstvu"). In the four republics of Serbia, Croatia, Slovenia, and Bosnia-Herzegovina, 12,897 party members served in Communist brigades in 1949–50; many others refused to go, particularly when the brigades were revived in 1951 (Djokanović, "Članovi partije i uključenje u radne brigade").

[124] For the speech, see Tito, "The Real Reasons behind the Slander of the Cominform Countries toward Yugoslavia."

[125] Mustabegović, Jankelović, and Bajramović, "Uključenje radne snage u privredi u zeničkom srezu."

routes to filling their labor quotas, mobilizing anyone they could find, sometimes crudely and with force. The peasant labor cooperatives, with their concentrations of labor and ideological commitment, were particularly vulnerable targets of searches for "voluntary" labor in construction and the forests; the result was great harm to local agricultural production.[126]

The real innovations in this period were a response to the consequences that high labor turnover, "anarchic" increases in wages and bonuses, and political labor-recruitment campaigns had for internal stabilization. Kardelj began to assert ever more frequently, for example, that the essence of socialism was that individuals should be paid according to their labor, not their market price, and should be defined by the social relationship surrounding remunerated labor (radni odnos). If wages directly linked workers' effort and reward, output and purchasing power, then productivity would rise because workers would be able to see the link between their labor and standard of living immediately; the aggregate effect would be to balance monetary funds outstanding and consumable goods. The public sector, where such relations prevailed, had to be consolidated further; and factories had to become ever more self-sufficient, building housing for their workers, covering 45 percent of their own consumption, and growing more vegetables on their own farms. The peasant labor cooperative would become a "socialist work community" of permanent members who "feel it as their own socialist holding."[127] Greater regularity in wages and production would be sought through the introduction of individual employment contracts. On April 27, 1949, a ruling (rešenje) offered special benefits to agricultural workers who were willing to sign contracts obliging them to remain at the same job for at least one year. Higher benefits went to those willing to include their family. Workers' employment cards were also revised, and there was a campaign to get industrial workers to sign similar employment contracts tying them to a factory or a mine.

These measures were only a prelude to the more-radical changes in workplace organization and to the campaign against officials and managers that took place in April 1949. For leaders such as Vukmanović-Tempo, now chief at Mining, the shortages of skilled labor and low productivity provided ample reason to attack the "prewar experts" in the ministries who interfered with "workers' initiatives" in the factories; those on district party committees who robbed factories of their best foremen to do administration and threatened disciplinary action against directors who pro-

---

[126] Kidrič, "Tekući zadaci u borbi za izvršenje Petogodišnjeg plana," speech at the third plenum of the CPY central committee, in Petranović, Končar, and Radonjić, Sednice, 384–89.

[127] Kardelj, speech on agricultural policy at the second plenum of the CPY central committee, ibid., 32.

tested; and party members who refused to do heavy labor. Ridiculing the claims to expertise made by bureaucrats glued to their desks, Vukmanović-Tempo extolled the "devotion" and "ambition" of production workers who, like "the field soldier," go into the trenches and "fight." The path to increased productivity without wage inflation was a democratic reconstruction of factory life. Directors would share managerial authority with the party and union secretaries (the "Soviet troika") to eliminate the waste of parallel command hierarchies and to check willful factory managers. Labor inspectors would again be elected, this time jointly by the union and the Popular Front. Productivity conferences and workers' advisory commissions would be revived to identify loyal workers who would help find "internal reserves," improve productivity, and make the daily adjustments to supply bottlenecks so that they would save on engineers, who were in short supply, and keep workers in production.[128]

The centerpiece of this democratizing process was the reorganization of production on the shop floor and in the mines according to a system of autonomous production brigades. According to Vukmanović-Tempo, the problem with the current system was that skilled workers were demoralized because no matter how great their own effort to surpass the norms and thus bring greater reward to their brigade, their individual pay was the same as that of everyone else. Pay depended on actual output, and when output fell through no fault of their own—such as because of production bottlenecks that had led to delays by a previous shift of workers—they were effectively penalized for the work performance of others. Workers thought factory administrators (especially foremen who recorded results that determined actual pay) should accept responsibility and not take away from workers' incomes. They also blamed foremen for the delays caused when workers chose to stay away without notice for days.

The reform of production brigades into permanent, collective units of eight to twenty workers, led by a skilled worker but using group discipline and group evaluation of worker performance, took place in April. Basing the reform on the system in agriculture, the leadership aimed to reduce turnover of skilled workers without raising wage rates, by giving skilled workers control over production and payment decisions; and to attack the shortages of trained staff by making them superfluous in organizing work, discipline, and pay. After conferences to discuss labor organization collectively, the skilled worker (the *brigadir*, or brigade leader) would assign tasks, assist less skilled workers when necessary, and move among brigades to make sure that machines were operating at full capacity. Brigades could set up assembly lines to speed production so that each

---

[128] Discussion at the second plenum of the CPY central committee, especially by Vukmanović-Tempo and Kardelj, ibid., 159–73.

brigade pushed the next, and workers were encouraged to devise new tools that would do the work of several operations and to suggest organizational changes so that machines were not left idle. As the work of the brigade unit still determined output, the moral pressure of the brigade's "honor" and the disciplinary pressure of the group would act as powerful weapons to increase labor discipline and reduce the turnover that frequently halted production—in contrast to the previous method, by which the party organization would respond to a day's low output with a campaign for maximum effort the following day. Workers who wished to be absent would have to get prior approval from their fellow workers, so that their tasks could be reassigned in advance. The brigade leader and workers were free to redefine norms and fire slower workers. Foremen, now superfluous to the organization of production, could return to the line, which meant additional savings on administrative costs and fewer quarrels with local party committees. Party cadres would also be moved from staff positions to production brigades, where their political work with those who were not party members would be easier; and "Communist" brigade leaders would feel additional pressure to increase output through competitions held at party meetings where the results of fellow members were compared. The brigades would also serve as a system of on-the-job training to improve workers' technical skills and, through the communication of political information at brigade meetings, their ideological education as well.[129]

Enthusiastic reports from the field flooded party journals and newspapers in the middle of 1949. But the report from the coal mine of Breza, in Bosnia—where the new system began with one exemplary skilled worker, Alija Sirotanović, apparently playing the role of a Yugoslav Stakhanov—was less reassuring.[130] There the technical staff were opposed to the brigades, permitting only 10 percent of all workers to try out the new system; and the factory administration, party, and union organizations all continued to interfere with its extension even when its results argued otherwise. Other reports provide ample evidence of why staff might have been less than enthusiastic about the suggestions for improved organization that workers made at weekly brigade conferences and about workers' many criticisms of party and union organizations and technical staff for not implementing regulations.[131] Moreover, the bri-

---

[129] According to a union newspaper, the system "made a big difference in surpassing the plan in metallurgy" (at steel mills in Zenica, Smederevo, and Jesenice and at the Djuro Djaković factory, for example) and in raising productivity (*Bulletin du Conseil Central de la Confédération des Syndicats de Yougoslavie* 4, nos. 3–4 [1949]).

[130] Hadžić, "Zašto se i dalje razvija borba za visoku produktivnost rada u rudniku Brezi."

[131] For examples citing evidence of party resistance to the production brigades, see Hadžić, "Zašto se i dalje razvija borba"; and Trninić, "Kako je partiska organizacija u rud-

gades at coal mines contradicted the official policy of settling the workforce, for they migrated from one mine to another in highly publicized
productivity campaigns.

August 1949–June 1952: Economic Coercion and the Rise of Unemployment

The germ of reversal from the unusual twelve months of September 1948
to August 1949 was planted on February 17, 1949 (not at the party congress of 1952), with a shift in U.S. policy to "keep Tito afloat";[132] by August it had sprouted. The life raft was at first only a temporary relaxation
of export-licensing controls on most Cocom categories and permission to
apply for International Bank for Reconstruction and Development (IBRD)
loans, in exchange—at the insistence of the U.S. secretary of defense and
the Pentagon—for concessions that included no more aid for the Greek
guerrillas. But it did open the way to a longer-term trade and payments
agreement with Britain, full membership in the IMF, a European Cooperation Administration[133] agreement on February 22 to buy Yugoslav
copper and lead, and a trade agreement on March 22 with the Joint
Export-Import Agency of the Allied occupation in West Germany. In
July, the Yugoslav government closed its border with Greece. By August
1949, the trade blockade from the East had begun to take effect; domestic
riots and hints of a political underground suggested the extent of hardship
at home, arrests of White Guards in Slovenia brought an official Soviet
protest, and the Yugoslav ambassador to Washington, Sava Kosanović,
pled with Secretary of State Dean Acheson on August 16 and 22 to speed
action on Yugoslavia's loan requests to the IMF, IBRD, and U.S. Export-
Import Bank (including Tito's poignant request for toilet articles along
with mining and agricultural machinery). Also in August, the first World
Bank mission arrived, Yugoslavia joined the Coal Committee of the Economic Committee for Europe to replace Polish and Czech coking coal,

---

nicima 'Tito' učestvovala u organizaciji rada po novom metodu." The brigade system was
reintroduced in the Soviet Union in the late 1970s, but the production brigades did not
evolve into workers' self-management, as they did in Yugoslavia. According to Slider ("The
Brigade System in Soviet Industry") this was because factory and union officials effectively
opposed it. Andrea Rutherford proposes instead, in her 1988 thesis on the brigades (Yale
University), that the brigades were not as successful as they were said to be, especially in
resolving the supply situation. On a similar system introduced in Hungarian factories in the
mid-1980s, the ECWAs, see Stark, "Coexisting Organizational Forms in Hungary's Emerging Mixed Economy."

[132] The National Security Council directive was NSC 18/2. See Mugoša, "Odnosi Jugoslavije i SAD-a."

[133] On the ECA, see Hogan, *The Marshall Plan*, 102–4.

and the Ex-Im Bank credit of $20 million, which the Yugoslavs had sought doggedly for four years, was finally approved on the twenty-fifth.[134] U.S. policy now having been established, the Policy Planning Staff of the U.S. State Department confirmed these credits with a final change in policy on September 10 to "all-out support" in defense of Tito's leadership; and on November 17, the National Security Council pledged to assist Yugoslavia's defense against possible military attack.[135]

By the end of 1950, two-thirds of the Yugoslav current-account deficit was covered by U.S. loans (largely for American machinery), but the price of the long-sought foreign assistance to finance imports and the growing trade deficit would be high.[136] Two IMF drawings, $3 million approved on September 22 and $6 million on October 14, had to be repaid within two years; British loans in September were good for only ninety days, and on the condition that British-Yugoslav commodity-trade agreements balance first; the World Bank loan for $25 million was finally given on October 25, but on the condition that the new state first repay prewar debts to Britain, France, Belgium, and Italy; and immense U.S. pressure on Belgium to allow Yugoslavia to postpone repayment of its $6 million trade credit due in 1950 only persuaded Belgium to accept payment in kind rather than in hard currency. The Eastern bloc now canceled all treaties of friendship and mutual security; the Soviet leadership orchestrated both a campaign against Tito on the slogan that he had "sold Yugoslavia to Wall Street" and trials against "Titoists," beginning with that of László Rajk in September; and a second Cominform resolution on November 29, 1949, finalized the break.

By the end of August, foreign diplomats' field reports concurred with assessments at the highest levels in the Yugoslav party: the period between September 1949 and June 1950 would be unusually difficult. Stocks of fertilizer and agricultural machinery were exhausted and could not be replaced for at least one year and likely three; by early fall, grain reserves were dangerously low, and some republics had not bothered to store grain at all.[137] Kidrič calculated that rationing would have to con-

[134] Kosanović asked the United States to delay announcement of the credits until September 8 so as not to interfere with Yugoslavia's plan to seek further recognition with a seat on the UN Security Council, beginning with Kardelj's speech to the General Assembly on September 6 in which he denounced the USSR. The Yugoslavs, actively supported by the United States, were successful in their bid for the seat on October 20, 1949.

[135] NSC 18/4. "U.S. Policy toward the Conflict between the USSR and Yugoslavia," in *Foreign Relations of the United States, 1949* 5:978.

[136] *Foreign Relations of the United States, 1949* 5:926, 941–44, 959–78; and Duisin, "The Impact of United States Assistance on Yugoslav Policy, 1949–1959." See also Tomasevich, "Yugoslavia during the Second World War," 112.

[137] Kidrič, at the third plenum of the CPY central committee, in Petranović, Končar, and Radonjić, *Sednice*, 390–91.

tinue for another two years before free markets could resume. Budget outlays for national defense alone took 22 percent of the national income in 1949. Foreign-exchange earnings from exports were 36.3 percent lower than in 1948 (down from $302.2 million to $192.3 million), and imports had been cut by 8 percent, almost entirely from consumer goods.[138] Nonetheless, Kardelj told the third plenum of the central committee (meeting on December 29–30, 1949) that "the most important battle of socialism now"—national independence—had been won with the change in Western policy, for Yugoslavia was now considered worthy of material support and military defense as an alternative model of socialist democracy to Soviet "state capitalism" and "bureaucratic deformation."[139]

International recognition and a new foreign policy both allowed and required, in the views of Kardelj and Kidrič, a return to the Slovene model for the economy and government and to the political alliance with middle peasants and urban professionals—whose support, Tito complained, they had worked so hard to capture with policies of differentiation and which the "administrative methods" of a state census and political recruitment of labor had nearly cost them. The immediate economic tasks were to face the even greater demands of defense and the external-trade account, and thus further cuts in domestic consumption, that these new conditions required and to restore macroeconomic stability through massive cuts in employment, above all by returning people to the countryside. This policy shift would come to be identified in most socialist countries as an economic and political "reform program"; the Yugoslav leadership in December called it a "new strategic and tactical order," but its primary objective was to return to monetary incentives—what Kidrič now called "economic coercion"—to cut monetary demand further while increasing output.

Kardelj elaborated the "new" principles of foreign policy in December. The leaders would create "as wide a democratic front as possible"—a global version of their popular-front strategy during the war—to exploit conflicts within the camps of their enemies by appealing to the masses abroad; it would also be the ideological basis for nonalignment six years later. This strategy required unity on all foreign policy, which therefore had to be subject to party control, and a strong military deterrent.[140] They had to proceed *as if* there would be war tomorrow. All investment

[138] Tomasevich, "Yugoslavia during the Second World War."

[139] Petranović, Končar, and Radonjić, *Sednice*, 474.

[140] Kardelj, in his report on "Foreign-policy questions," at the third plenum of the CPY central committee, ibid., 480–81. As Kardelj put it, "All our internal political measures must today more than ever before be coordinated with our struggle for the masses in the world, with our foreign policy" (480). This course included giving the army separate representation in the central committee of the party.

not related to defense would be cut and the plan goals for the next two years revised downward (to the "key investment projects").[141] Exports would be expanded and imports cut a further 20 percent during 1950. Military conscription was renewed in October. Defense industries would continue to have priority in supply allocations (including one-third of permitted imports), and civilian construction firms would be obliged to undertake capital construction projects for the army. But because the reform also called for stabilization to reduce the trade deficit and repay loans—which meant cutting domestic consumption, especially federal expenditures—this continuing priority of defense-oriented production placed contradictory demands on federal policy. To continue these federal obligations, the leadership would slim down the federal administration and transfer back to the republics jurisdiction over their budgets and enterprises—or, as was said at the time, restore the republics' "sovereignty."[142]

The return to the pre-1948 federal contract was explained the same way as its suspension the previous December. At the third plenum in December 1949, Tito exploded in exasperated fury at republics that remained, despite the clarity of the January 1949 policy, "closed within their cocoons . . . of narrow-mindedness," objecting to every federal regulation, causing costly delays in execution of policy, and refusing to provide supplies to federal enterprises in their territory or to other republics at the same time that they demanded supplements from federal stocks for guaranteed provisions and failed to fulfill procurement quotas and labor plans.[143] Kidrič chose sarcasm: "Two times two is four, comrades, not six."[144] The tasks of production called for renewed attention to district-level party committees and planning commissions, but Ranković's regionalization plan was a failure, Kardelj argued at a conference in October 1949 called to discuss difficulties with republican party and ministerial cadres.[145] Instead of moving skilled cadres from republican capitals into the field to improve implementation, the plan had taken staff from localities, which they could not easily sacrifice, and created yet another layer of governmental bureaucracy. To enforce greater discipline on republics' use of labor and supplies and their budgetary expenditures, the leadership would require

[141] Tito, in discussion at the third plenum of the CPY central committee, ibid., 406; Kidrič, in his report on "current tasks in the struggle for completion of the five-year plan" (393–94). On the "key investment projects" strategy, see also Tomasevich, "Yugoslavia during the Second World War"; and Mladek, Šturc, and Wyczalkowski, "The Change in the Yugoslav Economic System."

[142] *Informativni Priručnik Jugoslavije*, 323.

[143] Vukmanović-Tempo at the third plenum of the CPY central committee, in Petranović, Končar, and Radonjić, *Sednice*, 417. Tito added, "No understanding for others' troubles."

[144] Ibid., 391.

[145] Blažević, at the third plenum of the central committee, ibid., 451; see also Kidrič's more general discussion of the problem (386–88) and Tito's comments (401–2).

republican governments to be financially self-sufficient, operating on principles of profit-and-loss accounting. On economic grounds, republics would be forced to release civil servants and professionals to the district committees and to firms, but the repossession of enterprises taken temporarily into federal ownership at the beginning of 1948 would also increase their revenue base, if they managed it well. Some relief would come from federal subsidies to local governments to help them hold onto skilled cadres and from the transfer of pensions for veterans and war invalids to the federal budget, in line with its jurisdiction over defense.

The restoration of the republics' property rights of 1946–47 also entailed the return of economic ministries, relieving the federal budget of substantial expenditures on salaries and offices. But planning offices would continue to be subordinated to territorial ones, for the planning commission became part of the economic council of each republic. The midlevel branch directorates for securing and distributing supplies for public-sector enterprises were to operate on profit-and-loss accounting and socialist commerce (marketing by producers), forming autonomous "higher economic associations" of enterprises in an industrial branch to prevent firms' commercial orientation from becoming "disloyal" competition among firms (that is, with profits gained by competitive market pricing rather than reduced costs of production).[146]

But the decentralization of most economic ministries and republican financial autonomy would require new instruments of coordination and control over the economy as a whole. A new administrative apparatus would defeat the purpose of decentralization, so coordination of the national economies would occur through *councils of representatives* from the government, party, and higher economic associations of each republic. In following the democratic principle introduced in local governments and agricultural cooperatives in the spring of 1949, the leadership hoped to reduce the constant complaints and quarrels with federal decisions by inviting republican leaders to "participate in the revisions" of the investment plan and adminstrative structure. Tito and Kidrič ceremoniously announced this reorganization of the state administration of the economy on February 8, 1950, calling it a "blow to bureaucratism." The implementing decrees between February and June aimed to leave to the federal government (the "state," in their speeches) "only as much operative,

---

[146] These associations were like the trusts in the Soviet case (see Carr and Davies, *Foundations of a Planned Economy, 1926–1929*). In this process of rationalizing the ministerial structure, there was an intermediate step during which the federal ministries, which had proliferated into ever more specific economic functions, were grouped by general function (such as light industry or heavy industry) and consolidated. The higher economic associations soon came to be called economic chambers (*privredne komore*) and, like the ministerial branch offices they replaced, were subdivided territorially.

personnel, and regulatory authority as is necessary (under the given level of material productive forces, social consciousness, and the general economic difficulties caused by the intense struggle for the five-year plan) to protect general planned proportions."[147]

Financial stabilization depends on real stabilization—the production and consumption of goods—and Kidrič chose to interpret that problem as excess employment in the public sector. The "change in social structure" had been excessive, in his view; the inattention of republican authorities and the depletion of cadres from the district state and party apparatus made it "thoroughly impossible to complete tasks related to industrialization and agriculture without making political mistakes"; and despite the policy of January 1949 to reduce the number of people on guaranteed provisions, the state was supplying more. The enemy of food production was no longer the kulak—the private trader hoarding grain in order to speculate—but a new social stratum he called "fluctuators," who speculated with their labor. These peasant-workers, who worked their land for food but took industrial jobs to obtain the right to guaranteed provisions for their families, were causing serious harm to industrial production with their irregular presence and turnover, and they consumed state provisions that ought to have been reserved for workers with no access to land and family food supplies. The volunteer labor brigades had also increased the demand for food—from people who should have been producing it but who were sent to the forests, construction sites, and mines instead. Still-higher procurement quotas for grain and industrial crops for 1950 and again for 1951 could be met (if republics no longer balked at federal quotas) by increasing the acreage sown, but there was insufficient labor for the task. Kidrič now argued that it was "completely un-Marxist" to think that industrialization could be achieved by "petty-bourgeois work brigades" rather than consolidation of the working class itself.[148] Economically, the brigades' low productivity, drain on state food reserves, and diversion of the true labor surplus away from permanent employment meant a net loss for the state; politically, they were clearly no longer voluntary, for youths broke their "legs and heads" trying to flee and peasants even lost their lives resisting.[149] Beginning in 1951, brigades would serve only local projects; once a year, for two or three months and with advance warning, people could contribute their labor where they could directly see its value to their own lives. As for peasant-workers, they had to choose. They were more than welcome to return to the village,

[147] Kidrič, "O reorganizaciji državne uprave privredom." The occasion was his speech on June 27, 1950, asking parliament to confirm the changes.

[148] At the third plenum of the CPY central committee, in Petranović, Končar, and Radonjić, Sednice, 392.

[149] Tito, ibid., 410.

whereas those who could not survive in agriculture without state provisions should leave for industry permanently. The only way to persuade village households to release surplus labor for industry, Kidrič argued, was the "economic coercion" that they understood. If denied the right to linked trade, they would leave for industry "naturally."[150]

At a conference in August 1949 on agricultural production, Tito and Kardelj reminded party cadres from the republics that the party line on "collectivization" was *not* all-out collectivization, let alone a forced pace—in Kidrič's words (at the third plenum in December), "we aren't creating cooperatives out of any *larpurlartisme*."[151] They had to concentrate machinery in existing cooperatives, intensify production, and permit labor cooperatives only where they made economic sense (in grain-growing regions and for cattle, a key export crop, but not in "passive regions"). It was also necessary to put public-sector labor cooperatives on self-financing terms (the regime of economic accounting) and replace all remuneration in kind by cash—either hourly wages or piece rates instead of the *trudodan*.[152] But official policy once again favored the general farmers' (marketing) cooperatives. The problem with agricultural productivity, Bakarić told the sixth party congress in November 1952 (four months after compulsory deliveries had come to an end), was that the peasant labor cooperatives had been "undermechanized and overmanned."[153] Although the core of Kidrič's argument for the change in labor policy had to do with food—cutting food imports, exporting more agricultural products, and restoring macroeconomic balances by reducing the size of the public sector—the third installment of the Ex-Im Bank loan in August 1950 ($20 million when the country's foreign debt was at $180 million, in mostly short-term credits) was used to purchase food. The formal request to the United States on October 20 for nonmilitary aid, again for food, was answered on November 21: over the following four months, 279,000 metric tons of food were shipped at a cost of $37.8 million (including transportation costs).[154] The new policy on agriculture was announced three days

---

[150] Kidrič, ibid., 391, 466.

[151] "Art for art's sake" (ibid., 389). Tito and Kidrič had already insisted, at an August conference of party cadres on peasant labor cooperatives, on strengthening the existing cooperatives and not increasing their numbers.

[152] The "labor day" of ten hours (the *trudodni* of Soviet practice) by which labor was organized and paid, in agriculture as in industry—with planned wage norms for output per unit of time—and by which the peasant labor cooperatives were to be organized.

[153] There were also two serious droughts, in 1950 and 1952.

[154] The political momentousness of this decision is perhaps reflected in the fact that on the same day, the public prosecutor was told to release Žujović from prison—after he had been willing, on November 11, to go before the central committee and confess to having engaged in enemy activity, and on condition that he write a public letter explaining that he had been wrong to believe in the USSR blindly (published in *Borba* on November 25, 1950,

later, on the twenty-fourth,[155] and the November issue of the party journal published an article justifying international loans in the transition to
socialism.[156] On December 29, President Truman signed the Yugoslav
Emergency Assistance Act of 1950 granting food up to $50 million.

The restructuring of public-sector enterprises to reduce labor turnover
and cut the wage bill also returned to the 1947 system. Enterprise management once again became responsible for employment and training; the
"economic coercion" of budget contraints aimed to regain discipine on
wages and provide incentives to improve workers' skills; and yet another
innovation in workplace organization to keep wages in line with real productivity began. In the fall of 1949, the time of this new policy, the country was at the height of the labor-brigade campaign (only the previous
April called the "new system of labor"); newspapers from September to
December 1949 contain little else than stories of brigades from all areas of
the country, accolades for the workers' advisory commissions that told
factory administrators how to increase productivity, and the location of
the hero of the hour, Alija Sirotanović, who was on tour with his brigade
to teach miners all over the country their new method for increasing output.[157] But the lesson leaders drew from the "Alija Sirotanović Movement
for Higher Labor Productivity" was that there remained immense "internal reserves" of labor in industry that justified a series of "revisions" in the
number of employed.

The new system was introduced in a campaign of three battles during
1950: the "battle to stabilize the labor force" with employment contracts;
the "battle to balance goods and monetary funds" through enterprise-
level balances among wages, labor plans, and guaranteed provisions; and
the "battle to execute the production plan with reduced quotas of labor."
Their sum was the system later known as self-management in workplaces,
which began in December 1949 with the election of workers' councils.

According to the Regulation on Settling Labor of early January 1950,
workers would not be permitted to work after March 1 without a written

---

p. 1). Žujović agreed to these conditions when he heard, in news reports of the period since
his arrest given him by Djilas, of attacks at the trial of László Rajk on persons he knew well
and on the Yugoslav party as fascist.

[155] Tomasevich suggests, in "Collectivization of Agriculture in Yugoslavia," that decollec-
tivization may have been a condition for food aid; but the argument of this book is that no
such condition was necessary.

[156] Guzina, "Medjunarodni zajmovi i socijalistička izgradnja." On September 6, 1950, the
Yugoslav representative to the IMF marked the country's election to the board with a
speech maintaining that international development aid to poorer countries was necessary for
world peace—an argument the Yugoslavs had been pushing since 1945 (Borba, September
15, 1950).

[157] See, for example, the front page of almost every issue of Borba from September 10 to
October 10.

employment contract, and enterprise directors would be held legally responsible for any workers who did. The contracts—which were set the
previous April for six months in basic industrial branches and three
months in others and which now defined employment, in Kardelj's language, as an "employment relationship" (*radni odnos*)—had to guarantee
workers a job commensurate with their skill levels. The law was thus used
to enforce direct relations between employment, skill level, and the legislated wage for each job classification. Unexcused absence from work was
reclassified as economic sabotage; workers were subject to criminal prosecution and could be punished by a monetary fine or up to three months'
compulsory labor doing repairs. Because the minister of labor and the
public prosecutor had been too cavalier about broken contracts, the
leaders argued, they would use the courts and the civil and criminal law
to protect workers' rights, enforce labor and wage regulations, and, not
incidentally, replace another government bureau with the initiative of
individual workers or managers in bringing claims. To enforce the wage
plan, they would turn to the National Bank, which controlled the cash
plans and wage funds of enterprises through its local affiliates.[158] While
rationing continued, control over the level of employment would be
through the state's allocation of guaranteed provisions; factories with
farms had their cash wage fund reduced, thus directly balancing wages
and goods within the firm.

Physical as well as financial stabilization was to be enforced by withdrawing the right to guaranteed provisions from workers who moved
among enterprises, calculating the size of workers' rations according to
the time they spent in steady employment, and forcing women "economically" into the labor force by denying guaranteed provisions to workers'
families. Insurance benefits would also be determined not by individuals'
contributions to the fund but by the length of time they had been regularly employed (one's *staž*, in which the government now included time
spent in war service, imprisonment, internment, or revolutionary activity), and benefits would be financed by a lump-sum state tax on enterprises.[159] It was assumed that to attract women to production and keep

[158] Despite preparations since 1946, the journal of the finance ministry, *Finansije*, conceded that the cash plans began seriously only in September 1949 ("Nekoliko zapažanja
povodom obilaska narodnih odbora," March–April 1950).

[159] The revised law on social insurance for workers, officials, and their families, promulgated January 12, 1950, was entangled in parliamentary debate the entire year; one reason
was its revision of old-age pensions. The previous law had included a waiting period before
the insured could draw benefits because long-term insurance had been enacted in prewar
Yugoslavia only in 1937, thus leaving older insured persons at a disadvantage. Another
weakness in the old law was the separate coverage and regulations for officials. The new law
included all employed persons and also those not in a *radni odnos* but doing "socially useful
and necessary activities, such as people elected to representative organs and certain social

them there, firms would have to take into account their needs, such as day-care centers. This regulation (Harmonization of Labor-Force Plans with the Wage-Fund Plan and the Guaranteed-Provisions Plan, also from early January) required enterprises and branch directorates (now higher economic associations) to draw up for approval, within eight days, dynamic labor plans with corresponding wage funds based on their general economic and production plans. Only when their maximum quota of employed persons was approved would authorization to issue consumer coupons be given. In the countryside, district labor offices signed the employment contracts for members of peasant labor cooperatives, issued consumer coupons to people who had the right to provisions but were without a public-sector contract, and withdrew that right from persons living in households with two or more hectares of cultivable land or an income per household member over three thousand dinars a year. The people's committees received discretionary authority to disallow the right to ration coupons to persons earning less that that. Their executive boards assessed eligibility for linked-trade coupons, denying them to households that held surplus labor (determined according to the number of a household's able-bodied members in relation to the size of its landholding and type and method of cultivation).

Finally, the long struggle to end workers' ability to bargain over wages and benefits through market strength entered its final battle. Leaders complained that the introduction of employment contracts in the spring of 1949 had only led workers to shift from wage demands to negotiation over working conditions and benefits, such as housing and food. But, Kardelj insisted, clauses on these matters *"cannot* be subject to negotiation in our conditions."[160] Such negotiations were also inflationary, encouraging frequent turnover and "disloyal competition" among enterprises for scarce labor—as well as perpetuating the incorrect idea, Minister of Labor Arsov wrote in June 1950, that management and labor did not have the same interests under social ownership, that somehow "the socialist firm is separate from its work collective rather than one unified whole."[161] Improvements in working conditions and workers' living standards had to be adjusted to the "real development of material forces."

The purpose of the workers' councils introduced at the end of Decem-

---

organizations." It also opened the possibility of insurance for independent professionals. The primary purpose of the new legislation, however, was to encourage retirements of older workers and soldiers by extending coverage to all workers insured before the war and raising the pension to 100 percent of the principal; thus the focus of debate was on old-age pensions (see Jelčić, *Socijalno pravo*, 18–20). The same system was in practice in the Soviet Union after 1934 (see Davies, *The Development of the Soviet Budgetary System*, 265).

[160] Quoted in Arsov, "Rešavanje pitanja radne snage," 30.

[161] Ibid.

ber 1949 was thus to gain workers' assistance in the wage restraint and employment cuts necessary to restabilize the economy and to restore the authority of enterprise management and technicians over production, including labor. The councils would combine the collective incentives and discipline of the production brigades with managerial accountability for enterprise budgets. At first, this substitute for collective bargaining in the market attempted simply to encourage an exchange of information about the economic conditions of the firm with managers' explanations for the business reasons behind their decisions so as to teach workers the "perspective" (long-run rather than short-run interests) appropriate to their position in socialism, and to train a new generation in managerial skills. The exchange of such information was intended to enhance incentives to higher productivity by making the link to output more transparent and managers more credible—in the language of rational-choice theory, by increasing commitment. At the same time, the councils would rationalize administration by consolidating into one elected body the functions of the labor inspectors, advisory commissions, production conferences, workers' inspectors, and state labor offices. As specified by the instructions for workers'-council elections issued jointly by the Federal Economic Council and the Central Board of the United Unions in December to republican union offices, "the formation of workers' councils does not lessen the significance of the director in managing the enterprise. . . . [His] authority, obligations, and responsibilities do not change in any way."[162] And although the councils' purpose was "to interest or activate ever-larger numbers of workers in solving problems of production," replacing the brigade system and Vukmanović-Tempo's devoted production workers, delegates would nonetheless only review the production plans, labor allocations, and work schedules formulated by engineers and technical staff, who knew best how to rationalize. Although the workers' councils would appear to replace the unions, union chief Djuro Salaj told the third plenum in December 1949 that the union leaders had been "blowing this horn for two years now."[163] In their view, production workers had received too much attention in relation to engineering and technical personnel and even, perhaps, exaggerated wages. It was engineers who had to be paid well; production workers were only recently arrived from the villages, and higher wages would only encourage their faster return to the land (since it would take less time to earn the cash they sought) and would reinforce their petty-bourgeois property-holding instincts rather than transforming them into industrial workers. The problem of the living standard came about not because inflation undermined production incen-

---

[162] "Uputstvo o osnivanju i radu radničkih saveta državnih privrednih preduzeća," in Petranović and Zečević, *Jugoslavija, 1918–1988*, 852–53.

[163] Petranović, Končar, and Radonjić, *Sednice*, 433.

tives as Kidrič had been arguing, but because of the moral economy of peasants.[164] Indeed, Salaj went so far as to say that workers needed to be led by engineers as well as by the party organization. Because skilled workers and engineers dominated the unions as in the prewar period, the line of descent for the workers' councils from the Knights of Labor and the Austromarxists was intact.[165]

The unions were assigned two functions: to organize council elections and nominate candidates, and to defend workers' rights to social insurance and benefits—which would now depend on the economic results of firms and on council deliberations, with the end of wage bargaining and the close of insurance bureaus. In the first round of elections, during the second half of January 1950, the councils were limited to the largest firms of the defense drive—215 state economic enterprises that had been under federal jurisdiction and had had brigades; these were firms in mining, machine tools, shipbuilding, printing, transport, gas and electricity, iron smelting, hosiery, and cement.[166] As the December instructions explained:

[164] Confronting the problem of turnover and absenteeism, Kidrič argued the importance of political work by managerial staff instead of economic incentives. Workers from the villages were absent to celebrate religious holidays, and because they were Orthodox, Catholics, and Muslims, this meant separate days for each he complained; to reduce such absences, mine workers were being given higher wages. "I think that it has no particular effect to offer him an ever higher wage, because as all can see, the higher the wage he receives, the less he works. He is accustomed to living on a chunk of bread and bacon, and when he has this, he's satisfied. Instead, it's necessary to do political work with such people . . . and first of all, enable him to know what his obligation is to the state . . . lift [his] cultural standard . . . and in some way tie him to the factory" (Kidrič, at the third plenum of the CPY central committee, ibid., 411). On this Chayanovian analysis, see J. Scott, *The Moral Economy of the Peasant*; and Cox's analysis of the Soviet debates in the 1920s (*Peasants, Class, and Capitalism*).

[165] On the Knights of Labor, see Hattam, "Economic Visions and Political Strategies"; and C. Martin, "Public Policy and Income Distribution in Yugoslavia," 27. In the Austromarxist scheme, the "chambers of labor" for workers and salaried employees were separate from the "chambers of commerce and industry," paralleling the distinction that developed in the Yugoslav case between the workers' councils within firms and the economic chambers, which associated firms by branch and republic. The model was clearly there in the similar distinction between the works' councils (organized according to the shopfloor) and the trade unions (organized by branch) in which the works' councils were subordinated to the trade unions and never achieved any important managerial functions (Gulick, *Austria from Habsburg to Hitler* 1:202, 213–14).

[166] Branko Horvat informs me that the idea for the councils began spontaneously in the cement factory in Split, although Kidrič's writings during World War II on workers' councils, the Weimar elements of the Slovene constitutional proposal of 1921, and the exposure of at least Slovenes and Croats to Austromarxism would suggest a longer gestation. The need to rationalize labor costs in heavy industry and export production was most immediate, however, as one can see in the beginnings of industrial reforms in other socialist states—for example, in Poland in the 1970s (see Woodall, *The Socialist Corporation and Technocratic Power*).

For now, until the necessary experience is gained, workers' councils will be founded only in a certain number of the best and most important collectives in our country. . . . Before the election of workers' councils, you need to organize conferences . . . inviting responsible ministers and directors of general, or main, directorates of the enterprises in which elections are being held, and also the enterprise directors, secretaries of the party organizations, and presidents of these enterprises' associations.[167]

From late January 1950 through 1951 and 1952, unions organized factory elections of delegates, from which representatives to branch-level workers' councils would then be chosen. These representatives would be, according to the newspaper publicity drive, the "best" workers, engineers and technicians, and workers honored as innovators and rationalizers.[168]

In the rationalizations of 1950, however, the most important task of the workers' councils was, as for the federal councils that replaced the ministries, to secure workers' cooperation—by being allowed to review management's decisions—in the upcoming employment revisions that would reduce "surplus labor" and "hoarding" and send "one part eventually [back] to the village." The labor quotas for 1950 were reduced by more than a million workers, leaving a total of only 1.3 million employed in the public sector. The cuts and reallocations were made in two waves: production workers in the spring, and primarily government administrative staff in the fall. Although leaders insisted on "political preparation" at the third plenum, 99,722 production workers were moved from one economic branch to another during March and April without explanation or choice. Fears of unemployment raised earlier in political circles were echoed in popular slogans such as "Surplus labor!" "Unemployment!" and "The crisis has begun!" Critics insisted that a return to the village was "a step backward" and "into unemployment."[169] Factory directors jumped at the opportunity to fire less-desired workers—invalids, women (especially pregnant women), ailing and older workers. Office staff cut workers by eliminating whole categories, such as repair workers, from factory employment rolls,[170] and local governments eliminated entire activities, such as artisanal and hostelry firms in Vojvodina. These cuts led to such

[167] "Popratno pismo uz uputstvo o osnivanju i radu radničkih saveta državnih privrednih preduzeća," in Petranović and Zečević, *Jugoslavija, 1918–1988*, 853.

[168] See, for example, *Politika*, January 28 and 29, 1950, on elections for workers' councils in the Breza coal mine in Bosnia-Herzegovina, the Rade Končar machine factory in Zagreb, the Čukarica shipbuilding firm, the Kultura printing firm in Belgrade, and seven firms (including those for hosiery, electric trams, and city gas) in Sarajevo.

[169] Arsov, "Rešavanje pitanja radne snage," 21–22.

[170] Ibid., 23. According to Has, giving this opportunity to managers led to overly "technocratic" evaluations in enterprises, although this seems to have been the leaders' intention ("Društveno-ekonomski osvrt," 148–49).

dislocation of services that workers had to be called back to their former jobs several years later. Many workers refused to move to their new assignments (for example, of the four hundred that the Subotica labor office sent during the spring to work in Pančevački Rit, only sixty went), and local officials sympathetic to those who shied from the mines or heavy industrial jobs found them other jobs rather than impose legal penalties.[171] On June 10, 1950, days after the basic and dynamic branch labor plans based on enterprise production plans submitted in January–February were due, Tito went to the national assembly with the new law on "the management of state economic enterprises and higher economic associations by the work collective." Although the work collective meant everyone in the firm, and the law assigned legal responsibility to enterprise management for labor and "direct operations," it was, in the hyperbole of the ideological struggle, a fulfillment of the historic promise of socialism that workers would run their factories: "Peasants in cooperatives, which they manage themselves, and workers in factories, which from now on they will manage themselves, today have their own fate truly in their own hands."[172] On June 27, the day before the second anniversary of the first Cominform resolution, the assembly enacted "workers' control."[173] By August and September, when the renewal of employment contracts offered another opportunity for dismissals, leaders were expressing confidence that "results will be even better because of workers' councils."[174]

Also on June 27, Kidrič asked the assembly to confirm the reorganization of state administration in the economy. Between September and December, the second labor revision cut an additional 122,500 workers and reallocated office workers and administrative staff, including 50,000 demoted into industrial or agricultural production (these were people whose lack of professional qualifications made them "incapable of performing administrative tasks successfully").[175] In this round the leaders were "especially careful,"[176] allowing the reallocations to drag on longer, discussing the transfers in broad consultations in the federal labor ministry, and setting up coordinating commissions of "interested parties" in districts and republics. "The problem of decentralization is to ensure the correct allocation of professional cadres," read the title of an article in the August–September issue of *Ekonomski Pregled*. Here, too, however, many who refused to take production jobs or return to the countryside were in-

---

[171] Arsov, "Rešavanje pitanja radne snage," 22–24.

[172] Tito, "Trudbeničko upravljanje privredom," 26.

[173] Ibid.

[174] Vjećeslav Holjevac, who took over from Arsov as federal minister of labor in July 1950, in "Problem radne snage: Neka iskustva iz prvog polugodišta."

[175] Dular, "Struktura osoblja zaposlenog u našoj privredi," 433.

[176] Has, "Društveno-ekonomski osvrt," 145.

dulged. Many others took matters into their own hands—such as the hundred-odd staff members of the Ministry of Light Industry who refused to accept their new assignments and, two months after the ministry's April dispersal to the republics, were seen going door-to-door in search of alternative offers in the capital.[177]

There were substantial criticisms of this reform program within the leadership, in spite of Tito's repeated attempts to sway critics with stories of political excess in the preceding year. The "narrowing on the labor front" was being done, Kidrič argued, *"for* socialism," while the "organizational measures" *must* be understood as "necessary in the given situation to secure the Plan"; if "they don't see them as socialism, then we can go to the devil and create a bureaucratic system."[178] For some senior party members, the change was being made too soon and too quickly; the leader of the Vojvodina party, Jovan Veselinov, was convinced that the peasants would want to join cooperatives if only the government's grain-requisitioning rules were less discouraging, and that the transition to economic and intensive methods and away from state responsibility for labor would not permit completion of the plan under prevailing conditions and could not be made overnight without serious economic consequences. Djuro Pucar continued to argue on behalf of many that labor problems would be better resolved by assigning people to jobs than by withdrawing guaranteed provisions, which would only cause the loss of labor already recruited. At one final conference in the Ministry of Labor on the eve of its elimination, in September 1950, participants agreed that this new system—in which labor was "a problem that only an economic organization can solve" with economic measures—had benefits, but "it did not bode well for employment 'at first.'"[179] The conflicts were particularly intense at the fourth plenum of the central committee in June 1951, when prices in retail markets for consumer goods were freed. Kidrič once again railed against the "bureaucratic mentality" that insisted on "socialist determination of planned prices" and that did not see that free prices and the operation of the "law of value" were essential incentives to increased production. On the other hand, former health minister Pavle Gregorić, addressing a dispute over the disposition of medicines held in federal warehouses, presented searing data on horrendous health conditions; he questioned the wisdom of freely selling instead of rationing scarce

[177] Arsov, "Rešavanje pitanja radne snage," 23.

[178] Kidrič, in Petranović, Končar, and Radonjič, *Sednice*, 394. He did add, however, that they would not "interfere with local initiative where it is truly based on local sources of materials."

[179] Has, "Društveno-ekonomski osvrt," 147. Arsov also reports that these reallocations raised fears of unemployment among some, but that the continuing shortages in mining and construction should have told them that "there was no danger of that in our economic system" ("Rešavanje pitanja radne snage," 21).

goods to people in need, and then predicted new horrors in health and social welfare as a consequence of ending all central authority for health. Others argued that financial methods would provide very weak incentives to labor recruitment and labor productivity, given the goods shortages and the prevailing "culture" of "transition from individual to socialist forms."[180]

The resolution to this conflict on the appropriate methods for the transition lay, in Kardelj's view, with the party. The transition would be made through "agitation and propaganda" by party activists to develop "socialist consciousness" (acceptance of sacrifices in the interest of long-term objectives); "initiative" (more effort with neither force nor immediate economic reward, on the promise of future gain); and "democratic relations in our production" through the forums for participation, such as the workers' councils. This would also be the best policy of national defense, because an international reputation for democratic participation "is just what will enable us to show the world the difference between us and them."[181] The return of control over education and culture to the republics in 1950 would "win sympathy in circles of intellectuals, scientists, etc."[182] People without a public-sector employment contract but who performed "socially useful and necessary activities, such as people elected to representative organs and certain social organizations," would receive rights to social insurance, as independent professionals probably also would later. And, Tito said, "because of our policy toward the imperialist world, we must now take special care, particularly with younger members of the Party, to see that they not forget that we are a socialist country."[183]

During 1951, Yugoslavia's reorientation to Western trade and aid also led to a reform that ended the monopoly of the Ministry of Foreign Trade over foreign-trade transactions, handed to the Economic Council the authority to regulate trade in particular products when the social interest (that is, defense) demanded it, gave jurisdiction over customs and tariffs to the finance ministry, and began an active exchange-rate policy by devaluing the currency from 50 to 300 dinars to the U.S. dollar. On November 1, the first $16 million installment of U.S. military aid under the two countries' Mutual Defense Assistance agreement[184] arrived in Belgrade, and American efforts to persuade the French and British to sell Yugoslavia arms and tanks materialized during that month.[185]

---

[180] Petranović, Končar, and Radonjić, *Sednice*, 662–67.

[181] Kardelj, at the third plenum of the CPY central committee in Petranović, Končar, and Radonjić, *Sednice*, 454; Arsov, "Rešavanje pitanja radne snage."

[182] Kardelj, in Petranović, Končar, and Radondjić, *Sednice*, 480.

[183] Ibid.

[184] Ibid., 478.

[185] Between mid-1951 and 1955, the United States coordinated aid from the United States, Britain, and France. By November 1952, the economic and military aid that had

Few months had passed before the prediction of the labor conference in September 1950 proved correct. Throughout 1951 and 1952, enterprises went overboard in the struggle for profitability (*rentabilnost*), guided by the "material interests of work collectives." Firms increased both accumulation and wages by firing all who did not "immediately produce an output," including those in maintenance jobs—who would clearly be needed later—and workers considered (as in the spring of 1950) less productive, such as women, the infirm, and the aged.[186] Two droughts within three years sent agricultural output plummeting, and the start of the Korean War in June 1950 brought a disastrous shift in global terms of trade against imported fuels, strategic materials, and machinery. Many industries simply came to a halt, and others reduced production significantly; the adjustments in the fields of energy and mining alone cut employment 14.6 percent between January 1951 and January 1952 and 17.4 percent by June 1952.[187] The leaders had declared an "end to unemployment" in September 1947; five years later, the official unemployment of public-sector workers had surpassed levels "normal for Western European countries" (referring to the monetarists' "normal rate" of 5 percent).[188] The "correctness of the new economic measures" was demonstrated, according to discussion at the sixth party congress in November 1952, by the completion of the production plan for industry "at the same time [that] the number of workers has notably lessened."[189] Delegate Simo Kokotić reported, "Not only has the Bor mine successfully completed its plan tasks, but it has also reduced its costs of production in proportion. The Bor mine now completes its plan tasks with about three thousand fewer workers than it had in 1938."[190]

CONCLUSION

The rhetoric of the Yugoslav-Soviet propaganda war of December 1948 to November 1952 encouraged an interpretation of the Yugoslav system as

---

arrived from the West totaled $286.6 million in grants, $267.2 million in credits (from the U.S. Export-Import Bank, IBRD, IMF, London Club, and individual countries), and $51 million in war reparations, mainly from Germany. Military aid continued until 1958; and by mid-1962, U.S. aid had reached $2.3 billion, of which $719 million was military aid (Mugoša, "Odnosi Jugoslavije i SAD-a"; Tomasevich, "Yugoslavia during the Second World War," 105–7, 112; Hoffman and Neal, *Yugoslavia and the New Communism*, 88–91).

[186] Has, "Društveno-ekonomski osvrt," 148–49.

[187] *Ekonomska Politika*, August 28, 1952, 422.

[188] Has, "Društveno-ekonomski osvrt," 141. See also Krstulović, "Stalno podizanje proizvodnosti rada."

[189] Čalić, "Ekonomska problematika na VI. kongresu saveza komunista," 325.

[190] Ibid.

an alternative to the Soviet system, an alternative characterized by workers' control, antibureaucratic socialist democracy, and decentralization. In its international position, it did differ substantially from the path followed in Eastern Europe from the end of 1947 (and especially early 1949) until 1953. The country created an independent and politically significant armed forces, received Western military and economic aid and trade, and as a result was able to return to the gradualist position on agricultural socialization and to the methods of economic control considered appropriate to light manufacturing and processed goods for domestic consumption and export. The new course reemerged in Hungary, Poland, and the USSR in 1953 and, following a detour, after 1956; and while their reforms and those in Czechoslovakia in the 1960s differed from the Yugoslav ones in political trajectory and international timing, the similarities in economic conceptions, the common legacy of Leninist institutions and the NEP's "regime of economy" in industry and agriculture, and even the parallels with Soviet industrial relations of the 1930s are usually ignored.[191]

Decentralization and workers' control were also not what they are claimed to have been. One of the purposes of decentralization was to "strengthen centralism by developing its democratism,"[192] and one of the purposes of workers' control was to reduce the power over wages that tight labor markets and then the production-brigade system had given to workers. The dynamic of the period was not between central and local power and authority, or between more or less party power; it involved the different *kinds* of authority possessed by each of the three levels—federation, republic, and commune (as localities began to be called)—with each change of policy. The "economic" methods of what I have called the Slovene model of Kardelj and Kidrič were more centralized and "administrative"— in the sense that they emphasized central regulations on wages and capital-labor ratios, vertical links in economic and political coordination, and managerial-technocratic authority—than were the "political" and "campaign" methods during 1948–49 of the Foča model, with its radical democratization in production, popular supervision and checks against all administrators through local assemblies, media, and voters' meetings, and *local* impress of party cadres and military. The difference in the role of "bureaucracy" in these two approaches was more a matter of where than how much. The system of workers' councils transferred authority from workers themselves back to staff—managers, engineers, and unions. "Economic" methods led to the concentration of plant and a reduction in

---

[191] For the years of direct parallels, see Carr and Davies, *Foundations of a Planned Economy, 1926–1929*, vol. 1, no. 1; and Dobb, *Soviet Economic Development since 1917*.
[192] *Informativni Priručnik Jugoslavije, 1950*, 323.

the proportion of workers actually in production (to reduce costs of production). And the general farmers' cooperatives, restored to the center of agricultural policy as the leadership had intended in 1946, employed primarily administrators, not farmers: in 1955, of 51,393 permanent "workers," only 8,471 worked exclusively in agriculture; 4,593 worked in shops connected to agriculture, while 38,329 were employed in non-production tasks.[193] The idea that "economic" methods represented a choice for the "market" was true only in the sense that prices were freed in retail goods markets; and in contrast to the extensive labor mobility and turnover of the 1948–49 extractive policies, there was no market allocation of factors of production in the "new economic system"—the employment contracts, concept of socialist work communities, and workers' councils all aimed to *im*mobilize the workforce.

The real aim of these changes was to diminish the federal government: to reduce its bureaucratic offices and move ministries to the republics, to cut the size of public-sector employment in order to cut the cash-wage bill and the number of people provisioned by state supplies, to eliminate central supply allocations and give authority to firms and their branch associations,[194] to cut the federal budget for stabilization purposes by transferring tasks and jurisdictions to lower levels, to return responsibility for labor supplies and authority over hiring and firing to enterprises, to cut further the federal government's role in production and investment, to use "lean" monetary instruments of economic direction, and to nudge forward the process of the "withering away" of the state. And whereas historically, as Joyce Appleby writes, "the society's dependence upon the food supply provided, after all, the rock bottom reason for political control of economic activities,"[195] the leaders' commitment to a gradual transfer of labor from agriculture to industry—temporarily reversed in 1948–49 by their even greater commitment to build a strong defense, through their own efforts if necessary—led in the opposite direction: to reducing

---

[193] *Privreda FNRJ u periodu 1947–1956*, section on the agricultural population, 164–65.

[194] Although prices were freed in retail markets in 1951, the former directorates—now branch producer organizations, or economic chambers (*privredne komore*)—assumed authority over allocating scarce production materials because, as an article in *Ekonomska Politika* reported ("Sporazumna distribucija," December 17, 1953, p. 1012), the "market" would give cement, steel, wool, etc. only to the economically strongest rather than to those whose need was greatest. The *privredne komore* would act as intermediaries among producers, creating a forum to establish agreements among them on priorities (what came to be called in the 1970s the contractual, or *dogovorna*, economy), while leaving some room for contracts between individual firms ("though also not forgetting the peasant market"). They would "eventually" solve the problem of supplies with imports in the first half of 1954 and then, by exporting production in the second half of the year, pay for the imports. According to Ward, these producers' associations were especially important in "controlling the allocation of foreign exchange among firms" ("Industrial Decentralization in Yugoslavia," 171n).

[195] *Economic Thought and Ideology in Seventeenth-Century England*, 101.

political control and cutting the public sector in the face of near famine, a reversal made possible with American credits.[196]

To the extent that there was an "administrative period" in the immediate postwar years, it began in January 1948 with the creation of a labor ministry and temporary federal control over labor, supplies, and many industries in order to build defense with domestic resources, and it ended with the closing of the state labor offices in September 1950 after completion of the labor revisions ordered the previous December. The fundamental difference between that period and the policy on either side of it was the approach to the employment of labor.

But there did emerge, out of what was in fact a more complex founding period of constantly changing methods and institutions, two tendencies that would resurface alternately in the next forty years. These tendencies were defined by the different emphases in production—with their differing systems of economic incentives, employments, and political organization—that resulted as in the founding period, from policy responses to changes in international conditions. The availability and requirements of foreign financing, shifts in terms of trade and market access as they affected both foreign demand for Yugoslav goods and factor prices for domestic manufacturers, and the needs of defense alternately favored the conditions of supply contracts (military procurement, producers' inputs, bilateral trade agreements, or adverse terms of trade under which gains could come only through increases in supply) and the conditions of demand in retail markets (both domestic and export, and therefore market niche and price more than quantity adjustments).

In the first cluster, the emphasis was on the production of fuel and food grains, the extraction of minerals and other primary products, capital goods, and military equipment and stockpiles; in the second cluster, the emphasis was on processed goods and light manufacturing, garden farming, and other consumer goods. The Slovene model preferred the production profile of the second cluster, and that model continued to shape the dominant economic and political institutions for the entire period. Nonetheless, the importance of an independent defense, the privileged position of manufacturers of final goods, and the unpredictable fluctuations in foreign demand also kept alive the Foča model. Political disagreements over policy continued, and the differential effects on regions and employment sectors were significant. But it was the uncontrollable international environment that remained decisive for governmental policy.

[196] The leaders gave two reasons for not wanting to unite with Bulgaria (despite Stalin's pressure) that reinforce the interpretation in this book of their long-term strategy; that Bulgaria was on the less industrialized and poorer end of the Yugoslav spectrum and would shift the domestic balance away from the developed northwest; and that as a more urban party of industrial workers, the Bulgarian Communist party was more willing to collectivize agriculture (see, for example, Kardelj in V. Dedijer, *Novi prilozi* 3:302).

Chapter 5

A REPUBLIC OF PRODUCERS

THE CHANGES in the organization of the economy in 1950 and of foreign trade in 1951 had to be confirmed constitutionally, because economic recognition of Yugoslav sovereignty permitted normalization at home and because economic restructuring (the "new economic system") required political restructuring. The Basic Law adopted by the national assembly on January 13, 1953, was only the second of five constitutions; a battle over the sixth, beginning in 1982, led to the final disintegration of the Yugoslav state in 1990. Most analysts of its collapse, particularly domestic critics of the regime, ascribe its economic and political downfall to the 1974 constitution and the related constitutional document on labor relations of 1976, the Law on Associated Labor (colloquially called the "workers' constitution"). But the principles of the 1974 constitution had already been established before 1953, in the period chronicled in the previous chapter; and each successive constitution after 1953 was a further step in the process of realizing the original leaders' *idea* of a socialist society—a system in the process of becoming through constitutive laws.

The differences in the constitutions and in systemic laws in intervening years reflect the unfolding of this idea as the leadership confronted different international conditions—in the areas of national security, terms of trade, and terms for finance, refinance, and export earnings—by alternating between two basic approaches to production with respect to labor incentives, industrial organization, and priority sectors. This is because the institutions of the domestic order continued to be defined by the conditions of its origin, when national independence was defined in terms of military threats to territory and when the capital needed for industrialization was in short supply—both machinery and trade finance, and human capital (skilled technicians, managers, and workers with steady industrial habits). This scarcity defined a mentality toward the economy that never changed.[1] Despite the one-party state and the political purges

---

[1] A continuing dispute in the literature on socialist systems, primarily those of Eastern Europe and the USSR, concerned whether they were best understood by Hungarian economist Janos Kornai's concept of "shortage economies." I do not enter this discussion here, except to remark that there is persuasive empirical evidence against the argument (see

of opponents, disputes over how to resolve those shortages and how to increase capital continued because of the persistent conflict between the Slovene model, which won institutionally, and the Foča reality arising from the leaders' multiple goals, the country's heterogeneity, and its complex international position. The political system became critical to the leaders' objectives because changes in the approach to production required institutional adjustments and because the political system was expected to manage and harmonize the remaining conflicts.

Understanding that political model is particularly important to understanding Yugoslav unemployment, as well as the ultimate collapse of the system itself, because most explanations of both focus on the political system. For adherents of the original Ward model (elaborated in the next chapter), Yugoslav unemployment was greater than it needed to be because of the decision-making rights at the workplace—because of the institutions for consultation between management and production workers in the public sector (whether economic enterprises or social services and institutions) over wages, benefits, investment, and employment. For others, the bargaining among republican delegates within councils of the federal government as a result, it is argued, of the 1974 constitution caused the decline of the entire economy and with it the system itself (although we have seen that these councils had already begun to replace the ministerial structure by 1950 and eventually would replace all other governmental offices in the economy). In the first instance, it was market socialism (as the Yugoslav system was often labeled) that failed; in the second it was decentralization—to the great disappointment of the many who continue to support both.

This book argues that it was neither workers' councils with an inability to impose wage restraint nor the conflicts among the republics' political elites with their inability to agree on policy that was the cause of unemployment and disintegration; it was instead the effect of contradictions in the leaders' strategy for development and national independence on economic policies, social organization, and political action. To understand these outcomes, the workers' councils and federal decision making must be seen in that broader context, as the leaders intended them and as they interacted with other parts of the system.

Burkett, "Search, Selection, and Shortage," for a discussion and references to the empirical research by Richard Portes and others). A large part of the actual shortages was a result of rationing in response to international problems—a problem that might or might not have been resolvable by open market economies. The postcommunist period will provide better answers. More important to this study is the early experience in the history of socialist regimes with shortages of production inputs and skilled labor and the institutionalized *structuring* of these societies thereafter as if the primary problem were such shortages.

MISUNDERSTANDINGS

The first thing that must be clarified about this new system is that it was not, and never became, a system of workers' control. The concept of a labor-managed firm and an economy organized around labor-managed firms, on which an entire theoretical literature later arose, does not accurately reflect the rights and powers assigned to production workers in Yugoslav enterprises or the purpose of worker participation in enterprise management. In fact, the system no longer recognized unpropertied wage earners, either as a class or a status. The concept of labor as an actor separate from capital ceased to exist. It was replaced by the central concept of a property owner who was a producer of value and by its operative principle—the *incentive to increase produced value* (that is, productivity, or net value), an incentive that would derive from rights of political and economic decision making.

These units of property-owning producers were actually associations of people defined individually by their employment contract placing them in a long-term employment position (*radni odnos*), which was a right to receive income in proportion to work as defined by the legally regulated job classification of that contract. The essence of socialist employment (the *radni odnos*), Kardelj told the second plenum of the central committee in January 1949, was "the method of payment."[2] As collectivities, these associations of producers were defined by the producers' political rights to participate in decisions on the creation and disposition of net *income* ("surplus value," or gross receipts minus costs). Their particular "labors" that they joined together in an *organization of associated labor* distinguished them according to functions within the organization and according to the rights and relative shares to income and benefits within the work (capital) collective (*radna zajednica*). But the reference in policy debates to direct producers or to the workers' collective meant not workers but enterprises, whose representatives were almost always from management or the party organization. Moreover, alongside this organization of the public sector, there was a private sector of producers—individuals or households also defined by the right to draw income on their net earnings and limited in their rights to dispose of capital assets—but they could "join their labor" (associate and contract) only with social-sector firms, and their political rights to participate with other producers in the allocation of surplus were confined to the local level where they paid fees and income tax.

What joined these producers/working people conceptually was the core idea of this economic and political system: the early liberal idea of

---

[2] Petranović, Končar, and Radonjić, *Sednice Centralnog komiteta KPJ (1948–1952)*, 32.

economic interest as the motive of social good (an idea often associated with Adam Smith, although currently alive in rational-choice theories of behavior) and therefore the source of right. The property-rights school, in the Austrian school version of Carl Menger, defined the philosophical underpinnings of this individualist-societal link:

> The state can greatly harm the citizen's interest by interfering too much. . . . Being responsible and caring for the well-being of one's self and family is a powerful incentive for work and industry. The discharge of these duties becomes the purest joy and truest pride of the free citizen. . . . Any incentive which makes the workers work harder may be regarded as a gain to the economy. The most effective inducement for the workers lies in their recognizing that their reward depends on their own diligence.[3]

Tito preferred to call this inducement "perspective":[4] workers' effort and short-term wage restraint followed from the knowledge that they had political control (the "people's power" that, Kidrič insisted in 1946, distinguished their socialism from state capitalism). The conflict between capital and labor was now only one of time horizons (and therefore investment), as classical theorists often saw it.[5]

It is the case, as the labor-management literature stresses, that the effective focus of property rights, and thus the work collective's economic incentive to maintain and enhance the value of its assets, was the collective's *income* (whatever the source—production realized in sales, or budgetary grants from corporate tax revenues).[6] But the purpose of budgetary autonomy (the core idea of "self-management") was what that literature treats as its consequence—to increase gain by cutting costs of production so that income rose only in proportion to real gains in productivity. Moreover, the assignment of responsibility for budgetary discipline to managers and the banks, to protect against the moral hazard possible given this freedom, created the potential for conflicts between workers and

---

[3] These excerpts are from the primary source of Menger's ideas, the 1876 lecture notebooks of Crown Prince Rudolf of Austria, cited by Streissler in "What Kind of Economic Liberalism May We Expect in 'Eastern' Europe?" 198. Streissler identifies these ideas with the property-rights school within liberal thought.

[4] Tito, at the third plenum of the CPY central committee, in Petranović, Končar, and Radonjić, *Sednice*, 404.

[5] In the ever-developing, specialized language for this system, capital was increasingly referred to after the mid-1960s as *minuli rad* ("past labor"); the term became official with the 1974 constitution. On the dispute critical to theories of labor management over what constituted the objective function for workers under self-management, and whether workers would take a long time horizon, see Tyson, "A Permanent Income Hypothesis for the Yugoslav Firm."

[6] The latter source would be for governments (called "sociopolitical communities") and financially autonomous providers of public goods and services such as education or roads (eventually called "communities of interest").

their elected representatives, between workers' council and management board, and between the entire work collective and outside regulators, such as the social accounting service within the banks and other administrators of legislated rules. Self-management meant financial independence (the word *sovereignty* was used for republics)—as it did in 1927, when the government withdrew its contribution from financing for unemployment compensation and left workers' chambers solely responsible, and in 1937, when Tito strove to put the CPY on its own financial footing because the Comintern refused to support it further. Interference with that independence, whether the "dependence" of debt or the reduced freedom of public claims on the collective's income, came to be seen as a limit on that sovereignty, on self-management. The leaders' purpose after 1947 in localities, republics, enterprises, and social services, however, was to enforce economic responsibility without resort to state power, using (as the language of the early 1950s called the budget constraint of an enterprise's net realized income) the "automatic control of the market."[7]

"Workers' control" was only one aspect of the return to "economic coercion" after August 1949 in order to stabilize the "market"; the behavioral principle of individual economic interest was, in the explanation offered in May 1952 by economist and party replacement at Finance Kiro Gligorov, intended to bring consumption of wage goods back into line with existing (dwindling) supplies while stimulating production, and to restore value to the currency as an instrument of economic calculation and policy. "By the logic of his own interest," the peasant who was forced to pay cash for industrial goods and meet higher tax obligations would increase production for the market, and this increased supply would in turn bring prices down. Similarly, Gligorov explained, devaluation of the dinar would act as a stimulus to increased production for export, given the obligation to keep expenditures (including wages and benefits) within the limit of a firm's receipts.[8] Cuts in public expenditures (investment, officials' salaries, and guaranteed provisions) would automatically release resources for manufacturers.

Indeed, the argument that financial accountability was more effective than state control was the reason given for ending the "administrative period" and transferring "concern for finding labor from state organs to

[7] A typical example can be found in Gorupić, "Uloga ekonomista u našoj privredi"; see also Mladek, Šturc, and Wyczalkowski, "The Change in the Yugoslav Economic System." Enthusiasts in the northwest, particularly, criticized the "dominant note in the contemporary economic thought of bourgeois countries"—the demand for a "strengthening of the economic functions of the state"—as "an expression of the growing disharmony between productive forces and production relations in capitalism and a reflection of the general crisis of capitalism" (Dabčević, "Neki suvremeni ekonomisti o ekonomskoj ulozi države," 37).

[8] K. Gligorov, "Factors in Our Economic Stabilization."

the firm, which undertakes measures for the more correct utilization of labor."[9] As an official in the Ministry of Social Policy explained, the state labor offices "had led to the expenditure of financial resources for the employment in the economy of new labor that after a short stay left the firm, often not even contributing enough to cover the costs of its engagement."[10] The first instance of extending the financial discipline of self-management to social services and public utilities that did not "create value" but used that created by others, called social self-management, was in social insurance, because "the office of social insurance and economic enterprises that had use of these funds had not been materially interested in the rational expenditure of these resources. Thus it occurred that there were firms that misused the funds, taking from the social-insurance account sums that they could not justify and that they used as their own working capital."[11]

It is also misleading to call this system "market socialism." The leaders' concept of *socialist commodity production* was not a market economy, although final goods ("commodities") markets operated largely by a free price mechanism and consumer demand was meant to be the primary incentive to producers. Increasing price liberalization also occurred in the foreign sector—particularly after 1961, when the second stage of reforms for GATT (General Agreement on Tariffs and Trade) membership replaced multiple coefficients with a uniform tariff, duties were progressively liberalized, and, after 1972, the exchange rate became an active instrument of policy.[12] But the market did not apply to factors of production—labor, capital and intermediate goods, raw materials, credit in the form of working and venture capital—although monetary prices were assigned to facilitate allocation and comparative valuation and a rent was charged on fixed capital and borrowed funds. This was not the model of market socialism identified with Oscar Lange, Frederick Taylor, E. Barone, and others, for there was no central calculation of shadow prices to imitate a market and investment choices were increasingly decentralized. Price regulation was used in place of a production plan in order to achieve balanced development as well as monetary equilibrium by influencing incentives to producers,[13] so that the government kept the

[9] Has, "Društveno-ekonomski osvrt na problem zaposlenosti," 146.

[10] Maričić, "Neki problemi organizacije i rada biroa za posredovanje rada," 662.

[11] Matović, "Samouprava u socijalnom osiguranju," 430.

[12] There is much dispute about how liberalized the foreign transmission of prices actually was; see Tyson and Neuberger, "The Transmission of International Disturbances to Yugoslavia." On the inappropriateness of price mechanisms as a policy instrument for foreign trade, see Dyker, *Yugoslavia: Socialism, Development, and Debt*, 97–101 and passim.

[13] See Lange and Taylor, *On the Economic Theory of Socialism*; and Heimann, "Literature on the Theory of a Socialist Economy." Also, contrast the more contemporaneous ac-

price of factors of production, necessities (such as grains), and strategic goods relatively low and allowed prices of manufactured and consumable goods to respond to demand. The macroeconomic conception of an economy behind the market-socialist model (the "Keynesian revolution") did not inform its institutional construction, nor does the model pay much attention to the goals assigned to the Yugoslav state (the federal government): directed development for structural change in economic capacity, and management of foreign relations (including defense).

Part of the confusion lies in what to call a socialist economy that is not a planned economy. The planning system that emerged by 1952 was only a set of policy goals for production and investment in the coming plan period (goals were set annually until 1956 and at five-year intervals thereafter, but with interruptions) that were supposed to define credit, price, and foreign-trade policies, and a forecast of the actual growth path of economic aggregates based on the production plans of firms and development plans of localities and republics. It was not a set of commands, quantity controls, or directed allocations, nor was it the apparatus to effect them,[14] although the government did resort to ad hoc quantity controls when the need for immediate response precluded use of financial instruments (which took longer to show results). Enterprises were operationally autonomous, although subject to substantial regulation; but the monetary system did continue to operate on the same principles as monetary planning in the Soviet system, including nonconvertibility, accounting principles in the public sector,[15] and attempts both to maintain social control over money and finance and to capture resources from the private sector and foreign sources for public use in order to insure public determination of investment. A nonplanned socialist economy is not necessarily a market-socialist economy, and its principles of allocation may even vary across time and economic sectors (as we saw in the previous chapter).[16]

Another part of the confusion over characterizing the Yugoslav system arose from the system's use of many market elements and from its frequent references to the market, references that in fact had varying mean-

---

count from a Chinese author, which parallels more directly the Yugoslav practice (Jiang, "The Theory of an Enterprise-Based Economy").

[14] The planning commissions became advisory committees to republican governments, and the plan's goals were not legally binding.

[15] See Lavigne, "The Creation of Money by the State Bank of the USSR," for a clear discussion of this system. Portes, "Central Planning and Monetarism," gives an interesting interpretation of the relation between this system of monetary planning and monetarism.

[16] This variation and the unsettled character of the Yugoslav system in the 1950s are made particularly clear in Ward's doctoral dissertation, "From Marx to Barone." On the argument that the Yugoslav system was a form of market socialism, see also Nove, *The Economics of Feasible Socialism;* and Bideleux, *Communism and Development.*

ing for different people and at different times. Most commonly, the *market* meant the operation of the "law of value" on which Kidrič insisted, siding with Lenin against Bukharin in arguing that the "equilibrium conditions of reproduction" would hold under socialism as well.[17] They believed, namely, that to balance demand and supply one must stimulate supply as well as, in the short run, limit demand and ration supply; for that, consumer demand in retail markets (with free prices for finished goods) was fundamental as the economic incentive to producers. The enthusiasm for the "market" at the first congress of the new professional association of economists in 1952 was for such "economic laws" (and an increased role for their science),[18] although some economists, like many party leaders at the third plenum in December 1949, worried that it might be too soon because of severe shortages.[19] But the *market* could also mean what Kidrič called the "capitalist principles of accumulation" (commercial profit) and "economic coercion," which would continue to govern economic behavior in relations with Western markets and in the private sector of individual producers. In a third use of the word, *market* was in fact applied to decentralization, perhaps on the assumption that ever less central direction and ever more autonomy for actors within the economy necessarily meant that market principles would emerge. It was this idea that led teams of economic advisers from the IMF to insist on decentralization as a Trojan horse for marketization (especially in the 1950s and 1960s), and it could explain in part why each IMF program was followed by further decentralization of some kind.[20] But decentralization in the sense of subsidiarity was also critical to the leaders' idea that the incentive of individual economic interest operated better when the decision making and supervision necessary to macroeconomic stabilization were closer to those who actually produced. Checks and balances operated best within budgetary units, where financial accountability was assessed, not in the society at large. Decentralization along budgetary lines (according to work units that produced market value), profit-and-loss accounting in the economy, and balanced budgets in "nonproductive" activ-

[17] See Sutela, "Ideology as a Means of Economic Debate."

[18] Gorupić, "Uloga ekonomista u našoj privredi." This theme weaves through the economic journals in 1952–54 and also through the discussion on employment policy in 1954 (reported in Has, "Društveno-ekonomski osvrt").

[19] Author's interviews in 1982 with economists who were present at the third plenum; see *Ekonomski Pregled* 3, nos. 1–2 (1952). This concern is one of the reasons that Milenkovitch argues that the rapid dismantling of planning in 1950–52 must have been political (*Plan and Market in Yugoslav Economic Thought*, 73–77).

[20] Jan Mladek, personal communication in Washington, D.C., 1987; Sanja Crnković, personal communication at the Institute of Economics in Zagreb, on her studies of this pattern, 1982. See also Mladek, Šturc, and Wyczalkowski, "The Change in the Yugoslav Economic System."

ities did not mean that this "hard budget constraint" was achieved by a market-clearing price mechanism or was immune to contradiction for other policy priorities. They did mean that macroeconomic equilibrium was conceived as a sum of microeconomic behaviors.

The political links among the socialist units of the economy were not horizontal, but vertical, as Dragoljub Jovanović complained in the debate over farmers' cooperatives in 1946. The institutions were based on Kardelj's image of autonomous socialist communities—whether a village-based cooperative, a commune, or an organization of associated labor (workplace and unit of account)—linked by representation in assemblies and the party hierarchy. Economically, autonomous producers were linked partly through the hierarchy of the banking system and monetary control, and partly through cooperative contracts. These bilateral relations were primarily for the exchange of raw materials and industrial goods between farmers' cooperatives and public-sector enterprises, so as to bind private suppliers to the social sector and eventually incorporate them into it; or, after the mid-1970s, for investment and joint ventures between enterprises in the developed republics and enterprises in the republics or regions classified as less-developed. But there was also horizontal consultation among functional groups within territorial units. For example, the chambers of commerce and industry, the unions, and local governments consulted on incomes policies, and producers within an industrial branch conferred (cartel-like) over price policy, rationing priorities when essential inputs were scarce, and economic-policy recommendations. But these organized "interests" would then aggregate territorially through the hierarchy of the federal system to participate in policy-making or to implement central policies locally. Goods would naturally flow across borders, and there was a divisive debate over citizenship before the constituent assembly, in order to facilitate labor mobility, chose to make Yugoslavs citizens of the country as well as of their republic (as in Swiss cantons) or their ethnic nationality and country (as in the USSR).[21] Nonetheless, the budgetary system intended limits on the horizontal flow of money and credit; and, as the official complaints from the labor ministry in 1949 show, there continued to be political resistance to border crossings by producers or localities to find cheaper sources of labor or higher profits (in contrast to the purchase of raw or finished goods). The

---

[21] I thank Carol Lilly for information about this debate. Hondius elaborates on the history of citizenship laws and their outcome in 1946 (*The Yugoslav Community of Nations*, chaps. 1–3); he makes clear that citizenship in a republic was considered primary because the federal government did not maintain citizenship lists separate from republican rolls (184). But he appears to be unaware of the debate that led to the reason for what he calls "federal state allegiance." This debate occurred, of course, before the leaders' strategy was politically secure (before the 1946 politbureau meeting and 1948–49 purge).

leaders' concern for social stability through settling labor and households was, however, superseded by the mid-1950s by local and republican governments' concept of economic interest, which aimed to protect their tax base and prevent "expatriation" of profits or the influx of unwanted migrants.

One might say that the Yugoslav system was a mixture of liberal and socialist assumptions about economic behavior and goals for economic and political life. Organizationally, it was a hybrid,[22] based on an idea of social-property rights that were simultaneously economic and political; its methods of allocating economic resources and of making and enforcing public choices relied on neither the competitive price mechanism of capitalist society nor the planning bureaucracy of statist society, but on the idea of democratic consultation and agreement among autonomous and self-interested but also cooperative property owners (governments and the work collectives with rights to manage social assets) on common rules for value and distribution.[23]

EMPLOYMENT

The new constitutional order was based on the authority of labor—"all power derived from working people," which meant persons employed in producing value. The constitutional right to work was not a right to a job, but a right of persons already employed to participate in decisions on the use of assets they helped create and to receive an income on the basis of their labor.[24] Guarantees of this right to work lay not in governmental policy but in the property rights guaranteeing subsistence (and thus preventing the unemployment associated with proletarianization) that underlay the leaders' two-sector strategy. By law, firms in the *public sector* had

[22] In describing the Hungarian system this way, Hankiss assumes that it was a composite of inherited systems, spontaneous changes, and ad hoc adjustments ("In Search of a Paradigm"). There was some of that also in the Yugoslav case, but I believe that far more pattern can be discerned in these two cases of reformed socialism if one starts with the ideas of economic and political strategy that guided them both—with some identifiable differences, such as that one was a unitary and the other a federal system and the differences in agricultural policy and organization resulting from the differences in agricultural organization at the time of the formation of domestic political alliances by their respective Communist parties (I thank Juhasz Pal for this information on Hungary). The Yugoslav economist Branko Horvat approached the issue in the 1960s from the standpoint of the organization of authority in a system designed to eliminate bureaucracy and hierarchy, which he portrayed with a circular chart.

[23] According to Kardelj, the key social question was how national income (sometimes called surplus product) gets distributed. For one of his numerous statements of this point, see *Problemi naše socijalističke izgradnje* 2:133. In the language of social-choice theory, this is the contractual (in contrast to the exploitative) concept of the state.

[24] Krajger, "Dohodak preduzeća u našem sistemu."

to pay the guaranteed wage first, after material costs were paid. This minimum wage was calculated in terms of the prevailing prices of a bundle of
basic commodities (an index that the government adjusted downward
when stabilization pressure was intense). Laws also required firms to
maintain a reserve fund for basic wages and to contribute to a commune
solidarity fund on which firms could draw temporarily if they were short
of cash to pay the basic wage. Adjustments to the business results of a firm
were made within the annual accounting period by varying income rather
than jobs, until a decision to rationalize led to dismissals or transfers. The
private sector, as a reserve to collect and release labor for the public
sector as the latter adjusted, was guaranteed subsistence by government
regulations to protect smallholdings and shops against the concentration
and differentiation that this sector's capitalist principles would otherwise
effect on landholdings and private capital.

The key to employment expansion, and therefore to moving persons
from the private to the public sector, was rising productivity. Although
productivity was defined in its Marxist sense of declining socially necessary labor time, and although social control over investment was intended
to expand capacity and productivity, the system of industrial relations
assumed that the primary source of growth was rising labor productivity
in existing firms, supplemented by local initiative. In his parliamentary
address introducing "workers' control," Tito spoke of the "particular importance for the councils of the working collectives to use their influence
to ensure as rational a distribution of labour as possible, so as not to allow
unproductive labour to become ensconced in their enterprises . . . [and
to] prevent the infectious disease known as bureaucracy becoming en-
demic in our country."[25] In a 1951 closed-door session of the Economic
Council (which was assigned what little federal concern for employment
would remain), Kidrič specified this right to fire as well as hire: "An enterprise can execute a rationalization in the interests of savings and the goal
of realizing greater production and, as a consequence of that, can fire
surplus labor."[26] The party organization (*aktiv*) in the firm was tasked
primarily with teaching workers the "habit of intensification." If a firm
failed to cover costs and depreciation with receipts, it would have to accept the force of "economic law" and close shop. Similarly, private artisanal and farming households would release their "surplus labor" for
industrial, public-sector employment when they could not sustain family
members with their own production and the free-market earnings that
constituted the household "budget." Like workers, they would be taught
by "economic coercion" to calculate the use of their own labor in indus-

[25] Tito, *Selected Speeches and Articles, 1941–1961*, 111.
[26] Mirjana Pavlović, "Boris Kidrič o principima tržišne ekonomije," 1188. The first law on
bankruptcy was introduced in 1954 (Ward, "From Marx to Barone," chap. 1).

trial rather than agrarian terms: they would perceive a direct relation between their consumption preferences and their contribution to real (and realized) output.

Labor's price (incomes) in the public sector should, it was believed, be a direct measure of its contribution to productivity (in the real sense of output above what workers consumed, and in value terms defined by savings on the costs of production), not a measure of its scarcity and bargaining power on an external market. In fact, labor turnover and competition among firms for workers only raised costs of production without contributing to increased output. In place of labor mobility, there would be a contract with a work community for long-term, stable membership; and in place of the market wage, there would be legislated job classifications and wage scales to reward those who remained with the firm (the criterion of seniority), increased their skills (the criterion of certified qualifications), or took on managerial responsibility. In accordance with the principle of self-management, each firm's rule book on wages, although based on republic-level legislation on jobs and wages, had to be approved by the workers' council; the proportion of profits (also affected by accounting regulations) distributed as wages and social benefits would be discussed by the work collective at the end-of-year accounting; and managers' proposals for hiring or firing employees would be submitted for approval to the management board (and eventually the workers' council) along with the plan for production and modernization for the following year.

The new wage system that passed the assembly in December 1951 and was in practice by April 1952 formally ended all central determination of wage norms and labor quotas (although the system had never applied to more than a handful of federal industries).[27] Already in the first round of free decisions by workers' councils in 1950–52, skilled production workers on the management board did not protest firings of unskilled workers (who "contributed less to productivity"), and workers' councils approved the wage scales developed by engineering staffs that gave raises to administrative and technical staff and skilled workers and then cut the wages of unskilled workers.[28] The resulting wage explosion led authorities to backtrack and assign regulatory authority to local governments, including the authority to set a firm's statutory wage rates (with the "active participation" of the union organization and the firm's management). In

[27] Wage norms remained on the statute books until 1955, not as the guaranteed wage and profit share that succeeded them, but as a minimum wage and proportional (piece) rates for output.

[28] Ward, "From Marx to Barone," 160–65, 169. See also his discussion in "Industrial Decentralization in Yugoslavia" on the separate treatment of administrators, which protected them from dismissal.

1955, the last distinctions between wages, salaries, and profits fell. Wages were redefined as income; they were no longer considered a cost of production but were paid after material costs, and they were composed of three separate elements: (1) output norms, differentiated as incentives to productivity; (2) bonuses for contributions above the average (norm), measured for production workers by increased effort, cost efficiencies, or technical innovations; in services, by budgetary savings; and for managerial and technical staff, by market profits; and (3) a share in net profits, distributed at the end of the year after the firm had paid taxes and contributions to social services and employee benefits (for example, the housing fund). Basic wage rates were set for each industry by the economic chambers (*privredne komore*, the association of producers' branch associations), unions, and republican governments, and the profit share in individual wages might well be negative—a reduction in income over several months until budgets recovered losses and were again balanced.

Responsibility for preventing unemployment lay with the unions and local governments. Managers were obliged to consult the union if they planned to dismiss more than five workers at once, and when a shortage of cash to pay minimum wages was clearly only temporary, they could draw on the commune's solidarity fund to prevent unnecessary layoffs and dismissals. Because the problem of unemployment was viewed in terms of the pace at which persons from agriculture could get jobs in industry and in terms of the redundancies caused by a firm's rationalization, it was assumed to be primarily a question of local judgment and capacity: localities should assist firms in finding new labor and help persons temporarily made redundant; and where the pace of aggregate economic growth was too slow, they should intervene to develop smaller local industries and services that would be both labor-intensive and consumption-oriented. The regulatory and tax powers granted local governments were extensive: to license all productive and trade activities of the private sector; supervise the accounts of local enterprises and hold managers of public-sector firms legally responsible for these accounts, assuming emergency authority over internal restructuring if necessary to forestall bankruptcy; use revenue from the profits tax on public-sector enterprises and from the income tax on private-sector households to finance new enterprises, grant credits and guarantee bank loans for firms wishing to expand, and invest in local housing, roads, sewers, elementary schools, and other infrastructural needs; formulate social policy; and even regulate prices and wages if needed to stabilize the local economy.

Because the leaders saw frictional unemployment as normal, they reopened the "labor mediation bureaus" (employment service) in 1951 to aid dismissed workers in finding new jobs and to reduce the "long-term disharmony" between the needs of firms and the supply of labor. Open unemployment was acknowledged, but as a matter of social, not economic, policy; it was thus assigned to the Council for Public Health and Social Policy and to the province of social insurance for the "involuntary, temporarily unemployed," including health insurance for those registered as looking for work. This attitude was thoroughly consistent with the overall strategy. No charity, sympathy, or welfare for the unemployed was appropriate, for it would only reduce the resources going to real accumulation and give monies to people who were not contributing to real output. Moreover, as Tito put it in his attack on the system of guaranteed provisions in January 1949, "budgets create dependence."[29] Only persons who had been employed for a minimum period were eligible for unemployment compensation, since they had contributed to the tax on the wage fund of enterprises that financed it; and it was paid only for six months, on the assumption that reemployment might take that long. But if they had alternative means of support—in practice, it was usually women and youth, whose "families" (employed male heads of households) were assumed to provide for them, that were considered to have such support—they were eligible only for health insurance because their subsistence was not threatened, and they were therefore not considered truly unemployed.[30]

By the same reasoning, public works were not considered an appropriate response to unemployment because they were not "economic"—they drained budgets rather than earning their way. Although the volunteer labor brigades mobilized the unemployed in 1945 and 1948–49, these were seen not as social measures, to be reinstituted when open unemployment rose in 1952, but as economic measures—a source of labor for short-term demands for capital construction and a way to protect the public sector from resorting to a policy of extensive employment—and as an instrument of cultural revolution for the young. Tito sought an end to the brigades from 1946 on, first for fear that the deteriorating physical conditions of the camps interfered with this revolutionary objective, and then because the brigades' demand on supply stores threatened supplies for the army and exacerbated budgetary deficits and inflation. Because they consumed more wage goods than they produced, they had in effect be-

---

[29] Tito, at the second plenum of the CPY central committee, in Petranović, Končar, and Radonjić, *Sednice*, 93.

[30] When the economic assumptions about productivity combined with the cultural prejudices of the period, however, and a rash of dismissals in 1951–53 fell largely on war invalids, women, and unskilled workers, the government chose to ignore its grant of autonomy to firms. It decreed prohibitions against the dismissal of workers needing "special consideration of personal, family, and other circumstances" and, as early as April 12, 1952, imposed fines on enterprises that fired women because they were pregnant (Maričić, "Neki problemi organizacije," 663).

come institutions of "welfare" (ironically, given the horrendous decline in youth health).[31] Finally, the employment bureaus had to be self-managing as well—free to manage as they saw fit the local grants they received, but responsible for balancing their budget.

This approach to unemployment gave the employment bureaus[32] a dual identity: as the local social-welfare agency, they determined eligibility for unemployment compensation, health-care rights, and grants for retraining and for travel to prospective jobs; and as the agent of society's interest in rational employment, they were to collect and publish data on jobs and to work with local firms and policymakers to improve employment opportunities. Their location, however, reflects the system's organization around producers. Firms were the best judge of employment, and the bureaus, like the state labor offices in 1948–50, were services for firms in their search for labor. They could contract labor for public-sector firms only, and officials recommended locating them at the point of labor demand, not supply—where industries were concentrated and where their "economic interest" would generate links between the bureaus and local authorities in neighboring areas in which employment levels were lower and where "by nature there ought to exist surplus labor." Exceptions accommodated, instead of correcting, the developmental conditions of the period: where there were no professionals trained to perform its tasks (a problem everywhere outside of Slovenia and parts of Serbia), a bureau could not be established; on the other hand, the very poor state of inter-district transportation links in the less-developed republics, especially Macedonia and Montenegro, required the proliferation of bureaus (despite the administrative costs) to every locality, so that workers were effectively assured their rights to unemployment assistance and so that temporary unemployment did not prevent people from continuing to live where they wished.

Local approaches to unemployment varied substantially in these first years. In Croatia and Bosnia, employment bureaus favored the first strategy: setting up in an industrial center or in a locality where industry was concentrated and then creating a network with the bureaus of three or four neighboring districts in which a rural labor surplus prevailed. In Macedonia, district employment bureaus frequently faced the problem of substantial seasonal unemployment; they sought to resolve it by collective contracts with enterprises in other republics, sending hundreds of workers to construction jobs lasting under two months. In Serbia, many

---

[31] Tito, at the third plenum of the CPY central committee, in Petranović, Končar, and Radonjić, *Sednice,* 433–34.

[32] In a later stage of self-management, these were called "communities of interest for employment."

local bureaus organized conferences with local businesses to obtain "much greater understanding and willingness to cooperate" on the part of firms, and to "take greater account of firms' real needs for workers and staff with specific skills and qualifications." In the Serbian town of Niš, the bureau engaged local firms to organize multiservice workshops to employ unemployed skilled artisans, and it called meetings of the unemployed to ask them to establish priorities for who should be hired first. A number of other districts also invited the unemployed to discuss solutions for their employment. The republic-level employment service in Croatia devised a plan with the cooperation of management boards of public enterprises to solve two problems at once by substituting female labor for male: creating jobs for women and a supply of "essentially technically qualified and physically able" men needed for priority investment projects. Otherwise, republican governments were accused of doing little to assist coordination; even though some published regular bulletins of employment data (Serbia, Croatia, and Slovenia), the information was of little use because it was incomplete, obsolete, or inaccurate.[33]

The bureaus' resources were hardly in proportion to their mandate, which was to "eliminate the consequences of structural and long-term disharmony." In addition to the shortage of trained professionals and usable data, the budgetary constraints of their self-management status led frequently to choices that further localized activities. Outlays legally required for the costs of travel and lodging for job searches in other localities were often considered wasteful because the bureaus estimated the risk that jobs would not materialize as too high, thus also making the collection of data on job openings of little use.[34] Furthermore, unemployed persons hesitated before looking for work away from home because of the serious shortage of housing, without which one could not accept new work at any wage.[35] Because new housing construction was a local responsibility, financed by a tax on the wage fund of those currently employed in local public-sector enterprises, this problem also had no ready solution. The number of technical training schools declined sharply after 1950–51 for the same reason—local governments saw no reason to spend scarce funds on training workers who might move elsewhere; and even though job vacancies remained because the specific skills that local firms sought could not be found in the area, local governments invested

---

[33] Maričić, "Neki problemi organizacije."

[34] Ibid.

[35] In November 1947, Minister of Labor Vicko Krstulović told the fifth plenum of the central committee of the unions, "The most difficult problem [in the employment of new labor] is that of housing. Until that is resolved, we cannot solve the labor problem. It is one of the main reasons for people leaving their jobs, and the problem of instability in the labor supply" ("Stalno podizanje proizvodnosti rada," 194).

instead in schools for general education.[36] The managerial side of self-
management—the government of social-service institutions by a management board composed of representatives of "social interests" (the staff,
local firms, and local administration)—did not appear to overcome these
constraints with cooperation and initiative, as was intended. In Slovenia,
the boards reportedly dealt largely with clerical tasks; the Split (Croatia)
authorities rejected the idea of a social-management board entirely; and
most boards found their time taken up with hearing appeals from persons
denied eligibility for unemployment compensation by the bureau.

THE STATE

The economic reforms of 1950–51 did not resolve political disagreements
over methods of economic allocation or political organization—despite
the political purge of the inner circle and of the entire party, which left
large numbers of persons languishing in prison on Goli Otok and in central Bosnia and sent many others into permanent retirement or exile.[37] A
revised constitution, because of quarrels over it, took more than a year to
negotiate through committees and the national assembly. In December
1951, Kardelj instructed Moša Pijade, the ideological elder of the prewar
party, to prepare this revised constitution on the basis of Kardelj's suggestions and consultations with a committee of legal experts. Intending to
bring it to the assembly in June (probably for the symbolic echoes with
June 1948 and 1950), Kardelj presented the draft to the politbureau in
April 1952. Pijade, substituting for an ill Kardelj, took it to the central
committee on May 27, where he was bombarded with criticisms and suggested amendments rather than the veneration and applause one might
have expected. Even Tito admitted indecision on several matters, including the choice between direct and indirect elections, and Pijade was unable to present a revised draft to the constitutional commission of the
national assembly until November. While Tito and Kardelj expressed increasing exasperation over the character of debate in the press (including
the party newspaper, *Borba*) and the public's proposals (which "smell of
enemies" but are "prettily masked"), once the path of public discussion

[36] Itsidor Izrael, speaking at the discussion on the labor force held at the Belgrade Institute of Economics in 1954 (Has, "Društveno-ekonomski osvrt," 157–58).

[37] Aleksandar Ranković later admitted that fifty-one thousand persons had been caught
up in the purge and either killed, imprisoned, or sentenced to hard labor (Petranović, Končar, and Radonjić, *Sednice*). See also Banac's study of this group, who were collectively
labeled "Cominformists" (*ibeovci*) even though only a certain portion of them actually sided
with the Cominform resolution or Stalin (*With Stalin against Tito*).

had been taken, it had to be allowed to run its negotiated course. Closure was reached only by postponing definition of the property system.[38]

Although obliged by the party statute adopted at the fifth congress in July 1948 to call a meeting again in 1951, Tito did not open the question until the fifth plenum of the central committee on May 27, 1952—and not for statutory reasons, but because they were "completing our Five-Year Plan" and nearing completion of the "entirety of our internal social construction, and particularly the question of power [vlast]"; and despite repeated assurances that it would convene on October 19, the sixth congress finally met on November 7–9. Indecision delayed a new party program, although Djilas admitted that the current one "obviously . . . no longer fits."[39] With the exception of minor "corrections" in the program, such as extending the period between party congresses beyond three years, a new one was not adopted until 1957.

The sixth party congress did affirm the political defeat of all those who had argued for centralized allocation of scarce professionals, skilled labor, and consumer goods, and it reinforced the tactic of justifying or combating on political grounds—above all, nationalism—what were in fact choices between economic models and growth strategies, and the assignment of rights and powers each entailed. Speeches at the congress gave short shrift to the economic and political reforms and to domestic policy (despite the continuation in 1952–53 of extraordinary defense expenditures and stabilization austerities required by reorientation to Western markets and military and food aid), so as not to distract from its main theme: Tito's sermon on their relations with the Soviet Union and the Cominform and the importance of their national independence. Where Hebrang had been tarred with Croat nationalism,[40] Žujović with treason,[41] and all dissenters and waverers with "Cominformist" loyalty to Stalin rather than Tito, the charge was now Serb nationalism—the penalty

---

[38] Discussion at the fifth plenum of the CPY central committee, in Petranović, Končar, and Radonjić, Sednice, 661.

[39] Ibid., 646.

[40] In Kardelj's speech at the fifth party congress in July 1948; see also Banac, With Stalin against Tito. In addition to the many quarrels over Hebrang's leadership of the Croat party during the war, the main examples cited of his nationalism were his insistence, while he was minister for industry in the provisional government, on a better exchange rate in the purchase of Croatian wartime currency and his insistence, as head of the planning commission, that a "Slovene" aluminum factory be moved closer to its source of bauxite ore, which happened to be in Croatia.

[41] There is much evidence that Žujović was reporting to the Soviet embassy in Belgrade, though the matter is in dispute. The argument here is that the more consequential conflict was over substantive policy, and that these disagreements—rather than the charges of treason—were far more significant for Yugoslav development.

being a purge (as of Rade Žigić and Duško Brkić, Serbs from Croatia and allies of Hebrang who argued at the second plenum in January 1949 that central allocation of scarce professionals was economically more rational and that decentralization would inevitably demand *more* administrators)[42] or marginalization (as of Pavle Gregorić, who thought health care should be a question of economic investment and federal concern, not just social policy and local concern).[43]

No proposals for central solutions to the question of labor—whether shortage or surplus—ever again received a hearing. The antagonism to state economic power in the liberal Marxism of the northwest parties and the definitive 1928 vote on the national question against the party central-izers prevailed, and the party was renamed the League of Communists of Yugoslavia (LCY), to signify its confederal essence. Tito had insisted that the sixth congress be held in Zagreb—"in the spirit of our decentralism," Milovan Djilas explained to the central committee, to which Tito added, "because of the role of the working class of Zagreb in the prewar period."[44]

The slogan for the labor revisions of 1950 that aimed to make the state lean again and to return to the land or the family unskilled labor, peas-ants, and peasant-workers employed in the public sector (the "fluctuators" who speculated with their labor)—a slogan as well for the workers' coun-cils that would instill habits of labor rationalization—was "the consolida-tion of the working class." The congress affirmed it by convening on a Sunday—"so that," Tito insisted, "it can be arranged a little more ceremo-niously, and more delegations of workers will be able to come."[45] Beyond such ceremony, workers were to focus their economic and political inter-ests within their "working communities" and to view their common inter-ests in the struggle for labor productivity and restraint on demands for higher wages and benefits within its bounds.

The vision of the state in the Slovene model was that of the national democratic revolution by a substitute bourgeoisie discussed in chapter 2. The state would defend territorial integrity and national property against

---

[42] Petranović, Končar, and Radonjić, *Sednice*, 144–50. On the still-unresolved questions surrounding the case of Žigić and Brkić, including the Lika-Kordun affair in the summer of 1950 over the Cazin revolt, see Roksandić, *Srbi u Hrvatskoj*, 147–50.

[43] At the second plenum of the CPY central committee (Petranović, Končar, and Radon-jić, *Sednice*, 254–59); see also his remarks at the third plenum on training new doctors (336–39) and his warning at the fifth plenum about the "unusual difficulties" in Switzerland re-garding health care "because they have no central authority that decides" and "each canton is a state of its own" (662).

[44] At the fifth plenum of the CPY central committee, in Petranović, Končar, and Radon-jić, *Sednice*, 647.

[45] Ibid.

foreign occupation, ownership, or dictate. As a coercive, feudal, mercantilist, and bureaucratic force, it would disappear. Assemblies of delegates from a "league" of Communists would debate policy goals, and assemblies of producers' representatives would decide on the distribution of monies they created. Central, societywide institutions would consist of a bank, an assembly, and a party. All other functions would be "socialized": in the shift in this concept that Charles Gulick attributes to Karl Renner, it meant that the "functions previously performed by the state (police, courts, government intervention) [would be] 'regained' by society."[46] Public services should be financed separately, as institutions independent of state budgets.

Producers had to control finance, not financiers producers. Therefore, the tasks of commerce and finance should, it was believed, be integrated into firms; income from market power (whether due to market advantage or to natural monopolies, such as in mining) should be taxed for provision of public goods;[47] and interest charges on money advances should be low and stable to reduce currency arbitrage. Since bond or capital markets could give governments leverage over producers, opening the way to financial crises, and currency convertibility would open the door to foreign definition of domestic values produced, both were abjured. Instead, the system of production incentives and financial accountability meant that economic interest and political right had to be joined, just as in the workers' councils. There could be no taxation without representation of those who produced value, and fiscal illusion should be avoided by earmarking all budgets by their purpose and preventing any later shift of monies to purposes or territories other than what the creators of those funds (elected representatives of taxpayers) had intended. The federal division of the budget, as minister of social policy Anton Kržišnik explained it in 1945,[48] and the autonomy of social-insurance funds (and later of all social services) were to prevent such drift and give political control over funds to those who had a direct economic interest in their rational use. The same principle would later be used to prevent the investment of

---

[46] Gulick, *Austria from Habsburg to Hitler* 1:222 n. 120, citing Renner's *Wege der Verwirklichung.*

[47] Bakarić spent much time on the problem of rents in agriculture (see "O zemljišnom rentu"), and it was decided quite early to abandon a tax on natural monopolies because of the difficulty in calculating it. But the principle remained in wage regulation, where net personal incomes substantially above average were taxed at a progressive rate above the industry average—not to equalize incomes, as is usually asserted, but on the assumption that high incomes must include windfall profits and would therefore distort direct incentives (which is a different issue from whether the average citizen reacted to such incomes with a populist sense of a "just wage").

[48] See chap. 3, p. 72.

child-allowance funds in day-care centers or the investment of the local reserve fund for wages in new workplaces;[49] by the same logic, subsidies to export producers had to come from customs duties.

To implement this innovation in producers' control over finance capital, the 1953 constitution created a second chamber in all legislative bodies where elected delegates from public-sector work collectives would debate and review all economic-policy documents (prepared by technical staff in the executive branch)—the state budget, the social plan and annual resolution on the economy, tax laws, rulings of the price office, and decisions on subsidies, tax credits, and premiums. Kidrič introduced this idea to the fifth plenum in May 1952 with great enthusiasm—these councils of producers would realize the "dictatorship of the proletariat," taking the place of the bureaucracies of planning and finance.[50] Seats would be apportioned by industry, according to each one's contribution to national wealth (a contribution measured at the time by the proportions set for that sector in the social plan of the upcoming period). But given the great disparities in industrial development at the time, the strict application of this electoral principle would give unfair advantage to the more-developed republics—with the result, Kidrič warned, that at the federal level the chamber would be composed almost entirely of Slovene and Croat workers. Therefore, proportional representation would be determined by wealth within each republic, but each republican delegation would receive equal representation in the assembly (this corporate principle of republic quotas, called *nacionalni ključ*—literally, the "national key"—applied after the 1963 constitution to positions in federal government organs as well).[51]

In time, specialized, autonomous investment funds proliferated, each managed by representatives of producers with tax obligations and therefore interests in that specialty from each republic (for example, delegates of the League of Agricultural Chambers managed the Fund for Agricultural Modernization). Social services funded from tax monies were managed by a board with trilateral representation—from government

[49] See the complaint of Milan Vujačić in 1967 in "Dečija zaštita ili zaštita fondova."

[50] Petranović, Končar, and Radonjić, *Sednice*, 677–79.

[51] The principles of representation, electoral laws, and organization of parliaments changed with each constitution (there were new ones in 1953, 1963, and 1974 and draft amendments in 1987). The 1963 constitution, for example, replaced the councils of producers with four functional chambers—for the economy, education and culture, social welfare and health, and organizational-political questions—to which delegates from workplaces were still elected; the federal chamber was composed of two sections—delegates from municipal assemblies and delegates of republican and provincial assemblies. See Hondius, *The Yugoslav Community of Nations*, 286–91; and Burg, *Conflict and Cohesion in Social Yugoslavia*, passim. On the changes in electoral laws, see Seroka and Smiljković, *Political Organizations in Socialist Yugoslavia*.

(representing society's interests) and public-sector firms (which had financial interests as the creators of the value taxed) as well as employees of the service. Banks reflected the cooperative principle more directly, being managed after 1964 by representatives of their depositors—that is, enterprises—with votes in proportion to their deposits. By 1958, the territorial principle of the federal system had priority over all sectoral organization of capital—banks, funds, transfers.

Autonomy for producers and socialization of state functions radically narrowed the sphere of public choice to questions of distribution and redistribution of monies. It was essential that the state maintain the value of the currency, but disputes remained over how best to organize a banking system to do that.[52] Because a stable value depended in large part on the financial discipline of producers, the government could regulate principles of distribution (such as for wages), supervise budgetary accounts, and adjust accounting rules when that discipline was lacking (for example, it could determine what could be counted as a cost, establish the order in which obligations were to be paid, or make changes in the reserve requirements and depreciation allowances). It had no instrument of deficit finance or other countercyclical policy to wield power over macroeconomic aggregates; it could only cut money in circulation (for example, by adjusting the turnover tax, altering jurisdictions for public expenditures, setting higher requirements for self-financing or cash reserves, performing end-of-year tax reassessments to balance government budgets, or altering the exchange rate with foreign currencies) and raise production incentives.

The federal government, as Žujović complained, had no ownership of productive activities (except temporarily in 1948 and 1949) and therefore no revenue "from production."[53] Its revenues came directly from its jurisdictions: the turnover tax, to regulate aggregate demand and supply on an all-Yugoslav market;[54] customs duties, to manage the foreign-trade balance; foreign loans guaranteed by the central bank; and a portion of enterprise taxes granted to the federal budget from the republics.[55] Because of this responsibility for the "market" (final consumption), the lower cham-

---

[52] See Gedeon, "Monetary Disequilibrium and Bank Reform Proposals in Yugoslavia," on the various schools, ranging from proponents of an independent central bank to those using the real-bills doctrine to defend decentralized, cooperative banks (the latter school was largely based in Zagreb).

[53] The constitution gave specific powers to the federation and all residual powers to the republics.

[54] The turnover tax was replaced between 1964 and 1967 by a retail sales tax on consumer goods, for budgetary revenue more than as an instrument of price policy (Horvat, "Yugoslav Economic Policy in the Post-War Period," 237).

[55] In 1986, the last quarrel over financing for the federal budget produced a reform that limited its financing to federal revenues only.

ber of the federal assembly (the Federal Chamber) had jurisdiction over questions of labor and social welfare and its delegates came from local governments; and localities whose per capita income was below the countrywide average and whose personal income tax was thus insufficient received grants-in-aid from the federal budget.[56] The upper chamber—the Chamber of Republics and Provinces, with representatives from republican assemblies—reviewed the social plan, federal budget, and economic policy, in accordance with the return in 1950 to republican jurisdiction over transportation, energy, and education alongside light manufacturing, agriculture, and labor. Businesses and farms in the private sector, which paid fees and income tax to localities, had corresponding political rights to elect delegates to local assemblies. Persons in private employ and households could also, as a "political manifestation" of citizenship "most significant after that of elections," contribute to state revenues in bond issues—such as the second National Bond for the Five-Year Plan of June 12, 1950 (the first was in June 1948), organized by the popular front and trade union in all branches.[57]

Socialization of the state—its "withering away"—implied devolution of its administrative functions to lower governments, civilian supervision through assemblies representing property owners (governments and public-sector workplaces), and as much as possible the automatic operation of "economic laws" through self-managed budgets. Conditions in the 1950s, however, required some state intervention, administrative powers, and selective credit. Socialization would be a process adjusted to "material conditions"; but such conditions, as Kidrič explained the application of proportional representation of enterprises *within* republics, required supplemental adjustments to the long-term goal, not a change of institutions or their underlying assumptions. These temporary conditions were two: the developmental disproportions in the economy among sectors and regions, and a still-hostile world of atomic (later nuclear) powers, closed trade, and defense alliances. Thus industrialization required some redistribution of capital for investment in less-developed areas and sectors, and some administrative intervention—but not an apparatus. The General Investment Fund, financed at first by federal monies and later by

[56] These grants began in July 1964, when the communes became financially responsible for social services, although by 1967 responsibility had shifted to separate "self-managed communities of interest" for education, child care, child allowances, and other social services (see Turčinović, "Financing Socio-political Units"). In 1971, the federal chamber's jurisdiction was reduced to international treaties, courts, and the few other remaining federal responsibilities (Burg, *Conflict and Cohesion*).

[57] *Informativni Priručnik Jugoslavije*, 1950, 363–87. Subscription lasted until September.

a direct capital tax on republics,[58] would therefore be managed by republican governments. It would distribute monies from republics above the average in gross domestic product (a measure of development and also of market advantage that could be fairly taxed) to those below it, redefining republics and provinces as "more-developed" (richer) or "less-developed" (poorer).[59]

"Socialism in one country" also meant interacting in a world that was not socialist, so the federal government would retain responsibility for managing that interaction. Foreign trade would be liberalized gradually; foreign assistance would be needed for some time to supplement domestic savings; and national independence under conditions of hostility from the two ideological camps required trade diversification to lessen the vulnerabilities of 1946–50. Thus, while foreign-trade firms and other enterprises could engage directly in Western markets, the government would remain active in foreign trade because of its responsibility for debt repayment and therefore for implementing the conditionality programs for IMF credits; and it would have to negotiate official loans, many commercial credits, and bilateral trade agreements. In trade contracts with the clearing area of the Eastern bloc and in the bilateral exchanges more common with developing countries, it would have to serve as intermediary, advancing monies from the federal budget to domestic firms operating abroad (for example, in construction) until payment arrived. But the adjustment of the model to this global reality remained problematic; as Croat economist Ivo Perišin wrote in the early 1980s, the system regulating international economic relations and integration into the international division of labor was "still in the process of transformation."[60]

National-defense doctrine also combined two separate forces and principles: the goal of demobilization to civilian militias under the control of the republics, and the maintenance of an all-Yugoslav standing army under central command and federal jurisdiction. Prepared to deter and ultimately defend against a "massive nuclear attack of blinding power and aerial onslaught on Yugoslav territory,"[61] the army would also be

[58] At that time, it was renamed the Federal Fund for More Rapid Development of Less-Developed Republics and Regions.

[59] By 1975, enterprises were permitted to fulfill up to half of their contribution to their republic's obligation to the fund by investing directly in another enterprise—forming a joint venture—in a less-developed area. By 1980, the fund's board was even composed of delegates from enterprises (taxpayers) in order to give producers control over the former sphere of public investment itself, on the grounds that governments wasted enterprise tax monies in bad investments. In the early days of the fund, certain regions within a more-developed republic (as in the case of Croatia) could also receive aid.

[60] Perišin, "The Banking System and Monetary Policy."

[61] *Les forces armées de la RSFY*, 75, 79.

equipped with advanced light arms for conventional warfare to support the territorial defense forces, which would be prepared to wage a "people's war" with armed citizens defending localities. Accordingly, the federal budget included the pensions and benefits for veterans and salaries for the Yugoslav Peoples' Army (YPA); the secretary of national defense[62] controlled a federal council for trade in special goods and let contracts with domestic manufacturers for military equipment and supplies; and the federal government maintained a national food policy and energy controls for strategic self-sufficiency. The leaders' policy of neutrality between blocs included a one-third rule on all military equipment and armaments in order to guard against dependence on a single supplier (a rule that also kept them in several global markets): one-third of equipment and supplies could come from NATO countries (eventually primarily licenses), one-third could come from the Warsaw Pact (eventually heavy artillery and equipment from the USSR), and one-third must come from domestic production (under the budget of the federal secretary for national defense). The process of demilitarization of the economy that began in 1953 affected not only investments, plant conversion, and economic models, but also the police, state security, industrial (party) militias, and intelligence services. The devolution of these functions to civilian sectors or lower governments also occurred in stages, in response to changes in perceived security threats—in 1955–56, 1965–66, 1968, and 1974.[63]

In the leaders' view, unemployment was a short-term inevitability of development and problems in foreign trade, but it would not result from their system of social ownership and producer control once these conditions evaporated. Thus, although the social plan for investment specified a target for the rate of employment growth, it was only a residual of the

[62] Although cabinet ministers were still referred to colloquially as ministers, officially they were renamed secretaries, and their bureaus called secretariats instead of ministries, to symbolize their antibureaucratic and anti-Soviet revolution.

[63] For example, border tasks were divided between the YPA and the civilian police and customs officials in 1953; the National Army Act of 1955 appointed national-defense committees in republics and commissions in districts; the Internal Affairs Act of 1956 subdivided state security (intelligence, alien control, etc.) between the party and police; and the Basic Act on Internal Affairs of 1966 devolved to republics and localities administrative jurisdiction over state security, public peace, fire protection, passports, border control, and other matters. Alongside devolution came socialization: party militias became the core of the territorial defense forces in 1968, and after 1974 defense was incorporated into production. The center of the new defense system based on territorial militias—the committees for social self-protection of the "all-national defense" (općenarodna odbrana)—were the primary units of economic organization in the public-sector workplace, the basic organizations of associated labor (BOALs). See Bebler, "Yugoslavia's National Defense System"; Hondius, The Yugoslav Community of Nations; Dean, "Civil-Military Relations in Yugoslavia, 1971–75"; Les forces Armées; and chap. 7.

calculations made for projected growth in productivity and in total industrial output. This target was adjusted for expected demographic change,
on the argument that it was in society's interest to have the public sector
grow fast enough to employ youth as they entered the workforce. None of
the consultative or legislative institutions, of course, represented the unemployed. The unemployed did not fulfill the conditions for economic
decision makers because they created no value and therefore had neither
an "interest" in economic policy nor the right to participate. To the extent
that unemployment occurred, it was a question of local jurisdiction.

The LCY and the United Unions organization had the organizational
capacity to represent the virtual interests of the unemployed, in the sense
that social democracies with full employment are said to be successful
because unions are comprehensive, centralized peak organizations that
can implement proemployment policies chosen when the workers' party
controls the government. But the principle officially linking political voice
to economic interest, defined as belonging to those who created value and
therefore financed public goods, applied to these organizations of labor as
well. Membership in the union was in principle obligatory, but only for
those employed in the public sector (of whom 80 to 95 percent actually
joined, depending on the year and the industry). Although unified within
branch, then republic, and finally countrywide federation, and although
officially represented in policy forums that touched on employment and
incomes, the union was nonetheless confined in its official responsibilities
to implementing agreements and regulations on these matters within enterprises. Its control over elections of workers' councils and management
within the firm might influence hiring decisions, but it primarily had the
right to redistribute—to review and winnow the list of projected layoffs
prepared by technical staffs and to assist in the retraining or reassignment
of "surplus labor."

Membership in the LCY, in contrast to the union (and the Socialist
Alliance of Working People, which succeeded the Popular Front in 1950),
was limited to 5 to 7 percent of the population above the age of eighteen
and was subject to rigorous admission and continuation standards. The
party's task was not to represent separate interests of labor, which no
longer existed, but to provide the bond of common purpose that would
replace the coercive instruments of the state and "harmonize interests"
that might temporarily appear in conflict. As the state administration devolved or socialized, the party apparatus would as well: to the republics,
localities, and workplaces that would pay its members' salaries and social
insurance.[64] According to Djilas, Kidrič ended the party's special privi-

---

[64] The number of party functionaries was cut drastically in 1952–54 and again in the
second half of the 1960s; by 1964, republican party congresses were held before the all-

leges and stores in 1951 because they were an "anomaly of financial accounting."[65]

Over time, therefore, the state would be replaced by the societywide rules negotiated by property owners (representatives of republics and firms), central monetary policy, and, where necessary, the enforcement power of party loyalty and "conscience" in localities and workplaces. The leaders saw no need for supplementary political institutions to forge consensus and resolve conflicts among cooperative producers in this cooperative state when the producers' interests did not immediately dictate it.[66]

Yugoslav congress, and in 1965 the central control and cadre commissions were moved to the republics. Whether party organizations were to be located in enterprises or in communes remained a point of persistent conflict between Croatia and Serbia that reflected the developmental conflict between the Slovene and Foča models. The conflict lay in the degree of industrialization and incorporation of the working-age population into the socialized sector and the corresponding degree of need for commune-level coordination of a population that included many employed in services and administration outside enterprises, as well as a larger private sector.

[65] Djilas, *Rise and Fall*, 18.

[66] The model of Lenin's *State and Revolution* was not by accident.

Chapter 6

UNEMPLOYMENT

THE EXPECTATION of the Yugoslav party leaders that they had set in motion by 1952 a system in which unemployment might be a temporary problem of development but not an outcome of the system itself proved wrong. People moved increasingly out of private, subsistence agriculture; but the public sector did not grow at a pace sufficient to give them, or youth entering the workforce for the first time, the jobs they sought.

Although there were periods of rapid growth in employment, the total growth in employment contracts in the social and private sectors between 1957 and 1982 was only 0.52 percent, because of the decline in private agricultural employment.[1] The average annual rate of increase in employment in the social sector was 4.0 percent, and the rate of decline in private-sector employment was 3.1 percent. Much of the change was due to transfer of people from wage-labor status under private hire to social-sector employment; and the gap between the two rates, representing the ability to absorb the labor surplus, grew wider. The number of people registered with employment bureaus as looking for work rose without cease after 1950, at an average of 11.4 percent a year in the precrisis period of 1952–75. This official measure of unemployment continued to rise for the entire postwar period, from about 5 percent in 1952 to 17 percent in 1988.[2]

The image of a population neatly divided into two settled communities of secure subsistence—the public and private sectors—hid from view the growing groups of people in neither world: workers who had been judged superfluous by management and workers' councils yet who wished to remain in industry or had no land to which they could return; a highly mobile collection of unskilled laborers traveling from one short-term construction job to another; the unemployed who gathered at dawn to wait for recruiters in informal day-labor "markets" on the outskirts of major cities; a large number of peasant-workers who continued to live in the

---

[1] Primorac and Babić, "Systemic Changes and Unemployment Growth"; figure in original ms. version (available from Emil Primorac), 11.

[2] Data are available in the many studies and journals of the Federal Bureau of Statistics (Savezni Zavod za Statistiku), Belgrade, and in the OECD *Yearbook on Economic Statistics*. See also Malačić, "Unemployment in Yugoslavia from 1952 to 1975"; Primorac and Della Valle, "Unemployment in Yugoslavia: Some Structural and Regional Considerations"; and Mesa-Lago, "Unemployment in a Socialist Economy: Yugoslavia."

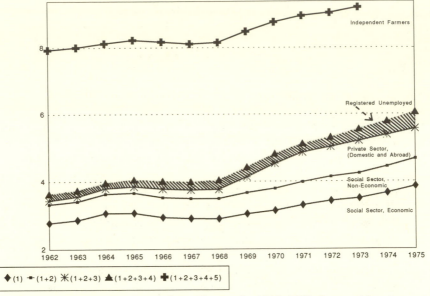

Figure 6-1. Employment Growth, in Thousands, 1962–1975. *Source:* Mencinger, "Utjecaj privredne aktivnosti na zaposlenost." *Note:* (1) social sector, economic; (2) social sector, nonecomonic; (3) private sector (domestic and abroad); (4) registered unemployed; (5) independent farmers.

village and migrate seasonally to industry and mines; and an ever-larger percentage of the younger generation waiting at home for a first job. As late as 1955, the *polutani* (peasant-industrial workers) formed a majority of the labor force employed in the textile, wood, brickmaking, and construction industries, a significant number of the workers in the chemical and agro-industrial branches of the economy, and three-fifths of the miners in Serbia and Bosnia.[3] The final countrywide census of 1981 showed a population of twenty-two million Yugoslavs, including thirteen million between the working ages of nineteen and sixty; of these, only seven million were employed in a regular employment position (*radni odnos*). Of the remaining six million, only one million were registered at an employment bureau as unemployed (at least half of these one million were actively looking for work), while another one million were working temporarily in foreign countries. This stark picture was drawn in October 1988 by the sitting president of the LCY during the debate over conditions for yet another IMF loan, enacted two months later. He concluded, "If an efficiency-oriented reform were put in place, 2 to 2 and one half million would be thrown out of work."[4]

[3] Kostić, *Seljaci-industrijski radnici*, 21–22.
[4] Stipe Šuvar, at the international roundtable "Socialism in the World," Cavtat, Yugoslavia, October 1988, cited in Denitch, *Limits and Possibilities*.

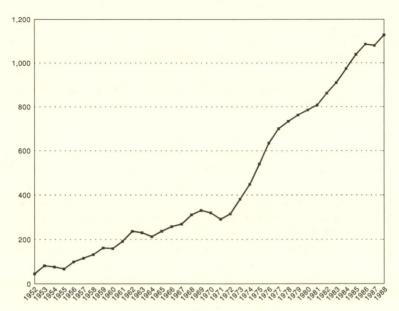

Figure 6-2. Unemployment, in Thousands, 1952–1988. *Sources:* For 1952–58: Macura, "Employment Problems under Declining Population Growth Rates and Structural Change," 496; for 1959–88: Mencinger, "Privredna reforma i nezaposlenost," 36.

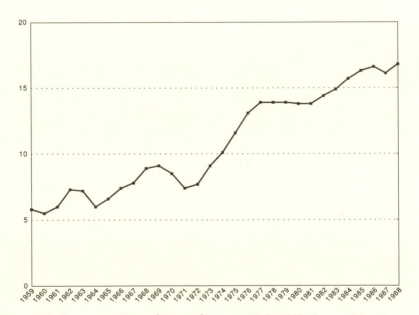

Figure 6-3. Percentage Rate of Unemployment, 1959–1988. *Source:* Mencinger, "Privredna reforma i nezaposlenost," 37.

These figures led many to question their meaning, to reduce the numbers with estimates of "real" unemployment, and to emphasize the rapid rate of job creation over the period. Little attention was given to the faster rate of growth in unemployment, the disproportionately high numbers among women, youth, and unskilled workers, and the shift over time from frictional to deeply structural causes, whereas it became ritual to acknowledge the very high rates in the southern and eastern parts of the country as if there were nothing to explain. Explanations for unemployment came largely from economists, divided between a smaller group of developmentalists and a large school of economists of mainly marginalist persuasion who saw in the labor management of firms a built-in bias against employment. Specialized journals filled with data analysis for employment-bureau administrators arose in the republics when the bureaus gained full self-management status in the 1970s, and a few statisticians and sociologists not directly paid for such work did analyses of the unemployed;[5] but the subject never attracted political analysts. In comparative historical terms, studies of the unemployed themselves—living conditions, methods of getting by, extent of social marginalization—were in 1990 at the point John Garraty assigns to the 1850s and 1860s in western Europe.[6] Although unemployment was classified as a question of social policy, enterprises—which financed social science research after the early 1970s—were not interested in the systematic study of poverty. Political harassment followed the few independent studies, such as those done in Serbia—including the work of lawyer-activist Srdja Popović. The Yugoslav Booths, Mayhews, Jahodas, and Lazarfelds had yet to emerge.

THE MEANING OF UNEMPLOYMENT DATA IN YUGOSLAVIA

Despite their quantitative representation, which makes them appear comparable across time and space, unemployment data represent very different realities in different societies and in the same society at different times. Because there were no household surveys in Yugoslavia, the reliability of the data had no test; but it is clear that their coverage varied substantially, as did the methodological instructions to statistical-bureau surveyors.[7] The data's relation to the labor supply could be assessed only

[5] Examples of such journals are *Zapošljavanje i Udruženi Rad*, a monthly in Croatia; and *Socijalna Politika*, formerly the house journal of the Ministry of Social Policy and Health (adopted wholescale from the Croat ministry of the 1939 Cvetković-Maček Agreement period) but long an autonomous publication of the federal Institute for Social Policy. There are also the rare empirical studies such as the one by Mladen Žuvela and Josip Županov, reported in Žuvela, "Grupe stanovnika pojačeno izložene nezaposlenosti;" and Filipović and Hrnjica, "Psihološki aspekti nezapošljavanja omladine."

[6] Garraty, *Unemployment in History*, 91–115.

[7] This is a characteristic of unemployment data in general, not of the highly professional Yugoslav Federal Bureau of Statistics.

once a censual decade. The one constant derived from the official and popular consensus that employment must be voluntary and that unemployment was short-lived. The unemployed were those people who voluntarily registered with a local employment-service bureau (renamed "communities of interest for employment" in 1969)[8] as "looking for work" in the public sector.

The reason to register as unemployed was to obtain health insurance and child allowances, some cash assistance, and access to retraining programs. Unemployed people who did not need or were ineligible for the bureau's services would not register. Over the entire postwar period, the employment bureaus found work, on average, for only 22 percent of people newly employed each year, and this number declined to 8.3 percent a year by 1973–80. Unemployment compensation, as a payment for *past labor*, was available only for those who had held a legal employment contract in the public sector (and only if they had no alternative means of support, judged according to family income or ownership of agricultural property), and the amount paid was in proportion to the time employed and the position's legislated wage rate. The local bureau made such determinations, on the basis of central principles and local monies. The right to health insurance also belonged only to those previously employed in the public sector (until 1960, when coverage was extended to independent farmers).[9] The proportion of the registered unemployed who qualified for compensation varied over the period 1952–85, from a high of 18 percent to 3.5 percent in 1984—only 11.6 percent of those with previous employment; and the amount was so meager (an average of 6,500 dinars a month when average salaries were 200,000) that it could scarcely be considered assistance. Its average duration was only 25–27 days, in accord with the view (inaccurate by the 1960s) that unemployment was frictional and short-term and that "welfare" was uneconomic dependence.[10] The effect of these restrictions was to discourage registration in the first place.

[8] "Communities of interest" was the label given public and social services once they became, after 1969, fully independent funds and agencies for employment, roads, housing, social insurance, etc.; they were managed by employees and an annual assembly of delegates from their direct financers in enterprises and from government.

[9] See Parmalee, "Medicine under Yugoslav Self-Managing Socialism," 97–100, 216–18. Between 1952 and 1960, independent professionals became covered by health insurance, to which they made payments; in 1959–60, as part of a program to encourage farmers to contract with social-sector marketing and processing firms, they received basic care as part of long-term delivery contracts. Beginning in 1973, Slovenia mandated unification of workers' and farmers' insurance, followed by Bosnia-Herzegovina, Montenegro, Serbia proper, and Vojvodina during the 1970s and by Croatia in 1980. Inequalities in the kind and amount of coverage between the two sectors remained, however, as Parmalee discusses extensively (passim).

[10] These data are calculated from the official federal statistics published annually in *Statistički Godišnjak Jugoslavije;* see also Malačić, "Unemployment in Yugoslavia from 1952 to 1975."

Moreover, to register one had to be in generally healthy condition, be of working age (15–60 for men, 15–55 for women), and reappear regularly to maintain active status—an obstacle for people who lived far from a bureau, particularly in rural and mountainous areas. One also had to sign an affidavit agreeing to accept whatever position the bureau staff offered, regardless of where it was. Sophisticates knew that the bureaus had no means to enforce this rule, but many unemployed who were unable to resettle (such as married women) or those with poor prospects for housing (such as youth who relied on their parental home and sustenance) would be deterred.[11]

The official rate of unemployment says more about the leaders' concept of employment than the reality of unemployment. Based on Kardelj's concept of employment as a stable "employment position" in a public-sector work collective and its separation from a world of stable subsistence in the private sector, the rate was actually a measure of the nonsubsistence population; in contrast to the standard measure in developed capitalist economies, where the rate is a proportion of the total population or of the potential labor force,[12] it was the unemployed portion of the social-sector employment pool—those currently employed in the public sector *with rights to self-management* and those formally registered as seeking work. Thus the base of this ratio excluded people working permanently abroad, those in the employ of the state secretariats for national defense and internal affairs, and those working in diplomatic establishments in foreign countries. On the other hand, the data made no distinction between full-time, permanent contracts and part-time or temporary contracts,[13] even though the latter did not fit Kardelj's definition; the numbers of such contracts rose significantly after the mid-1960s. Wage earners on legal contract in the private sector were counted as employed in some periods only, but the numbers excluded those with no cash income. For example, although in 1948 all rural women of official working age were counted as economically active because it was known that they shared fully in family farming activities, by 1953 women in agricultural households were no longer counted among the employed.[14] The narrower definition of employment that was first systematized in the instructions for unemployment surveys in 1954 tended to prevail,[15] but fluctuation in

---

[11] On the unwillingness to move in Croatia, see the study by Jureša-Persoglio, "Neke značajke socio-ekonomskog položaja nezaposlenih u SRH."

[12] Myers and Campbell, *The Population of Yugoslavia*. See the discussion of alternative measures in Mulina, *Nezaposlenost, uzroci i karakteristike u sadašnjoj fazi razvoja privrede*.

[13] Moore, *Growth with Self-Management*, 117–18.

[14] Myers and Campbell, *The Population of Yugoslavia*.

[15] Savezni Zavod za Statistiku, *Uputstva za polugodišnji izveštaj o zaposlenom osoblju* (1954). See also Savezni Zavod za Statistiku, *Uputstvo za sprovodjenje izveštaja o zaposlenom osoblju* (1958).

the definition of economically active persons was enough to make any assessment of the rate of unemployment or of the proportion of the active population that found employment over time extremely rough.

It was common for individuals to move on and off the unemployment rolls, depending on their level of discouragement and the need they felt for income. Following a pattern in many countries, registered unemployment tended to rise when price inflation or falling real wages cut into households' real income, forcing additional members to protect consumption levels by seeking paid employment. Unemployment figures also rose when employment grew, providing some indicator of the numbers of discouraged job seekers who returned to the registers when there was hope of finding work.[16] The seasonal rhythm of agricultural labor was in part captured because registered unemployment always increased in off-seasons, but the extent of the rural labor surplus was surveyed only in the decade after 1953, by developmental economists continuing prewar practice; it was estimated that year at 3.2 to 3.3 million persons (31 percent of the farming population) and in 1960–64 at 1 to 2 million.[17] Although all regions except Vojvodina still had substantial labor reserves in the countryside and in agriculture into the mid-1970s (despite the precipitous decline in the proportion of the active male population that was engaged in agriculture, from 69 percent in 1953 to 21 percent in 1981),[18] these reserves did not enter into the measures of employment and unemployment used by planning authorities and policymakers.

Attempts to assess the real extent of unemployment were rare, and they occurred at moments when sharply rising unemployment (during the severe recession of 1966–68 and the economic crisis of the 1980s) motivated officials to *reduce* the count of the "truly" unemployed. Yet the official studies actually found that the rate understated their numbers. For example, a 1967 study by the Federal Council on Labor (made public in April 1968) estimated that the official rate of 7.2 percent (269,000 persons) understated unemployment by almost 3 percent. Another 153,000 persons actively looking for work had not registered with an employment bureau; the hidden surplus among the employed added an estimated 200,000 to 250,000; and latent unemployment in agriculture was 1,400,000. On top of that were 400,000 persons (an additional 10 percent) officially working abroad but not considered unemployed. The study also

---

[16] Rašević, Mulina, and Macura, *The Determinants of Labour Force Participation in Yugoslavia,* 23.

[17] Macura, *Stanovništvo kao činilac privrednog razvoja Jugoslavije;* Nikola Čobeljić and Kosta Mihailović, speaking at the 1954 seminar discussion on the labor force held at the Belgrade Institute of Economics and reported in Has, "Društveno-ekonomski osvrt na problem zaposlenosti," 157–62; Puljiz, *Eksodus poljoprivrednika.*

[18] Myers and Campbell note that the 69 percent figure for 1953 was "one of the highest rates in the world" (*The Population of Yugoslavia*). For the 1981 figure (based on the 1981 census), see *Statistički Godišnjak Jugoslavije,* 1983.

estimated that the figures for the previous year (1966) undercounted the number of persons without work and actively looking by 20 percent; those for 1967, by 57 percent; and those for 1968, by 82 percent.[19] In 1981, a revision by the Federal Bureau of Employment of the criteria of "true" unemployment concluded that, despite popular belief to the contrary, 82 to 90 percent of the registered unemployed in that year did meet these criteria.[20] And because such periods of concern were also times when campaigns to reduce the cost of labor by rationalization and open unemployment were under way, attention focused on the additional unemployment *hidden* in the workplace. A semiofficial study during a campaign to intensify labor use in 1961–62 estimated hidden unemployment at 10–15 percent of industrial jobholders,[21] and the 1967 study put the number at slightly less than the number of registered unemployed; but more often the estimates of redundancy (such as in the studies for the long-term stabilization program of 1982–92) were so consistently set at 20–30 percent—without supporting evidence—that one doubts they represented systematic analysis. Equally difficult to judge was the extent of employable resources lost to employed persons who held second jobs, did overtime work, or received consulting fees for work at another workplace, although officials estimated in the 1980s that such resources would create 300,000 additional positions.[22] But nowhere was there an attempt to identify the actual labor supply, and of all the categories of people not captured by the unemployment data—those who were discouraged, at a distance from an employment bureau, culturally inhibited from registering, among the agricultural surplus, or resigned to the world of noncontractual, casual labor—official attention was paid only to redundancies among the employed and to workers temporarily employed abroad.

This latter category was the focus of a long-running, important debate about whether to classify workers in foreign countries (*gastarbeiter*, or guest workers) as unemployed at home. Periods of emigration always lowered the unemployment rate. For example, its sharp drop in 1955–57 can be attributed almost entirely to the permanent exodus of ethnic minorities and political malcontents when borders opened, and the fall in unemployment in 1961 corresponded to the federal government's organization of temporary labor migration abroad. The number of workers who left in 1969–73, about 500,000, was almost equal to the increase in

[19] *Zaposlenost i Zapošljavanje*, April 1968. See also Livingston, "'Yugoslavian Unemployment Trends."

[20] Author's interviews with top officials of the Federal Bureau of Employment (Savezni Zavod za Zapošljavanje) in Belgrade, November–December 1982; and data from the bureau's in-house reports.

[21] Livingston, "Yugoslavian Unemployment Trends," 756.

[22] Mencinger, "Otvorena nezaposlenost i zaposleni bez posla."

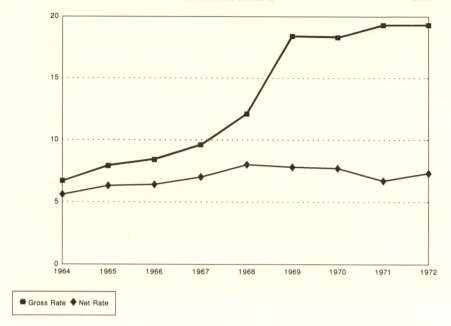

Figure 6-4. Unemployment Percentages: Gross and Net Rates, 1964–1972. *Source:* Babić and Primorac, "Analiza koristi i troškova privremenog zapošljavanja u inoz-emstvu," table 2. *Note:* Gross rates refer to both domestically employed and those registered as working abroad. Net rates refer to domestically employed only.

social-sector employment during the same period. The serious jump in unemployment during the 1970s was due in part (although less than is often asserted) to the expulsion from recession-plagued northern Europe of less-skilled Yugoslav laborers; in 1974–75 alone, 150,000 workers returned (30 percent more than the natural increase in the labor force that year).[23] The data on temporary workers abroad capture only those who went through official channels, although personal networks and the underground of informal and illegal labor burgeoned after receiving countries imposed stricter criteria in 1974–75. Before this sharp rise, in the census of 1971, the official total of those employed abroad was 672,000 (17 for every 100 persons employed at home); semiofficial estimates spoke confidently of more than 800,000, and experts close to the subject ventured a figure closer to one million.[24] Both Jože Mencinger and Emil

[23] Schrenk, Ardalan, and El Tatawy, *Yugoslavia: Self-Management Socialism and the Challenges of Development*, 266–70.

[24] Rašević, Mulina, and Macura, *Determinants*, offers an easy summary, but the data are extensive. See *Statistički Godišnjak Jugoslavije* and the publications of the Institute of Migration (Institut za Migraciju), Zagreb, including its journal, *Migracije*.

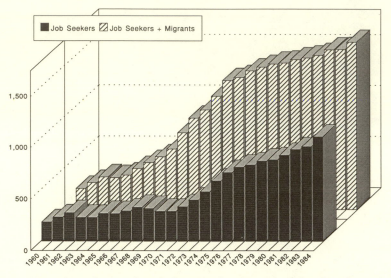

Figure 6-5. Job Seekers and Yugoslavs Working Temporarily Abroad, in Thousands, 1960–1984. *Sources:* For job seekers: *Statistički Godišnjak Jugoslavije*, various years; for migrants, 1960–64: Zimmerman, *Open Borders, Nonalignment, and the Political Evolution of Yugoslavia*, table 4.4; for migrants, 1965–84: Primorac and Babić, "Systemic Changes and Unemployment Growth in Yugoslavia, 1965–1985," table 3.

Primorac argue that they should be included in unemployment figures, while William Zimmerman maintains that their exodus also provided a political safety valve.[25]

THE UNEMPLOYED

During the 1950s, the Federal Bureau of Statistics gathered detailed data on the characteristics of persons in public employment and those who were fired from their jobs. But by 1964, data conformed to the new system of *income relations*, a system that identified people not by occupation or former employment, but according to social categories defined by the system of wage differentials and that system's assumptions about individual capacity to produce—that is, according to age, certified skill and educational qualifications, and gender. Societal measures of productivity and labor use had disappeared. The data do show significant change over time in the characteristics of individuals affected by unemployment, although

[25] See, among others, Zimmerman, *Open Borders, Nonalignment, and the Political Evolution of Yugoslavia;* Mencinger, "Privredna reforma i nezaposlenost"; and Primorac and Babić, "Systemic Changes."

these shifts do not correspond to the common benchmarks of political discussion—the 1965 economic reform and the 1974 constitution.[26] There is a first period, between 1950 and the end of 1957, when both dismissed industrial workers and the agricultural surplus were largely unskilled or semiskilled laborers, more than half of them women. Industries hardest hit by supply bottlenecks due to harvest failures or the difficulties in foreign trade, such as textiles and tobacco processing, and cyclical activity in construction accounted for most layoffs. Overall, this was a period of high growth in demand for labor, lasting until 1964; but it would be inaccurate to characterize it, as many do, as one of extensive employment, and unemployment also rose in 1956–57. Waiting time for jobs was usually short (between one and six months after first registration), and a higher proportion of workers found jobs through employment bureaus in comparison to later periods. There were also stark regional differences: Macedonia had a very high rate of unemployment, followed closely by Kosovo; more moderate rates prevailed in a middle group of industrializing republics (Montenegro, Bosnia, and Serbia proper, in that order); and the three former Habsburg regions of Vojvodina, Croatia, and Slovenia (lowest of all) enjoyed relatively low rates.

A second period, in the decade 1958–68, began with very high levels of layoffs from industry (in 1958 and 1961), followed by a recessionary stagnation in new employment in 1964–67 that was so severe as to reduce the absolute size of the employed population. Job vacancies grew after 1957, with a peak in 1963–64 and a dramatic drop to their low in 1967–68. The first political concern for unemployment occurred in Serbia in 1962, when the Socialist Alliance of Working People convened a conference on the problem and quarrels over economic policy erupted between party factions. Unemployment lasted substantially longer, unemployment compensation declined—in part because of the rising proportion of youth under the age of twenty-five seeking their first job who did not qualify and also because eligibility criteria tightened—and after 1963–64, employment bureaus placed an ever-smaller proportion of those who sought their services. The rate of increase in unemployment actually flattened out in 1964–68 because many workers withdrew from the pool out of discouragement or in order to leave the country. Women continued to be harder hit than men. An even more blatant sign of structural unemployment was the worsening regional inequalities according to the "historical" ranking mentioned above for 1950–57.[27]

The decade of the third period in the data, 1968–78, was similar: a gradual rise in unfilled vacancies beginning in 1967–68 peaked at the

---

[26] Both were, in fact, formal markers of previous changes.
[27] Primorac and Della Valle, "Unemployment in Yugoslavia."

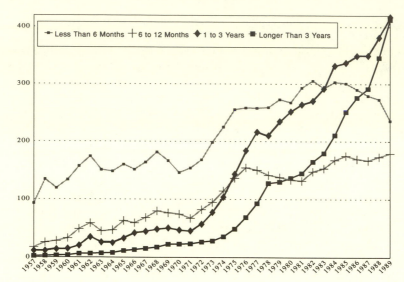

Figure 6-6. Length of Time Waiting to Be Employed, 1957–1989 (by thousands of job seekers). *Source: Statistički Godišnjak Jugoslavije,* various years.

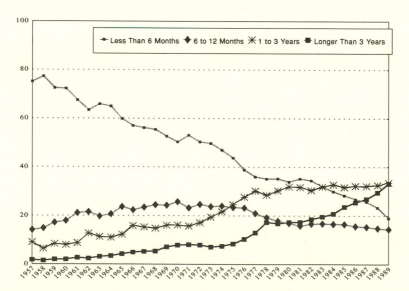

Figure 6-7. Length of Time Waiting to Be Employed, 1957–1989 (by percentages of job seekers). *Source: Statistički Godišnjak Jugoslavije,* various years.

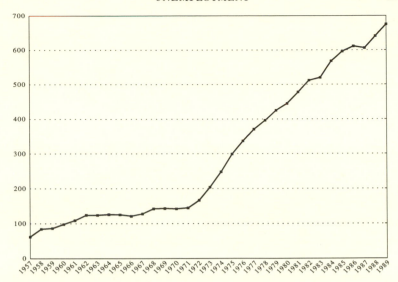

Figure 6-8. Women among the Registered Unemployed, in Thousands, 1957–1989. *Source: Statistički Godišnjak Jugoslavije,* various years.

same time as layoffs in the recession of 1978–79. After a lull in 1968–71 in official unemployment growth, when discouraged applicants sought jobs outside the social sector—in private-sector agriculture, crafts, tourism, and homework and in "guest" (temporary) employment abroad—the rate of unemployment rose 1 percent each year. Declining participation rates as one went from one republic to the next told a story of continuing regional inequality: by 1973, Slovenia, with effectively full employment at 1.8 percent unemployment, had 35 persons employed for every 100 inhabitants and even faced labor shortages in a number of industries, such as construction and mining; in the same year, registered unemployment in Kosovo and Macedonia was at 25 percent, while only 9 persons per 100 inhabitants were employed.[28] Figure 6-11 and Table 6-1 show the contrast among republics in the broader categories of economically active population and proportion of the labor force employed. The majority of the unemployed after 1971 were youth under the age of twenty-five, usually without work experience or claim to compensation; they accounted for almost 80 percent of the rise in unemployment between 1972 and 1983.[29] Women continued to form the majority of the unemployed, but after 1968 this could not be attributed to their educational level because they no longer differed from men in that respect; they increasingly fell

[28] Rašević, Mulina, and Macura, *Determinants,* 28.
[29] Primorac and Charette, "Regional Aspects of Youth Unemployment in Yugoslavia."

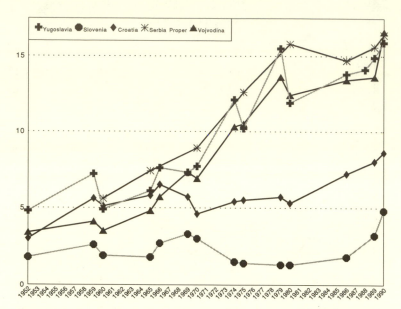

Figure 6-9. Unemployment Percentage Rates by Republic: The North, 1952–1990. *Sources:* For 1959–88: Mencinger, "Privredna reforma i nezaposlenost," table 1; for 1989–90: *Statistički Godišnjak Jugoslavije* (1990), 16.

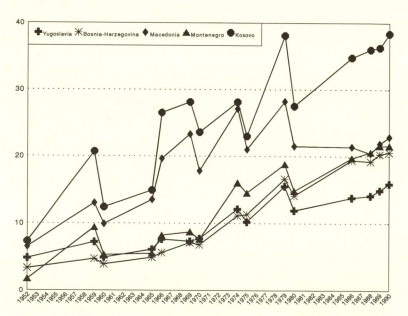

Figure 6-10. Unemployment Percentage Rates by Republic: The South, 1952–1990. *Sources:* For 1959–88: Mencinger, "Privredna reforma i nezaposlenost," table 1; for 1989–90: *Statistički Godišnjak Jugoslavije* (1990), 16.

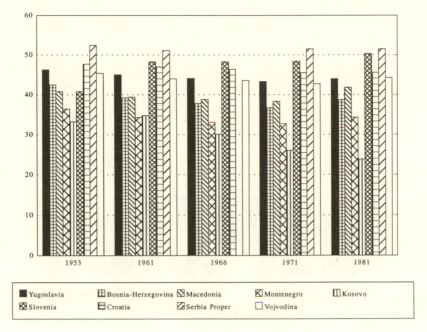

	Yugoslavia	⊞ Bosnia-Herzegovina	▧ Macedonia	▨ Montenegro	⊞ Kosovo
	▨ Slovenia	⊟ Croatia	▨ Serbia Proper	☐ Vojvodina	

Figure 6-11. Percentages of Economically Active Population by Republic or Province. *Source: Statistički Godišnjak Jugoslavije*, various years.

TABLE 6-1
Rate of Employment by Republic or Province
(percentages of working-age population)

	1960	1965	1970	1975	1980	1986	1990*
Yugoslavia	26.4	30.6	30.1	35.2	40.1	45.8	45.3
Less-developed regions							
Bosnia-Herzegovina	21.8	24.4	23.5	27.6	30.2	37.3	37.5
Macedonia	23.7	27.2	26.6	31.1	35.9	41.1	39.5
Montenegro	22.7	25.8	25.5	29.9	34.1	41.4	40.2
Kosovo	14.4	16.0	16.0	19.0	20.8	23.1	22.2
Developed regions							
Slovenia	43.2	50.6	50.7	60.5	68.2	71.6	68.5
Croatia	29.7	35.2	34.0	39.7	46.8	54.0	53.9
Serbia	21.3	25.1	26.0	31.4	37.0	42.0	42.4
Serbia proper	22.7	26.6	28.1	33.1	39.3	44.8	46.1
Vojvodina	29.3	34.7	31.5	36.7	41.4	47.8	48.4

Source: Statistički Godišnjak Jugoslavije, various years.

Note: The rate of employment is defined as the relation between the number of employed persons in the social and private sectors and the working-age population (women ages 15–59 and men ages 15–64).

* Estimate

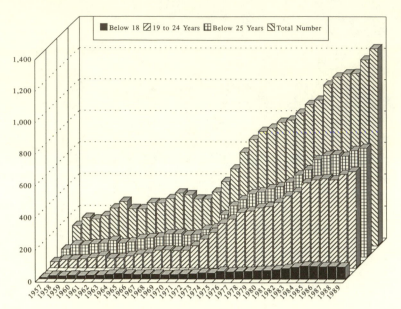

Figure 6-12. Unemployment by Age Category, 1957–1989 (by thousands of job seekers). *Source: Statistički Godišnjak Jugoslavije*, various years.

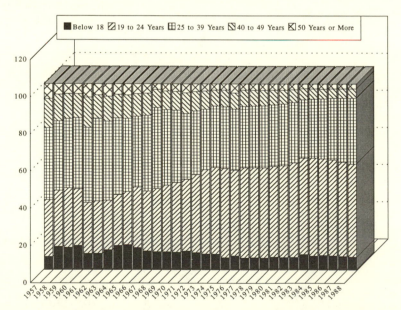

Figure 6-13. Unemployment by Age Category, 1957–1988 (by percentages of job seekers). *Source: Statistički Godišnjak Jugoslavije*, various years.

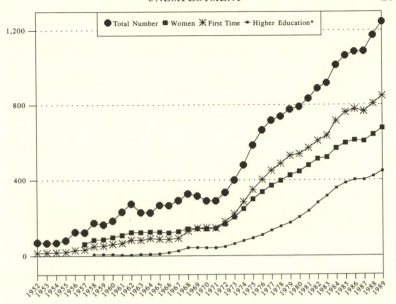

Figure 6-14. Women, New Entrants, and the Educated among the Registered Unemployed, 1952–1989 (by thousands of job seekers). *Sources: Statistički Godišnjak Jugoslavije,* various years; *Yugoslav Survey,* various issues. *Note:* "Higher education" refers to those with a university, college, intermediate, or secondary education.

into the categories of highly skilled workers and college-educated or above. The employment bureaus were ever less helpful, placing on average only 8.3 percent of the newly employed each year from 1973 to 1980.

The increasing displacement of the costs of unemployment onto the younger generation was beyond any doubt by 1985, when 59.6 percent of the registered unemployed were under the age of twenty-five. While only 15.4 percent of their cohort were unemployed in 1972, 38.66 percent were looking for work by 1985.[30] When firms raised requirements after the late 1970s for previous work experience to two to five years, only 11 percent of the unemployed had experience of more than one year, and 71.4 percent of the registered unemployed in 1985 (youth leaving school or housewives forced to work by the depression) had none at all. Although employers also sought ever more highly schooled job candidates, this did not diminish their numbers among the unemployed: 43.3 percent had technical-college or university diplomas in 1980, and 56.3 percent did in 1985. Beginning in 1965, the wait without work was ever longer as well;

[30] Ibid., 30.

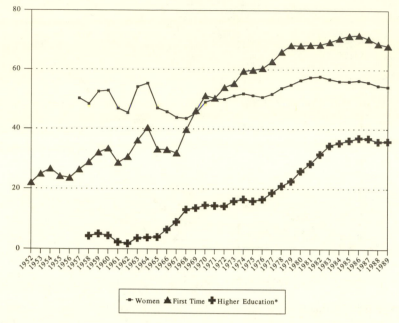

Figure 6-15. Women, New Entrants, and the Educated among the Registered Unemployed, 1952–1989 (by percentages of job seekers). *Sources: Statistički Godišnjak Jugoslavije*, various years; *Yugoslav Survey*, various issues. *Note:* "Higher education" refers to those with a university, college, intermediate, or secondary education.

in that year, 16.6 percent of the unemployed sat one year or longer. In 1985, 55.3 percent remained on the registries for two years or longer, and fully a fifth of the unemployed had found no job after three years. The exclusion of youth also exacerbated regional inequalities. In 1984, regis-tered unemployment was 1.7 percent in Slovenia, 7.2 percent and declin-ing in Croatia, 19.1 percent in Montenegro, 21.1 percent in Macedonia, and 33.3 percent in Kosovo.

EXPLANATIONS OF YUGOSLAV UNEMPLOYMENT

Yugoslav unemployment has a special place in the theoretical literature of neoclassical economics, where Benjamin Ward's thesis of 1958 on the backward-sloping supply curve for labor in "labor-managed firms" (a theo-retical construct) created a veritable industry, particularly for the many who value the idea of a decentralized economy with worker participa-tion[31] or sought a way to combine the efficiency of markets with the wel-

[31] See Ward, "The Firm in Illyria"; its elaboration by Domar, "The Soviet Collective Farm as a Producer Cooperative"; and the criticism by J. Robinson, "The Soviet Collective

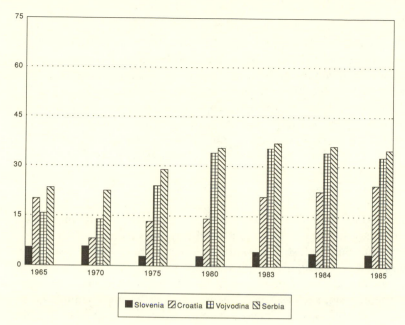

Figure 6-16. Youth Unemployment Percentage Rates: The North. *Source:* Primorac and Charette, "Regional Aspects of Youth Unemployment in Yugoslavia," 218. *Note:* "Youth" refers to persons aged 27 years or younger.

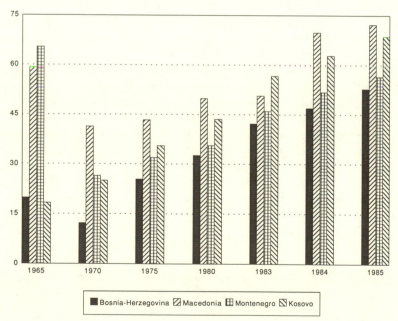

Figure 6-17. Youth Unemployment Percentage Rates: The South. *Source:* Primorac and Charette, "Regional Aspects of Youth Unemployment in Yugoslavia," 218. *Note:* "Youth" refers to persons aged 27 years or younger.

fare of socialism. This fascination also characterized a larger literature on the consequences of Yugoslavia's special institutional setting—a literature that was strangely divorced from issues of development, as if the leadership's dual strategy toward labor had infected scholarly research. I will follow that division by classifying approaches to Yugoslav unemployment into two catchall schools: "developmentalists," concerned with the transformation of an agrarian society; and "liberals," focused on institutions and mechanisms of "rational" allocation of resources that are largely given.

Agrarian Exodus

The developmentalists conceived of development as did the Yugoslav leadership, in terms of time and the absorption of an agricultural surplus population into industry and industrial habits. In the early years, developmentalists in Yugoslavia fell into two groups: (1) the demographers, statisticians, and developmentalists who continued the interwar focus on overpopulation, such as Miloš Macura, Rudolf Bićanić, Vladimir Bakarić, Ivan Krašovec, Zoran Pjanić, Vladimir Obradović, Dragan Vogelnik, Zoran Tasić, Ivo Lah, Milica Šentić, and Dušan Breznik; and (2) the economists who turned their attention more to the problem of inadequate demand, a problem that lay in the underdevelopment of productive resources within the country (for example, Nikola Čobeljić and Kosta Mihailović). Both groups focused on the pace of rural exodus, which was faster than the leaders' gradual strategy intended, and on the necessity of expanding productive capacity.

There was a tendency, however, for analysis to reflect political context; for example, certain perspectives became increasingly identified with certain republics (though not necessarily the nationality of the individual expert) and with views on the role that central policy could and should play in growth. This tendency began in the late 1950s, as republican jurisdiction over research centers and development policy brought the reappearance of prewar legacies, particularly the demographic and agrarian traditions of the Croatian school of rural sociology and the influence of economists from the Croat Peasant party on the one hand, and the tendency of developmentalists to congregate increasingly in Serbia (and later in Macedonia and Montenegro) on the other. This difference became more pronounced after 1962–64, when the political victory of economic reformers led to a purge of many developmentalist economists in Belgrade and to the declining influence on policy of federal research institutions. At the same time, concern over excess labor supply became a

---

Farm as a Producer Cooperative: Comment." Outside of a few Yugoslav commentators, however, little of this huge literature actually discusses unemployment.

preoccupation with demographic explosion in southern regions (particularly Kosovo and Macedonia), but the possible economic causes took a back seat to cultural explanations. A 1960 conference on population policy revealed clearly the kernel of a growing antagonism—already present in the conflicting arguments at a 1954 conference on the results of the 1953 census—between the perspectives of northerners (in Croatia and Slovenia) and those of the rest of the country, and the success of the former in defining the nature of the unemployment problem.[32] From then on, developmentalists of liberal persuasion and many economists of a sociological bent (such as Branislav Šoškić in Belgrade) who still wrote about external causes of rising labor supply or about developmental obstacles focused in their policy analyses on the need for microlevel efficiencies, on rationalizing labor cuts, and on structural barriers to a functioning labor market, while those who attributed rising unemployment instead to the marketizing economic reform and the abandonment by the late 1950s of societywide developmental policy were increasingly marginalized.

By the 1970s and 1980s, the issue of capital investment reduced to political distortions of rational investment choices, and the issue of surplus labor focused on areas of the country and their governments where unemployment was high. The concern was over improper investment of development credits transferred from north to south and excessive birthrates in the south (the Muslim communities in Kosovo and Macedonia were singled out for the greatest attention). There was even a tendency to worry more about the growth of employment, which economists were inclined to explain as a political response to the rising social protest in 1968–69 that encouraged featherbedding and job protections. Although the older developmentalist tradition persisted, especially in the south—in Macedonia, Montenegro, and to a certain extent in Bosnia and Serbia—these voices were only weakly heard, as in the development plans of these republics and in the negotiated compromises in the subcommissions set up to work out the stabilization program in 1984.

Although researchers outside Yugoslavia tended to fall into the second

---

[32] Ante Novak, who first organized the Federal Bureau of Statistics for Boris Kidrič in 1948 and who was present at the 1960 conference, argues that the absence of discussion at this conference on the aching need for a population policy has a political explanation—that southerners, especially from Kosovo, saw the idea of such a policy as national discrimination and an implied threat of genocide (Author's interview with Novak, Ljubljana, October 1982). But there was also the view that Malthusian concerns would disappear automatically with economic development (see, for example, Stupar, *Praktikum za socijalnu politiku*). Besemeres writes that "population policy is dominated by northern liberalism disproportionately" and that "even if the republics followed appropriate family planning policies now, they could not make up in decades for consequences in the age structure of differential fertility rates created by past 'policy'; the time to make a difference in demographic composition has long passed" (*Socialist Population Politics*, 237).

camp, those who might be classified as developmentalists brought the Todaro paradox to the Yugoslavia of the 1970s and 1980s in order to explain the continuing rise in its unemployment rate despite economic development. The Todaro and Harris-Todaro models of rural-urban migration argue that economic growth itself induces unemployment in industrializing countries because of their dual structure of employment and wages. Since wages are higher in the urban industrial sector and investment tends to be lower in rural areas, people move more rapidly than economic growth from the rural to the urban sector in search of higher wages and opportunities. The paradox enters because they adjust their migration to the probability of obtaining urban jobs, making policies that aim to reduce urban unemployment by expanding the number of urban jobs self-defeating. Testing the hypothesis on Yugoslav data for 1957–74, William Bartlett found a strong positive correlation between migration and intersectoral income differentials. But in place of the predicted elasticity of migration in response to urban employment opportunities, he found a pattern of unstable equilibrium as urban vacancies oscillated.[33] Arnold Katz, on the other hand, argued on the basis of data for 1965–80 that the paradox of growth-induced unemployment held so well for the less-developed republics and provinces that it could explain the pattern of regional variation in the unemployment rate almost entirely, and he concluded that macroeconomic policy to favor employment would be ineffective in reducing unemployment.[34]

Industrial Unemployment

Most analyses of Yugoslav unemployment have focused on firms' decisions to employ labor more or less efficiently, not on the need for structural change of the economy as a whole. This liberal school contains three separate approaches—the labor school originating with Ward's Illyrian model, the capital school, and the institutionalists. Ward's objective was to discover whether firms managed by workers instead of a private owner would exhibit different economic behavior because their business decisions would take into account the likely effect on employees' wages as well as overall profits. Controlling for extraneous factors by assuming that the two types of firms operate in the same environment, Ward focused on the firm's response to a change in demand for its products. Assuming further that workers' objective function would be the same—to maximize their income, or share of net profit—he suggested a contrasting world: assuming

[33] Bartlett, "A Structural Model of Unemployment in Yugoslavia."
[34] Katz, "Growth and Regional Variations in Unemployment in Yugoslavia, 1965–80," particularly 41–45. See also Sapir, "Economic Reform and Migration in Yugoslavia."

that net profit is fixed at the moment of distributing income, then the fewer workers who receive income, the larger the individual share. Uncertain about the outcome of their decision to expand or restrict production, workers would take fewer risks and show more caution than the capitalist who could freely fire labor or cut wages to protect profits if revenue declined. Ward concluded that labor-managed firms would tend to restrict output when faced with an increase in market demand because expansion would require taking on more workers and potentially leaving everyone worse off than before. This perverse outcome—that the Pareto-optimal decision under labor management was the opposite of that under private ownership—also led to monopolistic behavior by worker-managed firms: reducing risk and seeking gain through increases in price rather than output. The aggregate result for a society of labor-managed firms, from the irrational decisions on investment and from the market-distorting consequences of monopolistic behavior, *ceteris paribus*, would be less expansion of employment than in a capitalist society.

An entire school of debate and analysis emerged from this thesis as well as from its implications for producers' cooperatives in general.[35] In the Yugoslav case, James Meade, for example, argued that Ward's results would disappear if one removed his assumption that incomes are distributed equally within the firm or that workers seek to maximize their income rather than something else.[36] Laura Tyson argued that workers with virtual tenure in their firms might well have longer time horizons (Tito's reference to workers' "perspective" comes to mind) and could, even given their objective function of maximizing individual income, choose to risk a less-than-maximum income in the short run in order to spend resources on investment that expanded productive capacity.[37] Saul Estrin estimated a long-run model of Ward's argument with Yugoslav data for 1957–73 and found support for it: when enterprises were freer to allocate their earnings after the reform of 1965, the capital intensity of production rose sharply in the aggregate and in all industrial branches. He inferred that workers did choose to raise their wages in the long run, but with invest-

[35] See Fusfeld, "Labor-Managed and Participatory Firms: A Review Article"; and the special issue on participatory economics of the *Journal of Comparative Economics* (March 1986), especially the articles by Putterman ("Self-Management and the Yugoslav Economy") and Milanović ("The Labor-Managed Firms in the Short-Run: Comments on Horvat's 'Theory of the Worker-Managed Firm Revisited'").

[36] Meade, "The Theory of Labour-Managed Firms and of Profit-sharing"; idem, "Labour-Managed Firms in Conditions of Imperfect Competition." Roger McCain uses implicit-contracts theory to show that there is no reason to expect wages to be sticky in a labor-managed economy and therefore no reason to expect Ward's results necessarily ("The Economics of a Labor-Managed Enterprise in the Short Run: An 'Implicit Contracts' Approach."

[37] Tyson, "A Permanent Income Hypothesis for the Yugoslav Firm."

ments in fixed capital stock to raise their productivity rather than through more employment. Estrin also used this posited behavior of labor management to explain the failure to absorb rural labor, by showing that the urban-rural wage gap *widened* in the mid-1960s when unemployment rose sharply. Such insensitivity of the firm in its decisions on wages and employment to the presence of surplus labor outside it and the downward rigidity of public-sector wages also explained regional inequalities, he argued: the richer regions with lower unemployment tended to set the reservation wage for poorer regions, while the inflexibility of wages under self-management had more severe consequences for regions with lower overall savings.[38]

The tendency of Yugoslav firms toward capital intensity stimulated a second school of argument on unemployment. This capital school maintained that unemployment was caused not by labor management, but by the absence of a true capital market and thus a means to evaluate the relative opportunity costs of capital and labor. The artificially low price of capital, despite the relative abundance of labor and scarcity of capital, caused firms to favor capital-intensive investment over the employment of labor. Some analysts combined the two schools to argue the opposite: that a rise in the price of capital, or other nonlabor costs, would lead firms to employ more labor in order to spread the burden of higher costs by reducing the marginal increase per worker.[39] More important than whether existing firms expanded or not, Stephen Sacks argued, were the barriers to entry of new firms when capital markets did not exist. Since credit was channeled primarily to public-sector firms, and the only founders who had rights to draw a return on invested capital alone were governments, there were neither incentives nor resources to create new firms outside this channel that might employ more people.[40]

One need not choose between labor and capital schools, according to Branko Milanović's application of Austrian theory (especially Wicksell) to cooperative (labor-managed) firms. Such firms, he concluded, respond to

[38] Estrin, "The Effects of Self-Management on Yugoslav Industrial Growth"; idem, *Self-Management: Economic Theory and Yugoslav Practice*.

[39] See Vanek and Jovičić, "Uloga kapitalne opremljenosti rada u formiranju i raspodeli dohotka u Jugoslaviji"; and Vanek, *A General Theory of Labour-Managed Market Economies*. Eirik Furubotn and Steve Pejović's property-rights subgroup of the capital school argues that any firm operating with less than absolute property rights for owners will be less efficient than a pure capitalist firm in its use of production factors. But others argue that this is true only by their definition of property rights and capitalist firms, unrelated to firms' actual operation, while F. Drèze disproves it formally (see Fusfeld, "Labor-Managed and Participatory Firms," 772; C. Martin, "Public Policy and Income Distribution in Yugoslavia"; and Petrin, "The Potential of Small-Scale Industry for Employment in Yugoslavia").

[40] Sacks, *Entry of New Competitors in Yugoslav Market Socialism*, passim.

an increase in the rate of interest on capital, or to technological progress, in ways that lead to higher unemployment than when equivalent capitalist firms make wage and employment decisions.[41]

The more varied school of institutionalists focused on other organizational barriers to the mobility of labor and capital. For some, the federal system exacerbated the effect of labor management in protecting higher wages in richer republics and urban areas from lower-wage competitors in poorer republics and rural areas, by imposing political and cultural barriers to movement outside one's republic of origin.[42] Others examined the effect of the organization of credit. In a survey of attitudes to reconcile other survey data showing that firms chose to increase total income (including capital) with Ward's assumption that they aimed at maximizing individual income per worker, Janes Prašnikar found in Slovenia that firms differed according to their size. From surveys of three strata of decision makers (managers, workers'-council members, and production workers) in forty Slovene firms, he argued that large firms of five hundred workers or more sought to increase total income in order to increase their bargaining power over the allocation of bank credit and governmental price concessions, whereas smaller firms of fewer than five hundred workers, unable to hope for such influence, aimed to increase total income so that they could pay higher personal incomes per employee. Both strategies raised unemployment. Smaller firms restricted employment, as Ward posited, while larger firms expanded through mergers with other firms that would increase their economic weight; the consequences were growing industrial concentration, potential for monopolistic behavior, and aggregate employment lower than it might otherwise be. In analyzing Slovene firms that operated in an essentially full-employment environment, Prašnikar also measured an effect of the republics' economic autonomy of the federal system, for he found that these firms aimed to pay ever-higher wages—because they were competing to hold on to workers who moved among firms within the tight labor market of Slovenia in search of higher incomes and living standards—instead of attracting cheaper labor from other republics. This effect thus contributed to the lower than necessary level of employment in the country as a whole.[43] Whether or not these results applied in the different conditions in other parts of Yugoslavia, they did caution against assuming that all firms were

[41] Milanović, "The Austrian Theory of the Cooperative Firm"; but see also his critique of the "income school" (dohodoci, or dohodovna škola) of Yugoslav economists for ignoring the necessity of a macroeconomic policy for an economy of labor-managed firms ("Labor-Managed Firms in the Short Run").

[42] On ethnic barriers to mobility, see Hawrylyshyn, "Ethnic Affinity and Migration Flows in Postwar Yugoslavia."

[43] Prašnikar, "The Yugoslav Self-Managed Firm and Its Behavior."

alike. Finally, Tyson, applying a version of János Kornai's argument that socialist economies were based on soft budget constraints, focused on the inflationary consequences of the political unwillingness of governmental or bank authorities to enforce hard budget constraints on firms; to protect the incomes and jobs of employed workers, she argued, these authorities extended credit to cover losses, which then worsened unemployment in the long run.[44]

Although all three schools of argument concentrated on the economic distortions and efficiency loss of not pricing labor and capital in competitive markets, they also had political implications. The arguments on the effect of labor management resembled those about the role of trade unions in creating structural unemployment in capitalist economies.[45] According to Estrin, after 1965 labor management became a vehicle for urban-sector workers to monopolize their control over their jobs and wages and maintain an artificial scarcity against any reserve-army effects, although he never specifies the agents or process by which this political struggle occurred. For liberal economists within Yugoslav political circles, unemployment was a concern only after the social unrest of 1968–69, because it seemed to lead the party leadership to suppress the market reform of the 1960s in favor of a proemployment, proworker policy of job protection. But, like Estrin, these economists never provided the political details of this backlash and its relation to the 1974 constitution and 1976 labor legislation to support their assertion. By the 1980s, more and more economists were focusing on the apparent wage rigidity and inflationary pressure of self-management as the primary cause of unemployment. Some went so far as to say that only a true labor market would grant the unemployed their rights.[46]

The first analysis of unemployment in the postwar socialist period—the dissertation by Vladimir Farkaš that appeared in 1955, the same year as the new wage regulations for self-management and the extension of workers' councils from the higher economic associations (which replaced the branch directorates) to individual firms—was also the last analysis of any kind to step outside the constraints defined by the new system and official policy.[47] On the developmentalists, Farkaš argued that they were simply continuing the dominant interwar approach, defining unemployment as overpopulation or hidden unemployment—whether measured in

[44] Tyson, "A Permanent Income Hypothesis."

[45] A survey can be found in Piore, *Unemployment and Inflation*. The insider-outsider hypothesis would seem to apply only to the Slovene firms; see Lindbeck and Snower, *The Insider-Outsider Theory of Employment and Unemployment*.

[46] Letica, "Pravo na rad i nacrt zakona o udruženom radu."

[47] Farkaš, "Naša tzv. prenaseljenost i naš problem nezaposlenosti"; idem, "Odredjivanje osnovnog uzroka nezaposlenosti u FNRJ"; Panić, "Radna snaga i zaposlenost u Jugoslaviji."

Malthusian terms of too many people for the amount of food, or in neo-classical terms of technical coefficients for the optimal quantity of labor to increase marginal output as measured by labor's cost (wage). He argued that in contrast to Marx's law on population, according to which unemployment depended on the character of the social order, the developmentalists conceived unemployment as necessary in all economic systems, a variable quantity taking the form of overpopulation in agriculture or the level of employment (and therefore profit) in industry. In Farkaš's view, the socialist idea was to build an order based on the assumption of full employment, in which the population was the constant and the level of its productivity the variable subject to social correction. Unemployment was then a measure of the gap between people's needs and their ability to satisfy them, so that registered unemployment as one measure of the demand for earnings was only one small symptom of unemployment. Others were increased productivity (hence its great variability) or the search—whether registered or not—for paid work. One indirect measure of unemployment was the negative correlation in 1953–54 between household income and expenditures for most Yugoslavs (far more among rural than urban households); but much more relevant to the decision to seek work was the gap between individuals' expenditures and their theoretical list of needs (what Farkaš called psychological poverty, in contrast to material poverty). Indirect measures of this gap were such everyday phenomena as rural-urban migration, both periodic and permanent; multiple jobs, moonlighting, and supplementary work; the movement of women on and off unemployment rolls in direct relation to shifts in the cost of living; and economic crime.

This concept of unemployment together with Yugoslav conditions led Farkaš to criticize ruling policy as a "mechanical" application of Keynes's general theory ("fashionable" at the time) to the profoundly non-Keynesian conditions of underdeveloped and socialist Yugoslavia. Underdevelopment meant that, contrary to Keynesian assumptions, (1) the cost curve was distorted and employment did not depend primarily on costs of production, so that real wages and employment were not in direct relation; (2) the propensity to consume was greater than one, so that the multiplier and the accelerator did not work to translate higher investment into higher employment; and (3) Keynesian policies in developed countries continually worsened the gap between desires and the capacity to satisfy them in the less-developed countries with policies to increase demand for developed countries' products through foreign aid, continued international inequality in the distribution of national income, and support for the production of raw materials in less-developed countries in place of domestic industries that might satisfy those needs at home. The socialist character of the country, moreover, meant that (1) the guaranteed minimum wage was paid regardless of the success of a firm; (2) social management of the conflict between wages and employment occurred within production units rather than in macroeconomic policy; and (3) user costs of capital were widely regulated by society. Applying a Keynesian calculus to conditions in which production costs might regularly exceed expected revenue and in which the criterion for investment of effective demand conflicted with the basic welfare assumption of satisfying basic needs led to a range of negative economic results, such as inflationary pressure, income spillover in certain fields, poor quality and assortment of goods, monopoly, and dishonest competition.[48] As long as employment was treated as a matter of profit levels and incentives to invest and expand productive capacity in relation to the number registered as looking for work, Farkaš argued, there would continue to be wrong investment choices and underutilized capacity; as long as the method for raising productivity was income incentives, it would exacerbate inflationary pressures.

Unemployment was above all an international phenomenon that could only be resolved internationally, Farkaš maintained. The roles left for domestic policy could only be to try, in the economic sphere, to bring production closer to its theoretical potential of social productivity so that needs were more completely satisfied and the demand for jobs *declined;* in the social-policy sphere, to distribute national income so as to harmonize the individual's interest in rising wages and the society's interest in lowering unemployment within domestically given constraints; and, in the cultural sphere, to redirect aspirations from the developed world's consumption standards (which international competition encouraged) to a more realistic assessment of needs.

Clearly, Farkaš was too radical politically to be heard; at the time, the point was to become more like the developed world, not less, although to do it without capitalist crises and foreign exploitation. But his analysis was apposite nearly forty years later. Both the consequences of focusing largely on demand mechanisms—and eventually that meant adjusting to shifts in international demand—and the pertinent institutional factors he cited reveal difficulties with the dominant schools of thought.

As for those standard schools of explanation for Yugoslav unemployment, they had the opposite problem. They criticized the Yugoslav system from the theoretical perspective of a market economy rather than the system as it was constituted, as if the leaders had not had reasons to construct an alternative in the economic crises and unemployment that market economies produced. The possibility that the elements those schools criticized were part of an integrated conception and strategy of economic development and sustained growth was ignored.

[48] Farkaš, "Naša tzv. prenaseljenost," 59.

The obstacles to a market for capital and credit were placed not out of some blind antagonism to markets but in order to have some domestic control over the *developmental* consequences of investment. Since capitalist market economies continued to exhibit unemployment, inflation, and underdevelopment in ways that Marxian analysis could explain, the arguments supporting such institutional changes had not lost their power. Moreover, the capital intensity of production was *encouraged* by myriad acts of policy. A market price for labor would have undermined the system of incentives and the gains from workers' proprietary responsibility for limiting wages within real accumulation. For that reason also, the comparison of opportunity costs between capital and labor was to be made by firms. The apparent protection of urban workers from the competition of rural labor was intended to favor rising productivity and was not a cause of unemployment, leaders would argue, as long as the guarantees of limited property in the private sector were protected. The two sectors did not operate on the same principles. Moreover, in addition to the economic causes of rapid turnover in conditions of underdevelopment, there were noneconomic reasons of social order and national defense for settling the population.

Questions of efficient allocation of capital and labor were faced within the firm, and this made it doubly important to have central control over the financial system that would give economic information to firms and to have central guidelines on labor and incomes through accounting regulations. Contrary to the literature on labor-managed firms and "workers' control," wage rates were "set outside the firm," by accounting rules on incomes, local solidarity funds, rules on enterprise reserve funds for guaranteed wages, and rules on the guaranteed minimum wage.[49] Data on wages and unemployment showed no mutual relationship or evidence of any Phillips curve. Wages did correlate highly with productivity, rising as productivity rose (as one might expect with the indexing of job classifications and income).[50] Rules also required that taxes for social funds and investment be paid before income shares could be paid, and rules on depreciation and reserves were varied to prevent depletion of savings to augment incomes. Negotiated social compacts in the 1970s restrained wages while unemployment grew, so that after 1978 real wages fell without relief.[51] Extensive research on participation and decision making in labor-managed firms concluded that managers and their technical staff

[49] C. Martin, "Public Policy and Income Distribution," 110–11, 137. See also Adizes, *Industrial Democracy, Yugoslav Style*, 50ff.; and Mates, "Recent Tendencies in the Regulation of Income Distribution."

[50] Gapinski, Škegro, and Zuehlke, *Modeling the Economic Performance of Yugoslavia*, 139–41, 122.

[51] C. Martin, "Public Policy and Income Distribution"; Gapinski, Škegro, and Zuehlke, *Modeling*, 23.

made most decisions, and that workers' councils debated but had little influence on choices between higher incomes and employment-expanding investment.[52] At the same time, critics of the federal institutions should have included the effect of real goods markets within this institutional context; as Estrin argues, the richer republics were able to affect the actual reservation wage for the country, and Farkaš's analysis of the effect of Keynesian policies in developed countries—artificially raising demand in less-developed countries by worsening psychological poverty and increasing the gap he called unemployment—had its analogue in the Yugoslav space.

It is interesting to consider that Ward's formal result runs directly counter to the expectations for "workers' control" implied in the political speeches of the Yugoslav team of Kidrič, Kardelj, Tito, Bakarić, and others in 1949–50. The leaders counted on socially owned firms to make economically rational decisions in response to market demand for their output, if firms were free to make the decisions on factor mix, source of inputs, and expansion or restriction of production in pursuit of market profit (subject to some regulations known in advance). The conflict lies in part in different assumptions about workers' behavior, the educational role of party activists, legal regulations, and the obligation of managers and technical staff to explain their decisions on production and internal distribution to workers' representatives in socializing workers to think as the creators and owners of capital (officially called *minuli rad*, or "past labor," by 1973). As long-term, stable members of a workplace with a direct stake in its real growth, workers would, as Tyson proposed, take the long-term perspective. But there was also a conflict between the political rhetoric and the intention behind workers' control. The primary objective of worker self-management was to have workers accept the consequences of declining productivity or net revenues and limit their incomes, and to have them decide which of their peers were not sufficiently productive. The circumstances of its introduction as an alternative to market determination, moreover, were the difficulties of pursuing a *developmental* policy in the presence of major *external* shocks to the firm, from drought, revolutionary transition, and especially foreign-trade difficulties.

No assessment of the Yugoslav economy in the socialist period can be limited to employee-managed firms, for it would ignore the far more limited rights of all those in "nonproductive" and administrative positions, the very large portion of the economy outside the social sector (the unemployed or independent farmers and artisans), and the economy's openness

---

[52] A good summary of this research, done by Yugoslav sociologists such as Josip Obradović, Josip Županov, and Vladimir Arzenšek, can be found in Comisso, *Workers' Control under Plan and Market;* and Rawin, "Management and Autonomy in Socialist Industry."

to the international economy and its reliance on foreign capital to supplement domestic resources.[53] One might add, with F. Drèze, that the wage regulations defined substantial differentials within firms, and that the demographers' level charge against the Yugoslav south or the economists' campaign against investment choices in the south can be maintained only if economic evaluation is confined to highly aggregated data and the boundaries of republics (for the entire postwar period, for example, Serb households had on average 1.1 children, and in Macedonia there was, even more than fifty years ago, substantial variation in birthrates among communes). Levels of investment efficiency and productivity also varied within republics.[54] Heterogeneity across republics and localities in the level of unemployment, heterogeneity within republics according to the nature of production and historical paths, and differences in conclusions depending on the periodization of statistical series all suggest the need to move to the level of policy. What needs explanation by the politics of power is the failure to respond when the system did not meet expectations—not expectations that it would operate as markets should, but that it would operate as the leaders intended.

[53] On this last, critical element, it is perhaps ironic that Ward takes Horvat to task, in "Marxism-Horvatism: A Yugoslav Theory of Socialism," 516.

[54] Connock, "A Note on Industrial Efficiency in Yugoslav Regions."

Chapter 7

THE FAUSTIAN BARGAIN

THE CORE conclusion of the scholarship on full employment is that political variables define success: a commitment by public authorities to promote employment; a political consensus on the necessity of a macroeconomic, or systemwide, policy; and the political institutions to implement effective policies of international adjustment.

The failure of the Yugoslav socialist government to prevent rising unemployment cannot be attributed to a lack of political commitment. The strategy that defined governmental institutions and policy gave to government the priority of promoting economic growth in the sense of an ever-rising societal capacity to employ—without the financial crises that led to unemployment in market economies. Explicitly aimed at preventing capitalist unemployment, this strategy favored an expanding realm of social ownership of productive assets so that investment choices would serve the public interest in rational use of economic resources, not just private gain; and so that the competition between wages and profits would be eliminated. In contrast to centrally planned approaches to economic growth, the state was to diminish in size over time so as not to waste resources on nonproductive employment that reduced real growth. And in contrast to Keynesian approaches, the primary economic role of the state was to regulate the value of money and credit to prevent financial crises at their source—by maintaining a stable currency; by keeping costs low on credit for investment "to expand productive forces" and ensure sectoral proportions; and by regulating economic incentives to rising labor productivity *directly*, not through independent capital markets and wage bargaining.

The concept of planning was retained in the role and institutions of monetary control and financial instruments, but otherwise central policy had no need to represent the separate interests of wage earners or society against capital. A society organized around autonomous producers who controlled the use and distribution of earned capital would obviate the need for countercyclical policies and require instead a liberal, or "pro-business," policy of monetary stability and fiscal conservatism to provide the favorable climate for savings and investment decisions by the republics, localities, and firms that would expand employment. Despite the views of critics who attributed governmental policies that diverged from

this model to the ruling party's commitment to job security and employment protection (such as their charges that the reversal of marketizing
economic reforms after 1972 was a conservative reaction to unemployment in the 1960s, that indebted or nonprofitable firms were kept alive
with "soft budget constraints," and that investments in southern republics
were "politically" motivated instead of economically rational), this model
explicitly rejected any direct federal role in promoting or protecting
employment.

Although there were also critics of this Slovene model, as we have been
calling it, there was a broad consensus on this economic role of government within the ruling circles of the party and among mainstream economists. The problem lay with adjustment to international conditions.

The irreducible role of the federal government was in foreign affairs;
yet in this regard its economic record was dismal. The trade account was
in deficit every year between 1952 and 1983 except one (1965). Both
monetary-fiscal policy and credit policy gave priority to reducing that deficit. Like the orthodox, anti-inflationary, demand-restricting monetary
policy of business-oriented governments in capitalist economies, the
Yugoslav government's macroeconomic policy had a recessionary bias, ex-
acerbating unemployment and fueling the very financial crises (of enterprise debt, foreign debt, and rising inflation) that its monetary system was
designed to prevent. Cycles of restrictive, anti-inflationary policy were
followed by involuntary expansion (rather than Keynesian-like, or delib-
erate "soft budget constraints") as monetary authorities were forced to
monetize the debts accumulated in the restrictive phase. Instead of providing a buffer against international downturns, domestic policy exacerbated global trends, becoming restrictive when global demand fell and
truly expansionary only with the inflow of new foreign money.

The primary goal in the annual economic resolution in thirty-two out of
the forty-two years between 1949 and 1990 was external stabilization—
and, as Kiril Miljovski wrote in 1983, "unemployment [in Yugoslavia] is a
direct consequence of the idea by which every stabilization begins with
restrictions in employment regardless of the effects for economic
growth."[1] Every five-year economic plan from the second (1957–61) to
the last (1985–90), moreover, gave priority in investment policy to restoring liquidity to the current account, whatever the consequences for employment or for the sectoral balance of the domestic economy considered

---

[1] "Economic Development, Long-Term Goals, and Needs" (paper presented at conference of the Serbian Academy of Sciences and Arts, Belgrade, January 27–29, 1982). Miljovski was one of the country's most respected economists. A Macedonian trained in Zagreb
before World War II, he was a Partisan "first fighter," wrote extensively on economic development and regional inequalities, was elected to parliament and held posts in the federal
government, and was eventually elected to the Macedonian Academy of Sciences and Arts.

necessary to steady growth. Investment and labor policies alternated between the Slovene and Foča models, not because of a politics of liberal pressures and conservative reaction, but because of the requirements of trade and defense policy, just as had been the case in the initial periods of socialist rule.

In the debates over sources of capital for initial industrialization and over the policy of "socialism in one country" in 1946–48, the winning coalition in the leadership had laid its bets on "people's power" and on peaceful coexistence. In the context of the cold-war division of trade and defense blocs, "national communism" became a Faustian bargain. Playing on their independence of Moscow and availability to Western military strategy, signaling to each side their willingness to switch to the other, the Yugoslav leaders came to depend on the domestic means for this diplomatic independence and military strength that gave them special access to Western loans and capital markets and to favorable trade agreements in the nonaligned bloc. In place of full access to Western markets and export revenues, the source of their comparative advantage internationally became the army and Yugoslavia's global position outside the blocs. Tito understood this advantage and pursued it consistently for reasons independent of his personal power and glory, despite what critics charged.

In spite of the perverse effect on the operation of the monetary institutions and industrial policy that were designed to prevent unemployment, the government gave priority to maintaining access to foreign capital and leverage in foreign trade. This then began to undermine the basis of the party's political commitment to unemployment as well. The initiative for policy came from the international environment, and the political strength of the federal party was related not to the bargaining strength that comes from low unemployment, but to its bargaining strength with capital abroad. At the same time, the country's vulnerability to external shocks made it even more important to guard the bases of economic sovereignty at home: the principles of "people's power"—social ownership, no market for factors of production (capital and labor), and nonconvertibility of the currency—that defined the institutions of international adjustment. Openness required greater domestic control—not less, as Western economists insisted there should be.

THE YUGOSLAV STRATEGY IN THE CONTEXT OF INTERNATIONAL OPENNESS

The strategy chosen in 1946, and made possible by Western credits after 1949, was to use monetary instruments (such as price regulations, credit policy, special funds and subsidies, and exchange-rate policy) to direct a Ricardian growth path. Manufacturing and processing firms producing final goods for sale at home and abroad would be encouraged with the import of advanced technology and capital equipment and with cheap wage goods and raw materials. Foreign trade offered the most rapid path to increased productivity. Capital for initial industrialization would come from the inherited domestic capacity of manufacturing (largely in the northwest of the country)—the "wager on the strong"[2]—and from foreign supplements. This strategy would also protect the leaders' domestic political base in the northwest parties, among the middle peasantry that was to be gradually incorporated into the socialist sector of industrial work and remuneration, and among urban worker and middle strata whose standard would otherwise fall dramatically because of industrial investments. At the same time, the federal government had to guard the needs of production for a strong defense (on which access to foreign capital depended): it had to maintain the one-third rule of domestic origin for military equipment and armaments, as well as the national food policy and strategic stockpiles of fuel, food, and other necessities that would be produced at home if they could not be imported.

Until the 1980s, the country was able to sustain a very high rate of capital formation. But in contrast to the initial reliance on foreign credits only, growth was increasingly based on foreign borrowing.[3] The rate of overall economic growth varied with the availability of foreign supplements.[4] Impressive growth rates in the 1950s were largely due to foreign credits,[5] while the recessions of the 1960s reflected both business downturns in the United States and Western Europe and the retreat in official lending. The growth of the 1970s (like that of most developing countries) was "import-led."[6] Such borrowing, the refinancing of debt already after 1961, and the substantial increase in commercial credit to banks and firms after 1969 (which the National Bank did not borrow but had to guarantee) together led to a debt-service obligation so high by the late 1970s that it cut directly into domestic growth. On the basis of their econometric analysis of the Yugoslav economy between 1953 and 1984, James Gapinski,

[2] Maier, "The Two Post-War Eras," 343.

[3] Babić and Primorac, "Some Causes of the Growth of the Yugoslav External Debt," is an accessible work among a wide literature on the subject in former Yugoslavia.

[4] Oskar Kovač argues, in *Platnobilansna politika Jugoslavije*, that the use of foreign finance was always determined by supply in Yugoslavia. See also Babić and Primorac, "Some Causes of the Growth of the Yugoslav External Debt."

[5] Foreign sources provided about 33 percent of the funds for domestic investment in the 1950s (Ljubomir Madžar, personal communication, from research at the Yugoslav Institute for Economic Research in Belgrade).

[6] Babić and Primorac, "Some Causes of the Growth of the Yugoslav External Debt." In 1970–75, foreign funds accounted for 31.9 percent of the annual gross expenditures for investment in fixed and working capital (Gapinski, Škegro, and Zuehlke, *Modeling the Economic Performance of Yugoslavia*, 110).

Borislav Škegro, and Thomas Zuehlke concluded that "Yugoslavia's performance at home crucially depends upon its performance abroad."[7]

The "habit for rationalization" that Hebrang expected from workers in socially owned firms became instead an enduring inclination on the part of investors—whether enterprise management or officials—to seek the solution to growth and global competitiveness in imports of the most modern capital equipment and in technological modernization. The economy became increasingly dependent on imports of machinery and especially intermediate materials and spare parts for domestic production; by the early 1980s, 99.6 percent of imports were essential to production.[8] Despite Yugoslavia's maneuverability among global markets, moreover, the credits, capital goods, and intermediate materials on which the economy relied came largely from Western, hard-currency markets. The result was an impenetrable imbalance in the commodity composition and terms of trade among the country's trading areas that seemed to require further borrowing. It is not surprising that Laura Tyson and Egon Neuberger find that, for the 1960s and 1970s, "a 1.0 percentage point decline in average growth rate in Western Europe produces a 1.0 to 1.6 percentage point decline in Yugoslav exports."[9] In the 1970s, between 75 and 89 percent of the deficit on both trade and capital accounts was with countries of the OECD (Organization for Economic Cooperation and Development);[10] and between 1950 and 1975, foreign credits covered 90.7 percent of the deficit on current account.[11]

As a result of the increasingly structural dependence of production on imports and because of the importance of a well-defended national sovereignty for the leaders' strategy and for access to foreign markets, federal policy gave priority to maintaining trade liquidity for firms—to protecting the level of foreign-currency reserves and the balance of foreign payments—in an effort to sustain the confidence of foreign creditors. The federal government's preoccupation with the trade deficit, foreign debt, and conditions for access to foreign capital affected domestic employment in two ways. First, it undermined the operation of federal macroeconomic policies that were meant to foster employment growth: the preferences for investment in new capacity laid out in the federal and republican so-

[7] Gapinski, Škegro, and Zuehlke, *Modeling*, 21.

[8] Borislav Škegro, personal communication, fall 1982 (at the time, Škegro was an assistant at the Zagreb University Institute of Economics; in 1993, he became deputy prime minister of Croatia). Even farming was import-dependent: agricultural economist Vladimir Stipetić reported at the October 1982 annual meeting of the Yugoslav Association of Economists in Opatija, Croatia, that milling was one-third dependent, cooking-oil production was 48 percent dependent, and cattle raising was 65 percent dependent.

[9] Tyson, *The Yugoslav Economic System and Its Performance in the 1970s*, 92n.

[10] Ibid., 87.

[11] Gapinski, Škegro, and Zuehlke, *Modeling*, 156.

cial plans (which were to guide bank credit policies, subsidies, decisions of the price office, and grants) were determined by the trade balance and availability of foreign capital, and the stabilizing function of monetary and fiscal system (to maintain clear and direct incentives to increase productivity and to invest) was oriented toward external stabilization. The second effect on employment came through the government's method of restoring external equilibrium and repaying debt.

The Slovene model, like most economic models, presumed a closed system—not one embedded in a world economy and (in the case of a socialist economy) also embedded within a domestic economy in which a large segment of activity, including most of agriculture, was also external to the model because it was private. The task of monetary, fiscal, and exchange-rate policy in the ruling paradigm was to prevent the financial crises that could lead to industrial unemployment—by keeping money in circulation tied to actual production. According to the logic of monetary planning, by which governance through "economic instruments" was meant to operate, the normal balancing of monetary demand and actual supply was to occur at the microeconomic level of self-management accounts. All budgets in the public sector (in the economy, social services, and government) were legally obliged to balance accounts quarterly; if this was not sufficient, the federal authorities mandated changes in accounting regulations. Policy to correct an imbalance between monetary holdings and goods available for purchase (that is, inflationary pressures) worked simultaneously on the demand side and the supply side. It began with short-term limits on consumption, achieved by cutting money in circulation, and an attempt to stimulate increased output through productivity incentives in public-sector firms. Tight money might be effected through limits on credit and on prices, regulations tying wages more strictly to productivity, or rules raising reserve ratios in banks and firms. Supply incentives were both generalized and specific, directed at both firms (managers) and workers; they included liberalized prices, tax cuts, lower depreciation allowances, wider wage differentials, and targeted subsidies. Because employment was the province of autonomous firms and local governments, it was critical that the federal government maintain monetary control as the system prescribed, providing the economic environment for simultaneously growing productivity and employment.

Although there were domestic sources of inflationary pressure (above all the consistently low productivity of agriculture), the government's ability to perform this task of macroeconomic management—of keeping control over the quantity of money in circulation and therefore over the value and clarity of wage and income incentives to production—was seriously weakened by foreign borrowing, the contractual obligations of bilateral trade, and imported prices. The inflow of foreign credits (and on those rare occasions of a current-account surplus, of net earnings) expanded the money supply in the same potentially inflationary way as the printing of new money, and the lender of last resort became in fact not the National Bank but the IMF. Although both had the same ideological approach to stabilization, the IMF could be ignored less easily. Nonconvertibility made the economy more vulnerable to the effects of business cycles in the two countries to which the currency was tied—the United States and, after the mid-1960s, the Federal Republic of Germany as well. Balance-of-payments supports provided by U.S. aid and loans in the 1950s and 1960s and by worker remittances from Germany after the early 1960s thus became vulnerable at the very time they were most needed because foreign demand for commodities was down. Trade contracts in the clearing region and bilateral trade, on the other hand, operated on the same accounting principles as the domestic monetary system, which meant that the National Bank was the intermediary between the foreign contractor and the domestic producer. But since a promised trade contract was sufficient to demand cash from the Bank, any delay in a foreign partner's payment resulted in a monetary emission without cover. Finally, domestic prices could not be protected from the influence of import costs, which were responsible for one-fourth to one-half of a domestic inflation that averaged 22 percent by the early 1970s, moderated momentarily, shot up to 40 percent in 1979, and continued to rise until triple-digit hyperinflation hit in 1985.[12] On the one hand, the GATT and the IMF demanded price liberalization as a means to reduce the trade deficit. On the other hand, enterprises were permitted to accommodate imported costs in prices so as not to distort productivity-related incentives with the market. Despite the constant political theme that wages were the primary cause of domestic inflation, which justified further cuts in employment as well as incomes, Gapinski, Škegro, and Zuehlke found that price inflation was affected more by the money supply and import prices than by wages. The rise of import prices actually forced the real wage down.[13]

Throughout the post-1952 period, the government faced a nearly constant deficit in trade in the convertible-currency area and, after the early 1960s, nearly constant inflationary pressures. A vicious circle thus arose between external stabilization and domestic stabilization, each one requiring and simultaneously undermining the other. But the choice of stabilization policy was driven by pressures for external stabilization and by

[12] Organization for Economic Cooperation and Development, *Economic Survey: Yugoslavia* for the relevant years. See Macesich, *Yugoslavia: The Theory and Practice of Development Planning*, on the critical role of import costs in domestic inflation and the limited ways that Yugoslavia, as a global price taker, had for adjustment.

[13] Gapinski, Škegro, and Zuehlke, *Modeling*, 138.

the need to adjust to external conditions over which the government had little control. The solution to the trade deficit was to seek new short-term credits and to resort periodically to IMF loans. Resort to the IMF reinforced the restrictive monetarism (in effect) and fiscal conservatism of the demand-management side of the leaders' policy: to reduce the trade deficit, repay debt, and reduce inflation by restricting domestic consumption (including imports) and promoting exports. The effect of tight monetary policy and cuts in imports was almost immediately felt in production; nonessential imports were only a tiny portion of the total. Firms were told to exploit internal reserves, cut production costs (and therefore labor), and use internal savings for new investment. Government budgets had to be cut, and then essential imports—if necessary, through administrative controls for a short-run effect. The effect at first was always a domestic recession like those that occur in market economies under orthodox stabilization, which the policy came to resemble.

Because working capital for public-sector enterprises came only from the cash accounts and advances of banks, the first effect of tight money was a liquidity crisis, affecting payment for delivered production supplies even before payment of the guaranteed wage to workers. To keep production going, firms created new instruments of payment, usually writing IOUs to suppliers (a form of involuntary trade credit). The banks, which were both cooperative (managed by enterprise depositors) and organized territorially (each republic being responsible for economic policy on its own territory), felt obliged to acknowledge these IOUs—in large part because the situation disadvantaged all producers of primary and intermediate goods whose incomes depended on payment by producers of final, marketable goods. Thus, the cash-flow problems of the former clearly had to do with stages of production rather than inherent profitability, and there was no reason to penalize them with bankruptcy. Moreover, such firms tended to concentrate in poorer regions, which would be devastated by wholesale bankruptcies. As lender of last resort in the domestic economy, however, the National Bank was then presented by its member banks with *faits accomplis* that it had to monetize through primary emission in order to avoid threatening countrywide economic crisis and thus defeating the purpose of monetary restriction.[14] The alternative (as occurred in the early 1980s when the National Bank, under IMF pressure, refused to bail out such republican banks) was for networks of managers and republican politicians to choose to forestall bankruptcy by socializing the debt over the territory of the bank among all of its enterprise depositors.

The control by producers over finance—through cooperative banks and

[14] Shirley Gedeon, personal communication; see also her "Monetary Disequilibrium and Bank Reform Proposals in Yugoslavia" and "Post-Keynesian Theory of Money."

contractual relations with suppliers—therefore made it possible for larger, processing and manufacturing firms to try to keep production going and wages paid in the face of central restrictions by shifting costs to others. The bias in favor of large firms to the detriment of smaller and poorer firms was compounded by the territorial organization of the banking system. Two highly publicized examples in the 1980s—when the Zagreb Bank and the Belgrade Bank were near bankruptcy as a result of the debts of their largest depositors (the Croatian oil producer INA and the Smederevo steelworks, respectively)—demonstrate that firms considered of major consequence to a republic's economy were more likely to benefit from this socialization of debt.[15]

Firms also responded to the external shocks of overnight rises in imported costs due to devaluation and the frequent administrative controls on imports (imposed when price instruments were ineffective or too slow) by seeking greater security of supplies outside the channels affected by monetary regulation. Long-term contracts and informal relationships between suppliers and final producers (the "network" against which Kidrič railed in 1947–48 because it made producers less susceptible to central control and reinforced nonprice mechanisms of allocation), as well as vertical integration in order to internalize suppliers or gain market leverage, increased industrial concentration and monopolistic tendencies. Even short-term shortages enhanced the power of the branch-level economic chambers in rationing and allocating supplies among member producers and enforcing price agreements.

The overall effect of firms' response to anti-inflationary policy, therefore, was to undermine not only the policy, but also the effectiveness of the instruments of financial regulation and the long-term authority of monetary and fiscal policy.

Macroeconomic stabilization policy, in fact, followed a stop-and-go pattern of restriction and expansion that created recessions but did not coun-

[15] The system of proportionality in decision making gave large producers with large accounts the primary influence over bank policy in any case. As members of the banks' governing boards, the managers of large firms were often personally (and politically, through party membership or connections) vulnerable to political pressure from a republic's leadership to take decisions said to be necessary to protect the republic's economy, rather than decide on the basis of banking criteria alone; see the 1982 *Start* interview with Tomislav Badovinac, the temporary manager appointed to restructure the Economic Bank of Zagreb (Privredna Banka Zagreba) after the affair that nearly bankrupted this primary bank of Croatia. In analyzing the bank's liquidity crisis, Badovinac (and others) focused on the lack of independence in banking and on the effect of federal price and trade regulation of the strategic oil industry (84 percent of the bank's $1.1 billion foreign debt was due to the losses of the primary oil producer in Croatia, INA, and the primary electricity producer, Electroprivreda). On the other hand, little attention was paid to the trouble that Citibank decided to cause for the Economic Bank when it was twenty-four hours late on repayment of outstanding loans on March 3, 1982.

teract them with Keynesian-like new credit to increase employment because the transactions being monetized had already occurred. Instead of counteracting global movements, policy exacerbated their effect. It became restrictive when global demand fell, tightened further until enterprise debt forced monetary expansion, and was truly expansive only when new foreign money was available. The first consequence of expansion being a surge in imports, however, the resulting trade deficit would start the cycle anew.[16] The analysis by Gapinski, Škegro, and Zuehlke found that unemployment grew when the money supply expanded because expansion created a trade deficit. Increases in nominal government expenditures lowered unemployment in a "Keynesian-like . . . big, real effect," but generated a new round of unemployment and foreign debt because of the effect on the foreign sector.[17]

Fiscal policy could not be intentionally expansionary in support of employment because its purpose was to supplement monetary policy in maintaining balanced budgets and because deficit financing through domestic instruments was not institutionally possible. As an accounting mechanism, taxation increased when revenues declined.[18] Because stabilization policy combined demand repression with trade liberalization and supply-side tax cuts on firms, its effect was to reduce dramatically federal revenue—customs duties, the turnover tax (later the sales tax), and grants from the republics' taxes on enterprises. Cuts, not increases, in public expenditures had to follow. To cover essential expenditures (particularly for defense, which was the largest item of the minimalist federal budget) that could not be cut, the federal government had to search for other sources of revenue. It had three self-defeating choices: to demand more from republican budgets, reducing monies for developmental investment and employment expansion in the republics; to borrow more monies abroad, only creating the need down the road for renewed stabilization policy; or to print money, thus also reviving the impulse for anti-inflationary policy. The federal government did have means to spend outside the budget that could expand employment, and it was constitutionally obliged to do so for purposes of national security and basic infrastructure. But where these monies did not come from republican

[16] See Dyker, *Yugoslavia: Socialism, Development, and Debt*; Horvat, *The Yugoslav Economic System*; and Bajt, "Lessons from the Labor-Management Laboratory." Horvat cites a 1973 study by Marko Kranjec that shows that fiscal policy after 1965 exacerbated cyclical activity 66 to 99 percent (251).

[17] Gapinski, Škegro, and Zuehlke, *Modeling*, 211–12.

[18] Without a bond market, the government could not use fiscal policy to counteract the effects of the market, foreign or domestic. Not only could the government not borrow from the population, it actually was the lender to the population, through intergovernmental transfers (from republics and provinces to the federation and from the federal government— through credits—back to producers and lower-level governments).

contributions in a direct trade-off with republican investment and employment promotion, they were largely foreign credits (above all, World Bank development loans for infrastructure). The cycle shows up in the Gapinski, Škegro, and Zuehlke analysis: a period of foreign borrowing was always followed by a period of domestic taxation, and the availability of foreign credit determined the current marginal tax rate on enterprise income ("profits").[19]

The conflict between the monetary instruments designed for a closed, socialist, and industrializing economy and the demands of international openness becomes particularly clear when one considers the burden that exchange-rate policy should have borne in international adjustment. The question of its role also introduces a more fundamental problem: whether the government's policies were appropriate to the conditions it faced. A constant feature of macroeconomic stabilization policy and the "stop" side of the stop-and-go cycle of international adjustment was devaluation of the dinar. In the language of Kiro Gligorov's explanation of the 1952 devaluation, it was an instrument of "economic coercion" to force producers to increase supply.[20] The failure of devaluation as a way to resolve trade deficits and of exchange-rate policy in the 1970s, when the dinar was allowed to float but became overvalued, was attributed to a mercantilist protection of domestic manufacturers. Such protection could be seen to originate in the leaders' early strategy for industrialization and then to be perpetuated over time, in manufacturers' economic power and the favoritism shown to exporters because of persistent trade deficits. But the problem of devaluation and, later, of a market-clearing exchange rate as instruments to manage foreign trade had far more to do with Yugoslavia's particular niche in the international economy.[21]

The country's primary problem was not fluctuating demand for its exports in which price mattered most, but supply shocks—in the price of credit, the prices of imports necessary to production (raw materials, fuels, equipment, and spare parts), and the political barriers imposed unpredictably against Yugoslavia's exports, regardless of price. Its primary export markets, moreover, operated not on competitive demand principles but on bilateral contracts in the East, the South, and even the West (financed by suppliers' credits or, by the 1970s, on countertrade terms). The import dependence of most production for export to Western markets not only made exchange-rate policy largely ineffective where it might have operated, but also meant that devaluation always fueled inflationary pressures at home. Because Yugoslavia was a small country in the global economy,

[19] Gapinski, Škegro, and Zuehlke, *Modeling*, 97, 215–16.

[20] K. Gligorov, "Factors in Our Economic Stabilization."

[21] On the reasons that devaluation and exchange-rate policy were ineffective and inappropriate instruments, see especially Dyker, *Yugoslavia*, 97–101.

with no control over the price of imports or terms of trade, producers could increase revenues only by increasing supply. But this ran up against the supply bottlenecks caused by import restrictions. The primary way producers adjusted to the shift in price structures due to devaluation was thus not to expand exports but to cut production or shift temporarily to domestic suppliers where possible. As was the case with monetary policy, the segmentation of markets, accounting character of financial institutions, and pervasive use of supply networks among firms or vertical integration made reliance on price mechanisms for adjustment less than effective.[22]

Instead, the conjunction of the leaders' guided Ricardian strategy with foreign creditors' insistence on foreign-trade liberalization and on the benefits of foreign competition had the effect (without any need for political pressure on the part of firms) of transforming exchange-rate policy into an instrument of industrial policy. An overvalued dinar favored manufacturers with cheap imported supplies so that they could be more competitive in foreign markets, just as domestic price policy favored them with regulated raw-material prices. Price liberalization exposed domestic producers of production inputs (such as farmers) to foreign competition, forcing them to produce at lower cost (or go out of business).[23] The aim of foreign-trade protection, however, was primarily to safeguard national-security concerns (such as the food and energy policy and sectors such as shipbuilding, iron and steel, and machine building—all of which were also export producers, though more often for markets in the East and South than for hard-currency Western ones). The aim of liberalization was to force down prices of raw materials at home.

As for employment, the effect of repeated devaluation of the currency was instead to feed the inflationary spiral of domestic prices; in raising the nonlabor costs of production, particularly where supply bottlenecks made an immediate supply response difficult, it required firms to adjust by lowering labor costs—that is, by cutting (or not expanding) employment.

The leadership was not oblivious to the ineffectiveness of its instruments to reduce the balance-of-payments deficit and restore growth, but its interpretation of the problem (often aided by IMF advisers) was that "financial discipline" was missing and that the economic incentives had

[22] Commander, in "Inflation and the Transition to a Market Economy," analyzes the inflationary consequence of stabilization policy from the special perspective of socialist economies in transition to market economies in the early 1990s, where institutional particularities (such as a segmented financial system) and the burdens left from the previous regime (such as a stock of interenterprise debt) must be taken into account in applying such policy.

[23] Author's discussions with Živko Pregl and Ferdnand Trost in Ljubljana, 1982, and with Božo Marendić and Borislav Škegro in Zagreb. Most economists criticized the country's nearly always overvalued exchange rate.

become distorted. To restore both discipline and the effectiveness of production incentives, the government would initiate another round of decentralizing institutional reforms, extend the realm of "self-management" to include more activities in the regime of economic accounting and fiscal responsibility, and attempt to reassert the role of enterprises in keeping wages and expenditures within the constraints of actual earnings, against contrary developments in the interim since the last reforms. For example, in place of cutting government expenditures whole categories of expenditures would be removed from the federal budget and handed to budgetary authorities closer to producers or to independent agencies with autonomous, self-managed funds (as in the case of social services). By 1975, public expenditures and tax authority were shared by more than eight thousand parastatal "self-managing communities of interest."[24] Even the federal fund for less-developed areas—the sole remaining direct role of the central government in economic development—was restructured in the late 1970s to improve financial discipline over the use of the monies by giving republics more control over their contributions. Republics could be absolved from up to half of their tax obligation to the fund if their firms invested directly in firms in the southern republics and provinces targeted by the fund (bypassing federal, republican, and provincial authorities). In the 1980s, authorities replaced the fund's managing board with representatives elected from enterprises instead of republican governments. In other words, the response to ineffective policy was to decentralize and to reduce further the scope of governmental policy.

An unusually difficult problem was to settle on a system for allocating foreign exchange that would allow it to reach those most in need of Western imports (and that would resolve bitter political fights over access) while not worsening the deficit. The primary principle that enterprises were most likely to be financially responsible gave to firms that earned foreign exchange the right to retain a certain (and growing) percentage as an export incentive. But this left many domestic producers of raw and intermediate materials, who nonetheless could not produce without imports or could do so more profitably with cheaper foreign supplies, without access to foreign exchange or in the position of having to bargain for it in producers' associations. Bankruptcy was no solution (regardless of the consequences for unemployment) because such firms often supplied goods essential to export producers as well as those serving the domestic market.[25] Proposals to lower retention quotas and give more control to

---

[24] "Fiscal System and Fiscal Policy," 27–28.

[25] The primary demand of the student demonstrators during the events of 1970–71 in Croatia was an increase for Croat firms in the retention quota for foreign exchange; although

the National Bank succumbed to the politics of economic power within the system, defeated by the objections of powerful export producers and the republics (especially Slovenia and Croatia) into which the largest share of hard currency flowed.

The government's response was to give firms and territorial banks greater freedom to borrow abroad, so as to increase the supply of foreign currency while getting it into the hands of those best able to guarantee repayment as judged by the foreign lender. Yet, as a consequence of international changes after the early 1970s in its regime toward foreign borrowing, the federal government had to guarantee most of this debt and therefore repay a mounting foreign debt that it had had no part in borrowing. By 1976, the government had divided the balance of payments into separate republican accounts in order to hold each republic directly responsible for repayment. Republic-level "self-managing communities of interest for foreign economic relations" were established to give producers' organizations greater control over export policy and foreign-exchange allocation, on the basis of a fund created with half of the federal customs revenues.[26]

In contrast to the pressures toward concentration and financial centralization found in open market economies, the Yugoslav government sought further decentralization, deconcentration, and producer control. The reasons for this choice multiplied with time. In making enterprises responsible for stabilization, the leadership remained committed to its

---

the political leadership was removed, the demand was granted. On the difficulties that domestic producers selling on the domestic market had in obtaining foreign exchange to pay for imports of essential inputs, and the resulting bottlenecks for other producers—including those earning foreign exchange through exports—see, for example, the article in *Borba* (June 26, 1982) on the rubber and chemical industry "Balkan" in Suva Reka, Kosovo; and Škrbić, "Manjak—četiri milijarde," on the steel industry and iron metallurgy complex at Zenica, Bosnia-Herzegovina. A 1982 article in *Ekonomska Politika* ("Prerada metala: Strah od neizvesnosti") discusses the pressure from the metal-processing industry—complaining of rising uncertainty over supplies from the domestic steel industry because of foreign-exchange shortages—to give steel the same priority status as oil in access to foreign exchange. This pressure led the federal "self-managing community of interest for foreign economic relations" to propose that $80 million be set aside for steel mills; the National Bank opposed this move unless the resulting export production was sold to convertible-currency countries.

[26] In 1977–78, banks were permitted to issue securities. The Agrokomerc scandal of 1987 can be traced to this regulation; the Bosnian conglomerate issued bonds far in excess of its cover, which were purchased in large amounts by banks throughout the country—above all Ljubljana Bank—apparently on the assumption that the important political connections of the Agrokomerc director and the political assurances of the Bosnian political elite were sufficient guarantee. Major Western commercial banks made a similar mistake in lending to Eastern Europe on the assumption that the Soviet umbrella was sufficient guarantee of repayment.

strategy of dismantling the state and combining political right with economic interest. The IMF campaigned for decentralization and reduced governmental interference in the economy, ostensibly because these would encourage market forces. The interests of profitable producers and wealthier republics in gaining greater autonomy over their resources (above all, foreign exchange) were even stronger after periods of restrictions and recession. And the further decentralization proceeded, the more the political representatives of the republics and enterprises saw a vested interest in keeping rights over assets, reducing further the competence and finances of the federation, and opposing any proposal for re-centralization, even if it meant a more effective policy. Nonetheless, these reforms did continue to reduce the federal government's capacity for monetary control and macroeconomic management, and therefore for producing the noninflationary growth necessary to prevent industrial unemployment.

Alongside the recessionary bias of macroeconomic policy, therefore, there was a decline in the federal role in preventing unemployment of the developmental kind by seeing to the developmental investment and sectoral proportions necessary to absorb the agricultural surplus and demographic increase; and this role was in any case also subordinated to foreign policy. The first stage of decentralizing reforms after 1952 was the transfer (by 1958) of federal sectoral-investment funds and responsibility for developmental investment to territorial banks and planning offices in the republics. By 1971, federal authorities had lost all control over credit policy.[27] As the vacuum in federal investment funds was filled by foreign monies, influence on the policies (if not always the consequences) of developmental investment came increasingly from multilateral and public lenders—above all the World Bank—as one can see clearly in the Green Plan for agriculture, which was initiated in 1973, and the priorities of the social plan for 1976–80.[28] From the early years, however, priority sectors of the social plans were defined by the priority placed on reducing the balance-of-payments deficit and guarding national security (with actual investment preferences depending on particular international conditions). In place of planners' calculations of investment to protect the sectoral balance of domestic production and maintain steady growth, the

[27] Dyker, *Yugoslavia*, 120, 147.

[28] On the Green Plan of 1973, by which the World Bank made available 1 billion dinars for investment credits in agriculture—channeled through contracts with the social sector but available only for approved development projects in the private sector—see Miller, "Socialism and Agriculture in Yugoslavia," 38 n. 64; and Dyker, *Yugoslavia*, 155–56. On the notable similarity between the Yugoslav social plan of 1976–80 and the World Bank proposals for structural adjustment, see the discussion in the World Bank's *Yugoslavia: Adjustment Policies and Development Perspectives*.

federal plan emphasized a combination of export promotion and import-substituting investments, when national security and the external terms of trade for manufacturers' key production supplies favored domestic production. Employment remained a residual of the plans—but, as we will see in the next chapter, the preferred means for international adjustment directly affected the use of labor in the same way that they had in the first decade of power.

POLITICAL CONFLICT AND POLICY CHOICE

The influence of international openness and adjustment did not only undermine the governmental capacity to implement the leaders' strategy for economic growth and full employment; it was equally important in its effect on the lines of political conflict over policy. Critics of Yugoslavia's failure to adopt successful policies of international adjustment and to reverse the mounting foreign debt, persistent trade deficits, and dependence on borrowing, refinancing, and the IMF and foreign banks tend to focus on elite conflict.

Some argue that the problem lay in the lack of consensus (surely exacerbated by—though not originating in—a voting system at the federal level that required consensus and gave each republic a veto). Disagreements caused prolonged delays in formulating policy and diffident implementation. Yet countries renowned at the time for their success at international adjustment, such as Japan and Sweden, also were known for prolonged gestation periods for formulating policy and reaching consensus. The weakness of enforcement mechanisms discussed in the previous section was due not to elite conflict but to the strategy on which the leaders agreed.

Others argue that political leaders were divided between economic reformers and conservative antireformers, and that the failure of economic policy was due to the success of conservative forces in preventing full promulgation of liberal market reforms. This obstruction, it is said, grew largely out of conservatives' reaction to the unemployment threat from "efficiency-oriented" reforms. According to this argument, economic policy in the postwar period had two major turning points: the marketizing economic Reform of 1965 (it is always capitalized, to distinguish it from other reforms) and the constitution of 1974 legislating its reversal at the hands of party conservatives. Yet, as with the great divide attributed to 1948 and the Tito-Stalin conflict, as well as with the "end of the administrative system" in 1952, a closer examination of economic policy reveals a different chronology than is suggested by political rhetoric. As with 1946–52, the conflict is better portrayed as one between opposing economic institutions and policies intended to facilitate microeconomic adjustments to a change in international conditions—the tension identified in chapters 2 and 4 between the Slovene and Foča models—than as one between liberal reformers and conservative reactionaries.

The difficulty was that the existence of elite political conflict did not bring forth policy alternatives to counteract the effect of openness on the economic strategy chosen in the early period. In contrast to the historical origins of proemployment policy in the West, no political group organized to challenge the center's growth policy on the grounds that it caused unemployment—not even when this policy of macroeconomic stabilization, workplace-centered measures of productivity, and antigovernment (decentralizing and "socializing") reforms failed to achieve its explicit objective of restoring noninflationary growth and reducing trade deficits.

Instead, elite conflict focused primarily on the distributive consequences of such stabilization policy: contributions to the federal budget and to the federal development fund, the nature of expenditure cuts, and the regime for allocating foreign exchange. More significant than elites' disagreement was their common solution to such conflicts over money. By increasing the pie through more foreign credits or federal seigniorage and by compensating for cuts with greater autonomy over the use of funds, they only increased the difficulties in controlling the money supply, fed inflation, and added to the financial segmentation that resulted from autonomous, self-managed budgets.

The vicious circle of such economic policy and conflict over distribution was intensified by the political outcomes. The more unsuccessful international adjustment was, the more openness and flexibility among foreign markets were valued. The more the criteria of international participation dominated federal policy choices, the less room there was for genuine policy debate among domestic actors and the less effective became the political institutions necessary to successful international adjustment. The more unsuccessful that adjustment was, the more important federal policy was to the economic fate of republics and localities, and the less economic authority it retained. Whereas Peter Katzenstein argues that Austria's and Switzerland's success "continuously relegitimize[s]" the political institutions necessary to national policy and strengthens the "compatibility of views" between the bargaining parties that precedes such cooperation,[29] one can see the mirror image in the Yugoslav case. Failure continuously delegitimized federal institutions and weakened consensus and cooperation. In contrast to the view that there were sharp policy divides in 1965 and 1974, the findings of the literature on social democratic regimes fit Yugoslavia as well: the institutions of political and economic power adopted by 1952 limited later choices.

---

[29] Katzenstein, *Corporatism and Change*, 29.

Thus, although liberals accused conservatives of obstructing market reforms, they were unwilling to abandon the rights of republics and enterprises to control economic assets (rights that increased with each stage of treform, including stages called reactionary) in favor of market-oriented policy on the grounds that this was recentralization; nor would they renounce the policies favoring final-commodity producers (called "profitable" firms) and export production in favor of a real market economy. Although they promoted "westernization" and accused conservatives of an eastward inclination, the economic power of most liberals lay in their access to all three trading spheres. Even if full membership in Western organizations had been within the country's reach (through the European Community and NATO or the neutral states' European Free Trade Association), the most successful manufacturers were those producing for both civilian and military needs[30] and able to arbitrage their participation in all three foreign markets when international conditions changed. Unwilling to recognize the consequences of their preferred reforms for domestic producers of raw and intermediate goods and for areas lacking a well-developed commercial infrastructure or geostrategic advantage in foreign markets, and able to obstruct market allocation of foreign exchange and impose territorial restrictions on the movement of labor and capital, most liberals contributed both to the political necessity of Kaldorian compensations to the less profitable firms and areas (compensations that they often condemned) and to the ineffectiveness of central policy.[31]

While it is true that conservatives had no love for marketizing, westernizing economic reform because it resulted in unemployment in 1950–52 and the 1960s and also in economic inequality, their influence on economic policy was secondary once the decisions on the form of the state had been made. And although the decisions of 1965 were politically significant, not for economic reform but for security policy, only a minority among the conservatives would have preferred joining the Warsaw Pact and the Council for Mutual Economic Assistance (CMEA) as full mem-

[30] Such manufacturers were identifiable by their membership in the association of firms producing on military contract created in the 1980s, the Community for Armaments and Military Equipment of Yugoslavia (ZINVOJ).

[31] In the (Nicholas) Kaldor version of the compensation principle in welfare economics, "gainers compensate losers": there is compensation "of potential losers by gainers, so as to leave the former with at least the same real income as they had enjoyed under the *original* distribution of income before the change." The second version is the (Tibor) Scitovsky principle of "losers bribing gainers": "The payment of a compensation or bribe by those likely to be damaged by a change to the gainers from it: a payment adequate to dissuade the latter from advocating the change and still leave the potential losers better off than they were destined to be if the change were to be made" (Dobb, *Welfare Economics and the Economics of Socialism*, 84–85). Dobb also discusses the possible contradictions in both versions, as well as in the proposal by Scitovsky to join the two (86–118).

bers. Conservatives were in conflict with liberals primarily over investment preferences—favoring domestic producers of fuels, grains, and
capital goods—but not over the country's international position. They
were unwilling to challenge the Faustian bargain of "national communism" that traded independence of Moscow for a special role in world
diplomacy and access to Western finance. For most conservatives and
liberals, the risks of abandoning this international comparative advantage
were too great. Yet the policy consensus on a macrosystems approach to
international adjustment to which scholars attribute much of the success
with full employment, from Austria to Sweden,[32] surely had its source in
the choice in the immediate postwar period to orient those countries toward the U.S.-organized trading and security regimes while retaining sufficient independence for that macroeconomic policy.

Contrary to the findings of the literature on economic policies of labor-
oriented governments, then, the initiative for Yugoslav policy came not
from domestic pressures but from international developments. Because
those events were largely unpredictable, felt mainly through a crisis in
foreign accounts or a threat to national security, they tended to preempt
systematic organization of domestic political pressure as well. The federal
government attempted to represent the interests of labor—in Kardelj's
redefinition, income recipients in socialist communities of work—but its
bargaining was with international capital, not domestic organizations of
capital. To prevent unemployment—which was defined as being left
without means of subsistence—the government adjusted regulations in
the microeconomic sphere to increase labor's productivity and to rationalize employment in accordance with international conditions. (The consequences of these adjustments for unemployment are the subject of
chapter 8.)

The data on unemployment discussed in chapter 6 reveal the path of
central economic policy more clearly than does the political rhetoric of
domestic party factions and independent economists. Policy cycles can be
identified roughly each decade, as changes in national security, foreign
trade, and the supply of foreign capital led to domestic policy shifts. The
transitional period continued after 1950 until 1957; the next period was
1958 to 1967, then 1968 to 1978, and finally 1979 to 1989. If there were
defining moments, such as 1965 and 1974 were said to be, they were
rather 1961, when the proportion of the labor force employed was at its
maximum and after which incremental capital-outputs ratios continued to
rise,[33] and 1971, after which the already-rising rate of unemployment escalated sharply and unemployment was clearly structural.

[32] See especially Lehmbruch, "Liberal Corporatism and Party Government"; and
Scharpf, "Economic and Institutional Constraints of Full-Employment Strategies."
[33] Pavle Sicherl, personal communication, Ljubljana, October 1981, based on un-

1953–1957

Policy in this first postwar period was governed by the availability of foreign credits (particularly U.S. food and military aid) and the gradual reduction of regional security tensions. They made it possible for the leadership to shift away from the investments of military self-reliance, to proceed with demobilization and cut the defense budget, to increase investments in consumer goods and light manufactures for the urban and industrial population and for export, and to increase trade relations substantially. The end of the Korean War ameliorated international shortages and price inflation of defense-related raw materials, and the country's terms of trade began to improve. The death of Stalin in 1953 revived debates throughout the Eastern bloc on "new-course" policies like the ones the Yugoslavs had begun several years earlier. Regional peace seemed secured in 1954 with the end of the Allied occupation in Germany, the resolution of the Trieste crisis (which was largely responsible for delaying demobilization of the Partisan army), and the neutralization of the Truman Doctrine in the Balkans, marked by the Balkan Pact between Yugoslavia, Greece, and Turkey. In 1955 the peace treaty was signed in Austria, and Yugoslav membership in the Organization for Economic Cooperation opened the possibility of better trade relations with Western Europe and removed barriers to emigration. The government agreed to issue passports upon demand, making open borders a reality for citizens. The founding conference of the nonalignment movement the same year brought favorable agreements for oil and strategic materials from developing-country allies.[34] Rapprochement with the new Soviet leadership of Georgy Malenkov and Nikita Khrushchev brought an end to the Eastern blockade; trade agreements with the Soviet Union for import of heavy weaponry, other military equipment, and a nuclear reactor; and, in 1956, observer status in the CMEA.

These international conditions made possible a continuation of the pol-

---

published studies done on contract in possession of the author. Dyker summarizes a number of studies over the postwar period (*Yugoslavia*, 46, 104, 140).

[34] The move to petroleum fuels occurred in Japan and the USSR as well; but in Yugoslavia the switch caused a major debate among technocrats in 1955–58 because there were substantial domestic sources of energy (coal and especially hydroelectric power, for which Yugoslavia's technical innovations were internationally respected) and because of the costs of user conversion and external dependency. The debate began with an engineer at Elektroprivreda and continued with a 1963 study for the federal Economic Chamber (Privredna Komora) on capacity use (see the report on the engineering study in *Ekonomski Pregled*, nos. 3–5 [1968]). Many accused the main oil company, INA (Zagreb), of making profits by importing more crude oil than was needed domestically and stimulating demand by getting people to switch. The debt problems of the 1970s and the persistent political problems with coal miners, especially in 1968–70, were unforeseen.

icy toward labor outlined in the program of the sixth party congress in
November 1952. Able to reduce the defense budget's drain on the economy from its high of 22 percent of GNP in 1952 down to 8.5 percent in
1957, the government oversaw a boom period from 1954 to 1957 based on
foreign credits that enabled the cheap import of grains, other foods, and
raw materials from the West (52.2 percent of the deficit on current account up to 1955 was covered by grants and only 16.2 percent by loans).[35]
Thus "the number of workmen [could] be reduced in agriculture" with
mechanization of state and cooperative farms to improve yields. In the
rest of agriculture, credits, tax relief, and government regulations aimed
to encourage intensive cropping and the development of small industries
to process agricultural goods "in which part of the relieved labor could be
engaged."[36] This policy also made possible the idea of a settled citizen
soldiery for the territorial defense forces, essential to demobilization of
the standing army. In March–May 1953, a second agrarian reform legalized the end of the peasant labor cooperatives and also limited private
landholdings to ten hectares (over Bakarić's objections), transferring land
above that amount to remaining cooperatives to compensate them for
land withdrawn by peasants returning to private ownership. As the avenue to socialization through market control, the general farmers' cooperatives in the villages were given a monopoly over the purchase of private
farmers' produce and their access to fertilizers, machinery, and improved
seeds.[37] Although the key projects of the five-year plan of 1947–51 were
not completed until 1956, in 1953 the leadership confirmed the shift in
investment policy to light manufacturing and consumer goods and to what
Kardelj called a "preference" for agriculture. The adoption of this policy
by the party's executive committee in 1954 was accompanied by the transfer of investment planning to independent funds at each level of government (the federal fund was called the General Investment Fund, or GIF).

Nonetheless, unsettled international conditions required the policy's
reaffirmation at a high-level meeting of party leaders (*savjetovanje kod
druga Tita*, or conference with Tito—the informal gathering of close advisers used for the decisions of December 1948) on September 25, 1955,

[35] Macesich, "Major Trends in the Postwar Economy of Yugoslavia." "Wheat imports rose
to an annual average of 700,000 tons in 1952–54 as against only 100,000 tons in 1948–51 . . .
[and] in 1955–58 . . . [to] the very high rate of over a million tons per annum" (Warriner,
Revolution in Eastern Europe, 71). An agreement in January 1956 for American wheat,
cotton, and lard was the largest Public Law 480 program for any country to that date.

[36] Kardelj, in his address to the sixth congress of the LCY in 1952.

[37] Tomasevich, "Collectivization of Agriculture in Yugoslavia"; Rusinow, review of *Die
Kooperation zwischen den privaten Landwirtschaftsbetrieben und den gesellschaftlichen
Wirtschaftsorganisationen*, by Ivan Lončarević; "Poljoprivredna stanovništvo," in *Privreda
FNRJ u periodu 1947–1956*; Savez Komunista Jugoslavije, *Borba Komunista Jugoslavije za
socijalističku demokratiju*; Warriner, *Revolution in Eastern Europe*.

followed in October by a formal consultation with economic experts. The next year, the leaders' assumptions about the international political conjuncture of regional security and peaceful coexistence were again interrupted. The formation of NATO in 1948 and the Warsaw Pact in May 1955 had already revived internal party disputes over international alignments that the nonalignment movement had not fully dispelled. The liberals' pressure in favor of the territorial defense forces in the republics, which would allow the standing army to be cut, and in favor of republican authority over manufacturing and investment was undercut by the global debate on nuclear warfare and deterrence, which gave renewed life to the YPA and to the institutes and personnel engaged in the domestic atomic-energy program.[38] The prospect that American military aid would end in 1957,[39] the growing hostility of the U.S. Congress at Yugoslavia's rapprochement with the USSR and the organization of the nonalignment movement, and then the Suez crisis—which endangered both oil supplies and the principle of nonalignment—seemed to bring a renewal of the threats of war and isolation of the late 1940s. Unrest in Poland, the occupation of Hungary in October 1956, and Soviet cancellation once again of new trade agreements and credits the next February[40] forced a delay in the second five-year plan (intended for 1957–61), and the leadership reverted to some elements of forced self-reliance and defense preparedness. This included the reinstitution, between 1956 and 1958, of the volunteer youth brigades that had been disbanded "forever" only three years before. There was a renewed effort in the spring of 1957 at the "socialist transformation" of agriculture, called a "break-through on a narrow front" in the party platform written at the end of the year.[41] Common or uncultivated lands were taken into the public sector (a form of "enclosures").[42] Farmers' cooperatives received exclusive control over new in-

[38] Until 1961—the high point of investment in nuclear energy—this program received 60 percent of the country's expenditures for research and development. S. Dedijer, "Tito's Bomb," discusses the origins of the program and gives some data on it. On the Soviet nuclear-warfare debate, see Garthoff, "The Death of Stalin."

[39] Most studies (for example, Lampe, Prickett, and Adamović, *Yugoslav-American Economic Relations since World War II*) argue that the Yugoslavs requested termination of U.S. aid. But this must have been only a formality to protect the idea of independence, for they knew aid was being ended (as it was at the same time for similar recipients, from Spain to South Korea).

[40] They were reinstated in July 1957, and Tito and Khrushchev met secretly in Bucharest in August. But in November an "antirevisionism" resolution was read at the Moscow celebration of the October Revolution and the draft program of the LCY platform was criticized strongly—and in December the credits were again retracted, for another five years.

[41] Warriner, *Revolution in Eastern Europe*, 79; the reference again is to Stalin's 1928 speech on collectivization.

[42] This was accomplished with two laws on land use in 1957, the Uncultivated Land Act and the Expropriation Act.

vestment in the private sector, to encourage their extension from marketing into production. And private farmers were required to join district marketing boards (business leagues, or *poslovni savezi*)[43] and encouraged to form joint ventures with social-sector farmers in order to get access to development credits, agricultural services, and machinery.

Nonetheless, at the end of 1956, Kardelj argued that the "lessons of Hungary" required a new "liberalization." The economic growth in 1957–61 would eventually be based largely on foreign commercial loans and suppliers' credits that had to be repaid with interest (in 1956–60, 10.7 percent of the trade deficit was covered by grants, 43 percent by loans) and on revenues from commodity exports. The latter seemed to require trade liberalization.[44]

1958–1967

The difficulties with aid now forced to a head a debate already in progress about the primary cause of the persistent trade deficits. Liberals among the politicians, influential economists, and industrialists from the more-developed western republics (above all Slovenia, personified by Boris Krajger) were convinced that the solution was export orientation and linking up with the process of European trade integration that was taking a leap forward in 1958 with the Treaty of Rome (a policy they called "integration into the international division of labor").[45] Fearing the consequences of exclusion from this process on the basis of Yugoslavia's particular neutrality and government-negotiated trade, liberals pointed to the boom in processing industries that favorable prices and cheap imported raw materials had brought. This was also the era of fascination in socialist countries with the potential for economic growth and human liberation promised by the "scientific-technological revolution," a view already present in Kidrič's Slovene model. Yugoslav liberals accordingly argued that growth should be based on technological modernization through imported Western machinery and cheaper production supplies. The latter would eventually be replaced by domestic supplies when foreign price competition forced domestic producers of raw materials and wage goods to raise their productivity and cut costs. In opposition to this

[43] See chap. 3, n. 67.

[44] Ljubomir Madžar, personal communication.

[45] On the consequences for Yugoslavia of the decisions by Western European countries to make their currencies convertible, end the European Payments Union, and create the European Monetary Fund in 1958, see the article by B. Filipović in the journal of the National Bank, *Finansije* (May 1959). Filipović also discusses the change in 1958 in the role of the U.S. dollar and the major influence this change had on world trade, on the IMF, and on economic aid.

view, the developmentalists, whose professional base was most closely identified with Belgrade, had been arguing throughout the 1950s that the root cause of the trade deficit was the importation of food, especially wheat,[46] as a result of low agricultural productivity at home.[47]

In 1958, as the liberals had hoped, the decision was taken to seek membership in the GATT, to obtain IMF standby credits to cover the difficult transition of trade liberalization (in 1958 and again in 1961 and 1965), and to begin a new stage of economic reform and institutional change necessary to meet the GATT conditions. Arguing that by 1958 Yugoslavia had reached the "middle level of development," by which they meant that its natural resources were fully utilized, its economy stable, and its industry able to satisfy most domestic needs,[48] the leaders also announced that there was no longer any need for federal investment in development. The republics should assume responsibility for their own development policy, and territorial allocation of investment, foreign exchange, and supplies should accordingly replace the sectoral plans. The socialization of investment (as it was called) transferred funds from the GIF and sectoral banks (for industry, agriculture, and foreign trade) to republic-level (territorial) banks operating on commercial terms within their territory. Communes assumed responsibility for financing social services in place of federal grants-in-aid.

By 1961, liberalization had replaced the multiple exchange coefficients in foreign trade and differential tax rates appropriate to sectoral planning with uniform customs tariffs and tax rates, removed agricultural protection, and reemphasized enterprise profitability. Because full "economic independence"[49] was being granted to the republics while substantial differences in levels of development remained, the leaders also agreed to create a compensation mechanism through low-interest loans to republics

---

[46] In 1951–54, food made up 26 percent of total imports—the third-highest percentage in Europe, after Germany and the United Kingdom, and the highest per capita (*Privreda FNRJ, 1957*, 280). *Privreda FNRJ u periodu 1947–1956* laments, "It's a shame that, in the return to the earlier position [on cooperatives], the results achieved weren't used at least to combine farmsteads of former cooperants." The agrarian law of May 1953 did include *arondacija* (consolidation of a single farmer's parcelized holdings) for new estates and enclosures of existing ones, but it was not executed. Investment in agriculture in 1947–56 represented 9 percent of economic investments and 7 percent of total investments in the economy (*Privreda FNRJ u periodu 1947–1956*, 161).

[47] See, for example, the compendium by economists of the developmentalist school edited by R. Stojanović, *Yugoslav Economists on Problems of a Socialist Economy*; Čobeljić, *Politika i metodi privrednog razvoja Jugoslavije, 1947–1956*; and particularly *Privreda FNRJ, 1957*.

[48] Cited in *Les forces armées de la RSFY*; this language also permeates the speeches of the eighth party congress in 1964 (see *Osmi kongres SKJ*).

[49] Tito, address to the eighth party congress, December 1964, in *Osmi kongres SKJ*, 38.

and regions designated as less developed.[50] It would be based on a 2 percent (in place of the previous 6 percent) capital tax on public-sector firms, and because these firms were within republican jurisdiction, the new federal fund would be financed by republican taxation. In the third social plan of 1961–65, emphasis was placed on "regional growth."

The dual push for imported technology and export promotion also affected the army. It chose to modernize technologically by purchasing armaments and licenses in world markets and, in order to pay for this investment, to increase the export of arms. The policy of export promotion extended to services as well, most importantly the further development of the tourist industry on the Adriatic coast, commercial extensions of the maritime fleet, and the export of labor (remittances from Yugoslav workers abroad soon came to cover more than half of the deficit on current account).

While the domestic reforms of 1958–61 were preoccupied with the liberalizations demanded by GATT membership and the orientation toward European trade, international price competitiveness, and export promotion, Tito entered his most determined phase of nonalignment. This included advocating economic assistance for poorer countries as a faster road to peace than military blocs and (Tito himself having decided not to pursue a nuclear force) campaigning against nuclear weapons. The painful domestic adjustment to global markets and to the criteria of foreign competition coincided, as in 1950–52, with two bad harvests (in 1960 and 1961) and with unfavorable conditions abroad. A serious recession occurred in Western economies in 1960–61 and again in the mid-1960s, and relations with the superpowers were anything but calm in 1960–63. The Yugoslavs' party program of 1958 and their choice for liberalization and a human-capital approach in response to Soviet rejection brought a repeat of the propaganda war of 1948–49, with the Moscow Declaration of December 1960 and then the sustained Chinese attack on the Yugoslav "way."[51] But the United States also objected to the Belgrade conference of nonaligned nations in 1961 by cutting off the economic aid it had only just granted when Yugoslavia's quarrel with the USSR revived. World

---

[50] It was called the Fund of the Federation, later changed to the Federal Fund for More Rapid Development of Less-Developed Republics and Regions and then to the Federal Fund for the Crediting of the Insufficiently Developed Republics and Provinces to emphasize its shift from grants-in-aid to repayable credits; finally, "regions" or "provinces" was replaced with "Kosovo". The GIF continued to operate until January 1, 1964, however, until quarrels about the new fund could be stilled.

[51] The new party platform of 1958 was published in English as *Yugoslavia's Way*. Criticism of Moscow's attack was taken up in particular by Veljko Vlahović in his speech to the fourth party plenum in 1962; Edvard Kardelj responded to the Chinese in his 1960 *Socialism and War*.

tensions skyrocketed with the Sino-Soviet split of 1961, the conflict between Khrushchev's pronuclear and aggressive third-world policies on the one hand and Kennedy's conventional-force buildup and focus on Europe on the other, and then the 1962 Cuban missile crisis and 1963 nuclear-force disputes within NATO.

Once again the government reacted by shifting the emphasis in investment policy back to basic industries during 1960 and 1961, and in 1963 the five-year plan for 1961–66 was abandoned in midstream. Moreover, the combination of domestic stagflation in response to the economic reforms, rising trade deficits after 1960, and disquiet over international events gave new life to the bitter political debate over the reform, the federal government's investment policy and its role in directing the rate and structure of developmental investment, and the remaining monopoly of the YPA over defense financing. This debate ended soon after relations improved with the United States and the USSR during 1963 and after the signing of the partial Nuclear Test Ban Treaty in January 1964.

At the momentous eighth party congress of December 1964, Tito rose to chastise party delegates for failing to complete the economic reform, "although a decision on this matter was arrived at a long time ago." Despite one last effort by representatives of Serbia to have agricultural production valued "adequately," the congress documents referred to federal transfers for agriculture and developmental investment as "wasted aid" to less-developed republics that should be limited to the completion of current projects and to the kind of "technical and personnel assistance" that Yugoslavia was sending to less-developed countries. Domestic capital-goods industries, many built largely for military self-reliance with government funds, were labeled "political factories" that ought to be closed. A reduction in government investment expenditures, accomplished by transferring to enterprises far greater responsibility for their own investment (primarily from internal funds), was called a victory for "workers' control" over "political forces" in investment decisions that properly belonged to "direct producers."[52]

With the end of the political battle over reforms in 1964 and the completion of the two-stage liberalization for GATT membership, the year 1965 is usually identified as a watershed—the year of the Reform, when the campaign surrounding two currency devaluations, two price revisions, and a new dinar brought the liberal policies home to the urban public. The consequences of the reform were also felt in a severe recession in 1965–68. Probably far more important than economic reform, though, were the drastic worsening in Yugoslavia's terms of trade and the

[52] *Osmi kongres SKJ.* (See "Practice and Theory," English version of congress proceedings, p. 55.)

Western recession, which dimmed hopes for export-oriented growth.[53]
The removal of tariff protections after 1961 did cause a mass closure of
private farms unable to compete with cheap imports. The resulting concentration of landholdings received a boost from the export-oriented policy of agro-industrial complexes and the intensification campaign for
economic rationalization in 1965–67, which brought further enclosures,
commassation, and mechanization of state farms.[54] Restrictions on the
purchase of agricultural machinery for private use came to an end in
1964.[55] The government chose to end its reliance on farmers' cooperatives
as intermediaries between the social and private sectors, removing all
remaining federal rebates, subsidies, and investment credits to agriculture and encouraging direct contracting between processing industries
and private farmers to support agro-industrial complexes (*kombinats*).
The federal fund for loans to less-developed regions began to operate
(after quarrels among the republics over redistribution had delayed it four
years), but the effect was to reduce sharply interrepublican transfers for
investment after 1965.

At least as important a part of the liberal victory sealed by the eighth
party congress was its decision on defense: to forgo nuclear deterrence
and orient military forces to the choice of conventional deterrence in Europe. Defense policy would thus place the territorial defense forces on a
near-equal footing with a smaller, more technologically sophisticated
standing army (a move marked by forced retirements of senior army officers in 1964) and would choose in 1965 to keep the country outside the
Warsaw Pact (a decision revealed by the absence of Yugoslav delegates at
the Warsaw Pact consultative political meeting in 1966). A massive political purge and demotions of military, internal-security, and party personnel (identified with the fall of Aleksandar Ranković at the fourth plenum
in July 1966 but in fact having begun in 1964) followed the sharing of the
last province of federal independence—jurisdiction over foreign affairs
and defense—with the republics.[56]

---

[53] Recessions in the U.S. economy occurred in 1948–49, 1953–54, 1957–58, 1960–61,
and 1965–67—all years of difficulty in the Yugoslav economy (Shonfield, *Modern Capitalism*, 10–18).

[54] See Miller, "Socialism and Agriculture in Yugoslavia"; and Rusinow, review of *Die
Kooperation*.

[55] Purchases then skyrocketed (Olga Supek, personal communication). To judge by
farmers' complaints in parliament that they found imported agricultural machinery less
suited to their conditions than domestic products, which had become less available, this was
not a policy to sell domestic inventories when external demand was falling.

[56] See Hondius, *The Yugoslav Community of Nations*, 270–72, 331–32. The story behind
Ranković's fall from power remains to be told, but the conventional wisdom—that it was due
to unhappiness with the excessive power he was said to wield domestically through the
secret police (there were charges that he was even bugging President Tito's private cham-

At the same time, the policy toward foreign aid and finance entered a new era as a result of the mounting foreign debt and the substantial loss of federal revenue due to the successive devolution and socialization of budgetary expenditures and the effect of trade liberalization on customs duties. Instead of a declining dependence on foreign capital, as the economic strategy had intended, there was a growing demand for it. The federal government's increasing reliance on foreign monies for domestic investment and its ever more frequent resort to refinancing and recycling of its foreign debt led it to seek new sources of foreign capital—one recourse being liberalization of rules on foreign investment. A new round of World Bank loans provided the bulk of the credits for investment in new or modernized infrastructure—roads, harbors, and railroads (the credits were distributed, after negotiation, to republic projects).[57] Enterprises, commercial banks, and republican governments gained the right to enter international capital markets independently. Legislation revised rules on social ownership to encourage joint ventures that would bring foreign equipment and capital directly to domestic producers, without the need for hard currency or new government debt.

After 1965, the dependence of domestic production on imports of raw materials and intermediate goods (including capital equipment) also grew. These purchases, however, were supported not by the favorable terms of public assistance enjoyed in the 1950s, but with commercial and Eurodollar short-term loans.[58] Not alone among developing countries in facing the decline of public, long-term loans in the 1960s, the maturation of debt assumed in the 1950s, trade deficits, and the need to seek debt relief, Yugoslavia managed to delay payment of Export-Import Bank debt until 1968–71 by consolidating its debt from 1950 and the 1961 program loans. It reduced the amount of its Public Law 480 obligations and deferred them to 1968–72, and gained new assistance of $1.2 billion from the U.S. government (to be repaid after 1970). In 1967 it obtained another IMF loan, and during 1965–68 managed to persuade many European governments to refund debt until 1970.[59]

---

bers) and with his iron-fisted rule over Kosovo province—ignores important events for Yugoslav foreign policy and in the domestic conflict that linked domestic economic policy with foreign-trade and defense policy (for example, the conflict in the USSR over nuclear vs. conventional forces; the termination in September 1964 of Khrushchev's *sovnarkhoz* reform and the replacement of the regional councils with the ministerial and branch-industry structure; and the beginnings of Yugoslav participation in Warsaw Pact committees in mid-1965, which was reversed the next year at exactly the time of Ranković's purge).

[57] Data and background can be found in Lampe, Prickett, and Adamović, *Yugoslav-American Economic Relations*, 35–38, 64, 174–76.

[58] See M. Unković, "Inostrani kapital u jugoslovenskoj privredi."

[59] Bitterman, *The Refunding of International Debt*; see also Lampe, Prickett, and Adamović, *Yugoslav-American Economic Relations*. On the availability of new monies because

1968–1978

If there were any lingering doubts about the advisability of the devolution of authority over foreign affairs, particularly defense (and the army certainly had them), they were erased by external events in 1967–68. The Arab-Israeli war broke out in 1967, with firsthand participation by a Yugoslav contingent in the UN peacekeeping force. In August 1968, Warsaw Pact troops invaded Czechoslovakia to put a stop to an economic reform similar to the Yugoslav one. Finally, there was an escalation of the war in Vietnam. Kardelj's parliamentary address at the end of 1967 opened the next stage of "socialization," which would culminate in the 1974 constitution; that stage began with the army as concern rose over national security. The new strategic doctrine of "all-national defense" (a relabeling of the "people's war" concept from wartime and 1948–50) gave the republican territorial forces equal status with the YPA and set in motion the next stage of decentralization of national security and socialization of the coercive functions of the state (military and police). All-national defense (initiated in 1964 but formally adopted by the party leadership only in November 1968 and enacted in February 1969) would make firms and local governments the core of the defense and security system. According to the system's principles, this integration of military functions into civilian institutions at the popular level—the next stage in the "withering away of the state" through its socialization—also required fuller party supervision of the army and coordination with it in central party councils.[60] The process of amending the 1963 constitution between 1967 and 1971 confirmed the change in foreign affairs. It also finalized the transfer to republican party committees of control over cadre appointments (in 1969) and the transfer of the remaining federal bureaucracies to the republics (in 1971), with coordination at the federal level by committees of republican delegates.

Successful postponement of the foreign debt until 1969 meant that economic policy could concentrate on rebuilding foreign hard-currency reserves. Export promotion to Western markets continued to have priority, so much so that in 1967 exporters were even required to get prior approval to export to the clearing area. A continuing decline in Western demand for Yugoslav exports and the slow growth in developed countries in 1970–71,[61] however, led firms to seek markets in developing countries

---

of growing competition between U.S. and European banks, see Griffith-Jones, "The Growth of Multinational Banking."

[60] The use of intelligence from the party unit within the army to bring trumped-up charges against Ranković in 1966 and justify his forced resignation suggests that party control over the army had been won earlier.

[61] This period also saw the steepest rise in commodity prices since 1950 (International Labor Office, *Employment, Growth, and Basic Needs*, 26–27).

instead (especially India and Egypt). But the global expansion of U.S. and European commercial banks in the late 1960s provided a new source of trade financing, and in 1970 Yugoslavia succeeded in negotiating a trade agreement with the European Community. In 1971, the government further liberalized the rules on foreign investment and took another IMF standby loan with its condition of a stabilization policy. To promote exports, it devalued the currency annually from 1971 to 1974 (twice in 1971), and it raised the proportion of foreign-exchange earnings that firms did not have to sell to the National Bank.

Although the new constitution was not promulgated until 1974, the fundamental changes in the international environment in 1973—with the unilateral abandonment of Bretton Woods by the United States in the summer and then the first OPEC oil-price shock that fall—reinforced the shift already taking place after 1970 among Yugoslav firms to domestic suppliers or to suppliers and export markets in the East and nonaligned world. These changes also brought a sharp change in economic policy. At first the government continued on the road to currency convertibility, creating a limited foreign-exchange market in May and shifting in July to a managed floating exchange rate. But the oil-price rise alone increased the trade deficit for 1974 by 22 percent. The rise of Western European protectionism, with unforeseeable nontariff barriers against Yugoslav goods (such as the outright ban on Yugoslav beef imports in 1974 and ad hoc prohibitions on textiles, steel, ships, and beef in 1975), followed by the West German recession of 1975–76, which sent ever-larger numbers of Yugoslav *gastarbeiter* (guest workers) packing, wreaked havoc with the balance of payments and the westward orientation of governmental policy. In contrast to the concerted effort in the 1960s to reduce the proportion of trade on clearing accounts and increase trade in convertible-currency markets,[62] the trade deficit and the needs of domestic manufacturers forced Yugoslav firms to look east, especially to the Soviet markets, for import of production supplies (above all oil) and for export of the machinery, ships, footwear and clothing, electrical equipment, and processed foods excluded from Western markets.[63] The altered global terms of trade also made domestically produced raw materials, energy, basic chemicals, and minerals less costly than imports and more saleable in Western markets, as evidenced by the rising share of primary commodities in relation to higher-value-added goods in Yugoslav exports after 1974.[64]

[62] Exports to clearing-account countries were virtually stagnant in 1965–69.

[63] Exports to OECD countries fell from an average of 55.2 percent of total Yugoslav exports in 1971–73 to 40.5 percent in 1974–78; exports to CMEA countries rose from an average of 35.6 percent in 1971–73 to 43 percent in 1974–78 (Tyson, *The Yugoslav Economic System*, 88-91).

[64] Economic Commission for Europe, "The Relative Performance of South European Exports."

This shift in investment priorities has been wrongly billed as a conservative political reaction to the unemployment of the 1960s and as a policy of import substitution over export promotion. Instead, it represented a shift in the kinds of exports the country could and did sell. Moreover, the interruption of detente in Europe and growing international tensions revived the government's concern for defensive self-sufficiency. The resulting shift in investment priorities to defense-related industries and stocks concurred with the rising demand from alternate export markets and Yugoslav manufacturers for cheaper domestic supplies.[65] By 1969, these international tensions already had the YPA general staff concerned about defense preparedness and financing for modernization. In 1974, the tenth party congress emphasized "the necessity of building up and developing the YPA as the armed force of the working class and all the nations and nationalities of the SFRY [Socialist Federal Republic of Yugoslavia]."[66] Nor was there any reversal in the perceived threats to national security. In 1977, the new American administration refocused defense policy onto Europe and NATO began another buildup of conventional troops (matched by the Warsaw Pact the next year); the Soviet Union invaded Afghanistan in 1979; and the superpowers failed to complete a nuclear-nonproliferation treaty. These events heightened the YPA's interest in new weapons systems and its concern over the preparedness of the territorial defense forces; by 1980–81, there was even renewed interest in a domestic nuclear force and nuclear energy to reduce oil dependence.

In contrast to the unfavorable conditions in capital markets during the similar policy shifts in 1948–49, 1956–58, and 1960–61, the supply of recycled OPEC dollars in Western capital markets made it possible after 1973 for Yugoslavia to service its debt and finance balance-of-payments deficits with escalated foreign borrowing in place of commodity-trade earnings from the West. That supply also favored the investment policy of the period. World Bank loans after 1975 supported investment in transportation and agriculture,[67] and U.S. and European banking consortiums

[65] The 1976–80 social plan, adopted a year late because of conflicts among republican leaders, aimed to correct the deficit and reduce the import dependence of domestic production by investing in shipbuilding, agro-industry, tourism, ferrous and nonferrous metals, basic chemicals, equipment, synthetic rubber, infrastructure, electric power, coal, petroleum, and gas (Schrenk, Ardalan, and El Tatawy, *Yugoslavia: Self-Management Socialism and the Challenges of Development*, 209; Chittle, *Industrialization and Manufactured Export Expansion in a Worker-Managed Economy*, 106).

[66] *Les forces armées*, 86ff. Just as the all-national defense doctrine was publicly proclaimed only five years after its adoption in 1964–65 (at the ninth party congress in 1969), the formal announcement of this course came only five years after the shift in policy (Bebler, "Development of Sociology of *Militaria* in Yugoslavia," 59–68).

[67] Such loans amounted to $750 million in 1977 and 1978 alone.

financed joint ventures in energy and petrochemicals.[68] Even greater freedom was granted to banks (in 1975) and enterprises (in 1977) to increase their foreign reserves by borrowing directly in foreign capital markets, leading major European banks to complain loudly about the rapid proliferation of unregulated borrowing requests and to demand that the federal government rein them in.[69] After 1975, as an incentive to improve trade performance and debt repayment, the government transferred control over half of customs revenues to manufacturing and foreign-trade firms through social funds at the federal and republic levels ("self-managing communities of interest for foreign economic relations"). As the system's principles required, management of these funds, and therefore a share in foreign-trade policy, was handed to the representatives of firms earning export revenues. The balance-of-payments account was also subdivided among the republics, each of which was assigned a proportion of foreign credits to which it had a "right" and which it was obliged to repay. A further trade agreement with the European Community was signed in December 1976, and talks began with the European Free Trade Association in 1979.

1979–1989

Both legs of economic policy after 1973—foreign trade and foreign finance—buckled under the external shocks of 1979–80. The short-run response was, as usual, to seek further assistance from the IMF. The EC trade agreement of 1976, up for renewal in 1979, unexpectedly ran into difficult bargaining. Talks on greater cooperation between the CMEA and the EC that had encouraged thoughts of a real end to trade barriers in Europe came to an abrupt halt with the invasion of Afghanistan. In spring 1980, the jump in interest rates on the U.S. dollar sent Yugoslavia's debt-service obligations soaring, as most of its debt was denominated in U.S. dollars and 58 percent of that debt was in high-interest commercial loans.[70] At the same time, Yugoslav trade in markets in the East and South was hit by the second price rise for OPEC and Soviet oil (by then

[68] Petrol Ljubljana financed a natural-gas pipeline in the Eurodollar market through Bankers' Trust International; INA, the Zagreb oil company, formed a joint venture with Dow Chemical in 1978 to build a petrochemical-processing plant on the Croatian island of Krk; and a joint venture with Westinghouse built a nuclear-power plant (Krško) in Slovenia.

[69] Green, "Comment," 248–49.

[70] Ledić, "Debt Analysis and Debt-Related Issues." The debt went from $2 billion in 1969 to $20 billion in 1982; the hard-currency debt-service ratio jumped to 24 percent in 1978 and to 35 percent in 1980; and the average burden of repayment in the period 1983–86 was $5 billion a year. The country began repaying principal in 1985. See Dyker, *Yugoslavia*, 114–28; and Lampe, Prickett, and Adamović, *Yugoslav-American Economic Relations*, 148–89.

Yugoslavia was paying for it in convertible currency). The collapse in the prices of primary commodities, in part because the United States, France, and others were dumping massive stockpiles of strategic raw materials onto the world market, sent prices of Yugoslav mineral exports such as copper and aluminum plummeting.[71] The trade deficit reached a record high in 1979, wholesale bankruptcy threatened domestic industry as capacity utilization fell under 70 percent, and foreign reserves were so low that an IMF credit of $340 million was drawn in May, followed by a request for a compensatory loan facility.[72]

This time, however, Western commercial banks chose to stop lending to Eastern Europe—including in that category Yugoslavia—on the grounds that the Polish crisis of 1980–81 would spread. Despite the world recession in 1980–83 (which reduced the net contribution of remittances from Yugoslav workers abroad to only 25 percent of the trade deficit by 1981), there was no choice but to reemphasize commodity exports to hard-currency markets and to negotiate with the IMF (now also taking a much firmer stance on debt-repayment conditions) to "restore foreign confidence," as new prime minister Milka Planinc's mandate read in 1982. While negotiations proceeded on what was to become the first of the IMF's three-year standby facilities to developing countries, the government sought once again to refinance and reschedule existing debt (against vocal opposition within the assembly and sections of the party).[73]

The all-out campaign after 1980 for debt repayment through stabilization and export promotion included another "economic reform" to reorient domestic institutions to Western markets and foreign price competition ("integration into the international division of labor") and to increase productivity in manufacturing, again by technological modernization through imports. Just as in 1959–60, planners in Slovenia had become increasingly worried after 1975 over their loss of world market share, their technological obsolescence relative to Western traders, and a brain drain of technically skilled professionals to Austrian firms that paid higher salaries, while the drop in world market prices for most raw materials once again made it cheaper to import than to buy from domestic producers. A long-term stabilization program, written by a committee

[71] Anton Bebler (Slovene political scientist and defense expert), personal communication.

[72] The Yugoslavs made the request on the grounds that the poor harvest that year, the earthquake in Dalmatian tourist areas, and the decline in remittances from workers abroad were beyond their control.

[73] Substantial long-term loans were obtained in 1981 and 1982. After difficult negotiations organized by the U.S. ambassador and State Department among fifteen Western countries, the IMF, the World Bank, six hundred commercial banks, and the Bank of International Settlements, a $2 billion loan package was arranged in January 1983. The IMF standby loan of 1981–83 was followed by a second one in April 1984.

chaired by the Slovene Sergej Kraigher,[74] was adopted by the federal assembly in July 1983, and a new constitutional commission established in 1983 produced a set of 130 altered articles and 29 amendments to the constitution to be debated first by the public, then within the party, and then in the assembly, beginning in January 1986.[75]

The debate over reorientation to the West was, as it had been in 1961–63, complicated by the international situation. On the economic side, there were again signs of opening in the West. In 1985, the EC began a new stage of monetary integration (scheduled for completion in 1992), the CMEA and the EC resumed the negotiations stalled in 1979, commercial banks reversed their lending policies dramatically, and in the USSR President Mikhail Gorbachev sped up the process of economic reform with *perestroika* and then *glasnost*. But national security remained problematic. The Croatian assembly and public opinion in Slovenia (especially through the Socialist Alliance-financed maverick youth weekly *Mladina* and the opposition intellectual journal *Nova Revija*) began to insist that under the prevailing international conditions there was no longer any need for a standing army and that the territorial defense forces within the republics were sufficient. The army perceived a very different world. Engaged in maintaining martial law in the rebellious province of Kosovo, alarmed at the rising social disorder and political discontent over the austerity policies of debt repayment, and fearing the attempts by the northern republics to transform the territorial defense forces into "parallel armies"—to the extent that the minister of defense redrew military districts to cut across republican borders in 1985 and urged the reintegration of major infrastructure such as railroads, electricity grids, and postal and telephone services[76]—the general staff also saw no apparent reduction in the hostility of the external environment. An escalating arms race and increasing NATO attention to the southern European theater (including

[74] Not only was this program an obvious parallel with the market-oriented economic-reform policy adopted because of difficulties with foreign trade in 1958–61, but that program was written by a committee chaired by a Slovene liberal of the same name (though no relation), Boris Krajger.

[75] The commission was initiated by a letter from Najdan Pašić—a political scientist, party member, and at the time chief justice of the supreme court—to the party presidency in September 1982, although a committee along these lines had been set up by the twelfth party congress in June of that year. It was eventually named for Josip Vrhovec, the chair of the commission that drafted the final report. The amendments were based on an analysis of the political system by the commission and on its 1985 report, *A Critical Analysis of the Functioning of the Political System of Socialist Self-Management* (Burg, "Elite Conflict in Post-Tito Yugoslavia," 192 nn. 56, 57).

[76] Facing funding problems for defense from 1976 on, the armed forces sought ways to simplify, improve coordination, and streamline, including the decision taken in 1983 to become self-sufficient in arms by 1990 (Gow, *Legitimacy and the Military*, 97–103).

its maneuvers in 1985 and 1986) seemed to demand greater expenditures for defense when the decline in federal revenues, slow economic growth, and the stabilization program demanded cuts.

Although political disagreements over the best way to repay the debt led the federal cabinet to abandon the IMF program temporarily in 1985–86, the return to the IMF in 1988[77]—and with it the institutional changes to implement economic liberalization—culminated in eighteen new laws that declared an end to the system of self-management and associated labor,[78] opened the economy to full foreign ownership and repatriation of profits, and legalized market allocation of labor and capital. But while the IMF supported prime minister Ante Marković's "shock-therapy" stabilization program in the spring of 1990, the Slovene electorate voted that December to seek full national independence by June 1991. Demands by the Slovene and Croatian governments for complete control in their territory over remaining federal jurisdictions—the police, military, courts, and laws—succumbed, in the act of implementation, to civil war.

CONCLUSION

The first part of an answer to the paradox of Yugoslav unemployment lies with the role of government in a socialist state. No longer a political force representing labor alone—not only because it had created a one-party state but, more importantly, because of the assumptions and institutional consequences of social ownership—the government aimed to represent the collective interests of society as a whole in ever-improving economic conditions and a territory free from war. The Yugoslav party leadership's choice of economic strategy and its political prerequisites made this task one of representing the country's interests globally: securing capital for growth, responding to the consequences of global business cycles for domestic growth, and protecting national security.

The dynamic of public policy was driven neither by electoral competition between political parties representing labor or capital at home, nor by a domestic business cycle, but rather by the federal response to international events: regional security concerns and the superpower contest, changes in foreign demand for Yugoslavia's goods and in its terms of trade, and changes in the supply of foreign capital to finance imports and supplement federal revenues and infrastructural investment. The data on unemployment show particularly clearly that the initiative for and path of central policy originated outside the country, and that elite conflict and

[77] The federal cabinet chose to return to the IMF in February 1987, but the new program—called the May Measures—was not adopted until May 1988.

[78] Primary among them was the Law on Enterprises of January 1989.

factional debates would follow a policy decision in which the disputants had little say—except over when it would be ratified and what political purges might be necessary. Economic adjustments required political adjustments, not the other way around.

Because policy decisions were made in response to international conditions over which the leaders had no control, their implementation was often interrupted unexpectedly, such as when an export-oriented liberalization was undercut by a Western recession or by global tensions that demanded a temporary retreat to the needs of defense. Far more significant in explaining the failures of Yugoslav policy than the common accusations about elite dissensus is the uncertainty engendered by this vulnerability, which made it very difficult to plan a response and implement it consistently. The fact that policies were driven largely by crisis also made it extremely difficult to organize domestic opposition to government policy and to act strategically.

Yugoslavia's international niche and its increasing dependence on foreign creditors for domestic production and employment did put the country in a structural position comparable to that of wage earners in capitalist countries. Instead of contesting this structure, however, President Tito's solution was to seek from within it as much gain as possible through nonalignment and through third-world forums demanding redistribution of wealth. This strategy appeared to be succeeding until the late 1970s, but with so much of domestic production dependent on imports (including production for export), what one might call a Keynesian-type deficit financing was inappropriate to the country's position. Even with another refinancing in 1982–85, the conditions of foreign-debt repayment and a long world recession demonstrated its limits. The government remained beholden to Western capital.

The consequence for policy and politics was a series of vicious circles. The fundamental trap lay in the leaders' Faustian bargain between their strategic position internationally and access to foreign capital (both credits and trade). The symbiosis between the two increased the probability of unpredictable external shocks, because trends in global capital and trade on the one hand and superpower conflict on the other did not run parallel. As if struck by a series of hurricanes, the country might not recuperate from one shock before the next one hit, and policies to deal with one were not the same as for another. Yet to abandon one half of the bargain would have been to abandon the other. This would have required a fundamentally different internal order and the overthrow of one in which otherwise opposing political factions had developed vested interests.

The vicious circle of foreign policy translated into political conflict. The primary difference between liberal and conservative policies and interests was defined by the industrial policy (and its organizational prerequisites)

required by each side of this foreign-policy bargain (foreign-trade earnings in Western markets on one side and military self-reliance on the
other). This meant that factional politics and elite dissensus were inevitable. Because policy shifts were defined by unpredictable external events,
however, neither side could ever claim a total victory, and consensus was
unachievable. This is scarcely unusual for any country, but it negated the
fundamental premise of the leaders' political strategy and institutions.
Instead of political harmony and unity against the outside, there was continuing tension and weakness.

Unable to resolve the policy stalemate, elite conflict focused instead on
redistribution and control over capital. The result was to translate the
political conflict back into economic conflict in a continual competition for
funds—competition between federal revenues and republican taxes,
among potential recipients of foreign loans, between republics or firms
benefiting from foreign economic policy and those demanding compensation. One way to resolve this conflict temporarily was with foreign credits.
But this built-in, insatiable demand for foreign credits returned the country full circle to its original vulnerability to external conditions and the
need to protect its international bargaining strength as a precondition for
domestic stability.

The political choice of a gradualist path to protect the party's domestic
coalition and ease the costs of initial industrialization by supplementing
domestic savings with imported credits and equipment was in time
turned on its head. Because domestic production became more rather
than less dependent on imports, it also became more difficult to change
defense policy as liberals demanded, while economic policy was shaped
more and more by the particular supply of foreign-trade finance and its
conditions. Instead of a temporary solution to economic development,
this strategy became an economic trap, and the difficulty of escaping it (as
witnessed by the many other developmentalist countries in the world that
had similar difficulties with shifts in military and development aid, global
recessions, external shocks, and foreign debt) was nonetheless then compounded by the political consequences. The idea of "socialism in one
country" was to provide a second logic of collective action in domestic
economic institutions in favor of a country of wage earners, as opposed to
the first logic of capital internationally. Instead, the openness to foreign
capital distorted the functioning of those institutions and the capacity of
the government to adjust internationally and facilitate economic
growth.[79]

---

[79] As Vladimir Gligorov observes, however, the idea of socialism in one country was for
the Bukharinist side the decision not to export revolution, there thus being no justification
for a standing army (*Gledišta i sporovi o industrijalizaciji u socijalizmu*). This fundamental
problem for liberal reformers, mentioned in chapter 1, was not resolved by the Yugoslavs in
the international conditions of the cold war.

The effect on the leaders' strategy for full employment was adverse. Instead of preventing the financial crises that lead to industrial unemployment, the government was preoccupied with external stabilization and therefore built a recessionary bias into policy without the institutional capacity to prevent further inflation and to regenerate growth. The greater the openness to foreign capital and to price liberalization as the mechanism for adjustment, the less the monetary institutions of the socialist economy were able to function as intended. Instead of providing the conditions for growth that would absorb surplus labor from agriculture as well as new generations, the government responded to these financial crises by seeking to improve the financial discipline of economic actors through decentralization, socialization, and financial autonomy. This undermined further the capacity of macroeconomic policy to maintain a stable currency. In place of governmental guardianship over sectoral balance and infrastructural investment for sustained growth and declining regional inequality, there were social plans and developmental investments oriented to the needs of the foreign sector and the projects for which external financing could be found.

Here, too, there were vicious circles. The IMF policies were particularly inappropriate, and each failure required a new dose of IMF credits and policies. Monetary and fiscal policy followed stop-and-go cycles, imposing restrictions to fight inflation that only fueled inflation and required further restrictions. Expansionary policies were able to increase employment in the short run if they were the result of government expenditures rather than simply an increase in the money supply, but because the initial result was a jump in imports, such a policy could not be sustained. The government would then return to cutting demand by placing restrictions on credit and imports that required firms and lower governments to adjust by cutting production, nonproductive expenditures, and labor costs.

These cuts all implied cuts in employment or its redistribution. At each point, the federal government had to face the vicious circle by adjusting with labor. Although it had no jurisdiction over employment, the federal policy had direct consequences—to which we turn in the next chapter.

SLOVENIA AND FOČA

LABOR-ORIENTED governments, according to the scholarly literature, have been able to approach full employment not only because of their explicit political commitment to bringing about full employment through the instruments of government policy (particularly in regard to international adjustment), but also because they have the political capacity to support those policies with discipline in the labor market. Centrally bargained social pacts between organized labor and organized business (usually mediated by government representatives) can implement incomes policies that overcome the inevitable trade-off between wages and jobs. The key to these "corporatist" pacts is labor's promise of wage restraint—in exchange for lower unemployment, governmental assistance in retaining and relocating workers when adjustment to shifts in market demand creates redundant labor, a share in profits when they improve, and other benefits.

Controversy surrounds the claims made for voluntary wage restraint and centralized bargaining mechanisms as guarantees of fuller employment. One of the more telling criticisms is the ease with which monetary and exchange-rate policies can undo the effect of incomes policies.[1] Incomes pacts did restrain wages in Yugoslavia, moreover—real wages fell without reprieve from 1978 on, at the same time that unemployment was rising fastest. But this fact did not influence the reigning explanation of Yugoslav unemployment: labor management of firms gave workers power over the trade-off between wages and jobs, and the incentive was to choose higher incomes over investment in new employment. There was no mechanism for disciplining labor's demand for ever-higher wages without the threat of unemployment from profit-maximizing private owners (and therefore an end to self-management). Governments then

[1] Therborn, for example, warns against evaluating such corporatist mechanisms apart from foreign-trade policy. Finding that wage restraint was not correlated with either full employment or successful international competitiveness and, further, that the cost of labor per unit of output as expressed in national currencies had no statistical relation to that cost expressed in international currency, he concludes that for OECD countries in 1973–84, as least, "incomes policies can be made as well as unmade by currency policies and changes in the exchange rates" (*Why Some Peoples Are More Unemployed than Others*, 17). Wallerstein, "Centralized Bargaining and Wage Restraint," also questions the corporatist arguments about wage restraint.

compounded the error by softening the budget constraints on firms and by making new investments that were politically motivated and uneconomic—both policies aimed, it was said, at protecting jobs.

In fact, a primary goal of the introduction of workers' councils in 1949–50 was to deprive unions of their bargaining power over wages in export-producing firms at a time when skilled labor was scarce. Elected representatives of skilled production workers were to be consulted by managers on how to *cut* labor costs. The aim was to have workers accept limits on wages and benefits within enterprise net revenue, approve capital investments even if they cut into incomes, and sanction dismissals of workers when required by budgets or modernization programs. The essence of self-management as it was extended to ever more public-sector workplaces over time was this attempt to enforce incomes policies and financial discipline without state involvement or central regulation. The trade-offs between wages and investment (or, as the Yugoslavs put it, between short-term pay and long-term income) were to be left to the "work collectives" of public-sector workplaces.

Moreover, consulting workers on their wages and on employment questions within the firm was only one aspect of the Yugoslav leaders' program for full employment. This program aimed both to utilize labor throughout the income-paying public sector in ways that kept productivity rising above consumption (creating capital and thus the capacity to employ) and to provide, temporarily, subsistence in a free private sector for all those who could not be employed immediately in the public sector without defeating the first goal.

Within the public sector, according to the leaders' economic ideology, investments would promote capital by expanding productive capacity within a territory or capital intensity within a firm. In investment choices, labor productivity and a rising gross national product would take priority over employment if the two were in conflict.[2] Firms were to increase labor productivity—by keeping their bill for wages and benefits in line with productivity gains, capitalizing labor through machinery and education, and intensifying the use of labor to cut relative costs. "Revaluation" of labor, rather than its "devaluation" (falling wages and unemployment), required investment as well in improving the skills and education of employed workers and in retraining workers in line with technological modernization.

The system of direct economic incentives also had to be protected. Thus, the rights to self-management of work collectives had to be periodically reviewed and revived. Income inequalities within branches,

---

[2] Burger, Kester, and den Oudem, *Self-Management and Investment Control in Yugoslavia*, 208.

windfall profits, market-driven rather than productivity-driven wages, and labor turnover all had to be counteracted to prevent market allocation of labor, which would undermine these incentives. While firms were not to be penalized by imported costs over which they had no control, they also had to transfer to social use (through taxation for investment, local wage funds, and social services) a portion of their income that reflected a market advantage of which they were chance beneficiaries. Government standards for wage differentials and job classifications aimed to bring income shares into line with individual "capital" (the capacity to raise productivity, called "each according to his abilities" and "equal share for equal work under equal conditions").[3] Redundant labor was not to be fired, but "reassigned"—where possible—to jobs more in line with the person's skills.

Society also needed to be reorganized periodically to prevent the accumulation of unproductive employments—such as government bureaucracy and administrative positions—and reduce them instead to a minimum. Social services were to be financed by firms (through direct grants, local taxation, their provision within the firm, or contract) so that expenditures on nonproductive activities would be governed by the limits of achieved productivity. Ever-expanding socialization, by which employment in the public sector would expand and government budgets decline in favor of autonomous (self-managed) financing, would incorporate ever more of society into the economic regime of "income relations." That is, more and more people would be employed in the system of productivity-oriented work incentives of industrial organization and financial discipline, in which earnings and benefits would reflect one's relative capacity to produce and would represent a share of realized income (though not more).

Job security, therefore, was not a right to a job, but a right to a guaranteed minimum wage for people who had public-sector jobs. (Temporary job security, however, aimed to protect the direct link between economic interest and political rights: there were prohibitions against firing people while they held elected positions—as managers, members of workers' councils, or delegates to assemblies.) Protection against unemployment lay only in the legal limits on private employment and on the sale of land, so that smallholdings in the private sector could act as a safe haven when public-sector growth was not sufficient to accommodate all those desiring employment (that is, a public-sector job). In other words, because new employment was to be limited by real economic growth but unemployment was to be avoided, the relevant trade-off was seen not as the one between wages and jobs, but as one between public-sector employment

---

[3] Law on Labor Relations of 1965, cited in *Yugoslav Survey* 8, no. 3 (August 1967): 22.

and the private reserve. Instead of adjusting wages and the level of employment according to profits, firms and government regulations would adjust by moving people between the two sectors. People who had guaranteed smallholdings in agriculture or crafts, were supported by families, or were working abroad could await expansion of the public-sector without fear for their subsistence.

Unemployment under Yugoslav socialism was not a result of wage pressure, guaranteed job security, or insufficient savings (the savings rate was comparatively high[4] and investment generally ran around 40 percent of gross material product).[5] Its explanation lies with the disconnection between the program for full employment and the two sets of conditions within which it was operating—its international environment on the one hand (as discussed in the previous chapter) and the domestic labor supply on the other. Governmental policy to adjust to that international environment was in fact a set of parameters for labor use. If trade deficits required cutting domestic demand and expanding exports—the stabilization policy for thirty-two years out of forty-two—then incomes and employments had to adjust. If difficulties in foreign markets or national security required shifts in production or limited growth, then the entire organization of society might be affected, not just particular firms. Instead of the condition posed in Benjamin Ward's Illyrian model of the backward-sloping supply curve of labor under labor management—how workers' councils would respond to an increase in demand for their products—a far more common condition facing self-managed firms was the opposite: how would management and workers' councils respond to a drop in demand or to stabilization-oriented restrictions on money, credit, and imports intended to force firms to use internal reserves more efficiently and finance more of their own investments? Shifts in the country's terms of trade in foreign markets—such as the market demand most common in trade with the West and long-term supply contracts in trade with the East and South—and in the kinds of commodities in demand affected the measure of productivity and the accompanying incentives of government regulations.

Alongside the need for international adjustment, economic development led to a rural exodus and population increase. The leaders' goal of a technologically advanced, highly productive, administratively lean, full-employment economy within the context of the country's international position came to be realized in only a small part of Yugoslav territory—above all in Slovenia. There the norm throughout the postwar period was labor shortages rather than surplus; the agricultural labor surplus had

---

[4] Bergson, "Entrepreneurship under Labor Participation," 207.
[5] Babić and Primorac, "Some Causes of the Growth of the Yugoslav External Debt," 78.

been exhausted by early commercialization of agriculture and early industrialization, and population increase was low as a result of women's employment and rising wages and household incomes. In most of the country, however, the norm was a growing disharmony between governmental policies and/or international conditions on the one hand and the labor-supply conditions of the locality or republic on the other. Institutional reforms that aimed to improve financial discipline increased this disharmony. Decentralization and socialization parcelized labor markets and created ever-greater differences between the size of a local labor surplus and the economic resources for its employment. The result was growing unemployment, which was unevenly spread across regions and social groups.

Promoting Productivity

Kidrič's early insistence on the "law of value," on an economy that respected the "equilibrium conditions of growth," occurred at a time of dire international conditions and a severe drought. As the previous chapter argued, however, these two conditions—insufficient export earnings in relation to import needs or debt obligations, and low productivity of agriculture—continued to require policy adjustments to restore equilibrium conditions. Thus, the reason that data on unemployment reflect the chronology of policy aimed at adjusting to international conditions (affecting trade, capital availability, and national defense) is that those conditions set the limits of public-sector employment and the policies toward labor that, in restoring external equilibrium, aimed to reestablish conditions for economic growth at home.

In the very specific adjustments to agricultural policy, government employment, lines of industrial production, and income regulations, there nonetheless operated two very different ideological approaches, sometimes in combination and sometimes in opposition. These two approaches—the models of Slovenia and Foča that emerged from the wartime and immediate postwar period—had differential consequences for localities, regions, and economic interests because of the territorial organization of economic management and investment.

The Slovene model, a "liberal" approach to economic growth within a socialist economy, focused on the incentives to manufacturing and processing firms of export markets and consumer demand in retail markets. It emphasized "world-market standards of productivity," price competition, and commercial orientation with its pressures for technological modernization—lowering unit labor costs while capitalizing labor with machines and higher skills. Intensification and concentration (through cartels or vertically integrated firms) were pushed both by policy and by firms' strategies to gain market advantage. Policy encouraged the flexibility to hire and fire in response to market demand and the market provision of collective consumption (benefits, welfare, and social services) in the interest of enterprise savings and demand-oriented efficiencies.

The Foča model, a developmentalist approach, focused instead on the production of raw material, energy, infrastructure, producers' goods, and food for home consumption as well as export, largely on long-term contract or in response to price-inelastic demand. It therefore emphasized quantity increases that depended more on steady work, labor discipline, skills adapted to production, and shop-floor flexibility. Goods were to be allocated within workplaces as incentives to commitment, and economic and administrative functions were to be incorporated ("socialized") into firms to cut transaction costs and nonproductive services. Decentralization and divisionalization aimed to break-up industrial concentration (even where policy in a liberal phase had encouraged it) so as to improve the directness of work incentives, the visibility of the relation between productivity and reward, and accountability for budget constraints.[6]

The face of self-management in the first model was autonomy: the rights of work collectives (enterprises) to retain their earnings and the authority of managers and professional staff. In the second, it was participation: the rights of production workers to discuss ways of raising their productivity while limiting their aggregate income. But in both approaches to the organization of production and the concept of productivity, the societal approach to economic growth through increasing productivity required a progressive reduction or socialization of nonproductive activities—that is, the state and public services. Alternation between these approaches and their corresponding labor policies follows the periodization set out in the previous chapter for international adjustment.

1952–1957

The mixture of the Slovene and Foča approaches was particularly clear in the first period of the new regime because of the continuing insecurity of international conditions. The government proceeded with its hopeful commitments to demobilize the army and shift to civilian production and light manufacturing for export and domestic consumer goods, but external threats interrupted on occasion. The capital investments of the five-year plan and foreign credits provided the conditions for the leaders' preferred liberal policy toward labor within a context of capital develop-

---

[6] The push for decentralization and divisionalization in the 1970s parallels similar developments in other countries. See, for example, Shapiro and Kane, "Stagflation and the New Right"; and Howell, "The Dilemmas of Post-Fordism."

ment: to increase domestic savings and growth by industrializing both manufacturing and agriculture in the socialized sector, favoring mechanization, fewer workers, and a smaller federal budget. The fulfillment of Kardelj's prediction that agricultural machinery would begin to roll off production lines in 1953 made it possible to reduce the labor force on state farms and in labor cooperatives. The 1953 agrarian reform and government subventions encouraged intensive cropping and small rural industries so as to be able to return the "relieved" labor to the private sector. Private artisans were granted the right to employ up to five wage laborers (other than family members), as were private farmers (subject to special taxation). In factories, workers' councils (still only at the level of branch associations) gained more freedom in decisions on wages and employment in order to make the necessary labor cuts and improve wage incentives to productivity. A bankruptcy law entered the books, and the discussion of wage norms and labor rationalization in journal articles betrays the Taylorist ideology of engineers and skilled workers at the time.[7]

Although the social plan for 1954 proposed a growth rate of 8 percent for employment but 17 percent for output,[8] the skilled workers and engineers on the workers' councils had been so zealous in their firing in 1950–52 that employment expanded instead when factories found they had to rehire essential maintenance workers. The explosion of aggregate wages, due to the higher wages voted for managerial staff and skilled workers and unplanned increases in actual employment, led the government to reintroduce wage regulations. In line with constitutional jurisdictions, local governments were given the authority to impose limits on personal incomes where necessary.[9]

But local governments were at the time faced with two huge tasks: finding employment for demobilized soldiers and sacked political functionaries,[10] and providing for the benefits, housing, construction work, and other services performed until then by the military.[11] To economize on local finances, governmental reforms were introduced. Smaller communes were consolidated into larger units, local social services such as elementary education were divested onto "self-management" footing, and the many local offices created in the fall of 1948 to implement the five-year plan were closed. Even so, local expenditures soared with the de-

[7] See, for example, Dereta, "O nekim osnovnim pokazateljima radne snage."

[8] *Ekonomska Politika*, March 4, 1954, 191.

[9] See especially Ward, "From Marx to Barone."

[10] The number of party functionaries was halved in 1952–54, and the federal bureaucracy was reduced from 47,310 workers in 1948 to 10,328 in 1956 (Hondius, *The Yugoslav Community of Nations*, 191).

[11] For example, the military-party commissions on national security, the KNOJ, were disbanded between the end of 1952 and March 1953, and the functions of state security were transferred to civilian agencies.

mand for new housing, pensions, and public-sector jobs. Because localities coped by imposing tax rates so high that enterprises were left without working capital, the federal government reimposed controls on local fiscal authority.[12]

Federal legislation formalized the new system in 1955 with a new wage system and a proposed new Law on Labor Relations. The previous wage norms and piece rates were translated into general regulations to guide the writing of enterprise statutes on pay, which were then subject to approval by workers' councils in order to institutionalize further the self-disciplining role of "workers' control" in wage decisions. Workers would receive a guaranteed minimum wage "advanced" each month, but beyond that, incomes in the socialized sector would no longer be treated as a cost of production but as a share of the net value added in production. Moreover, personal incomes could not be paid (or docked, if the net was negative) until all costs, taxes, and depreciation had been deducted from the market value of that output in the end-of-year accounting. Thus, three years before the government abandoned sectoral investment and planning by global proportions in favor of territorial banks and planning within republics, the basis of economic calculation shifted to enterprise profitability (net revenue) and ended the means for economywide calculation of labor productivity.[13] Accordingly, workers' councils were extended to the enterprise itself, and the right to hire and fire workers—not management staff—was transferred from the director to the workers' council (which had two standing commissions, one for hiring and firing and one for discipline).

Although the decisions had been made and were being implemented, political quarrels over this change in development strategy and the victory of the income school and its marginalist approach did not fully abate, delaying until 1957 the first congress of workers' councils (it had been planned for 1954 to celebrate the new system) as well as the new Law on Labor Relations codifying the changes since 1948.[14] Opposition also de-

---

[12] See Ward's discussion of the "dead brigades" used in enterprises as a way of reducing their accounting profits and therefore their taxes under the steeply progressive profits taxes before 1955 ("The Firm in Illyria," 584–85).

[13] This new wage system is called the victory of the income school (*dohodovna struja*, or *dohodoci*) over the developmentalists; see Dabčević-Kučar et al., *Problemi teorije i prakse socijalističke robne proizvodnje*. But this Croatian faction also had many members from Serbia.

[14] The law was enacted in March 1957. It codified each period of labor regulations on the rights and statuses of employed persons, and thus the principles of income distribution, job classification, and hiring and firing according to which enterprise statutes, rule books, and compacts with other firms and governments were written and enforced. Researchers in Belgrade complained, however, that many people, such as shepherds (*čobani*), still had no regulated employment status, or *radni odnos* (*Privreda FNRJ u periodu 1947–1956*, 161).

layed the seventh party congress, scheduled for 1956, until 1958. According to political leaders, this opposition came from those who considered the renewed emphasis on labor productivity as the measure of growth to be a strike against the countryside. But international security also played a role; there was a brief return to defense mobilization in 1956–57 because of revived insecurities on the eastern front and the impending end of U.S. military aid. The youth labor brigades were brought back, and the employment of professional party cadres increased in factory subunits. A steep jump in output norms for coal production at the same time that incomes declined under the stabilization of 1957 led to the first acknowledged postwar labor strike—at the Trbovlje mine in Slovenia—at the end of the year.[15]

1958–1967

Nonetheless, by January 1958, institutional changes in the system of wages and investment were reaffirmed by international conditions, and the liberal policy came much more clearly into its own. The application to GATT, the further opening to Western trade in line with Western European developments, and the modernization of industrial production through imported technology to improve productivity in existing plants all required massive changes in the employment structure of the social sector to make it more competitive and productive. Under the code word "the human factor" and the slogan of the "revaluation" rather than "devaluation" of labor, the labor force in the public sector was to be "modernized" as well by improving skills through retraining and workers' education. Policies aimed at increasing the ratio of skilled labor and engineers "to operate the new machines"[16] allowed wage differentials to rise and, in order to keep a lid on the aggregate wage bill, allowed the firing of unskilled and otherwise redundant labor. Postwar demobilization expanded to the economy with the replacement of members of the older,[17] "Partisan" generation (who had entered industrial and managerial positions with the meager education of their prewar opportunities and on the basis of their war record) by "skilled, schooled cadres." The army also

[15] The party leadership responded by changing the union leadership, installing Svetozar Vukmanović-Tempo. He had been minister of mining in the mobilization of 1948–49 and the champion of production workers and of the brigade system in 1949, but he was also a convinced "liberal" on economic reform and opening. As a prominent "first fighter" and organizer of the Partisan struggle in Macedonia, he could oversee the dismissals of unskilled laborers and Partisan veterans. On this and subsequent strikes, see Jovanov, *Radnički štrajkovi*.

[16] *Yugoslav Trade Unions*, 1964. In 1957, a special tax ("contribution") was assessed on firms to pay for training programs (doprinos za kadrove u privredi).

[17] In the sense of perspective, not age (although this was not always made clear).

made massive cuts in personnel (especially in the more highly paid officer corps) in order to pay for its initial investments in technological modernization—the purchase of armaments and licenses in the world market.[18] Factories built largely under federal jurisdiction for defense self-reliance and the production of capital goods had either to close or restructure to meet the criteria of market profitability for international "competitiveness" and the GATT-defined program of liberalization. All firms had to adjust to the market by cutting labor costs.[19] By 1960, price, tax, and accounting regulations rewarded increases in fixed assets and penalized employment.[20]

The effect of these policies to increase growth by cutting labor, rationalizing its use, and investing in new capacity and equipment could be seen in rising unemployment already in 1956–57 and again in 1958–59. But the opening of borders after 1955 provided an outlet—first permanent emigration, then temporary work. By 1960, the government's jurisdiction over foreign affairs had led it to reenter the field of employment concerns. A Federal Bureau of Employment was established with the sole responsibility of facilitating and regulating the cross-border flow of Yugoslavs wishing to work temporarily in West Germany, Austria, Belgium, or Sweden, because of the government's interest in capturing workers' hard-currency remittances and negotiating their welfare rights in foreign countries and also because of the receiving countries' requirements that the flow of workers be carefully regulated.[21] An additional outlet for the unemployed came with the push for tourist dollars in the early 1960s and the new demand for services that could be provided by the private sector.

The most common form of restructuring in this period was vertical integration. Competitive pressures abroad and especially supply difficulties at home due to declining agricultural productivity and recurring stabiliza-

[18] See the discussion in weekly articles throughout 1957 in the army newspaper, *Narodna Armija;* and Tito's speech to the federal assembly in April 1958 (Tito, *Tito u Skupštini*, 295).

[19] In Vojvodina, 50 percent of the firms were "nonaccumulative"; they, along with others (such as the machine industry and crafts), complained about this damaging shift, which would undervalue their output even more (*Narodna Armija*, issues for August 1957).

[20] Horvat argues that until 1960 taxation created capital-saving inducements but after 1964 stimulated labor-saving practices, making thousands of workers redundant; that the shift to payroll taxation in 1965, together with social-insurance contributions, made labor 60 percent more expensive "than necessary"; and that the flat rates introduced a rigidity into economic behavior that tended to intensify business cycles (he cites a study by the economist Pero Jurković in 1972 showing that the levy of taxes on factors of production rather than on business results prevented "elastic cushions in recessions and booms") (*The Yugoslav Economic System*, 236–38, 244).

[21] The 1963 constitution added a new federal agency, the Council for the Question of Expatriates, which essentially dealt with workers abroad (see Hondius, *The Yugoslav Community of Nations*, 295).

tion restrictions on credit and imports led firms to concentrate assets and to increase technical and commercial economies of scale for more effective competition in foreign and local markets. The stabilization policy of 1961, which included a moratorium on new investment, tightened credit, and the expectation that firms would finance their own capital investments (above all from internal funds), was even accompanied by a political campaign for integration in 1961–62.[22] To guarantee supplies and prices over a longer period when import restrictions, currency devaluation, and rising costs in agriculture were creating production bottlenecks, firms integrated their suppliers or established long-term contractual relations, and the producers' associations that were organized around supply and pricing functions (the branch cartels in each republic) were strengthened. Successful conglomerates, particularly the lucrative export-import trade firms, "saved" failing firms by assuming their debts in easy takeovers. Industrial firms enlarged to increase their bargaining power over the new commercial banks, which now allocated credit—but they did so through mergers and buyouts instead of by hiring new employees. In their supervisory role over public firms, local governments permitted firms with losses to remain in business if they merged with profitable ones and accepted cuts in administrative staff and workers.[23] The same process of rationalization of resource use through concentration occurred in governmental administration, as the number of communes was reduced from 3,811 to 759 in 1962. Burdened with ever-greater tasks in relation to their resources, however, communes became in fact more dependent on republican and federal funds. The 1963 constitution therefore encouraged the pooling of budgetary funds among associations of communes; in 1964, richer and poorer communes were encouraged to unite so as to increase their ability to finance the local infrastructure and social services for which they were now responsible. In 1964, the republics of Bosnia-Herzegovina, Serbia, and Macedonia abolished district governments entirely.[24]

In support of the liberal orientation to the economic incentive of consumer demand, and in part to relieve some of the burden of liberalized

---

[22] This campaign was identified especially with Tito's November 1961 speech in Skopje (see Macesich, *Yugoslavia: The Theory and Practice of Development Planning*, 87).

[23] Such moves were usually resisted, sometimes successfully, by workers' councils; see *Yugoslav Trade Unions*, no. 12 (April–June 1964): 66–67, 70–71. Workers in a profitable firm in Macedonia staged a strike lasting forty-five days in August and September 1985 when the commune government (and party organization) decided to merge it with an unprofitable firm to resolve the latter's economic difficulties (author's interviews in Belgrade, 1985).

[24] See Carter on the confusion and competition that this introduced into the elections of 1967 because cadre decisions had previously been made by the district party committee (*Democratic Reform in Yugoslavia*, 61–62).

(that is, higher) prices on the population, the government introduced consumer credit in 1960–61. But such an increase in money independent of production put an even greater premium on controlling labor costs. A semiofficial study in 1961–62 supported the campaign to intensify labor use in existing firms with estimates of hidden unemployment among industrial jobholders of 10 to 15 percent.[25] In the recession of 1961–62, when "factory employment opportunities declined as economic activity slowed [and] unemployment rose," the government "became reluctant to continue to open new, high-cost, labor-intensive industrial capacities . . . [thus] layoffs of surplus labor were sanctioned, political organizations advising enterprises that workers who owned land or had other nonwage income should be discharged first."[26]

Fighting inflationary pressures further in 1962, the government began to negotiate incomes policies at the federal and republican levels in a process that was to become the prime method of wage regulation. Although it still set central guidelines for enterprise statutes on income distribution, the government began with proposals from the producers' associations for wage rates for industrial sectors, sent them for review to the United Unions organization, and then sent them to the republics to be adapted into republic-level social compacts. Enforcement was included in the supervisory role of local governments, which inspected the cash accounts of enterprises from which incomes were paid and periodically sent inspectors from the banks' social-accounting office to examine enterprise books.

To cut public expenditures and leave enterprises with greater resources for investment, a new round of socialization extended self-management to public services such as education and health care. Expected to respond to consumer demand ("strengthening the role of personal income in financing social requirements"),[27] employees in social services were given rights of self-management as an incentive to greater efficiency through voluntary wage rationalization. That is, they were now free to adjust salaries within the limits of their budget (according to the principles of the "income" system and "pay according to results").[28] In turn, greater efficiency and the market allocation of social services would make it possible to cut enterprise taxes and reduce internal funds set aside for "collective consumption goods."

[25] Livingston gives the source of these estimates only as "unpublished official data" in his careful article ("Yugoslavian Unemployment Trends," 757; see also 760).

[26] Ibid., 756–57. At the same time that massive layoffs occurred in May 1962, taxes on the private sector increased sevenfold, eliminating ten thousand artisans—"barbers, blacksmiths, cobblers, tailors, pastry makers" (Macesich, *Yugoslavia*, 203).

[27] The social plan of 1964–70.

[28] *Yugoslav Trade Unions*, no. 10 (September 1963): 30–35.

The most explicit statements of the conception underlying the liberal system are found in the speeches of the eighth party congress, held in December 1964, because it marked the end of the liberals' domestic political battles against the developmentalists. The leaders began with the announcement that Yugoslavia had entered the ranks of the moderately developed countries because per capita income had reached about $500. Higher wages and a shorter workday were victories of the workers' movement, Tito claimed in justifying the campaign to intensify the use of existing capacities. The reduction of the official workweek after 1963 from forty-eight to forty-two hours was their "second industrial revolution" because it replaced the rural day schedule with industrial ("standard European") working hours and forced peasant-workers and moonlighters to make a choice for one "work relation."[29] The workweek was reduced further to forty hours in 1965 (with one hour overtime permitted), to thirty-eight (plus one) in 1966–69, and to thirty-six (plus one) in 1970.

The congress was followed at the beginning of 1965 by a new Law on Labor Relations that codified the changes since 1957 and extended legal protections to workers in private hire. The first federal ("basic") law on employment attempted to rationalize the organization and financing of employment bureaus and the principles of job classification and retraining. The liberal approach was even clearer in the policy objectives of the social plan for 1966–70. It proposed that "in order to ensure optimal proportions with regard to the rate of employment, available accumulation, the level of labour productivity and living standards, it will be necessary to decelerate the rate of employment in relation to preceding periods, especially in the first years of the planned period, when, as a result of the reform, existing relative surpluses of manpower will be the first to be absorbed and more economically employed."[30]

The emphasis on commercial profitability in foreign and domestic markets intensified in response to the severe recession of 1965–66 and declining Western demand. With respect to labor, this emphasis was manifest in pressure on firms to increase middle-management staffs and marketing departments and give them more autonomy to respond to market conditions.[31] The guiding policy line was "to reduce costs of production in general and costs of production per unit of output, reducing above all the participation of labor, in order to increase the competitiveness of the Yugoslav economy on the international market."[32] The managerialist trend was reflected in constitutional amendments that sought to free man-

---

[29] Hondius, *The Yugoslav Community of Nations*, 321, n. 561.

[30] *Yugoslav Federal Assembly* 4, no. 7 (1966): 12.

[31] For a study of two Belgrade manufacturing firms during this period, see Adizes, *Industrial Democracy, Yugoslav Style*, 95.

[32] Šoškić, "Tržišni sistem socijalističke privrede i reforma."

agers from the oversight of the management board (with its two-thirds representation of production workers).[33] University reform and expansion aimed to train professional strata while diverting youth's demand for jobs into longer education. A new push for vocational education at the high-school level received foreign assistance.[34] Labor regulations reemphasized the responsibility of enterprises as well in training and retraining their employees, and the legal obligation to accept one trainee for every fifty employees and to employ them after two years was reinstated.

Yet the rise of skill credentials pushed up aggregate wages, because wage rates were tied to skill level and educational certification. Thus, additional dismissals were necessary.[35] The greater reliance on market allocation of social services and benefits was also cutting the purchasing power of wages. Less well paid blue-collar workers responded with wage strikes, and the union opened a fight to reassert the principle of "socialist distribution according to work" (that is, in terms of output productivity and thus adjusted for inflation).[36] Conflicts between market-oriented directors and workers opposed to their disciplinary decisions,[37] and between union leaders and their rank and file over wage inequalities and dismissals, culminated at the end of 1967 with the removal of Svetozar Vukmanović-Tempo from the presidency of the unions when he polemicized publicly against market-oriented managerial interests.[38]

---

[33] The trend was reflected above all in Amendment 15, adopted in December 1968. It permitted the transfer of authority over hiring and firing to the director and professional organs within management—such as the *stručni kolegijum*, or council of expert advisers to the director. That authority was reversed in the amendments of 1971 and in the 1974 constitution.

[34] OECD technical assistance through the Mediterranean Project initiated discussions on reforming secondary education to increase vocational training, discussions that bore fruit in experiments in Split and Vojvodina in 1969–71 and in a major reform of secondary education after 1972. There were similar developments in university expansion and secondary-school reform in Western Europe at the time (for example, in France and Italy). These reforms presumed an ability to plan manpower effectively, but the linear assumptions of the manpower-planning model on which the OECD project was based precluded such an ability, according to the critical analysis by Doran and Deen, "The Use of Linear Difference Equations in Manpower Planning."

[35] Adizes's study of two Serbian enterprises during this period provides rarely available information on the choices firms made. While workplaces paid the costs of employees' extra training, Adizes reports that in one of the textile firms he studied in 1967, anyone who had not acquired the desired training by 1970 was to be transferred automatically to another workplace or job classification (*Industrial Democracy, Yugoslav Style*, 50).

[36] *Yugoslav Trade Unions*, no. 11 (January–March 1964). See also Rusinow, *The Yugoslav Experiment;* Carter, *Democratic Reform in Yugoslavia;* and Jovanov, *Radnički štrajkovi.*

[37] The trade-union newspaper was filled with stories of such conflicts during 1964.

[38] His criticism appeared in the pages of *Ekonomska Politika* (Economic Policy), the liberal Belgrade weekly similar in style and views to *The Economist* of London.

New employment stagnated from 1964 to 1967 and the labor surplus in the social sector rose, as a result of the policies of export orientation, economic liberalization, and macroeconomic stabilization as well as the response to these policies in industrial concentration, administrative rationalizations, and "modernization."[39] While more and more people found incomes in the private sector or abroad, many others simply withdrew in discouragement from the unemployment rolls. Revised labor legislation in 1968 attempted to reverse the situation by requiring firms to give preference in hiring to the unemployed (not new registrants but those previously employed and let go) when persons of otherwise equal qualifications applied. The law also required firms to rehire within one year persons laid off as a result of business losses if conditions improved. Both in 1960 and in 1969, legislation sought a way around this problem of a prior obligation to persons employed in the social sector when labor costs dictated dismissals by revising pensions to encourage earlier retirements. It is also striking, given the legal obligations of firms to employed pregnant women, that a law permitting abortions was enacted in 1960 and that in 1969 women gained the right to contraception.

At the same time, however, the changes in defense policy in 1964 favoring the territorial defense forces and purging the state security police (the highlight being the purge of Ranković in July 1966), as well as the constitutional amendments of 1967–69 to republicanize the remaining federal administration (followed necessarily by the republicanization of party personnel and finances), increased the number of people looking for jobs in enterprises. These decentralizations, induced in part by stabilization to cut spending on "nonproductive" salaries, were accompanied by another consolidation of communes; their number fell from 759 to 501 in 1968. The "socialization" of parliament, in which representation shifted to "delegates" from self-managed workplaces (introduced in 1967 but effective only after the last multicandidate elections in localities in 1969), transferred financing for delegates' salaries and perquisites from government budgets to enterprise income.[40] This change was followed by the extension of self-management autonomy in 1969–70 to the bureaus of civil servants and experts responsible for social services.[41] The effect of cutting public expenditures, however, was to shift costs back to firms and reverse

[39] On the latter process, see Adizes, *Industrial Democracy, Yugoslav Style*, 65.

[40] The "delegate system" referred to social-sector workplaces as the "base" (*baza*) of the sociopolitical system.

[41] These "self-managing communities of interest" for schools, hospitals and clinics, theaters, roads, and public utilities were to manage their services autonomously and receive a budget directly from enterprises, which would send delegates to review expenditure plans and budgets and to pledge "contributions" in annual meetings.

the process of cutting taxes on enterprise income begun in the early 1960s. Instead of creating a leaner public sector, moreover, decentralization actually accelerated the employment of administrators, as Wagner's law would predict.[42]

1968–1978

Workers' strikes, peasants' pressure to form their own cooperatives, nationalist eruptions after 1967 in Kosovo, Slovenia, and especially Croatia (the "mass movement"), and student rebellions in Sarajevo, Belgrade, and Priština in 1968 and in Zagreb in 1970 occupied public attention in these years. The social unrest led most Yugoslavs to assume that the change in economic policies (which they date from 1972, when liberal party leaders in Croatia and Serbia were purged) was a political reaction against this decline in civil order. But the conditions for a major change in policy toward labor preceded the political crackdown and had been developing outside the country. The shift in foreign trade after 1969 to markets in the East and South (most of which was governed by long-term bilateral contracts) and the shift in domestic production to greater concern with energy, raw materials, producers' goods, and strategic supplies for domestic processors and manufacturers, for the army, and for Western markets[43] (and therefore greater concern with transport for domestic supply routes) meant that increasing revenues depended on increasing quantities more than on price competition and marketing. What was identified as a conservative reaction was in many ways a return to the production profile of the developmentalist model and its political correlates—the Foča model. But because the changes were a result of liberal policies and in no way implied a reversal of commitments to foreign trade, openness, and continuing decentralization, this was not an institutional or ideological victory for the developmentalist faction as much as it was a de facto, practical one that created, as in the 1950s, a mixed system.

The restructuring and refinancing of foreign debt throughout the 1960s made external stabilization even more critical after 1969, and policymakers now identified the cause of domestic inflation with the unregulated market of the 1960s, particularly during 1965–68. Complaints from enterprises and unions about high turnover and absenteeism among

[42] Goati reports that the number of officials grew 0.6 percent annually in 1965–72, when social-sector employment grew less than 2.0 percent a year; but it rose 7.4 percent annually in 1972–87, when social-sector employment grew 4.2 percent a year ("Savetovanje").

[43] Yugoslav exports in the 1970s were increasingly composed of primary commodities and lower-value-added goods; see Economic Commission for Europe, "The Relative Performance of South European Exports."

skilled workers who earned second incomes in the informal market contributed to this view,[44] while the anti-inflationary program took particular aim at managers' high salaries and the bonuses they received for turning a commercial profit. The export of labor services had probably reduced political discontent over unemployment and provided critical hard currency, but by 1970 the government had become increasingly concerned about the brain drain of technical experts and skilled workers to Western Europe. It sought ways to persuade them to return and attempted to limit labor emigration to unskilled workers for whom there were no jobs at home.[45]

The numerous reasons for renewed attention to production skills, including a rising rate of job vacancies in the midst of rising unemployment, converged in a raft of new legislation on labor and education. The 1974 Law on Employment expressed renewed concern for manpower planning, legally obliging firms to project their manpower needs and develop training plans, increase the number of trainees, and give them permanent positions after they completed their training period. The new defense doctrine of all-national defense reintroduced universal conscription and obligatory military-training courses in high schools and universities.[46] Firms and local governments became the center of the system of defense; they were obliged to maintain stockpiles of necessities and weapons and to require persons employed in the public sector to undergo regular, active training in the reserves. A reform of secondary education ended the traditional two-track system of *gimnazije* (the university-directed liberal-arts high schools, similar to the lycée or gymnasium) and technical schools (for vocational education directed at immediate employment). A comprehensive system extended general education two years beyond elementary

[44] See Dyker on the rules against private-sector activity, such as the ban on import of semifinished goods for private businesses in July 1971 and the prosecution of "business crimes" in 1973 (*Yugoslavia: Socialism, Development, and Debt*, 83).

[45] Public discussions on emigration began in early 1970, and legislation appeared in February 1973 (Tanić, "Yugoslavia"). Many forces converged in this concern: the Slovene government faced shortages of technical expertise and was concerned about the replacement of Slovene emigrants with people from other regions of Yugoslavia; Croat émigrés in Germany reputedly had a role in the nationalist "mass movement" of 1967–71 (a primary charge by the federal party leadership against Croatian leaders Savka Dabčević-Kučar and Miko Tripalo at the Karadjordjevo "accounting" of December 1971); the YPA leadership was apparently concerned about the depletion of essential domestic skills; and debates in the federal assembly were dominated by the general view that the social costs of educating these skilled migrants were not being recouped. The 1973 law on labor migration gave preference to the unemployed and forbade those who had not completed their military service to emigrate.

[46] The outflow of reserve and retired officers into the civilian sector was not sufficient to meet the demand for trained military instructors, so that five universities opened departments for national-defense studies in 1975 (Bebler, "Development of Sociology of *Militaria* in Yugoslavia").

school and required universal vocational specialization thereafter in order to increase the supply of production-related and technical skills and reduce the supply of skills for which demand was declining.[47] Firms offered high-school youth contracts that would pay their schooling and guarantee them jobs if they trained as technicians or skilled workers.

Authorities also argued that incentives to productivity had been seriously diluted by managerial independence and the monoliths of industrial concentration and integrated conglomerates. To revive the pressures that self-management was intended to exert on workers to increase output while keeping wages within the limits of their productivity and enterprise revenue, and to reduce transaction costs further, a campaign for divisionalization began. Enterprises and cooperatives were subdivided into the smallest production units capable of independent accounting because they produced a marketable product; these units were named "basic organizations of associated labor" (BOALs).[48] In a two-decade-long quarrel among economists over valuation of labor, the "specific cost of production school" won a momentary victory, in 1974–76, over the hegemony of the "income school" (dohodoci) that had lasted since 1955. The latter was strongest in Croatia and Slovenia (although there were also members in Serbia), where the treatment of income as a share in value-added favored firms producing final goods for the market; the "specific cost of production" school, on the other hand, had long decried official disregard both for the prices paid raw-material and intermediate-goods producers and for the need to calculate labor costs in relation to fixed assets and other production inputs as a measure of efficiency within the firm. Labor legislation in 1974–76 refocused attention on skilled production workers and the reduction of turnover. Increases in the salaries of managers and other administrative or social-service staff ("nonproductive" employees) were indexed to the gains of production workers.

Although this legislation included more-secure guarantees for produc-

---

[47] This program was initiated by the OECD-funded Mediterranean Project in the mid-1960s and taken up by school reformers, first in Vojvodina and then in the Croatian littoral. Its model in the final stages was a mixture of, ironically, the educational systems in Sweden and the German Democratic Republic—the countries with the highest employment rates in Europe—although its origins are found in the polytechnical ideas of Napoleonic reforms. Later, however, it came to be identified with the unpopular sociologist-politician Stipe Šuvar, who was minister of education for Croatia at the time it was fully implemented. The "šuvarica" angered middle-class parents, required local budgetary resources to provide a full range of vocational schools in accord with a freedom of occupational choice that was unrealistic, and suffered from the planning assumptions that (as discussed in n. 34 above) characterized all such educational reforms (author's interviews in Croatia, Slovenia, and Serbia in 1975, 1978, and 1982).

[48] See Sacks, Self-Management and Efficiency, on divisionalization and the similar trends in other countries at the time.

tion jobs, leading many to call the Law on Associated Labor of 1976 a "workers' constitution" that protected workers against unemployment, its primary focus was the stabilizing objectives (also seen in 1949–50) of reasserting direct incentives to labor productivity and reducing costly turnover and market-influenced wage and salary inflation. Accordingly, it strengthened rules requiring parity between a person's individual qualifications and job classification, and it stiffened penalties against workers who threatened productivity through absenteeism, damage to social property, laziness, or lack of work discipline (in 1977, absence five days running without prior notice *required* dismissal, according to Article 215 of the 1976 law; a prison sentence or reformatory confinement of three months or more—after 1976, six months or more—was sufficient grounds for "termination," as was any official decision declaring a person unable to work). Services that had moved out of enterprises into autonomous bureaus or retail markets during the 1960s, such as marketing and services provided by accountants, lawyers, and doctors, were now reintegrated into enterprises to get more control over costs and, in the case of doctors, to prevent workers' use of paid sick leave as a cover for moonlighting.

Moreover, despite the belief that there was greater job security, enterprises were increasingly cautious about employing new permanent labor. Labor regulations permitted more flexibility to hire on temporary, part-time, or specific-project contracts when a firm's need for labor was likely to be temporary—such as when it had to replace employees on military or training leave, respond to an abnormal rise in market demand or a limited-production contract, or do seasonal work.[49] Firms did not fill positions vacated by retiring employees. The government attempted to get greater control over aggregate wages by reviving societywide and republic-negotiated social compacts on incomes policies (largely ignored in the emphasis on managerial autonomy), even though the shift to a flexible-exchange-rate regime and rising import prices undercut the effectiveness of such policies.[50] The voluntary character of the compacts also made them unenforceable if firms were unwilling.[51] Furthermore, workers' real incomes began to fall steadily, since prices rose faster than wages and enterprise income was barely sufficient to pay the contractual

[49] Specific-project work was done on freelance terms (*honorarno*), often by retired professionals. The amount of part-time, contractual, seasonal, and overtime work jumped significantly after the early 1970s (see Zukin, "Practicing Socialism in a Hobbesian World").

[50] Incomes policies were ineffective worldwide in the stagflation of the 1970s (William Nordhaus, commentary in discussion at the Yale University Conference on the World Economy, June 1988).

[51] In 1977, according to the Zagreb daily *Vjesnik*, 80 percent of all enterprises in Croatia disregarded the social compacts they had signed; *Privredni Vjesnik* (Business News) reported in 1978 that 50 percent of the enterprises it surveyed in Croatia ignored the compacts.

wage (sometimes not even that), let alone bonuses or profit shares. The rate of unemployment shot skyward.

While the private sector had been intended as a refuge for surplus labor expelled from the social sector, during the 1960s it began to generate increasing wealth, which the government, strapped for funds, attempted to capture for investment in new workplaces. The Green Plan of 1973 encouraged private farmers to pool their resources in cooperatives in exchange for financial assistance to purchase modern equipment; the plan was in fact largely aimed at getting World Bank loans that gave priority to the private sector.[52] It was also, however, one of a number of efforts to encourage Yugoslav workers abroad to return and invest their savings in productive activities—in agriculture, services, and small businesses—in order, authorities said enticingly, "to obtain work more quickly." Employment plans within the annual federal economic resolutions reserved a specified number of jobs for returnees, giving priority in employment to some of their occupations. New laws on property rights permitted returning migrants to invest their own funds in small factories in the public sector in exchange for employment—essentially, to buy themselves a job. In 1978, the government began to look to foreign loans specifically for employment by establishing a special federal fund "for credits to increase employment in economically less developed regions"; the fund was to be based entirely on foreign monies and would encourage joint ventures "where unemployment was grave."[53] A 1977 law on credit and banking opened municipal savings institutions to capture private savings, established favorable rates on loans to marginal firms to protect employment, and guaranteed deposits and raised interest on individual accounts through the National Bank. Private persons were permitted to open foreign-exchange accounts in banks and were paid interest in dinars. Local governments financed infrastructural projects, such as new elementary schools and hospitals, with bond issues and local campaigns to "increase savings."[54]

[52] The first of these loans was offered in 1971 by the World Bank along with the UN Food and Agriculture Organization; it was granted in 1976 after much difficulty. The second loan came in 1978. The story of these loans tells much about the Yugoslav system; see Dyker, *Yugoslavia*, 156–57.

[53] The fund was established by the Law on the Procurement and Use of Foreign Resources for the Purposes of Increasing Employment and Providing Jobs for Those Returning from Work Abroad. Its basic task was to collect resources from other countries on a grant-in-aid or credit basis to finance employment in economically underdeveloped regions and areas of marked emigration. See the press conference of Kiro Gligorov, then president of the federal assembly, on June 18, 1977, cited in RFE:RAD Background Report no. 114 (June 21, 1977) from the story in *Borba* (Belgrade), June 19, 1977.

[54] The citizens of Bosnia-Herzegovina voted to pay a 3 percent tax on their personal incomes for the 1984 winter Olympic games.

The political coloration of these labor reforms and their obvious parallels to those of the 1950s—together with the delay until 1974 in promulgating a new constitution to codify the decentralizing amendments of 1967–71 and the delay of the revised law on labor relations until 1976—contributed to the perception that the changes were a reactionary response to political and social turmoil. Yet, as early as 1977, managers began a revolt against the labor regulations, revisions were made, and party leaders insisted that managers be given greater flexibility in disposing of labor. By 1981, enterprises had taken their demands to the legislatures and won. The return to an IMF-conditioned stabilization in August 1979 also initiated a new series of wage controls and devaluations.

1979–1989

Between 1979 and 1982, the full-fledged return to economic reform and exports to Western markets in order to repay convertible-currency debt necessitated rewriting labor legislation. Although the language of rationalization and dismissal continued to refer to the need for discipline on the job, this now meant the threat of unemployment. In the words of an economist on the Kraigher Commission, set up to draft a long-term stabilization program acceptable to the IMF, "a position of employment is not a privilege." If no profit, then bankruptcy.[55]

Revised legislation now allowed firms to terminate a trainee's employment contract after one year and to fulfill their legal obligation by putting multiple trainees into one position and choosing among them according to performance on the job. Lower budgets for social services and the military due to declining growth forced cuts in their staffs. Limits were placed on university enrollments in fields with the greatest surplus of skills—which happened to be liberal (noneconomic) professions, such as medicine, dentistry, and the liberal arts and social sciences. Firms resisted the pressure to hire additional family members and generally excluded women and youth from consideration by adding the qualification in the obligatory advertisements of job openings that candidates "must have completed their military service."[56] New full-time positions carried ever-higher requirements for prior work experience, often of a specialized nature, and demanded a host of special internal qualifications and equivalents of formal schooling. By 1989, the Law on Enterprises, written to encourage foreign investment, gave managers full rights to hire and fire labor and erased the system of self-management. Prime Minister Ante Marković gave top priority to privatization of public-sector firms.

---

[55] Author's interview in Ljubljana, October 1982. Laws facilitating bankruptcy appeared in 1987; see Knight, *Financial Discipline and Structural Adjustment in Yugoslavia.*

[56] Ruža First-Dilić first alerted me to this practice.

During the 1980s, just as in the early 1960s, official concern for the employment consequences of stabilization restrictions and export promotion led to yet another reduction in the workday, calls for multiple work shifts, revisions of pension laws to encourage earlier retirement, and some increase in the minuscule monies for unemployment compensation. Taxation also shifted back from enterprises to personal incomes, and social services, housing, and utilities were again to be financed through user fees and retail markets instead of enterprise funds. Social compacts on incomes were revised to permit lower taxes on enterprises' gross wage bill on the argument that Yugoslavia's comparative advantage in exports was in low labor costs. The basket of commodities defining the guaranteed minimum wage rate became smaller in 1982. At the end of 1984, the terms of agreement with the IMF produced a nationwide compact on incomes policy, signed by republican governments and sent to all basic organizations of associated labor.

The primary proposals for expanding employment also relied, as before, on the encouragement of small firms and services in the private sector (*mala privreda*) and on calls for redundant labor to return to agriculture. This time, however, attempts to remove the limits on landholdings succeeded in Croatia, and later in Serbia. Only Slovenia explicitly held out, arguing that its borderlands were already in danger of depopulation and that smallholdings plus tax relief to private peasants were necessary incentives to keep the peasants there. Many republics also structured tax-relief packages to encourage employment. In Serbia, for example, beginning in 1979–80, tax authorities excused from taxation people in traineeships, small firms in their first year or two of business, and firms that employed the handicapped.[57] In 1987, the government negotiated grants from France (30 million francs) and the Federal Republic of Germany (33 million marks) to assist the return of Yugoslav professionals working abroad by creating projects that would provide them with jobs.[58]

A new policy on federal aid to less-developed areas of the country allowed republics to fulfill up to 50 percent of their obligations by encouraging their firms to invest directly in joint ventures in these areas. Like the arguments made at the eighth party congress in 1964—when liberals and developmentalists clashed on the necessity of a fund to aid less-developed areas and Tito argued for the latter to receive technical assistance of the kind Yugoslavia was then giving to third-world countries— the new policy differentiated the economic space of the country accord-

---

[57] T. Raičević, personal communication, Belgrade, November 1982. See Mates, "Recent Tendencies in the Regulation of Income Distribution," on changes in accounting rules for taxation of personal income.

[58] "Rates of Employment and Unemployment, 1980–1987," 40.

ing to export specialization and corresponding comparative advantage. The more-developed regions of the north, as an area of "highly modern, technically advanced export industries," would invest in the south as an area of low-wage, labor-intensive industries "to absorb the problem of employment."[59]

DISHARMONIES

The rhetoric of central policy rarely stepped away from employment, but responsibility for implementing central policy and for employment resided with republican and local governments. The primary investors were these republican and local governments, enterprises, and, in most cases, the territorial banks, which lay at the intersection of the three by providing credit in response to governmental social plans and enterprise applications. The expansion of productive capacity and developmental investment was the jurisdiction of republican governments after 1958, and even where federal investments continued, the republics were handed the completed projects and thus the obligation to maintain them. Economic planning was therefore a republican affair, in which the industrial and sectoral policies of structural change were focused on regional development using the financial resources that a republic could capture—in its territorial bank, from federal grants and subsidies, and from the foreign monies earned or borrowed by its enterprises. At the same time, republican authorities, like the federal government, saw employment promotion as a commitment to growth in general. Local governments, particularly through the activities of employment services that put pressure on local officials and worked with enterprise directors, performed the function of a market wage in capitalist countries—adjusting the (local) supply of labor to the demand for it.

The consequence was a growing disjuncture over time between policies addressed to the external environment, guided by a particular model of growth, and the reality of the labor supply in the country. It was manifest in an increasing disparity between the demand from the social sector of labor and the pattern of both agrarian exodus and generational turnover. As a result especially of the territorialization of capital flows (within republics and in federally mediated transfers between republics) and of human-capital formation (system of schooling), there were "vastly different labor market conditions among the various republics."[60] And the in-

---

[59] Proposals from the Kraigher Commission's working group on employment (unpublished version); Branislav Šoškić, speech at the annual meeting of the Yugoslav Association of Economists, Opatija, Croatia, October 1982.

[60] Schrenk, Ardalan, and El Tatawy, first draft of their analysis of the World Bank mission; but see their *Yugoslavia: Self-Management Socialism and the Challenges of Development*, 244–45, and the detailed elaboration at 245–49 and 286–315.

creasing disparity over both time and space between demand and supply created an ever-greater disproportion between need and resources for new investment at the local level.

In the republic-centered world of statistical data and political representation, however, the reality of growing unemployment contrasted sharply with conditions in Slovenia. There the model underlying governmental policies—an industrially advanced, lean socialist core of skilled workers and commercially attuned manufacturers participating fully in Western trade, a settled labor reserve of private farmers and artisans, and a government of experts and a local militia—seemed to be the cause of full employment. It was easy to conclude that the choice of growth strategy and accompanying institutions (including republican economic sovereignty) was correct, and that unemployment in other republics, rising as one went east and south, was due to political interference with that model or to "cultural" differences. But Slovenia was also the one republic where the initial developmental and labor-supply conditions and existing plant on which the original Slovene model was based actually held.[61]

The first problem in all the other areas was the imbalance between the pace of industrial demand for labor and the pace at which surplus labor was released from the countryside. The historical dimension of differences among the republics remained clearest. The contrast was particularly sharp between labor-importing Slovenia, with its early commercialization of agriculture and development of light manufacturing and its universal elementary education, and areas untouched by industry even in the 1930s. The areas of greatest population density were those where industry was least developed before the war and where land was scarcely arable, such as the Dalmatian hinterland and the Dinaric range of Herzegovina and Montenegro (where population density in the 1930s was as high as in China or Java). The exodus of Partisan veterans onto the plains of Vojvodina and Slavonia in 1946–47 was insufficient to prevent the poorly developed regions from remaining "regions of emigration." People continued to emigrate according to prewar traditions and access to external routes—to the West, to urban centers in the poorer republics, and, eventually, to Slovenia.

Policy contributed to this disharmony. A development strategy based for political reasons on a gradual approach to capital accumulation that took advantage of imported capital and existing capacity in processing and manufacturing and on federal investment in new capacity in heavy indus-

---

[61] In 1945, 78 percent of industry in Yugoslavia lay north of the Danube-Sava line. By 1968, the proportion of industry in the central and eastern parts of the country had grown from 22 percent to 45 percent, but much of that was heavy and defense-oriented industry; it was not sustainable in the economically difficult decades after 1965, while light manufacturing in the north could be modernized (Hamilton, "The Location of Industry in East-Central and Southeast Europe," 177, 183).

try, raw-material extraction, and infrastructure for defense needs directly intensified the inherited differences. State policies toward defense, in 1938–39 and again in 1947–49, located strategic industries in the interior and left vulnerable borderlands declared as security zones with little industry (such as Vojvodina and Croatian Medjumurje) or with only administrative towns (as in Macedonia) until the 1960s.[62] Investments in infrastructure also reproduced inherited geopolitical profiles: federal projects (including the volunteer brigades) and monies were dedicated to defense-oriented infrastructure, largely in the interior, whereas republican expenditures and foreign loans for infrastructure after 1960 were more oriented to foreign-trade earnings and favored areas with more-developed transportation and communication links to Western Europe, the tourist and shipping industries of the Dalmatian coast, and inherited infrastructure in river valleys.[63] Even in the 1970s and 1980s, offshore processing and assembly were purposely located near Western markets, in Slovenia and parts of Croatia,[64] whereas the energy, mining, and heavy-industry sectors were in areas of Bosnia, Kosovo, Serbia, and Macedonia—which were more isolated from foreign markets, particularly convertible-currency markets. Foreign credits and investment for various purposes flowed to more-developed areas with better infrastructure and international contacts.[65]

[62] Borders closed to economic exchange by the split with the Cominform in 1948–49 were doubly affected—by both federal policy and external hostility. While Croatia and Serbia benefited from Hungarian and Romanian openness during the 1960s, Macedonia was particularly harmed by the effects of poor political relations—not only the Eastern blockade (and the fact that Bulgaria was fully oriented to its Eastern markets until the mid-1980s) but also the closing of the border with Greece when Yugoslav authorities conceded to Western demands in 1949 and again in the 1960s, as relations between Yugoslavia and Greece under the junta turned hostile. The tensions over the border transformed market towns on the Macedonian side into administrative centers (for political control, customs inspection, radar stations, and watchtowers) without their own economic base, discouraged firms from developing commercial and export activities, and led many firms to use Slovene intermediaries for the processing and marketing of Macedonian raw materials. Of the thirty communes in Macedonia, fifteen were in border areas; of the fourteen least developed, seven were on the border itself and the others were mountainous, food-deficit districts. Across two of Macedonia's three foreign borders were areas even less developed, moreover—Pirinsko Macedonia in Bulgaria and Albania (author's interviews with Dobri Dodevski and others at the Institute of Economics in Skopje, December 1982).

[63] Rusinow describes the policy conflict produced in the early 1960s by the clash between the "Danubian" and "Adriatic" concepts of economic development—the first favored by Serbia, with its river transport and links to the east, the second by Croatia, with its maritime transport and access to the west (*The Yugoslav Experiment*, 133–34; see also Wilson, "The Belgrade-Bar Railroad").

[64] Slovenia and Croatia joined a grouping initiated by northern Italian provinces in the 1980s to discuss regional cooperation in the "Alpe-Adria" area (the name taken by the association) for tourist, economic, and cultural development.

[65] The western republics had far greater success in international capital and Eurodollar markets once republics and firms were free to borrow (the former after 1965 and the latter

The sectoral distinctions in agricultural policy and property also followed the historical pattern of geographical differences—between private-sector, small-scale and household production of fruits, vegetables, and livestock for retail markets, with few regulations and free prices, on the one hand; and the social-sector, large-scale production of basic food-stuffs (such as grains and oils) and industrial crops in Bosnia and in the plains of Vojvodina, Slavonia, and Macedonia on the other. Social-sector agriculture received government credits, which the private sector did not, but it was also regulated by a defense-oriented national food policy that set prices, required permission for export, and tied the areas where it prevailed far more to the domestic market and negotiated prices.[66]

Consequently, labor-intensive activities in industry and agriculture tended to predominate in areas with more-developed industry, diversified activities, and lower agricultural surpluses and birthrates. Highly capital-intensive activities in energy, mining, and heavy industry were located in less-developed areas with large labor surpluses in the country-side and high birthrates. The extreme that demonstrates the pattern was the province of Kosovo, with birthrates comparable to those of south Asia but industrial investment in sectors that are highly capital-intensive, such as energy, metallurgy, and smelting.[67] The availability of investment resources was in inverse proportion to the demand for jobs as a result of price policy, which regulated industries and producers that happened to concentrate disproportionately in poorer areas and which allowed prices and goods to roam freely for final manufacturers and processing firms that tended to concentrate in more-developed areas. The policy of firing women first in a recession, unless they were pregnant, compounded the problem, because of the interactive effect and inverse relation between female employment and birthrates.[68]

The incongruence between policy and domestic conditions was not only geographic and demographic but temporal as well. In place of grow-

---

after 1974); foreign direct investment also favored Croatia and Slovenia (including major energy and petrochemical projects by Dow Chemical and Westinghouse). Even research monies to firms and institutes tended to flow along well-established networks; a World Health Organization study of population control in the early 1980s, for example, was done in Slovenia rather than Kosovo or Macedonia because the Slovene research team was known in international social science and aid circles.

[66] The differences between Vojvodina and Slovenia are discussed in Bookman, "The Economic Basis of Regional Autarchy in Yugoslavia."

[67] The birthrate for Kosovo declined from 43.5 per 1000 population in 1950–54 to 30.0 per 1000 in 1985–89, in comparison to 28.8 and 15.2 per 1000 for all of Yugoslavia in the same periods. But the rate of natural increase was 25.5 per 1000 for Kosovo in 1950–54, rising to 28.9 in 1965–69 and falling to 24.1 in 1985–89; the Yugoslav average had declined from 17.0 to 6.1, while in 1985–89 Slovenia was at 3.1, Croatia at 1.5, and Serbia proper at 2.4 (*Statistički Godišnjak Jugoslavije* for the relevant years).

[68] For Yugoslav data on this effect, see Mihovilović et al., *Žena izmedju rada i porodice*.

ing demand in industry for surplus labor released "naturally" from agriculture, restrictive policies occurred in all spheres at once—in monetary and fiscal policy for macroeconomic stabilization and in labor policy in social-sector industry, agriculture, and public services aimed at increasing productivity and reducing labor costs; the released surplus was thus pushed in the other direction. Unskilled labor expelled from industry in the 1950s and 1960s did not find the countryside receptive because central policy—in 1955–57, in 1965–68, and again in 1970—was also aimed at raising agricultural productivity through concentration of landholdings, mechanization, and incorporation of more land as well as marketing activities into the social sector. These were the same years in which imports of grain, cotton, and oil substituted for domestic production of coal and grains, releasing even more labor from the land and primary industries. The demobilization and then "socialization" of the security apparatus and the army (in 1955, 1958–64, after 1966, and again in the 1970s) sent veterans, police, and retiring officers home to areas that, because of the pattern of wartime fighting and recruitment into the Partisan army, were more agrarian and less well equipped with a range of manufacturing and tertiary employments (particularly Bosnia-Herzegovina, Montenegro, and the former military border of Croatia).

Instead of absorbing the agricultural labor surplus and reducing the problem of developmental unemployment after the 1950s (according to the justification for joining GATT in 1958, this was no longer an issue), the openness of the economy during the 1960s and 1970s made the country vulnerable to serious Western recessions that affected export commodities and then labor—at the same time that the rural outflow was growing.[69] Moreover, although government policy in the early 1970s was to induce skilled labor to return from abroad, the receiving countries changed their policies at the time in the opposite direction, expelling less-skilled labor and accepting only more highly skilled workers and technicians in their lower quotas. The pace of agrarian exodus actually quickened after 1971, only a few years before opportunities in Western Europe disappeared and Yugoslav *gastarbeiter* flooded back.[70] Thus, despite em-

[69] Such recessions took place in 1960–61, in 1965–67, and more or less continuously after 1974. U. S. recessions in 1953–54 and 1957–58 were also significant in Yugoslav policy shifts during the 1950s, when Yugoslav trade with the United States was higher (see Shonfield, *Modern Capitalism*, 10–18).

[70] Between 1971 and 1981, the agricultural population countrywide declined 18 percent, from 38.2 percent to 19.9 percent of the total population. By republic, the 1981 figures were 9.2 percent in Slovenia, 13.0 percent in Montenegro, 14.5 percent in Croatia, 16.6 percent in Bosnia-Herzegovina, 19.2 percent in Vojvodina, 20.5 percent in Macedonia, 24.0 percent in Kosovo, and 26.6 percent in Serbia proper (calculated from "The Non-Agricultural Population," 5).

ployment growth in 1973–75,[71] the resident labor force increased in absolute terms for the first time since the mid-1960s recession, and there was an explosion in the unemployment rolls. By 1982, Macedonia was employing twelve thousand new workers a year—but the demand was for eighteen thousand jobs.[72]

In addition to the disparity between industrial demand for labor as defined by official policy and the rate of rural outflow, a second problem for areas outside those fitting the initial conditions of the Slovene model was the cumulative impact of macroeconomic stabilization and development policy. Despite the early commitment to female equality, which urged women into the industrial labor force, equalized wages for a job regardless of who held it, and emphasized universal education, the approach to welfare and unemployment sent women packing first. As a result, women's participation rates were (except in Slovenia) closer to those of southern Europe than those of socialist countries. Yet the secular rise in demand for jobs, independent of demographic change and agrarian exodus, was primarily a response to stabilization policies, as falling household incomes and living standards pushed second and third family members into the labor force in search of supplementary wages. At the same time that women and youth were being fired, in other words, they were more likely to be seeking employment.

In contrast, the liberals' enduring battle to demilitarize the state, the economy, and society was in practice often legitimized by the official approach to external stabilization. Deflationary policies, which aimed at reversing the balance-of-payments deficits and building up hard-currency reserves, emphasized reducing federal expenditures by cutting competences and the military budget. But the achievement of such cuts came at the price of rising burdens on local governments—and thus an ever-greater drain on resources where effective investment for employment had to occur. Moreover, the world environment was not always so accommodating as to reduce military threats when Western demand for exports fell and capital markets were tight. More often—such as the late 1960s, after the mid-1970s, and throughout the 1980s—both situations demanded a policy response simultaneously. The contradictory demands on central policy had to be implemented, however, at the local level, and the effect was to magnify the existing disparities between investment resources and employment needs among localities. According to Pavle Sicherl's dynamic analysis of economic inequalities in the country—a measure of the time needed by the less-developed republics to catch up

[71] 1974 was a good year for employment, and employment growth in 1975 was the highest in ten years (Mencinger, "Utjecaj privredne aktivnosti na zaposlenost").

[72] Tripo Mulina, personal communication, Belgrade, October 1982; Kiril Miljovski, personal communication, Opatija, October 1982.

to the more-developed ones in various economic indicators—the "most important single factor" in the differences in gross material product (GMP) per capita was the level of industrial, social-sector employment.[73] The discrepancy accruing from early advantages widened substantially between 1961 and 1971.

The policy-generated temporal disjuncture between labor demand and supply also had a generational aspect. The great value placed on the "human factor" in growth led to substantial attention to education and training, but again the cycles were at odds. Attempts to retire the Partisan generation to make room for a better-educated, younger generation in the second half of the 1950s and the early 1960s sent these often still young veterans into local economies at a time when investment in the economy and in schooling was being decentralized to republican and local budgets.[74] The postwar baby-boom generation entered the labor market in exactly the same years as the serious employment recessions surrounding the 1960s economic reforms, especially after 1965. Instead of the needed expansion, job creation was nearly at a standstill, dismissals were rising, and policy required firms to hire first those whose jobs had been made redundant by the reforms, so that turnover was strictly within the cohort of persons already employed.[75] The more importance that formal educational qualifications took on for employment and incomes, the higher was the incentive to leave rural towns and villages. The ever-larger contingent of the rural exodus were youth who left, they told rural sociologists, not

[73] Sicherl, "Time-Distance as a Dynamic Measure of Disparities in Social and Economic Development." In 1971, according to Sicherl's measure of time distance between the "more developed republics" and the "less developed republics," the latter needed five years to "catch up" in measures of productivity, fifteen years to reach the same levels of employment, and forty years to equalize demographic rates. The time distance for per capita income (GMP per capita) between the two groups of republics was 11.5 years, of which employment levels explained 5.1 years, productivity 4.4 years, and the demographic component 2 years (ibid.).

[74] The commune budget for Mostar, Bosnia-Herzegovina, gave first priority and substantial monies to housing and schools; the least-funded categories were "intervention in the economy" and "investment in the economy," and funding for them declined after 1965. In 1969, the budget for education was 23 million new dinars; for noneconomic investment, 7,293,400; and for the two economic categories, a total of 431,400 (Rosenblum-Čale, "Appropriation Politics," 31 n. 41). In the 1980s, Macedonian towns with high female unemployment did invest heavily in textile industries, however, because credits favored export-oriented processing and these industries were deemed more suitable for women (author's interviews with Dobri Dodevski and Olga Dimitrieva of the Institute of Economics in Skopje and Tripo Mulina of the Institute of Economics in Belgrade, fall 1982).

[75] This was the period when, according to Estrin, freer wage determination in firms made it possible for urban-sector workers to monopolize control over their jobs (*Self-Management: Economic Theory and Yugoslav Practice*, 204–5). Adizes gives a far better picture of the actual decisions being made by managers for modernization and markets at the time (*Industrial Democracy, Yugoslav Style*).

because of lower wages and insufficient investment in jobs (as the Todaro model would argue), but because of the lack of educational opportunity.[76]

The reform and expansion of university education in the 1960s yielded a cohort in the 1970s that sought jobs commensurate with their certification, but economic policy had shifted in favor of skilled production jobs for which they had neither the skills nor the volition. The reform of secondary education in the mid-1970s to encourage vocational training in needed technical skills gave localities the responsibility for providing the full range of occupational training that local youth desired at exactly the point when the next round of governmental decentralization, combined with the new defense role of localities, weighed heavily on local budgets for jobs, housing, and unemployment assistance. Most localities simply could not provide a full range of choice, thus either limiting the skills that employers could find locally or encouraging a further exodus from smaller to larger towns. Secondary-school students had a choice of either studying in the one or two technical schools their town could afford or emigrating to cities, which could offer a fuller range but were accumulating ever-larger pools of unemployed residents and migrants. This reform continued into the period of sharp monetary contraction with debt repayment in the 1980s.

Moreover, decentralization reduced only the number of "unproductive" administrators employed at one level, while it increased the total number. Although the expansion in employment in services, government, and other administrative tasks in 1976–79 was able to absorb some of the younger generation and its skills, it was cut short by the renewed economic reform and stagnation in new employment after 1979—a reversal intended in part to cut back on such "overemployment."

These various disharmonies in the path of development played themselves out, however, within separate universes in each republic. Most republics contained internal differences. For example, there were wide differences among Macedonian towns that had traditionally specialized in specific crafts and that varied substantially in birthrates, commercial opportunities, and administrative obligations. In Croatia, regional differ-

---

[76] Dilić, *Seoska omladina danas*. Studies in both Croatia and Serbia have shown that young women left at an earlier age than men because their disadvantages in employment, even more than prospects for a successful marriage, drove them to seek better education in the towns (author's interviews with Olga Supek and Zagorka Golubović, anthropologists who did field research in villages of Croatia and Serbia). To send them to secondary school, parents spent household savings that would in the past have been a marriage dowry. On the beginning of this change, see Trouton, *Peasant Renaissance in Yugoslavia*. Sociologists also recorded the increasing aging of the agricultural population at the time (see the articles by Svetozar Livada and Edhem Dilić in Department of Rural Sociology, Institute of Agricultural Economics and Sociology, *The Yugoslav Village*; on the same process elsewhere in Eastern Europe, see H. Scott, "Why the Revolution Doesn't Solve Everything").

ences were substantial, between the interior (the former military border, where timber, mines, and railroads provided work), the industrial complex of the Zagreb region, the tourist industry of Dalmatia, and the rich agricultural fields and agro-industry of Slavonia and Baranja.[77] Federal investment in the 1940s and 1950s had an overall conception not limited to particular republics, and military production not only was spread throughout the country, for strategic reasons, but also followed a policy requiring integration of production phases among plants dispersed throughout the country.

Nonetheless, the economic autonomy of republics over the policies directly affecting labor—in education, investment monies, regional development, incomes and welfare, and military conscription—and the fact that capital for investment flowed vertically among governmental budgets and the banking system meant that republics had greater influence over employment outcomes. The allocation and concentration of capital and credit, whether derived from federal subsidies, foreign credits, taxation, or other transfers, were territorially organized rather than sectoral or market-driven. In contrast to the flow of semifinished and finished goods, the cross-regional flows of capital and credit were low.

All of the differential consequences of central policies on inherited capacities, geographical position, and composition of population had their effect on the monies available for investment. When the republics first gained autonomy over investment credit and began to define their separate development strategies after 1958, for example, the cuts in overall investment rates, in the proportion devoted to heavy industry and agriculture, and in federal investment were made on the argument that the country had reached the middle levels of development and that domestic industry was now able to satisfy domestic needs. In fact, the republics were at vastly different levels of development. The less-industrialized republics were left to face the unfinished task of massive infrastructural and industrial development when policy favored technological modernization, fuller utilization of existing capacity, and reorientation to Western trade. In addition, the GATT-defined liberalization between 1958 and 1961 eliminated the capacity for differentiation in federal policy, replacing multiple coefficients with uniform tariffs, progressive taxation with pro-

---

[77] The policy shift in Croatia after 1972 to investment in the poor interior—such as in the aluminum plant at Obrovac, to take advantage of local bauxite (already on long-term contract, it turned out, to the Soviet market)—received heavy criticism as irrational, "political" investment by the new, more conservative Croatian leadership to buy back the allegiance of local Serbs after the Croatian nationalist tensions in 1967–71. But a more straightforward economic explanation is suggested by the pattern of similar investment choices elsewhere in Yugoslavia and in the rest of the world as a result of the sharp rise of commodity prices on world markets after 1969, which made the aluminum appear to be a cheaper source for domestic producers and a more profitable export.

portional rates, and sectoral priorities with foreign price competition for producers of raw materials and intermediate goods.[78] The fact that larger concentrations of capital and longer gestation times were needed for capital investments than for equipment modernization meant that the problem of temporal disjunctures between federal policies of international adjustment and domestic employment became ever greater the farther one moved away from the northwest of the country.

In 1963, for example, the "entire economic leadership of Serbia" was preoccupied with "how to put a stop to Serbia's further decline into relative economic backwardness."[79] Losing the fight to change the price structure more in favor of agriculture and its contribution to GDP (gross domestic product) and all measures based on it, planners turned to major capital projects of "strategic" importance for Serbian development, such as the Belgrade-Bar railroad,[80] the completion of the Danube-Tisza-Danube canal (linking Hungarian agriculture and the Iron Gates hydroelectric plant on the border with Romania), the oil refinery in Pančevo, the steelworks at Smederevo, the hydroelectric plant at Djerdap, and regulation of the Velika Morava River. These projects, treated as the "to be or not to be" for Serbia, were completed only in 1979, however, when the country was on a course of global-market integration favoring light manufacturers and processors.[81] Similarly, massive investment in Macedonia in the 1970s went, with the aid of federal funds, to several large capital projects (including the Feni nickel plant and the Skopje steelworks), which came on stream just when producers faced world recession, adverse terms of trade, liberal economic reforms, and, shortly thereafter, the collapse of the Eastern market altogether. Substantial capital investment in mining and metallurgy in the interior of Croatia in the early 1970s (such as the aluminum-processing plant in Obrovac) depended on a global price structure and Eastern markets that had already changed by the 1980s. The serious business losses that resulted were only one of the reasons for the deindustrialization of entire regions in the 1980s, similar to what occurred in the central industrial belt of Bosnia-Herzegovina. It was a problem not only of capital, but also of thousands of workers who became unemployed when the mines and plants closed but who had long ago been displaced from the land.

Structurally more vulnerable to recession, the less-developed republics

---

[78] Gapinski, Škegro, and Zuehlke found that linear equations were very successful in modeling taxes of all kinds, including sales and personal income taxes, and thus revealing that rates were effectively proportional, not progressive (*Modeling the Economic Performance of Yugoslavia*, 154).

[79] Pešaković, "Niško savetovanje ekonomista Srbije, 1963 i danas."

[80] See Wilson, "The Belgrade-Bar Railroad."

[81] Pešaković, "Niško savetovanje."

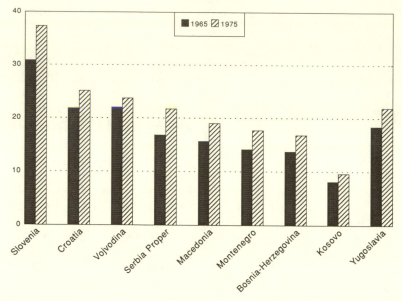

Figure 8-1. Percentage of Employment in the Social Sector by Republic. *Source: Statistički Bilten Jugoslavije* (1977), cited in Pleskovič and Dolenc, "Regional Development, in a Socialist, Developing, and Multinational Country," 12.

also saw the time necessary to catch up in employment capacity lengthen with the ever more frequent resort to macroeconomic stabilization policy and its approach to structural adjustment. Because the "comparative advantage of regions [was] crucially determined by the credit potential of specific territorial banks,"[82] policies to tighten discipline over banks by increasing their reserve ratios and limiting credit for working capital also had the effect of penalizing poorer regions and weaker banks, causing particular hardship for enterprises with seasonal credit needs. The republican control over credit tended to lead as well to duplication of facilities and a resulting excess industrial capacity.[83] This increased the tendency to idle capacity (with its effects on unemployment) and the tendency for

[82] Kovać et al., *Privreda Jugoslavije do 1985*, 212–14.

[83] Technical capacity was far too great for the domestic market after 1958, as each republic built its own steel mills, oil refineries, and consumer-goods factories for refrigerators, textiles, and footwear. By 1965, for example, there were five steel miles in four republics producing 2.2 million tons per year altogether, although one mill had to produce at least 2 million tons annually to break even (Hondius, *The Yugoslav Community of Nations,* 319). This duplication of capacity was a primary theme in the mounting public criticism of the republicanization of the economy attributed to the 1974 constitution at the time of the foreign-debt crisis and the more general economic crisis beginning in 1979–1982.

large firms to find ways to stimulate domestic demand for their unsold inventories (even when federal policy aimed to restrict demand). Moreover, republican banks' control over credit was disadvantageous for employment because of the bargaining power in these banks of large industrial firms, which were more likely to enlarge by merger than employment expansion. Smaller, more labor-intensive firms tended, therefore, to be more risk-averse and more dependent on internal resources for both rising incomes and employment expansion.

Internally generated resources (whether for firms or republics) were also differentially affected by federal policy as a result of the structural differences in production across territories. Price regulation favoring industrialization worked to the disadvantage of the less-developed areas, ironically, because prices for raw materials and intermediate supplies were kept artificially low while industrial prices were high. Tariff policy and foreign-trade liberalization were used to expose producers of such materials to foreign competition while protecting manufacturers. Policies to promote exports with subsidies and rights to retain foreign-exchange earnings benefited the more-developed republics (especially Slovenia and Croatia), where export producers and hard-currency earnings concentrated; so did advances on clearing trade if one includes Serbia. Export producers tended to be price setters domestically also. The flow of prized foreign exchange from guest workers' remittances and tourist earnings, in addition to foreign-employment alternatives for absorbing the rural surplus, disproportionately benefited Slovenia and Croatia, which for reasons of geographical proximity and cultural tradition (especially in Croatia) had the largest contingent of temporary foreign migration.

The role of wages in limiting savings for investment was also disproportionately harmful to the areas with higher unemployment. Wages in social-sector firms tended to be more equal across republics than would be predicted by differences in their gross social product per capita. As a result, in the less-developed republics a higher proportion of republican and local budgets and of enterprise earnings went to wages and benefits than in the more-developed republics, thereby reducing local resources for new investment and jobs—particularly when stabilization policies required more reliance on internal resources. Contrary to the literature on labor management and the regular criticism from northern economists and politicians (particularly in Slovenia), this was a result of the productivity-oriented wage regulations—which had an equalizing influence across republics—and the fact that the reservation wage for the country was set by upward pressure on wages in full-employment Slovenia, where the wage was highest. Wages in the less-developed republics also were the target of protests against budgetary subsidies and development credits from economists and politicians in the more-developed republics, even though the higher aggregate demand that resulted from such wage levels disproportionately benefited those more-developed republics and in effect created a built-in domestic market for their goods. The problem was compounded by the concentration in poorer regions of low-wage industries, which tended to distribute a higher portion of their net receipts to wages, and a far larger proportion of "nonaccumulative" firms (basic industries) that depended on budgetary subsidies.[84] While social-sector wages were higher than strictly marginal rules within firms would predict, they were not as high as in richer areas, making it difficult for firms to pay the wages (and particularly benefits) necessary to attract and retain skilled labor. Those who emigrated from poorer areas, whether to the more-developed republics or abroad, were not the least-productive "surplus," but the most skilled and ambitious.

Aware of the biases of these policies, the leadership and the representatives of richer firms and regions conceded to compensation for those who were losers. It became ritual for Tito to point out that the more-developed republics had an economic interest in the rapid development of the others.[85] But the political system was organized around questions of allocation and distribution, and without economic growth, the consequence of the socialist monetary system was that "what [was] a plus in one region [was] necessarily a minus in another."[86] The federal transfers for development in the form of low-interest, long-maturing loans became the subject of constant criticism, even though they amounted to less than 2 percent of GDP annually. Political debate could, and did, occur over actual taxes and transfers, but not over the effects of invisible redistribution due to the regulation of economic activity through, for example, regulated prices, special funds, selective credits, export incentives, and tariffs—all of which worked to the net advantage of firms in the more-developed regions.[87] And it was at the moment of declining growth and restrictive macroeconomic policy for stabilization and debt repayment—when such

[84] Vojvodina complained frequently about this problem; see the discussion as early as 1956 in the pages of *Narodna Armija* (see n. 19 above).

[85] See the citation from his address to the ninth party congress in 1969 in Wilson, "The Belgrade-Bar Railroad," 377–79; and his speech to the eighth party congress in 1964, in which he outlined the new policy for development of the less-developed republics through "technical and personnel assistance from the community" of the kind Yugoslavia was providing other countries. He also laid out the trickle-down arguments underlying the policy (*Osmi kongres SKJ*, 41–42).

[86] Miljovski, "Possibilities for the Development of Underdeveloped Areas," 10.

[87] Evidence was widespread that the effect of price regulations "was relatively unfavorable to the less developed republics" (Dubey et al., *Yugoslavia: Development with Decentralization*, 193–94); on the bias of investment and liberalization against the less-developed republics, see 200ff. Dyker cites Macedonian research on the effect of the policy-dictated price structure that draws the same conclusion (*Yugoslavia*, 77).

compensatory transfers mattered most to poorer and less foreign trade-oriented enterprises and areas and when the demand for employment was rising—that the fight to reduce taxation and federal redistribution was at its height. At the least, this wrangling meant long delays in disbursements while conflicts over priorities and funds were negotiated.

Alternative monies, either from direct federal investment or from foreign credits, were always project-specific. Because federal monies were limited by jurisdiction to capital projects, infrastructure, and defense, this avenue reinforced the bias of investments toward capital intensity, single-industry towns, and production of strategic raw materials. Moreover, these projects—such as the Feni nickel plant in Macedonia, the Obrovac aluminum plant and Knin railroad line in Croatia, and the Smederevo steel plant in Serbia—were eventually transferred to republican "management" after completion, often becoming heavy, long-term burdens on republican budgets.[88] Foreign credits through joint ventures were often given on the condition that the Yugoslav firm import technical personnel from the supplier, and they fed import dependence and foreign debt without necessarily enhancing domestic capacity.[89] Even though such credits increased local employment in places, the republicanization of responsibility for foreign debt after 1977 obliged poorer republics to repay with their own resources in a period of very rapid dinar devaluation and dollar revaluation. The Agrokomerc financial-corruption affair of 1987, in which the Bosnian conglomerate was found to have floated unsecured promissory notes totaling $865 million to at least fifty-seven banks in four republics between 1984 and 1987, illustrates the use of one of the rare domestic alternatives (given the tendency of republics to hoard monies where possible), for it was occasioned by the denial of federal funding for the conglomerate's proposed development projects.[90] Moreover, during periods of liberalization when capital and labor began to move across republican borders, richer republics and towns instituted protectionist policies in the interest of tax revenue to prevent the entry of new producers from other localities or republics (to which, as final owners, they paid their "income" taxes); argued against policies that would allow capital to circulate outside their grasp, such as a market would imply; imposed reg-

[88] Author's interviews. On Smederevo, see Burger, Kester, and den Oudem, *Self-Management and Investment Control.*

[89] The joint venture between Dow Chemical and INA Zagreb to build a petrochemical plant on the Croatian island of Krk imported everything it needed, did not use or intend to use local labor, and had the effect of displacing many local occupations (such as tourism, fishing, and agriculture) while bringing in a stratum of more educated outsiders that created local tensions (Cichock, "Reevaluating a Development Strategy").

[90] At the same time, the General Accounting Service reported that there was $8.5 billion in unsecured enterprise credits in the country (Remington, "Yugoslavia").

ulations on immigrants (whether from other republics or surrounding rural areas); revived discussion about local posting during army service so as to keep desired skills at home; and in the main acted in ways that furthered the segmentation of capital and labor markets in territorial enclaves.[91]

Slovenia began the postwar period with shortages of skilled labor. It was able to achieve full employment rapidly and sustain it for forty years (unemployment never exceeded 1.5 percent until 1985). Its planners assessed progress in terms of international standards of productivity and growth, and they succeeded in persuading central policymakers to adopt these criteria.[92] They argued, for example, that technological modernization should receive priority because by 1958 the country had reached the middle levels of development and the domestic raw-material base was being exhausted; and that declining rates of relative productivity growth in the 1970s—felt with particular intensity in Slovenia because it was losing skilled professionals across its northern border and having to fill shortages of production labor with temporary migrant Bosnian and ethnic Albanian (Kosovar) workers in the late 1970s and early 1980s—created a desperate need for renewed technological advantage in the 1980s.[93] Slovene planners worried about a serious labor shortage in the 1980s. The republic's unions and firms tended to lead the country in labor strikes, protesting wage controls and restrictive policies; they were the first to break ranks over federal wage controls, arguing that because they had shortages of labor, they should not be prevented from raising wages to keep and attract labor. As a result, they set the reservation wage for the country.[94] The first instance of a parliamentary vote of no confidence in the country, in December 1966, forced the resignation of prime minister Janko Smole when the Slovene assembly failed to pass the government's bill to reduce the level of social-insurance contributions by enterprises and increase workers' share. In 1982, under similar reform-oriented and

[91] As owners of capital and primary "venture capitalists" in the country, the republican governments sought federal regulation in ways similar to those used by private firms in Stigler's analysis of regulation in market economies; those with greater resources won rights to exclude competitors, while those with fewer resources settled for grants of money ("The Theory of Economic Regulation").

[92] The following information was obtained through the author's interviews in October 1982 with Živko Pregl (then director of the Slovene planning bureau); Emil Pintar (author of the bureau's report on the Slovene Development Plan to the Year 2000); and other Slovene research economists and sociologists, including Jože Mencinger, Stane Saksida, and Pavle Sicherl.

[93] They estimated that the migration of skilled Slovenes abroad in the 1970s was equivalent to the loss of thirty thousand units of schooling, while they considered the budgetary costs of encouraging migrants from other republics too great by 1980 (interviews cited in n. 92 above; *Informativni Bilten*).

[94] C. Martin, "Public Policy and Income Distribution in Yugoslavia."

restrictive policies, Slovene accountants made a successful public protest against the government's attempt to reduce the minimum wage by changing the measure of subsistence (the price of a basket of consumables) on which it was based. Slovenians were also the most insistent voices for local postings during military service; in the early 1980s, they went to the extreme by demanding "national armies" in which there would be no service outside one's republic. Capital investment in Slovenia as well as Croatia in the 1980s focused on a transportation network connected with international routes—the "Brotherhood and Unity" trunk highway connecting Europe with the Middle East through Yugoslavia, the Zagreb-Maribor links, the Adriatic coast highway (*magistrala*), and the highway to Dalmatia through Bosnia.

Croatian planners, on the other hand, faced far greater internal variation among subregions and communes than existed in Slovenia because the process of development had been one of "polarization and concentration of economic activities."[95] Development plans consistently favored the valley of the Sava, the Zagreb-Rijeka link, and the Adriatic coast, whereas 80 percent of the employed in the less-developed interior areas of the republic worked in traditional branches (lumber, textiles, food, and industrial construction materials). Firms in these branches, although labor-intensive and more efficient in the use of materials than firms in the more-developed areas, had low levels of net profit and therefore insufficient resources for new investment and local development. Zagreb-centered industrialists had succeeded in blocking policy change,[96] while politicians focused on the loss of Croat workers to foreign markets and on declining Croat birthrates in comparison with the higher rates among national minorities and potential migrants from the south.

In Serbia, planners and politicians focused far more on intra-Yugoslav comparisons and, after losing the fight over development strategy in 1958–64, on the capital and infrastructural projects necessary to the republic's industrialization and consistent with its geographic position (in the center of the Balkan peninsula and dependent on river and rail transport, for example). Studies in 1979 for the republic's long-term plan discovered that for Serbia proper, despite the massive capital investment after 1964 to reduce disparities, the "degree of development of its production capacities is at the level of the three underdeveloped republics and [its] social product per capita is 5 percent below the average for the coun-

[95] Baletić and Marendić, "Politika razvoja privredno nedovoljno razvijenih područja S. R. Hrvatske," 357.

[96] On the study of Croatian regional economic development in 1976–80 that was made for the long-term plan to the year 2000, see *Ekonomski Pregled* 32, nos. 7–8 (1981), especially the articles by Marendić, Turčić, and Mates, "Mjerenje i analiza razvijenosti općine"; and Baletić and Marendić, "Politika razvoja."

try." Its tax obligations, however, ranked with those of the developed republics, with which it was still officially classified.[97] Evidence that it was "lagging behind" the rest of the country continued to appear in 1981–84. And, amid serious levels of unemployment, planners foresaw a new rural exodus because farmers still made up 28 percent of the population in 1981—a proportion they expected to continue falling until it reached the Slovene level of 10 percent.[98]

The developmental profiles of the republics in the 1980s and the level and character of their unemployment, despite fundamental economic and social change, reflected the decisions of the late 1950s—to participate fully in global markets, to favor the Slovene model of developed economies, and to end economywide development planning except as a by-product of foreign economic and defense policy. The farther an area was from northern markets, developed transportation networks, and the benefits of early industrialization (light manufacturing, industrial habits, and literacy), and the larger the proportion of its population employed in agriculture, in "nonproductive" occupations (such as the army, security forces, and civil service), in low-wage and "nonaccumulative" industries, and, most important, in the private sector, the greater its unemployment. Although there was much variation across towns within a republic, official unemployment figures surpassed 20 percent in Kosovo, Macedonia, Serbia proper, and Bosnia-Herzegovina by the mid-1970s, and they continued to rise. But by the 1980s, the registered job seekers were increasingly urban—often men assumed to be heads of household with skills appropriate to public-sector industry, or educated youth from urban homes. The rural basis of unemployment and the official remedy had been substantially replaced by rapid urbanization and by long-term industrial recession—except in Kosovo. There people were indeed returning to the land. With the pooled resources sent home by youth working temporarily in the northern republics (primarily in private shops) or abroad, extended families in the Albanian community were buying up land.

SURPLUS LABOR

The principles guiding the Yugoslav leaders' approach to labor set in 1948–50 retained their force throughout the period of socialist rule. Cen-

---

[97] Milovan Marković, speech before the Chamber of Republics and Provinces of the federal assembly, February 28, 1985 (printed in *Foreign Broadcast Information Service*, March 1, 1985, I 4).

[98] These data did not take into account the immigration of Serbs and Montenegrins from Kosovo at the time. The numbers of these immigrants were far less significant than their potency as emotional and political symbols for segments of the Serbian population and the leadership in Belgrade.

tral policy would establish guidelines and standards for employment. Republics could not be considered economically sovereign without final authority over where and how their population was employed. But those responsible for the issue of employment had to be attuned to the vast variety of local conditions and had to recognize the point at which political grievances about unemployment would first appear and when they could best be addressed so that they did not accumulate and threaten the system. Whether it was a matter of state-directed mobilization in 1948–49 or of stabilizing employment through workers' participation in local assemblies and workers' councils after 1949, local authorities (in the government, the economy, and the party) were most suited to this highly sensitive political task. When local firms did have to fire people "in the interests of rationalization" or when "material conditions" did not permit a sufficient pace in the transfer of labor from agriculture to industry and from private to socialized sector (at the time of these justifications by Kidrič and Kardelj, in 1949–52, local authorities had the opposite problem in most of the country, except Macedonia), then the resulting unemployment was seen not as an economic problem but a social one. And welfare, too, was the responsibility of local communities.

Consonant with the leaders' decentralized, enterprise-based approach to macroeconomic stabilization, the commitment to what is called in capitalist countries an "active labor-market policy" was also to be fulfilled at the local level. In line with the distinction between industrial and agrarian unemployment, there was a division of labor among local agents. To minimize industrial unemployment (that is, dismissal of persons already employed), workplaces were legally obliged to find new positions for workers made redundant by rationalization or technological change. To minimize agrarian unemployment, local authorities were responsible for economic development within their territory that was attuned to employment conditions and the pace of deagrarianization and socialization.

Within firms, for example, investment plans for modernizing production included funds for improving workers' skills or reassigning them, and the union branch lobbied firms to contribute to local retraining programs. When layoffs of more than five persons were economically necessary, management was obliged to consult the union branch within the firm on who should go and how to find them new assignments. The trade-union journal *Rad* (Labor) is filled with such cases: for example, when workers from a small craft enterprise that closed in Toplica, Serbia, were transferred to a local construction firm in 1963, or when the integration of two firms into the pharmaceutical giant Galenika the same year created a surplus of 160 workers in the Belgrade area. The union's self-congratulatory retelling of the latter transfer process illustrates well the principles at work (see the appendix to this chapter). Youth in traineeships and women were let go first (with the exception of pregnant women, whose employment was protected by law) on the grounds that their families could support them.

Despite the social norm valuing consultation where possible prior to firing and reassignment, there were legally acceptable conditions for involuntary dismissal.[99] Employees could be fired if a work unit was eliminated, if there was no equivalent job in the organization for a person whose position was being eliminated, if the firm's business volume declined for an extended period, if an expert commission ruled that a person's abilities did not meet the needs of the job, or if a person slated for reassignment refused to undergo retraining. All were instances that upheld the formal principles of parity (between a person's qualifications and job classification) and labor productivity.

Local employment bureaus thus spent most of their time and monies on retraining programs. Their staffs negotiated employment contracts for retrained workers with local firms. In areas of high unemployment, they also pressured firms to hire university-educated youth and the apprentices from vocational schools whom firms had agreed to train but then did not employ. Local governments would, understandably, take a wide range of measures to prevent the bankruptcy of a large local employer because they were responsible for solving the resulting problems of unemployment. More burdensome in normal times than local dismissals, however, was the responsibility for absorbing people released from federal jobs or administration by the policies of decentralization and socialization. The return to localities of demobilized, purged, or "retired" veterans or army officers—in 1955, after 1965, and again in the 1970s during the socialization and localization of defense—and the return of middle-level civil servants and administrative staff from farm cooperatives presented local pension boards, housing funds, and employers with a difficult task. These surplus government employees were frequently encouraged to enter elections—in 1955, when the newly created school boards opened local posts, and in 1967 and 1969, when there were multicandidate elections for parliament. But the delegate system, which "socialized" political representation (elections were based in enterprises, which then

---

[99] However, these conditions on dismissal did not represent the real restraints on managers, who had far more flexibility. In interviews with the author, enterprise directors consistently denied the commonly held view that "with the exception of cases of criminal or severe personal misconduct affecting the whole working community, workers cannot be laid off" (Schrenk, Ardalan, and El Tatawy, *Yugoslavia*, citing Article 19 of the 1976 Law on Associated Labor). It was necessary to follow legal procedures preventing arbitrary dismissal, they admitted, but it simply was not the case that workers and employees could not be fired. Articles insisting that there was no "right to employment" or even to a particular job appeared frequently in the specialized literature on employment and in the social sciences as well.

paid delegates' salaries), erased this opportunity after 1969. The poorer the area, the more likely it was that many people had left for jobs in the civil service or army and that it would bear a disproportionate burden in their reintegration. Behind the frequently heard complaints about the ethnic disproportions in governmental bureaucracies lay a hard reality: as a result of the concentration of wartime combat in poorer regions, the decentralization of the security apparatus placed a higher burden, per capita, on local employment in poor towns or regions in the interior, which were more often ethnically mixed. In conditions of declining growth and rising unemployment generally, choices in the rationing of ever-fewer jobs in relation to the number of job seekers could (in fact or in perception) be made according to ethnic criteria.[100] Even in the fall of 1948, when localities were handed many "'federal and republican tasks" to "readjust the disproportion between capital construction and living standards," party leader Vladimir Bakarić worried about the disproportion in the location of local industries—worst, he said, in Croatia, where 56.8 percent of "local businesses" were in Zagreb and there were "none at all" in thirty-five districts or towns.[101]

Živan Tanić's analysis of the 1973 federal legislation to "stimulate the return of workers from abroad and their employment in Yugoslavia through programs of intensified economic development" applies more generally. The program ran into problems, he writes, because the employment bureaus were not up to the task of retraining returnees, poor communes lacked the resources for development programs, and information to migrants was insufficient. In many places, the local authorities simply had not implemented the policy—not for lack of agreement among political elites but for lack of economic resources.[102]

The most difficult employment-related problem for local governments was actually the problem of housing. Factories that chose to expand production when they expanded their markets tended to open new plants in neighboring communes so that they did not have to build more housing at the existing plant.[103] Time spent in commuting long distances to work continued to be a problem for productivity long after 1949–50.[104] The

[100] This was not a topic on which systematic research could be done, however, because of its political sensitivity. Such bias was largely inferred from highly aggregated data on ethnic disproportions in particular occupations, or was simply an untested perception.

[101] Bakarić, "Vezana trgovina poljoprivrednih i industrijskih proizvoda," 106.

[102] Tanić, "Yugoslavia."

[103] Such stories from Serbia and Bosnia are told in *Yugoslav Trade Unions*, April–June 1964, 71.

[104] There is a large literature on the extent and costs of "daily migration" (*dnevne migracije*) and the phenomenon called "peasant-workers" (*seljaci-radnici*). Hawrylyshyn calls them a "landed proletariat"; for a summary, see his "Yugoslav Development and Rural-Urban Migration," 341–42.

veterans' organization (SUBNOR) became infamous for its political pressure on localities to build housing for retired Partisans. The shortage of housing was a particularly serious obstacle to labor migration, discouraging both individuals' search for jobs elsewhere and expenditures by employment services on travel costs to facilitate that search (despite the rights of the unemployed to such assistance).

The result was that enterprises were vulnerable to pressure from their employees to hire family members or local friends. The more difficult the economic times, moreover, the greater the pressure. Legally required to pay local tax obligations first, before wages and contractual obligations, firms were often faced with rising taxes at the same time that they were under this pressure to employ, because local welfare and investment needs were rising. When the employment services became "self-managing communities of interest" after 1967, and thus (along with other public services) financially autonomous of local budgets, this meant additional taxes for enterprises. "Insurance in case of unemployment" was then paid by firms out of the personal income of each employed worker, but at rates that varied among republics because of differences in levels of unemployment. In 1982, the rate was lowest in Slovenia and highest in Kosovo (1.5 percent).[105]

To keep local industries and the communal tax base alive, the commune's office of the social accounting service also required firms to pay the claims of other local firms before those of distant suppliers. Local monopolies on trade, agricultural purchasing, and exporting firms often arose for the same purpose—to prevent firms from outside the territory from capturing "local resources." To compensate for higher tax rates or to forestall a firm's decision to move, a variety of concessions to local public-sector firms were often necessary, as well as lax enforcement of accounts and price regulations. The search for credits as an alternative to internally generated revenues encountered the same vicious circle that produced growing inequalities among republics: the lower the value of a firm's fixed assets, the lower the chance of obtaining bank credit and the more circumscribed the selective investment funds to which firms or governments could apply for building up local fixed assets. Investment choices were thus even more likely to be driven by the source of credit (and especially by the official priority on investments that sought to develop exports for foreign exchange) rather than by market criteria. When using local resources for explicit employment promotion, local governments tended to choose investments according to the characteristics of the people in need of jobs (for example, building textile plants to employ women) instead of according to the likely profitability of the products or services.

[105] Author's interview with Tripo Mulina, Institute of Economics, Belgrade, November 3, 1982.

The conflict between central policy and local resources over employment promotion was most striking in the central role played in both by the private sector. In all federal proposals after the mid-1960s, and for most leading economists, the only available (and, many thought, the best) solution to growing unemployment was to develop the *mala privreda*—the sector of small-scale, "independent" firms in services and manufacturing. Most local governments, however, usually resolved increasing pressure on local revenues by raising license fees and taxation on private-sector businesses.[106] This was not for ideological reasons of antipathy to private activity, as was often asserted, but for lack of sufficient resources to perform the tasks assigned. To reduce tensions with public-sector firms, local authorities sought monies where they were available, from household savings and private firms that were less able to exit. At the local level, therefore, there was a growing conflict between policies to minimize industrial unemployment and those designed to employ the rural surplus and demographic increase.

The sector of independent smallholdings and trades remained essential to full employment in the leaders' strategy. "Private agriculture collects workers from [industry, social-sector agriculture, and other social-sector activities] when they are redundant and releases them . . . when they are needed," according to Gapinski, Škegro, and Zuehlke.[107] But the most common response to unemployment was migration. Within Yugoslavia, day-labor exchanges in large cities served newcomers and unskilled laborers, and construction projects attracted migrating unskilled workers from all parts of the country. Youth left rural towns for higher education and employment in cities, primarily in the republic of their nationality because republics defined school curricula and family networks provided housing. Skilled workers and professionals sought the higher incomes (and especially the benefits) available in Slovenia, where labor shortages prevailed during most of the socialist period.[108] But the most important outlet for domestic unemployment was foreign migration. In 1948–53, roughly 100,000 persons left the country, followed in the next four years by another 195,000 (equivalent to 10 percent of social-sector employment

[106] An economic explanation of local authorities' attitude toward private entrepreneurs seems sufficient, but the tendency to explain it as ideologically based antagonism nonetheless prevailed. Sacks focuses on the limits to entry in the Yugoslav economy, which are partly explained by the level of fees and taxes; these fees and taxes usually absorbed the first year's profits for small firms (Sacks, *Entry of New Competitors in Yugoslav Market Socialism*).

[107] Gapinski, Škegro, and Zuehlke, *Modeling*, 133.

[108] By the late 1970s, one-quarter of the labor force in Slovenia was from elsewhere. The figure was lower than it would have been had the Slovene government not regulated the flow carefully to minimize "social costs" (it feared social intolerance if non-Slovenes exceeded an acceptable level, and it would have to expend additional resources on infrastructure that could otherwise be directed to improving Slovene living standards).

in 1957).[109] After 1960, both permanent and temporary migration to Western Europe and the United States compensated for the decade of labor-cutting economic reform.[110] After 1974, when Yugoslav unemployment was no longer frictional or cyclical but structural, Western recession pushed the emigrants back home.

CONCLUSION

The last Yugoslav policy toward labor appeared in the supplementary documents of the long-term stabilization program adopted in 1983. It reflected what Claus Offe labeled the "realist position" emerging in the 1980s on the European ideological left as well as in the center. Although he was discussing Germany, his description of the policy goal also applied to Yugoslavia: "State policy should cease aspiring to the impossible, such as political guarantees of (the restoration of) full employment." Arguing not only that Keynesian instruments had "become blunt" but also that "there are no *alternative* ways of achieving this goal," the realists, according to Offe, abandon the orthodox goal of integrating the unemployed into the "stable army of employed" and think "more in terms of *excluding* labour from the market." First immigrants, then women, older workers, and young people should be encouraged to drop out of the labor force by policy measures such as a "flexible reduction" of paid working time, more "freedom of action" in self-help, "redundancy payments" through family policy and the "symbolic currency of 'social recognition'," and a redefinition of work so as to maintain families.[111]

In Yugoslavia, this policy was in effect an open admission—the first since the employment bureaus were reestablished in 1952—that the socialist commitment to full employment could no longer be met. Yet there was nothing new for Yugoslavia about the solutions proposed by this "realist" position in Western Europe. This had been the Yugoslav policy to protect individuals' subsistence in periods of unemployment since 1952, and it had shaped the structure of Yugoslav society, its moral economy regarding subsistence and the right to work, and political attitudes about unemployment and the unemployed. As the next chapter discusses, the social, cultural, and political consequences of the policy toward unem-

---

[109] Such data were not collected for 1948–53, but indirect calculations from the census yield very rough estimates. The largest contingent after 1955 were ethnic Turks, while the earlier exodus also appears to have been national in motivation. Germans, Italians, Turks, and Jews left, largely as a result of World War II (Macura, *Stanovništvo kao činilac privrednog razvoja Jugoslavije*, 69).

[110] Gapinski, Škegro, and Zuehlke, *Modeling*, 135.

[111] Offe, "Three Perspectives on the Problem of Unemployment," 90–91. He goes on to demonstrate the lack of relation between these proposals and the characteristics of unemployment, and thus that this approach is no solution (92–95).

ployment in turn became obstacles to political action that might have demanded or proposed alternative solutions. The realism became self-fulfilling, in that unemployment remained hidden. That did not, however, prevent its effects from having major political consequence, as will be discussed in the final chapter.

APPENDIX
"GALENIKA TACKLES THE PROBLEM OF REDUNDANT WORKERS"

At the beginning of this year, the planned task having been completed, the workers' council ordered the services in the management to make a new systematization of jobs (a scheme indicating precisely the jobs needed in the factory, the number of workers and employees, and the qualifications they must have) and services needed in the new enterprise. After a month, having completed the systematization, the services concluded that the factory would have a surplus of 160 workers and employees.

The workers' council informed the factory trade union committee, the People's Youth committee and other organizations about this, and asked them to give their views on the proposed systematization, i.e., the reorganization of the enterprise. After close discussions at their sessions, the leaderships of these organizations accepted the changes suggested. But they again pointed out the seriousness of the problem, and asked that it should be systematically and carefully tackled. In the view of the political activists of the factory, including the factory trade union committee, the workers' council should pay attention to certain principles when transferring workers to other economic organizations or institutions, and stick to them when deciding which man should go to another collective.

The first of these principles was to avoid transferring workers who had been working in these factories for many years. The second principle was to transfer inferior workers, i.e., those who had been negligent in their duty. Suggestions were also made that when transferring people attention should be paid to whether he or she was the only earner in the family, and if so, to transfer primarily those whose husband or wife worked. Among the workers there were some who had retired and had pensions but, benefiting by the legal regulations, they continued to work. The standpoint of the political activists was that such workers should be the first to be transferred, and that those with the right to a pension should retire in any case.

Of course there were other suggestions too, one of the most significant among them being that the transfer of workers must be discussed by their comrades in their economic units.

The workers' council adopted these suggestions and worked out a list of workers that were supposed to go to other enterprises. The list was submitted to the factory trade union committee with a request for remarks, if any. In order to have a clearer picture of every worker proposed for transfer, the trade union immediately organized the distribution of a questionnaire to all these workers and employees. Thus these trade union

Reprinted from *Yugoslav Trade Unions*, no. 10, (September 1963): 42–44.

members had to say what their vocational qualifications were, what kind of job they had done and for how long, whether they were married, whether the wife (or husband) worked, how many children they had, what the family income was, whether they had received awards in the factory, or had been punished for lack of discipline, and if so why, and whether they had been elected to the workers' council.

Having received these data, the trade union organized meetings of workers in the economic units, at which they gave their opinion of this or that worker who was proposed for transfer.

According to the original plan of the management, P.B., a worker in the sales unit, was to be transferred. Meanwhile, the economic unit held a different view, saying that he was a very good worker and that there were inferior workers in this service, and it proposed such a worker to the workers' council for transfer. This view was supported by the political activists of the factory, and of course it was adopted by the commission of the workers' council in charge of transfers.

In another economic unit R.K., an office employee, was also on the list for transfer. But at the meeting of the economic unit it was said that she was pregnant and therefore protected by the law. The change was made.

O.M. was also to leave the factory. Her economic unit said that she really did not work satisfactorily, but added that she had been a good worker at her previous job, and that she might be sent back there. However, it was stated that her previous post was already filled, and so she was entered on the list for transfer.

The worker D.S. was also on the list for transfer, but his economic unit stressed that he was very conscientious and industrious and that he should remain in the factory. This view was adopted by the commission.

It should be added that in normal conditions the opinion of the economic unit on dismissal or transfer, as well as on admission of workers, is valid and final. As the situation was exceptional in these cases, the economic units could only make suggestions, while the final decision was taken by the workers' council through its commission. Nevertheless, the views and suggestions of the economic units considerably influenced the final decision of the commission. According to the original plan, 160 workers were redundant. After discussion in the economic units this number was reduced to 148, because work was found in the factory itself for some workers and employees who had been proposed for transfer.

Although the action for transfer had been extensively examined and carried out, fifty-four workers and employees who had to leave the factory appealed to the management board of the factory. To decide on these grievances as fairly as possible, the management board submitted them all to the trade union, with a request for its opinion. The trade union convened new meetings in the economic units, and the workers reconsidered each case. The trade union then submitted the workers' views to the management board, which had been authorized by the workers' council to make the final decision. After a detailed study of the complaints, the management board allowed thirteen, so that finally the number of those who had to go to other collectives was 135.

But this completed only one part of the business. The other part was to find work in other collectives for the workers who had to leave the factory owing to redundancy. The workers' council therefore ordered the expert services of the enterprise to contact immediately the neighboring factories and institutions to find jobs for these workers and employees. Two months later this task was completed successfully. Here are a few examples [of] how it was carried out.

After the reorganization of the new enterprise, the factory was left with some empty business premises. The Prokupac enterprise for the sale of spirits was interested in these premises—it wanted to use them for the bottling of wine. Evidently Prokupac was expanding its business. The Galenika expert services learnt of this and agreed to hand over these premises to Prokupac on condition that it should employ a number of Galenika's workers. Prokupac agreed and took over twenty workers.

The institute for the training of workers in Zemun was another partner with whom an agreement was reached on the employment of redundant workers. A sideline of this institute was packing, and it did this for Galenika. Since Galenika increased its production after the integration, it needed greater quantities of packing material, and this meant in practice greater production in the institute, i.e., employment of a greater number of workers. Thus an arrangement was made with the institute for the employment of a group of redundant workers from Galenika.

Similar arrangements were made with the Metalac enterprise and some other collectives, so that all 135 workers and employees got new jobs with the help of their factory. After three months of intensive work on the problem of redundant manpower, the question was finally solved.

Meanwhile the workers' council was interested in what the workers in the factory thought of its action. At its request, the factory psychologist made a form of inquiry in the collective: he talked with sixty workers and asked them three questions: why a number of workers had to leave the factory; what they thought of the transfer procedure; and what, in their view, was the role of the trade union in this action.

The answer to the first question was that the transfer of workers had been demanded by integration, i.e., the economic interests of the enterprise. The answer to the second was that the procedure was democratic, that everybody in the factory could say what he or she thought of the redundant workers. However, some were of the opinion that the weaknesses of the individuals who were proposed for transfer should not have been spoken of in public, but communicated to them personally. As for the trade union role, the reply was that it was a good thing that the trade union had been constantly consulted in this whole matter; that it played its part successfully; and that its authority in the factory had risen since then.

Chapter 9

DIVISIONS OF LABOR

THE ASSOCIATION of socialist governments with full employment begins in the nineteenth century, when workers vulnerable to unemployment saw that it was in their economic interest to demand governmental redress and eventually employment promotion. By the second half of the twentieth century, governments of all political persuasions were watching the unemployment figures because of the potential for political consequences: strikes, civil unrest, or at least protest votes. In an analogy to the economists' concept of a natural rate of unemployment, according to which a market economy must expect between 4 and 7 percent of the labor force to be "frictionally" unemployed at any time, there is an unspoken assumption that there is also a natural level of social tolerance for unemployment, above which such tolerance evaporates rapidly. Although Communist parties ruling socialist states were not vulnerable to electoral defeat, this did not prevent them from being concerned as well about possible discontent and maintaining their authority as working-class parties. The party's power and the regime's political stability, it was generally argued, rested ultimately on the political legitimacy that came from full employment: on the basis of a tacit *social contract* between government and wage or salary earners, citizens remained politically passive in exchange for job security. If socialist parties originated in the struggle against unemployment in capitalist societies, surely unemployment in socialist societies would lead to political opposition and demands for a change in policy.

The failure of socialist government in Yugoslavia to prevent unemployment from rising above frictional rates or to alter policies that led to not only cyclical but even structural unemployment by the mid-1960s can be explained by the leaders' continuing belief in their strategy (reinforced by foreign creditors), the vested interest of influential producers and republican governments in their particular international niche, and the vicious circles of policy and politics described at the end of chapter 7. But these cannot explain the virtual silence about unemployment[1] and the absence

---

[1] Writing in 1982, two years after Yugoslavia had achieved the highest level of unemployment in Europe, Tijanić and Andjelić reported, "There are economists who think we were late by a quarter of a century in putting employment into midterm [economic] plans, but it was still pushed to the bottom of the list of goals and tasks" ("Obično nezaposleni mladi").

of political protest by the unemployed or by persons vulnerable to unemployment who recognized their interest in common cause. Why did groups that were systematic losers economically in Yugoslav society—such as women, youth, unskilled urban labor, the rural reserve, poorer communities, and the less-developed regions and republics—not choose to improve their economic position through, following the model of labor parties, political organization and mutual alliances to press for change in central policies?

This paradox arises from the final element of the leaders' approach to labor. Although their strategy failed to prevent unemployment, it succeeded in its goal of eliminating *capitalist* unemployment. There were certainly obstacles to political organization in the constitutional privileges of the Communist party and the limits on independent political associations, but far more significant in explaining the absence of a politics of unemployment were the characteristics of socialist unemployment and the acceptance in Yugoslav society of the official attitude toward it.

By aiming to avoid mass layoffs and to prevent proletarianization with a public guarantee of subsistence, the regime transformed the public's view of unemployment. In place of the oppositional logic of private property and class solidarity of labor against capital, moreover, the system of employment, reward, and reassignment created a logic of individual competition and status achieved according to regulated criteria for membership and exclusion. Conflict occurred over those criteria and over competition to improve individual "capital" as a means to employment—whether through schooling, personal or political contacts and loyalties, or migration.

The division of society into public and private sectors, to protect the strategy's commitment to a lean public sector and rising labor productivity, also eliminated the reciprocal relation between economic and political power that is found in market economies with private ownership and that formed the basis of a common interest between the employed and the unemployed. The dual face of capitalist unemployment discussed in chapter 1, which limited workers' power but also provided the political incentives to organize societywide against unemployment, was thereby eliminated as well. Because labor markets were primarily local or republican, the countrywide level of unemployment had little influence on labor's strength in bargaining with managers or governments over jobs and wages, and the level of unemployment had little influence on the political strength of a party whose power depended not on electoral support but on international leverage (and, in local and republican committees, on control over economic resources). The reason labor governments pursue full employment in market economies—that it serves both the economic interest of their constituents and the political interest of their political organizations—did not hold.

The socialist communities of Kardelj's vision, ironically, did not create societywide solidarity but instead segmented society into separate universes of decision making on employment and income—by the division of property rights between the two sectors, the separate labor and capital markets of the republics, and the long-term employment contracts and autonomous bargaining over wages and benefits within self-managed workplaces. Extensive decentralization and the absence of a formal market for labor (so as to maintain direct incentives to productivity) were substantial barriers to the perception of a common interest in reducing unemployment and to the construction of societywide social alliances necessary for effective pressure. As some intellectuals complained in the 1960s, this was a society composed of many distinct "reservations."[2]

In sum, social identities, moral economy, and political organization were shaped by the leaders' strategy toward labor—and in turn sustained that strategy.

SOCIAL INVISIBILITY OF UNEMPLOYMENT

The official concept of unemployment in socialist Yugoslavia was to be without means of subsistence; as Bakarić said in 1982, the unemployed were "people with nowhere to go."[3] Hence the political importance of the mechanisms that aimed to prevent this: the guaranteed minimum wage for people in public-sector jobs and protected smallholdings in private-sector agriculture and services. Popular opinion reflected this official conception. The most common response of both citizens and specialists when confronted with the facts of unemployment was that it was "not the English kind." In this view, unemployment did not mean the penury or proletarianization of classic industrialization; anyone who wished could always return to the land and survive.

This attitude was reinforced by the official solution to unemployment: to move truly surplus labor from agriculture into industry and, when economic rationalization created surplus labor in industry, to fire those who had sources of subsistence such as land or a family—thus making dismissal decisions a family affair involving the farm household or workers' organizations within the socialist-sector work community. Although the goal of these transfers was to incorporate an ever-larger proportion of the population into the *income relations* of industrial organization and principles of socialist accumulation (direct incentives to increase individual and collective productivity), the effect was to build society around social rela-

---

[2] See M. Mirić, *Rezervati.*

[3] Bakarić, who was speaking with a delegation from Titograd University (Montenegro), is quoted in Tijanić and Andjelić, "Obično nezaposleni mladi." Tijanić and Andjelić add that Bakarić must have been "thinking they're a minority."

tions and concepts of welfare more closely resembling those of the prein-
dustrial household. Kardelj's model of socialist communities harks back to
an earlier age of agrarian moral economy, particularly in the ideal type
associated with the theories of A. V. Chayanov, author of the classic study
of Russian smallholding and peasant economy, or with the populist glori-
fication of the *zadruga* in the Balkans.[4] The socialist community was likewise centered on production, guaranteed subsistence to its members,
and—only after the basic survival of individuals and the collectivity was
assured, and on the basis of democratic consultation among adults—
distributed net earnings to members according to their seniority, managerial authority, and contributions to output. In socialist Yugoslavia, the
public-sector enterprise (divided into basic organizations of associated labor), the farm household, the urban family, and the migrant keeping close
ties to family at home all practiced collective solidarity to provide subsistence.[5] Only "when a work collective cannot guarantee the constitutional
right to work"[6] from its reserve fund and the commune's standing solidarity fund would the larger social community enter to provide temporary
relief for people made unemployed as a result of industrial restructuring.
Unemployment was a social, not an economic, problem of redistribution
after a production cycle. It was as if the populist elements of the 1940
alliance and the private, small-property sector defined the model for social relations in the urban socialized sector, rather than the other way
around.[7]

According to this concept of unemployment, people differed not in
their vulnerability to unemployment (except for the few months' waiting
time that was considered normal for a first job or for reassignment), but in
their disposable incomes. The problem of joblessness was supplanted by
that of living standards, so that unemployment itself did not arouse much
sympathy. Although families differed substantially in the vulnerability of
their members to unemployment, its consequences were seen only as
part of the more general personal struggle to improve living standards and
as part of the continuum of income inequality, which depended on many
factors. The discrimination against women and youth in hiring and firing

[4] On this moral economy, see J. Scott, *The Moral Economy of the Peasant;* on the role of
Chayanov's views in Soviet debates, see Cox, *Peasants, Class, and Capitalism;* and on the
zadruga, see Byrnes, *Communal Families in the Balkans.*

[5] The mixed farmer-worker households of Slovenia, where an extensive network of good
roads and diversified local industries and services made it possible for households to engage
in a variety of economic activities while remaining settled, may have been the unconscious
model instead.

[6] The Law on Labor Relations of 1967, cited in *Yugoslav Survey* 8, no. 3 (August 1967):
21.

[7] In this and many other situations, Yugoslavs familiar with the programs of the Croat
Peasant party in the interwar period have seen many parallels.

was accepted because the "family" (the cash earnings of the employed member) would take care of them, redistributing what it had to ensure the survival of all members. Unemployed urban youth remained in parental homes while they waited for public-sector jobs. Urban and rural families relied on networks of kin and ritual kin for private exchange of agricultural produce and connections with urban schooling and jobs. Migrant workers—whether Croat engineers in Germany, Bosnian factory workers in Slovenia, Serb villagers in Austrian and German construction, or Albanian confectioners in the northern Yugoslav republics—sent money home to sustain their families and contribute to their means of domestic subsistence: the house, farmland, and bank account for durable goods. The underlying solidarity on subsistence and income—not on employment and its associated rights in the socialized sector—even led to unions' willingness to fire persons who could earn second incomes in the private sector, as well as to a widespread but largely incorrect view that much higher incomes could be earned in the private sector.

The consequence of this approach was to make the truly unemployed invisible. The relative absence of sociological and psychological studies on the unemployed helped to nurture the prevailing view. Popular opinion mirrored the nineteenth-century idea in the official presentation of unemployment data—that unemployment was voluntary or short-lived, a choice for leisure instead of work made according to household standards of consumption. Open unemployment was equated with foreign migration—citizens' choosing to work temporarily abroad for the higher incomes they could earn in the more industrialized north of Europe.[8] Official job seekers at home were dismissed as persons who registered with employment bureaus in order to get health insurance and still be at leisure—a view that was a poorly disguised prejudice against "women who don't really want to work" and who bloated the unemployment figures. The more prevalent image was of the "unemployment of the employed"[9] in public-sector offices, an image based on the milling throngs on urban streets during working hours—people who ought to be at their desk but were enjoying a coffee or a stroll instead. The physiocrats' "leeches" were alive and well in popular culture.

In the search for higher income, unskilled and semiskilled blue-collar

---

[8] While some economists in the 1970s and 1980s began to include this foreign migration in measures of "true" unemployment at home (see Primorac and Babić, "Systemic Changes and Unemployment Growth"; and Mencinger, "Utjecaj privredne aktivnosti na zaposlenost"), official views pointed to the large number of migrants abroad who had been employed as professionals and skilled workers before they left. The fact of joblessness (the problem of "filling empty bellies") was, in these views, separated from the motivation to migrate outside the country for higher incomes or to solve the migrant's "housing problem" at home (which, according to opinion surveys, was a more frequent reason for migration). See "Some Basic Features of Yugoslav External Migration."

[9] Mencinger, "Privredna reforma i nezaposlenost."

workers did resort to work stoppages and strikes. But skilled production workers, who had whatever market leverage there might have been over wages because they were more often in shortage and were politically represented, were more inclined to improve their prospects in the unofficial economy, where opportunities for moonlighters (electricians, repair workers, and those in the building trades) could be lucrative. The stratum of "fluctuators" so harshly criticized by Boris Kidrič in 1949 stretched from peasant-workers to the core of the industrial class. Skilled industrial workers did the opposite of what Kardelj planned for the kulaks: to end their control over rural markets—without destroying their productive capacity—by gradually incorporating them into the socialist sector and its industrial mentality and thus weakening their foot in the private sector. Instead, skilled workers kept one foot in the secure and benefit-granting public sector and stepped with the other into a second, private job to supplement their income and protect themselves against unemployment. Middle strata in cities and tourist areas, too, entered the world of private profits by renting to subtenants or foreigners, dealing in foreign currency, or taking on work in private-sector tourism, retailing, or agriculture.[10]

The diluted principles of the socialist sector were not replaced, however, by those of the market, for the markets in which these people participated were local, specialized, and unregulated. As with the reversion to a more traditional institution in the concept of the work community, a halfway house between agrarian and socialist society seemed to emerge in which personal connections, early advantages in urban housing and socialist-sector employment, and nonmarket allocation of goods replaced Kidrič's idea of the rational calculation of economic incentives to increased productivity and production for market demand. When villagers sent their children to live with urban cousins for education beyond elementary school and in exchange provided their relatives with food, the urban household's consumption of agricultural produce expanded, diverting that produce from the market; the effectiveness of monetary incentives to both farmers and their urban relatives was diluted; and local balances between labor supply and demand were disrupted by outsiders seeking access to socialist-sector jobs through their relatives. Migrants without family in the cities formed urban clubs of people from their own region or republic, creating a network of mutual assistance for housing and jobs along regional and ethnic lines; or they relied on political avenues—party membership and political activism—to improve their access to housing and a job. Those without rural ties and direct access to food, such as the descendants of the core of the prewar industrial working class, felt more intensely the fall in the value of their incomes.

The principles of selection for deciding whom to fire first in a rational-

---

[10] See I. Bićanić, "The Inequality Impact of the Unofficial Economy in Yugoslavia."

ization also perpetuated the social attitudes and habits that originally shaped those principles. The assumption that women or rural residents would not lack for housing and material support (despite the large number of single or divorced women and the many villagers without land) reinforced traditional attitudes toward women's employment and family roles. Rural households held onto land as insurance, leaving aged women to cultivate it alone and thus reinforcing the low productivity of the land and the prejudices against peasant-workers—that their mentality remained that of small property owners "tied to their land."[11] Women were more likely to accept downward reassignment and retraining and to refuse nomination to elective positions (such as in the workers' council or parliament) so that they would have more time for the additional household duties—above all child care—imposed by the traditional division of household labor and the inadequate development of public services.[12] The result was to diminish further their political influence on spending priorities and employment and to reinforce prejudices about their productivity.

Rules designed to protect workers—such as the obligation of management to inform the union when dismissing five or more workers at once, the assignment of jobs commensurate with skills, and the prohibition against layoff of workers who were on leave for military service or vocational training, were pregnant, or had infants up to age one—became reasons not to employ certain persons in the first place: youth who had not completed their military service, women who might become pregnant, and the disabled, the unskilled, and others of presumed lower productivity (especially recent migrants from the countryside), all of whom filled the unemployment rolls in such high proportions. Enterprise directors insisted that there were no restrictions on dismissing a worker, as long as they followed the rules on prior warning and kept good records; but the long and involved process may have encouraged caution in hiring. Faced with high rates of female unemployment, local authorities and employment bureaus also reinforced occupational divisions of labor by channeling women into jobs for which they were "suited"—textiles, food processing, health care, education, and office work. But these were low-wage sectors more vulnerable to fluctuation in world market price and demand and to labor cuts for rationalization in government and enterprise budgets.[13]

[11] Like so much else in this social portrait, this was a widespread characteristic in socialist Eastern Europe. See H. Scott, "Why the Revolution Doesn't Solve Everything."

[12] Mihovilović et al., *Žena izmedju rada i porodice.*

[13] This strategy was particularly explicit in Macedonia (Tripo Mulina, interview with author, October 1982). In 1978, women made up 78 percent of the labor force in the production of finished textiles and 61 percent in linen and textiles (Woodward, "The Rights of Women," 246).

The concept of employment as a bundle of rights attached to a "social relation of work" (*radni odnos*) in the public sector also created a world of social distinctions and competition within that sector that were based on status. Employment was regulated by statutory rules in the constitution, legislation, and negotiated agreements on eligibility, incomes, and reassignment. It defined a status in society, one's *relative* prestige and share in income and benefits, based on the assumptions about productivity built into these rules. Most important, it defined a status legally separate from that of the unemployed person or person employed in the private sector. Protests against threats to employment took the form, as the official system expected, of individualized appeals—to fellow workers on the injustice of a dismissal or unwanted reassignment, or to law courts, lawyers, and paralegal bodies on its legality.

Despite the political rhetoric praising the worth of production workers, the statutory rules on income distribution and job-related perquisites (including rules formulated in bargained "compacts" among government, business, and labor) actually reinforced earlier values as well. The emphasis on formation of human capital and on parity between job classification and formal skill qualification gave those with higher education a higher social status, wage rate, and priority for benefits such as housing, and it maintained the importance that formal education was accorded in the prewar culture.[14] Those who achieved the appropriate educational qualifications came to expect employment, often viewing their school diplomas as a right to a job of a particular category. Anecdotal evidence is rich with instances of unemployed youth who refused job offers because the position was beneath the status of the occupation for which they had trained. Education was particularly important to parents in the private sector, who saw investment in their children's education as the avenue to public-sector jobs, upward social mobility, and a family's inheritance. At the same time, it was commonplace to explain unemployment in poorer regions as the "overproduction of intellectuals" trained in liberal professions (a phrase also used by the king to justify closing rural *gimnazije* during the depression of the 1920s and 1930s) and to attack as irrational the investment in proliferating universities in provincial and regional towns (such as Priština, Rijeka, and Niš) in the 1970s. But at an individual level, this strategy for upward mobility was rational.

The Slovene model of Kardelj and Kidrič envisioned the state as a body of rule-making experts that needed no authority with independent producers other than that afforded by expertise and professional competence. But the leaders' need to build authority rapidly after 1950 led them to draw heavily on the symbols of status in the culture of the 1940s. The fourth plenum of the central committee in June 1951 devoted most of its

[14] See Trouton, *Peasant Renaissance in Yugoslavia.*

agenda on the design of the new state to the authority of the law courts
and judges ("one of the strongest weapons we had and that a state can
have in its own hands," Kardelj explained). They would gain the public's
respect, Tito and Kardelj insisted, if professional standards were raised
and prewar qualifications revived, and if their social status were improved
with higher salaries, better housing, and a return to the offices in their
prewar buildings, where possible.[15] Liberal campaigns in the 1950s,
1960s, and 1980s that aimed to replace an "older, poorly schooled Partisan
generation" holding down positions of authority on the basis of war service (and by implication, all those in the army and police apparatus) with
the younger generation on the basis of formal skill qualifications also im-
puted greater authority to formal criteria of expertise. Their language of
productivity and modernity reinforced the perception of a privileged status for human capital and education and the lower social worth ascribed to
the realm of the "political." This began early, as can be seen in the skepti-
cal reception given Ranković's proposal at the second party plenum in
January 1949 for improving the authority of party cadres by upgrading
their perquisites (and thus status).

This conflict in values was exacerbated in those cases in which job competition did occur—when youth waiting for ever-scarcer openings competed with the administrators, security police, and military personnel
sent into the economy with the successive waves of demobilization and
decentralization, and when educated youth who chose not to join the
party competed with their peers who did. A national survey in 1971 of the
Partisan elite (the "first fighters," who had joined the Partisans in 1941)
found that more than half had been retired before pension age, that 27
percent had incomes below the legal minimum, and that they "complained most of social isolation, inactivity, and lack of prestige." In 1972,
of 437,709 veterans in Serbia, only 32 percent were employed.[16] This
perception of competition and relative worth was nurtured by the regulations on employment and reward, because they specified *differentials*
among legally defined groups to which individuals belonged according to
their job qualifications. Qualitative improvements or upward mobility
came not with increased effort but by moving up through categories of
relative status. There were generally two legitimate means: educational
advance (through special courses, training abroad, or night school)[17] or

---

[15] Petranović, Končar, and Radonjić, *Sednice Centralnog komiteta KPJ (1948–1952)*, 565;
see also Ranković's report, p. 534. This was the same reason Ranković gave, in his report on
the party to the second plenum of the central committee in January 1949, for improving
what he called the miserable living conditions of party cadres; this argument was reversed in
1952 (ibid., 202–6, 251).

[16] Dean, "Civil-Military Relations in Yugoslavia, 1971–75," 54 n. 34, 50.

[17] One especially common path was to take a master's degree in middle age so that the
category of one's position, and therefore one's pension, was raised.

political activism. Although many combined the two routes, the growing unemployment of educated youth after 1972, the greater direct party involvement in decisions on managerial and professional appointments during the 1970s, and the further "'socialization" of political cadres in the party, security forces, and army reinforced the belief that there was a contest between educational achievement and the political reliability of party membership. Moral-ideological commissions created to review appointments in education and the mass media after 1974, although they rarely overturned the recommendations of peer-review personnel commissions judging professional qualifications, gave new life to this belief. When youth did not secure the job their schooling had ordained, the language of employment regulations and political campaigns made it natural to assume (and difficult to refute) that the rules had not been applied, that there was discrimination. Rival candidates had won, they assumed, only because of party membership or political connections—or, in areas of mixed nationality, because of national quotas (the *ključ*) or ethnic prejudice and protection.[18]

At the same time, the demand for production workers of all kinds in the 1970s often went unfilled. Heavy physical labor in low-paying jobs, such as mining, was perennially short of takers. Unskilled and semiskilled industrial workers had no prospect of anything more than marginal improvements in pay. Their wage gains from work stoppages and strikes did not compensate for the depressive effect of stabilization policies, incomes compacts, and growing inflation (especially after the mid-1970s) on their real incomes; and the system of individualized layoff and reallocation marginalized them politically. Training in industrial skills was unpopular. As the Serbian labor secretary Marija Todorović complained in 1982, the "greatest problem of harmonizing personal and collective interests" in the Yugoslav system lay "in the contradictions expressed in the field of employment and reassignment to more-complex tasks"; its most frequent manifestation was the "many who argue for the education of youth in productive tasks and highly skilled [technical] education but who send their children into occupations for which there are already tens of thousands of unemployed." Stipe Šuvar, the Croat sociologist-politician most closely identified with the reform of secondary education, warned the same year that the country was "in for difficult times in this decade" because of the conflict between a slowing economy and the "expectations" of

[18] The president of the Serbian League of Youth complained in 1982 that a "greater problem than unemployment itself is the competition, myth, corruption, familiarity, connections, etc., in finding a job." Reflecting on the additional role of social status, he continued, "A youth will wait patiently for four to five years, knowing the economic situation and low demand for his profession, but his patience is lost if someone who graduated after him with poorer grades but from a better social position gets a job first" (quoted in Tijanić and Andjelić, "Obično nezaposleni mladi").

youth, which had led to a "hyperproduction of 'nonproductive' intelligentsia in the towns" and an "explosion of higher education to a patho-
logical extent." He complained that "peasant children and workers'
children will do anything to avoid their parents' fate and want to leave
direct production, whereas those in the middle classes are striving to
maintain or improve their position. Any petty office work is to be chosen
over factory work."[19]

The official rhetoric promoting increases in capital, including human
capital, was imbued with the idea of achieved, not ascribed, status. But
access to employment became ever less an issue of the expansion of the
public sector to incorporate a primarily peasant population and ever more
a matter of internal turnover within the socialized sector and of the personal or political influence that an urban younger generation had with
individuals already employed. While parents in the private sector viewed
education expenditures as their children's patrimony, fathers in the public sector were reported to see their legacy to their children as having a
job waiting for them. In a comparison of the unemployed in Split,
Croatia, in 1968 and 1981, sociologists Josip Županov and Mladen Žuvela
found the same groups represented: youth, women, the unskilled or disabled, migrants, and poorer strata. But their social origins had changed
significantly. People of peasant stock were less well represented, because
their numbers had dropped in the population at large. Children of professionals or white-collar workers were no better represented in 1981 than in
1968, reflecting their continued good position and political power in society. Similarly, workers' children had opportunities for work abroad if they
did not already have access to public-sector enterprises. But two groups
suffered particularly for their lack of influence in the public sector of the
economy. The children of private artisans depended for their opportunities on continuing their schooling, but they could not compete with
workers' or professionals' children after graduation because their parents
had no connections with a public-sector job that they could pass on or use
as an entree to another. The children of parents in the defense establishment, in which there was no more demand for personnel, fared worst;
their parents' influence was outside economic enterprises in the socialist
sector.[20]

POLITICAL EXCLUSION

A second consequence of the system created by the leaders' strategy and
its approach to unemployment was to segregate the political world of the

---

[19] Šuvar, "Plave i bele kragne."

[20] Županov and Žuvela, "Kriteriji inferiornosti nezaposlenih." The mothers of children in
the latter category had lived with a double disadvantage in access to jobs—on top of their

employed from that of the unemployed. In addition to social invisibility, there developed a form of political invisibility as a result of the end to unemployment in its mass, involuntary form and as a result of the dual-sector approach to unemployment, with its distinction in political rights that arose from a political system structured around the economic system. The level of unemployment significantly affected bargaining power in the economy—but in bargaining over money and credit between collective units of property owners (republics, enterprises, and banks), not between workers and employers, or among workers in ways that could lead to the political solidarity of workers with the unemployed.

The threat of unemployment in the socialized sector was individualized, and employment and wages were regulated according to measures of individual capital (economic, political, and social). Whether the loss of a job in the socialist sector led to retraining, reassignment, or expulsion into the private sector, it was executed by workers' organizations (the workers' council, its disciplinary committee, the union, or the self-management courts), not by managers or political authorities. Social ownership bound employed persons' interests in higher wages and secure jobs to the economic results of their employers, even if those results were not sufficient to guarantee their continued employment.

In the political system, as described in chapter 5, "economic interest" was a constitutional concept, granting political rights to participate in economic decisions and policy in proportion to economic value produced in the public sector. Those who did not produce value (the unemployed) did not have such official rights, while those who did had no need to organize. Interest was not an unstructured political incentive defined by labor-market competition or workers' organizational resources. To be unemployed meant above all to be politically excluded from the full citizenship accorded to the status of employment in the socialized sector of the economy. People employed in the private sector could be represented politically only in local and neighborhood assemblies of voters and could organize according to economic interests only through contractual relations with a socialist-sector enterprise.

Central policy was formulated by a host of councils, assemblies, parliaments, and corporatist negotiations, all of which represented only social-sector producers (though variously called workers, organizations of associated labor, or enterprises). Alliances to influence policy occurred

---

gender, they were often outsiders in their communities because they moved frequently to accompany their husbands.

In a survey of attitudes in Macedonia in 1981, respondents ranked unequal employment opportunities as the "first and most painful source of social inequality," far more important than housing, education, wages, and other material goods (Kimov, "Da li se povećavaju socijalne razlike?").

among managers of enterprises, along industrial-branch lines within the economic chambers (*privredne komore*), and among elected delegates in the halls of parliaments. Such alliances were highly influential—above all those of the exporters, on whom the country's capacity to import (and increasingly to produce) depended. But if such virtual representation did not meet the interests of workers or of the unemployed waiting for openings, then the institutional assignment of jurisdiction over labor and employment to republics, localities, and firms and the vertical, territorial organization of the political system meant that the independent interests of labor or the unemployed could be represented only by the single voice of their enterprise or republic. The institutional avenues of political influence and bargaining gave no way to assess the economic costs of unemployment in the country at large, or to formulate political trade-offs between wages and jobs.

In all these ways, the dual face of capitalist unemployment had been sundered—by the system of economic democracy that linked political representation to producer-centered economic organization and by the property division between public and private sectors (instead of between labor and capital). The two organizations explicitly representing the interests of labor—the Communist party and the union organization—are usually dismissed in the literature as having failed this task because they also became official organizations, guaranteed political power constitutionally instead of having to compete with other parties and unions for it. But this view is insufficient to understand the roles they did play, which (as with competitive parties in a market economy) were defined by the particular organization of the economy and the state that resulted from the leaders' ideology.

The idea of social ownership means that the party should represent the collective interests of all working people—of society as a whole—above their particular interests (served by the many other official forms of representation, such as firms, localities, industries, and professional groups). In Kardelj's model of progressive socialization and decentralization to eviscerate federal (state) power and to cut social expenditures on "nonproductive" labor, the Communist party's importance and its presence in social life were supposed to grow in proportion as the state (the bureaucracy, army, and police) was dismantled and its functions integrated into firms and communes. But because the party did not have a separate administrative bureaucracy or the formal system of *nomenklatura* found in countries of "bureaucratic socialism," it increasingly depended for its power on the ability to influence who held authoritative positions within society.

Because the economic criteria of professional competence and productivity-related skills could not be ignored, the party's solution was to recruit managers and professionals into its membership. Industrial workers never composed more than 36 percent of LCY membership, a figure from the height of the recruitment campaign of 1960–64 to favor skilled workers; two years later, rising unemployment sent that proportion plummeting, the most frequent cause for expulsion being nonpayment of dues.[21] Peasants had composed half the party's membership after the war, but their numbers declined with the campaign of the fifth party congress to recruit workers in 1948 and then dropped drastically after 1952, from 22 percent in 1954 to less than 5 percent by 1976.[22] By 1964, the party had become an organization of administrators and professionals. A Yugoslav contributor to a study of "workers' management" for the International Labor Office gave this explanation: "The proportion of League members is generally higher in managerial organs and in delegations than among the workers who elect them. Membership in the League is, in fact, a criterion for election to such bodies in some cases, since League members are deemed to be motivated to defend and develop the management rights of workers."[23] Managers were elected by employees in a firm (though approved by the local party committee and government), unless the firm was under temporary local governance in a prebankruptcy restructuring; a firm's representatives in the assembly were also chosen by employees. But to prevent conflicts of interest in the decisions they took, those performing elected functions were granted job security. The law prohibited their involuntary dismissal, and it protected the jobs to which they would return if they were voted out or when their tenure expired.[24] Labor regulations also required firms to hold open the jobs and continue the salaries of employees on leave for official business or military service. Managers with demonstrated loyalty to the local party committee would, if temporarily unemployed, receive a salary from party coffers until a new position could be found.

These protections for party-approved managers were the source of widespread criticism, from the accusation that the party had created a privileged "new class" (Milovan Djilas's thesis in his revival of a classic socialist theme in the 1950s) to the charge that it had reproduced an informal *nomenklatura* indistinguishable from that of state-socialist regimes of the Soviet type. Members of this stratum of managers who owed their positions to party membership or approval defended these protections, however, as the basis of independence from popular pressures within a firm when hard economic decisions had to be made (along the lines of theories of insulated bureaucracies).[25] No mention was made from either

[21] See Seroka, *Change and Reform of the League of Communists in Yugoslavia*, 29–33.

[22] *Yugoslav Survey* 17, nos. 1,2 (February, May 1976).

[23] International Labor Office, *Employment, Growth, and Basic Needs*, 164.

[24] Tenure was limited after 1963 to two terms, but the limitation was often ignored in practice.

[25] See the *Start* interview with Tomislav Badovinac, the man sent in to oversee the restructuring of the indebted Economic Bank of Zagreb (the republican bank of Croatia).

camp of the fact that elected representatives in parliamentary bodies were immune from unemployment and therefore any personal economic interest in solidarity with the fate of the unemployed.

Moreover, the effect of growing unemployment, as well as the party's rationalizing response to it, was not to create a political opportunity to revive its identity as a labor party or its collective interests in the potential threat to social order from the unemployed, but to further narrow its power. The party's dependence on managerial loyalty grew over time as it gave up other instruments of control and as the expansion of educational opportunity increased the number of people capable of holding such posts. Party membership was only an additional qualification and not always necessary for positions of authority, but it became an increasingly important distinguishing device after the early 1970s, when unemployment rose among the university-educated. Although membership was once meant to be a mark of achievement and honor, its selectivity forming the primary basis of the party's claim to authority from the civic virtue of its members,[26] it more and more became an instrument of exclusivity to limit entry to political and managerial posts and to raise their value by creating an artificial scarcity.

The factors promoting this development came into play only shortly after the political campaign surrounding the economic reform of 1958–65. Because the very public display surrounding the purge of Ranković and the central cadre commission in 1966–67 seemed to promise greater openness, the disappointed expectations bred resentment in those excluded. As the number of new jobs narrowed, rules were introduced to check power within this managerial network through limited tenure within specific posts and obligatory rotation among those already employed. At the same time, the market-oriented economic reform, which rewarded managers for turning a commercial profit, had undercut the vertical lines of party accountability and led to a purge of managers most conspicuous for creating trade-based empires and expanding outside their republic of property registration (through horizontal rather than vertical organization).[27] The result was that in fact an ever more closed, narrow

[26] Pusić argues that the party still represented "virtue" in the early 1980s as the dominant criterion in choosing representatives; there were election slogans of "Elect the best!" and committees to assess "moral-political suitability" of individuals for positions of responsibility in political, managerial, and social functions ("Uloga kolektivnog odlučivanja u realizaciji radničkih interesa," 223).

[27] Informal explanations attribute this purge to nationalism, on the argument that firms crossing republican lines tended to be export-import based conglomerates originating in the administrative period in Belgrade (such as Genex) that expanded toward profitable opportunities in the 1960s, such as tourism on the Dalmatian coast. In this case, the Croatian government and Dalmatian towns (such as Dubrovnik) opposed their intrusion on the

group circulated among directorships in the economy and government. The effect of growing unemployment on the LCY, in sum, was its metamorphosis into a craft union of managers and politicians and a further decline in its governing role apart from its managerial function.

The union's success in preventing mass unemployment also had the paradoxical consequence of weakening, not strengthening, its political resources. This was because its success narrowed the basis for solidarity on economic interest and for political action and included the loss of labor's traditionally powerful weapon, the general strike. The political alliance between peasants and workers that was critical to the party's revolutionary strategy did not survive the institutional separation of the private and public sectors that originated in the policy against rapid socialization of agriculture. Despite the protections in labor regulations against competition from this private-sector "reserve of the unemployed," the unions tended to see the subsistence guarantee of property ownership in the private sector as reason to give preference to their membership—urban dwellers, usually men assumed to be heads of household, with industrial or administrative skills and work habits appropriate to public-sector jobs, and with no source of income or housing should they become unemployed. Unions had little sympathy for those who could earn money in the private sector, for wealth earned through market advantage or what they considered speculation, or for workers absent from work, on the assumption that they were off working on their own land or at second jobs and therefore in no need of a job when others were truly unemployed.

Labor-market competition largely took the form of migration to places with labor shortages or higher incomes and benefits, such as Slovenia and the Dalmatian coast. Thus it was governments (local and republican) rather than unions that acted to protect social-sector wages and jobs by erecting formal or informal barriers between residents and immigrants, or by importing "foreign" labor (from outside the area) on limited contract for specific projects.[28] Confined to temporary work and dormitory housing, classified as newcomers on local rolls, and subjected to informal pressures where there were differences in language and culture, immigrants

---

grounds that they were Serbian. No systematic study has tested this hypothesis against the one offered here. See also Djodan, *The Evolution of the Economic System of Yugoslavia;* and Šošić, *Za čiste račune.*

[28] Throughout the socialist period, local and republican governments acted to prevent competition for their industries and populations with myriad limits on entry of labor, industries, or goods (such as the Serbian boycott of goods from other republics, especially Slovenia, in 1990), in ways analyzed by Stigler for capitalist societies—except that in the Yugoslav case there was no need for separate pressure from industries for governmental regulations because of social ownership and the fiscal system. See Stigler, "The Theory of Economic Regulation."

without familial connections often found it difficult to overcome initial disadvantages in residence and schooling.[29]

When the system of workers' councils replaced collective union bargaining affecting the trade-off between higher wages on the one hand and investment and jobs on the other with debate and review of managerial proposals within the firm, the unions' new task confined them to the public sector of the economy. Like the LCY, they were to represent social interest (in overall growth and its derivative, rising employment); their role was to participate in the discussions about central rules on productivity-based wages and wage increases and then to implement those rules. At the same time, they were to represent the interests of workers against managers in reviewing and implementing managerial decisions within firms on rationalizations and dismissals. Contrary to the conception of unions as "transmission belts" for central policy that dominates the literature on Communist-governed states, this dilemma between their official and representative roles led, according to Ellen Comisso, to alternating pressure between "plan" (central regulations) and "market" (enterprise autonomy).[30] In fact, the unions resolved the dilemma in a way that distanced them even more from any societal role regarding unemployment. On the one hand, they fought to protect their authority to implement central regulations through their legal right to nominate candidates to enterprise decision-making councils, therefore fighting for the authority of workers' councils in general against managerial encroachment. At the same time, they fought to increase the economic resources available for the firm's wage bill, working in collaboration with management and against central authority in support of greater enterprise autonomy over disposition of its income and of taxation for the commune's solidarity fund (which provided firms with insurance to pay the guaranteed wage).

As a result, however, the authority of the union organization at the firm depended on implementing central labor regulations and policy, making it difficult to support a worker's appeal against regulations. Workers who appealed dismissal complained frequently that they received no union

[29] Author's interviews with Josip Županov on the fate of migrants to Split from villages in its hinterland; with Slovene sociologists and Silva Mežnarić on the restrictions Slovenia imposed on labor from other republics; with Ivo Banac and Olga Supek on the activities of local authorities in Dubrovnik to protect local labor against the influx of employers from other republics who would bring labor with them; and with Radoslav Stojanović on local reactions against the expansion of Serbian foreign-trade firms, such as Genex, into domestic markets in the 1950s (on the same conflict in the 1960s, see also Šošić, *Za čiste račune*). On the introduction of a distinction in some municipal statutes after the 1963 constitution between long-term residents and recent settlers, see Hondius, *The Yugoslav Community of Nations*, 308–10.

[30] Comisso, *Workers' Control under Plan and Market.*

support and were inclined as a result to take their complaints individually to self-management courts, where town lawyers outside the firm were more likely to come to their defense.[31] The unions' influence, on the other hand, grew out of the social bonds of relatively stable membership and personal relations with the director, management board, and technical staff within the firm, making it difficult to contest a managerial decision. Instead of organized militancy, the unions chose vagueness and dissembling so as to protect the personal relations underlying their influence. In place of collective bargaining in the interest of workers against managers or government, they fought to increase economic resources within the firm. The union-led "Battle for Incomes" in 1957–58, as it was called at the time,[32] for example, was not a battle for higher wages (although it had that consequence in some firms), but a joint battle with liberals to reduce enterprise taxation, increase the portion of earnings retained, free firms to make decisions on profit allocation that affected jobs and incomes (decisions regarding personal incomes, investment in new equipment and plant, funds for collective consumption goods, and expansion of employment), and transfer authority over hiring and firing from the management board to the workers' council. That alliance fell apart in 1968, however, when liberals took the next step and sought to transfer the unions' authority over hiring, firing, and income distribution by way of the workers' council to the director and appointed council of technical advisers. Although the conflict cost Vukmanović-Tempo his leadership of the union, the union won restoration of its authority (in the constitutional amendments of 1971 and 1974) when central policy shifted after 1969.

THE DIVISIONS OF SELF-MANAGEMENT

A third consequence of the leaders' strategy and the resulting structure of economic and political organization was to make solidarity and alliances across social divisions on issues of governmental policy that influenced employment and unemployment extremely unlikely. In the classic case of social democracy, the Keynesian political revolution had two elements: a new consciousness about the need for a macroeconomic conception of economic activity and for active governmental policy to counteract the

---

[31] Hayden, "Labor Courts and Workers' Rights in Yugoslavia." Hayden writes that in an analysis of the self-management courts (courts of associated labor) in 1977 and 1978 by the federal cabinet in preparation for a proposed reform of these courts, "the passive role of the trade unions was castigated, particularly insofar as the unions do not protect individual workers (and, by extension, organizations) from improper activities by management and management organs" (254).

[32] See Rusinow, *The Yugoslav Experiment*, 116.

aggregate paradoxes of autonomous, microeconomic decision making and laissez-faire; and the formation of broad electoral alliances—among political parties representing industrial labor, and other wage-earning, salaried, or small-property groups—in opposition to the unemployment-causing policies of orthodox stabilization and business protectionism. Collective opposition to such policies in Yugoslavia was difficult to forge because both elements were lacking: a societywide conception of collective interest in macroeconomic policy to counteract the powerful forces for decentralization and segmentation, and a social alliance across groups and economic interests sufficient to exert pressure from below for policy change.

The example of social democracy is usually considered irrelevant to the socialist states because their single-party systems did not operate by the competitive logic of elections. The defining characteristic of social democracy, after all, was its historic compromise with capitalism in accepting a parliamentary road to power and social change. Are not the privileged position of the ruling party and police harassment of dissident and opposition groups sufficient to explain the failure of effective political demand for change in socialist regimes? But they prevented neither the broad horizontal alliance against the party leadership in the case of the Solidarity movement in Poland after 1979—which joined trade unions, intellectuals' clubs, farmers' associations, the Catholic church, and local party officials (the "horizontalists")—nor the grand alliances, however, momentary, of revolutionary protest against Communist regimes in Eastern Europe in 1989.

At first glance, a Keynesian political alliance (which Adam Przeworski calls a compromise with capitalism to nationalize consumption rather than production)[33] would seem to have been possible in the Yugoslav case, where, as was argued at the beginning of this chapter, the concept of employment as subsistence and "income relations" had replaced political solidarity on employment with solidarity on income. Since social ownership meant that few held wealth-producing assets and that everyone in the public sector of the economy was a wage or salary earner, and since private ownership was limited to smallholdings, one might expect that a broad political alliance could have been formed among consumers against the demand-cutting restrictions imposed by macroeconomic policy on their purchasing power, in opposition to those who might support an anti-inflationary policy to restore external liquidity (such as the strongest firms or the political elite in the more-developed regions).

However, despite the principles of political and economic unity on which the Communist party built the state and social order—a single

[33] Przeworski, *Capitalism and Social Democracy*, 36–38.

party and union, a popular front with allied social strata, social ownership, a single accounting and monetary system, a common market, and uniform central rules—the leaders' methods of gaining flexibility through foreign capital, a private sector, and extensive operational decentralization created a society riven by divisions and factional conflict. There was no absence of social conflict or political protest over economic policies in this society. Alliances could be formed and reformed among enterprises and even governments on policies concerning monies and credit, and governments were able to mobilize social protest in support of their demands. But no alliances emerged across social groups to pose, in Claus Offe's words, a counteracting logic to defend labor in opposition to this logic of capital[34]—or, to put it in Yugoslav terms, to reverse the localization or privatization of questions of employment and make unemployment an issue of economic policy.

The massive evidence about wage formation and investment decisions showing how little say workers had over their incomes and job creation argues against the thesis that unemployment in Yugoslavia was a result of workers' power over wages in labor-managed firms. The system of self-management did contribute substantially to unemployment, on the other hand, as a political obstacle to a change in macroeconomic policy because it was the means to shift the locus of bargaining over wages and jobs to the level of the firm or lower, even though its system of wage discipline was phrased in terms of rights and political power. The political consequences of self-management had far less to do with the nature of decisions that could be made within self-managed units than with the character of society composed of such units and the nature of the links connecting them. The ostensible freedom of self-managed firms with respect to labor, revenues, and individual incomes focused political energies on the firm rather than the state—in the same way that in Poland the *central* setting of prices and wages helped to focus political energies instead against the government and to foster organization across social groups, in opposition to the rising price of food and the negative consequences for labor norms and wages in export industries.[35]

The presence of a retail market and free prices for consumer goods also was not sufficient to create a basis for political action among consumers (as it was in the successful alliances between workers and farmers in the case of the Swedish Social Democrats in 1932–34 and in the case of Solidarity in Poland) because that market was only one among multiple, unlinked

[34] Offe, "Two Logics of Collective Action."

[35] See Woodall, *The Socialist Corporation and Technocratic Power*, on similarities with the Yugoslav case in Edward Gierek's "import-led" growth strategy in the 1970s and the origin of both economic-reform oriented industrial policy and reorganization and worker protests in export sectors, such as steel, textiles, shipbuilding, coal, and chemicals.

modes of exchange. Consumer goods might be obtained through family reciprocity or with cash purchase—in nonconvertible domestic currency, in foreign currencies earned working abroad or bought either legally or illegally, or in credit or goods in kind from a place of employment in the socialist sector. Economic solidarity on falling standards of living did not lead to political solidarity where people operated in separate distributive and exchange networks. What political organization could bridge the differences between those who had a hedge against inflation in foreign-currency holdings from foreign emigration or in private links to Western markets and those who did not? between those who had access to food from private farmers through family ties and those who had no source of food outside what their money wage could buy? between those who received benefits (such as housing credits, health and accident insurance, vacation stays, meal coupons, and winter food staples) from a social-sector job and those who had to purchase everything on the open market? and between those for whom the effect of monetary and exchange-rate policy was to increase their purchasing power and those for whom it meant a sharp decline in what they could buy?

The end of the "wage struggle" with the introduction of self-management, which replaced unions' rights and attempts at collective bargaining with the rights of workers' councils to debate, be consulted, and discipline workers, did not end bargaining over wages. It only pushed that bargaining into the workplace, creating conflicts rather than solidarity among workers in their "socialist communities." The most contentious decision within firms was the adoption of the rule book on wage and income scales. Not only did actual personal incomes vary as a result of changes in production costs, profits, and taxes, but they also depended on the rate assigned a person's job classification. This created divisions between blue-collar and white-collar wage earners and across strata defined by skill certification. That conflicts over purchasing power erupted within the Yugoslav firm is demonstrated by the dismissals and rising wages of skilled workers in 1950–53, by the wage-push inflation in the 1960s when regulations were eased substantially and unemployment skyrocketed, and by the frequent work stoppages against the union leadership and management within a plant to protest wage cuts or forced job-saving mergers with unprofitable local firms.[36]

In contrast to Hungary, where managers of autonomous enterprises could choose, for example, to alter internal salaries as long as they kept within the limits of the assigned wage bill (such as by hiring more low-cost, unskilled labor in order to increase wage payments to skilled labor),

---

[36] Such work stoppages grew more frequent after 1958. In August–September 1985, a strike in Macedonia by workers from a profitable plant protesting such a decision lasted forty-five days.

in the Yugoslav system rank-and-file discontent over visible inequalities within the workplace alternated with the inflationary pressures of the aggregate wage bill on the money supply or price levels. The government responded to wage and price inflation by alternately regulating and deregulating wages and contributions for social benefits. Work stoppages usually had managers running to the factory floor and governments conceding to wage demands in order to protect the myth of self-management (as worker control) and to prevent strikes from spreading beyond the confines of the firm. But these immediate solutions preempted broader political mobilization (as they were intended to do) while feeding inflation and eventually requiring a new round of anti-inflationary restrictions and labor rationalization.

The authorities' solution to the wage demands of professionals and civil servants, who were so contentious in 1947–49 (for example, in the attack on the Ministry of Finance under Sreten Žujović), was administrative decentralization and socialization of government services (and thus employees)—transferring the activity to the budgets of firms or to independent agencies financed by enterprise taxation. In the 1970s, salaries for those in administrative positions and the "nonproductive" sphere of social services (referred to as people on "guaranteed salaries") were indexed to the wage rates and gains of production workers.[37] Politically, this indexation created a silent alliance, in no need of organization, among public-sector employees; but it also made wage restraint difficult to implement when administrators responsible for discipline benefited directly from wage increases, and it transposed the trade-off between economic and social investment and jobs into escalating tax rebellion. Both mechanisms of wage control in the public sector refueled inflationary pressures as well as rounds of intensification and stabilization restrictions that increased unemployment. But there was no political mechanism for bargaining over the trade-off except to lobby for tax concessions that had the effect of shifting taxation onto the private sector.

Economic-policy shifts created other conflicts among income earners that also inhibited political alliances. In addition to the divisions according to skill categories mentioned above, tensions between the separate decision-making hierarchies of production workers on the one hand and technical and administrative staff on the other intensified whenever new labor regulations shifted favor from one to the other. Because the accounting rules required that taxes to finance public services be paid be-

---

[37] The categories of federal expenditure were also indexed as a *percentage* of gross domestic product (a category excluding services), which put additional pressure on the capacity to collect federal tax revenues to meet the legislated percentage. This is why the military increasingly complained in the 1980s about the instability and unpredictability of its actual budget.

fore workers' net-income shares, the jobs of civil servants and employees in social services were in direct conflict with workers' incomes. Conflicts arose between economic enterprises and nonprofit cultural and social services when enterprises responded to the austerities of stabilization policy with an attack on the cost of financing public services and lobbied for their taxes to be cut by adopting user fees, relying more on market purchase, or cutting the defense budget and the number of parastatal agencies (the self-managing communities of interest).

A fundamental role of political organizations is to create the perception of common interest that is necessary to collective action even in the presence of seemingly insurmountable conflicts of interest. In theory, the unions had the organizational basis to play this role—to fashion broad alliances within and across industrial branches or to propose policy change on the occasion of writing labor and wage regulations or negotiating incomes-policy agreements. Alliances between industrial-branch unions and those in the social services were difficult to form, however, because there was no role for union bargaining in workplaces whose budgets were the result of grants (as with social services) instead of being "earned." In fact, the powerful professional and civil-service unions of the 1940s were no longer unions as a result of this transformation, and they performed functions with little relation to those of unions in the enterprises. They served as welfare organizations for visiting sick colleagues, sending birthday greetings, or organizing festivities within the workplace (such as for International Women's Day), and they joined local, republican, and federal associations to promote professional development and define policies for reskilling and benefits. The incentives discussed above for union officials to focus on increasing their firm's total revenues and collaborate with management made alliances between the unions and enterprise directors or economic liberals possible—until these allies turned against union authority and workers' decision-making rights within the firm.

Although the country's international position and its stop-and-go macroeconomic policy created an unpredictability of conditions that made it difficult to act strategically, the conflicts over trade liberalization in the 1960s did demonstrate the possibilities of broader alliances on matters of federal economic policy. For example, at the end of 1967, students and workers in some republics organized marches in sympathy with miners' strikes protesting government neglect of their industry. An open fight at the sixth union congress in June 1968 over the damage to the textile and mining industries caused by the decade-long trade liberalization and repeated recessions produced a full union resolution of solidarity.[38] The

---

[38] On the congress and floor fight, see Carter, *Democratic Reform in Yugoslavia*, 165.

party's choice to replace Vukmanović-Tempo, Dušan Petrović-Sane—who was another Partisan "first fighter," was not known for his liberal views, and was from Bosnia, where the strikes began—suggests that union opposition *was* compounding on several fronts. Nonetheless, more important than this change to more loyal leadership in preventing the development of a broader social alliance was the unions' ambiguity on employment. In response to rising youth unemployment and the massive social protest in the universities only weeks before, the union congress gave only a tepid nod to the students' own plight. In its Resolution on Employment, it chose to "condemn . . . work organizations closing in on themselves . . . conserving the existing qualification structure . . . [in] opposition to the employment of all categories of schooled cadre. . . . The unions must be engaged in the correct application of the law on obligatory admission of trainees and [must] fight for implementation of the rulebook on trainees."[39]

The unions and the youth wing of the party had been the Communists' most radical and committed activists in the days of revolution, but as employment questions were funneled into the self-managed workplace and union authority outside the firm into setting the principles of labor regulations, the two were driven into separate "reservations" with no stable grounds for political alliance. In the period after 1968, when unemployment became increasingly the plight of youth who could not get a first job, the primary demand of the League of Youth (Savez Omladina) was that high-school youth and university students be given the constitutional classification of "worker" and thus rights to representation and participation in economic decisions in their schools and localities. The attempt failed, and the league became known for its inaction at the grass roots; it was used instead as an avenue of individual advancement for political careers in the party leadership. Dependent on funding from the party's front organization, the Socialist Alliance of Working People, and assured of employment as long as they remained loyal activists, youth leaders continued to perform their assigned task of organizing youth labor brigades and, when unemployment became severe in the 1980s, of making strident pronouncements in youth journals and at congresses. To the extent they were heard at all outside these forums, these protests were relegated to the category of "problems of youth." Nor did they lead to the mobilization of "troops" among youth or to sustained pressure, because of quarrels among the youth league's separate republican branches over the priority of their different demands and concerns.

Perhaps the most significant effect of the system of workplace decision making called self-management was to end the party's identity with the

[39] *Yugoslav Survey*, 1968, p. 638.

working class and its interest separate from those of enterprises or governments. Although informed observers within the country insisted that
the party never lost the loyalty of industrial workers and emphasized the
importance to its ruling power of the web of personal and political connections among party politicians throughout the country, neither this informal network nor workers' silent loyalty was the same as creating political
alliances across the various divisions within society in support of labor.

Whereas the progressive socialization of the state and of economic functions was intended to give the party a more important role in governance
by resolving differences and "harmonizing" conflicts, the party itself was
not immune to the divisive effects of decentralization and socialization.
The "socialization" of the party meant that members belonged to units at
their workplace (which paid their salary) and were active there. The rank-
and-file party members thus identified with and owed their first loyalty
to their work collective (employer).[40] Party membership offered no special privileges and required payment of dues (at 12 percent of salary); and,
unlike the time spent in self-management meetings, time spent on party
meetings and duties did not receive compensation as time worked.
Studies of dissent within party organizations found far more criticism in
the villages—where private-sector employment dominated and party
organizations were territorial, rather than enterprise-based—than in
public-sector firms and institutions, where party membership did not
protect individuals from being fired.[41] Party members were no different
than non-party members in their conflicts of economic interest with
people employed in offices and services supported by enterprise taxes.
The primary means of enforcing party policy was by influencing appointments to managerial positions, but the appointment and accountability of
enterprise directors was an additional source of conflict between the commune and enterprise party committees. Conflicts between commune and
enterprise party organizations over tax revenues and retained earnings
might be resolved by common cause against the private sector, but the
shift of taxes and fees was guided not by the prejudices of socialist ideology (as it was usually alleged) but by economic interest. Divisions within

[40] Comisso writes, "The roots of the LCY's recruitment dilemma seems [sic] to lie in a
lack of incentives for blue-collar workers to pay the costs of political action party membership entails for them. When workers as a group derive benefits from party actions, the
benefits take the form of 'public goods' which accrue to the work collective as a whole, or to
workers in general, regardless of party affiliation or the lack of it." This encouraged free
riding and made the party responsive to the worker's needs when "his interests coincided
with those of society or with those of the enterprise," but "should they conflict, he could
hardly turn to the party of the working class for support" ("Can a Party of the Working Class
Be a Working-Class Party?" 72, 86).

[41] See Carter, *Democratic Reform in Yugoslavia*, 71.

the party thus occurred in line with the budgetary divisions of the economy where employment and wage decisions were made.

Behind the frequent criticism that delegates elected to political office were primarily party cadres was the presumption of party unity, discipline, and common purpose that in fact did not exist on questions of money and employment capacity, unless the productivity of the firm rose or an infusion of capital from outside provided resources to redistribute. The politics of producivity in a redistributive regime, as Charles Maier has argued for the United States, depends on prior economic growth to circumvent conflicts.[42] Party leaders in the various republics and provinces competed for resources; after 1969, their own employment and power depended on the proportion of resources they could control and keep at home. With rare exceptions, the basis of political representation in units of autonomous ("self-managed") budgets had little relation to policy positions and factions on federal policy toward foreign trade, defense, and investment. Instead, the former came to define the latter: conflicts over substantive policy were redefined as conflicts over the distribution of money—over budgetary revenues and tax policy, transfers and subsidies, and the locus of control over monetary policy, foreign-exchange allocation, and banking.

Studies of effective political organization in other socialist states emphasize the critical role that intellectuals play in forging broad social alliances, by explaining the links between particular and general interest and providing a language and symbols for political action.[43] In the Yugoslav leaders' vision of the state, professional experts had substantial authority. They wrote the rules for the legislative and executive branches of government, performed the analyses in research institutions to propose or justify investment projects, and wielded substantial critical influence in journals, universities, and party forums. In their criticism of public policies, the economists, sociologists, and party leaders with social science backgrounds who presented professional studies to party forums or spoke at public gatherings did, over time, identify and make public many immediate causes of unemployment. They pointed out, for example, that government policy and enterprise demand did not correspond to the traits of the labor supply; that the preoccupation with small-property firms as a panacea to unemployment assumed a category of resident skills and resources that were in deficit, not surplus; that allowing earlier retirement with full

---

[42] Maier, "The Politics of Productivity."

[43] This theme runs through the literature on economic reform in socialist countries and why it failed politically in Czechoslovakia but brought revolution in Poland, for example. A good representative of this literature from the more recent period is Staniszkis, *Poland's Self-Limiting Revolution.* For a critical view of the thesis, see Laba, *The Roots of Solidarity.*

pension in the 1970s and 1980s would only worsen the shortage of workers with industrial skills; that enterprise demands for several years' prior work experience were unrealistic, and certainly would do little to reduce unemployment among youth; and that labor regulations for reassignment discriminated against new entrants to the labor force.

Yet the republican jurisdiction over education, research institutes, and development planning, made effective by budgetary autonomy, centered such analyses within republics, whose very real differences in labor markets led to separate worlds and perceptions. A planner from full-employment Slovenia and a planner from Kosovo or Macedonia facing open unemployment of 15 to 30 percent had little in common. With rare exceptions, the common ground across republics of the various proposals for remedying policy mistakes was no different from previous policy: focusing on alternative methods of adjusting and allocating the supply of labor or finding new avenues for employment in the private sector.

Like the unions, professionals proposed nothing that would challenge the basis of their own authority, focusing largely on qualifications and productivity. In the early 1980s, as in the early 1960s, they criticized barriers to the employment of "young, schooled cadres" and the monopoly over existing jobs by workers with less skill, work effort, and creativity than unemployed youth, which kept productivity suboptimal; and they argued for "differentiation" in favor of "those who work and against those who do not."[44] But in cases where their proposals extended to societywide economic policy, the differences in approach among expert communities in the republics prevailed. For example, one proposal originating in Serbia in the late 1970s, for long-term social planning (1985–2000) for the entire Yugoslav space, was resisted by Slovenia because the Serbs insisted on using their method of planning and the Belgrade Institute of Economics, while the Croats insisted on their method and the Zagreb Institute of Economics; the Slovenes preferred a third method—one combining social, economic, and demographic aspects. Slovene economists argued that the Serb proposals for devoting greater attention to developmental planning, setting proportions among key sectors, recognizing the links among phases and sectors of production in final output, introducing a federal investment fund, and strengthening the revenue base of federal functions were a return to the system of the 1950s and that improved macroeconomic management could not make up for microeconomic defects in the efficiency of capital when investors were not free to manage and earn a return on capital.[45]

[44] Serb sociologist Silvano Bolčić, in *Razvoj i kriza jugoslovenskog društva u sociološkoj perspektivi*, 192. The "basic condition for overall progress" in Yugoslav society, Bolčić continues, is an "affirmation of labor."

[45] Review of economic proposals from Ljubomir Madžar and his group at the Yugoslav

Experts and intellectuals were not defined by their republican origin. Schools of thought crossed republican lines, and both formal and informal professional contacts maintained the frequent exchange of ideas. But the progressive transfer of federal funds and competencies to the republics gradually deprived experts of a base independent of the republics where they were employed, and residences and spheres of political action had to be chosen. By the 1980s, social scientists' proposals for change in labor-market institutions varied largely with their republic's milieu.[46] In Serbia, for example, Silvano Bolčić proposed greater government involvement in the problems of employment, but within the local context:

> Effective social action to conquer unemployment requires each commune to complete a concrete analysis of the possibilities for employment in every work organization in its territory . . . and work out a precise annual plan of employment . . . with specific schedules of who will be employed in that period. . . . Commune organizations of the League of Youth could form "committees for employment" in which representatives of unemployed youth would actively participate. With the collection of ideas for employment and constant social pressure on all institutions and organizations that can contribute to opening new positions, more favorable possibilities would be created.[47]

In the northwestern republics, in contrast, economists and sociologists spoke increasingly of the de facto existence of a labor market and the need to recognize not only its existence but its superiority as a method of allocating labor and resolving the irrationalities that produced unemployment.[48] In full-employment Slovenia and in Croatia, where unemployment had fallen below 5 percent by the first half of the 1980s, the consequence of tighter labor supply and even shortages had been the creation of marketlike conditions; surveys on labor turnover by the Yugoslav Institute on Productivity demonstrated that for many years, professionals in these republics had been moving frequently among

---

Institute of Economic Research in Belgrade (by then a section of the Institute for Social Sciences) by Jože Mencinger (first minister of the economy for Slovenia after the multiparty elections of 1990) in *Ekonomska Politika* (1987). No republic or province in Yugoslavia can be treated as a "unitary actor," for economists and politicians within republics divided among schools of thought and economic-policy advice. But at any moment there were also differences among republics, and the two positions cited here from Slovenia and Serbia best represent the main alternatives of influential opinion in 1987–91.

[46] Verdery analyzes a Romanian version of intellectual competition with a nationalist component in *National Ideology under Socialism*.

[47] Bolčić, *Razvoj i kriza*, 216–17.

[48] The Slovene sociological association held a conference in Ljubljana on the "labor market" in October 1982. Among those most prominent on the subject in Croatia were Branko Horvat, Slaven Letica, and Josip Županov.

firms in search of higher incomes and better conditions. By 1990, experts in these republics had equated their belief in the remedy of real labor markets with abolition of the system of worker consultation in firms (self-management) and had demanded full privatization of the public sector. If managers were not free to hire and fire, they argued, and if foreign investors were not assured of these rights, the economic crisis of the 1980s would not end.

The difficulties of forging cross-republican political alliances on questions of employment were most apparent in the group in which conditions for collective action were best and that was most prone to political protest: university students. Within two years of the decline in absolute numbers of persons employed, the universities exploded in Priština (in 1967 and repeatedly thereafter), in Belgrade and Sarajevo (in 1968), and in Zagreb (by 1971). But because university education and employment conditions were under republican jurisdiction, students differed in their perception of the cause of their potential unemployment. As a result, they pursued quite different demands and political tactics, despite many personal and professional connections among student leaders and the professors and critical intellectuals who inspired them.

In Belgrade and Priština, the capitals of Serbia and its province Kosovo, surplus labor came largely from the rural exodus as youth attempted to enter the public sector by way of the universities, and protests were led by poorer students from village backgrounds whose excellent grades were not sufficient to win them either party membership or good prospects of employment.[49] Their attack on the state centered on the LCY as a system of spoils in employment, whose monopoly on access to jobs conflicted with the open and egalitarian ideals of the system. Their slogan, "down with the Red Bourgeoisie!" demanded a change in who controlled access to jobs, not an alternative program for unemployment. Nonetheless, despite these common interests and political programs within the same republic, the two groups could not ally because of the budgetary system and the ethnonational legitimation of its division. In Kosovo, for example, the students defined the struggle as one against Belgrade for greater control over both local education and government budgets; the primary cause of unemployment was seen as the absence of such local control, which made possible national discrimination favoring Serbs over ethnic Albanians in education and in jobs in the socialized sector of the economy and government. Few discussed who actually benefited from the policy of investment in raw-material extraction and capital-intensive heavy industry in the province that generated so few jobs.

In Croatia, as rural surplus labor emigrated for work in Europe and as

[49] Tomanović, *Omladina i socijalizam*, 73–100.

the economic reform for greater integration with Western markets favored many areas of the republic, students in Zagreb in fact agreed with
their republican party leadership that unemployment was the result of
"Belgrade's" taxation of Croat resources (above all foreign-exchange receipts from tourism, transport, and guest-worker remittances). They took
to the streets to add force to their leaders' demands for greater autonomy
over resources that they claimed belonged to Croatia. Although their revolt began with a university reform in 1970–71, by the time they were in
the streets, they were focusing their demands on higher retention of
foreign-exchange receipts than allowed by the quotas set by the National
Bank, a decentralization of the banking system to give local producers
greater access to bank credit,[50] and an end to the capital tax for development aid for other republics. In full-employment Slovenia, similarly, students allied with party leaders and unions who saw the drain of "Slovene"
resources to Belgrade and the poorer republics as reducing their potential
for higher wages and social welfare.[51]

These differences also held for alliances that students in one republic
might create with others: students in Belgrade and Sarajevo could organize support for workers in coal mines and textile factories, but they were
unable to extend this alliance to republics that benefited from Western
market liberalization.

THE ORIGINS OF POLITICAL CHANGE

Where pressure for political change in socialist Yugoslavia did occur and
originated at least partially in economic interest, social forces, and popular demand, it came from the country's two outliers on unemployment.
Full employment in Slovenia and nearly full *un*employment in Kosovo
were the two exceptions that prove the rule of this chapter's arguments
about the relation between political demand and the society created by
governmental economic policy.

In Slovenia, where nearly full employment and spot shortages of skilled

[50] Gedeon identifies the differences in the banking proposals of the Croat, Serb, and
Slovene economic schools in "Monetary Disequilibrium and Bank Reform Proposals in
Yugoslavia."

[51] The first government to resign in postwar Yugoslavia was the Slovene government of
Janko Smole in December 1966, when the chamber on health and welfare of the Slovene
parliament rejected its program for cutting enterprise contributions for social insurance and
shifting the tax onto workers' wages (the vote was later reversed, however, and the government withdrew its resignation). In 1985, the "catalyst for nationwide abandonment of wage
austerity" under the IMF program was the rapid midyear rise of wages in Slovenia; the
"Slovene government claimed that wage compression had reached the limits of social tolera-
tion, although its wages had fallen least and were the highest above average" (Henderson,
"The International Monetary Fund and Eastern Europe").

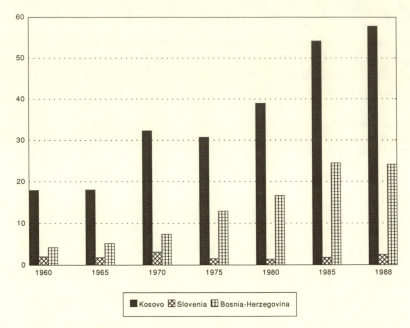

Figure 9-1. Percentage Rate of Unemployment: Kosovo, Slovenia, and Bosnia-Herzegovina. *Source:* Mencinger, "Privredna reforma i nezaposlenost," table 1.

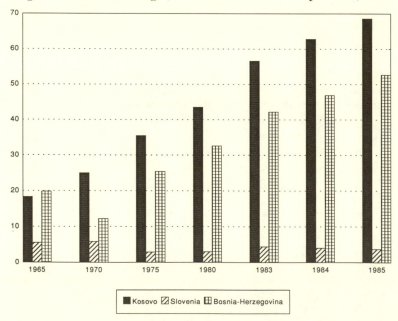

Figure 9-2. Percentage Rate of Youth Unemployment: Kosovo, Slovenia, and Bosnia-Herzegovina. *Source:* Primorac and Charette, "Regional Aspects of Youth Unemployment in Yugoslavia," 218. *Note:* "Youth" refers to persons aged 27 years or younger.

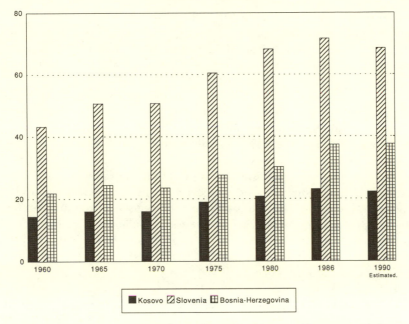

Figure 9-3. Percentage Rate of Employment: Kosovo, Slovenia, and Bosnia-Herzegovina. *Source: Statistički Godišnjak Jugoslavije,* various years. For the numbers, see table 6-1. *Note:* The rate of employment is defined as the relation between the number of employed persons in the social and private sectors and the working-age population (men ages 15–64 and women ages 15–59).

workers and professionals prevailed throughout the postwar period, a society had been created in which labor had real bargaining power over incomes, benefits, and jobs. Despite arguments that such power came from the institution of "workers' control" and "labor management" of firms, labor did not have such power in the other republics, where self-management also prevailed. The exercise of that power at the level of enterprises and in republic-level politics had led in time to a pluralist politics as well—a burgeoning "civil society." (It is necessary to note, however, that the financing for most of these activities came from the party-affiliated Socialist Alliance of Working People). Full employment had created de facto labor-market conditions within the republic, leading to the development of the social and political relations that accompany labor markets. Slovene political activity increasingly resembled that found in market economies: parliamentary responsiveness to popular pressure, governmental concessions to loosen federal restrictions on wages and social welfare, multicandidate elections, and, when democratic elections occurred in 1990, competitive party politics in which the spectrum of political tendencies resembled central European traditions. Peter

Katzenstein's argument for Austria and Switzerland applied equally well for Slovenia: the very fact of economic success "continuously re-legitimized" the political institutions necessary to governmental policy and strengthened the "compatibility of views" between the bargaining parties, whether labor and government or labor and management.[52]

This situation depended, however, on protecting the conditions for full employment, which were republican jurisdiction over labor and control over the economic resources necessary to Slovenia's choice of development policy. During the 1980s, as will be discussed in the final chapter, the Slovene government was able to strengthen its ability to act as a sovereign unit by giving political activities within the republic freer reign and by directing Slovene society's capacity for collective action against the outside. The goal was to protect these conditions—by adopting protectionist labor policies, organizing a successful rebellion against the federal government when Slovene control over capital and employment and the internal political system appeared threatened, and in the end pressing for total national independence.

The other outlier was Kosovo. It also demonstrates the reciprocal relation between employment conditions and political action. Here unemployment was so high and the opportunities for socialist-sector employment so few that nearly 80 percent of the republic's population, and an even larger proportion of ethnic Albanians, was confined to the private sector—working in agriculture, trades, household labor, and family businesses (particularly in other republics or abroad in temporary economic migration), or registered as unemployed. While this lack of opportunity for public-sector employment excluded them from the full enjoyment of political rights, it provided the economic basis for an alternative community centered in family-based social organization and ethnically based political identities. Extended families lasted longer than in other parts of the country and among other national groups, serving in part as a vehicle for strategies of economic diversification.[53] Migrant workers and entrepreneurs sent earnings home, and families used the income to buy up land. Eventually, their economic and therefore political exclusion produced a political network in families and villages—an entire parallel society alongside the formal economy of the Serbs, Montenegrins, and a few Albanians—which gave the leaders an impressive capacity for mobilizing collective action.

[52] Katzenstein, *Corporatism and Change*, 29.

[53] According to research on the *zadruga* in several areas of the country in the late 1960s by the anthropologist Zagorka Golubović and her students at the University of Belgrade, households of a hundred members were not rare in Kosovo (Golubović, personal communication). In contrast to the rest of the country, where the *zadruga* had died out, it appeared to be alive and well in the early 1970s among Albanian families in Kosovo. This basis for

Although this political network was not in a position to ignore federal rules on wages and benefits in the socialist sector (as full employment allowed the Slovenes to do), its political capacity to mount lasting sedition and to threaten a major rebellion became clear after 1981 when Albanian nationalists began another round in their efforts for political independence (at the time, for a separate republic). Although the response of Serbian and federal authorities to the internal war was to intensify political and police repression—arresting suspected troublemakers, closing schools, purging Albanian leaders from the party, and eventually imposing martial law in the province with federal troops—the provincial authorities' political capacity also enabled them to extract ever-larger compensatory grants and credits from the federal government. This bribe (or blackmail), when no one in the country was willing to accede to their political demands, reflected the redistributive foundations of Yugoslav politics, which would grant money rather than change the development strategy and the investment, foreign-trade, and price policies that were the cause of the unemployment. In addition, while politically counterproductive for Serbia and the country as a whole and in complete violation of both domestic and international declarations of human rights, this governmental response strengthened the internal political unity of Albanian nationalists that had originated in their economic condition outside the public sector of employment.

The Albanian uprising helped create popular support for nationalist intellectuals in Serbia, providing the glue of anti-Albanian sentiment for a social movement in Serbia of the East European type. When a similar alliance among Communist party leaders, parliamentary delegates, nationalist intellectuals, and popular sentiment in Slovenia made the choice for full independence, the crucial political moment came in a momentary alliance between Slovenia and Kosovo against Serbia. In February 1989, three months after the Slovene government had refused to participate in an all-Yugoslav referendum on a new federal constitution, arguing that this was a matter of republican and parliamentary authority and that it intended to institute a multiparty system instead, the Slovene Communist party leader Milan Kučan told a mass meeting—which took place in Ljubljana in support of striking Albanian miners at Stari Trg, Kosovo—that the strike was a defense of "AVNOJ Yugoslavia." The previous October, Slovenia had bargained for federal concessions on the constitutional amendments in exchange for approving the retraction of Kosovo's autonomy in Serbia's republican constitution. But by throwing down the gauntlet to Serbian nationalists, for whom the 1943 commit-

---

diversified economic strategies across many economic environments and countries became important in the 1970s and 1980s.

ment to a postwar federal state of six republics represented the disem-
powering of Serbia through the federal division of its nation, Kučan was
able to consolidate his support with the Slovene public, defend Albanian
political rights with the constitutional principles of territorial sovereignty
and the republics' and provinces' right of secession, and identify Serbia
and its leader, Slobodan Milošević, as the enemies of Slovene democracy
and of Yugoslavia. While this did not prevent Slovenia from voting in the
federal presidency to impose emergency rule over Kosovo in March 1989,
it did help push increasing numbers of Serb citizens into open support for
Milošević and Serbian nationalism.

Open nationalist confrontation between intellectuals and then governments in Slovenia and Serbia broke the rules of Kardelj's political system
and severed irreparably the alliances of convenience between Slovenes
and Serbs that had kept the country together under similar economic
conditions in the interwar period. Nonetheless, this political dynamic was
a result of governmental policies of international adjustment to those conditions, with the aim of restoring growth and preventing capitalist unemployment. It was a return to policies of global market integration and
Westernization, and the requisite changes in employment and in social
and governmental organization, that led to this confrontation and to the
systemic breakdown discussed in the final chapter of this book.

Chapter 10

BREAKDOWN

THE DECADE of the 1980s began with a shift in governmental policy, a return to an explicit program of marketizing, "efficiency-oriented" economic reform—the pure version of the Slovene model. It closed in 1989 with legislation ending the property rights of the socialist system and with a declaration by Slovenia's government of its intention to "dissociate" the republic from Yugoslavia. Economic crisis had led to political crisis, then to a siege of the federal government, and by 1991 to implosion and multiple civil wars.

There were competing explanations. President Tito's death in May 1980—which, fortuitously, occurred within months of this return to the IMF and economic reform—retrospectively confirmed the popular view that the system had been held together by his charismatic leadership and could not survive it. He himself had been inclined to tell foreigners, in Louis XV fashion, "after me, there will be chaos."[1] A second line saw an anticommunist revolution paralleling events throughout the region: a popular revolt from below demanding free enterprise and democracy and reflecting an ideological crisis—a loss of faith in communism and in the legitimacy of the ruling party. A third explanation repeated the political rhetoric that accompanied all "liberal" economic reform within the country, citing opposition to reform from Communist conservatives and centralist Serbian nationalists.

Instead, the period and its outcome are better understood as politics as usual in unusual times. The government attempted to adjust to changing international conditions in the same way it always had, but both the international and the domestic conditions on which the leaders' strategy had been based until then no longer held. The international system underlying their Faustian bargain of national communism was breaking down, and the society that had to respond with the employment adjustments had been transformed by their strategy of economic development since 1946 and by previous governmental policies of international adjustment.

---

[1] Personal communication from Pamela Harriman (1993), to whom Tito said this when she was staying as a guest at his villa near Split in 1979 after attending the funeral for Edvard Kardelj with her husband, Ambassador Averell Harriman, as official U.S. representatives. Lenard Cohen gives the political scientist's explanation: "Tito's death not only removed the principal symbol of the regime's legitimacy, but also the only public figure able to forge—or if necessary force—a working consensus among the increasingly divided political elite" (*The Socialist Pyramid*, 441).

With means used for decades to buy time ever less available, the political requirement of a new round of stabilization, structural adjustment, and systemic reorganization was not charismatic leadership. It now mattered crucially that the political institutions of the leaders' strategy could not, as was argued in chapter 7, perform their intended tasks of enforcing financial discipline, regenerating growth, and managing political conflicts over economic resources. In contrast to the thesis that there arose out of this economic crisis an ideological crisis and a popular, anticommunist movement for political change, the existing political system—for reasons discussed in chapter 9—could not generate such collective action countrywide, let alone an alternative policy more appropriate to the changed conditions. Whereas the outcome had elements of conservative reaction by Communist party leaders and elements of Serbian nationalism, the movement for systemic change was initiated by party leaders in the northwestern republics, primarily Slovenia, who were reacting to the threat to their power over capital that was posed by the institutional reforms being demanded by international creditors and by a policy of macroeconomic stabilization. They justified their opposition, moreover, with the system's ruling ideology. But in contrast to the liberal Marxist vision of the state critical to that ideology, the withering away of the Yugoslav state did not bring harmony.

Unemployment remained far down the list of public concerns in this period of economic and political crisis, politically invisible to the end—as it had been in the previous three decades. But the collapse of the Yugoslav socialist system cannot be understood without reference to it. As the Salais group found in the case of France at the same time, the institutions set up to deal with unemployment in the 1920s and 1930s retained their force into the 1980s, but they could no longer do the job.[2] The severity of the adjustment program had finally brought the threat of socialist unemployment—which meant a fall in social status and political rights—to the core of the most privileged in the public sector: the administrative stratum and its children. Their response was to attack the institutions of employment allocation for such positions—the party's influence over managerial positions, the affirmative action of national quotas, and the educational reforms. Republican governments assailed the governmental functions financed by the federal budget—the army, federal offices, military pensions, and welfare subsidies to local governments—so as to reduce the heightened burden on their incomes. Yet another shift in labor policy for international reorientation disproportionately affected poorer localities in the interior, where populations were more ethnically mixed and defense industries concentrated, and the result of the sectoral

---

[2] See Piore, "Historical Perspectives and the Interpretation of Unemployment."

and geographical biases common to such market reorientation (as discussed in chapter 8) had a pronounced territorial (and thus governmental) dimension. Finally, the approach to labor rationalization—to cut labor costs in the public sector and raise productivity by excluding "less productive" persons who had alternative, private sources of subsistence—introduced a new category of differentiation between public and private employment: a person's national identity. For all these reasons, the leaders' strategy toward unemployment led to nationalism and the destruction, rather than transformation, of the Yugoslav state.

INTERNATIONAL ADJUSTMENT

The pressure for change in Yugoslav economic policy and for political reform in the 1980s came as it had in the past—not from domestic political forces but from the international system. There were three crucial moments: in 1979, 1985, and 1989. To review the situation as discussed in previous chapters, problems began in 1979 when the trade deficit and skyrocketing foreign debt forced the government to draw emergency credit from the IMF. When the Croatian delegate Milka Planinc became prime minister in 1982, her mandate was to restore the confidence of foreign creditors. By 1982, negotiations with the IMF had also brought a three-year standby loan that was conditional on economic reform. A long-term stabilization program aimed not only to cut domestic demand sufficiently to reduce the foreign debt and trade deficit to manageable levels, but also to make the institutional changes necessary for more effective financial discipline and greater exports to Western markets in the long run. That is, external stabilization was once again aimed at lowering labor costs; in order to reduce inflation, improve the competitiveness of manufactured exports, increase production efficiency and invest the savings in technological modernization, and cut the drain of state expenditures (administrative employees, defense, and federal subsidies and transfers for local welfare and development credits) on productive investment.

Economic reform cut short the expansion in employment that occurred during the 1970s; after 1979, employment stagnated and public rhetoric emphasized the problem of "'overemployment." Unlike in the early 1960s, when the previous such economic reform took off and registered unemployment was around 6 percent, the official unemployment rate was now close to 14 percent. Concealed within this number were the structural character of unemployment, its unequal regional distribution, and the fact that more than half of the jobless were under the age of 25 and had engineering or university diplomas. Moreover, while the problem of unemployment had most affected the peasantry and unskilled workers in the 1950s, the pensioned officers and security police and the university students from poor (usually rural) origins in the 1960s, and rural migrants to the cities (especially Belgrade and Skopje) and the children of private artisans and military personnel in the 1970s, by the 1980s unemployment was threatening industrial workers and especially the children of the urban middle class. The prospect of additional unemployment thus faced the beneficiaries of socialism—industrial workers and budget-financed administrators, professionals, and office workers.

Unlike in 1947 or 1950, moreover, the proportion of the population working in agriculture had dropped dramatically, from 78 to 19.9 percent by the 1981 census. The pace of urbanization had been particularly rapid in the 1970s as individuals left rural areas and poorer towns in search of economic opportunity. The realism of the government's domestic solution for surplus labor—to send an increasingly urban strata of unemployed back to the villages and private-sector agriculture and trades—had thus been reduced substantially. The foreign demand for labor, the primary outlet for the rural labor surplus and children of private-sector parents, had been on the decline since 1975 (cutting the contribution of workers' remittances from one-half to only one-fourth of the trade deficit by 1979, for example).[3]

As in the previous periods when foreign-trade conditions required such economic reform (in 1949–52 and 1958–64), adjustment again began with substantial cuts in public investment, the leaders relying on internal savings and domestic sacrifices for recovery because a global recession was hindering export trade, Western protectionism was again on the rise, and Yugoslavia's terms of trade had deteriorated. Fresh capital was available only to refinance debt. But while there was a short-term economic recovery in 1985–86 and a resumption of lending to Eastern Europe by foreign banks, both of which allowed the government to abandon the IMF program in favor of more moderate sacrifice and some growth stimulus, foreign trade and domestic growth did not recover, unlike in the earlier periods. And instead of a reduction in international tensions or a military threat from the Warsaw Pact (which would favor conventional-war doctrine and decentralization to the territorial defense forces)—either of which would have been compatible with the ongoing cuts in the federal defense budget—the threat from NATO continued to mount, requiring attention to the air and naval defense of the seacoast and cities against a possible blitzkrieg attack and stimulating a new arms race in sophisticated weapons.[4] While a coalition of economic liberals and international credi-

[3] Debates in the federal assembly in 1975–76 gave vent to anger at the workers who were returning. See *Politika*, October 10, 1975, 7; and April 11, 1976, 8 (cited in Besemeres, *Socialist Population Politics*).

[4] Military expenditures in developed countries, particularly NATO members, peaked in 1987; in Yugoslavia (as in other developing countries, including Greece and Turkey), the high point was 1983 (Isaković, "The Balkan Armies," 2).

tors worked throughout the decade to restore value to the currency and the authority of financial indicators and monetary regulation, by 1985 a spiral toward hyperinflation had begun with double-digit inflation. The dinar was replaced in domestic transactions by foreign hard currencies, and by the end of 1989, a new prime minister had initiated a "shock-therapy" program aimed toward immediate stabilization and currency convertibility within the year.

The government did succeed, as it had in the 1960s, in negotiating a debt-refinancing package during 1983–85, which was coordinated by the U.S. State Department to support Prime Minister Planinc and the economic reform. But this help was premised on the cold–war assumptions of Yugoslavia' special status—on its Faustian bargain. By 1985, these assumptions were seriously challenged as a result of changes in Europe. The moves toward greater European integration after 1985—in the West with the program for EC monetary unification in 1992, and in the East with Gorbachev's economic reform in the USSR, the resumption of negotiations between the CMEA and the EC, and the move in CMEA trade away from long-term bilateral trade agreements toward world market pricing—suggested that the division of the world economy into separate markets, which had given Yugoslav manufacturers some flexibility, might end. While foreign economic opportunities emerged for Slovenia and Croatia in tourist and trade associations with neighboring countries, the perception of a rising military threat due to NATO's posture in the eastern Mediterranean prolonged the army's concerns for defensive self-reliance.

Throughout the country, but particularly in the northwest, the debates that originally shaped the leaders' strategy during the 1920s and 1930s, as discussed in chapter 2, were being revived. The issues of identity and boundaries, including international economic and military alliances, once again revolved around the question, "Who are we in Europe?" And because all regions and social groups were experiencing declining standards of living and rising unemployment as a result of the debt and trade crisis—even though differences were also being exacerbated—the questions of what common economic program and constitutional form would fit their heterogeneous conditions were also raised again. The answers given to the second question by the long-term stabilization program of 1983 and the party commission's report on constitutional reform (made public in 1985) still reflected the compromises that had characterized the political-economic mix of the Slovene and Foča models. But the pressure from the international system for homogenization and a choice for the Slovene model was intensifying.

By 1989, the collapse of the Warsaw Pact, the political revolution in Eastern Europe, and the termination of Yugoslavia's special relationship with the United States had removed the rationale for the country's neu-

trality and defensive strength in the Balkans. Although negotiations with
the EC and the European Free Trade Association had not been as expansive as the Yugoslavs had hoped, and although their neutrality had left
them as outsiders in the East-West rapprochement in security and economic relations, there was a consensus within the federal government
(including the army) in favor of westernization and liberalization. There
no longer seemed to be any purpose to the roles played in the past by the
Yugoslav People's Army, the nonalignment movement, and domestic production to support military independence. Even had Tito lived, the
global era in which he had created his primary function as a leader—his
international role in balancing among foreign blocs and his domestic role
in balancing between the institutions and political factions of the Slovene
and Foča models—was coming to an end.

The real question facing the government was how to manage politically
this task of implementing economic reform and policies for debt repayment. What domestic political resources would compensate for the loss of
the customary sources of temporary flexibility and maneuverability in the
strategy for economic growth—access to foreign capital and export markets and expulsion of labor into the private sector and agriculture?

The federal government proceeded to implement macroeconomic stabilization in the usual manner, introducing institutional reforms of the
public sector that would increase financial discipline and labor productivity by improving producers' economic incentives to use resources more
efficiently (to be profitable) and by strengthening the vertical links of control through monetary institutions and uniform (central) rules appropriate
to a single market. According to Yugoslav economic liberals, IMF economists, and foreign creditors, the extreme decentralization and segmentation of the economy in the 1974 constitution and subsequent legislation
on foreign borrowing and debt obligations had become counterproductive, causing constant delays, financial indiscipline, and an immobilized
government. Focusing first on the need to create a renewed capacity for
effective monetary policy in the hands of an independent central bank, by
1985 the IMF in particular began to insist on a strengthened federal administration as well.[5] By 1987, the IMF and World Bank placed priority
in negotiations for new loans on this political capacity for macroeconomic
policy, referring to "radical surgery" to remove the remaining socialist
elements inhibiting market allocation of capital and labor. The constitu-

[5] It is difficult to assess the influence of the IMF and other foreign creditors (such as the
Bank of International Settlements) in the political quarrels of the time, although the IMF's
credits and imprimatur were more critical than ever before. But it is perhaps ironic that,
after a half century of urging "decentralization" as a precondition for marketization (and even
using it as a code word for the same), the IMF and other Western advisers would now be the
proponents of a strong federal administration and a renewed economic center.

tional amendments embodying the resulting federal program called these institutions of a neoliberal market economy "functional integration."

The goal of monetary discipline and reduced inflation not only gave authority back to the National Bank (evident in, for example, its refusal to bail out indebted republican banks); it also required greater diligence with respect to the constitutional obligation to balance government budgets. Because federal tax revenues were declining as a result of trade liberalization and macroeconomic stabilization policies, the outflow of taxes from republican coffers increased. At the same time, the republics' revenues from businesses were being reduced by the supply-side incentives to enterprises (which cut their taxes and shifted financing of services to user fees and retail markets). A federal fiscal crisis necessarily implied a local fiscal crisis in all communes below the average in per capita GDP, and the question of whether republican governments would have to assume their welfare role was left open.

Finally, structural adjustment to Western markets was being facilitated by wage restrictions and new labor legislation giving managers a freer hand to hire and fire in the pursuit of commercial profits and lower labor costs. Industrial policy guiding credit policy and labor regulations reemphasized both demand for manufactured commodities in Western markets and technological modernization to compete with international standards of productivity. The employment program within the long-term stabilization policy brought the dual labor-sector strategy into the public sector, proposing to divide the country territorially into a high-wage, technologically advanced, export-oriented North and a low-wage, labor-intensive South. The search for foreign investment in a more competitive international environment soon began to drive labor legislation as well— to encourage foreign investment by removing the last limits on foreign ownership and all self-management curbs on managerial authority over labor. By 1988, legislation for privatization—private-property rights for foreign capital, the end of workers' rights to consultation, and the end of the division of firms into basic organizations of associated labor—was being enacted. World Bank recommendations were formulated into bankruptcy legislation.

The effect of new banking regulations was a political crisis in Croatia and Serbia when the debts of the largest depositors in their republican banks (particularly the oil producer INA and the steel industry at Smederevo) could be reduced only by spreading the debt among other depositors, thus socializing it across smaller firms within the republic. By 1987, the limits on new federal credit had spread the banking crisis to Bosnia-Herzegovina, where the largest conglomerate—Agrokomerc— attempted to recoup its losses with unsupported promissory notes bought by banks throughout the country, most heavily by the still-solvent, successful republican bank of Slovenia. A real-interest-rate policy (the last holdout of the federal authorities against the IMF stabilization program) made borrowing too costly for the small businesses that were the primary hope of the government's employment policy. Tax rebellions by republican parliaments, which simply refused to pay the federal government, led the latter to make up the shortfall in minimum legislated funds for the army and other federal obligations by ignoring limits on the money supply and accepting seigniorage.[6] Declining subsidies to local governments unable to pay their welfare commitments led to rising taxes on the already-squeezed private sector. Plant closures in declining industries (often in one-industry towns) brought the first real appearance of unemployment resulting from mass layoffs. By 1990, estimates of economic redundancies for the year (unemployment due to bankruptcies and closures, not including technological redundancies due to the introduction of new equipment or labor-saving procedures) numbered 445,000 in a labor force of 10 million (6.6 million in the public sector) and were expected to be even higher in 1991.[7]

THE POLITICAL CONSEQUENCES OF UNEMPLOYMENT

The economic success of this program, according to the government's strategy, depended on the renewed gains in productivity and profit from the rationalizing and commercially oriented reforms of the public sector of the economy and on the enforcement power of economic interest. The strategy, however, like all those based on classical or neoclassical models of economic growth, had always presumed not only a closed economy but full employment. In the presence of high unemployment, its consequence was to undermine the political bases of the system. Just as the political assumptions of the strategy intended, there was no politically mediated relation such as a political movement to protest the threat, and then the reality, of even higher unemployment or to propose alternative policies; the effect was direct.

The first effect of unemployment was on the capacity to enforce policy goals. The vertical links of monetary control and economic interest in Kardelj's political system ran on two tracks: the Communist party, and the parliamentary and conciliar representation of economic interests. The two enforcement mechanisms were the hierarchical discipline of the LCY and its affiliated organizations and their powers of persuasion with non-

---

[6] The relation between the federal budget and the money supply in such a hybrid economic system is a complex and technical subject. See Mates, "Inflation in Yugoslavia" and "Measurement of Government Budget Deficit"; and Commander, "Inflation and the Transition to a Market Economy."

[7] Crosslin, "Labor Related Programs in Yugoslavia," 8.

members to accept the rules established by experts and by social consultation as being in their collective, long-run interests; and the natural cooperation and "harmonization of interests" in deliberative councils and elected assemblies by delegates from self-governing, public-sector producers (republican governments, and enterprises) whose economic interest lay in rational choices on economic policy. Both mechanisms became ineffective as a result of unemployment.

As access to public-sector employment became ever more restricted and unemployment grew particularly among those aspiring to administrative positions (the category of "guaranteed salaries") because of their education, the authority of the party was increasingly undermined by its transformation into a gatekeeper for such positions—a form of craft union for managers and politicians. The reality of declining employment and increasing individual competition reinforced individual strategies to improve personal capital—skills and years of education, party activism, and networks of reciprocal personal obligations. Those who failed to obtain employment commensurate with their formal qualifications, as the principle of parity required, perceived an increasing competition between political and educational criteria. Resentment over the party's influence (or perceived influence) over high-status jobs intensified, while the ever more frequent resort to personal and political connections further corrupted application of the rules.[8] Within enterprises, where conflicts over incomes intensified with declining incomes and federal restrictions (the number of work stoppages and strikes rose 80 percent between 1982 and 1983; by 1987, 1,570 work stoppages involving 365,000 workers were reported officially),[9] relations between industrial workers and the party were also strained because the party's role in supervising wage restrictions placed it increasingly in the role of strikebreaker.[10] Since the program for marketization once again made professionals—no longer contractual employees of enterprises—respond to consumer demand for their services, they became an independent source of support, separate from the party hierarchy, for workers challenging a firing or wage regulations (as discussed earlier in regard to Slovene accountants and lawyers in the communes' labor courts). The adjustment to changing international conditions and for economic stabilization over the years by altering regulations on money, labor, and constitutional jurisdictions—and when the required adjustment could not occur fast enough, by further altering the rules and convoking new agreements—had begun to undermine the le-

---

[8] An especially popular proverb after the late 1960s was "A law exists so as to have a loophole" (Zakon postoji da ima rupu).

[9] Ramet, "Apocalypse Culture and Social Change in Yugoslavia," 9; Remington, "Yugoslavia."

[10] See Jovanov, "Pledoaje za dijalog o državi u socijalizmu," for this assessment.

gitimacy of those rules. Deprived of their essential attributes of stability and predictability, the rules lost authority; this could not help translating into degrading the authority of the party that was supposed to supervise their implementation. Citizens did not enjoy the security of enforceable rules applied regardless of station.

The party's commitment to the general interest—a commitment embodied in federal rules—was also strained by the party's "socialization" in an economy without full employment because its members depended for their livelihood on their workplaces.[11] The leaders' discipline over the party rank-and-file that was essential to the enforcement aspect of democratic centralism was so weakened as to appear nonexistent. In a period of sharply declining resources, the national committees (republican party organizations) that composed the LCY were in competition for the economic resources necessary to their patronage on jobs and credits within their republic.

The second means of enforcing policy goals—the commitment of representatives of republican governments and organizations to the agreements they had participated in making—thus began to unravel as well, because their responsibility for the economic development of their territory and its capacity for employment and rising standards of living depended on the resources they could keep from being taxed away or could capture from federal funds. The idea of a contractual state based on mutual interests, cooperation, and "harmonization" of differences (rather than the electoral choice of winners and losers) was in conflict with the economic reality. The role of parliaments was to decide issues over which the governments that were represented had fundamental differences of economic interest—budgets, taxes and transfers, and reform legislation. Unable to agree, plagued by delays in decision making and growing instances of vote trading, logrolling, and deadlock resolved only by temporary decrees of the federal cabinet, the federal government exhausted the patience and lost the confidence of an ever-growing number of Yugoslav citizens and foreign creditors. But the problem was not, as many observers insisted, that there was no consensus among political leaders. The problem was that political consensus was the only mechanism available for resolving these conflicts and making hard choices. Forced to come to some agreement by the risk of losing foreign credits or by the constitu-

---

[11] Although criticized by self-management advocates as well as Western economists, the party's practice of "sanitization"—the procedure for restructuring a firm to forestall bankruptcy—made some sense. The local government and party committee appointed a temporary outside manager who was, of course, part of the circulating stratum of the party's managerial cadres. Asked about the basis of his virtues in attempting to restructure the Economic Bank of Zagreb in 1982, Tomislav Badovinac emphasized his "independence" and therefore his freedom to make necessary but unpopular decisions (*Start* interview).

tional timetable according to which executive decrees would become law unless overridden by the assembly, the members tended to achieve "paper unity," as it was called—but it was agreement that could not be implemented.

A second effect of the leaders' strategy in a situation of high unemployment was to undermine the delicate balance in constitutional jurisdictions of the federal system because of the intensified competition among property owners to protect their capital assets from declining further. In this system of socialist property rights, those owners were the republican governments. Conflicts in federal-republican relations over implementing federal policy occurred in all three aspects of the reform that affected control over capital and employment—the recentralization of control over monetary policy, the banking system, and foreign exchange; the restrictions to cut excess demand, embodied in control on wages, salaries, and credit and in the rising taxation of republics to reduce the federal deficit; and the proposals to improve federal administrative capacity for effective macroeconomic policy. All three would deprive the republics and provinces of the sovereignty over economic resources that they had gained between 1968 and 1978. Although most republics opposed this diminution of sovereignty, because of the consequences for their resources for local investment and employment expansion (and therefore political power), their bargaining strength in this contest varied according to their level of unemployment and their flexibility in international adjustment to prevent unemployment from rising. While the decline of the federal party's international bargaining position gave the republican parties the illusion of more freedom to go their own way, that freedom would also depend on international leverage.

It was not the republics in the south with unemployment of 20 percent or more that took the political lead, but Slovenia—with full employment, labor shortages in industry, and only recent threats to living standards. Full employment in Slovenia meant that the costs of liberalization and technological modernization were much lower. The republic's extensive export orientation (in both Western and Eastern markets) and share of military industries also made it able to adapt more readily to changes in foreign economic policy, even when it opposed a particular policy as less favorable to Slovene interests. In a context of frequent labor shortages, government economists were more inclined toward comprehensive planning over Slovene space, taking into account social and cultural as well as economic factors in development policy; and Slovene unions and firms consistently objected to the maximums placed on wages. When stabilization policies required cuts in wages and social expenditures, the republican government tended to respond to workers' and managers' protests by ignoring the controls.

Although an export-oriented, marketizing reform would seem to have been most advantageous to the republics earning the largest export revenues in Western markets, the Slovene government objected strongly to its loss of rights to retain those revenues in Slovenia implied by the new requirements for depositing foreign exchange with the National Bank. Without that foreign exchange, Slovenia's program to raise worker productivity back to European standards and to resolve labor shortages in industry with imports of more-advanced equipment and technology was in danger. In view of declining standards of living in the republic and wage competition with foreign countries for professional labor, its enterprises began to campaign against the rules on redistribution of a portion of market earnings from "above-average" to "below-average" firms and localities to replenish solidarity funds for guaranteed wages and the federal fund for credits to less-developed republics. In their view, this redistribution was weakening the incentives to higher productivity in Slovene firms.[12] Objecting to federal taxation on similar grounds—that resources were being wasted on the less efficient or unproductive—the republican government began to protest against the visible beneficiaries of the federal budget: the federal army, the less-developed republics, and the federal administration.[13] (Firms receiving selective credits and subsidies, such as for export promotion, escaped criticism.) In a campaign directly counter to the reform proposals to restrengthen the federal administration, Slovene authorities began to press for erasure of the last vestiges of federal power—the YPA, the federal fund, the federal constitutional court, and all federal legislation that was in conflict with its republican legislation. An early step in this project was to prevent a political coalition from mobilizing against it; the Slovenes proposed transforming the federal League of Communists into a confederation along the lines of the conciliar federal government, with multiple-candidacy elections for the party's presidium and a shift in voting rules from majority principles to

[12] The research by Vodopivec to demonstrate this point originated in this political climate, most pronounced in Slovenia ("Productivity Effects of Redistribution in a Socialist Economy").

[13] In the first stages of the return to economic reform and emphasis on overemployment, in 1982, the press in Croatia and Slovenia paid much attention to the rapid growth of employment in the federal administration. According to an article in the Zagreb daily *Vjesnik* on September 8, 1982, the average annual increase in the previous "few years" was 16 percent, in contrast to the 2.5 to 4.5 percent for the country as a whole; and the party organization within federal offices held meetings (presided over by Slovene party leader Marjan Rožič) to reverse the growth, the "special concern" over the rising proportion of "employees with low qualifications," the hiring according to "personal interest" instead of by competition, the rising proportion of administrative categories in which "income is determined exclusively by established coefficients" regardless of "work contribution and results of labor," and the rising number of persons employed part-time, on contract, and after retirement (p. 5).

parity by republic and consensus (a system they called asymmetric federalism). By 1985, Slovenia was proposing that the country itself become a confederation of sovereign republics.

The turning point in Slovene demands came after 1985, when economic developments in Europe suggested new opportunities—independent of the federal government—for foreign capital, Western trade, and eventually, it was hoped, integration with central Europe. The resumption of commercial-bank lending to Eastern Europe gave profitable exporters a way to get around federal restrictions on foreign exchange; foreign investment began to flow into Slovenia and Croatia; and both Italy and Austria expanded economic ties eastward, including the opening of affiliates of four Austrian banks in Ljubljana. For the same external reasons that caused a decline in the bases of federal authority—the party's bargaining power in a cold-war environment that had given the government and firms access to Western capital markets, fuels, and multiple export markets—the Slovene party and government saw its options multiply. At the same time, the Slovene economy benefited less than in the past from federal government policies. The advantages to Slovene firms of federal price regulations that favored manufacturers had diminished substantially with domestic price liberalization, while the global decline in prices of primary commodities after their rise during the 1970s now made foreign raw materials cheaper than domestic products.[14] This, together with the decline in the strategic threat on Slovenia's own borders and its policy of keeping them populated with settled farmers, made it even easier to argue against the federal defense budget and federal protection of domestic producers of those raw and intermediate materials that were integral to the country's strategic policy of self-reliance. Moreover, even the Slovene unemployment rate had risen to 5 percent by 1985, although the government continued to focus on the problem of labor shortages.

The Slovene government was not alone in opposing the reforms in property rights to economic resources earned by producers on a republic's territory. The Croatian assembly was more vocal in refusing to support the defense budget with its tax monies. Vojvodina and Macedonia were as often leading the opposition to recentralization of the "planning system" (control over investment funds and industrial policy) and to the idea that the federal government should have some key economic functions necessary to a macroeconomic policy, even though their economies were dependent on domestic markets for both supplies and sales.[15] Conditions in the labor markets of all the republics and provinces except Slo-

---

[14] On the greater integration of the Slovene economy with international markets than with the domestic economy in the 1980s, see Bookman, "The Economic Basis of Regional Autarchy in Yugoslavia."

[15] Bookman contrasts the situation in Vojvodina with that in Slovenia (ibid.).

venia (and Kosovo, whose case was discussed in the previous chapter) at a time when unemployment could climb further gave them even more incentive to maximize the funds under republican control (including federal grants and budget subventions). Nonetheless, because their lack of independent resources in international capital and goods markets (in contrast to Slovenia) kept them dependent on the federal government's good relations with foreign creditors and its access to foreign capital and trade, the other republics and provinces could obstruct the changes but not initiate alternatives.[16]

The only exception was Serbia. While Slovenia was locked in a struggle with the federal government, the political economy of Serbia was in the opposite position. Whereas Slovenia had never had to take federal aid and its citizens felt penalized for their economic success, Serbia was also ineligible for aid, considered a more-developed republic. But its economic indicators in the 1980s told a different story. It had fallen below the average on all measures, but it was still paying federal taxes at rates assessed on those classified as more-developed; its GDP was declining, its unemployment rising, and a rural exodus continuing. The 1974 constitution had given its provinces control over their economies, including the federal grants-in-aid to Kosovo. Along the same lines as the federal proposals for increasing federal economic capacity, liberals in Belgrade were attempting to reverse the autonomies granted by the 1974 constitution and regain constitutional powers over the whole of the Serbian economy—in opposition to those in Vojvodina demanding continuing autonomy and an increasingly determined Albanian population demanding a separate republic for Kosovo. With unemployment in Belgrade above 25 percent, a large portion of it due to the rapid influx from rural areas and other republics after the late 1970s, proposals for a restrengthened federal administration were also clearly in Serbia's interest; Slovene proposals to end it entirely would, if enacted, add substantially to local unemployment rolls.

---

[16] This position was confirmed by the actions of Yugoslavia's foreign creditors in 1990–91 when the country's breakup seemed ever more likely. As late as May 1991, bankers urged support for the economic-reform program of the federal government (under Prime Minister Ante Marković) and therefore its capacity to service its foreign debt—the primary purpose of the reform. They insisted that the country should be held together because only with the export-earnings capacity of Slovenia and Croatia were the other four republics able to get reasonable credit terms in international capital markets; and without those two republics, banks had little prospect of having their outstanding loans to the other four republics paid. (personal communication from Charles Meissner, U.S. member of the debt-refinancing teams of the 1980s and early 1990s). But as early as 1982, when the IMF adopted a far more rigid policy toward conditionality than with previous programs, a member of the IMF's team in Yugoslavia proposed talking directly to republican leaderships because it was clear to him that the power of implementation lay with them. He was told that this was not possible because the IMF could negotiate only with sovereign authorities; he resigned from the mission (author's interview with that member).

In all the republics except Slovenia, however, the reform policies divided party leaderships, enterprises, and populations. There was no identifiable, single republican interest or party faction where economies combined socialist and private sectors; export and domestic-market orientation; links with Western, Eastern, and nonaligned markets; commercial and productive activities; and distinct areas of manufacturing and primary-commodity production. Because of the strong localization and territorial patterns of economic activity, party committees and leaders were directly affected by these differences. The most striking example was the "great silence" said to reign during the 1980s in Croatia. The party leadership had been elected after the 1972 political purge of party leaders accused of nurturing mass nationalism (the so-called mass movement, or *maspok*) in order to win Croatian interests at the time of the previous marketizing, Western-oriented reform in the 1960s. They were said as a group to fear the consequences of a repeat of the social turmoil and, in the case of some individuals, to represent areas of ethnically mixed (mainly Serb and Croat) population in the poor interior and the Dalmatian hinterland. But these areas were objectively suffering from the shift in policy and deindustrialization, with particularly hard-hit local industries—railroads, construction, timber, and mining. It was of some consequence politically that the areas with better prospects from the economic reform in central Croatia and Dalmatia had a more purely Croatian population, while the areas with declining prospects and severe unemployment had mixed populations. The same was true in Macedonia, although here as in Bosnia-Herzegovina, there was little difference among towns and areas of the republic in their exposure to serious economic hardship as a result of declining demand for their products, both at home and in export markets near collapse in the Middle East and in CMEA countries.

While Slovenia and, to a certain extent, Croatia were in the anomalous position from the point of view of economic reform of benefiting from market principles while refusing to abandon their rights of "economic sovereignty" to allow the free, countrywide, flow of labor, capital, and foreign exchange that a market economy implies, so the other republics and provinces sought compensatory federal expenditures and foreign credits for developmental infrastructure, capital industries, and welfare transfers to local budgets at the same time that they were resisting any loss of their constitutional authority over capital resources to the federal government. The result was constitutional deadlock and no sign of a compromise position.

A third political consequence of unemployment was its effect on the system's capacity to adapt politically to the requirements of new economic and social conditions. Whereas the Slovene rebellion against the constitutional aspects of the economic reform remained within the vertical hierarchy of Kardelj's institutional system—taking the path of territorial decentralization and republican sovereignty that the Slovene Communist party had been pursuing since 1934 to its final conclusion—the consequences of governmental policy were beginning to break down the rigid divisions of republican borders, just as they had during the liberal reforms in the 1960s until the constitutional amendments of 1967–71 interfered. For example, as early as 1982, the economic emergency led Planinc to insist that she be allowed to ignore the rule on ethnonational parity in cabinet appointments; Slovenia traded concessions on the reform in 1985 for an exception to the constitutional order of rotation for prime minister, giving the post to Branko Mikulić from Bosnia; and by 1986 the IMF had successfully pressured the government to adopt a majority-decision rule in place of consensus for the board of governors of the National Bank. As part of a major reform of defense policy, Minister of Defense Branko Mamula redrew the borders of military districts in 1985 to cut across republican lines, and the federal army stepped up a campaign to reintegrate the major infrastructural systems of the country (transportation, communications, and energy). There were discussions in the mid-1980s (in which all republics except Slovenia participated) about establishing a countrywide core curriculum, with selections from all national literatures, for primary and second education, in order to break down educational barriers to labor mobility and to improve awareness and appreciation of cultural pluralism. Regional development groups to regenerate areas devastated by industrial decline or shifts in investment priorities began to form, such as the one made up of local planning authorities and economic experts in the *krajina* (an area shared by Croatia and Bosnia-Herzegovina). By 1988, workers from large industries in Croatia, Serbia proper, and Vojvodina had taken their wage protests out of their factories and republics to the doors of the federal assembly.[17]

Moreover, while full employment in Slovenia had created marketlike conditions and the beginnings of pluralist politics, elsewhere the extent of rising unemployment and falling wages, savings, and household incomes, as well as the ever-harsher prospects of international adjustment, was such that one could imagine the fall of political barriers as well in a counterforce of Jacksonian character against the Madisonianism of the smaller, richer states of Slovenia and Croatia. Throughout the country, economic hardship, a ceiling on upward social mobility, stricter criteria for employment in the public sector, rising internal economic migration, and cultural shifts to justify keeping women and youth at home were bringing a

---

[17] Carter discusses the attempts by party organizations to obstruct workers' efforts to create cross-republican alliances in the 1960s (*Democratic Reform in Yugoslavia*, 164–67, 204–7).

profound social upheaval. There was a kind of Brownian motion of ex-cluded groups—either discarded politically in some previous purge or never given entry into the public sector—though there were no obvious signs of how they might coalesce. The deaths of Kardelj in 1979 and Tito in 1980 removed the last taboos on political speech and reactivated voices calling for a reassessment of the war and of those purged after the war—from Archbishop Stepinac in Croatia to the many Serbs and Mon-tenegrins charged as Cominformists in 1948–50 or forced into retirement as generals in 1958–64 and members of the security apparatus in 1966. Unemployed youth in many regions gave support to millenarian and fun-damentalist religious movements and to right-wing ideas (such as revivals of Chetnik, Ustasha,[18] and Nazi memorabilia and loyalties). Churches be-came more politically active. Unemployment pushed many urban dwellers into "gray" or even criminal activities, and it increased tensions between long-time residents (favored by Kardelj's policy of settled com-munities) and newcomers (such tensions dated back to the population resettlements on the northern plains in 1947, but they had shifted to the cities through individual migrations since then). Signs of social disloca-tion, "strains of pessimism, gloom, resignation, escapism of various kinds," and "critical reevaluation . . . of the central underlying myths and heroes of the state" appeared everywhere.[19]

Nonetheless, such a political revolution from this social upheaval would have to overcome the segmentation by status, the republican divisions, and the personalistic, familistic, and informal channels for coping that resulted from the system of employment. Any new arrangement required new political forms. But political response to economic difficulty was still institutionalized around the system's two forms of political action: redis-tributing people among existing jobs or between property sectors, and redefining rights to assets and incomes in the direction of greater auton-omy (with the obligation of balancing accounts and in the hope that there would be a resulting initiative in increasing those assets). This was what Yugoslavs had learned to do. But this system also favored the republics, enterprises, or individuals that had higher initial capital assets. Those who organized the political path after 1985 were not the unemployed but the employed who feared unemployment. In the society described in this book, this fear was the fear of property owners that they would lose value and status. Their fight was organized around a language of rights.

The first of the two arenas of this political fight, against redistribution of

[18] The Chetniks were the armed bands formed around Serbian royal army units during World War II; the Ustashe were the elite paratroopers of the Croat fascist state. Both fought against the Partisans.

[19] Ramet, "Apocalypse Culture and Social Change in Yugoslavia," 3, 15; for a good sam-ple of political and cultural manifestations, see 3–26, passim.

labor in response to international conditions, was centered in the core of the public sector—the core of privilege. Even more than in the 1960s, the economic reform in the 1980s was an attack on "nonproductive" expenditures, budgetary financing, and administration of any kind outside the enterprises—for defense, local subsidies, social services. Efforts to rationalize and regulate through governmental policy in the 1970s had led the party to assert influence over managerial and professional appointments, to the growing resentment of those whose education did not guarantee them employment of the status they expected, as was discussed above. Such efforts also had led to educational reform, which by the 1980s (as in the 1960s) had moved from elementary and secondary education to the universities. This reform struck at the heart of the middle class and its capital—its individual bases in formal education and its ability to pass on this inheritance (its cultural capital) to its children.[20] The major reform of secondary education after the late 1970s was, in effect, an attempt at social revolution from above at a time of declining opportunity. The abolished *gimnazije* had been a preserve of social privilege and exclusive access to university enrollment. The extension of general education to youth in vocational schools, giving them the equal right to enroll in universities and putting all youth on the same track of universal and vocational training, became a lightning rod for the discontents of urban middle-class parents (although the competition over enrollments in preferred specializations still benefited those with cultural capital and created a new hierarchy of elite and less-privileged schools and students).[21] By the early 1980s, limits were placed on university enrollments in liberal-arts and medical faculties because such professionals were already in surplus. Professional parents saw these limits as political discrimination against the humanistic intelligentsia; similarly, they viewed the expanded opportunities for university education in new regional universities as the party's attempt to dilute standards and their status.[22]

This urban middle-class discontent was also manifest in an increasingly open conflict between the civilian and military halves of public-sector "nonproductive" employment. The largest component of the remaining federal budget after 1958–64, the federal army and defense industry were obvious objects of criticism, while the army was also facing the need to

---

[20] This was a widespread phenomenon, not limited to Yugoslavia. Hirsch identified it for Western Europe in the 1970s, in *Social Limits to Growth;* Dahrendorf returned to it in the 1980s in *Life Chances.*

[21] In Slovenia, however, the bureau of education soon quietly reversed the reform because of parents' protest and experts' evaluations.

[22] On the other hand, students from rural areas who failed their course exams (held all at once at the end of the year, in European tradition), assumed they were victims of an explicit policy to cut unemployment by returning them to their farms (even if they owned no land, as parents complained to me in Vojvodina).

rationalize resources without endangering defense preparedness. Army leaders sought several reforms in their concern about the declining quality and availability of military recruits,[23] about the difficulty of attracting Slovenes and Croats to the officer corps because pay was higher in civilian jobs in their economies, and about the economic costs of conscription. In the early 1980s, young men were required to complete their military service before attending university. By 1985, there was a shift to the idea of a professional army (as in many other countries at the time). Within the army, there was a growing threat of rebellion among the middle ranks of officers, whose salaries and benefits were declining; a majority of them were of Serb nationality, and they began to resent the limits on their prospects of promotion and higher salaries set by the rules on national quotas and proportions for senior officers. Outside the army, a primary focus of youth political activity in Slovenia (and to a certain extent Croatia) was a campaign against the army and conscription—to cut the defense budget on pacifist grounds, to gain the right to conscientious objection, and to realize rights to use one's own language in the army and be posted at home.

The second arena of political response to the threat of economic decline, the struggle for autonomy over capital, was dominated by the republics in response to the institutional reforms concerning money and credit and the constitutional reform that followed. This struggle was led by Slovenia, which had the most to lose and the greatest organizational and economic resources for the fight. The language used by its party leadership, as well as by enterprises resisting taxation of market profits and by most republican assemblies, was one of rights and restoration of what they considered rights to fight recentralization and redistribution. Federal taxation was seen as governmental interference with the constitutional rights of enterprises and republics to "self-management" and "sovereignty"—an interference, it was insisted, with the "freedom" of enterprises and of "workers." The Slovene government even rejected the defense minister's proposal to resolve their mutual financial conflict with autonomy by extending self-management to defense, creating a separate, autonomously managed defense budget with a legislated portion of the income tax.[24]

[23] The concern over foreign emigration and loss of a large cohort of youth was particularly manifest in the defense establishment for this reason, although the support of Croat guest workers in Germany for Croat nationalism in the 1960s and the ability of rebels from the Croat community in Australia to penetrate into Bosnia and attempt to spur an armed uprising in 1972 also influenced the military's perception of national security. Émigrés played a similar role in 1990–91 funding the election of a nationalist to the Croatian presidency in 1990 and providing arms, mercenaries, and financing for the war that began in 1991.

[24] The compromise established in 1985 was to divide the federal budget into three parts: one for the army, one for export incentives and material reserves, and one for all other beneficiaries. In November 1986, however, the government agreed to finance the federal budget from federal revenues alone, breaking all remaining links to the republican budgets.

Thus, this political fight, contrary to the claims that it was a democratic revolution against the Communist system and the result of the party's loss of ideological legitimacy, was in fact led by Communists to justify the claims of property owners on economic resources in terms clearly reflecting the ideological hegemony achieved by the parties in the more industrialized northwest in the 1930s. The language of the conflict reveals how firmly the ideology underlying the party's original strategy (as was argued in chapter 9) had been implanted. Using the language of productivity, it was claimed that monies transferred through the federal fund were employed less productively in the southern republics than they were in the north or when northern enterprises invested directly.[25] Such transfers should be assessed in terms of the "differential contribution of each republic" to gross domestic product and the extent to which the "survival" of each republic was aided or endangered (*ugrožen*). The proliferating autonomous public services and utilities were "bloated bureaucracies," and military salaries were an "unproductive" drain on the economy. Even the program of the Communist party leadership in Serbia during the renewed process of constitutional reform after 1985—which aimed to reunify Serbia by ending the near-republican status of its two provinces and to increase its influence on federal policy, by means of mass demonstrations that brought political allies to the party leaderships in its provinces and in Montenegro—was called by Milošević an "antibureaucratic revolution," as Tito and Kidrič had called the firings in ministries aimed at stabilization in 1950. And although this attempted Jacksonian revolution stayed within the Madisonian rules and used methods similar to those of Croatian nationalists in the 1960s, Slovenia and Croatia declared it to be against the constitution.

The final political consequence of unemployment was its effect on the country's ability to continue to manage unemployment itself. The constitutional assignment of labor questions to the republics in 1946 survived all subsequent changes in policy and institutional reform. As discussed in chapter 8, the territorial decentralization of the economy and vertical lines of the formal political system, property rights, and capital flows had created and maintained separate labor markets within each republic. Individuals emigrated to cities or different republics to improve their prospects, because those prospects depended on the budgets that financed particular employments. The politics of employment and unemployment revolved within the republics and localities.

As in the leaders' strategy for economic growth, protecting achieved status required more than autonomy over capital; it was also necessary to

---

[25] On the inaccuracy of this charge, see Connock, "A Note on Industrial Efficiency in Yugoslav Regions."

adjust the supply of labor to declining demand with reorganization and downsizing of the public sector and with expulsion of the less productive back to the land, to the family, or into emigration, even if only temporarily. The "realism" (to use Claus Offe's term) of the last federal resolution on employment, in 1983—which, as part of the long-term stabilization program, deferred until the twenty-first century any attempt to employ those now unemployed—was up to the republics and localities to implement, for labor fell within their jurisdiction. The political methods these authorities chose for implementing a "realistic" approach dealt the final blow in the process of systemic breakdown—an exclusivist nationalism that destroyed the country.

In the early 1980s, even before the Slovene campaign to reduce the YPA to "national armies," Slovenia's government sought to send home Bosnian and ethnic Albanian workers and to restrict entry by new migrants. The planning bureau argued, on the basis of research studies, that their number had reached the maximum of social tolerance for non-Slovenes and that the economic costs of additional infrastructure and social benefits for any newcomers would lower standards of living in Slovenia.[26] But Slovene authorities justified this decision on the grounds that their "national distinctiveness" and cultural identity were "threatened."[27]

In Serbia, the political rebellion in the province of Kosovo that began again in 1981 expelled many Serbs and Montenegrins, who left because of fear or pressure. Combined with the growing immigration of Serbs from other republics (particularly from smaller towns with declining industry in Bosnia-Herzegovina), who sought economic opportunities in Belgrade or claimed refuge from job discrimination as Serbs, these waves of migration threatened to bring lower living standards and even higher unemployment in Serbia proper. It was not long before such immigration became a focus of the discontents of middle-class professionals and intellectuals who attributed Serbia's declining economy and status to the (con)federal Titoist system, which had, in their view, followed a policy of "divide and conquer" against the Serbian people since the AVNOJ principles for a federal constitution declared in 1943.[28] The complex struggle over the autonomy of the provinces and over Albanian rights in Kosovo

[26] Non-Slovene labor made up about 25 percent of the republic's labor force at the time. This measure of "social tolerance" was also popular at the time in France, where it was said that the proportion of North African immigrants in a town should not exceed 20 percent.

[27] Author's conversations with officials and social scientists in Ljubljana. Such language also pervaded the journals, press, and politicians' speeches by 1986–87; for a typical example, see Foreign Broadcast Information Service, Eastern Europe, for April 17, 1987, I4.

[28] A committee of the Serbian Academy of Sciences and Arts wrote a Serbian "national program" in 1986, though it was not published until 1993 (except for excerpts from a draft, on which much speculation about a political program was based; see "Memorandum SANU"). Slovene opposition intellectuals issued theirs in 1987.

could not be separated from the tendency to reconstruct republican interests as "national interest," any more than this tendency could be avoided
in Slovenia. The Albanians' demand for a separate republic was a demand
for their "national rights to self-determination," and in Serbia proper
there were rising calls to defend the "honor" and restore the "long-
aggrieved rights" of the Serb nation.

In Croatia, the assembly openly joined Slovenia in the fight against the
federal government and the army, casting it as a struggle for Croatian
national rights. The army's pressures for the reintegration of basic infrastructure and for a restrengthened Communist party, and the proposals
from the federal government and the IMF to strengthen macroeconomic
administration, were identified with what were called the historical "centralism" and "unitarism" of Serbs. Serbs in Croatia were said to have been
privileged in governmental employment in the police, army, and local
administration, so that cuts in government bureaucracies and a shift of
resources away from the ethnically mixed interior to central Croatia and
Dalmatia began to be justified with an anti-Serb campaign in the same
way that the purge of party leaders had been in 1949–50.

Even in Bosnia-Herzegovina, demographic shifts in the ethnic composition of local communities as individuals left economically declining villages and towns for work abroad (a pattern more characteristic of Bosnian
Croats) or for schooling and possibly work in other republics (more characteristic of Bosnian Serbs, who tended to go to Serbia) had also changed
the ethnic composition of those who held local political and administrative
positions, resulting in growing ethnic tensions. And just as in the 1960s,
the higher birthrate of Muslims in Kosovo, Macedonia, and Bosnia-
Herzegovina provided an excuse for the prejudice and scapegoating that
arose from resentments over job competition and declining status and
income.

The regulation of statuses for the productive use of labor and the politics of exclusion from the public sector to protect the rights of those who
remained there culminated with the alteration of citizenship itself in
1989. Obliged to bring their republican constitutions into harmony with
the intended 1988 economic-reform amendments to the federal constitution, republican assemblies in Slovenia, Croatia, and Macedonia redefined their republics as states of their majority nation. The rights of
national self-determination and equality that adhered to individuals'
membership in any constituent nation within the country, regardless of
residence, and the requirement for national quotas in governmental positions were de facto abolished. To confirm this final step toward full "national sovereignty" of the republics, Slovenia and Croatia held democratic
elections in April 1990, and those who campaigned on nationalist plat-
forms gained pluralities. Particularly blatant about this goal was the na-

tionalist campaign of Franjo Tudjman, a retired general of the federal army and former Communist, who won the Croatian presidency by combining an anticommunist platform with anti-Serb rhetoric. Equating "decommunization" with "de-Serbianization" of government employment, he rallied political support behind the banner of job dismissal, to purge everyone associated with the Communist regime—including not only party members but any Serbs as well.

The nationalist exclusion of people relegated by the constitutions to minority political status became the goal of rewritten citizenship rights in all the republics, in some more openly than in others. Instead of the liberal political goal of transforming the delegate system—replacing the system of representation of producers with a state of "equal citizens and workers" and the principle of one person, one vote, which many proposed in 1987–89—"national preference" in jobs and housing won out. As each republic's economic capacity to guarantee subsistence to all its citizens declined, the group receiving full citizenship rights diminished further.

CONCLUSION

As with the capitalist system it aimed to replace, the underlying contradictions of the Yugoslav reform-communist system and its main lines of sociopolitical conflict cannot be understood apart from unemployment and the particular manifestation of its threat. This book does not argue that socialist unemployment played the same economic or political role as does capitalist unemployment. But its causes and characteristics do reveal the primary mechanisms and dynamic by which socialist Yugoslavia functioned—and declined. The politics of socialist systems, and of their postcommunist transition, mirrored their economic system. Under social ownership of productive capital, individuals' employment defined their personal identities, economic interests, and social statuses; social and political conflict, competition, and collective action were organized according to the criteria for individuals' access to employment and the criteria for financing those jobs.

The social and political system that Kardelj constructed (and repeatedly reconstructed) according to a particular ideology of economic growth and its approach to the use of human labor—called in this book the Slovene model—presumed full employment. It could not function as intended under unemployment. As real and threatened unemployment increased during the 1960s and especially after the mid-1970s, the key elements of the system began to crumble from within. The vertical lines of authority—the LCY, federal rules and regulations, and the banking system—were ineffective in enforcing policy decisions; in the presence of unemployment or its threat, loyalty to an employer or potential employer—workplace, locality, or republic—took precedence. When there was a threat of unemployment, with its immediate loss of status and all that that entailed, a state based on the cooperation and discipline of mutual interest among political representatives of autonomous producers and property owners (in economy and government) was not conducive to—indeed, was likely to be in conflict with—the "financial discipline" of "economic interest" of the system of self-managed budgets. The legitimacy of the LCY as the representative of the common interest suffered irreparably from its transformation into a craft union for managers, as well as from competition between political and educational routes for managerial and professional ("middle-class") employments in the public sector. And the delicate constitutional balance of the federal system and the rights of national equality could not survive the effect that financial reforms and the sustained fiscal crisis surrounding debt repayment had on the capacity of republican governments to employ and to negotiate wages.

By the early 1980s, the official solution to unemployment itself was reaching its limit—the institutions of family, farm, schooling, and foreign migration could not absorb the level of unemployment generated, and the society to which this approach was adapted had been irrevocably changed by the program of economic growth. Yugoslavia was no longer an agrarian, industrializing country. People could still talk about "going back to the farm," but this psychological reassurance (if it was applied to oneself) or complacency (if it was applied to others) had little basis in reality. Kardelj's model of stable socialist communities combining the productive incentives and distributive solidarity of industrial wage earners and small property owners (the alliance of workers, peasants, and free professionals) applied to an ever-diminishing number of people, and the social protections of that model (unemployment was still defined as a social question, not an economic one) no longer served a society characterized by rapid urbanization and internal economic migration. There were instead a growing urban underclass of unskilled workers and rural migrants; an ever-larger stratum of managerial and professionally trained people seeking public-sector, nonindustrial employment; and deindustrialization in poorer regions. Although no political organization of the unemployed occurred, nor was there any such organization around the problem of unemployment, the result was an escalating social upheaval of revolutionary proportions by the late 1980s.

Declining prospects, lower relative incomes, and increased competition for employment commensurate with educational achievement and status expectations all led to open and growing resentment within the established managerial, professional, and urban white-color stratum against the system's policies of redistribution. Manifest in many groups, across social layers and regions, this unorganized discontent at public, intended (*namenjeni*) redistribution was focused on several fronts: the educational reform, which appeared to threaten privileged social position; the privileges of party membership, the LCY's presumed control over high-status jobs, and its network of informal connections and aid; the taxes and contributions from earnings that went to local solidarity funds for guaranteed wages and to the federal budget for the army and for credits and subsidies to poorer localities and less-developed republics; and the national quotas for government employment. Demographic shifts, particularly the rising birthrate of Muslims in Kosovo and Bosnia-Herzegovina, evoked fears and prejudice from many sides. In place of Kardelj's settled communities with their sense of proprietorship, latent conflicts rekindled into open tension between longtime residents and migrants—recent migrants in urban areas and earlier migrants in towns and villages. And in the private sector of rural, unskilled, and unemployed persons, there was resentment at their second-class status and sense of inferiority—a resentment waiting to be exploited.

Despite the exhaustion of the approach to unemployment and this growing social discontent, there was not yet pressure for the system to adapt politically. Those with the greatest economic and organizational resources could still benefit from demands for change along the lines defined by the existing economic system and its ideology: further autonomy over income, justified as the right of those who earn (and who have a direct interest in financial accountability) to decide on the allocation of income; and further rationalization of "nonproductive" labor by cutting governmental expenditures (personnel) and expelling less-productive workers into the private sector. Others continued to pursue individual and familial strategies for gaining employment, with its status and benefits. No political counterforce was being generated to demand changes that might bring action on unemployment. Instead, the stabilization program to repay debt took the final step of abolishing the entire system of protections against unemployment—the rules against mass layoffs and dismissal for reasons of economic rationalization; the limits on the free sale of land and hiring of labor that were intended to provide guaranteed smallholdings for farmers and artisans; and the guaranteed minimum wage.

And despite the economic failure with regard to full employment and guaranteed subsistence, the political system of Kardelj's Slovene model had survived intact: demands for change and reform aimed to strengthen the hierarchical organization of political and economic power, the vertical lines of communication and conflict between federal and republican political authorities, and the states' rights and property rights of territorially organized governments and firms and their contractual relations. This perpetuated the dominance of relations between international creditors and the federal government, between federal and republican governments, and between republican and local authorities, as against the horizontal, cross-republican, and nonofficial associations and lines of communication that are more common to a market economy (and so-called civil society). Competition remained focused on *rights* to income and economic assets. Although the prevailing economic ideology was antagonistic to the state, periodic rounds of liberalization led not to a market-based political system but to ever-greater decentralization, regionalism, and disintegration. The logical conclusion of this process was the dissolution of the country itself.

EPILOGUE

In 1989–90, the cold war ended. The conditions supporting socialist Yugoslavia's Faustian bargain went with it. It was historically appropriate that the bargain, contracted in the events surrounding Germany's division in 1948–49 and Stalin's retreat from the reform option, should lose its raison d'être at the time of Germany's reunification and Gorbachev's reforms.

Within Yugoslavia, the debate on economic and political reform between 1982 and 1990 had, ominously, returned to the original bases of political unity in the Partisans' wartime alliance—the struggles for national independence and against foreign economic exploitation. "Nations" were "threatened" with cultural extinction and linguistic contamination; and they were "suffering" from the economic "exploitation" of others. But this time, the nation was a republic or constituent people. The Slovenes suggested replacing the slogan "brotherhood and unity" with "togetherness" and "asymmetric federation." The rhetoric of mutual accusations prepared people mentally for civil war, instead of a war of resistance against the outside. Nationalism—this time of independent states—turned inward, as if in an attempt to destroy all that had been accomplished in forty-five years.

A war did indeed follow, of vicious proportions. Contrary to the commentary by foreign journalists and politicians, which guided external policy and public opinion on the wars in the former Yugoslavia, the historical memory of antagonisms among its separate nations was at best a tertiary factor—and it dated only to World War II. Although the argument in this book did not foresee a violent outcome of the path it analyzed—evergreater disintegration for reasons of economic ideology and international adjustment—it does portray the real nature of the conflict. Even in the country's dissolution, the Slovene and Foča models defined the parameters. On the one hand was the internationally negotiated retreat of the federal army from Slovenia and the recognition of its secession from the federation (taking "decentralization," autonomy over capital, and sovereignty over economic assets to their logical conclusion). On the other hand was a bloody civil war, unleashed by politicians and persons employed by public budgets and feeding off the disconnected but mounting resentments (described in chapter 10) that raged among secessionists, sections of the army, groups claiming national preference, and old and new settlers in the farming villages of Croatia where Partisans from "passive regions" had been resettled after World War II, as well as in the poor, deindustrializing interior of Croatia and Bosnia-Herzegovina (which had been dependent on the production of primary commodities, infrastructure, and defense industries).

In place of the uneasy symbiosis of the Slovene and Foča models that had lasted nearly half a century, international conditions finally forced a choice. The requirements of economic reorientation westward to repay foreign debt and then the loss of Yugoslavia's strategic role between the superpowers together forced a process of homogenization. But except in Slovenia, the internal political economies of the federal units were not homogeneous. Moreover, until a new European (or international) defense and economic order evolved to define the country's new options and provide the basis for a lasting, stable outcome in the region, domestic politicians, regardless of political camp, were continuing to take the initiative along the lines of strategic behavior in the socialist period: demanding political autonomy over economic assets and redistributing persons among jobs and sectors.

With the socialist constitutional and welfare systems removed from the reform-communist system, however, the national layer of the wartime alliance was free to operate unfettered. Political action centered on the demand for national control over territory and the physical expulsion or reduction in status of persons of other nationalities. In the wars over land and local community that resulted, it was predictable, according to the analysis in this book, that the latent conflict of the underlying division of socialist Yugoslavia—between the public and private sectors of employment—would explode into class war.

It is commonly said that the end of the cold war in eastern and central Europe, including the disintegration of Yugoslavia, was the result of an ideological crisis of disillusionment. In fact, the economic ideology of reform communism was triumphant. In the midst of war and mutual accusations of genocide, aggression, and destruction of a country, governments in Slovenia, Croatia, the federal republic of Yugoslavia (consisting of Serbia and Montenegro), and Macedonia were all implementing an identical macroeconomic program—a business-oriented, orthodox stabilization policy to cut domestic demand (incomes, jobs, and public expenditures). Their primary problems remained foreign debt and effective foreign-trade and exchange-rate policy. The leaders elected in 1990 were still in power in every state in 1994.

The same could be said of postcommunist economic policy throughout Eastern Europe. Despite the introduction of competitive elections, the alternation in power between renamed communists and liberals, with their respective approaches to economic growth and to labor, was remarkably reminiscent of the alternations in Yugoslavia in response to changing international conditions chronicled in this book. The breakup of Czechoslovakia and the Soviet Union followed paths nearly identical to the Yugoslav one of the constitutional conflict, demands for national sovereignty over economic assets, and conflict over macroeconomic policy that accompany socialist economic reform.

Moreover, the successful exit of Slovenia (in contrast to the rest of the country) and its pluralistic politics made possible by full employment and a favorable trading position was not a complete victory for the Slovene model. The conditions that made the Foča model a constant factor in Yugoslavia began to confront Slovenia as an independent state. Whereas unemployment had been below 2 percent in 1988, it increased fivefold between 1989 and 1991 and stood at 14 percent by mid-1993.[1] This reflected the loss of much of Slovenia's former internal (Yugoslav) market for goods, an uncertain international position economically, and substantial governmental defense expenditures to build a new army and appeal politically to local nationalists. In response to the influx of fifty thousand displaced persons and refugees from Bosnia-Herzegovina[2] (though this was a small number compared to the more than half a million refugees in both Croatia and Serbia), there was a rise in antiforeigner activities; and a far-right, xenophobic, nationalist party won 10 percent of the vote in the elections of November 1992, which also saw a loss by the anticommunist coalition to the former Communists.[3] In September 1992, the Slovene government closed its borders to further refugees.

To an even greater extent in Croatia and Serbia, the consequences of insistence on "states' (national) rights" included the economic drain of substantial defense budgets and the growing power domestically of the police and army. In Croatia, unemployment was being kept at bay by the fact that mobilized soldiers were not seeking work. But it was only a matter of time before demobilization would confront the government with the choice between dealing with a serious social crisis and formulating a real policy toward unemployment. The war protected the government's convenient segregation between the ministries of economic technocrats negotiating with international creditors and the ministries and lobbies of the defense establishment. But eventually there would be either confrontation or accommodation between these local versions of the Slovene and

[1] Milan Andrejevich, RFE/RL Daily Report, no. 166, August 31, 1993, citing a study by the respected Economics Institute in Ljubljana (renamed the Bajt Institute after its founder, Aleksandar Bajt).

[2] Zerdin, "Tokens of Slovene Sovereignty," 4, citing data from UN High Commissioner for Refugees' Office of the Special Envoy for former Yugoslavia, External Relations Unit, Zagreb.

[3] The recipient of this 10 percent (well above the 5 percent minimum for parliamentary representation), Zmago Jelinčič, included in his campaign speeches the accusation that Bosnian refugees were fleeing economic deprivation rather than war (*Financial Times*, December 8, 1992, 2).

Foča models. Yet, in contrast to other areas of the former Yugoslavia, Slovenia and Croatia were being offered relatively favorable international conditions.

In the meantime, as war continued in Bosnia-Herzegovina, threatened to resume in Croatia, and had not yet been avoided in Macedonia and Serbia, the autonomist impulse was still alive. As nationalist governments centralized power and economic control in the new capitals, they were countered by regionalist movements.

In neither economic ideology nor political response had there been much change as a result of the end of socialist Yugoslavia. Despite the terrible tragedy of war in the name of nations, there was only a holding action until a different approach to labor and employment could be found.

Appendix

STATISTICAL DATA

THE RAW DATA used to create the figures in this book are presented here. Each table of data corresponds to the figure(s) of the same number (for example, table 6-1 corresponds to figure 6-1). All the data were gathered by the Federal Bureau of Statistics, which was created by Ante Novak at the request of Boris Kidrič in June 1948 and which maintained a consistently high standard of professional expertise. Unemployment series were hampered, however, by changes in measurement and definition, and the analysis of rates of change is hindered by the absence of household surveys on unemployment and by the fact that data on the population and on the actively employed are available only for census years. Statistical-yearbook data and the data of the OECD and the ILO (International Labor Organization) are not consistent, but the differences are not substantial enough to affect interpretation; I chose to stay with the longer series and more comprehensive data of the Federal Bureau of Statistics. In some cases, I have taken advantage of the hard work of gathering and analyzing the bureau's raw data that was done so carefully by economists Jože Mencinger, Miloš Macura, and Emil Primorac; and I am grateful for their generous assistance at several stages in this work. Dan Turner did the tedious work of putting my many piles of confusing data into computer files and performed what remain to me miracles in transforming them into graphs and tables.

APPENDIX TABLE 6-1 AND 9-3
Employment and Unemployment, 1962–1975

	Social Sector, Economic Activity (1)	Social Sector, Noneconomic Activity (2)	Subtotal A (1+2)	Private Sector, Home and Abroad (3)	Subtotal B (1+2+3)	Registered Unemployed (4)	Subtotal C (1+2+3+4)	Independent Farmers (5)	Subtotal D (1+2+3+4+5)
1962	2775	549	3324	114	3438	202	3640	4292	7932
1963	2862	549	3411	144	3555	187	3742	4265	8007
1964	3064	571	3635	161	3796	172	3968	4160	8128
1965	3070	595	3665	186	3851	206	4057	4173	8230
1966	2942	588	3530	252	3782	230	4012	4164	8176
1967	2908	588	3496	256	3752	238	3990	4122	8112
1968	2898	599	3497	269	3766	280	4046	4111	8157
1969	3043	626	3669	463	4132	295	4427	4060	8487
1970	3140	650	3790	737	4527	294	4821	3950	8771
1971	3299	683	3982	872	4854	264	5118	3842	8960
1972	3424	713	4137	882	5019	289	5308	3741	9049
1973	3497	742	4239	958	5197	354	5551	3663	9214
1974	3658	779	4437	935	5372	418	5790		
1975	3854	818	4672	890	5562	502	6064		

Source: Mencinger, "Utjecaj privredne aktivnosti na zaposlenost."

APPENDIX TABLE 6-2 Unemployment, 1952–1988		APPENDIX TABLE 6-3 Unemployment Rate, 1959–1988	
	Unemployed (in thousands)		Percentage Unemployed
1952	44.7	1959	5.8
1953	81.6	1960	5.5
1954	76.2	1961	6.0
1955	67.2	1962	7.3
1956	99.3	1963	7.2
1957	115.9	1964	6.0
1958	132.0	1965	6.6
1959	161.0	1966	7.4
1960	159.0	1967	7.8
1961	191.0	1968	8.9
1962	236.0	1969	9.1
1963	240.0	1970	8.5
1964	212.0	1971	7.4
1965	236.0	1972	7.7
1966	257.0	1973	9.1
1967	269.0	1974	10.1
1968	310.0	1975	11.6
1969	330.0	1976	13.1
1970	319.0	1977	13.9
1971	291.0	1978	13.9
1972	315.0	1979	13.9
1973	381.0	1980	13.8
1974	448.0	1981	13.8
1975	540.0	1982	14.4
1976	635.0	1983	14.9
1977	700.0	1984	15.7
1978	734.0	1985	16.3
1979	762.0	1986	16.6
1980	785.0	1987	16.1
1981	808.0	1988	16.8
1982	862.0		
1983	910.0		
1984	974.0		
1985	1039.0		
1986	1086.0		
1987	1080.0		
1988	1128.0		

Source: Mencinger, "Privredna reforma i nezaposlenost," 37.

Source: For 1952–58: Macura, "Employment Problems under Declining Population Growth Rates and Structural Change, 496; for 1959–88: Mencinger, "Privredna reforma i nezaposlenost," 36.

APPENDIX TABLE 6-4
Unemployment: Gross and Net Rates (percentages)

	1964	1965	1966	1967	1968	1969	1970	1971	1972
Net unemployment	5.6	6.3	6.4	7.0	8.0	7.8	7.7	6.7	7.3
Percentage change		12.5	1.6	9.4	14.3	−2.5	−1.3	−13.0	9.0
Gross unemployment	6.7	7.9	8.4	9.6	12.1	18.4	18.3	19.3	19.3
Percentage change		17.9	6.3	14.3	26.0	52.1	−0.5	5.5	0.0

Source: Babić and Primorac, "Analiza koristi i troškova privremenog zapošljavanja u inozemstvu," table 2.
Note: The net rates include only the domestically employed; gross rates include those registered as working abroad as well.

APPENDIX TABLE 6-5
Job Seekers and Migrant Workers (thousands)

	1952	1953	1954	1955	1956	1957	1958	1959	1960	1961	1962	1963	1964	1965
Registered job seekers	71.4	68.0	69.2	81.7	126.3	123.7	174.2	164.8	185.4	232.6	274.0	229.0	228.0	266.9
Percentage change		−4.8	1.8	18.1	54.6	−2.1	40.8	−5.4	12.5	25.5	17.8	−16.4	−0.4	17.1
Migrant workers									18.0	28.0	42.0	80.0	105.0	130.0
Job seekers plus migrant workers									203.4	260.6	316.0	309.0	333.0	396.9

	1966	1967	1968	1969	1970	1971	1972	1973	1974	1975	1976	1977
Registered job seekers	265.3	291.5	326.8	315.6	289.7	289.5	333.5	398.7	478.5	583.8	665.2	716.7
Percentage change	−0.6	9.9	12.1	−3.4	−8.2	−0.1	15.2	19.6	20.0	22.0	13.9	7.7
Migrant workers	190.0	220.0	260.0	430.0	600.0	680.0	770.0	860.0	810.0	770.0	725.0	705.0
Job seekers plus migrant workers	455.3	511.5	586.8	745.6	889.7	969.5	1103.5	1258.7	1288.5	1353.8	1390.2	1421.7

	1978	1979	1980	1981	1982	1983	1984	1985	1986	1987	1988	1989
Registered job seekers	737.9	775.0	789.2	833.2	887.8	916.3	1012.9	1063.9	1084.5	1087.1	1173.0	1244.9
Percentage change	3.0	5.0	1.8	5.6	6.6	3.2	10.5	5.0	1.9	0.2	7.9	6.1
Migrant workers	695.0	690.0	693.0	675.0	675.0	650.0	625.0					
Job seekers plus migrant workers	1432.9	1465.0	1482.2	1508.2	1562.8	1566.3	1637.9					

Source: For job seekers: *Statistički Godišnjak Jugoslavije*, various years; for migrant workers, 1960–64: Zimmerman, *Open Borders, Nonalignment, and the Political Evolution of Yugoslavia*, table 4.4; for migrant workers, 1965–84: Primorac and Babić, "Systemic Changes and Unemployment Growth in Yugoslavia, 1965–1985," table 3.

Unemployment by Length of Time Waiting on the Employment Service Register (thousands)

	Total	Less Than 6 Months	Less Than 6 Months (% Total)	6–9 Months	6–9 Months (% Total)	9–12 Months	9–12 Months (% Total)	1–3 Years	1–3 Years (% Total)	Longer Than 3 Years	Longer Than 3 Years (% Total)
1957	123.7	92.9	75.1	9.5	7.7	7.9	6.4	11.2	9.1	2.2	1.8
1958	173.7	134.2	77.3	13.9	8.0	11.8	6.8	11.2	6.4	2.6	1.5
1959	164.5	119.2	72.5	14.6	8.9	13.6	8.3	13.8	8.4	3.3	2.0
1960	184.9	133.5	72.2	17.8	9.6	15.2	8.2	14.7	8.0	3.7	2.0
1961	232.6	157.0	67.5	23.6	10.1	25.4	10.9	20.3	8.7	6.3	2.7
1962	274.0	173.9	63.5	29.4	10.7	29.4	10.7	34.8	12.7	6.5	2.4
1963	229.0	150.8	65.9	22.5	9.8	22.6	9.9	25.9	11.3	7.2	3.1
1964	228.0	148.1	65.0	23.4	10.3	23.6	10.4	25.1	11.0	7.8	3.4
1965	266.9	159.8	59.9	30.7	11.5	32.3	12.1	32.7	12.3	11.4	4.3
1966	265.3	151.2	57.0	29.9	11.3	29.3	11.0	41.9	15.8	13.0	4.9
1967	291.5	163.6	56.1	33.4	11.5	34.8	11.9	44.5	15.3	15.2	5.2
1968	326.8	181.2	55.4	40.7	12.5	39.1	12.0	48.3	14.8	17.5	5.4
1969	315.6	166.2	52.7	38.2	12.1	38.2	12.1	50.5	16.0	22.5	7.1
1970	289.7	145.8	50.3	35.6	12.3	38.8	13.4	46.7	16.1	22.8	7.9

1971	289.5	153.6	53.1	32.8	11.3	34.3	11.8	45.5	15.7	23.3	8.0
1972	333.5	167.9	50.3	40.0	12.0	42.1	12.6	57.0	17.1	26.5	7.9
1973	398.7	198.3	49.7	46.6	11.7	48.1	12.1	77.3	19.4	28.4	7.1
1974	478.5	224.9	47.0	57.6	12.0	56.8	11.9	103.5	21.6	35.7	7.5
1975	583.8	255.3	43.7	68.5	11.7	67.7	11.6	143.2	24.5	49.1	8.4
1976	665.2	258.3	38.8	75.4	11.3	78.9	11.9	183.7	27.6	68.9	10.4
1977	716.7	257.8	36.0	75.2	10.5	74.9	10.5	216.0	30.1	92.9	13.0
1978	737.9	259.0	35.1	68.6	9.3	72.8	9.9	210.0	28.5	127.5	17.3
1979	775.0	272.8	35.2	68.4	8.8	69.4	9.0	234.5	30.3	129.9	16.8
1980	789.2	267.5	33.9	64.0	8.1	69.4	8.8	251.7	31.9	136.6	17.3
1981	833.2	293.1	35.2	66.4	8.0	65.2	7.8	264.0	31.7	144.5	17.3
1982	887.8	305.5	34.4	74.7	8.4	72.8	8.2	270.3	30.4	164.5	18.5
1983	916.3	292.4	31.9	77.7	8.5	75.3	8.2	291.7	31.8	179.2	19.6
1984	1012.9	303.4	30.0	84.0	8.3	83.4	8.2	331.7	32.7	210.5	20.8
1985	1063.9	301.0	28.3	86.6	8.1	88.1	8.3	337.0	31.7	251.2	23.6
1986	1084.5	290.3	26.8	82.9	7.6	86.2	7.9	349.1	32.2	276.0	25.4
1987	1087.1	279.4	25.7	83.8	7.7	82.7	7.6	349.5	32.1	291.7	26.8
1988	1173.0	273.0	23.3	85.3	7.3	87.6	7.5	381.2	32.5	345.9	29.5
1989	1244.9	235.8	18.9	96.5	7.8	82.4	6.6	417.4	33.5	412.8	33.2

Source: Statistički Godišnjak Jugoslavije, various years.

APPENDIX TABLE 6-8
Unemployment—Women

	Registered Job Seekers (thousands)	Percentage Change
1957	62.1	
1958	84.2	35.6
1959	86.5	2.7
1960	97.9	13.2
1961	108.9	11.2
1962	124.2	14.0
1963	123.9	−0.2
1964	126.0	1.7
1965	125.2	−0.6
1966	121.2	−3.2
1967	127.7	5.4
1968	142.1	11.3
1969	143.0	0.6
1970	141.9	−0.8
1971	144.8	2.0
1972	166.6	15.1
1973	203.8	22.3
1974	248.1	21.7
1975	299.0	20.5
1976	337.0	12.7
1977	370.8	10.0
1978	396.4	6.9
1979	425.2	7.3
1980	445.0	4.7
1981	478.0	7.4
1982	512.0	7.1
1983	520.0	1.6
1984	568.0	9.2
1985	596.0	4.9
1986	611.0	2.5
1987	606.0	−0.8
1988	641.0	5.8
1989	675.0	5.3

Source: Statistički Godišnjak Jugoslavije, various years.

APPENDIX TABLE 6-9, 6-10, AND 9-1

Unemployment Rate by Republic or Province (percentages)

	1959	1960	1961	1962	1963	1964	1965	1966	1967	1968	1969	1970	1971	1972	1973	1974
Yugoslavia	5.8	5.5	6.0	7.3	7.2	6.0	6.6	7.4	7.8	8.9	9.1	8.5	7.4	7.7	9.1	10.1
Less-developed regions																
Bosnia-Herzegovina	5.5	4.2	4.5	6.3	5.8	4.8	5.2	5.7	6.5	8.1	8.5	7.4	6.0	6.7	8.5	10.9
Macedonia	10.5	11.5	15.0	15.5	12.0	10.0	15.6	19.3	19.9	22.8	22.5	21.9	21.2	20.8	23.0	25.0
Montenegro	8.5	6.1	5.9	6.3	6.5	5.8	5.7	6.9	8.0	9.2	8.8	8.3	6.5	7.2	11.3	15.0
Kosovo	17.9	15.4	19.3	22.7	31.6	14.6	18.0	26.6	25.4	26.9	28.4	32.3	23.9	22.8	26.6	27.0
Developed regions																
Slovenia	2.4	2.0	1.7	2.0	1.8	1.4	1.8	2.4	3.1	3.8	3.5	3.1	2.7	2.2	1.8	1.5
Croatia	5.1	5.6	5.8	6.7	6.2	5.6	6.1	6.4	6.6	7.2	6.2	4.9	4.3	4.6	5.2	5.1
Serbia	7.0	6.1	6.9	8.6	9.8	7.8	7.8	8.4	8.6	9.8	10.9	10.7	9.2	9.6	11.7	13.2
Serbia proper	7.3	6.2	6.9	8.5	9.4	8.4	8.2	7.9	7.9	8.9	10.2	9.9	8.7	9.1	11.1	12.9
Vojvodina	4.2	4.0	4.3	6.1	6.2	5.2	4.9	5.4	6.2	7.6	8.4	7.6	6.7	7.4	9.2	10.0

(continued)

APPENDIX TABLE 6-9, 6-10, AND 9-1 *(Continued)*

	1975	1976	1977	1978	1979	1980	1981	1982	1983	1984	1985	1986	1987	1988	1989	1990*
Yugoslavia	11.6	13.1	13.9	13.9	13.9	13.8	13.8	14.4	14.9	15.7	16.3	16.6	16.1	16.8	14.9	15.9
Less-developed regions																
Bosnia-Herzegovina	12.9	14.8	15.2	15.8	16.5	16.6	16.7	17.9	20.3	23.0	24.4	24.3	23.1	24.1	20.3	20.6
Macedonia	26.8	28.2	26.8	27.2	27.5	27.9	29.0	28.1	26.4	26.7	27.6	27.7	27.3	27.1	21.9	22.9
Montenegro	17.3	17.8	17.3	19.0	19.3	17.5	18.1	19.3	21.6	23.5	24.6	24.6	23.6	26.3	21.6	21.6
Kosovo	30.7	34.1	35.7	36.8	37.8	39.0	39.1	41.0	44.5	49.9	54.2	57.1	57.0	57.8	36.3	38.4
Developed regions																
Slovenia	1.5	1.8	1.7	1.5	1.3	1.4	1.6	1.7	2.0	1.9	1.8	1.7	1.8	2.5	3.2	4.8
Croatia	6.0	7.1	7.1	6.5	5.8	5.7	6.1	6.9	7.4	7.7	7.9	7.9	7.8	8.5	8.0	8.6
Serbia	15.1	17.3	19.4	19.6	19.5	19.4	18.7	19.1	19.1	19.5	20.2	20.8	20.3	20.8	17.6	19.1
Serbia proper	14.6	16.5	19.0	19.9	19.5	18.9	17.7	17.9	17.3	17.0	17.4	17.9	17.8	18.1	15.6	16.4
Vojvodina	12.0	14.4	15.8	13.9	13.8	14.4	14.6	15.1	15.6	15.7	15.7	15.6	13.9	14.3	13.6	16.6

Source: For 1959–88: Mencinger, "Privredna reforma i nezaposlenost," table 1; for 1989–90: *Statistički Godišnjak Jugoslavije* (1990), 16.
Note: The rate of unemployment is defined as the relation between the number of unemployed (registered job seekers) and the total number of employed and unemployed persons.
*Estimate

APPENDIX TABLE 6-11

Socioeconomic Structure of the Population by Republic or Province (percentages of total population)

	Economically Active Population						Agricultural Population						Urban Population			
	1953	1961	1966	1971	1979	1981	1953	1961	1966	1971	1979	1981	1953	1961	1971	1981
Yugoslavia	46.3	45.0	44.1	43.3	43.3	44.0	60.9	49.6	44.9	38.2	29.3	19.9	21.7	28.3	38.6	46.5
Less-developed regions																
Bosnia-Herzegovina	42.5	39.2	37.8	36.7	36.7	38.7	62.2	50.2	45.1	40.0	28.9	17.3	15.0	19.5	27.9	36.2
Macedonia	40.8	39.4	38.8	38.3	38.2	41.8	62.7	41.3	45.8	39.9	28.9	21.7	26.1	34.9	48.1	53.9
Montenegro	36.4	34.3	33.1	32.7	32.7	34.3	61.5	47.0	41.0	35.0	26.0	13.5	14.2	21.1	34.2	50.7
Kosovo	33.2	34.8	30.1	26.0	25.9	23.8	72.4	64.2	58.4	51.5	42.2	24.6	14.6	19.5	26.9	32.5
Developed regions																
Slovenia	40.8	48.3	48.3	48.4	48.4	50.3	41.1	31.1	26.0	20.4	12.5	9.4	22.0	28.9	37.7	48.9
Croatia	47.7	47.0	46.4	45.5	45.5	45.6	56.4	43.9	37.7	32.3	24.1	15.2	24.3	30.8	41.0	50.8
Serbia	48.4	47.3	51.4	45.7	51.5	45.4	66.7	56.1	50.2	44.0	34.5	25.4	22.5	29.8	40.6	46.6
Serbia proper	52.4	51.1	n.a.	51.5	n.a.	51.8	67.2	56.2	n.a.	44.1	n.a.	27.6	21.2	28.6	40.8	47.8
Vojvodina	45.4	44.0	43.6	42.7	42.7	44.3	62.9	51.8	40.6	39.0	32.0	19.9	29.5	38.3	48.7	54.1

Source: Statistički Godišnjak Jugoslavije, various years.

APPENDIX TABLE 6-12 AND 6-13
Unemployment by Age Structure (thousands)

	Total	Below 18 Years	Below 18 Years (% Total)	19 to 24 Years	19 to 24 Years (% Total)	Below 25 Years
1957	123.7	8.8	7.1	37.5	30.3	46.3
1958	173.7	21.7	12.5	52.1	30.0	73.8
1959	164.5	19.8	12.0	52.3	31.8	72.1
1960	184.9	24.1	13.0	56.1	30.3	80.2
1961	232.6	20.3	8.7	63.3	27.2	83.6
1962	274.0	24.2	8.8	76.8	28.0	101.0
1963	229.0	24.6	10.7	60.6	26.5	85.2
1964	228.0	29.7	13.0	62.1	27.2	91.8
1965	266.9	36.0	13.5	75.9	28.4	111.9
1966	265.3	31.7	11.9	85.8	32.3	117.5
1967	291.5	29.4	10.1	93.6	32.1	123.0
1968	326.8	31.6	9.7	110.6	33.8	142.2
1969	315.6	30.7	9.7	112.6	35.7	143.3
1970	289.7	27.4	9.5	108.2	37.3	135.6
1971	289.5	29.3	10.1	111.2	38.4	140.5
1972	333.5	31.1	9.3	139.0	41.7	170.1
1973	398.7	34.1	8.6	180.1	45.2	180.1
1974	478.5	40.4	8.4	222.1	46.4	262.5
1975	583.8	38.6	6.6	279.1	47.8	317.7
1976	665.2	50.3	7.6	305.3	45.9	355.6
1977	716.7	45.9	6.4	346.8	48.4	392.7
1978	737.9	48.8	6.6	356.0	48.2	404.8
1979	775.0	49.7	6.4	375.1	48.4	424.8
1980	789.2	54.5	6.9	383.9	48.6	438.4
1981	883.2	55.5	6.7	410.2	49.2	465.7
1982	887.8	60.2	6.8	450.5	50.7	510.7
1983	916.3	68.1	8.6	476.0	51.9	544.1
1984	1012.9	75.7	7.5	532.0	52.5	607.7
1985	1063.9	83.1	7.8	551.1	51.8	634.2
1986	1084.5	81.9	7.6	558.3	51.5	640.2
1987	1087.1	79.0	7.3	550.7	50.7	629.7
1988	1173.0	80.4	6.9	584.9	49.9	665.3
1989	1244.9	77.6	6.2	602.7	48.4	680.3

Source: Statistički Godišnjak Jugoslavije, various years.

Below 25 Years (% Total)	25 to 39 Years	25 to 39 Years (% Total)	40 to 49 Years	40 to 49 Years (% Total)	Above 50 Years	Above 50 Years (% Total)
37.4	48.0	38.8	19.4	15.7	10.0	8.1
42.5	64.9	37.4	25.1	14.5	9.9	5.7
43.8	61.5	37.4	22.1	13.4	8.8	5.3
43.4	70.8	38.3	23.9	12.9	10.0	5.4
35.9	94.1	40.5	37.9	16.3	17.0	7.3
36.9	121.8	44.5	34.7	12.7	16.5	6.0
37.2	97.5	42.6	30.7	13.4	15.6	6.8
40.3	94.2	41.3	28.9	12.7	13.1	5.7
41.9	105.2	39.4	33.7	12.6	16.1	6.0
44.3	101.4	38.2	32.4	12.2	14.0	5.3
42.2	119.0	40.8	34.8	11.9	14.7	5.0
43.5	142.9	43.7	31.9	9.8	9.8	3.0
45.4	128.4	40.7	31.7	10.0	12.2	3.9
46.8	113.0	39.0	29.3	10.1	11.8	4.1
48.5	102.5	35.4	32.6	11.3	13.9	4.8
51.0	114.9	34.5	34.7	10.4	13.8	4.1
45.2	130.0	32.6	39.1	9.8	15.4	3.9
54.9	158.9	33.2	41.2	8.6	15.9	3.3
54.4	194.2	33.3	52.2	8.9	19.7	3.4
53.5	219.1	32.9	58.1	8.7	32.4	4.9
54.8	236.5	33.0	63.6	8.9	23.9	3.3
54.9	245.0	33.2	63.0	8.5	25.1	3.4
54.8	259.0	33.4	64.8	8.4	26.4	3.4
55.5	261.9	33.2	62.4	7.9	26.5	3.4
55.9	277.5	33.3	62.3	7.5	27.7	3.3
57.5	288.4	32.5	61.2	6.9	27.5	3.1
59.4	290.0	31.6	56.8	6.2	25.4	2.8
60.0	322.3	31.8	56.2	5.5	26.7	2.6
59.6	344.7	32.4	55.8	5.2	29.2	2.7
59.0	361.1	33.3	55.2	5.1	28.0	2.6
57.9	374.3	34.4	55.0	5.1	28.1	2.6
56.7	416.9	35.5	60.3	5.1	30.4	2.6
54.6	258.9	20.8	249.0	20.0	56.7	4.6

APPENDIX TABLE 6-14 AND 6-15
Unemployment, 1952–1989 (thousands)

	1952	1953	1954	1955	1956	1957	1958	1959	1960	1961
Total registered job seekers	71.4	68.0	69.2	81.7	126.3	123.7	174.2	164.8	185.4	232.6
Percentage change		−4.8	1.8	18.1	54.6	−2.1	40.8	−5.4	12.5	25.5
Registered job seekers—Women	n.a.	n.a.	n.a.	n.a.	n.a.	62.1	84.2	86.5	97.9	108.9
Percentage change							35.6	2.7	13.2	11.2
Percentage of total						50.2	48.3	52.5	52.8	46.8
Persons seeking a job for the first time	15.7	16.9	18.4	19.7	29.8	32.6	50.2	52.7	61.8	66.6
Percentage change		7.6	8.9	7.1	51.3	9.4	54.0	5.0	17.3	7.8
Percentage of total	22.0	24.9	26.6	24.1	23.6	26.4	28.8	32.0	33.3	28.6
Job seekers with univ., college, intermediate, or secondary education*	n.a.	n.a.	n.a.	n.a.	n.a.	n.a.	7.5	8.3	8.2	5.3
Percentage change								10.7	−1.2	−35.4
Percentage of total							4.3	5.0	4.4	2.3
Migrant workers	n.a.	n.a.	n.a.	n.a.	n.a.	n.a.	n.a.	n.a.	18.0	28.0
Job seekers plus migrant workers									203.4	260.6
Job seekers receiving unemployment compensation	n.a.	n.a.	n.a.	n.a.	n.a.	21.2	23.1	22.8	20.5	29.1
Percentage change							9.0	−1.3	−10.1	42.0
Percentage of total						17.1	13.3	13.8	11.1	12.5

Sources: Statistički Godišnjak Jugoslavije, various years; Yugoslav Survey, various years; for migrant workers, 1960–64: Zimmerman, Open Borders, Nonalignment, and the Political Evolution of Yugoslavia, table 4.4; for migrant workers, 1965–84: Primorac and Babić, "Systemic Changes and Unemployment Growth in Yugoslavia, 1965–1985," table 3.

*Annual averages

1962	1963	1964	1965	1966	1967	1968	1969	1970	1971	1972	1973
274.0	229.0	228.0	266.9	265.3	291.5	326.8	315.6	289.7	289.5	333.5	398.7
17.8	−16.4	−0.4	17.1	−0.6	9.9	12.1	−3.4	−8.2	−0.1	15.2	19.6
124.2	123.9	126.0	125.2	121.2	127.7	142.1	143.0	141.9	144.8	166.6	203.8
14.0	−0.2	1.7	−0.6	−3.2	5.4	11.3	0.6	−0.8	2.0	15.1	22.3
45.3	54.1	55.3	46.9	45.7	43.8	43.5	45.3	49.0	50.0	50.0	51.1
83.8	82.6	91.9	88.3	87.4	92.8	129.8	145.6	148.2	145.7	179.8	220.4
25.8	−1.4	11.3	−3.9	−1.0	6.2	39.9	12.2	1.8	−1.7	23.4	22.6
30.6	36.1	40.3	33.1	32.9	31.8	39.7	46.1	51.2	50.3	53.9	55.3
5.0	8.3	8.7	10.7	17.2	26.3	43.0	43.2	42.3	41.8	47.7	63.5
−5.7	66.0	4.8	23.0	60.7	52.9	63.5	0.5	−2.1	−1.2	14.1	33.1
1.8	3.6	3.8	4.0	6.5	9.0	13.2	13.7	14.6	14.4	14.3	15.9
42.0	80.0	105.0	130.0	190.0	220.0	260.0	430.0	600.0	680.0	770.0	860.0
316.0	309.0	333.0	396.9	455.3	511.5	586.8	745.6	889.7	969.5	1103.5	1258.7
34.6	23.8	21.8	32.7	31.5	32.8	27.5	16.8	10.6	10.5	10.2	11.5
18.9	−31.2	−8.4	50.0	−3.7	4.1	−16.2	−38.9	−36.9	−0.9	−2.9	12.7
12.6	10.4	9.6	12.3	11.9	11.3	8.4	5.3	3.7	3.6	3.1	2.9

(continued)

APPENDIX TABLE 6-14 AND 6-15   (*Continued*)

	1974	1975	1976	1977	1978	1979	1980
Total registered job seekers	478.5	583.8	665.2	716.7	737.9	775.0	789.2
Percentage change	20.0	22.0	13.9	7.7	3.0	5.0	1.8
Registered job seekers—Women	248.1	299.0	337.0	370.8	396.4	425.2	445.0
Percentage change	21.7	20.5	12.7	10.0	6.9	7.3	4.7
Percentage of total	51.8	51.2	50.7	51.7	53.7	54.9	56.4
Persons seeking a job for the first time	284.4	349.1	401.7	449.5	486.9	528.5	537.7
Percentage change	29.0	22.7	15.1	11.9	8.3	8.5	1.7
Percentage of total	59.4	59.8	60.4	62.7	66.0	68.2	68.1
Job seekers with univ., college, intermediate, or secondary education*	79.4	93.4	110.3	134.2	155.0	174.8	204.7
Percentage change	25.0	17.6	18.1	21.7	15.5	12.8	17.1
Percentage of total	16.6	16.0	16.6	18.7	21.0	22.6	25.9
Migrant workers	810.0	770.0	725.0	705.0	695.0	690.0	693.0
Job seekers plus migrant workers	1288.5	1353.8	1390.2	1421.7	1432.9	1465.0	1482.2
Job seekers receiving unemployment compensation	11.3	17.1	18.7	17.2	18.4	21.1	19.7
Percentage change	−1.7	51.3	9.4	−8.0	7.0	14.7	−6.6
Percentage of total	2.4	2.9	2.8	2.4	2.5	2.7	2.5

1981	1982	1983	1984	1985	1986	1987	1988	1989
833.2	887.8	916.3	1012.9	1063.9	1084.5	1087.1	1173.0	1244.9
5.6	6.6	3.2	10.5	5.0	1.9	0.2	7.9	6.1
478.0	512.0	520.0	568.0	596.0	611.0	606.0	641.0	675
7.4	7.1	1.6	9.2	4.9	2.5	−0.8	5.8	5.3
57.4	57.7	56.7	56.1	56.0	56.3	55.7	54.6	54.2
569.2	607.3	635.1	714.3	759.7	776.4	764.7	806.2	846.5
5.9	6.7	4.6	12.5	6.4	2.2	−1.5	5.4	5.0
68.3	68.4	69.3	70.5	71.4	71.6	70.3	68.7	68.0
236.6	280.0	315.6	357.7	384.6	401.0	400.5	420.0	446.3
15.6	18.3	12.7	13.3	7.5	4.3	−0.1	4.9	6.3
28.4	31.5	34.4	35.3	36.2	37.0	36.8	35.8	35.9
675.0	675.0	650.0	625.0	n.a.	n.a.	n.a.	n.a.	n.a.
1508.2	1562.8	1566.3	1637.9					
28	27.4	50.5	28.3	27.6	29.4	34.9	44.6	41.4
42.1	−2.1	84.3	−44.0	−2.5	6.5	18.7	27.8	−7.2
3.4	3.1	5.5	2.8	2.6	2.7	3.2	3.8	3.3

APPENDIX TABLE 6-16, 6-17, AND 9-2
Youth Unemployment Rates by Republic or Province (percentages)

	1965	1970	1975	1980	1983	1984	1985
Yugoslavia	20.6	15.3	22.2	27.7	33.0	35.1	37.3
Less-developed regions							
Bosnia-Herzegovina	19.8	12.2	25.4	32.6	42.2	46.9	52.7
Macedonia	59.2	41.3	43.3	49.8	50.6	69.8	72.2
Montenegro	65.4	26.4	31.9	35.6	46.0	51.7	56.4
Kosovo	18.3	25.0	35.5	43.5	56.6	62.8	68.6
Developed regions							
Slovenia	5.5	5.8	2.9	3.0	4.4	4.0	3.7
Croatia	20.1	8.2	13.3	14.2	20.8	22.4	24.3
Serbia	23.4	22.5	28.9	35.5	37.0	36.1	34.9
Vojvodina	15.7	13.9	24.0	34.0	35.4	34.1	32.7

Source: Primorac and Charette, "Regional Aspects of Youth Unemployment in Yugoslavia," 218.

Note: "Youth" refers to persons aged 27 years or younger.

APPENDIX TABLE 8-1
Social Sector Employment by Republic or Province
(percentages of total employment)

	1965	1975
Yugoslavia	18.4	21.9
Less-developed regions		
Bosnia-Herzegovina	13.7	16.8
Macedonia	15.6	19.0
Montenegro	14.1	17.7
Kosovo	8.1	9.6
Developed regions		
Slovenia	30.8	37.3
Croatia	21.8	25.1
Serbia	16.8	20.2
Serbia proper	16.8	21.7
Vojvodina	22.0	23.7

Source: Statistički Bilten Jugoslavije (1977), cited in Pleskovič and Dolenc, "Regional Development in a Socialist, Developing, and Multinational Country," 12.

BIBLIOGRAPHY

Adam, Jan. *Employment and Wage Policies in Poland, Czechoslovakia, and Hungary since 1950.* New York: Macmillan, 1984.

———, ed. *Employment Policies in the Soviet Union and Eastern Europe.* New York: St. Martin's Press, 1982.

Adamić, Louis. *The Eagle and the Roots.* Garden City, N.Y.: Doubleday, 1952.

Adizes, Ichak. *Industrial Democracy, Yugoslav Style: An Organizational Study of Decision-Making.* New York: Columbia University Press, 1971.

Adler-Karlsson, Gunnar. *Western Economic Warfare, 1947–1967: A Case Study in Foreign Economic Policy.* Stockholm: Almquist and Wicksell, 1968.

Allcock, John. "'The Socialist Transformation of the Village': Yugoslav Agricultural Policy since 1945." In Ronald A. Francisco and Betty A. Laird, eds., *Agricultural Policies in the USSR and Eastern Europe.* Boulder, Colo.: Westview Press, 1980.

Alt, James. "Political Parties, World Demand, and Unemployment: Domestic and International Sources of Economic Activity." *American Political Science Review* 79, no. 4 (1985): 1016–40.

Anderson, Benedict. *Imagined Communities: Reflections on the Origins and Spread of Nationalism.* London: Verso, 1983.

Antal, László. "Conflicts of Financial Planning and Regulation." *Acta Oeconomica* 30 (1983): 341–65.

Antifašističko Veće Narodnog Oslobodjenja Jugoslavije (AVNOJ). *Zakonodavni rad Predsedništva AVNOJa i Predsedništva Privremene narodne skupštine DFJa* (November 19, 1944–October 27, 1945). Belgrade, 1945.

Appleby, Joyce Oldham. *Economic Thought and Ideology in Seventeenth-Century England.* Princeton, N.J.: Princeton University Press, 1978.

Arsov, Ljubčo. "Rešavanje pitanja radne snage." *Partiska Izgradnja* 2, no. 6 (June–July 1950): 17–33.

———. "Mobilizacija nove radne snage za izvršenje privrednog plana." *Narodna Država* 2, no. 6 (June 1948): 3–11.

Auty, Phyllis. "Yugoslavia and the Cominform: Realignment of Foreign Policy." In Wayne S. Vucinich, ed., *At the Brink of War and Peace: The Tito-Stalin Split in a Historic Perspective.* New York: Brooklyn College Press, 1982.

Avakumović, Ivan. *History of the Communist Party of Yugoslavia.* Vol. 1. Aberdeen: Aberdeen University Press, 1964.

Avramović, Dragoslav. "Odnos izmedju spoljnih i unutrašnjih finansija socijalističke privrede." *Finansije* 6, nos. 11–12 (November–December 1950): 30.

Babić, Mate, and Emil Primorac. "Some Causes of the Growth of the Yugoslav External Debt." *Soviet Studies* 38, no. 1 (January 1986): 69–88.

———. "Analiza koristi i troškova privremenog zapošljavanja u inozemstvu." *Ekonomski Pregled* 26, nos. 11–12 (November–December 1975): 667–86.

Badovinac, Tomislav. Interview. *Start,* October 23, 1982.

Bahry, Donna. "Perestroika and the Debate over Territorial Economic Decentralization." *Harriman Institute Forum* 2, no. 5 (May 1989): 1–8.

Bajt, Aleksandar. "Lessons from the Labor-Management Laboratory." Unpub. ms. 1987.

————. "Investment Cycles in European Socialist Economies: A Review Article." *Journal of Economic Literature* 9, no. 1 (1971): 53–63.

Bakarić, Vladimir. Interview. *Start,* January 2, 1982, 11–18.

————. "Problemi zemljišne rente u prelaznoj etapi." In *O poljoprivredi i problemima sela: Govori i članci.* Belgrade: Kultura, 1960.

————. "O radu narodnog fronta na selu." In *O poljoprivredi.*

————. "Vezana trgovina poljoprivrednih i industrijskih proizvoda i njeno ograničavanje porasta kapitalističkih elemenata na selu: Stanje zadrugarstva." In *O poljoprivredi.*

Bakić, Ljubomir. "Politika bržeg razvoja privredno nedovoljno razvijenih republika i autonomnih pokrajina." *Sociologija* 19, nos. 2–3 (1977): 397–411.

Baletić, Zvonimir, and Božo Marendić. "Politika razvoja privredno nedovoljno razvijenih područja S. R. Hrvatske." *Ekonomski Pregled* 32, nos. 7–8 (1981): 355–67.

Baletić, Zvonko, and I. Baučić. *Population, Labour Force, and Employment in Yugoslavia, 1950–1990.* Vienna: Verein Wiener Institut, 1979.

Balog, Nikola. "Uredbe vlade FNRJ u 1948 godini." *Narodna Država* 3, no. 1 (January 1950): 97.

Banac, Ivo. "The Fearful Asymmetry of War: The Causes and Consequences of Yugoslavia's Demise." *Daedalus* 121, no. 2 (Spring 1992): 141–74.

————. *With Stalin against Tito: The Cominformist Splits in Yugoslav Communism.* Ithaca, N.Y.: Cornell University Press, 1988.

————. *The National Question in Yugoslavia: Origins, History, Politics.* Ithaca, N.Y.: Cornell University Press, 1984.

————. "Yugoslav Cominformist Organizations and Insurgent Activity: 1948–1954." In Wayne S. Vucinich, ed., *At the Brink of War and Peace: The Tito-Stalin Split in a Historic Perspective.* New York: Brooklyn College Press, 1982.

Bartlett, William J. "On the Dynamic Instability of Induced-Migration Unemployment in a Dual Economy." *Journal of Development Economics* 13, (1983): 85–96.

————. "Economic Development and Institutional Reform: The Introduction of Workers' Self-Management in Yugoslavia." *Economic Analysis and Workers' Management* 14, no. 4 (1980): 429–43.

————. "A Structural Model of Unemployment in Yugoslavia—An Alternative to the Institutional Hypothesis." Unpub. ms. University of Southampton, 1980.

Basom, Kenneth E. "Socialism as National Liberation: Edward Kardelj's Classic Work on the National Question." Unpub. ms. N.d.

Beard, Charles, and George Radin. *The Balkan Pivot: Yugoslavia. A Study in Government and Administration.* New York: Macmillan, 1929.

Bebler, Anton. "Development of Sociology of *Militaria* in Yugoslavia." *Armed Forces and Society* 3 (November 1976): 59–68.

————. "On Civil-Military Relations in the European Socialist States." Unpub. ms. N.d.

————. "Yugoslavia's National Defense System." Unpub. ms. N.d.

Begović, Nada. "Zaposlenost." In *Privreda FNRJ u periodu od 1947–1956 godine* Belgrade: Ekonomski Institut FNRJ, 1957.

Begović, Vlajko. "Naša poljoprivreda i pitanje njenog socijalističkog preobražaja." *Komunist* 3, no. 1 (January 1949): 76–102.

————. "Problem obezbjedjenja radne snage i stručnih kadrova u petogodišnjem planu." *Narodna Država* 1, no. 6 (September 1947): 18–32.

Berend, Ivan T., and György Ránki. *The European Periphery and Industrialization 1780–1914.* Translated by Éva Pálmai. Budapest: Akadémiai Kiadó, 1982.

Bergson, Abram. "Entrepreneurship under Labor Participation: The Yugoslav Case." In Joshua Ronen, ed., *Entrepreneurship.* Lexington, Mass.: Lexington Books, 1982.

Besemeres, John F. *Socialist Population Politics: The Political Implications of Demographic Trends in the USSR and Eastern Europe.* White Plains, N.Y.: M. E. Sharpe, 1980.

Bićanić, Ivo. "The Inequality Impact of the Unofficial Economy in Yugoslavia." In Sergio Alessandrini and Bruno Dallago, eds., *The Unofficial Economy: Consequences and Perspectives in Different Economic Systems.* Brookfield, Vt.: Gower, 1987.

Bićanić, Rudolf. *Kako živi narod* (1935). Reissued posthumously as *How the People Live.* Edited by Sonia Bićanić and Joel Halpern. Department of Anthropology, University of Massachusetts. Amherst: University of Massachusetts Press, 1981.

————. "Agrarna kriza od 1873–1895 i njezin utjecaj na ekonomsku i socijalnu strukturu Hrvatske." Parts 1–3. *Ekonomist*, nos. 3–5 (1937): 97–108, 151–59, 199–204.

Bideleux, Robert. *Communism and Development.* London and New York: Methuen, 1985.

Bitterman, Henry J. *The Refunding of International Debt.* Durham, N.C.: Duke University Press, 1973.

Bjeladinović, Andro. "O privrednim preduzećima." *Finansije*, yr. 2, vol. 4, no. 6 (June 1947): 373.

Blaug, Mark. *Economic Theory in Retrospect.* 3d ed. Cambridge: Cambridge University Press, 1978.

Block, Fred. "Postindustrial Development and the Obsolescence of Economic Categories." *Politics and Society* 14, no. 1 (1985): 71–104.

Bolčić, Silvano. *Razvoj i kriza Jugoslovenskog društva u sociološkoj perspektivi.* Belgrade: Radionica SIC, 1983.

Boltho, Andrea, ed. *The European Economy: Growth and Crisis.* New York: Oxford University Press, 1982.

Bombelles, Joseph T. *Economic Development of Communist Yugoslavia, 1947–1964.* Stanford, Calif.: Hoover Institution, 1968.

Bonacich, Edna. "The Past, Present, and Future of Split Labor Market Theory." In Cora Bagley Marrett and Cheryl Leggon, eds., *Research in Race and Ethnic Relations.* Vol. 1, Greenwich, Conn.: JAI Press, 1979.

Bonnell, Victoria E. *Roots of Rebellion: Workers' Politics and Organizations in St. Petersburg and Moscow, 1900–1914.* Berkeley and Los Angeles: University of California Press, 1983.

Bookman, Milica Žarković. "The Economic Basis of Regional Autarchy in Yugoslavia." *Soviet Studies* 42, no. 1 (January 1990): 93–109.

Bošnjović, Ilijas. *Razvoj i zaposlenost (Razvoj i politika zaposlenosti u Bosni i Hercegovini).* Sarajevo: Svjetlost, 1980.

Brajić, Vlajko. *Problemi zapošljavanja u uslovima tehnološkog progresa.* Monograph no. 64. Belgrade: Institut za Uporedno Pravo, 1972.

Braun, Rudolf. "Taxation, Sociopolitical Structure, and State-Building: Great Britain and Brandenburg-Prussia." In Charles Tilly, ed., *The Formation of National States in Western Europe.* Princeton, N.J.: Princeton University Press, 1975.

Brewer, Anthony. *Marxist Theories of Imperialism: A Critical Survey.* London: Routledge and Kegan Paul, 1980.

Burg, Steven L. "Elite Conflict in Post-Tito Yugoslavia." *Soviet Studies* 58, no. 2 (April 1986): 170–93.

———. *Conflict and Cohesion in Socialist Yugoslavia: Political Decision Making since 1966.* Princeton, N.J.: Princeton University Press, 1982.

Burger, Willem, Gard Kester, and Guus den Oudem. *Self-Management and Investment Control in Yugoslavia.* The Hague: Institute of Social Studies, 1977.

Burkett, John P. "Search, Selection, and Shortage in an Industry Composed of Labor-Managed Firms." *Journal of Comparative Economics* 10, no. 1 (March 1986): 26–40.

———. *The Effects of Economic Reform in Yugoslavia: Investment and Trade Policy, 1959–1976.* Research Series no. 55. Berkeley: Institute of International Studies, University of California, 1983.

Byrnes, Robert F., ed. *Communal Families in the Balkans: The Zadruga. Essays by Philip E. Moseley and Essays in His Honor.* Notre Dame, Ind.: University of Notre Dame Press, 1976.

Čalić, Dušan. "Ekonomska racionalnost, sociološki i politički zahtjevi samoupravnog socijalizma." Paper presented at conference of the Serbian Academy of Sciences and Arts, Belgrade, 1982.

———. "Ekonomska problematika na VI. kongresu Saveza komunista." *Ekonomski Pregled* 3, no. 6 (1952): 321–29.

Cameron, David R. "The Colors of a Rose." Unpub. ms. 1988.

———. "Does Government Cause Inflation? Taxes, Spending, and Deficits." In Leon Lindberg and Charles Maier, eds., *The Politics of Inflation and Economic Stagnation.* Washington, D.C.: The Brookings Institution, 1985.

———. "Social Democracy, Corporatism, Labour Quiescence, and the Representation of Economic Interest in Advanced Capitalist Society." In John H. Goldthorpe., ed., *Order and Conflict in Contemporary Capitalism.* Oxford: Clarendon Press, 1984.

Campbell, John C. *Tito's Separate Road: America and Yugoslavia in World Politics.* New York: Harper and Row, 1967.

Cardoso, Ferdinand Henrique, and Enzo Faletto. *Dependency and Development in Latin America.* Berkeley and Los Angeles: University of California Press, 1979.

Carlo, Antonio. "Capitalist Restoration and Social Crisis in Yugoslavia." *Telos*, no. 36 (Summer 1978): 81–110.

Carr, Edward Hallett. *Socialism in One Country: 1924–26.* Baltimore: Penguin, 1970.

———. *The Bolshevik Revolution, 1917–1923.* Vol. 1. New York: Macmillan, 1951.

Carr, E. H., and R. W. Davies. *Foundations of a Planned Economy, 1926–1929.* 2 vols. Part 1 of *A History of Russia.* New York: Macmillan, 1969.

Carter, April. *Democratic Reform in Yugoslavia: The Changing Role of the Party.* Princeton, N.J.: Princeton University Press, 1982.

"Čelik kao nafta." *Borba,* October 29, 1982.

Chepulis, Rita. "Migration Policies and Return Migration with Particular Reference to Yugoslavia." *Studi Emigrazione Études Migrations,* 18, no. 63 (September 1981): 319–35.

Chichilnisky, Graciela. "Terms of Trade and Domestic Distribution: Export-Led Growth with Abundant Labor." *Journal of Development Economics* 8 (1981): 163–92.

Chirot, Daniel. *Social Change in a Peripheral Society: The Creation of a Balkan Colony.* New York: Academic Press, 1976.

Chittle, Charles R. *Industrialization and Manufactured Export Expansion in a Worker-Managed Economy: The Yugoslav Experience.* Tübingen: Mohr, 1979.

Chowdhury, Abdur R., Stephen G. Grubaugh, and Andrew J. Stollar. "Money in the Yugoslav Economy." *Journal of Post-Keynesian Economics* 12, no. 4 (Summer 1990): 636–46.

Cichock, Mark A. "Reevaluating a Development Strategy: Policy Implications for Yugoslavia." *Comparative Politics,* January 1985, pp. 211–28.

Clark, Cal, and Karl F. Johnson. "Variations in the Policies of Yugoslav Communes: Developmental Imperatives versus Regional Style." *Comparative Political Studies* 16, no. 2 (July 1983): 235–54.

Clissold, Stephen, ed. *Yugoslavia and the Soviet Union, 1939–1973: A Documentary Survey.* London: Oxford University Press for the Royal Institute of International Affairs, 1975.

Čobeljić, Nikola. *Politika i metodi privrednog razvoja Jugoslavije, 1947–1956.* Belgrade: Nolit, 1959.

———. "Proizvodni faktori i proizvodna orijentacija Jugoslavije." *Ekonomist* 11, nos. 1–2 (1958): 1–24.

Cohen, Lenard J. *The Socialist Pyramid: Elites and Power in Yugoslavia.* Oakville, N.Y., and London: Mosaic Press, 1989.

Cohen, Lenard, and Paul Warwick. *Political Cohesion in a Fragile Mosaic: The Yugoslav Experience.* Boulder, Colo.: Westview Press, 1983.

Cohen, Stephen. *Bukharin and the Bolshevik Revolution: A Political Biography.* Oxford: Oxford University Press, 1980.

Čolaković, R. "Rešenje nacionalnog pitanja u Jugoslaviji." *Komunist* 4, nos. 4–5 (July–September 1950): 65–67.

Comisso, Ellen. "Can a Party of the Working Class Be a Working-Class Party?" In Jan F. Triska and Charles Gati, eds., *Blue-Collar Workers in Eastern Europe.* London: Allen and Unwin, 1981.

Comisso, Ellen. *Workers' Control under Plan and Market*. New Haven, Conn.: Yale University Press, 1979.

Commander, Simon. "Inflation and the Transition to a Market Economy: An Overview." *World Bank Economic Review* 6, no. 1 (1992): 3–12.

Communist Party of Yugoslavia. Central Committee. *Statement of the Central Committee of the Communist Party of Yugoslavia in Regard to the Resolution of the Information Bureau of Communist Parties on the Situation in the Communist Party of Yugoslavia*. Belgrade: Jugoslovenska Knjiga, 1948.

Connock, Michael. "A Note on Industrial Efficiency in Yugoslav Regions: Some Electrical Evidence." *Soviet Studies* 34, no. 1 (January 1982): 86–95.

Connor, Walker. *The National Question in Marxist-Leninist Theory and Strategy*. Princeton, N.J.: Princeton University Press, 1984.

Coulson, Andrew. *Tanzania: A Political Economy*. New York: Oxford University, Press, 1982.

Cox, Terry. *Peasants, Class, and Capitalism: The Rural Research of L. N. Kritsman and His School*. Oxford: Clarendon Press, 1986.

Crosslin, Robert L. "Labor Related Programs in Yugoslavia: Evaluation and Recommendations." Report for the World Bank, June 1990.

Dabčević, Savka. "Neki suvremeni ekonomisti o ekonomskoj ulozi države." *Ekonomski Pregled* 2, no. 6 (1951): 376–85.

Dabčević-Kučar, Savka, Miladin Korać, Miloš Samardžija, Jakov Sirotković, Rikard Štajner, and Tihomir Vlaškalić, *Problemi teorije i prakse socijalističke robne proizvodnje u Jugoslaviji*. Zagreb: Informator, 1965.

Dahrendorf, Ralf. *Life Chances: Approaches to Social and Political Theory*. Chicago: University of Chicago Press, 1979.

Damjanović, Pero, Milovan Bosić, and Dragica Lazarević, eds. *Peta zemaljska konferencija KPJ (19–23. oktobar 1940)*. Izvori za Istoriju SKJ, ser. A, vol. 1. Belgrade: Komunist, 1980.

Dautović, Mirko. "Nagradjivanje u preduzećima kao stimulativ za povečanje produktivnosti rada." *Ekonomski Anali* 3 (1956): 131–47.

Davidović, Milena. "Nezaposlenost i društvena nejednakost u Jugoslaviji." *Gledišta* 27, nos. 7–9 (July–September 1986): 3–35.

Davies, R. W. "Soviet History in the Gorbachev Revolution." *The Socialist Register*, edited by Ralph Miliband and John Saville, pp. 37–78.

———. *The Development of the Soviet Budgetary System*. Cambridge: Cambridge University Press, 1958.

Day, Richard. "Democratic Control and the Dignity of Politics: An Analysis of *The Revolution Betrayed*." *Comparative Economic Studies* 29, no. 3 (Fall 1987): 4–29.

———. ed. and trans. *N. I. Bukharin: Selected Writings on the State and the Transition to Socialism*. Armonk, N.Y.: M. E. Sharpe, 1982.

Dean, Robert W. "Civil-Military Relations in Yugoslavia, 1971–75." *Armed Forces and Society* 3 (November 1976): 17–58.

Dedijer, Stevan. "Tito's Bomb: The Birth and Death of an R & D Policy in a Developing Country." Unpub. ms. 1972.

Dedijer, Vladimir. *Novi prilozi za biografiju Josipa Broza Tita (1945–1955)*. 3 vols. Belgrade: Rad, 1984.

————. *The Battle Stalin Lost: Memoirs of Yugoslavia, 1948–1953*. New York: Viking Press, 1971.

Deleon, Ašer. "Conclusion of the Congress of Trade Unions." *Yugoslav Review* 5, nos. 3–4 (May–June 1955): 18–19, 29.

Denitch, Bogdan. *Limits and Possibilities: The Crisis of Yugoslav Socialism and State Socialist Systems*. Minneapolis: University of Minnesota Press, 1990.

Dereta, B. "O nekim osnovnim pokazateljima radne snage." *Evidencija*, nos. 1–2 (1951): 8–10.

Dilić, Edhem, ed. *Seoska omladina danas: Rezultati istraživanja u S.R. Hrvatskoj*. Zagreb: Centar Društvenih Djelatnosti SSOH, 1977.

Dirlam, Joel B., and James Plummer. *An Introduction to the Yugoslav Economy*. Columbus, Ohio: Charles E. Merrill, 1973.

Djilas, Milovan. *Rise and Fall*. San Diego: Harcourt Brace Jovanovich, 1985.

————. *Tito: The Story from Inside*. Translated by Vasilije Kojić and Richard Haynes. New York and London: Harcourt Brace Jovanovich, 1980.

————. *Wartime*. Translated by Michael Petrovich. New York: Harcourt Brace Jovanovich, 1977.

————. *Memoir of a Revolutionary*. Translated by Drenka Willen. New York: Harcourt Brace Jovanovich, 1973.

————. *Conversations with Stalin*. New York: Harcourt, Brace, and World, 1962.

Djodan, Šime. *The Evolution of the Economic System of Yugoslavia and the Economic Position of Croatia*. New York: Casz, 1973. Reprinted from *Journal of Croatian Studies* 13 (1972).

Djokanović, Milovan. "Članovi partije i uključenje u radne brigade." *Partiska Izgradnja* 3, nos. 5–6 (October–December 1951): 18–22.

Djordjević, A. "O socijalističkom takmičenju." *Vjesnik Rada* 4, nos. 11–12 (November–December 1949): 447–75.

Djordjević, Jovan. "Državno uredjenje Federativne Narodne Republike Jugoslavije." *Informativni Priručnik Jugoslavije*, 1949, pp. 136–47.

Dobb, Maurice. *Theories of Value and Distribution since Adam Smith: Ideology and Economic Theory*. Cambridge: Cambridge University Press, 1973.

————. *Socialist Planning: Some Problems*. London: Lawrence and Wishart, 1970.

————. *Welfare Economics and the Economics of Socialism: Towards a Commonsense Critique*. Cambridge: Cambridge University Press, 1969.

————. *Soviet Economic Development since 1917*. 6th ed. London: Routledge and Kegan Paul, 1966.

————. "Full Employment and Capitalism." In *On Economic Theory and Socialism: Collective Papers*. New York: International Publishers, 1955. Originally published 1950.

Dodevski, Dobri. *Problemi strukture u procesu industrijalizacije nedovoljno razvijenih područja Jugoslavije*. Skopje: Ekonomski Institut na Univerzitot "Kiril i Metodij," 1975.

Domar, Evsey. "The Soviet Collective Farm as a Producer Cooperative." *American Economic Review* 56, no. 4, pt. 1 (September 1966): 734–57.

Doran, Howard E., and Rozany R. Deen. "The Use of Linear Difference Equations in Manpower Planning: A Criticism." *Journal of Development Economics* 8 (1981): 193–204.

Dubey, Vinod, et al. *Yugoslavia: Development with Decentralization.* Baltimore: Johns Hopkins University Press for the World Bank, 1975.

Duisin, Duško. "The Impact of United States Assistance on Yugoslav Policy, 1949–1959." Master's thesis, Columbia University, 1959.

Dukanac, Ljubomir C. "Novi poreski sistem FNRJ." *Finansije*, yr. 2, vol. 3, nos. 1–2 (January–February 1947): 4–8.

———. *Indeksi konjunkturnog razvoja Jugoslavije, 1919–1941.* Belgrade: Biblioteka Beogradske Trgovinske Komore, 1946.

Dular, Marijan. "Struktura osoblja zaposlenog u našoj privredi." *Vjesnik Rada* 5, no. 11 (November 1950): 433–36.

———. "Uvodjenje izveštajno-statističke službe o uposlenom osoblju, platnom fondu i radnom vremenu." *Vjesnik Rada* 3, no. 1 (January 1948): 16–19.

Dyker, David A. *Yugoslavia: Socialism, Development, and Debt.* London and New York: Routledge, 1990.

Economic Commission for Europe. "The Relative Performance of South European Exports of Manufactures to OECD Countries in the 1970's: An Analysis of Demand Factors and Competitiveness." *Economic Bulletin for Europe* 34 (1982): 503–61.

Eichengreen, Barry, and T. J. Hatton, eds. *Interwar Unemployment in International Perspective.* Dordrecht, Netherlands: Kluwer Academic Publishers, 1988.

Eichengreen, Barry, and Marc Uzan. "The Marshall Plan: Economic Effects for Eastern Europe and the former USSR." *Economic Policy* 7, no. 14 (April 1992): 13–76.

"Employment, 1977–1984," *Yugoslav Survey* 27, no. 1 (1986).

Engels, Friedrich. "The Tactics of Social Democracy." In Robert C. Tucker, ed., *The Marx-Engels Reader*, 2d ed. New York: Norton, 1978.

Erlich, Alexander. *The Soviet Industrialization Debate, 1924–1928.* Cambridge: Harvard University Press, 1960.

Erlich, Vera Stein. *Family in Transition: A Study of 300 Yugoslav Villages.* Princeton, N.J.: Princeton University Press, 1966.

Esping-Andersen, Gösta. *Politics against Markets: The Social Democratic Road to Power.* Princeton, N.J.: Princeton University Press, 1985.

Esping-Andersen, Gösta, and Walter Korpi. "Social Policy as Class Politics in Post-War Capitalism: Scandinavia, Austria, and Germany." In John H. Goldthorpe, ed., *Order and Conflict in Contemporary Capitalism.* Oxford: Clarendon Press, 1984.

Estrin, Saul. *Self-Management: Economic Theory and Yugoslav Practice.* Cambridge: Cambridge University Press, 1983.

———. "The Effects of Self-Management on Yugoslav Industrial Growth." *Soviet Studies* 34, no. 1 (January 1982): 69–85.

Estrin, Saul, Robert E. Moore, and Jan Svejnar. "Market Imperfections, Labor Management, and Earnings Differentials in a Developing Country: Theory and Evidence from Yugoslavia." *Quarterly Journal of Economics* 103, no. 3 (August 1988): 465–78.

Farkaš, Vladimir. "Naša tzv. prenaseljenost i naš problem nezaposlenosti." *Socijalna Politika* 5, nos. 7–8 (July –August 1955): 50–59.

———. "Odredjivanje osnovnog uzroka nezaposlenosti u FNRJ." *Socijalna Politika* 5, no. 9 (September 1955): 3–14.

Fehér, Ferenc, Agnes Heller, and György Márkus. *Dictatorship over Needs.* New York: St. Martin's Press, 1983.

Feiwel, George. "Causes and Consequences of Disguised Industrial Unemployment in a Socialist Economy." *Soviet Studies* 26, no. 3 (July 1974): 344–62.

Ferge, Zsuzsa. *A Society in the Making: Hungarian Social and Societal Policy, 1945–75.* White Plains, N.Y.: M. E. Sharpe, 1979.

Filipović, Velimir, and Sulejman Hrnjica. "Psihološki aspekti nezapošljavanja omladine." *Gledišta* 8 (1967): 1693–99.

Filtzer, Donald. *Soviet Workers and Stalinist Industrialization: The Formation of Modern Soviet Production Relations, 1928–1941.* Armonk, N.Y.: M. E. Sharpe, 1986.

Firković, Mirko. "Tržište." In *Privreda FNRJ u periodu od 1947–1956 godine.* Belgrade: Ekonomski Institut FNRJ, 1957.

"Fiscal System and Fiscal Policy." *Yugoslav Survey* 31, no. 3 (1990).

Fitzgerald, E. V. K. "Stabilization and Economic Justice: The Case of Nicaragua." In *Debt and Development in Latin America.* Kwan S. Kim and David F. Ruccio, eds., Notre Dame, Ind.: University of Notre Dame Press, 1985.

Flaherty, Diane. "Plan, Market and Unequal Regional Development in Yugoslavia." *Soviet Studies* 40, no. 1 (January 1988): 100–124.

———. "Economic Reform and Foreign Trade in Yugoslavia." *Cambridge Journal of Economics* 6 (1982): 105–43.

Fleming, J. Marcus, and Viktor R. Sertić. "The Yugoslav Economic System." *International Monetary Fund Staff Papers* 9 (July 1962): 202–23.

Foreign Relations of the United States, 1949. Vol. 5, Eastern Europe, the Soviet Union. Washington, D.C.: U.S. Government Printing Office, 1976.

Foreign Relations of the United States, 1948. Vol. 4, Eastern Europe, the Soviet Union. Washington, D.C.: U.S. Government Printing Office, 1974.

Freeman, Richard B., and James L. Medoff. *What Do Unions Do?* New York: Basic Books, 1984.

Fusfeld, Daniel R. "Labor-Managed and Participatory Firms: A Review Article." *Journal of Economic Issues* 17, no. 3 (September 1983): 769–89.

Gapinski, James H., Borislav Škegro, and Thomas W. Zuehlke. *Modeling the Economic Performance of Yugoslavia.* New York: Praeger, 1989.

Garraty, John A. *Unemployment in History: Economic Thought and Public Policy.* New York: Harper and Row, 1978.

Garthoff, Raymond L. "The Death of Stalin and the Birth of Mutual Deterrence." *Survey* 25, no. 2 (Spring 1980): 10–16.

Gedeon, Shirley J. "Monetary Disequilibrium and Bank Reform Proposals in Yugoslavia: Paternalism and the Economy." *Soviet Studies* 39, no. 2 (April 1987): 281–91.

———. "The Post-Keynesian Theory of Money: A Summary and an Eastern European Example." *Journal of Post-Keynesian Economics* 8, no. 2 (Winter 1985/86): 208–21.

Gedeon, Shirley J. "Yugoslav Monetary Theory and Its Implication for Self-Management." Ph.D. diss., University of Massachusetts, Department of Economics, 1982.

Gerschenkron, Alexander. *Economic Backwardness in Historical Perspective: A Book of Essays*. Cambridge: Harvard University Press, Belknap Press, 1962.

Ginić, Ivanka. *Dinamika i struktura gradskog stanovništva Jugoslavije: Demografski aspekt urbanizacije*. Belgrade: Institut Društvenih Nauka, 1967.

Gligorov, Kiro. "Factors in Our Economic Stabilization." *Ekonomska Politika* 1, no. 8 (May 1952): 143–45.

———. "Neki problemi u vezi sa izvršenjem opštedržavnog budžeta za 1947 god." *Finansije*, yr. 2, vol. 4, no. 9 (September 1947): 479–88.

Gligorov, Vladimir. *Gledišta i sporovi o industrijalizaciji u socijalizmu*. Belgrade: Institut Društvenih Nauka, 1984.

Goati, Vladimir. "Savetovanje [in honor of Najdan Pašić]." *Ekonomska Politika*, no. 1841 (July 13, 1987): 17–18.

Gogić, Janko. *Razvoj i strukturne promjene regiona Jugoslavije*. Belgrade: Privredni Pregled, 1977.

Gorupić, Drago. "Uloga ekonomista u našoj privredi." *Ekonomski Pregled* 3, nos. 1–2 (1952): 1–8.

"Govor Andrije Hebranga." *Narodna Država* 1, nos. 4–5 (June 1947): 10–25.

Gow, James. *Legitimacy and the Military: The Yugoslav Crisis*. New York: St. Martin's Press, 1992.

Gradska Samoupravna Interesna Zajednica Zapošljavanja. *Zaposlenost u Beogradu: Tendencije, problemi i perspektive do 1985*. Belgrade, 1981.

Granick, David. *Job Rights in the Soviet Union: Their Consequences*. Cambridge: Cambridge University Press, 1988.

Green, Donald W. "Comment." In Egon Neuberger and Laura D'Andrea Tyson, eds., *The Impact of International Economic Disturbances on the Soviet Union and Eastern Europe*. New York: Pergamon Press, 1980.

Gregory, Mary B. "Regional Economic Development in Yugoslavia." *Soviet Studies* 25, no. 3 (October 1973): 213–28.

Griffith-Jones, Stefany. "The Growth of Multinational Banking, the Eurocurrency Market, and Their Effects on Developing Countries." *Journal of Development Studies* 14, no. 2 (January 1980): 204–23.

Gross, Mirjana. *Radnički pokret u Hrvatskoj potkraj XIX. stoljeća: Izabrani izvori*. Zagreb: Školska Knjiga, 1957.

Gulick, Charles A. *Austria from Habsburg to Hitler*. 2 vols. Berkeley and Los Angeles: University of California Press, 1948.

Guzina, Vojin. "Medjunarodni zajmovi i socijalistička izgradnja." *Komunist* 5, no. 6 (November 1950): 21–78.

Hadžić, Branko. "Zašto se i dalje razvija borba za visoku produktivnost rada u rudniku Brezi." *Partiska Izgradnja* 3, no. 1 (February 1951): 61–63.

Hahn, Werner G. *Postwar Soviet Politics: The Fall of Zhdanov and the Defeat of Moderation, 1946–1953*. Ithaca, N.Y.: Cornell University Press, 1982.

Hall, Peter. *Governing the Economy: The Politics of State Intervention in Britain and France*. London: Oxford University Press, 1986.

Halpern, Nina. "Policy Communities, Garbage Cans, and the Chinese Economic

Policy Process." Paper delivered to the annual meeting of the American Political Science Association, 1987.

Hamilton, F. E. Ian. "The Location of Industry in East-Central and Southeast Europe." In George W. Hoffman, ed., *Eastern Europe: Essays in Geographical Problems*. New York: Praeger, 1970.

———. *Yugoslavia: Patterns of Economic Activity*. New York: Praeger, 1968.

Hammel, Eugene A. *The Pink Yo-Yo: Occupational Mobility in Belgrade, ca. 1915–1965*. Research Series no. 13. Berkeley: Institute of International Studies, University of California, 1969.

Hankiss, Elemér. "In Search of a Paradigm." *Daedalus* 119, no. 1 (Winter 1990): 183–214.

Harvey, David. *The Limits to Capital*. Chicago: University of Chicago Press, 1982.

Has, Zdenko. "Društveno-ekonomski osvrt na problem nezaposlenosti." *Ekonomist*, nos. 3–4 (1954): 127–62.

———. "Borba za poštovanje ugovora o radu." *Vjesnik Rada* 5, no. 3 (March 1950): 125–27.

———. "Proces uključivanja radne snage i naši neposredni zadaci." *Vjesnik Rada* 5, nos. 1–2 (January–February 1950): 26–33.

———. "Da li su jedinstveni sindikati državna organizacija? Odnos države i sindikata u Jugoslaviji." *Vjesnik Rada* 1, no. 7 (November 1946): 306–9.

Hattam, Victoria. "Economic Visions and Political Strategies: American Labor and the State, 1865–1896." Unpub. ms. 1988.

Hauslohner, Peter. "Gorbachev's Social Contract." *Soviet Economy* 3, no. 1 (1987): 54–89.

Hawrylyshyn, Oli. "Ethnic Affinity and Migration Flows in Postwar Yugoslavia." *Economic Development and Cultural Change* 26, no. 1 (October 1977): 93–116.

———. "Yugoslav Development and Rural-Urban Migration: The Evidence of the 1961 Census." In Alan A. Brown and Egon Neuberger, eds., *Internal Migration: A Comparative Perspective*. New York: Academic Press, 1977.

Hayden, Robert M. "Labor Courts and Workers' Rights in Yugoslavia: A Case Study of the Contradictions of Socialist Legal Theory and Practice." *Studies in Comparative Communism* 18, no. 4 (Winter 1985): 247–60.

Heimann, Eduard. "Literature on the Theory of a Socialist Economy." *Social Research* 6 (1939): 88–113.

Henderson, Anne. "The International Monetary Fund and Eastern Europe: The Politics of Economic Stabilization and Reform." Ph.D. diss., Department of Political Science, Yale University, 1989.

Hewett, Ed A. *Reforming the Soviet Economy*. Washington, D.C.: The Brookings Institution, 1988.

Hibbs, Douglas. "Political Parties and Macroeconomic Policy." *American Political Science Review* 72, no. 4 (1977): 1467–87.

Hirsch, Fred. *Social Limits to Growth*. Cambridge: Harvard University Press, 1976.

Hirschman, Albert O. *The Passions and the Interests: Political Arguments for Capitalism before Its Triumph*. Princeton, N.J.: Princeton University Press, 1977.

———. *National Power and the Structure of Foreign Trade*. Berkeley and Los Angeles: University of California Press, 1945.

Hoffman, George W. *Regional Development Strategy in Southeast Europe: A Comparative Analysis of Albania, Bulgaria, Greece, Romania, and Yugoslavia.* New York: Praeger, 1972.

Hoffman, George W., and Fred Warner Neal. *Yugoslavia and the New Communism.* New York: Twentieth Century Fund, 1962.

Hogan, Michael. *The Marshall Plan: America, Britain, and the Reconstruction of Western Europe, 1947–1952.* Cambridge: Cambridge University Press, 1987.

Holjevac, Vjećeslav. "Problem radne snage: Neka iskustva iz prvog polugodišta." *Vjesnik Rada* 5, no. 7 (1950): 289–91.

———. "Problemi radne snage." *Borba,* July 23, 1950.

Hondius, Frits W. *The Yugoslav Community of Nations.* The Hague: Mouton, 1968.

Horvat, Branko. "Neke teze postavljene su naopako." *Izbor* 11 (1981): 21ff.

———. *The Yugoslav Economic System.* White Plains, N.Y.: M. E. Sharpe, 1976.

———. "Short-Run Instability and Long-Run Trends in the Yugoslav Economy's Development." Translated by Helen M. Kramer. *Eastern European Economics,* Fall 1975, pp. 3–31. Originally published (in Serbo-Croatian) in *Ekonomist* 14, nos. 1–2 (1974).

———. "Yugoslav Economic Policy in the Post-War Period: Problems, Ideas, Institutional Developments." *American Economic Review* 61, no. 3 (June 1971): 71–169.

———. *An Essay on Yugoslav Society.* White Plains, N.Y.: International Arts and Sciences Press, 1969.

Horvat, Branko, and J. Michael Montias. "The Theory of the Worker-Managed Firm Revisited." *Journal of Comparative Economics* 10, no. 1 (March 1986): 9–25. Special issue on participatory economics.

Hoston, Germaine. *Marxism and the Crisis of Development in Prewar Japan.* Princeton, N.J.: Princeton University Press, 1986.

Howell, Chris. "The Dilemmas of Post-Fordism: Socialists, Flexibility, and Labor Market Deregulation in France." *Politics and Society* 20, no. 1 (1992): 71–99.

Hroch, Miroslav. "How Much Does Nation Formation Depend on Nationalism?" *East European Politics and Societies* 4, no. 1 (Winter 1990): 101–15.

Ikonić, Branislav. "The Yugoslav Economy Marked by Stabilization Efforts and Structural Adjustment." *Review of International Affairs* 23, no. 762 (January 1982): 3–6.

Institute of Agricultural Economics and Rural Sociology. *The Yugoslav Village.* Zagreb, 1972.

International Labor Office. *Employment, Growth, and Basic Needs: A One-World Problem.* New York: Praeger, 1976.

———. *Legislative Series, 1927.* Part 1, International and A–D. Geneva, 1930.

Irvine, Jill A. "Tito, Hebrang, and the Croat Question, 1943–1944." *East European Politics and Societies* 5, no. 2 (Spring 1991): 306–40.

———. "State Building and Nationalism: The Communist Party of Yugoslavia and the Croat Question, 1941–45." Ph.D. diss., Department of Government, Harvard University, 1989.

Isaković, Zlatko. "The Balkan Armies at the End of the Cold War." Unpub. ms. Belgrade, 1993.

Itoh, Makoto. "The World Economic Crisis." *New Left Review* 138 (March–April 1983): 93–95.

Ivin, Daniel. "Analiza 'Pregled istorije Saveza Komunista Jugoslavije' u vezi sa II i III plenumom CK KPJ u 1949 godini." *Putevi Revolucije* 2, nos. 3–4 (1964).

Jahoda, Marie. *Employment and Unemployment.* Cambridge: Cambridge University Press, 1982.

Jahoda, Marie, Paul F. Lazarsfeld, and Hans Zeisel. *Marienthal: The Sociography of an Unemployed Community.* Chicago and New York: Aldine, Atherton, 1971.

Jakšić, Božidar. "Jugoslovensko društvo izmedju revolucije i stabilizacije." *Praxis* 8, nos. 3–4 (May–August 1971).

Janos, Andrew. *The Politics of Backwardness in Historical Perspective: Hungary, 1825–1945.* Princeton, N.J.: Princeton University Press, 1985.

Jelčić, Vera. *Socijalno pravo: Prava u sistemu socijalnog osiguranja SFRJ.* Zagreb: Informator, 1982.

Jiang, Yiwei. "The Theory of an Enterprise-Based Economy." *Social Sciences in China* 1 (March 1980): 48–70.

Johnson, A. Ross. *The Transformation of Communist Ideology: The Yugoslav Case, 1945–1953.* Cambridge, Mass., and London: MIT Press, 1972.

Johnson, Chalmers A. "The Nonsocialist NICs: East Asia." *International Organization* 40, no. 2 (Spring 1986): 557–66.

———. *Peasant Nationalism and Communist Power: The Emergence of Revolutionary China, 1937–1945.* Stanford: Stanford University Press, 1962.

Jončić, Milorad. *Ustav SFRJ sa saveznim zakonima koji se i dalje primenjuju.* Belgrade: Finansijski Studio, 1971.

Jovanov, Neca. "Pledoaje za dijalog o državi u socijalizmu." *Socijalizam* 23, nos. 7–8 (1980): 79–103.

———. *Radnički štrajkovi u Socijalističkoj Federativnoj Republici Jugoslaviji od 1958. do 1969. godine.* Belgrade: Zapis, 1979.

Jovanović, Dragoljub. "Političke uspomene." Unpub. ms. Hoover Institution Archives, Stanford, Calif.

Jowitt, Kenneth. *The Leninist Response to National Dependency.* Berkeley: Institute for International Sstudies, University of California, 1978.

———. "Inclusion and Mobilization in European Leninist Regimes." *World Politics* 28, no. 1 (October 1975): 69–96.

———. "An Organizational Approach to the Study of Political Culture in Marxist-Leninist Systems." *American Political Science Review* 68, no. 3 (1974): 1171–91.

———. *Revolutionary Breakthroughs and National Development: The Case of Romania, 1944–1965.* Berkeley and Los Angeles: University of California, 1971.

Jureša-Persoglio, Djurdja. "Neke značajke socio-ekonomskog položaja nezaposlenih u SRH, te njihova spremnost za prostornu i profesionalnu mobilnost." *Revija za Sociologiju* 10, nos. 3–4 (1980): 145–48.

Kahler, Miles. "European Protectionism in Theory and Practice." *World Politics* 37, no. 4 (July 1985): 475–502.

Kalain, R. "Mao Tse Tung's 'Bukharinist' Phase." *Journal of Contemporary Asia* 14, no. 2 (1984): 147–55.

Kalember, Dragica. "Siromaštvo i pitanje besposličenja kroz istoriju i u savremenosti." Ph.D. diss., Faculty of Laws, University of Belgrade, 1981.

Karcz, Jerzy F. "Agricultural Reform in Eastern Europe." In Morris Bornstein, ed., *Plan and Market: Economic Reform in Eastern Europe*. New Haven, Conn.: Yale University Press, 1973.

Kardelj, Edvard. *Problemi naše socijalističke izgradnje*. Belgrade: Kultura, 1960.

———. *Socialism and War: A Survey of the Chinese Policy of Coexistence*. New York: McGraw-Hill, 1960.

———. "The Struggle for the Fulfillment of the First Five Year Plan." Speech delivered in the national assembly, April 25, 1948. Mimeo.

Kaser, Michael, and E. A. Radice, eds. *The Economic History of Eastern Europe, 1919–1975*. Vol. 2, *Interwar Policy, the War, and Reconstruction*. Oxford: Clarendon Press, 1986.

Katz, Arnold. "Growth and Regional Variations in Unemployment in Yugoslavia, 1965–80." Working Paper no. 159, Department of Economics, University of Pittsburgh, 1983.

Katzenstein, Peter J. *Small States in World Markets: Industrial Policy in Europe*. Ithaca, N.Y.: Cornell University Press, 1985.

———. *Corporatism and Change: Austria, Switzerland, and the Politics of Industry*. Ithaca, N.Y., and London: Cornell University Press, 1984.

Kertesi, Gábor, and György Sziráczki. "The Institutional System, Labour Market, and Segmentation in Hungary." In Roger Tarling, ed., *Flexibility in Labour Markets*. London: Harcourt Brace Jovanovich, Academic Press, 1987.

Keyssar, Alexander. *Out of Work: The First Century of Unemployment in Massachusetts*. Cambridge: Cambridge University Press, 1986.

Kidrič, Boris. *Socijalizam i ekonomija*. Zagreb: Globus, 1979.

———. *O novom finansiskom i planskom sistemu*. Belgrade: Rad, 1951.

———. "Ekspoze o Predlogu opštedržavnog budžeta za 1950 godinu." *Finansije* 5, nos. 1–2 (January–February 1950): 3–18.

———. "O reorganizaciji državne uprave privredom." *Komunist* 4, nos. 4–5 (July–September 1950): 27–32.

———. *Ekspoze povodom pretresa prijedloga općedržavnog budžeta za 1949 (godinu)*. Mala Ekonomska Biblioteka, no. 3. Zagreb: Naprijed, 1949.

———. "Ekspoze pretsednika Privrednog saveta i Savezne planske komisije Borisa Kidriča." *Finansije* 4, no. 1 (January 1949).

———. *O tekućim pitanjima naše privredne politike*. Zagreb: Naprijed, 1949.

———. "Govor na plenumu Glavnog odbora Jedinstvenih sindikata" (November 16, 1946). Reprinted in *Privredni problemi FNRJ*. Belgrade: Kultura, 1948.

———. "Govor na pretresu opštedržavnog budžeta za 1948 godinu" (April 23, 1948). Reprinted in *Privredni problemi FNRJ*. Belgrade: Kultura, 1948.

———. "Obrazloženje osnovnog zakona o državnim privrednim preduzećima." *Borba*, July 21, 1946. Reprinted in *Privredni problemi FNRJ*. Belgrade: Kultura, 1948.

———. "O karakteru naše privrede." *Komunist*, no. 1 (October 1946). Reprinted in *Privredni problemi FNRJ*. Belgrade: Kultura, 1948.

———. "O vezanim cenama." *Borba*, February 15, 1948. Reprinted in *Privredni problemi FNRJ*. Belgrade: Kultura, 1948.

———. "O nekim principijelnim pitanjima naše privrede." *Komunist* 2, no. 2 (January 1947): 45–55.

———. "Obrazloženje nacrta osnovnog zakona o zadrugama." In *Sabrana dela*. Vol. 3.

Kimov, Džordži. "Da li se povećavaju socijalne razlike?" *NIN*, November 29, 1981.

Kirschen, E. S. *Economic Policy in Our Time*. Vol. 1. Chicago: Rand McNally, 1964.

Kitaljević, B. "Istoriska Gradja." *Finansije* 7, nos. 1–2 (January–February 1952): 76–91.

Kitching, Gavin. *Development and Underdevelopment in Historical Perspective: Populism, Nationalism, and Industrialization*. London and New York: Methuen, 1982.

Kljaković, Vojmir. "The Legacy of the Anti-Fascist Council (AVNOJ), 1942–1945." Paper presented at conference "War, Revolution, and the Early Socialist Period in Yugoslavia: A Historical Retrospective," Yale University, April 1984.

———. "The International Significance of the Second Session of AVNOJ." *Socialist Thought and Practice* 23, no. 12 (1983): 63–76.

Knight, Peter. *Financial Discipline and Structural Adjustment in Yugoslavia: Rehabilitation and Bankruptcy of Loss-making Enterprises*. Staff Working Paper no. 705. Washington, D.C.: World Bank, 1984.

"Kogod hoće da radi biće zaposlen." *20 Oktobar*, May 18, 1945, p. 4.

Komisija Saveznih Društvenih Savjeta za Probleme Ekonomske Stabilizacije. *Polazne osnove dugoročnog programa ekonomske stabilizacije*. 1982.

Komunistička Partija Jugoslavije. Centralni Komitet. "Uputstvo C.K. K.P.J. o reorganizaciji oblasti." *Komunist* 4, nos. 4–5 (July–September 1950): 228–31.

Kongres radničkih saveta Jugoslavije, 25–27 juna 1957. Belgrade: Rad, 1957.

Kornai, János. *The Road to a Free Economy: Shifting from a Socialist System: The Example of Hungary*. New York: Norton, 1990.

———. *Contradictions and Dilemmas: Studies on the Socialist Economy and Society*. Budapest: Corvina, 1983.

———. *The Economics of Shortage*. Amsterdam: North-Holland, 1980.

———. "Resource-Constrained vs. Demand-Constrained Systems." *Econometrica* 47 (July 1979): 801–19.

Korošić, Marijan. *Antiinflaciona politika*. Belgrade: Ekonomski Institut and Borba, 1980.

Korpi, Walter. *The Democratic Class Struggle*. London: Routledge and Kegan Paul, 1983.

Korpi, Walter, and Michael Shalev. "Strikes, Power, and Politics in the Western Nations, 1900–1976." In Maurice Zeitlin, ed., *Political Power and Social Theory*. Greenwich, Conn.: JAI Press, 1980.

Kostić, Cvetko. *Seljaci-industriski radnici*. Belgrade: Rad, 1955.

Kostić-Marojević, Darinka. *Promena društvene sredine i promene u porodici: Jedno empirijsko ispitivanje dveju grupa domaćinstava iz Crne Gore*. Belgrade: Institut Društvenih Nauka, 1968.

Koštunica, Vojislav, and Kosta Čavoški. *Party Pluralism or Monism: Social Move-*

ments and the Political System in Yugoslavia, 1944–1949. Boulder, Colo.: East European Monographs, 1985.

Kovač, Oskar. *Platnobilansna politika Jugoslavije.* Belgrade: Institut Ekonomskih Nauka, 1973.

Kovač, Oskar, Ljubomir Madžar, Zoran Popov, and Dragoljub Stanišić. *Privreda Jugoslavije do 1985.* Belgrade: Ekonomika, 1982.

Kovačević, Ivan. *Ekonomski položaj radničke klase u Hrvatskoj i Slavoniji, 1867–1914.* Zagreb: Institut za Suvremenu Istoriju i NIP, 1972.

Kovačević, M. "Pripreme za organizaciju oblasnih poverеништava rada u NR Srbiji." *Vjesnik Rada* 4, no. 4 (April 1949): 121–23.

Kraigher, Sergej. "Dohodak preduzeća u našem sistemu." *Naša Stvarnost* 7, no. 2 (February 1953): 45–64.

Kranjec, Marko. "An Analysis of the Effects of Yugoslav Fiscal Policy in the Light of Some Newer Theoretical Concepts." *Eastern European Economics* 14, no. 1 (Fall 1975): 32–36.

Krstulović, Vicko. "Stalno podizanje proizvodnosti rada poboljšava radne i životne uslove radničke klase." *Vjesnik Rada* 2, no. 11 (November 1947): 699–705.

Kurbović, Branko. "Polugodišnji rezultati izvršenja planova za 1952." *Ekonomski Pregled* 3, no. 4 (1952): 193–201.

Kurzer, Paulette. "Unemployment in Open Economies: The Impact of Trade, Finance, and European Integration." *Comparative Political Studies* 24, no. 1 (April 1991): 3–30.

Laba, Roman. *The Roots of Solidarity: A Political Sociology of Poland's Working-Class Democratization.* Princeton, N.J.: Princeton University Press, 1991.

Laković, M. "Otkaz u novim odnosima u privredi." *Socijalna Politika* 2, no. 7 (July 1952): 421–27.

Lampe, John R., Russell O. Prickett, and Ljubiša S. Adamović. *Yugoslav-American Economic Relations since World War II.* Durham, N.C.: Duke University Press, 1990.

Lampland, Martha. "Working through History." Ph.D. diss. Department of Anthropology, University of Chicago, 1987.

Lane, David, ed. *Labour and Employment in the USSR.* Brighton, Sussex: Wheatsheaf Books, Harvester Press, 1986.

Lang, Nicholas R. "The Dialectics of Decentralization: Economic Reform and Regional Inequality in Yugoslavia." *World Politics* 27, no. 3 (April 1975): 309–35.

Lange, B. "Osnovni pokazatelji iskorišćenja fonda radne snage državnih privrednih preduzeća." *Teška Industrija* 2, no. 4 (April 1950): 132–40.

Lange, Oskar, and Fred M. Taylor. *On the Economic Theory of Socialism.* Minneapolis: University of Minnesota Press, 1938.

Lavigne, Marie. "The Creation of Money by the State Bank of the USSR." *Economy and Society* 7, no. 1 (February 1978): 29–55.

Ledić, Michèle. "Debt Analysis and Debt-Related Issues: The Case of Yugoslavia." *Economic Analysis and Workers' Management* 18, no. 1 (1984): 35–64.

Lee, Bradford A. "The Miscarriage of Necessity and Invention: Proto-Keynesianism and Democratic States in the 1930s." Paper presented at a Social Science Research Council conference, Harvard University, 1985.

Lehmbruch, Gerhard. "Liberal Corporatism and Party Government." In Philippe Schmitter and Gerhard Lehmbruch, eds., *Trends toward Corporatist Intermediation*. Beverly Hills and London: Sage, 1979.

Lenin, Vladimir Il'ich. *The Development of Capitalism in Russia*. Moscow: Foreign Languages Publishing House, 1960.

————. *The State and the Revolution*. Moscow: International Publishers, 1943.

Les forces armées de la RSFY. Belgrade, 1977.

Letica, Slaven. "Pravo na rad i nacrt zakona o udruženom radu." *Zapošljavanje i Udruženi Rad: Ogledi, Članci, i Rasprava* 1, no. 1 (October 1976): 52–55.

"Let's Organize the Struggle of the Unemployed." *Proleter* 10, no. 1 (January 1934). Reprint, 1968. Belgrade: Institut za Izučavanje Radničkog Pokreta.

Levy, Marion J., Jr. *Modernization: Latecomers and Survivors*. New York: Basic Books, 1972.

Lewin, Moshe. *Political Undercurrents in Soviet Economic Debates: From Bukharin to the Modern Reformers*. Princeton, N.J.: Princeton University Press, 1974.

Lewis, Paul G. "Political Consequences of the Changes in Party-State Structures under Gierek." In Jean Woodall, ed., *Policy and Politics in Contemporary Poland: Reform, Failure, Crisis*. New York: St. Martin's Press, 1982.

Lindbeck, Assar, and Dennis J. Snower. *The Insider-Outsider Theory of Employment and Unemployment*. Cambridge: MIT Press, 1988.

Livada, Svetozar, and Blažo M. Perović, eds. *Društvene promjene u selu*. Belgrade: Biblioteka Sociologije Sela, 1974.

Livingston, Robert Gerald. "Yugoslavian Unemployment Trends." *Monthly Labor Review* (U.S. Department of Labor, Bureau of Labor Statistics) 87, no. 7 (July 1964): 756–62.

Ljujić, Velibor. "Primanje u partiji i poboljšavanje socijalnog sastava." *Partiska Izgradnja* 1, no. 6 (August 1949): 31–39.

Lompar, Dušan. "O novom sistemu trgovine." *Narodna Država* 2, no. 3 (March 1948): 10–20.

Löwenthal, Richard. "Development vs. Utopia in Communist Policy." In Chalmers Johnson, ed., *Change in Communist Systems*. Stanford, Calif.: Stanford University Press, 1970.

Lukač, Dušan, Conka Nikolić, Berislav Šefer, and Rafael Tabor, eds. *Ljudski faktor u socijalističkoj robnoj privredi samoupravnog društva i problemi zapošljavanja*. Papers presented at conference "The Human Factor in a Socialist Commodity Economy and Self-Managing Society and the Problem of Employment," February 11–13, 1969, at the Institute for Political Studies, University of Belgrade, at the initiative of the Federal Bureau for Employment Affairs.

Lydall, Harold. *Yugoslav Socialism: Theory and Practice*. Oxford: Clarendon Press, 1984.

McCain, Roger A. "The Economics of a Labor-Managed Enterprise in the Short Run: An 'Implicit Contracts' Approach." In *Advances in the Economic Analysis of Participatory and Labor-Managed Firms*. Vol. 1. Greenwich, Conn.: JAI Press, 1985.

Macesich, George. "Major Trends in the Postwar Economy of Yugoslavia." In Wayne S. Vucinich, ed., *Contemporary Yugoslavia: Twenty Years of Socialist Experiment*. Berkeley and Los Angeles: University of California Press, 1969.

Macesich, George. *Yugoslavia: The Theory and Practice of Development Planning.* Charlottesville, Va.: University Press of Virginia, 1964.

————. ed., with the assistance of Rikard Lang and Dragomir Vojnić. *Essays on the Yugoslav Economic Model.* New York: Praeger, 1989.

Macura, Miloš. "Employment Problems under Declining Population Growth Rates and Structural Change: Case of Yugoslavia, 1952–1958." *International Labour Review* 109, nos. 5–6 (May–June 1974): 487–501.

————. *Stanovništvo kao činilac privrednog razvoja Jugoslavije.* Belgrade: Nolit, 1958.

Maier, Charles S. "The Two Post-War Eras and the Conditions for Stability in Twentieth-Century Western Europe." *American Historical Review* 86, no. 2 (April 1981): 327–52.

————. "The Politics of Productivity: Foundations of American International Economic Policy after World War II." In Peter J. Katzenstein, ed., *Between Power and Plenty: Foreign Economic Policies of Advanced Industrial States.* Madison: University of Wisconsin Press, 1978.

Malačić, Janez. "Unemployment in Yugoslavia from 1952 to 1975." *Eastern European Economics* 17, no. 4 (Summer 1979): 85–109.

————. "Yugoslav Economists on Unemployment in Yugoslavia." *Eastern European Economics* 15, no. 4 (Summer 1977): 60–72.

Malle, Silvana. *The Economic Organization of War Communism, 1918–1921.* Cambridge: Cambridge University Press, 1985.

Marendić, Božo, Ivan Turčić, and Neven Mates. "Mjerenje i analiza razvijenosti općina S.R. Hrvatske." *Ekonomski Pregled* 32, nos. 7–8 (1981): 291–311.

Marić, Dušan. "O problemima radnih odnosa posle donošenja Osnovnog zakona o upravljanju." *Vjesnik Rada* 5, no. 11 (November 1950): 427–33.

Maričić, Ratko. "Neki problemi organizacije i rada biroa za posredovanje rada." *Socijalna Politika* 2, no. 11 (November 1952): 662–69.

Marković, Branimir. *Kretanje narodna dohotka, zaposlenosti, i produktivnosti rada u privredi Jugoslavije, 1947–1967.* Belgrade: Savezni Zavod za Statistiku, 1970.

Marsenić, Dragutin, and Milovan Pavlović. "Teorijski sporovi o privrednom sistemu SFRJ: Povodom savetovanja ekonomista u Ohridu [1970]." *Ekonomist* 24, no. 1 (1971): 76–94.

Martin, Andrew. "The Politics of Employment and Welfare in Advanced Capitalist Societies: National Policies and International Interdependence." In Keith Banting, ed., *The State and Economic Interests.* Toronto: University of Toronto Press, 1986.

Martin, Christopher. "Public Policy and Income Distribution in Yugoslavia: A Case of Arrested Market Reform." Ph.D. diss. Department of Economics, University of California at Berkeley, 1986.

Marzorati, Gerald. "Living and Writing the Peasant Life." *New York Times Magazine*, November 29, 1987, pp. 39, 46, 50, 54.

Mastnak, Tomaž. "Civil Society in Slovenia: From Opposition to Power." *Studies in Comparative Communism* 23 (Autumn–Winter 1990): 305–17.

Mates, Neven. "Inflation in Yugoslavia: Specific Form of Public Deficit Caused by Parafiscal Operations of the Central Bank." Unpub. ms. Zagreb, 1990.

————. "Measurement of Government Budget Deficit, Losses of Central Banks, and the Impact of Aggregate Deficit of the Public Sector on Inflation." Unpub. ms. Zagreb, 1989.

———. "Recent Tendencies in the Regulation of Income Distribution in Enterprises." In G. Macesich, ed., *Essays on the Yugoslav Economic Model*. New York: Praeger, 1989.

Matović, M. "Samouprava u socijalnom osiguranju." *Socijalna Politika* 2, no. 7 (July 1952): 428–32.

Meade, James E. "Labour-Managed Firms in Conditions of Imperfect Competition." *Economic Journal* 84, (December 1974): 817–24.

———. "The Theory of Labour-Managed Firms and of Profit-sharing." *Economic Journal* 82 (March 1972): 402–28.

Meek, Ronald L. *Study in the Labor Theory of Value*. 2d ed. New York and London: Monthly Review Press, 1956.

"Memorandum SANU: Grupa akademika Srpske akademije nauka i umetnosti o aktuelnim društvenim pitanjima u našoj zemlji." *Duga* (Belgrade), special issue, June 1989, pp. 19–47.

Mencinger, Jože. "Privredna reforma i nezaposlenost." *Privredna Kretanja Jugoslavije*, March 1989, pp. 23–39.

———. *The Yugoslav Economy: Systemic Changes, 1945–1985*. The Carl Beck Papers in Russian and East European Studies, no. 707. Pittsburgh: University of Pittsburgh, Center for Russian and East European Studies, 1989.

———. "Komentar" [on Ljubomir Madžar proposals], *Ekonomska Politika*, no. 1829 (April 20, 1987): 28–29.

———. "Otvorena nezaposlenost i zaposleni bez posla." *Privredna Kretanja Jugoslavije* 128 (April 1983).

———. "Utjecaj privredne aktivnosti na zaposlenost i efekti mjera za zapošljavanje na stabilizaciju." *Ekonomski Pregled* 27, nos. 11–12 (1976): 829–37.

Mesa-Lago, Carmelo. "Unemployment in a Socialist Economy: Yugoslavia." *Industrial Relations* 10, no. 1 (February 1971): 49–69.

Mežnarić, Silva. "A Neo-Marxist Approach to the Sociology of Nationalism: A Quest for Theory." Colloquium paper presented to the Woodrow Wilson Center, Smithsonian Institution, Washington, D.C., July 24, 1984. Later published as "A Neo-Marxist Approach to the Sociology of Nationalism, Doomed Nations, and Doomed Schemes." *Praxis International* 7, no. 1 (1987): 79–89.

Mihailović, Kosta. *Ekonomska stvarnost Jugoslavije*. 2d ed. Belgrade: Ekonomika, 1982.

Mihovilović, Miro A., et al. *Žena izmedju rada i porodice: Utjecaj zaposlenosti žene na strukturu i funkciju porodice*. Zagreb: Institut za Društvena Istraživanja Sveučilišta u Zagrebu, 1975.

Milanović, Branko. "The Labor-Managed Firms in the Short-Run: Comments on Horvat's 'Theory of the Worker-Managed Firm Revisited'." Paper presented to Yale University Colloquium on Participatory Economics and Politics, May 3–4, 1985.

———. "The Austrian Theory of the Cooperative Firm." *Journal of Comparative Economics* 6 (1982): 379–95.

Milenkovitch, Deborah Duff. *Plan and Market in Yugoslav Economic Thought*. New Haven, Conn.: Yale University Press, 1971.

Milenović, Miodrag. "Unutrašnje migracije i medjurepubličko zapošljavanje." *Socijalna Politika* 33, no. 3 (March 1978): 25–29.

Miljovski, Kiril. "Neke ekonomske, paraekonomske i neekonomske pretpostavke privrednog razvoja." *Scientia Yugoslavica* 8, nos. 1–2 (1982): 65–81.

———. "Possibilities for the Development of Underdeveloped Areas." In Radmila Stojanović, ed., *Yugoslav Economists on Problems of a Socialist Economy*. New York: International Arts and Sciences Press, 1964.

Miller, Robert F. "Socialism and Agriculture in Yugoslavia." Paper presented to the 21st conference of the Australasian Political Studies Association, Australian National University, Canberra, 1979.

———. *External Factors in Yugoslav Political Development*. Occasional Paper no. 14. Department of Political Science, Research School of Social Sciences, Australian National University, Canberra, 1977.

Milward, Alan. *The Reconstruction of Western Europe, 1945–51*. Berkeley and Los Angeles: University of California Press, 1984.

Mirić, Jovan. *Sistem i kriza*. Zagreb: Cekade, 1984.

Mirić, Milan. *Rezervati*. Zagreb: Razlog, 1970.

Mirković, Nicholas, ed. *Jugoslav Postwar Reconstruction Papers*. 3 vols. New York: Office of Reconstruction and Economic Affairs, Government of Jugoslavia, 1943.

Miroljub, Hadzic. *The Wage-Push Inflation in Yugoslavia*. Working Paper Series no. 67. The Hague: Institute of Social Studies, 1989.

Mitrany, David. *Marx against the Peasant: A Study in Social Dogmatism*. Chapel Hill: University of North Carolina Press, 1951.

Mladek, J. V., E. Šturc, and M. R. Wyczalkowski. "The Change in the Yugoslav Economic System." *International Monetary Fund Staff Papers* 2, no. 3 (November 1952): 407–38.

Montias, John Michael. "Economic Reform and Retreat in Jugoslavia." *Foreign Affairs* 37, no. 2 (January 1959): 293–305.

Moore, John H. *Growth with Self-Management: Yugoslav Industrialization, 1952–1975*. Stanford, Calif.: Hoover Institution Press, 1980.

Morača, Pero. *Istorija Saveza Komunista Jugoslavije: Kratak pregled*. 2d ed. Belgrade: Rad, 1966.

Morawetz, David. "Employment Implications of Industrialization in Developing Countries: A Survey." *Economic Journal* 84 (September 1974): 491–542.

Moses, Joel C. "Worker Self-Management and the Reformist Alternative in Soviet Labor Policy, 1979–1985." *Soviet Studies* 39, no. 2 (April 1987): 205–28.

Mucciaroni, Gary. *The Political Failure of Employment Policy, 1945–1982*. Pittsburgh: University of Pittsburgh Press, 1990.

Mugoša, Dragiša. "Odnosi Jugoslavije i SAD-a izmedju 1945 i 1949." Master's thesis, Faculty of Law, University of Belgrade, 1982.

Mulec, J., and M. Glišić. "Problem radne snage u metalurgiji i rudarstvu." *Narodna Država* 1, no. 2 (November 1946): 107–10.

Mulina, Tripo. *Nezaposlenost, uzroci i karakteristike u sadašnjoj fazi razvoja privrede*. Studije i Saopštenja no. 3, Belgrade: Ekonomski Institut, 1968.

Mulina, T., M. Macura, and M. Rašević. *Stanovništvo i zaposlenost u dugoročnom razvoju Jugoslavije*. Belgrade: Ekonomski Institut, 1981.

Mustabegović, Ejub, Jelisava Jankelović, and Šefik Bajramović. "Uključenje radne snage u privredi u Zeničkom srezu." *Partiska Izgradnja* 1, no. 4 (April 1949): 28–31.

Myers, Paul F., and Arthur A. Campbell. *The Population of Yugoslavia*. U.S. Bureau of Labor Statistics, International Population Statistics Reports, ser. P-90, no. 5. Washington, D.C.: U.S. Government Printing Office, 1954.

Naljeva, Mara. "Neka pitanja partiskog rada medju ženama." *Partiska Izgradnja* 2, no. 1 (January 1950).

Narodna Skupština FNRJ. *See* Yugoslavia.

Narodni Front Jugoslavije. *Drugi kongres Narodnog fronta Jugoslavije*. Belgrade, 1947.

"Ne postoji pravo na rad." *Ekonomska Politika*, no. 885 (March 17, 1966): 14–15.

Nešović, Slobodan. *Privredna politika i ekonomske mere u toku oslobodilačke borbe naroda Jugoslavije*. Belgrade: Privredni Pregled, 1964.

"New Economic Course." *Yugoslav Review* 5, nos. 8–9 (October–November 1955): 8–12.

"New Ways of Yugoslav Economy." *Yugoslav Review* 5, nos. 8–9 (October–November 1955): 3, 12–13.

Nikolić, Miloje. "Politika zapošljavanja." *Socijalna Politika*, July 20, 1968, pp. 6–9.

Nikolić, Miodrag. "Rast produktivnosti rada u Jugoslaviji." *Statistički Dokumenti* 1, no. 8 (1976): 14–21.

Nishimizu, Mieko, and John M. Page, Jr. "Total Factor Productivity Growth, Technological Progress, and Technical Efficiency Change: Dimensions of Productivity Change in Yugoslavia, 1965–1978." *Economic Journal* 92 (December 1982): 920–36.

Noel, Alain. "Accumulation, Regulation, and Social Change: An Essay on French Political Economy." *International Organization* 41, no. 2 (Spring 1987): 303–33.

"The Non-Agricultural Population." *Yugoslav Survey* 28, no. 3 (1987).

Nove, Alec. *The Economics of Feasible Socialism*. London: Allen and Unwin, 1983.

———. *An Economic History of the U.S.S.R.* London: Penguin, 1969.

O'Donnell, Guillermo. *Modernization and Bureaucratic-Authoritarianism: Studies in South American Politics*. Berkeley: Institute of International Studies, University of California, 1973.

Offe, Claus. "Capitalism by Democratic Design? Democratic Theory Facing the Triple Transition in East Central Europe." *Social Research* 58, no. 4 (Winter 1991): 865–92.

———. "Three Perspectives on the Problem of Unemployment." In *Disorganized Capitalism: Contemporary Transformations of Work and Politics*. Edited by John Keane. Cambridge: MIT Press, 1985.

———. "Two Logics of Collective Action." In *Disorganized Capitalism*.

———. "The Future of the Labor Market." *Telos*, no. 60 (Summer 1984): 81–96.

Oleszczuk, Thomas. "Group Challenges and Ideological De-radicalization in Yugoslavia." *Soviet Studies* 32, no. 4 (October 1980): 561–79.

Olson, Mancur. *The Logic of Collective Action*. Cambridge: Harvard University Press, 1965.

Osmi kongres SKJ. Belgrade, 1965.

Panić, Miodrag Lj. "Radna snaga i zaposlenost u Jugoslaviji." Ph.D. diss., Faculty of Laws, University of Belgrade, 1987.

Parmalee, Donna E. "Medicine under Yugoslav Self-Managing Socialism." Ph.D. diss. Department of Sociology, University of North Carolina, 1983.

Pašić, Najdan, and Kiro Hadži Vasilev. "Komunistička partija Jugoslavije—1945–48." In *Pregled istorije Saveza Komunista Jugoslavije*. Belgrade: Institut za Izučavanje Radničkog Pokreta, 1963.

Pavlović, Milenko. "Employment in the Socialized Sector, 1979–1984." *Yugoslav Survey* 26, no. 3 (1985): 11.

Pavlović, Mirjana. "Boris Kidrič o principima tržišne ekonomije i višku radne snage." *Gledišta* 13, no. 9 (September 1972): 1185–92.

Pejnović, Mladen. "SSO i stabilizacija." *Pitanje* 11 (August 1979): 4–5.

Perić, Aleksandar. "Društveni prihodi i rashodi u FNRJ." In *Priručnik za ekonomiku FNRJ*. Belgrade: Rad, 1958.

Perišin, Ivo. "The Banking System and Monetary Policy." In Rikard Lang, George Macesich, and Dragomir Vojnić, eds., *Essays on the Political Economy of Yugoslavia*. Zagreb: Ekonomski Institut, 1982.

Pešaković, Milentije. "Niško savetovanje ekonomista Srbije, 1963 i danas." *Ekonomska Misao* 13, no. 1 (March 1980): 145–48.

Pešić, Ratko. *Radno pravo*. Belgrade: Naučna Knjiga, 1966.

———. "Materijalno obezbedjenje radnika i službenika za vreme privremenog prestanka radnog odnosa." *Socijalna Politika* 2, no. 5 (May 1952): 304–11.

———. "O ugovorima o radu." *Vjesnik Rada* 4, nos. 1–2 (January–February 1949): 14–19.

Pešić, V. "Za potpuno i blagovremeno izvršenje plana radne snage u N.R. Srbiji." *Partiska Izgradnja* 1, no. 4 (April 1949): 73–77.

Peti kongres Saveza sindikata Jugoslavije. Belgrade: Rad, 1964.

Petranović, Branko. *Revolucija i kontrarevolucija u Jugoslaviji (1941–1945)*. Vol. 2. Belgrade: Rad, 1983.

———. *Politička i ekonomska osnova narodne vlasti u Jugoslaviji za vreme obnove*. Belgrade: Institut za Savremenu Istoriju, 1969.

———. "Narodna vlast u periodu administrativnog rukovodjenja privredom." In *Pregled posleratnog razvitka Jugoslavije*. Belgrade: Zavod za Izdavanje Udžbenika Socijalističke Republike Srbije, 1966.

Petranović, Branko, Ranko Končar, and Radovan Radonjić, eds. *Sednice Centralnog komiteta KPJ (1948–1952)*. Izvori za Istoriju SKJ, ser. A, vol. 2, no. 2. Belgrade: Komunist, 1985.

Petranović, Branko, and Momčilo Zečević. *Jugoslavija, 1918–1988: Tematska zbirka dokumenata*. Belgrade: Rad, 1988.

Petrin, Tea. "The Potential of Small-Scale Industry for Employment in Yugoslavia." *Economic Analysis and Workers' Management* 12, nos. 3–4 (1978): 347–63.

Petrović, D. "Prelazimo od starog na novo." *Partiska Izgradnja* 1, no. 4 (April 1949): 32–35.

Petrović, Vojislav J. *Razvitak privrednog sistema FNRJ posmatran kroz pravne propise*. 5 vols. Belgrade: Ekonomski Institut FNRJ, 1955–57.

Piore, Michael J. "Historical Perspectives and the Interpretation of Unemployment." *Journal of Economic Literature* 25 (December 1987): 1834–1850.

———. *Unemployment and Inflation: Institutionalist and Structuralist Views.* White Plains, N.Y.: M. E. Sharpe, 1979.

Piore, Michael J., and Charles F. Sabel. *The Second Industrial Divide: Possibilities for Prosperity.* New York: Basic Books, 1984.

Pjanić, Zoran. *Problem stanovništva u ekonomskoj teoriji.* Belgrade: Nolit, 1957.

Pleskovič, Boris, and Marjan Dolenc. "Regional Development in a Socialist, Developing, and Multinational Country: The Case of Yugoslavia." *International Regional Science Review* 7, no. 1 (1982): 1–24.

Polanyi, Karl. *The Great Transformation.* Boston: Beacon Press, 1957. Originally published 1944.

Polovina, Svetislav. "Ciljevi i perspektive zapošljavanja." *Revija za Sociologiju* 10, nos. 3–4 (1980): 149–51.

Pop-Antoška, Hristina. "Podaci o licima koja traže zaposlenje u Jugoslaviji." *Statistička Revija* 26, nos. 1–2 (1976): 122–33.

Portes, Richard. "Central Planning and Monetarism: Fellow Travelers?" In Padma Desai, ed., *Marxism, Central Planning, and the Soviet Economy: Economic Essays in Honor of Alexander Erlich.* Cambridge: MIT Press, 1980.

"Potrebno je iskoristiti unutrašnje rezerve koje postoje na našim železnicama." *Narodna Država* 2, nos. 4–5 (April–May 1948): 70–76.

"Povodom ukidanja uredbe o ustaljivanju radne snage." *Socijalna Politika* 2, nos. 2–3 (February–March 1952): 163–65.

Prašnikar, Janes. "The Yugoslav Self-managed Firm and Its Behavior." *Eastern European Economics.* 22, no. 2 (Winter 1983–84): 3–43.

Pravda, Alex. "Poland 1980: From 'Premature Consumerism' to Labor Solidarity." *Soviet Studies* 34, no. 2 (April 1982): 167–99.

———. "East-West Interdependence and the Social Compact in Eastern Europe." In Morris Bornstein, Zvi Gitelman, and William Zimmerman, eds., *East-West Relations and the Future of Eastern Europe: Politics and Economics.* London: Allen and Unwin, 1981.

"Prerada metala: Strah od neizvesnosti." *Ekonomska Politika,* April 12, 1982, 13.

Pribičević, Branko. *Sukob Komunističke partije Jugoslavije i Kominforma.* Belgrade: Komunist, 1972.

Primorac, Emil, and Mate Babić. "Systemic Changes and Unemployment Growth in Yugoslavia, 1965–1985." *Slavic Review* 48, no. 2 (Summer 1989): 195–213.

Primorac, Emil, and M. F. Charette. "Regional Aspects of Youth Unemployment in Yugoslavia." *Economic Analysis and Workers' Management* 21, no. 2 (1987): 193–220.

Primorac, Emil, and P. A. Della Valle. "Unemployment in Yugoslavia: Some Structural and Regional Considerations." *Jahrbuch der Wirtschaft Osteuropas* 5, no. 2 (1974): 455–87.

Privreda FNRJ, 1957. Belgrade: Ekonomski Institut FNRJ, 1958.

Privreda FNRJ u periodu 1947–1956. Belgrade: Ekonomski Institut FNRJ, 1957.

Przeworski, Adam. *Democracy and the Market: Political and Economic Reforms in Eastern Europe and Latin America.* Cambridge: Cambridge University Press, 1991.

Przeworski, Adam. *Capitalism and Social Democracy*. Cambridge: Cambridge University Press, 1985.

Puljiz, Vlado. *Eksodus poljoprivrednika*. Zagreb: Biblioteka Sociologije Sela, 1977.

Pusić, Vesna. "Uloga kolektivnog odlučivanja u realizaciji radničkih interesa." Ph.D. diss., Faculty of Political Science, University of Zagreb, 1984.

Putterman, Louis. "Self-Management and the Yugoslav Economy." *Journal of Comparative Economics* 10, no. 1 (March 1986).

Radmilović, Jerko. "Karakter službe posredovanja rada i pitanje njene reorganizacije." *Vjesnik Rada* 3, no. 1 (January 1948): 10–13.

Radonjić, Radovan. *Sukob KPJ s Kominformom i društveni razvoj Jugoslavije, 1948–1950*. Zagreb: Centar za Kulturnu djelatnost S.S.O. Zagreba, 1979.

Radovanović, Miroslav. "Različita shvatanja uzroka i oblika nezaposlenosti." *Zapošljavanje i Udruženi Rad: Ogledi, Članci, i Rasprava* 1, no. 1 (October 1976): 44–55.

———. "Osnovne karakteristike položaja nezaposlenih i shvatanje jedne grupe nezaposlenih." *Gledišta* 9, no. 2 (February 1968): 246–58.

———. "Socijalno-psihološke posledice nezaposlenosti." *Gledišta* 9, no. 4 (April 1968): 581–87.

Radovanović, R. "Ukidanje poreza na dohodak radnika, nameštenika i službenika—Nov doprinos socijalističkoj privredi i pravilnom nagradjivanju." *Narodna Država* 4, no. 5 (May 1950): 50–52.

Ramet, Pedro. "Apocalypse Culture and Social Change in Yugoslavia." In Pedro Ramet, ed., *Yugoslavia in the 1980s*. Boulder, Colo.: Westview Press, 1985.

———. *Nationalism and Federalism in Yugoslavia, 1963–1983*. Bloomington: Indiana University Press, 1984.

Ranković, Aleksandar. "Referat o sindikalnom pitanju." In *Peta zemaljska konferencija KPJ*. Belgrade: Komunist, 1980.

Rašević, M., T. Mulina, and M. Macura. *The Determinants of Labour Force Participation in Yugoslavia*. Geneva: International Labour Office, 1978.

"Raspored stručnjaka treba pravilno izvršiti." *20 Oktobar*, April 20, 1945, p. 2.

"Rates of Employment and Unemployment, 1980–1987." *Yugoslav Survey* 29, no. 4 (1988): 27–42.

Rawin, Solomon John. "Management and Autonomy in Socialist Industry—The Yugoslav Experience." *Jahrbuch der Wirtschaft Osteuropas* 4 (1973): 351–67.

Remington, Robin. "Yugoslavia." In Richard F. Staar, ed., *Yearbook on International Communist Affairs*. Stanford, Calif.: Hoover Institution Press, 1988.

"Rise in Employment, 1957–60." *Yugoslav Survey* 2, no. 2 (April–June 1961): 647–59, 793–802.

Rivers, Douglas. "Micro-Economics and Macro-Politics." Unpub. ms., Department of Political Science, Stanford University, 1987.

Robinson, Joan. "The Soviet Collective Farm as a Producer Cooperative: Comment." *American Economic Review* 57, no. 1 (March 1967): 222–23.

Robinson, Sherman, and Laura D'Andrea Tyson. "Foreign Trade, Resource Allocation, and Structural Adjustment in Yugoslavia: 1976–1980." *Journal of Comparative Economics* 9 (1985): 46–70.

Roemer, John. *Free to Lose*. Cambridge: Harvard University Press, 1988.

Roemer, Michael. "Dependence and Industrialization Strategies." *World Development* 9, no. 5 (1981): 429–34.

Roksandić, Drago. *Srbi u Hrvatskoj od 15. stoljeća do naših dana*. Zagreb: Vjesnik, 1991.

Róna-Tas, Ákos. "The Second Economy in Hungary: The Social Origins of the End of State Socialism." Ph.D. diss., University of Michigan, 1990.

Rosenblum-Čale, Karen. "Appropriation Politics: Consensus-Building and Conflict-Management in Mostar Commune, 1965–1969." Unpub. ms. 1977.

Rothschild, Joseph. *East Central Europe between the Two World Wars*. Seattle: University of Washington Press, 1974.

Rucciardi, Joseph. "Rereading Marx on the Role of Money and Finance in Economic Development: Political Perspectives on Credit from the 1840s and 1850s." *Research in Political Economy* 10 (1987): 61–81.

Rusinow, Dennison. Review of *Die Kooperation zwischen den privaten Landwirtschaftsbetrieben und den gesellschaftlichen wirtschaftsorganisationen in der Landwirtschaft Jugoslawiens* by Ivan Lončarević. *Slavic Review* 36, no. 4 (September 1977): 527–28.

————. *The Yugoslav Experiment, 1948–1974*. Berkeley and Los Angeles: University of California Press, 1977.

Sabel, Charles, and David Stark. "Politics, Planning, and Shop-Floor Power: Hidden Forms of Bargaining in Soviet-Imposed State-Socialist Societies." *Politics and Society* 11, no. 4 (1982): 439–75.

Sacks, Stephen R. *Self-Management and Efficiency: Large Corporations in Yugoslavia*. London: Allen and Unwin, 1983.

————. *Entry of New Competitors in Yugoslav Market Socialism*. Berkeley: Institute of International Studies, University of California, 1973.

Sapir, André. "Economic Reform and Migration in Yugoslavia: An Econometric Model." *Journal of Development Economics* 9 (1981): 149–87.

Savez komunista Jugoslavije. *Borba komunista Jugoslavije za socijalističku demokratiju*. Belgrade: Kultura, 1952.

Savezni Društveni Savet. *Dugoročni program stabilizacije*. Belgrade, 1984.

Savezni Zavod za Statistiku. *Uputstvo za sprovodjenje izveštaja o zaposlenom osoblju*. Metodološki Materijali no. 96. Belgrade, 1958.

————. *Uputstva za polugodišnji izveštaj o zaposlenom osoblju (Metod i način sprovodjenja)*. Metodološki Materijali no. 39. Belgrade, 1954.

Scharpf, Fritz W. "Economic and Institutional Constraints of Full-Employment Strategies: Sweden, Austria, and West Germany, 1973–1982." In John H. Goldthorpe, ed., *Order and Conflict in Contemporary Capitalism*. Oxford: Clarendon Press, 1984.

Schierup, Carl. "Quasi-Proletarians and Patriarchal Bureaucracy: Aspects of Yugoslavia's Reperipheralisation." *Soviet Studies* 44, no. 1 (January 1992): 79–99.

Schlozman, Kay Lehman, and Sidney Verba. *Injury to Insult: Unemployment, Class, and Political Response*. Cambridge: Harvard University Press, 1979.

Schrenk, Martin, Cyrus Ardalan, and Nawal A. El Tatawy. *Yugoslavia: Self-Management Socialism and the Challenges of Development*. Baltimore: Johns Hopkins University Press for the World Bank, 1979.

Schumpeter, Joseph A. "The Crisis of the Tax-State." In Alan T. Peacock, Wolfgang F. Stolper, Ralph Turvey, and Elizabeth Henderson, eds., *International Economic Papers*, no. 4. London and New York: Macmillan, 1954.

Schurmann, Franz. *Ideology and Organization in Communist China*. Berkeley and Los Angeles: University of California Press, 1966.

Schwartz, Herman. "Can Orthodox Stabilization and Adjustment Work? Lessons from New Zealand, 1984–90." *International Organization* 45, no. 2 (Spring 1991): 221–56.

Scott, Hilda. "Why the Revolution Doesn't Solve Everything." *Women's Studies International Forum* 5, no. 5 (1982): 451–62.

Scott, James C. *The Moral Economy of the Peasant: Rebellion and Subsistence in South-East Asia*. New Haven, Conn.: Yale University Press, 1976.

Scriven, John Graham. "Yugoslav Business Operations: Distribution of Income and Taxation." Ph.D. diss., Cambridge University, 1981.

Selznick, Philip. *The Organizational Weapon: A Study of Bolshevik Strategy and Tactics*. New York: McGraw-Hill, 1952.

Sen, Amartya K. *Employment, Technology, and Development*. Study prepared for the International Labour Office. Oxford: Clarendon Press, 1975.

Seroka, Jim. *Change and Reform of the League of Communists in Yugoslavia*. The Carl Beck Papers in Russian and East European Studies, no. 704. Pittsburgh: University of Pittsburgh, Center for Russian and East European Studies, 1990.

Seroka, Jim, and Radoš Smiljković. *Political Organizations in Socialist Yugoslavia*. Durham, N.C.: Duke University Press, 1986.

Sesardić, Dražen. "Značaj reorganizacije narodnih odbora." *Narodna Država* 3, no. 1 (January 1949): 19–32.

Šesti Kongres S.S.J. Belgrade: Radnička Štampa, 1968.

Shanin, Teodor, ed. *Late Marx and the Russian Road: Marx and the Peripheries of Capitalism*. London: Routledge and Kegan Paul, 1984.

Shapiro, Ian, and John Kane. "Stagflation and the New Right." *Telos*, no. 56 (Summer 1983): 5–39.

Shapiro, Judith A. "NEP Unemployment: A Failure for Market Socialism?" Unpub. ms. 1987.

———. "Unemployment from Tsarism to NEP." Unpub. ms. University of London, Goldsmith's College, Birmingham, England, 1987.

Shonfield, Andrew. *Modern Capitalism*. Oxford: Oxford University Press, 1965.

Shoup, Paul. *Communism and the Yugoslav National Question*. New York and London: Columbia University Press, 1968.

Sicherl, Pavle. *A Dynamic Analysis of Regional Disparities in Yugoslavia*. Income Distribution and Employment Programme, Working Paper no. 84. Geneva: International Labour Organization, 1980.

———. "Značaj zaposlenosti u našim uslovima." *Ekonomski Pregled* 27, nos. 11–12 (1976): 897–903.

———. "Time-Distance as a Dynamic Measure of Disparities in Social and Economic Development." *Kyklos* 3 (1973).

Singleton, Fred, and Bernard Carter. *The Economy of Yugoslavia*. New York: St. Martin's Press, 1982.

Sirianni, Carmen. *Workers' Control and Socialist Democracy: The Soviet Experience*. London: Verso, 1982.

Škrbić, P. "Manjak—četiri milijarde." *Borba*, October 29, 1982.

Slider, Darrell. "The Brigade System in Soviet Industry: An Effort to Restructure the Labour Force." *Soviet Studies* 39, no. 3 (July 1987): 388–405.

Smith, Stephen C. "Does Employment Matter to the Labour-Managed Firm? Some Theory and an Empirical Illustration." *Economic Analysis and Workers' Management.* 18, no. 4 (1984): 303–18.

Solinger, Dorothy. *Chinese Business under Socialism: The Politics of Domestic Commerce 1949–1980.* Berkeley and Los Angeles: University of California Press, 1986.

"Some Basic Features of Yugoslav External Migration." *Yugoslav Survey* 13, no. 1 (February 1972): 1–9.

Šošic, Hrvoje. *Za čiste račune: Banke, Genex, Reeksporteri.* Zagreb: Matica Hrvatska, 1970.

Šoškić, Branislav. "Ekonomska politika zaposlenosti i zapošljavanja u Jugoslaviji." *Ekonomski Pregled* 27, nos. 9–10 (1976): 625–50.

————. "Tržišni sistem socijalističke privrede i reforma." *Ekonomska Misao* 1, no. 3 (September 1968): 519–23.

Spasojević, Nebojša. "Kako je partiska organizacija Tuzlanske oblasti izvršila zadatak uključenja radne snage u rudarstvu." *Partiska Izgradnja* 1, nos. 9–10 (September–October 1949): 53–56.

Staniszkis, Jadwiga. *Poland's Self-limiting Revolution.* Princeton, N.J.: Princeton University Press, 1987.

Stark, David. "Coexisting Organizational Forms in Hungary's Emerging Mixed Economy." In Victor Nee and David Stark, eds., *Remaking the Economic Institutions of Socialism: China and Eastern Europe.* Stanford: Stanford University Press, 1989.

Stigler, George J. "The Theory of Economic Regulation." In *The Citizen and the State: Essays on Regulation.* Chicago: University of Chicago Press, 1975.

Stojanović, Radmila, ed. *Yugoslav Economists on Problems of a Socialist Economy.* New York: International Arts and Sciences Press, 1964.

Stojanović, Slavko. "Karakteristike i specifičnosti problema zaposlenosti i zapošljavanja stanovništva na području Slavonije i Baranje." *Revija za Sociologiju* 10, nos. 3–4 (1980): 139–44.

Stojanovski, Jovan. *Privredni sistem i nedovoljno razvijene republike i SAP Kosovo.* Skopje: Ekonomski Institut Univerziteta "Kiril i Metodij," 1979.

Streissler, Erich W. "What Kind of Economic Liberalism May We Expect in 'Eastern' Europe?" *East European Politics and Societies* 5, no. 1 (Winter 1991): 195–201.

Stupar, Mihailo. *Praktikum za socijalnu politiku.* Belgrade: Naučna Knjiga, 1967.

Sugar, Peter E. *The Industrialization of Bosnia-Hercegovina, 1878–1918.* Seattle: University of Washington Press, 1963.

Sutela, Pekka. "Ideology as a Means of Economic Debate, or the Strange Case of Objective Economic Laws of Socialism." *Jahrbuch der Wirtschaft Osteuropas* 13, no. 1 (1989): 198–220.

Šuvar, Stipe. "Plave i bele kragne." *NIN*, February 28, 1982, pp. 14–16.

Szporluk, Roman. *Communism and Nationalism: Karl Marx versus Friedrich List.* New York: Oxford University Press, 1988.

Tajnikar, Maks. "The Coexistence of Market and Plan in the Development of

Yugoslav Economic Thought." *Eastern European Economics* 16, no. 1 (Fall 1977): 74–101.

Tanić, Živan. "Yugoslavia." In Ronald E. Krane, ed., *International Labor Migration in Europe*. New York: Praeger, 1979.

Tarschys, Daniel. "Curbing Public Expenditure: Current Trends." *Journal of Public Policy* 5, pt. 1 (February 1985): 23–68.

Taševski, Bojan. "Samovoljno napuštanje posla—osnov za prestanak radnog odnosa." *Vjesnik Rada* 4, nos. 1–2 (January–February 1949): 4–29.

Therborn, Goran. *Why Some Peoples Are More Unemployed than Others: The Strange Paradox of Growth and Unemployment*. London: Verso, 1986.

Thomas, Hendrik. "Personal Income Distribution in Yugoslavia: A Human Capital Approach to the Analysis of Personal Income Differences in the Industry of a Labor-Managed Market Economy." Ph.D. diss., Cornell University, 1973.

Thompson, Edward P. *The Making of the English Working Class*. New York: Vintage Press, 1963.

Tijanić, Aleksandar, and Teodor Andjelić. "Obično nezaposleni mladi." *NIN*, February 28, 1982, pp. 14–18.

Tilly, Charles, Louise Tilly, and Richard Tilly. *The Rebellious Century*. Cambridge: Harvard University Press, 1975.

Tilton, Timothy A. "A Swedish Road to Socialism: Ernst Wigforss and the Ideological Foundations of Swedish Social Democracy." *American Political Science Review* 73, no. 2 (1979): 505–20.

Tito, Josip Broz. *Tito u Skupštini socijalističke Jugoslavije, 1942–1977*. Belgrade: Skupština SFRJ, 1978.

———. *Selected Speeches and Articles, 1941–1961*. Translated by Dorian Cooke, Djura Ninčić, and Zvonimir Petnički. Zagreb: Naprijed, 1963.

———. "Govor na svečanosti prilikom puštanja u saobraćaj omladinske pruge Šamac-Sarajevo" (November 16, 1947). In *Govori i članci*. Vol. 3. Zagreb: Naprijed, 1959.

———. "Trudbeničko upravljanje privredom," *Komunist* 4, nos. 4–5 (July–September 1950).

———. "The Real Reasons behind the Slander of the Cominform Countries toward Yugoslavia." New Year's address to the national assembly, December 27, 1948. Typescript.

———. "On the National Question." *Proleter*, No. 16 (1942).

Tobin, James. "The Economic Pendulum: 1962 . . . 1982 . . . 1992 (?)" Interview by Richard D. Bartel. *Challenge*, March–April 1992, pp. 9–16.

Todorović, Marija. "Osnovne karakteristike izmena i dopuna Zakona o radnim odnosima." In *Zakon o radnim odnosima SR Srbije u praktičnoj primeni: Zbornik radova*. Belgrade: "Revije rada," 1981.

Tomanović, Velimir. *Omladina i socijalizam*. Belgrade: Mladost, 1977.

Tomasevich, Jozo. "Yugoslavia during the Second World War." In Wayne S. Vucinich, ed., *Contemporary Yugoslavia: Twenty Years of Socialist Experiment*. Berkeley and Los Angeles: University of California Press, 1969.

———. "Collectivization of Agriculture in Yugoslavia." In Irwin T. Sanders, ed., *Collectivization of Agriculture in Eastern Europe*. Lexington: University of Kentucky Press, 1958.

————. *Peasants, Politics, and Economic Change in Yugoslavia*. Stanford, Calif.: Stanford University Press, 1955.

————. "Postwar Foreign Economic Relations." In Robert J. Kerner, ed., *Yugoslavia*. Berkeley and Los Angeles: University of California Press, 1949.

————. "German Economic Penetration and Exploitation of Southeastern Europe." *Civil Affairs Information Guide: U.S. Foreign Economic Administration*. War Department Pamphlet no. 31-127. Washington, D.C., 1944.

————. "German Penetration of Corporate Holdings in Croatia." In *Civil Affairs Information Guide: U.S. Foreign Economic Administration*. War Department Pamphlet no. 31-129. Washington, D.C., 1944.

————. "German Penetration of Corporate Holdings in Serbia." In *Civil Affairs Information Guide: U.S. Foreign Economic Administration*. War Department Pamphlet 31-128. Washington, D.C., 1944.

Trninić, Milan. "Kako je partiska organizacija u rudnicima 'Tito' učestvovala u organizaciji rada po novom metodu." *Partiska Izgradnja* 1, nos. 9–10 (September–October 1949): 57–61.

Trouton, Ruth. *Peasant Renaissance in Yugoslavia*. London: Routledge and Kegan Paul, 1952.

Tucker, Robert C., ed. *The Marx-Engels Reader*. 2d ed. New York: Norton, 1978.

Turčinović, Slobodan. "Financing Socio-political Units, 1961–1967." *Yugoslav Survey* 9, no. 2 (May 1968): 59–64.

Tyson, Laura D'Andrea. "Investment Allocation: A Comparison of the Reform Experiences of Hungary and Yugoslavia." *Journal of Comparative Economics* 7 (1983): 288–303.

————. *The Yugoslav Economic System and Its Performance in the 1970s*. Berkeley: Institute of International Studies, University of California, 1980.

————. "A Permanent Income Hypothesis for the Yugoslav Firm." *Economica*, n.s., 44, no. 4 (November 1977): 393–408.

————. "The Yugoslav Inflation: Some Competing Hypotheses." *Journal of Comparative Economics* 1 (1977): 113–46.

Tyson, Laura D'Andrea, and Gabriel Eichler. "Continuity and Change in the Yugoslav Economy in the 1970s and 1980s." In *East European Economic Assessment*, pt. 1, country studies. Washington, D.C.: Joint Economic Committee, U.S. Congress, 1981.

Tyson, Laura D'Andrea, and Egon Neuberger. "The Transmission of International Disturbances to Yugoslavia." In Egon Neuberger and Laura D'Andrea Tyson, eds., *The Impact of International Economic Disturbances on the Soviet Union and Eastern Europe*. New York: Pergamon Press, 1980.

"U borbu protiv besposlice!" *Proleter* 2, no. 11 (February 15, 1930): 1.

Ulam, Adam. *Titoism and the Cominform*. Cambridge: Harvard University Press, 1952.

United South Slav Committee. *Tito Speaks*. London, 1944.

United States Department of State. *Yugoslavia: Titoism and U.S. Foreign Policy*. Washington, D.C., 1952.

Unković, Andrija. "Povodom organizacije oblasnih inspekcija rada." *Vjesnik Rada* 4, no. 4 (April 1949).

Unković, Andrija. "Zaključci konferencije inspektora rada od 1 i 2 decembra 1949 održane u Ministarstvu rada FNRJ." *Vjesnik Rada* 4, no. 4 (November–December 1949): 475–76.

Unković, Milorad. "Inostrani kapital u jugoslovenskoj privredi." *Ekonomska Analiza* 14, no. 1 (1980): 53–67.

Uvalić, Radivoj. "Stanje i razvoj ekonomske misli i prakse i njihov medjusobni odnosi u našoj zemlji." *Ekonomist*, no. 2 (1952).

Uzunov, Nikola. "Problem nezaposlenosti u uslovima stabilizacione politike Jugoslavije." *Kadrovi i Udruženi Rad* 12, no. 1 (1982): 8–13.

Vanek, Jaroslav. *A General Theory of Labour-Managed Market Economies.* Ithaca, N.Y.: Cornell University Press, 1970.

Vanek, Jaroslav, and M. Jovičić. "Uloga kapitalne opremljenosti rada u formiranju i raspodeli dohotka u Jugoslaviji: Teorijska i empirijska analiza." *Economic Analysis and Workers' Management* 6, nos. 1–2 (1972): 50–59.

Verba, Sidney, and Goldie Shabad. "Workers' Councils and Political Stratification: The Yugoslav Experience." *American Political Science Review* 72, no. 1 (1978): 80–95.

Verdery, Katherine. *National Ideology under Socialism: Identity and Cultural Politics in Ceauşescu's Romania.* Berkeley and Los Angeles: University of California Press, 1991.

———. *Transylvanian Villagers: Three Centuries of Political, Economic, and Ethnic Change.* Berkeley and Los Angeles: University of California Press, 1982.

"Višak nezaposlenih—i zaposlenih." *Ekonomska Politika*, no. 1567 (April 12, 1982): 16–18.

Vodopivec, Milan. "Productivity Effects of Redistribution in a Socialist Economy: The Case of Yugoslavia." Ph.D. diss., Department of Economics, University of Maryland, 1989.

Von Hagen, Mark. *Soldiers in the Proletarian Dictatorship: The Red Army and the Soviet Socialist State, 1917–1930.* Ithaca, N.Y.: Cornell University Press, 1990.

Vucinich, Wayne S., ed. *At the Brink of War and Peace: The Tito-Stalin Split in a Historic Perspective.* New York: Brooklyn College Press, 1982.

Vujačić, Milan. "Dečija zaštita ili zaštita fondova." *Gledišta* 8, no. 2 (February 1967): 217–19.

Vujošević, Božo. "O nekim problemima radne snage (Povodom donošenja Uredbe o ustaljenju radne snage)." *Narodna Država* 4, nos. 1–2 (January–February 1950): 24–31.

———. "Za bolji metod u našem radu." *Vjesnik Rada* 4, nos. 11–12 (November–December 1949): 446–47.

———. "O nedostacima službe radničkog snabdijevanja." *Vjesnik Rada* 3, no. 1 (January 1948): 14–15.

Vukmanović-Tempo, Svetozar. *Revolucija koja teče: Memoari.* 2 vols. Belgrade: Komunist, 1971.

Vuković, Miloš. "Uticaj svetske privredne krize, 1929–1939, na privredu stare Jugoslavije." In Srpska Akademija Nauka i Umetnosti, *Svetska ekonomska kriza 1929–1934. godine i njen odraz u zemljama jugoistočne Evrope.* Belgrade: Balkanološki Institut.

Vušković, Boris. "Social Inequality in Yugoslavia." *New Left Review* 95 (January–February 1976): 26–41.

Wachtel, Howard. *Workers' Management and Wages in Yugoslavia*. Ithaca, N.Y.: Cornell University Press, 1973.

Walder, Andrew. *Communist Neo-Traditionalism: Work and Authority in Chinese Industry*. Berkeley and Los Angeles: University of California Press, 1987.

Wallerstein, Michael. "Centralized Bargaining and Wage Restraint." *American Journal of Political Science* 34, no. 4 (November 1990): 982–1004.

Ward, Benjamin. "Marxism-Horvatism: A Yugoslav Theory of Socialism." *American Economic Review* 57 (1967): 509–23.

———. "Industrial Decentralization in Yugoslavia." *California Slavic Studies* 2 (1963): 169–87.

———. "The Firm in Illyria: Market Syndicalism in Yugoslavia." *American Economic Review* 48, no. 4 (September 1958): 566–89.

———. "From Marx to Barone: Socialism and the Postwar Yugoslav Industrial Firm." Ph.D. diss., Department of Economics, University of California at Berkeley, 1956.

Warriner, Doreen. *Revolution in Eastern Europe*. London: Turnstile Press, 1950.

Weiler, P. *British Labour and the Cold War*. Stanford, Calif.: Stanford University Press, 1988.

Weir, Margaret, and Theda Skocpol. "State Structures and the Possibilities for 'Keynesian' Responses to the Great Depression in Sweden, Britain, and the United States." In Peter Evans et al., *Bringing the State Back In*. Cambridge: Cambridge University Press, 1985.

Wexler, Immanuel. *The Marshall Plan Revisited: The European Program in Economic Perspective*. Westport, Conn.: Greenwood Press, 1983.

Wilson, Orme, Jr. "The Belgrade-Bar Railroad: An Essay in Economic and Political Geography." In George W. Hoffman, ed., *Eastern Europe: Essays in Geographical Problems*. New York: Praeger, 1970.

Wolff, Robert Lee. *The Balkans in Our Time*. New York: Norton, 1967. Originally published 1956.

Woodall, Jean. *The Socialist Corporation and Technocratic Power: The Polish United Workers' Party, Industrial Organization, and Workforce Control, 1958–80*. Cambridge: Cambridge University Press, 1982.

Woodward, Susan L. "Soviet Rehearsal in Yugoslavia? Contradictions of the Socialist Liberal Strategy." *The Socialist Register, Communist Regimes: the Aftermath*, edited by Ralph Miliband and Leo Panitch, 1991, 322–47.

———. "Reforming the Socialist State: Ideology and Public Finance in Yugoslavia." *World Politics* 41, no. 2 (January 1989): 267–305.

———. "Orthodoxy and Solidarity: Competing Claims and International Adjustment in Yugoslavia." *International Organization* 40, no. 2 (Spring 1986): 505–45.

———. "The Rights of Women: Ideology, Policy, and Social Change in Yugoslavia." In Sharon Wolchik and Alfred Meyer, eds., *Women, State and Party in Eastern Europe*. Durham, N.C.: Duke University Press, 1985.

World Bank. *Yugoslavia: Adjustment Policies and Development Perspectives*. Washington, D.C.: IBRD, 1983.

Yugoslavia. *The Constitution of the Socialist Federal Republic of Yugoslavia.* Ljubljana: Dopisna Delavska Univerza, 1974.

―――. *Law on the Five Year Plan for the Development of the National Economy of the FPRY, 1947–1951.* With speech by Josip Broz Tito. Belgrade: Jugoslovenska Knjiga, 1947.

―――. Narodna Skupština FNRJ. *Drugo redovno zasedanje: Stenografske beleške* (Belgrade, December 2–21, 1946).

―――. *Drugo vanredno zasedanje: Stenografske beleške* (Belgrade, March 10–April 1, 1946).

―――. *Prvo redovno zasedanje: Stenografske beleške* (Belgrade: May 15–July 20, 1946).

―――. Savezna Skupština SFRJ. *The Associated Labour Act.* Ljubljana: Dopisna Delavska Univerza, 1977.

Za bolju organizaciju, sadržaj i metod rada." *Vjesnik Rada.* 5, nos 8–9 (August–September 1950): 362–64.

Zeković, Velimir. "Razvoj i karakteristike privrednog sistema FNRJ." In *Priručnik za ekonomiju FNRJ.* Belgrade: Rad, 1958.

Zerdin, Ali. "Tokens of Slovene Sovereignty." *Yugofax*, October 12, 1991.

Zimmerman, William. *Open Borders, Nonalignment, and the Political Evolution of Yugoslavia.* Princeton, N.J.: Princeton University Press, 1987.

Žujović, Sreten. Confession. *Borba,* November 23, 1950, p. 1.

Zukin, Sharon. "Practicing Socialism in a Hobbesian World: Development and Persistence of the Yugoslav State." In Neil Harding, ed., *The State in Socialist Society.* Oxford: Macmillan, 1983.

―――. "The Representation of Working-Class Interests in Socialist Society: Yugoslav Labor Unions." *Politics and Society* 10, no. 3 (1981): 281–316.

Županov, Josip. *Marginalije o društvenoj krizi.* Zagreb: Globus, 1983.

―――. "Aktuelni društveni zadatak." *Naše Teme* 25 (1983): 1945–56.

―――. "Egalitarizam i industrijalizam." *Sociologija* 12, no. 1 (1970): 5–44.

Županov, Josip, and Mladen Žuvela. "Kriteriji inferiornosti nezaposlenih u nas i u svijetu." *Kadrovi i Udruženi Rad* 11, no. 4 (1981): 3–12.

Žuvela, Mladen. "Grupe stanovnika pojačano izložene nezaposlenosti i neke njene socijalne i psihološke posljedice." *Sociologija* 10, no. 4 (1968).

PERIODICALS

Bulletin du Conseil Central de la Confédération des Syndicats de Yougoslavie (Belgrade), 1949

Economic Survey: Yugoslavia (Organization for Economic Cooperation and Development, Paris)

Ekonomist

Ekonomska Politika (Belgrade)

Ekonomski Pregled (Zagreb)

Finansije (Belgrade)

Informativni Bilten (Zavod za Društveno Planiranje, Ljubljana), 1982

Informativni Priručnik o Jugoslaviji (Belgrade), 1950–51.

Migracije (Zagreb), 1973–82
Narodna Armija (Belgrade), 1955–57
Narodna Država Partiska Izgradnja
Službeni List (Belgrade), 1948–49
Socijalna Politika
Statistički Godišnjak Jugoslavije (Savezni Zavod za Statistiku, Belgrade)
Yearbook on Economic Statistics (Organization for Economic Cooperation and
    Development, Paris)
Yugoslav Federal Assembly (Belgrade)
Yugoslav Survey (Belgrade)
Yugoslav Trade Unions (Belgrade), 1963–
Zaposlenost i Zapošljavanje (Savezni Savet za Rad, Belgrade)
Zapošljavanje i Udruženi Rad (Zagreb)

INDEX

Acheson, Dean, 144
Adam, Jan, 11n.22
administrative period, 64, 66–97, 163, 168
agricultural policy: agrarian reform, 57–58, 60, 70, 90, 242, 266; change to gain labor for production, 117; gradualist socialization, 161; Green Plan, 236, 279; for productivity, 286; sectoral distinctions, 285–86; with self-reliance strategy, 108–21; Slovene and Foča models' adjustment to, 264–65
agricultural production: dependence on, 105–6; drought years, 160; for export, 96, 130; policy to control, 112–14; pressure to increase, 60–61, 75, 90
agricultural sector: employment decline, 191, 348; exodus from, 286–89; labor force surplus, 67, 102, 263–64; radicalization, 100; socialist transformation, 243; voluntary labor in, 140–41. See also farmers' (marketing) cooperatives; labor brigades; landholdings, agrarian; private sector; villages
Agrokomerc affair (1987), 295
aid, foreign: dependence on, 95–96; industrialization strategy based on, 77–80; from postwar Soviet Union, 80–81; requests for and receipt of, 81–83, 100, 121; UNRRA assistance, 83, 95, 99; U.S., 99, 150–51, 249; U.S. military, 159. See also credit, foreign; military sector
Albanians: land purchases, 298; nationalism, 40, 343, 358, 365–66; as political force, 342–44
Alt, James, 27, 28n
Antifascist Council for the Liberation of Yugoslavia (AVNOJ), 52–54, 57
Appleby, Joyce O., 17, 162
Arab-Israeli War (1967), 250
Arsov, Ljubčo, 123, 153
Austria, 9, 342, 357
Austrian unemployment theory, 214–15
Austromarxism, 35, 48–49, 52, 155

autonomy: budgetary, 73, 167; competition to retain, 23; conflict over provincial, 365; farmers' cooperatives, 89–91, 172; firms, 72; peasants, 91–92; producers and production brigades, 142–44, 151, 185; republic governments, 336–37; Slovene model, 59, 265; Yugoslavian territories, 52–53. See also decentralization; self-management concept
AVNOJ. See Antifascist Council for the Liberation of Yugoslavia (AVNOJ)

Bakarić, Vladimir, 137, 138, 150, 301, 312
balance of payments: commodity-trade account (1948), 129; current account liquidity, 223; deficits, 95, 129, 223, 226, 244, 247, 287; effect of U.S. loans on, 145; foreign aid supports for, 228; with remittances, 228, 246, 254, 269, 293; subdivided among republics, 235, 253. See also economic shocks; exchange-rate system; foreign policy; trade, foreign; trade deficit
Balkan Pact (1954), 241
Banac, Ivo, 32, 33n, 34n, 49n, 56n, 62n
banking system, 185; Austrian banks (1985), 357; autonomous producers linked through, 172; borrowing abroad, 235, 253; branches of National Bank, 123; cooperative principle, 185; crisis, 351–52; crisis (1987), 351; in liquidity crisis, 229–30; recentralization (1980s), 355; in republics, 290, 292–93; with socialization of investment, 245; territorial organization of, 230
bargaining, wage. See collective bargaining
barter system, 125
Bartlett, William, 212
basic organizations of associated labor (BOALs), 277
benefits: under constitution, 41–42; worker acceptance of limits on, 261
Bicanić, Rudolf, 44n, 47n
Blažević, Jakov, 109, 112, 113, 115
Bolčić, Silvano, 337, 336n, 337n

borrowing. *See* loans
Bosnia-Herzegovina: abolition of district government, 270; Agrokomerc affair (1987), 295; capitalist development, 38; deindustrialization, 291; employment bureaus, 178; large-scale agricultural production, 285; low level of development, 283; mines in, 94; as nation, 39; nationalism, 366; relocation of defense-related industries in, 139, 284; separate party organization, 40; unemployment rates, 201, 204–5, 298, 339–44. *See also* Foča model
Bretton Woods, 251
brigades. *See* labor brigades; Partisans; Popular Front; production brigades
Broz, Josip. *See* Tito, Josip Broz
budget deficits, 108, 131
Bukharin, Nikolai, 75, 90, 171
bureaucracy: critique, 30; differences between Slovene and Foča models, 161; reduction plan, 132; transfer to republics of federal, 250. *See also* employment bureaus

cameralism, 18, 28
Cameron, David, 10n
Cannon, Cavendish, 122, 129
capital: demand for foreign, 249; effect of scarce, 164–65; focus on need for, 66; foreign aid to supplement, 77, 79–80; formation, 225; government role in redistribution, 186; industrialization requirements, 79, 224–25; Marxist idea of formation, 18–20; plan for accumulation of, 68–69, 75–77, 110; producers' control of, 183–85, 229–30; redistribution through General Investment Fund, 186–87; strategy for access to foreign, 224. *See also* aid, foreign; credit, foreign; trade, foreign
capital flows: within autonomous republics, 290; to more developed areas, 284; Slovenia and Croatia (1985), 357; territorialization, 282, 290
capitalist theory: as applied in Yugoslavia, 76; Marxist analysis, 3
capitalist unemployment, 27; elimination of, 311; rejection of, 322
capital markets: direct borrowing by banks and firms, 253; independent institutional entrance into, 249; obstacles to, 219; separate from labor markets, 312; in separate republics, 296; unemployment without, 214
central bank (National Bank): control of enterprise finances, 152; credit policy, 123; foreign loan guarantees, 185, 225; renewed authority of, 351; socialization of debt under, 229–30. *See also* banking system
centralization: combined with decentralization, 130–44; of economic policy making, 119; under self-reliance policy, 130–33; in Slovene economic methods, 161–62
Chayanov, A. V., 313
class struggle, Yugoslav style, 114, 118–19
Čobeljić, Nikola, 210
Cocom Accords (1947), 95
collective bargaining, 88–89, 153–55, 261, 326
collective consumption goods, 271
collectives. *See* farm collectives; producers; work collectives
Comisso, Ellen, 15n, 33n, 326, 334n
commodity shortages: response to, 124–26, 145–46; U.S. food donations, 150–51. *See also* aid, foreign; rationing; trade, foreign
Communist Party of Yugoslavia (CPY): adoption of Slovene coalition principles, 59–60; alliance with Croat Peasant party, 55–56; authority shifted to, 133–34; becomes League of Communists, 64, 182; consolidation of power (1948), 126–27; fusion of party with military functions, 51–53; heterogeneous ideologies in, 35–38; interwar alliances, 32; nationalism of, 56; purge (1948), 119–20; strategy to encompass heterogeneity, 41–49. *See also* League of Communists of Yugoslavia (LCY)
community farms, 104–6
comparative advantage: conflict over importance of, 240; of regions, 292; source of, 224
competition: with declining resources, 354; labor market, 112–13, 175, 325–26, 337–38; in labor market and political system, 353–54; among party leaders, 335; among property owners, 355; socialist, 78, 96

Connor, Walker, 35, 41
conscription, military, 147
constitutions: amendments, 250, 274; Basic
    Law (1953), 164, 184; commission (1983),
    255; constitution and related workers'
    constitution (1974), 164–65, 237, 250–
    51; economic policy (1963), 270; of 1921,
    41–42; principles of representation
    (post-1963), 184; provisional adoption
    (1943), 36; regulation of employment
    by, 317; revised, 180–81. See also
    legislation
consumption, domestic: commmodity scar-
    city, 124–26, 145–46; plans for, 68–69;
    rationing, 104; regulated by incomes
    and employment, 263; socially necessary,
    69
cooperatives: capitalist focus of, 76; charac-
    terization of farmers in movement for,
    89–90; legal mechanism for, 90; local
    level, 74; requisitioning of agricultural
    products, 90; revised basic law (1948),
    136; subdivision of, 277; trade by linked
    prices, 113–15; tradition in Croatia and
    Slovenia, 43; village, 44, 92. See also
    farmers' (marketing) cooperatives; labor
    cooperatives
Council for Mutual Economic Assistance
    (CMEA), 29, 241, 349
Cox, Terry, 21n.42
credit: as alternative to revenues from pro-
    duction, 302; IMF, 187, 228, 229, 245,
    347; obstacle to access, 219; for public
    sector agriculture, 285; in regional and
    republican banks, 292; with socialization
    of investment, 245–46. See also debt, ex-
    ternal; loans, foreign
credit, foreign: dependence on, 163, 257;
    direct borrowing of firms and banks, 235;
    economic policy related to, 241–42, 265–
    66; Joint Export-Import Agency, Allied
    occupation, 144, 150; relation to current
    account deficit, 226; relation to domestic
    taxation, 232; from Soviet Union, 243;
    suspension of lending, 254. See also
    debt, external; International Monetary
    Fund (IMF); World Bank
Croatia: decline in economy and employ-
    ment, 359; demand for territorial con-
    trol, 256; employment bureaus, 178–79;
    foreign currency flows to, 235; industrial-

ization in, 94; investment in, 291; juris-
    dictions granted (1939), 69; mines in, 94;
    nationalism, 55–56, 366–67; national se-
    curity issue, 255; organized unions and
    working class, 41; plans for development,
    297; regional differences within, 289–90;
    surplus labor emigration, 338–39; unem-
    ployment rates, 201, 204–5, 208; unrest
    (after 1967), 275
Croatian Communist party, 36, 43, 55–56
Croatian Liberation Front (ZAVNOH), 50,
    55
Croatian school of rural sociology, 210
Croat Peasant party (CPP), 43–44; alliance
    with Communist Party of Yugoslavia, 55–
    56; influence of economists from, 210;
    withdrawal of Communist party support
    (1947), 107
currency: devaluation, 159, 232–33, 251;
    reform goals (1945), 70
Cvetković-Maček Agreement (1939), 69
Czechoslovakia, 14, 28, 82

Dalmatia, 43, 44, 283–84, 290, 325
data, employment and unemployment,
    194–208, 240, 264, 338–44, 375–94
Davies, R. W., 28, 73n, 153n
debt, external: federal government guaran-
    tee for, 235; postponement, 250; recyc-
    ling, rescheduling, and refinancing, 225,
    249, 252–54, 275, 348–49; refunding by
    European governments, 249; repayment,
    227, 372; republics' responsibility, 295;
    service of, 253. See also credit, foreign;
    loans, foreign
decentralization: combined with centraliza-
    tion, 130–44; cost at local level, 300–301;
    effect on labor markets, 264; effect on
    size of public sector, 274–75, 289; fail-
    ure, 165, 350; in Foča model, 265; IMF
    campaign for, 236; with openness to for-
    eign trade, 233–36; in perceived wither-
    ing away of the state, 171, 250; rationale
    for, 69, 331; to regional party headquar-
    ters, 52. See also government, local; lo-
    calization; villages
defense policy: changes, 274; conscription
    and military training, 276; effect of, 248;
    effect of political strategy on, 98–99; fac-
    tors in arms race, 348–49; firm and local
    government responsibility for, 250, 276;

defense policy (*cont.*)
  localization of government tasks as, 119;
  mobilization, 268; redrawing of military
  districts, 360; relation to access to foreign
  capital, 224–25; relation to foreign policy,
  146–47, 241; in response to foreign trade
  problems, 116–17; of security zones,
  139, 284; with socialization, 187–88
deficits, domestic, 108, 131
democracy: economic, 5, 322; local level,
  74; with party decentralization, 135–36;
  technocratic, 118
developmentalist school: approach to
  economic policy, 245; approach to unemployment, 210–12, 216–17; over-
  shadowed by liberal school, 272
developmentalist state, 17–18
development theory: contradictions in, 165;
  developmentalists' school, 210; liberal
  school, 210
discrimination: against employment of
  women, 104; by national origin, 338,
  347, 366–67; against new labor force entrants, 336; with rising unemployment,
  360–61; against surplus labor, 153;
  against training of professionals, 302. *See
  also* ethnic criteria
Djilas, Milovan, 40n, 73n, 75
Dolomite Agreement (1943), 51
Drèze, F., 221
dualism: economic/political, 127, 183, 189;
  of socialist/capitalist strategy, 76; of un-
  employment/employment concept, 8

economic coercion concept, 146, 150, 151,
  168, 174–75
Economic Council, Yugoslavia, 73, 122, 125
economic growth: based on foreign loans
  and credits, 244; Foča model, 265; government priority to promote, 222–23;
  Marxist ideology, 18–20; Ricardian
  growth path, 224–25, 233; strategy with
  openness to foreign trade, 224–37;
  Todaro and Harris-Todaro models, 212
economic interest concept, 321
economic performance: effect, 263; factors
  in rise and fall of, 225, 230–31
economic planning: five-year plan, 73–76,
  95–96; focus of, 84; as policy goal, 170;
  republican government level, 282

economic policy: adjustment to strategy
  for, 96–97; conflict over development
  strategy, 74–83; correlation with unemployment patterns, 240, 264; for development, 287; differences in approach, 336–
  38; factors changing (1973), 251; with
  focus on global economy, 244–53; to increase growth, 268–69; influence of foreign credit availability, 236, 241; to meet
  Tito's self-reliance policy, 108–9, 121–28;
  party role in coordination and control,
  134; political conflict over, 237–56; reforms, 247–48, 347; reforms, response of
  republics, 355–59; with renewed autonomy of republics, 148. *See also* aid, foreign; economic planning; export
  promotion; investment; monetary policy;
  Reform (1965); self-reliance policy; trade,
  foreign
economic shocks: external, 130, 230–33,
  253–54, 257–58; oil-price shocks effect
  (1973, 1979), 251, 253–54; from response
  to international conditions, 240
economy: nonplanned socialist, 170–73; organized around labor-managed firms, 12,
  15, 166, 208, 212–13, 215, 220, 263,
  266n, 267n; post–World War II local, 60–
  61
economy, global: effect of Yugoslav response to, 227–40, 244–53; national independence in, 28, 33–34, 38, 98, 146,
  164, 165, 256
education: economic status with, 318; as
  investment, 317; reform, 276–77, 289,
  362; republic policy and jurisdiction,
  271, 290, 336, 338; secondary and university, 289, 338; vocational, 273, 276–
  77
Eichengreen, Barry, 23–24
electoral laws, 184n.51
employment: adjustment by moving
  workers, 263; as bundle of rights, 317;
  demand for increased, 99; differentiation between private and public sectors,
  347; with economic reform (1980s),
  347; effect of trade deficits on, 263; factors affecting domestic, 226–27; hidden surplus, 197; incentive proposals
  (1980s), 281–82; of labor surplus, 66–
  67, 74, 102; lack of federal jurisdiction
  over, 259; narrowed definition of, 196–

97; national identity as criterion for public, 347; private sector in villages, 334;
productivity for expansion of, 174; projected public sector (1947), 96; rationing criteria related to, 152–53; regulation by allocation of provisions, 152–53;
relation to political action, 339–44; socialist concept of full, 3–11; socialization
through public sector, 262. *See also* overemployment; socialism; unemployment;
workers; workers, private sector;
workers, skilled
employment bureaus: functions and success
of, 86, 195; registration rates, 191; retraining programs, 300; self-management
by, 178–79
employment contracts: defining legally regulated job classification, 166, 174; effect
of, 162; growth (1957–82), 191; legal enforcement provisions, 151–53
employment rates, 192, 375–94; comparison of sectoral, 25–26; levels in socialist
and capitalist countries, 27
Estrin, Saul, 213–14, 216, 220
ethnic criteria: in job rationing, 301; in student and employee selection, 301, 338
Europe: integration, 349; postwar relations
with, 82; provision of coal for, 144
European Community (EC): monetary unification, 349; negotiations with (1980s),
349–50; trade agreements with (1970,
1976), 29, 251, 253
European Free Trade Association (EFTA),
253, 350
exchange-rate system, 159, 169; with openness to foreign trade, 232–35; recentralization (1980s), 355–56. *See also* foreign
exchange
export production: earnings from, 146; during economic crisis (1948), 122–25; effect
on balance of payments, 129; increased,
96–97, 99–100, 102; producer control of,
235
export promotion, 229, 246, 250–51

factors of production: allocation in socialist
societies, 22–23; price regulation, 169–
70; shortages, 130–31
Farkaš, Vladimir, 216–18, 220
farm collectives, 125
farmers, private sector: cooperative move-

ment, 89–90; policy to undercut market
power, 112–13; requirements of, 244
farmers' (marketing) cooperatives, 43–44,
89–91; conceived as autonomous socialist communities, 89–91, 172; employment in, 162; monopoly position (1953,
1957), 242, 243–44; organization of,
61; relation to standard of living, 73–74,
84; renewed favoritism for, 150; replacement of free markets, 113; speculators
in, 106
Federal Bureau of Employment, 269
federalism: confirmation (1924), 36, 63; economic, 72; effect on state's economic policy, 76; provisional government (1943),
39–40, 52
Feiwel, George, 12–13
financial system: liquidity crisis, 229; producer control, 183–85, 229–30; Yugoslav
argument for control of, 219, 222–24.
See also banking system
firms: autonomy of, 72–73; borrowing
abroad, 235, 253; conflicts within and between, 330–32; defense and security systems as responsibility of, 250;
development of private sector, 303; effect
of legislation on employment policies,
278–80; financing of social services, 262;
foreign exchange retention by, 234–35;
freedom to access foreign credit, 235;
privatization policy for, 280; relation to
workers' councils, 267; role in Slovene
model, 183; subdivision of, 277; unions'
authority in, 326–27. *See also* producers; production; productivity; self-
management concept; state-owned enterprises; work collectives; workers'
councils
firms, labor-managed, 4, 12, 15, 166, 208,
212–13, 215, 220, 263, 266n, 267n
fiscal policy: federal level, 231; federal-level
revenues with decentralized, 76; local
government, 267. *See also* spending, government; tax policy
Foča model, 34, 58, 60, 90; contradiction
of Slovene model, 22; with country's dissolution, 371–72; economic methods,
161–62; interference of Slovene model
with, 96; mix with Slovene model, 265–
68, 349; production, investment and labor policies, 224, 275; property rights,

Foča model (*cont.*)
    60; reality of, 165; survival of, 163. *See
    also* developmentalist school
Foča Regulations (1942), 60
food policy. *See* farmers' (marketing) coop-
    eratives; private sector; rationing;
    subsistence
foreign exchange: control policy, 96–97;
    firms' retention of, 234–35
foreign policy: federal government role,
    223–24; with international recognition,
    146; strategy, 100–101. *See also* aid, for-
    eign; foreign policy; trade, foreign
free markets: postponement of, 146; re-
    placement of, 113; under socialist com-
    modity production concept, 169
Fund for Reconstruction of War-Damaged
    Regions, 83

Gapinski, James, 225–26, 228, 231, 232,
    303
Gaži, Josip, 107
Gedeon, Shirley, 185n, 229n, 339n
General Agreement on Tariffs and Trade
    (GATT): effect on trade policy, 169, 290–
    91; membership, 29; trade liberalization
    conditions for membership, 228, 245–47,
    268–69
General Investment Fund (GIF), 186–87,
    242, 245
Germany, 14; Partisan against, 80; war in-
    demnities, 82; wartime occupation of
    Yugoslavia, 93
Gligorov, Kiro, 168, 232
Gomulka, Wladyslaw, 101
Gorbachev, Mikhail, 28, 245, 349
government, federal: centralization of con-
    trol, 130–32; changing role with unem-
    ployment, 355–58; conditions for
    reduction of scope, 234; conflict with re-
    public and local, 74–76; coordination
    with republics, 73; economic adjustment
    with labor, 259; foreign policy, 223; juris-
    diction of, 69; lack of control over em-
    ployment, 259; loss of confidence in,
    354–55; loss of control of economic pol-
    icy, 233–36; new instruments of coor-
    dination and control (1950), 148;
    recentralization policy, 355–67; reve-
    nues, 185; role in revised labor policy,
    110–11; role in socialization of the state,

187–88; sharing jurisdiction with repub-
    lics, 248
government, local: control over coopera-
    tives, 91; defense and security systems as
    responsibility of, 250; economic and po-
    litical planning of, 73–74; employment-
    related problems and policy, 282, 300–
    303; excise taxes of, 78; jurisdiction, 69;
    protection of public-sector wages and
    jobs, 325; regulation and tax authority,
    176; responsibility for unemployment
    prevention, 176; role of employment bu-
    reaus, 300; tradition of, 52. *See also* lo-
    calization; villages
government, republics: administrative role
    with socialization, 186–87; autonomy
    over labor policy, 282, 290; coordination
    with federal government, 73; credit con-
    trol by, 292; as enforcers of self-reliance
    policy, 130; financial self-sufficiency, 148,
    168; jurisdiction, 69, 336; management of
    General Investment Fund, 186–87; new
    role in foreign affairs and defense (1966),
    248; property rights', 147–48, 355, 357;
    protection of commerce, 295–96; protec-
    tion of public-sector wages and jobs, 325;
    responsibility for foreign debt, 295; re-
    turn of financial autonomy, 148; with ris-
    ing unemployment, 355–60, 363–65;
    role in revised labor policy, 111
government policy, federal level: to adjust
    to international environment, 263; de-
    centralized responsibility for implemen-
    tation of, 282; defense-oriented food
    policy, 285; differential effect on firms
    and republics, 293; labor policy, 298–
    303
Great Britain, 53–54, 80
Greece: aid to civil war rebels, 121; rela-
    tions with guerrillas in, 82, 144
Green Plan (1973), 236, 279
Gregorić, Pavle, 182
Gulick, Charles, 35n, 49n, 183

Harris-Todaro migration model, 212
Hatton, T. J., 23–24
health care, 271
health insurance, 177, 195
Hebrang, Andrija, 56, 70, 71–72, 102, 119,
    226; on increased collectivization and
    productivity, 75; opposition to union au-

thority, 83–85; people's government concept, 74

Herzegovina. *See* Bosnia-Herzegovina

Horvat, Branko, 155n, 173n, 221n, 231n, 269n

housing shortage, 301–2

human capital: formation, 282, 317, 320; status for acquisition of, 318; as substitute for machines, 111

Hungary, 12–13, 14, 28, 60, 243, 330

hyperinflation (1985), 228

ideology: Communist Party of Yugoslavia (CPY), 43–45; economic, 6, 16–20; Marxist, 16–23. *See also* capitalist theory; Foča model; Leninism; Marxism; Slovene model; socialism

ideology of smallness, 37

imports: capital equipment and technology, 225–26; with decline in export income, 146–47; dependence of production on, 226, 249; effect of cutting, 229; payment for, 130–31; price effect, 228

incentives: in choosing higher wages, 260–61; to direct raising of labor productivity, 222–23, 261–62; in Foča model, 265; to improve trade performance, 253; to join public sector, 133; for joint ventures, 249; for lower taxes, 302; for property owner, 166; in public-sector labor policy, 261–62; to reduce labor force mobility, 88, 103–4, 141–43; for republics to invest, 234; in Slovene model, 264; to work, 102–3. *See also* producers; production

income relations system, 200

incomes: effect of trade deficits on, 263; enforcement policy, 261–62; in socialized sector, 267. *See also* wages

indexation of salaries, 277, 331

industrialization: capital requirements for, 79, 224–25; industrial labor force growth with, 67; postwar problems of, 66; reform of union role with, 85–87; workers' and union roles, 84

inflation, 228, 275–76, 349; anti-inflationary policy, 223; conditions for and response to, 331; early 1970s, 228. *See also* hyperinflation

informal markets: commodities, 125; labor, 315

institutions: conflict among economic, 237–56; factors in definition of Yugoslav, 65–66; factors in development, 74–75; in Slovene model, 95, 165; social service, 177–80

interest groups: areas of inattention by, 329–30; firm managers as, 321–22; party as, 322; private sector workers as, 342–43; of students, 338–39; veterans, 302; of workers, 327, 329–30, 341. *See also* political opposition

International Monetary Fund (IMF): ambiguity toward program of, 256; decentralization advice, 171; effect of terms of agreement with (1984), 281; GATT membership to obtain credits from, 245; as lender of last resort, 227–28; loans from, 228, 229, 347; membership, 82, 144–45; negotiations with, 122, 254; policies of, 259; relations with, 82, 345, 348; requirements for new loans (1987), 350; stabilization program (1979), 280; standby facilities to developing countries, 254, 347

investment, domestic: bias in, 295; in capital projects, 291; effect of decentralization, 288; incentives against new employment, 260–61; in less-developed areas, 281–83; in more-developed areas, 284; related to kinds of workers needing jobs, 302; reliance on foreign capital, 226–27; republics' control of, 290; for self-reliance, 108–9; shift in priorities, 250–53; in Slovenia, Croatia, and Serbia, 297, 357; social control over, 174; socialization of, 245–46, 249; uneven distribution of capital for, 290–91; World Bank loans for, 236, 249

investment, foreign, 249, 251, 351

Istria, 57

Italy, 57, 357

Itoh, Makoto, 27n.51

job security, 223, 262, 277–78, 310

Johnson, A. Ross, 118n

joint ventures, 252–53, 295

Jovanovic, Dragoljub, 49, 91–92, 107

Kardelj, Edvard, 32, 36, 39; on agricultural policy, 138; conception of new state, 117–18; concept of farmers' coopera-

Kardelj, Edvard (*cont.*)
tives, 172; draft constitution, 180; employment concept, 196; on industrialization, 67; model of socialization and decentralization, 322; on national independence, 146; nationalism of, 32, 36, 39, 48; on new foreign policy (1949), 146; purpose of cooperatives, 90, 92; reform of local people's committees, 107; requirement for new liberalization (1956), 244; on role of unions, 48; Slovene model, 161–62, 317, 367–68; socialist communities model, 313; on socialist employment, 166; on trade, 116; on wages and productivity under socialism, 141

Katz, Arnold, 212

Katzenstein, Peter J., 10n, 238, 341–42

Keynesianism, 6, 170, 217, 257, 327–28

Kidrič, Boris, 68, 71, 76–77, 83; on agricultural quotas, 122; anti-farmer/kulak statements, 125; class-based arguments, 115; dictatorship of the proletariat, 184; economic coercion concept, 146, 150, 168; on economic planning, 120; excess public sector employment concept, 149; fluctuators, 149, 315; "law of value," 76–77, 132, 158, 171, 264; people's power, 167; Slovene model, 161–62, 244, 317; on social tansformation, 137

Knights of Labor, 155

Kornai, Janos, 11n, 13n, 216

Kosanović, Sava, 144

Kosovo: demographic explosion (1962–64), 211; development of society in, 342; industrial investment, 285; martial law in, 255; surplus labor, 338; unemployment rates, 201, 203–5, 208, 298, 339–44; unrest (after 1967), 275, 338. *See also* Albanians

Kraigher, Sergei, 255

Krajer, Boris, 240

Krstulović, Vicko, 87, 103–4

Kržišnik, Anton, 72

Kucan, Milan, 343–44

kulaks. *See* farmers, private sector; farmers' (marketing) cooperatives; landholdings, agrarian

labor brigades: as economic measures, 177; reallocation of voluntary, 149–50; recruit-

ment campaign (1949), 151; in reform of production, 142–44; as supplement to public-sector labor force, 77–78, 140; volunteer, 97, 111–12, 121, 125, 243, 268, 333

labor cooperatives: local level, 115; peasant, 90, 138–41, 242; public sector, 150

labor force: agricultural policy to gain labor, 117; assignment of redundant, 262, 306–9; distribution according to work, 273; employment of peasant-industrial workers, 192; government control of local, 114; incentives for return of overseas nationals, 93, 301; with industrialization (1921–38), 67; layoffs, 201, 203; mechanisms to prevent market allocation, 261–62; in mines, 93; mobility and lack of mobility, 88, 103–4, 141–43, 162–63, 175, 301–2; mobilization, 99–100, 122–28, 139–41, 268; modernization of public sector, 268; nonproductive segment, 262, 362–63; participation in decentralized economy, 208; politics of labor supply, 102; public sector labor books, 88–89; recruitment, 104, 118–19; redistribution with rising unemployment, 361–62; reduction on state farms and labor cooperatives, 266; relocation to Bosnia, 139; return of overseas nationals, 304; role of labor brigades, 77–78; shortages, 92–93, 110–11, 136–37; supply scarcity, 93–94, 103–5; women's participation rates, 287. *See also* employment; labor brigades; labor markets; unemployment; workers; workers, private sector; workers' councils

labor force surplus: absorption of, 210; employment of, 66–67, 102; government employees as, 300; location of labor-intensive industries to capture, 285; mobilization of, 74; release to public sector, 174; right to fire, 174; rise in public sector, 274; Slovenia, 263–64

labor inspectors, 88

labor legislation: Law on Associated Labor (1976), 278; Law on Employment (1974), 276; Law on Labor Relations (1965), 272; in 1974–76 period, 277–78; in 1979–82 period, 280; revised (1968), 274

labor markets: control of employment

levels, 152; with decentralization and socialization, 264, 295–96; demand for production workers, 319; demand in domestic, 287; demand in foreign (1980s), 348; differences among republics, 282–83; effect of decentralization and socialization, 264; effect of nationalization, 93; effect of separate decentralized, 364–65; government intervention in local, 114; incentives as instruments to allocate, 94–95; lack of demand for new entrants, 288–89; levels of demand in domestic, 201; local supply and demand, 315; policy with self-reliance strategy, 110; as political problem, 102; preoccupation with supply, 210–11; proposed changes, 337; quota reductions (1950), 156–60; reforms (1970s), 278–80; relation of unemployment to supply, 194–200; with rising unemployment, 352–58; separate from capital markets, 312. *See also* decentralization; employment; labor brigades; localization; overemployment; unemployment

labor markets, informal, 315

labor offices, district, 153

labor policy: with adjustment to international conditions, 99–100; effect of political strategy on, 99; federal level guidelines, 298–99; of full employment, 261, 263; intervention in local labor market, 114; as political problem, 102; within public sector, 261–62; reforms and revisions, 182, 275–80; response to shortages, 110–15; to structure labor market, 102–7

landholdings, agrarian: under agrarian reform (1953), 242; with loss of tariff protection under GATT, 248; parcelized, 102; by peasants, 242; prohibited sale of, 114

law of value, 75–77, 132, 158, 171, 264

Law on Associated Labor (1976), 164, 278

Law on Employment (1974), 276

Law on Enterprises (1989), 280

Law on Labor Relations (1955, 1965), 267, 272

Law on Workers' Social Insurance (1921), 41–42

League of Communists of Yugoslavia (LCY), 64, 182; effect of growing unemployment on, 324–25; effect of rising unemployment on, 368; effect of socialization on, 334; effect of unemployment on discipline, 352–53; membership limitations, 189, 322–23; fifth party congress, 126–27, 181, 323; sixth party congress, 150, 181–82, 242; seventh party congress, 268; eighth party congress, 247, 248, 272; tenth party congress, 252. *See also* party leadership; party policy; Popular Front

League of Communist Youth of Yugoslavia (SKOJ), 78, 126

League of Youth, 333

legislation: abortion and contraception, 274; credit and banking (1977), 279; to encourage return of nationals overseas, 301; ending property rights, 345; freedom for managers, 351; for privatization (1988), 351; on property rights, 279; related to education, 276–77; related to state-owned enterprises, 73, 85; for reorganization of localities, 74; unemployment-related, 274; wage rates, 71, 87. *See also* labor legislation

Lehmbruch, Gerhard, 10n.15

lender of last resort: IMF as, 228; National Bank as, 229

Leninism: economic growth and political radicalism, 74–75; international aspects, 28; of LCY five-year plan, 65; nationalism of, 69; regimes concept, 15–16, 161; slogans, 106; stages of cooperative development, 90; vanguard party idea, 44

liberal school: applications of concepts of, 270–72; approach to economic growth, 244–45; labor, capital, and institutionalist approaches to unemployment, 210, 212–20

List, Friedrich, 38

loans, foreign, 144–45, 150–51; to banks and enterprises, 253; effect on domestic economic policy with, 224–25, 227–28; from IMF, 249, 251, 254; to meet trade deficit, 229; from multilateral lending institutions, 145; World Bank loans, 232, 249, 252. *See also* credit, foreign

localization: consequences of, 91–94; of defense, 300–301; of financial management, 227; of government, 118–19; importance

localization (*cont.*)
  of, 78; labor cooperatives, 90–91, 115, 150, 242; of labor recruitment, 176; of party organization, 135; self-sufficiency, 106–7; of unemployment issue, 189. *See also* decentralization; employment bureaus; government, local
Löwenthal, Richard, 21n.44

Macedonia: abolition of district government, 270; capitalist development, 38–39; class divisions in, 39–40; demographic explosion (1962–64), 211; differences within, 289–90; employment bureaus, 178; employment in, 287; investment in, 291; large-scale agricultural production, 285; nationalism of, 39–40; opposition to recentralization, 357; separate party organization, 40; Serb-Macedonian disagreements, 39–40; unemployment rates, 201, 203–5, 208, 298
macroeconomic policy: effect with international openness, 29–30, 223, 226–37, 287; employment cuts to stabilize, 100, 146; enterprise responsibility for stabilization, 235–36; federal government stabilization plan (1985), 350; IMF and World Bank roles in, 350–51; macrosystems approach to full employment, 10; to reduce unemployment, 212; for stabilization, 228–32, 254–56, 270, 299; state role, 222–23, 227; undermining of, 226–27. *See also* fiscal policy; monetary policy
Maier, Charles, 98, 335
managers, firm: alliances to influence policy, 321–22; conflicts with unions and workers, 273, 327; election and job security of, 323–24; potential conflict with workers, 167–68; protection for party-approved, 323–24; responsibilities of, 176; wages of, 266. *See also* self-management
Marinko, Miha, 133
markets: effect of multiple unlinked, 329–30; local level, 73–74; segmentation, 233; various interpretations, 170–71
market socialism: economy under, 169–71; failure, 165; misuse of term, 169
Markovic, Ante, 5, 256, 280
Marshall Plan (1947), 98, 101, 102, 121

Marxism: focus of Communist party in Yugoslavia, 41–42; unemployment, 3, 322
mass participation concept, 118–19, 127
Meade, James, 213
Mencinger, Jože, 199
Menger, Carl, 167
Mežnarić, Silva, 36, 37
migration: to foreign jobs, 198–99, 241; as labor-market competition, 325–26; as response to unemployment, 303–4; unskilled labor, 191–92
Mihailović, Draža, 50
Mihailović, Kosta, 210
Mikulić, Branko, 360
Milanović, Branko, 214–15
military sector: conscription, 147; defense policy related to, 276, 360; effect of World War II, 51–53; equipment and supplies, 188; foreign aid to, 79, 159; purges, 248; during wartime, 49–55. *See also* national independence
Miljovski, Kiril, 223, 294n
Milosević, Slobodan, 344, 364
Minc, Hilary, 101
mines: before and after nationalization, 92–93; labor shortages and employment, 92–94, 192; nationalization, 57; shortages, 105; strikes, 268, 332–33, 343; voluntary labor in, 140–44
Mitrany, David, 21n.42
monetary policy: currency, 349; debt monetizing, 223; following Slovene model, 227–37; through price regulation, 169–70; recentralization, 355; relation to production requirements, 73; of Slovene National Liberation Front, 59; system reform, 70–71
money supply: expansion with inflow of foreign credits, 227–28; methods to reduce circulation, 104; relation to unemployment, 231
Montenegro: employment bureaus in, 178; low level of development, 283; separate party organization, 40; unemployment rates, 201, 204–5, 208. *See also* Foča model
Mutual Defense Assistance agreement, Yugoslavia/United States, 159

national communism principle, 33–34, 224, 240

national independence, 28, 33–34, 38, 57, 65, 98, 146, 164, 165, 256
nationalism: Albanians, 342–44, 358, 365–66; Croat, 43; exclusionary, 365; focus on, 32–41, 43; party ideology, 181; republics and regions, 275, 343–44, 365–67; Serbian, 346; sources of, 346–47
nationalization: of mines, 93; during 1944–45, 57–58, 69–70; of retail trade and local enterprises, 114, 117; second phase (1948), 71
nation concept, 38–40
Neuberger, Egon, 226
nonalignment movement, 241, 243, 246, 257, 350
nonproductive labor, 262, 362–63
North Atlantic Treaty Organization (NATO), 243, 349
Nuclear Test Ban Treaty (1964), 247

Offe, Claus, 23, 304, 329
Organization for Economic Cooperation and Development (OECD), 241
organizations of associated labor, 4, 22, 166, 172
overemployment, 289, 347
overpopulation, 67, 216–17

parliamentary organization, 184n.51
Partisans: brigades, 52–53, 77; campaigns to replace and retire, 288, 318; interest group pressure, 302, movement, 51–54; relocation, 88
party leadership: competition over declining resources, 354; in factory workplaces, 268, 354; primary policy role, 126–44; shift in dominance (1924), 36
party policy: education, 362; effect of World War II, 49–51; enforcement, 130, 334–35
people's committees, 153
people's power concept, 76–77, 167, 224
Perišin, Ivo, 187
Petrović-Sane, Dušan, 333
Phillips curve, 7, 219
physiocrats, 19, 22
Pijade, Moša, 60, 180
Planinc, Milka, 254, 347, 360
Poland, 9, 12–13, 14, 28, 82, 243, 328, 329

political opposition: to localization, 92; over policy, 237–56; to policy on cooperatives and agriculture, 91–94; of villages, 107. See also interest groups
political system: in achievement of economic objectives, 165; based on producers, 166–73; constitutional changes in representation, 184; criteria for exclusion from, 320–27; factors preventing consumer influence, 329–30; local level participation, 74; people's power concept, 76–77, 167, 224; power consolidation, 99; representation, 74, 300–301; response to economic reform (1980s), 361–63; with rising unemployment, 352–55; strategy for transformation to socialist state, 31–63; village level, 334; of Yugoslavia, 22–23
Popular Front: social transformation role, 78; succeeded by Socialist Alliance of Working people, 189; volunteer labor brigades, 77–78, 97, 111–12, 121, 125, 149–51, 177, 243, 268, 333
population: explosion, 211, 263; levels of rural, 43; policy (1960), 211; by republic or province, 387; surplus agricultural, 67; unemployment as overpopulation, 216–17
Prasnikar, James, 215
Pravda, Alex, 12–13
prices: central setting of, 329; effect of import costs on, 228; factors of production, 169–70; under Foča model, 61; food policy setting of, 285; mechanism under commodity production concept, 169; regulation of factors of production prices, 169–70; trade by linked or interdependent, 113–15, 133. See also rationing; regulation
Primorac, Emil, 199–200
private sector: with agrarian and currency reforms, 70; capitalism of, 174; coordination with local level public sector, 74, 89–92, 127, 166–67, 172; differentiation of employment from public, 347; economic performance, 279; effect of government control of cooperatives, 91; employment in villages, 334; interest group development in, 342–44; as labor supply pool, 174; limitations on private sales, 114; local level coordination with

private sector (*cont.*)
    public sector, 73–74; political represen-
    tation of employed in, 74, 321; require-
    ments of farmers in (1957), 244; as safe
    haven for surplus labor, 262–63, 279,
    325; subsistence for unemployed in, 261,
    312, 347; surplus labor, 303; tourist ser-
    vices, 269. *See also* farmers' (marketing)
    cooperatives; landholdings, agrarian;
    workers, private sector
privatization: legislation, 351; policy for
    public-sector firms, 279, 280
producers: adjustment to price shifts, 233;
    control over export policy, 235; control
    over finance and capital, 183–84, 222–
    23, 229–30; cooperative, 190; public sec-
    tor political rights, 166, 320–21
production: agricultural sector policy to
    gain labor for, 117; changes required by
    changed objectives, 165; commodity pro-
    duction concept, 169; dependence on
    imported materials, 249; differences in
    Slovene and Foča approaches, 163; focus
    of economic policy, 137–38; incentives
    for farms, 113; of new products, 109; re-
    organization under democratization,
    142–43; as source of income, 110
production brigades, autonomous, 142–44,
    151
productive labor concept, 18–19
productivity: divisionalization to increase,
    277; incentives in labor policy for, 86–87,
    100, 166, 261–62; as key to employment
    expansion, 174; Marxist definition, 174;
    priority over employment, 261; produc-
    tion brigade concept, 142–44; projected
    targets for growth, 188–89; strategy to
    increase, 68, 86–87; wages as measure of
    contribution to, 175
profit sharing, 175–76
proletarian brigades. *See* Partisans
property rights: division between public
    and private sectors, 312, 322; Foča
    model, 60; for foreign investors, 5, 351;
    guaranteeing subsistence, 173; legislation
    ending, 345; opposition to reform, 357;
    during and post–World War II, 56–57,
    69–70; of republican governments, 355;
    restoration of republics', 147–48; under
    Slovene model, 59; socialist, 355; worker
    as owner, 166

protectionism: republics and towns, 172–
    73, 295–96, 325; strategy of, 232–33;
    Western European, 251, 348
Przeworski, Adam, 328
Public Law 480, United States, 249
public sector: coordination with local-level
    private sector, 74, 89–92, 127, 166–67,
    172; differentiation of employment from
    private sector, 347; employment by re-
    public and region in, 291–92; factory
    management in, 85; growth with self-
    reliance strategy, 111, 274–75; guaran-
    teed minimum wage in, 262; labor
    books, 88–89; labor policy within, 261;
    local-level coordination with private sec-
    tor, 73–74; modernization of labor force
    in, 268; payment of guaranteed wage,
    173–74; in restructuring of society
    (post-1944), 68; socialization through em-
    ployment in, 262; supplements to capac-
    ity, 77; threat of unemployment, 321;
    unemployment (1952), 160. *See also* em-
    ployment; firms; state-owned enter-
    prises; unemployment; workers
Pucar, Djuro, 158
purges: of Albanian leaders, 343; Com-
    intern (1928), 36; of Communist Party of
    Yugoslavia, 119–20; of developmental
    economists, 210; party (1950–51), 180; of
    party members, 127; political and mili-
    tary (1964–66), 248; Rankovic, 274, 324;
    related to managers' market orientation,
    324

radicalism, Yugoslav, 80
Radosavljević, Dobrivoje, 139
Rajk, László, 145
Ranković, Aleksandar, 46–49, 147, 248,
    274, 324
rationing, 125, 145–46; with centralization
    of supplies, 132; control over employ-
    ment level through, 152–53; of jobs ac-
    cording to ethnic criteria, 301; for wage
    and salary earners, 104–5. *See also* com-
    modity shortages
Reform (1965), 237, 247
regions. *See* Kosovo; Slavonia; Vojvodina
regulation: local government, 176; to pre-
    vent unemployment, 240; prices of fac-
    tors of production, 169–70; of private-
    sector subsistence wage, 174; of public-

sector wage rates, 175–76, 271; of terms of trade, 90–91
Regulation on Settling Labor (1950), 151–52
remittances, 246, 254, 269, 293
republics: capital flows and investment within, 290–98; differences within, 289–90; effect of economic autonomy, 290–91, 338–39. *See also* Bosnia; Croatia; Macedonia; Montenegro; Serbia; Slovenia
revenues, federal government, 185, 231
rights: as basis for Slovenia's opposition (1980s), 363–64; of citizenship, 172, 186, 366–67; in concept of job security, 262; constitutional right to work, 173; of economic and political decision making, 166; to guaranteed minimum wage, 262; of private sector workers, 166; to self-management of work collectives, 261; of unemployed individuals, 4, 30. *See also* property rights
rights, political: of associations of producers (workers), 166, 320–21; of private sector, 186; of public and private sector worker-producers, 166, 173, 320–21
Rivers, Douglas, 9n.13
Roemer, J., 19n, 19n.38
Romania, 14, 101
Rucciardi, Joseph, 20n.40
rule of law, 136–37

Sabel, Charles, 12
Sacks, Stephen, 214
Salaj, Djuro, 154
Sarlo, Metodija Sator, 39–40
security system: firm and local government responsibility for, 250; republics' opinions on issue of, 255
security zones, 139, 284
segmentation: of the economy, 350; of markets, 233; obstacles to overcoming, 361; of society, 312
self-determination: of nations within Yugoslavia, 41; strategy for, 38. *See also* government, local; government, republics; localization; villages
self-management concept, 167–69, 175, 179–80; basic organizations of associated labor under, 277; conditions for extension of, 233–35, 271, 277; declared end of, 5; effect of, 330–34; for employment bureaus, 302; legislation ending system for, 256; by manufacturing and foreign-trade firms, 253; political consequences of, 329; in public-sector workplaces, 261; rights to, 196; in Slovene model, 264–65; with withering away of the state, 186; for Yugoslav workers, 12, 15. *See also* production brigades; work collectives; workers' councils
self-managing communities of interest, 234, 302
self-reliance policy: enforcement, 130; implementation (1948), 121–28; of Tito, 108–11
Serbia: abolition of district government, 270; developmentalists in, 210; economic development policy and outcome, 291, 296–97; employment bureaus, 178–79; immigration of Serbs and expulsion of non-Serbs, 365; mines in, 94; nationalism, 343–44; plans for development, 297–98; political rebellion, 365; response to recentralization, 358; separate party organization, 40; surplus labor, 38; unemployment rates, 201, 204–5, 298; unrest, 338
serfdom, 89
Shoup, Paul, 35
Sicherl, Pavle, 240n, 287–88
Sirotanović, Alija, 143, 151
Škegro, Borislav, 226, 228, 231, 232, 303
SKOJ. *See* League of Communist Youth of Yugoslavia (SKOJ)
Slavonia: emigration from, 283; large-scale agricultural production, 57, 285; peasant resettlement in, 93
Slovene model, 34, 58; challenge to, 83; confronts Foča conditions, 99; contradiction of Foča model, 22; with country's dissolution, 371–72; economic methods, 161–62; of economic role of government, 58–59, 222–23, 264–65, 298; full employment concept, 367–68; implementation in Slovenia, 283; institutions of, 96, 165; investment and labor policies, 224; mix with Foča model, 265–68, 349; nationalism, 56; populist, or agrarian socialist elements, 89; production focus, 163; requirement for closed economic system,

Slovene model (*cont.*)
227; return to pure version (1980s), 146, 345–46, 349; vision of the state in, 182–83, 317–18

Slovene National Liberation Front, 49, 51, 55–56, 58–59

Slovene People's party, 43

Slovenia: capitalist development, 38; contested land areas, 57; demands for productivity and growth standards, 283, 296–97; economic performance under government policy, 263–64; foreign currency flows to, 235; full employment record, 296, 339–41; industrialization in, 94; labor shortages and immigration, 263–64, 283, 303, 325, 339–41; nationalism, 365–66; national security issue, 255; organized unions and working class, 41; population flows into, 283, 303; protectionist labor policies, 342; response to recentralization and economic reform, 355–60, 363; secession, 371; skilled workers and professionals, 94, 296, 303; strikes, 296; unemployment rates, 201, 203–5, 208, 339–44; unrest (after 1967), 275; vote for independence, 256; wage rates, 293

Slovenian Communist party, 36

social democracy, 327–28

social insurance: centralization of funds for, 71–72; for certain unemployed, 177; determinants of benefits, 152–53; Law on Social Insurance (1921), 41–42; self-management, 169, 183; state regulation of, 86. *See also* benefits; health insurance

socialism: commodity production concept, 169; conflict on transition methods, 158–59; differences in Yugoslavian form, 24–28; distinct from state capitalism, 167; economy without planning, 170; employment method of payment, 166; full employment concept, 3–11; at local level, 90–91; of public sector, 74–79; transformation to (1948), 121–44; unemployment under, 4; workplace under, 4. *See also* labor brigades; market socialism

Socialist Alliance of Working People, 33, 189

socialization: of agriculture, 110–15; of debt, 229–30; of defense, 300–301; effect on Communist party, 334; effect on labor

markets, 264; through employment in public sector, 262; to extend self-management concept, 271; of investment, 245–46, 249, 271; rationalization for, 331; in Slovene and Foča models, 265; of the state, 186–89. *See also* public sector

social policy: open unemployment as, 176–78; unification and centralization, 71–72

social sector. *See* public sector

social services: financing by firms, 262; institutions, 180; self-management concept in, 271; self-management for bureaus of, 274; self-management of local, 266

social status: of public-sector employee, 23, 317; relation of education to, 317; of unemployed individuals, 3–4, 23, 30, 321; upward mobility, 317–19

social transformation: goals of, 70, 74; post-1944, 68–69; role of youth groups, 78

social unrest, 216, 255, 275, 338–39. *See also* strikes; work stoppages

society: divided into public and private sectors, 191, 311–12; effect of recentralization policy, 360–61; with Marxist ideology basis, 21–22; perception of unemployment in, 23, 311; periodic reorganization, 262; public-sector employment as status in, 317; redistribution of assets, 68–70; regains role of the state (Slovene model), 183; response to unemployment invisibility, 312–20; segmentation, 312; structure of socialist, 312–13; with unemployment in Kosovo, 342

Soviet Union: campaign against Tito, 145; economic reform, 28, 349; postwar trade agreements with, 81; post–World War II policy toward Yugoslavia, 80–81, 108; Yugoslavian conflict over Balkans policy, 107–8

spending, government: announced increases (1947), 109; for defense (1949), 146; effect on local governments of reduced, 287; increases in local, 266–67; by self-managing communities of interest, 234

Stalin, Joseph: postwar perceptions of Yugoslavia, 80–81; quarrels with, 100–101; wartime relations with Tito, 53

Stark, David, 12

state, the: anticentralist concept (1924), 36; disappearance of (Slovene model), 182–83; implication of socialization or withering away, 186; Marxist ideology, 20; new role (1948), 117–18; Yugoslav interpretation of role, 219, 222, 335–36. *See also* government, federal; government, local; government, republics

state-owned enterprises: economic link to farmers' cooperatives, 172; expansion of United Union organization to, 87; protection from private sector labor demands, 91; restructuring (1949), 151; role of, 73, 85

strikes, 86, 268, 273, 275, 296, 315, 343, 353

subsistence: in conception of economic growth, 66–67; as criterion for firing workers, 312–16, 347; education at local level against concept of, 74; employment as, 328; guaranteed, 68, 89, 313

Šuvar, Stipe, 319–20

Sweden, 31, 329

Switzerland, 342

Tanić, Živan, 301

tax policy: credits as incentives, 234, 302; to encourage employment, 281; of income (1980s), 281; local government, 78, 176; for private sector, 352; reform (1947), 78; relation to foreign borrowing, 232; by self-managing communities of interest, 234

territorial principle. *See* banking system; decentralization; government, local; government, republics; localization

Therborn, Goran, 6n, 24, 260n

Tito, Josip Broz, 32, 39; on Bosnia, 39; on distribution of labor, 174; on extension of socialism, 137–38; increased personal power, 109; independence from Stalin, 33–34; leadership, 33, 51, 53–56, 145; nonalignment policy (1958–61), 246; position on domestic industrialization strategy, 96; prediction of socialism, 134; on productivity, 84; relations with Stalin, 53, 65; relations with United States, 101; on rule of law, 136–37; self-reliance policy, 108–11, 130–31

Todaro paradox, 212

Todorović, Marija, 319

Tomasević, Jožo, 44n, 90n, 146n, 151n, 338n

trade, foreign: centralized policy management, 187; Cocom export-control regime, 95–96; economic growth strategy with openness to, 224–37; federal government policy, 223–24; industrialization strategy based on, 79; influence on economic policy, 347–49; openness of Yugoslavian economy to, 28–29; as path to increased productivity, 225; policy formation, 116–17; searching for, 121, 129; as source of income, 95–96

trade agreements: Joint Export-Import Agency, Allied occupation, 144, 150; with Poland and Czechoslovakia, 82; in shift to foreign trade strategy, 95; with Soviet Union, 81, 241, 243; with Western Europe, 122, 129; with Western European countries (1984), 122

trade deficit: conditions for, 231; effect of external shocks, 251, 253–54; effect on incomes and employment, 263; financed through borrowing, 252; post-1952 period, 228–29; stabilization to reduce, 147. *See also* balance of payments

trade policy: with change in terms of trade, 247–48; GATT membership, 245–46; implementation of self-management principle for, 253; liberalization, 187, 245–46; reorientation to Western trade, 159; with Western trade reorientation, 159

trade unions: functions under Regulation on Settling Labor, 154–55; leagues in state-owned enterprises, 87; organization of socialist competition, 78; planned effect of workers' councils on, 261; representation on workers' councils, 85; responsibility for unemployment prevention, 176; role under socialism, 85–88; unification (1944), 71

treaty of friendship, Soviet-Yugoslav, 83

Treaty of Rome (1958), 244

Trieste, 84

Trotsky, Lev, 68

Truman, Harry S, 151

Tudjman, Franjo, 367

Tyson, Laura, 213, 216, 220, 226

unemployment: analysis of postwar socialist period (Farkas), 216–18; capitalist, 3;

unemployment (*cont.*)
consequences of rising, 352–67; dual face of, 8; with economic growth policy, 269; effect of growing, 324–25; effect on ethnic composition, 366; factors causing, 165, 263–64, 278–79, 286–87; frictional and open, 176–77, 195; guarantee against, 173; hidden, 6, 191–94, 198, 216–17, 271, 314, 321; immunity from, 323–24; Marxist theory, 3–4, 322; migration as response to, 303–4; official concept of and solution to, 312–14; as overproduction of intellectuals, 317; political consequences (1980s), 352–67; political exclusion with, 320–27; prevention, 176, 240; protection against, 262, 278; relation to money supply, 231; social stigma of, 4, 23, 312–20; societal response to invisibility of, 312–20; standard explanation of Yugoslav, 218–20; structural, 194, 201, 310, 347; threat of, 3–4, 321; Ward model, 165, 208, 210; Yugoslavian brand, 12. *See also* capitalist unemployment
unemployment compensation: eligibility, 177–78, 195; funding of, 302; increase in amounts for (1980s), 281
unemployment rates: by age, 203, 206–7, 209, 388–89; with cuts in labor force, 269; increase (1952–88), 191, 193–94; interpretation of data, 194–208, 240, 264; in Kosovo, Slovenia, and Bosnia-Herzegovina, 339–44; levels and demographics of (1980s), 347–48; of public-sector workers, 160; regional differences, 201, 203–5; Todaro paradox to explain rising, 212; among women and youth, 287, 316, 333, 383
unemployment theory: Austrian school, 214–15; capital school, 214; developmentalist school, 210; liberal school, 210, 212–13
union leagues, 87
United Kingdom, 81
United Nations, 82
United States, 31; economic assistance (1950), 150–51; effect of containment policy (1947), 95, 99; loans from, 144–45, 150, 249; policy shift (1949), 121–22, 144–45; postwar relations with Yugoslavia, 81, 101; relations with, 121,
144–45, 246–47, 349; revised Yugoslavian policy, 144–45
United Unions of Yugoslavia, 45, 71, 88–87; membership in, 189–90; political resources, 325; relation to workers' councils, 154; role in public-sector firms, 326–27
urbanization, 348

Verba, Sidney, 9n.13
Verdery, Katherine, 22n.45
Veselinov, Jovan, 158
veterans' organization (SUBNOR), 51, 302
villages: agricultural labor surplus, 67; coexistence with labor cooperatives, 90–91; cooperatives, 44, 92; government intervention into autonomy of, 114; guaranteed subsistence at level of, 89; labor recruitment in, 128; political system of, 107, 135–36, 334; private-sector employment in, 334
Vojvodina: agricultural estates, 43, 57; emigration from, 283; large-scale agricultural production, 285; opposition to recentralization, 357–58; peasant resettlement in, 88, 93; unemployment rates, 201, 204–5
voluntary labor. *See* labor brigades
Vukmanović-Tempo, Švetozar, 55, 124, 141–42, 273, 327, 333

wage rates: central setting of, 173–76, 329; differences across republics, 293–94; across public-sector firms, 293–94; replacement of legislated, 112; setting of, 87, 91, 103, 176
wages: components of, 176; factors reducing competition for, 88; as incentive to increase productivity, 86–89; as measure of contribution, 175; paid in cash and coupons, 104; public-sector guarantee of, 173–74, 312; redefined as income, 176; with rise in import prices, 228; within-firm conflict over inequalities, 330–31; as work defined by job classification, 166, 175; worker acceptance of limits on, 261; worker control, 267. *See also* collective bargaining
Wagner's law, 275
Ward, Benjamin, 12, 15, 208, 212–13, 215, 220, 263, 266n, 267n

Warsaw Pact: choice against membership, 248; collapse (1989), 349; formation (1955), 243; troops invade Czechoslovakia, 250

women: discrimination in employment of, 104; employment of, 287, 316, 333; unemployment rates, 383; wages of, 123

work collectives, 111; as association of producers, 166; in public-sector workplaces, 261; self-management, 261–62; under Slovene and Foča models, 265

workers: allocation in public and private sectors, 88–89, 157–58; conflicts among, 330–32; effect of participation in central policy, 4–5, 321; exports of, 246; as interest group, 327, 329–30, 341; interest of, 87–88; job cuts and reallocation, 156–60; political rights, 166, 173, 320–21; shifting between public and private sectors, 263; surplus public sector, 300–301; unemployment in public sector, 160. *See also* producers

workers, private sector: political representation, 74, 321; rights, 187

workers, skilled: bargaining power, 84, 86; as brigade leaders, 142–43; competition for, 87; distribution of, 94–95; emigration, 276; emphasis on, 268–69; favored as party members, 322–23; in informal labor market, 315; policy to increase number of, 268, 276–77; scarcity, 102, 107, 110–12, 130, 141, 296; in Slovenia, 283; wages of, 266

workers, unskilled: day labor, 303; increase in, 368; in mines, 92–93; not in public or private sectors, 191–92; problems of, 286; return from abroad, 199; wages of, 319; weak position of, 86; work stoppages and strikes by, 314–15, 319

workers' constitution, 278

workers' councils: in assignment of redundant workers, 306–9; effect of, 161–62; to end collective bargaining, 88–89, 153–55, 261, 326; function, 156–57, 175, 266–67; introduction of, 64, 84–85, 261; rationale for, 28; relationship with unions, 155–56

work stoppages, 330, 331, 353

World Bank: development loans, 232, 236; effect of loans from, 279; loan for timber equipment (1948), 122; membership, 144; negotiations with, 122; requirements for new loans (1987), 350

Yugoslav Emergency Assistance Act (1950), United States, 151

Yugoslav People's Army (YPA): defense policy, 250–56; redundancy, 350; wages, pensions, and benefits, 188

ZAVNOH. *See* Croatian Liberation Front (ZAVNOH)

Zimmerman, William, 200

Zuehlke, Thomas, 226, 228, 231, 232, 303

Žujovic, Sreten, 48, 76, 119

Županov, Josip, 320

Žuvela, Mladen, 320

About the Author

Susan L. Woodward is a Senior Fellow in the Foreign Policy Studies Program at the Brookings Institution.